FIFTH EDITION

About Language

A
READER
FOR
WRITERS

William H. Roberts
University of Massachusetts at Lowell

Gregoire Turgeon

Houghton Mifflin Company
Boston   New York

For Patsy, my inspiration

For Sarah—delightful and in charge. Right, Dad?

Senior Sponsoring Editor: Dean Johnson
Editorial Assistant: Mary Furlong Healey
Senior Project Editors: Christina Horn, Rosemary Jaffe
Senior Production/Design Coordinator: Carol Merrigan
Senior Manufacturing Coordinator: Florence Cadran
Senior Marketing Manager: Nancy Lyman

Cover Design: Harold Burch, Harold Burch Design, New York City

Printed in the U.S.A.

Library of Congress Catalog Card Number: 97-72535

Student Text ISBN: 0-395-87463-7

1 2 3 4 5 6 7 8 9-HM-02 01 00 99 98

As part of Houghton Mifflin's ongoing commitment to the environment, this text has been printed on recycled paper.

Brief Contents

(An annotated table of contents begins on page vii.)

Preface	**xvii**
Introduction	**xix**

Chapter One   **Names and Naming**   **2**

From a World Without Surnames   *J. N. Hook*   4
A Strange Kind of Magick Bias   *Justin Kaplan*
   and *Anne Bernays*   13
from I Know Why the Caged Bird Sings
   Maya Angelou   20
Just Call Me Mister   *David Frum*   26
Putting American English on the Map
   W. F. Bolton   29
Playing the Name Game by Other Rules
   Chet Raymo   38
Aesthetics   *Felix Pollak*   41
Additional Assignments and Research Topics   43

Chapter Two   **Gender, Race, and Language Conflict**   **46**

Sexism in English: A 1990s Update
   Alleen Pace Nilsen   49
"Put Down That Paper and Talk to Me!":
   Rapport-Talk and Report-Talk   *Deborah Tannen*   60
Real Men Don't: Anti-Male Bias in English
   Eugene R. August   68
The Name Is Mine   *Anna Quindlen*   79
From African to African American
   Geneva Smitherman   82
On Black English   *James Baldwin*   87
Additional Assignments and Research Topics   91

Chapter Three **Right Words, Wrong Words, My Words** 92

Order Out of Chaos *Bill Bryson* 94
A Rarity: Grammar Lessons from Dad
  Robert Klose 107
Four-Letter Words Can Hurt You
  Barbara Lawrence 110
Goodbye to All T__t! *Wallace Stegner* 114
The E Word *Cullen Murphy* 117
Words with Attitude *Gerald Parshall* 122
English Belongs to Everybody *Robert MacNeil* 128
Additional Assignments and Research Topics 133

Chapter Four **Language Development: Personal and Social** 134

Everything Had a Name *Helen Keller* 136
Baby Born Talking—Describes Heaven
  Steven Pinker 141
The Word Weavers/The World Makers
  Neil Postman 154
A Brief History of English *Paul Roberts* 168
Old World, New World *Bill Bryson* 179
Yadda, Yadda, Yadda *Leslie Savan* 193
The Story of Writing *C. M. Millward* 196
Additional Assignments and Research Topics 206

Chapter Five **Language and Cultural Diversity** 208

Vanishing Languages *David Crystal* 210
Should English Be the Law? *Robert D. King* 218
Aria: A Memoir of a Bilingual Childhood
  Richard Rodriguez 227
Americanization Is Tough on "Macho"
  Rose Del Castillo Guilbault 238
Names in the Melting Pot *Justin Kaplan* and
  Anne Bernays 241
Learning English Good *Tara Elyssa* 246
Additional Assignments and Research Topics 255

Chapter Six   **The Language of Politics and Advertising**   **236**

The Rhetoric of Democracy   *Daniel Boorstin*   258
Empty Eggs: The Doublespeak of
   Weasel Words   *William Lutz*   268
Things Go Better with Quark?   *Chris Reidy*   278
Three Advertisements for Analysis   282
Unprotected Sex Talk   *Ellen Goodman*   288
Types of Propaganda   *Institute for*
   Propaganda Analysis   291
next to of course god america i
   E. E. Cummings   298
Two Presidential Speeches   *John F. Kennedy*
   and *Ronald Reagan*   300
Additional Assignments and Research Topics   309

Chapter Seven   **Technology and Language**   **312**

Flame Throwers   *Doug Stewart*   314
Gender Wars in Cyberspace!   *Nathan Cobb*   316
Getting Close to the Machine
   Ellen Ullman   321
C'est What?   *John Yemma*   326
Techniques of Coinage   *John A. Barry*   330
Additional Assignments and Research Topics   334

Chapter Eight   **Writers and the Writing Process**   **336**

Freewriting   *Chris Anderson*   338
from Bird by Bird: Some Instructions on
   Writing and Life   *Anne Lamott*   345
Holding Your Reader   *Maxine C. Hairston*   349
Writing Is Rewriting   *Donald M. Murray*   364
Concision   *Joseph M. Williams*   375
Computers and Writing   *Sharon Cogdill*   384
Additional Assignments and Research Topics   391

Appendix   **Writing and Documenting: A Brief Guide**   **394**

I. Essay Writing and Revising   395
Revision Checklist   395
A Sample Student Essay   401
II. The Documented Essay   408
Revision Checklist   408
Typical Works Cited Entries   412
A Sample Documented Essay   416

**Glossary of Rhetorical and
Linguistic Terms**   **426**

Credits   **432**

Index   **435**

Annotated Contents

Preface   xvii

Introduction   xix

Chapter One   **Names and Naming**   2

From a World Without Surnames   4
J. N. Hook

An author and teacher discusses how surnames reveal the history, geography, and unique character of America.

A Strange Kind of Magick Bias   13
Justin Kaplan and *Anne Bernays*

The authors of *The Language of Names* examine the illogical but persistent belief that personal names somehow influence character and personality traits.

***from* I Know Why the Caged Bird Sings**   20
Maya Angelou

In a personal reminiscence, the noted writer and civil-rights activist illustrates how the act of naming implies authority and why controlling a name signifies control over a great deal more.

Just Call Me Mister   26
David Frum

Even strangers address us by our first names today, but for this author, "it's not friendliness that drives first-namers; it's aggression," an attitude resulting from relative power and status and their effect on the ways that we address others.

Putting American English on the Map   29
W. F. Bolton

An author and philologist concludes that toponymics, the study of place names, can be a major factor in defining the linguistic character of America.

Playing the Name Game by Other Rules   38
Chet Raymo

Because naming and understanding are intimately connected, both forms of biological naming—scientific and common—are applauded by scientist and author Chet Raymo.

Aesthetics   41
Felix Pollak

Names don't always seem well suited to the things they identify, but, as this poem shows, sound and meaning clash only because we expect them not to.

Additional Assignments and Research Topics   43

Chapter Two   **Gender, Race, and Language Conflict**   46

Sexism in English: A 1990s Update   49
Alleen Pace Nilsen

In a carefully structured argument, the author offers a wealth of evidence on the continuing presence of sexist language and analyzes its implications for both men and women.

"Put Down That Paper and Talk to Me!": Rapport-Talk and Report-Talk   60
Deborah Tannen

As this researcher explains, men and women use language differently; they also rarely understand this fact, so mistaken assumptions and hurt feelings often result.

Real Men Don't: Anti-Male Bias in English   68
Eugene R. August

A professor presents evidence that anti-male bias permeates the language we use every day and thus affects the attitudes of both men and women—and probably the ways that men act.

The Name Is Mine   79
Anna Quindlen

After an emergency, a married woman comes to understand more fully the implications of her decision not to take her husband's family name.

From African to African American   82
Geneva Smitherman

The author traces four centuries of "Names for the race" and links this evolution with the continuing process of self-identification that it reflects.

On Black English   87
James Baldwin

For this distinguished writer, black English not only unifies its speakers but also provides security and control, which otherwise are rarely possible for African-Americans.

Additional Assignments and Research Topics   91

Chapter Three

Right Words, Wrong Words, My Words   92

Order Out of Chaos   94
Bill Bryson

Three landmark dictionaries of the English language—and the lexicographers responsible for them—constitute the subject of Bryson's vivid and entertaining historical sketch.

A Rarity: Grammar Lessons from Dad   107
Robert Klose

A well-received grammar lesson, offered while enjoying the companionship of his son, emphasizes for a father the lamentable state of grammar and syntax study in today's schools.

Four-Letter Words Can Hurt You   110
Barbara Lawrence

For this writer, editor, and teacher, American society's apparent indifference to sexually abusive language raises discomforting questions about values.

Goodbye to All T__t!   114
Wallace Stegner

A novelist and teacher argues that taboo language is a powerful literary resource only if used with restraint; excess is irresponsible and quickly becomes comic.

The E Word   117
Cullen Murphy

Stressing his reassuring belief that any euphemism actually draws attention to the truth, the author offers an extensive catalog of euphemisms that cause more amusement than anxiety.

Words with Attitude   122
Gerald Parshall

In this review of the first volume of the *Random House Dictionary of American Slang,* the author dispels many mistaken notions about this colorful, serviceable variety of language.

English Belongs to Everybody   128
Robert MacNeil

A well-known print and television journalist reminds us that language change does not necessarily imply decay but instead can imply vitality, and that setting language standards has always been the public's prerogative.

Additional Assignments
and Research Topics   133

Chapter Four   **Language Development:
Personal and Social**   134

Everything Had a Name   136
Helen Keller

A remarkable woman, blind and deaf from early childhood, describes how her acquisition of language finally opened the world to her and made possible those links with other people that are usually taken for granted.

Baby Born Talking—Describes Heaven   141
Steven Pinker

In this excerpt from his book *The Language Instinct,* the author details the various stages of language acquisition, a process completed before a child turns four.

The Word Weavers/The World Makers   154
Neil Postman

Definitions, questions, and metaphors, as well as today's schools and modern technology—all these receive the attention of a well-known critic of modern culture as he reflects on our mapping of the world through language.

A Brief History of English 168
Paul Roberts

This well-known essay describes how and why the English we speak today differs so from earlier forms, demonstrating how greatly an understanding of history can contribute to our understanding of the language.

Old World, New World 179
Bill Bryson

With wit and obvious delight in his topic, journalist Bryson reviews the process that created a distinctly American English.

Yadda, Yadda, Yadda 193
Leslie Savan

A well-known essayist criticizes the clichés generated by today's popular movies and television, stressing both their consistent hostility as well as how often they encourage not thinking at all.

The Story of Writing 196
C. M. Millward

As Millward reveals—with clarity and in an unmistakable voice—spoken and written language were invented to serve different purposes, a fact that helps explain why writing involves more than simply transcribing spoken language onto paper.

Additional Assignments and Research Topics 206

Chapter Five

Language and Cultural Diversity 208

Vanishing Languages 210
David Crystal

The author makes clear the alarming rate of language extinction (an unfamiliar topic for most people) and illustrates the political implications of deciding what to do about this worldwide phenomenon.

Should English Be the Law? 218
Robert D. King

Arguing against the many legal efforts to declare English our "official" language, King stresses benign neglect as the best approach to avoiding the serious social unrest that many other countries have suffered because of laws designed to control language use.

Aria: A Memoir of a Bilingual Childhood   227
Richard Rodriguez

A Hispanic author sensitively argues against bilingual education, maintaining that assimilation is a part of personal growth and that public language must be part of anyone's public identity.

Americanization Is Tough on "Macho"   238
Rose Del Castillo Guilbault

The Spanish *macho,* which has entered English with decidedly unpleasant connotations, illustrates well how cultural misunderstandings can create language which then reinforces those misunderstandings.

Names in the Melting Pot   241
Justin Kaplan and *Anne Bernays*

The authors examine the unexpected, sometimes unintended transformation of surnames that occurred as millions of immigrants arrived in the United States at the turn of this century.

Learning English Good   246
Tara Elyssa

The frustrating experiences of English as a second language (ESL) students reveal much about English and about all languages.

**Additional Assignments
and Research Topics**   255

Chapter Six   **The Language of Politics
and Advertising**   256

The Rhetoric of Democracy   258
Daniel J. Boorstin

While convincingly placing advertising at the center of American culture, one of America's foremost historians describes the social history of advertising, its qualities today, and its far-reaching implications.

**Empty Eggs: The Doublespeak of
Weasel Words**   268
William Lutz

A review of the most common language tricks employed by advertisers whose promises rarely commit them to everything that we at first might believe.

Things Go Better with Quark? 278
Chris Reidy

This newspaper article, which illustrates the journalistic style of writing, examines product naming as a commercial enterprise and details some notable naming successes and failures.

Three Advertisements for Analysis 282

Ads for three different automobiles invite readers to recognize and discriminate among three different voices with a common message: We're selling exactly what you want.

Unprotected Sex Talk 288
Ellen Goodman

Because of her blunt public utterances, Jocelyn Elders lost her job as Surgeon General; the reasons why Elders seemed so indiscreet to so many Americans are examined by the Pulitzer Prize–winning newspaper columnist.

Types of Propaganda 291
Institute for Propaganda Analysis

This important overview reveals the most common techniques for bending language so that it perpetrates deceptions for political (and other) purposes.

next to of course god america i 298
E. E. Cummings

In this well-known and striking sonnet, a poet satirizes the political voice.

Two Presidential Speeches 300
John F. Kennedy and *Ronald Reagan*

Their inaugural addresses exemplify two political figures' use of language to establish the tone of their administrations and to articulate their political philosophies.

Additional Assignments and Research Topics 309

Chapter Seven | ## Technology and Language 312

Flame Throwers 314
Doug Stewart

The author reacts to otherwise reasonable people who make embarrassing spectacles of themselves when they generate the flame, that emotionally overheated variety of electronic mail.

Gender Wars in Cyberspace!   **316**
Nathan Cobb

A journalist examines the clearly delineated, strongly contrasting male/female approaches to online communication.

Getting Close to the Machine   **321**
Ellen Ullman

A consultant, editor, and former programmer stresses her belief that computers have distorted our opportunities for human relationships and that "the computer's pretty, helpful face" actually expresses the typical programmer's contempt for us.

***C'est* What?**   **326**
John Yemma

A journalist reviews the current state of efforts to create translating machines, devices that would translate reliably from one human language to another.

Techniques of Coinage   **330**
John A. Barry

In an excerpt from his book *Technobabble,* the author reviews the confusing, ugly vocabulary that accompanies our ever-expanding stockpile of technological wonders.

**Additional Assignments
and Research Topics**   **334**

Chapter Eight   **Writers and the Writing Process**   **336**

Freewriting   **338**
Chris Anderson

A teacher of writing describes a proven technique that can help generate ideas and make it easier to begin the writing process.

***from* Bird by Bird: Some Instructions on
Writing and Life**   **345**
Anne Lamott

A novelist, critic, and columnist offers reassurance that almost all first drafts are badly flawed and should be accepted as opportunities for improvement, not as predictions of failure.

Holding Your Reader   **349**
Maxine C. Hairston

A well-known writing instructor offers guidance on titles, openings, sentence structure, transitions, and many other issues that contribute to the clarity that readers demand and deserve.

Writing Is Rewriting   **364**
Donald M. Murray

As Murray shows, revision is not mere editing or proofreading; rather, it is the discovery of meaning itself and forms an essential stage in the process of writing.

Concision   **375**
Joseph M. Williams

In a selection from his book *Style: Ten Lessons in Clarity and Grace,* the author shows why brevity, one key to clarity, requires that we recognize weak, bloated language, which at first might not look that way to us.

Computers and Writing   **384**
Sharon Cogdill

As was true of many earlier technological innovations, computers have affected the writing process in unexpected ways, and for student writers, a computer presents both new opportunities and potential pitfalls.

**Additional Assignments
and Research Topics**   **391**

Appendix   **Writing and Documenting:
A Brief Guide**   **394**

Revision checklists, concise explanations of important writing topics, and two sample student essays offer practical advice for student writers.

**Glossary of Rhetorical and
Linguistic Terms**   **426**

Credits   **432**

Index   **435**

Preface

As has been true of all previous editions, this fifth edition of *About Language: A Reader for Writers* is designed to help students become more conscious of language and better able to use it effectively and responsibly. The choice of reading selections was guided by our belief that an introduction to the complex, subtle, and manipulative nature of language will help students understand how often language shapes our world and our thinking about it. After more than twenty years of experience in the college writing classroom, each of us recognizes as clearly as ever the increasing skill and confidence of student writers as they become more conscious of language itself.

New Features of the Fifth Edition

- Twenty-six new reading selections
- The addition of an Appendix, "Writing and Documenting: A Brief Guide," which provides student writers with practical guidance through revision checklists and two sample student essays
- A new chapter on technology and language
- New material on many aspects of language, including English as a second language and language acquisition during early childhood
- A comprehensive updating of our unit on language and cultural diversity

Organization and Coverage

About Language is an anthology of fifty-two reading selections organized around eight language issues.

 - Chapter One, "Names and Naming," focuses on the psychological, historical, and sociological aspects of the names we give to people, places, and things. Included are works by such authors as Maya Angelou, Justin Kaplan and Anne Bernays, and Chet Raymo.

 - Chapter Two, "Gender, Race, and Language Conflict," examines gender-based differences in language use (Deborah Tannen), sexist language (Alleen Pace Nilsen and Eugene R. August), and language issues particularly troublesome for women (Anna Quindlen) and for African Americans (James Baldwin and Geneva Smitherman).

 - Chapter Three, "Right Words, Wrong Words, My Words," brings together several topics that address the issue of "correct" language: dictionaries (Bill Bryson), obscenity (Barbara Lawrence), euphemism (Cullen Murphy), and slang (Gerald Parshall). The chapter concludes with Robert MacNeil's "English Belongs to Everybody," a thoughtful, reassuring commentary on history, language, and resistance to language change.

 - Chapter Four, "Language Development: Personal and Social," presents essays on early childhood language acquisition (Steven Pinker) and on the history and evolution of the English language (Paul Roberts, Bill Bryson, and Leslie Savan). Also included are a far-ranging reflection on language, metaphor, and experience (Neil Postman), a selection from the autobiography of Helen Keller, and a selection detailing the origin of writing (C. M. Millward).

■ Chapter Five, "Language and Cultural Diversity," examines the links between language and culture. Included are personal reflections and reactions (Richard Rodriguez and Rose Del Castillo Guilbault), as well as informative discussion of the historical and political aspects of this timely language issue (Justin Kaplan and Anne Bernays, David Crystal, and Robert D. King). In "Learning English Good," an essay written especially for *About Language,* the increasingly important issue of English as a second language is addressed by Tara Elyssa.

■ Chapter Six, "The Language of Politics and Advertising," looks at persuasive language and its effects on our opinions, decisions, and desires. Relevant language issues include public discourse (Daniel Boorstin, Ellen Goodman, and E. E. Cummings) and advertising language (William Lutz and Chris Reidy). Primary source material for analysis includes sample advertisements and noteworthy presidential addresses by John F. Kennedy and Ronald Reagan.

■ Chapter Seven, "Technology and Language," reviews some of the language issues created or highlighted by today's technology. Reading selections examine electronic communication (Doug Stewart and Nathan Cobb), computer-based translation of human languages (John Yemma), and some effects, both subtle and painfully obvious, of the personal computer on human relationships (Ellen Ullman) and on our contemporary vocabulary (John A. Barry).

■ Chapter Eight, "Writers and the Writing Process," looks at prewriting, writing, and revising through the eyes of such writers as Chris Anderson, Anne Lamott, Maxine C. Hairston, and Donald M. Murray. Also included is "Computers and Writing" by Sharon Cogdill. This essay, written especially for *About Language,* addresses the effects of computers on student writing.

■ The text concludes with an Appendix, "Writing and Documenting: A Brief Guide," a new, practical instructional aid organized around revision checklists. Topics addressed include paragraph focus, essay form, grammar and punctuation, and manuscript form. Two sample student essays, one of them a short documented essay, provide useful models for student writers as they complete that almost traditional assignment, the five-hundred-word essay. Also included is an updated glossary of rhetorical and linguistic terms.

Acknowledgments

We thank, yet again, our colleagues at the University of Massachusetts at Lowell. Thanks also go, in abundance, to our wives Patsy and Susan for their advice and patience.

We also thank our students, who every year teach us new things about the power of words to discipline, to liberate, and to delight.

We also wish to thank the following individuals for their constructive comments and suggestions: Jennie Dautermann, Miami University, Ohio; Richard C. Norwood, Jr., University of South Carolina; Michael Given, Southern Illinois University; Jeannette Webber, Santa Barbara City College, California.

W. H. R. and G. T.

Introduction

All writing instructors eventually hear themselves telling student writers to "begin at the beginning." It thus seems only fair that we begin this fifth edition of *About Language: A Reader for Writers* with an introduction that describes some of the reasons why your instructor has directed you to buy a language reader. Instructors regularly disagree about the best approach to take when teaching writing, but those who adopt a language reader usually do agree on one thing—that concentrated attention to language issues serves vital purposes in learning to write well. *About Language,* which is *A Reader for Writers,* concludes with a chapter that addresses several of the most important aspects of the writing process, and every reading selection in this book should prove helpful to a student writer. This is true for many reasons, some of which deserve mention here.

A language reader benefits a wide range of college writing students. Some of you entered college well prepared to write unified, coherent prose. You also perhaps realize that words can bring unique pleasure to both writers and their audiences. If either of these descriptions fits you, you'll find that this language reader provides an unexpected, refreshing introduction to the ways in which language serves us. On the other hand, if your preparation for college writing has been less useful, you will benefit immeasurably from this reader's emphasis on *seeing* language, for doing so is always the necessary first step toward writing well.

Regardless of your experience, much of the pleasure of the language-based approach comes from its immediate relevance to the world that we all experience every day. For example, the first chapter of *About Language* is devoted to the issue of names and naming. You'll explore the idea that names, instead of serving only as identifying labels, actually possess immense power to categorize and to influence attitudes. Anyone who shudders at the thought of naming a child *Wilbur* or *Irma* already understands this fundamental truth about names. However, the same principle guides the naming of enemy missiles *Scuds* and U.S. missiles *Patriots.* Naming manifests an identical power for parents and for governments (and advertisers and many others), and examples of this power at work are all around us. Language and discrimination, language play, and the other language issues treated in *About Language*—they all connect directly with our daily lives.

A language reader focuses attention appropriately, that is, on writing itself. You might find that students in other writing classes are using readers organized according to the rhetorical modes, which include comparison, cause and effect, division and classification, and other tactics for structuring paragraphs and essays. However, because writing is not "about" comparison and the other modes, this approach sometimes encourages writers to mistake tactics for objectives. When asked to identify what they wrote in a previous semester's composition course, some students, ignoring topics and essay writing itself, declare that they "wrote a process analysis and a cause and effect." Although these students misconstrue the writing task, they simply remember what they were encouraged to remember. The language-based approach provides a more appropriate focus. Although writing is not "about" language, *writing about* language encourages writers to treat the rhetorical modes as valuable tactics, not as ends in themselves.

You also might hear about "writing across the curriculum," another increasingly popular approach to college writing. It, too, subordinates tactics. Its purpose is to remind students that people in all disciplines write so as to learn, and that writing well allows people to learn more effectively about any subject. Because language issues obviously play a role in studying every subject, study of language issues, presented as part of an English curriculum, can help any student to understand better the demands of "writing across the curriculum."

A language reader provides a focus appropriate to an increasingly diverse society. Regardless of their culture, all people are linked in their use of language, so the study of language issues inevitably reminds us that our society is multicultural. Studying language issues also facilitates the study of cultural similarities and differences. *About Language* includes a chapter titled "Language and Cultural Diversity," and many selections in other chapters explore this issue.

A language reader can unify writing topics without sacrificing freedom. A language reader can make writing easier for the student who asks, "What do I write about?" Usually you write about language. Moreover, because most aspects of human experience involve language, the language-based approach provides an almost unlimited supply of writing topics. As an example, suppose you have a special interest in writing about your grandparents. While exploring the issue of language and group identity, you might write about the ways that you and your grandparents use language to reflect membership in specific but different groups. The issue of public and private language might lead you to consider how language encourages or inhibits intimacy with your grandparents. Study of language development and discrimination could help identify historical and cultural influences evident in your grandparents' language and in your own. Writing about almost any subject can incorporate language study in similar ways.

Finally, a language reader serves a purpose that derives from the writing process. Although this process is always personalized by a writer's strengths, weaknesses, and disposition, it inevitably centers itself on the same frustrating yet intoxicating task: to find the right word. Experienced writers appreciate how many subtle implications are embodied in this description. For student writers, then, one fundamental purpose for a language reader can be summarized this way: *to focus attention on words and thus to reveal what "the right word" can mean.*

About Language

CHAPTER ONE

Names and Naming

People with a gloomy view of the future predict that someday our names will be replaced by numbers. Even now, social security numbers often seem as important as names. Why such concern over threats to our names, which, after all, can be untidy and cumbersome and difficult to spell and pronounce? Numbers, by contrast, seem neat, efficient, and in desirably infinite supply, eliminating the problem of asking or answering, "Which Michael?" or "Which Jennifer?"

Our appalled response is easy to understand when we recall that a gloomy view of the future usually implies a vision of a dehumanized future, a future in which human life is not valued as we believe it deserves to be. We identify ourselves with names and not numbers *because* we're human. We give names to other people, places, and things, and the impulse to name everything we live with also seems uniquely human. The names we have and give are the subject of this chapter, which examines what names reveal about our understanding of the world and our reactions to it.

Surnames are a storehouse of history, and the first selection, J. N. Hook's "From a World Without Surnames," looks at the origins of surnames and their value in tracing historical change. Justin Kaplan and Anne Bernays examine our often mistaken belief that names possess "A Strange Kind of Magick Bias" that guides those who bear them. In an autobiographical essay from Maya Angelou's *I Know Why the Caged Bird Sings*, we hear a story about naming and the power and control that the act of naming implies. Then, in "Just Call Me Mister," David Frum complains thoughtfully about the instant familiarity created when strangers address us by our first names, a common practice today and one that Frum believes is prompted by hostility rather than good will. All four selections remind us how often names do more than merely label people so as to distinguish one person from another.

The names we give to places and things are equally significant and revealing. W. F. Bolton's "Putting American English on the Map" discusses toponymics, the study of place names, and the apparently clean slate our country presented to its new inhabitants in the eighteenth and nineteenth centuries. Physicist and author Chet Raymo reflects on the connection between the two systems of biological naming, scientific and common, and emphasizes why human nature requires that both types of names coexist. Finally, the poem "Aesthetics," by Felix Pollak, humorously reminds us that attractive names sometimes identify decidedly unattractive realities.

A Chinese proverb declares, "The beginning of wisdom is to call things by their right names." Names identify, reveal, and classify our experience of the world, and the wise person learns to respect their significance and to use them with care. When identity seems threatened by anonymity, this is the declaration we hear: "I'm not a number. I have a name."

From a World Without Surnames

J. N. Hook

Imagine trying to function without a surname in our complex society. For many centuries in Europe, however, people had no surnames; surnames developed only as changes in society made them necessary. This is one of many issues examined in the following richly detailed selection by J. N. Hook, coauthor of twenty-one textbooks about English. Hook shows that surnames reveal history, geography, and the unique character of nationalities.

■ **J O U R N A L   P R O M P T** *Think about your surname and those of your family members, going back several generations. Write about what the names mean and what they reveal about your ancestry.*

1   When the world's population was small and even a city might hold only a few thousand people, and when most folks never got more than ten or fifteen miles from their birthplace (usually walking), and when messages were sent by personal messenger rather than by impersonal post, there was hardly a necessity for more than one name. Even kings got by with a single name. When someone referred to King David, there was no need to ask David who?

2   No one knows who first felt the need to apply any name at all to himself or any of his fellows. According to Pliny, some ancient tribes were *anonymi* (nameless) and it is barely possible that a few *anonymi* may still exist in remote corners of the world. But for the most part personal names of some sort exist wherever there are human beings. As British onomatist C. L. Ewen has said,

> The most general custom among the savage tribes was to give a child the name of a deceased ancestor, but any descriptive word which might indicate sex, order of birth, race, caste, office, physical feature, god, historical fact, or a more fanciful concept, served the purpose of a distinguishing label.

3   "A distinguishing label"—that of course is what a name is. It differentiates one person from another, allowing a mother to single out one child's attention, helping an officer to address a command to an individual, assisting any of us to carry out our daily tasks that depend on distinguishing one person from another.

4   Customs in naming have varied considerably, and some seem strange to us. Ewen mentioned an African tribe in which young boys had names that were changed to something else at puberty, and another tribe in which a father took a new name when his first child was born, his virility having thus been confirmed. Members of other tribes change their names after serious illness or when they get old. Some American Indians had different names for different seasons. People of Dahomey, in East

4

Africa, once had several names, including some that named guardian spirits and others that were kept secret except from intimates. Some names have been very long: *The Encyclopedia of Religion and Ethics* mentions a Babylonian name that can be translated "O Ashur, the lord of heaven and earth, give him life." To this day, the Balinese have no surnames, and as youngsters many often change their personal names. They do have caste and birth-order designations that stay with them all their lives.

5   The ancient Greeks generally used only single names (Sophocles and Plato, for example), but occasionally employed additional phrases for further identification. Thus Alexander, whom we describe as "the Great," was Alexandros o Philippon, Alexander the son of Phillip.

6   During Rome's centuries of greatness, Romans—especially those of the upper classes—were likely to have three names, like Gaius Julius Caesar. The *praenomen* (Gaius) corresponded to our given names. The *nomen* or *nomen gentilium* (Julius) identified the clan or tribe (*gens*), which usually consisted of a number of families sharing this name. The *cognomen* (Caesar) designated the particular family within the *gens*. There might even be a fourth name, called an *agnomen*, which could be a mark of distinction (like "Africanus" bestowed on Scipio after military victories in Africa), or just an additional mark of identification (for instance, Emperor Octavian, born Gaius Octavius, added the name Julius Caesar after Gaius, but retained Octavianus as an *agnomen*). During the period of Rome's decline, some persons adopted or were given even more names—as many as thirty-six.

7   In Roman times the *cognomens* were most like our surnames. They were hereditary, and they usually fell into the same classifications as English and Continental names. Some indicated the place from which the family had come or with which it was associated: Gnaeus Marcius Coriolanus, about whom Shakespeare wrote a play, is said to have won the battle of Corioli in 493 B.C. A few names are those of ancestors: Agrippa, the family name of some of the descendants of Herod the Great. Some plebeians bore *cognomens* that named their occupations, as Metellus (servant), Missor (archer). The Romans especially liked descriptive *cognomens*, as Sapiens (the wise), Crassus (the fat), or Marcellus (the little hammer).

8   After the fall of Rome, multiple names largely disappeared for a few centuries throughout Europe, although compound names were fairly frequent in some places. Thus Irish Faolchadh was a compound of *wolf* and *warrior*, and the German Gerhard was compounded of *spear* and *firm*.

9   In the tenth century Venetian noblemen began to adopt hereditary family names. This custom was to be followed later by the Irish, the French, the English, and then the Germans and other Europeans.

10   Suppose that you were living in England in the Middle Ages. Suppose further that your name was John. Not John Something—just John. The Somethings did not yet exist in England. King or commoner, you were just John.

11   Your male ancestors had also been John, or Thomas, Robert, Harold, Richard, William, or more anciently Eadgar or Eadwine or Aelfred, and their wives may have been Alice, Joan, Berthe, Blanche, Beatrice, Margaret, Marie, Inga, or Grette. Most

names of your day were Norman French, since the descendants of William the Conqueror and his followers ruled the land. Huntingdon, for instance, had only 1 percent recognizably Anglo-Saxon names in A.D. 1295.

12   The number of different names was not large. The same Huntingdon list shows that 18 percent of all males in that county were called William, 16 percent John, 10 percent Richard, and 7 percent Robert, and that only 28 other names made up the remainder. So over half of these men shared only 4 names. In Yorkshire in the fourteenth century, in a list of 19,600 mixed male and female names, C. L. Ewen found that John accounted for 17 percent of the total, followed by William, Thomas, and Robert, with Alice (5 percent) and Joan (4 percent in various spellings) the most popular names for women. There were some biblical names other than John—almost 2 percent Adam, for example—but the popularity of Peter, Paul, Abraham, David, and others was still in the future.

13   England, like other countries in the Middle Ages, was mainly a rural and male-dominated society. There were no large cities. Some groups of people lived within the walls of a castle or nearby; still others clustered in villages from which workers trudged short distances each day to tend the crops or the livestock, or where they remained to do their smithing, wagon making, tailoring, or other tasks. Women often worked beside the men in the fields, and in a family wealthy enough to have its own cow or a few pigs or sheep, the women were likely to be responsible for the animals' care. Women's liberation was centuries away and largely undreamed of—although older England had had some strong queens, and Shakespeare's plays would later reflect some influence of women on medieval national affairs. In general, women were subservient, and their subservience was to be shown in the naming processes getting under way.

14   Almost all the occupational names, for example, refer to work done mainly or entirely by men in the Middle Ages, and countless fathers but few mothers were memorialized in names that would become family names. Had women's prestige been higher we would today have many persons with names like Milkmaid, Buxom, and Margaretson.

15   If the Middle Ages had been urbanized, no doubt the use of second names would have accelerated. If a city has three thousand Williams, ways must be found to indicate which William one talks about. A typical medieval village, though, might have had only five or ten Williams, a similar number of Johns, and maybe two or three Roberts or Thomases.

16   Even so, distinctions often needed to be made. If two villages were talking about you (John, you remember, is who you are), misunderstandings would arise if each had a different John in mind. So qualifications were added, as in imaginary bits of conversation like these:

"A horse stepped on John's foot."
"John from the hill?'
"No. John of the dale."

"John the son of William?"
"No. John the son of Robert."

"John the smith?"
"No. John the tailor."

"John the long?"
"No. John the bald."

17   In the rush of conversation the little, unimportant words could drop out or be slurred over so that John from the hill became John hill, and the other persons could be John dale, John William's son, John Robert's son, John smith, John tailor, John long, and John bald (or ballard, which means *the bald one*). The capital letters that we now associate with surnames are only scribal conventions introduced later on.

18   Distinctions like those illustrated in the conversations were a step toward surnames. But the son of John the smith might be Robert the wainwright (wagon maker). That is, he did not inherit the designation *smith* from his father. There were no true English surnames—family names—until Robert the son of John smith became known as Robert smith (or Smith) even though his occupation was a wainwright, a fletcher (arrow maker), a tanner or barker (leather worker), or anything else. Only when the second name was passed down from one generation to the next did it become a surname.

19   That step did not occur suddenly or uniformly, although throughout most of Europe it was a medieval development. Ewen has described the details of the development in England, basing his scholarly analysis on thousands of entries in tax rolls, court records, and other surviving documents. He has pointed out that before the fourteenth century most of the differentiating adjuncts were prefaced by *filius* (son of), as in Adam fil' Gilberti (Adam, son of Gilbert), by *le* (the), as in Beaudrey le Teuton, by *de* (of, from), as in Rogerius de Molis (Roger from the mills), or by *atta* (at the), as in John atte Water (John at the water), which later might be John Atwater. These particles often dropped out. Thus a fourteenth-century scribe began writing his name as David Tresruf, but other evidence shows that Tresruf was simply a place name and that David de Tresruf was the way the scribe earlier wrote his name.

20   Almost all English and Continental surnames fall into the four categories I have illustrated:

Place names	John Hill, John Atwater
Patronyms (or others based on personal names)	John Robertson, John Williams, John Alexander
Occupational names	John Smith, John Fletcher
Descriptive names	John Long, John Armstrong

21   With a few exceptions the million-plus surnames that Americans bear are of these four sorts. If we were mainly an Oriental or an African nation, the patterns would be different. But we are primarily European in our origins, and in Europe it seemed natural to identify each person during the surname-giving period according to location, parentage, occupation, appearance or other characteristics.

22   It never used to occur to me that my name and almost everyone else's name has a meaning, now often unknown even to its possessors. My own name, I found, is a place name. A *hook* is a sharp bend in a stream or a peninsula or some odd little corner of land. My paternal ancestors, who came from Somerset in southern England, lived on such a hook, probably one of the many irregularly shaped bits of land in Somerset. The numerous Hookers, like General Joseph Hooker in the Civil War, lived in similar places in the name-giving period. Hocking(s), Hoke(r), Horn(e), and Horman(n) are other English or German names that share the meaning of Hook, so they are my cousins, by semantics though not by blood. So are the Dutch Hoekstra, van Hoek, and Haack, who lived in their own odd little corners in the Netherlands.

23   By coincidence, my mother's father (part Finnish, mostly German) bore a name that also referred to a bend or angle. He was Engel, and his ancestors had lived in Angeln, in Schleswig in northern Germany. The Angles who came in the fifth century to the British Isles with the Saxons, Jutes, and Frisians to help the Celts against the savage Picts (but eventually drove their hosts to the western and northern reaches of the islands) took their name from the same German area, and England—Angle-land historically—is named for them. Angeln got its name because it was shaped somewhat like a fishhook; the word is obviously related to *angle* and the sport of *angling*.

24   The fourfold identification of people by place, ancestry, occupation, or description has worked well, and only science fiction writers today ever suggest that our names may or should be replaced by numbers or number-letter combinations. Even an ordinary name like William Miller, George Rivers, or Anne Armstrong can acquire an individuality and a remembrable quality hard to imagine for 27-496-3821 or Li94T8633. I'd probably not enjoy a love affair with American names that looked like mere license plate identifications.

25   The proportion in each category of names may vary from one European language to another. Thus 70 percent or more of Irish, Welsh, and Scandinavian surnames are patronyms. Spanish families have also preferred patronyms, but place names are not far behind. In France patronyms lead once more, but names of occupations are in second place. In Germany, however, patronyms of the simple English sort are relatively few, although hereditary combinative descriptions like the previously mentioned Gerhard are common, occupational names are frequent, and place names not uncommon. In most countries personal descriptive surnames lag behind the others.

26   Elsdon Smith analyzed seven thousand of our most common American surnames and found these proportions:

	Percentage
Place names	43.13
Patronyms	32.23
Occupational names	15.16
Nicknames (descriptives)	9.48

27   In an analysis that I made of several hundred American surnames of English origin, I obtained the following percentages:

	Percentage
Place names	35.49
Patronyms	32.37
Occupational names	19.66
Personal descriptors	12.47

The fact that large numbers of American surnames are derived from England is reflected in the similarities between Smith's percentages and mine.

28   Often, superficially different American surnames turn out to be essentially the same name in meaning when translated from the foreign language into English. . . . Place names, often unique or nearly so, are not likely to be internationally duplicated except when they refer to geographically common features like bodies of water or land masses. We may illustrate the possibilities with the English surname Hill, whose German equivalent may be Buhl, Buehler, Knor(r), or Piehl, paralleled by Dutch Hoger and Hoogland (literally *high land*), French Depew and Dumont, Italian Costa and Colletti, Finnish Maki (one of Finland's most common names), Hungarian Hegi, Scandinavian Berg, Bergen, Bagge, and Haugen, and Slavic Kopec, Kopecky, and Pagorak, all of which mean *hill* or *small mountain*.

29   Differences in size or in skin or hair coloration are international, as many of our personal descriptive surnames confirm. English Brown and Black, for instance, may refer to either dark skin or brown or black hair. (*Black*, however, sometimes comes from the Old English *blac*, related to our *bleach* and meaning *white* or *light*, so Mr. Black's ancestors may have been either fair or dark.) Blake is a variant of Black. The French know the dark person as Le Brun or Moreau, the Germans as Braun, Brun, Mohr, or Schwartz, the Italians as Bruno, the Russians as Chernoff. Pincus refers to a dark-skinned Jew, Mavros to a dark Greek. Dark Irishmen may be named, among other possibilities, Carey, Duff, Dunn(e), Dolan, Dow, or Kearns. Hungarian Fekete has a dark skin. Czechoslovakian Cerny or Czerny (black) reveals his linguistic similarity to Polish Czarnik, Czarniak, or Czarnecki and Ukrainian Corney. Spanish Negron is a very dark person.

30   Many names spelled identically are common to two or more languages, and a considerable number of such names have more than a single meaning. So Gray, although usually an English name meaning *gray haired*, in a few instances is French for a person from Gray (the estate of Gradus) in France. Gray must therefore be classified both as a personal descriptor and a place name. Hoff is usually German for a farm or an enclosed place, but less often is English for Hoff (pagan temple), a place in Westmoreland. Many Scandinavian names are identical in Denmark, Norway, and Sweden, although spelling variants such as *-sen* and *-son* suggest the likelihood of one country rather than another. In general a person must know at least a little about his or her ancestry before determining with assurance the nationality and most likely meaning of his or her name.

31   A small percentage of names, few of them common in the United States, is derived from sources other than the basic four. For example, a few Jewish names are based on acronyms or initials. Thus Baran or Baron sometimes refers to *Ben Rabbi Nachman*, and Brock to *Ben Rabbi Kalman*. Zak, abbreviating *zera kedoshim* (the seed of martyrs), is often respelled Sack, Sacks, or Sachs, although these may also be place names for people from Saxony. Katz is sometimes based on *kohen tzedek* (priest of righteousness), and Segal (in several spellings) can be *segan leviyyah* (member of the tribe of Levi).

32   Other Jewish names are somewhat arbitrary German or Yiddish pairings, usually with pleasant connotations, like Lowenthal (lions' valley), Gottlieb (God's love), or Finkelstein (little finch stone). Some modern Swedes have replaced their conventional patronyms (Hanson, Jorgenson, etc.) with nature words or pairings of nature words, like Lind (linden), Lindstrom (linden stream), Asplund (aspen grove), or Ekberg (oak mountain).

33   Numerous Norwegian surnames are a special variety of place names called farm names. Many Norwegian farms have held the same name for hundreds of years, and people from a given farm have come to be known by its name. So Bjornstad, for instance, means *Bjorn's farm*, and Odega(a)rd means *dweller on uncultivated land*.

34   Japanese names are comparable to some of the Jewish and Swedish names mentioned a moment ago, in that they frequently combine two words, one or both of which may refer to nature. So Fujikawa combines two elements meaning *wisteria* and *river*, Hayakawa is *early, river*, Tanaka is *ricefield, middle*, Inoue is *well* (noun), *upper*, and Kawasaki is *river, headland*.

35   Chinese surnames are very few—perhaps nine or ten hundred in all—and endlessly repeated. A few dozen of them are especially widely used, like the familiar Wong, which may mean either *field* or *large body of water*, Chin (the name of the first great dynasty, of more than two thousand years ago), Wang (*yellow* or *prince*), Le (*pear tree*), and Yee (*I*).

36   The names given foundlings could readily provide material for a full chapter. Bastard as an appellation was once freely applied to foundlings or any illegitimate children even among royalty and the nobility, but today the name is opprobrious and there are few if any Bastards listed in American directories. Italian Esposito is the same as Spanish Exposita, for which the Italian spelling is generally substituted. Other Italian names suggest the blessedness or holiness of the foundling: De Benedictis, De Angelis, De Santis, and della Croce (one who lives near the cross).

37   The English Foundling Hospital authorities once conferred noble or famous names on foundlings, who thus might be named Bedford, Marlborough, Pembroke, or the like, or sometimes Geoffrey Chaucer, John Milton, Francis Bacon, Oliver Cromwell, or even Peter Paul Rubens. Some names were taken from fiction: Tom Jones, Clarissa Harlowe, Sophia Western. Other foundlings were given the names of places where they were found: e.g., Lawrence because the infant was found in St. Lawrence. A little girl in a waiting room of the Southern Railway was named Frances Southern.

38   Not more than one American surname in twenty, however, can be classified with assurance in any category other than the big four: places, patronyms, occupations, and descriptors.

Questions on Content

1. According to Hook, what is the single most important function of a person's name?

2. For many centuries in Europe, multiple names were unusual. Most people went by single names—*John* and *Eadgar* and *Alice* and *Inga*. Why did surnames finally become necessary?

3. Hook points out that the subservient position of women in the Middle Ages was reflected in the naming process. Explain why this is true.

4. Nearly all English and Continental surnames fall into one of four categories. What are they?

5. Explain the origin of the name *England.*

6. What do Japanese names have in common with Jewish and Swedish names?

Questions on Structure and Style

7. Hook discusses the origin of his own surname. What does this add to his presentation?

8. Why does Hook begin by discussing naming customs in ancient Greece and Rome and in certain African tribes?

9. Why do you think Hook wrote his book *Family Names* (from which this selection is taken)? What audience did he have in mind? Was the book designed as a reference tool or as some other type of work?

10. The selection is filled with examples. Are they confusing or interesting? Could Hook have written this selection effectively with fewer examples?

Assignments

1. In his book *Listening to America*, Stuart Berg Flexner lists these eighteen surnames as the most common in the United States:

   Smith

   Johnson

   Williamson

   Brown

   Jones

Miller

Davis

Wilson

Anderson

Taylor

Thomas

Moore

White

Martin

Thompson

Jackson

Harris

Lewis

All of these are English names, but not all the people bearing them are English. For example, many families named Smith were originally named Schmidt, Smeds, Goldsmith, or Smidnovics. Although the ethnicity of the bearers varies, not only the above-listed eighteen but also the forty most common names in the United States are English. This string is finally broken by the forty-first most common name, Cohen. This ranking is for the country as a whole, and it tells us a great deal about how the United States was settled. In many specific areas of the country, however, other names are more common, and these names provide a history of how a particular region was settled. Study the surnames in your region, and write an essay showing how they reflect its history.

2. Make a family tree for your family, tracing its history back several generations. What do the surnames tell you about your family? Write an essay discussing these names. Identify the nationalities they reflect, and tell whether the names were derived from place names, patronyms, occupations, or descriptions. (You probably won't be able to do this with every name, but gather as much information as possible. Interviewing relatives or people with the same surnames may help in difficult cases.)

A Strange Kind of Magick Bias

Justin Kaplan and Anne Bernays

History is not destiny, and our names don't control our future either. This reminder from the authors of *The Language of Names* might surprise, considering how often names give off unmistakable connotations of power or helplessness or other qualities that, of course, have no substantive connection with any person's name. However, as parents demonstrate, often unintentionally, the belief persists that names create a "magick bias" toward certain character and personality traits. That's why your brother might be Michael, but Elmo is a Muppet. But how do we explain philanthropist and community leader Ima Hogg?

■ **J O U R N A L   P R O M P T**   *Prepare a list of five first names that you like and five you do not like. Before reading this selection, think about why you listed the names you did.*

1   Much like Freud's "Anatomy is destiny," the shape and substance of a life, its varied activities and vicissitudes, are often seen as affected, if not predetermined, by a name. Carried to an extreme, those who believe that names are destiny—*"Nomen est omen"*—and interpret coincidence as magic find it unremarkable that someone named Scratch should be a dermatologist; Sleis, a butcher; Peake, a roofer; Sipper, a soft-drink magnate; Charles Hartwell Bonesteel, a military commander; Sir Ronald Brain, a neurophysiologist. Umberto Eco, eminent student of signs and symbols and author of *The Name of the Rose* and other international best-sellers, says that his surname is an acrostic derived from *"Ex caelis oblatus,"* Latin for "offered by the heavens." Like Eco, the others are all real people, not invented, but, of course, the argument doesn't account for all the similarly named people who ended up doing something quite different, and this, in turn, suggests an opposite conclusion. Names carry no more weight in governing an extended personal history than any other trait, physical or emotional, and perhaps less, although it would be gratifying to have one as apt as those just cited. It seems that, finally, so long as namers—mother, father, or both parents—remain within certain boundaries of taste, convention, common sense, and creativity, the names we end up with are what we make of them and not the other way around.

2   The names-are-destiny argument figures notably in Laurence Sterne's eighteenth-century novel *Tristram Shandy*. Tristram's father, Walter Shandy ("shandy," by the way, carries the meaning of "half-crazy") believed that "there was a strange kind of magick bias, which good or bad names, as he called them, irresistibly impressed upon our characters and conduct." "How many Caesars and Pompeys," he would say, "by mere inspiration of the names, have been rendered worthy of them? And how

13

many . . . are there, who might have done exceedingly well in the world, had not their characters and spirits been totally depressed and *Nicodemus'd* into nothing?" A child called something "neutral," like Jack, Dick, Tom, or Bob, could turn out to be either a fool or a sage, a knave or a good man. William stood "pretty high"; Andrew was "like a negative quality in Algebra"; while "of all the names in the universe, he had the most unconquerable aversion for Tristram . . . unison to *Nincompoop*." If you named the child Judas (or Iago or Adolf), in all probability, "the sordid and treacherous idea, so inseparable from the name, would have accompanied him through life like his shadow, and, in the end, made a miser and a rascal of him."

3   Father Shandy's argument holds a certain amount of water, especially for parents looking beyond the cradle into the future of their offspring. Your name is not necessarily your fate, but it's something you've got to live with all the same, just as Shandy's son, Tristram, had to live with a name a father loathed but for some "malignant" and perverse reason foisted on the infant.

4   In line with these general principles about "magick bias," a group of British psychologists asked their subjects to rank a list of first names by positive and negative traits. The consensus was: John is trustworthy and kind; Robin, young (as in A. A. Milne's Christopher Robin, "forever young"); Tony, sociable; Ann, nonaggressive; Agnes, old (as in David Copperfield's prudent, grave, and sisterly second wife, Agnes Wickfield); Matilda, definitely unattractive. Other studies put Michael, James, and Wendy in the active category; Afreda, Percival, and Isadore in the passive category.

5   Without thinking about it, many people are convinced that first names send out fervid, compressed messages: "Watch out for me," "Come closer," "Vote for me," "Buy my product," "Marry me," "Call the cops." Daily soap operas on television in particular rely on this primitive antenna system. The systematic study of names used in television dramas is relatively new; its results reinforce this unnuanced reading of the language of names. Until very recently soap operas rigidly upheld the prevailing social order and gender roles. For instance, a "bad" woman's true character is signaled by the fact that her name has been masculinized, so that thoroughly rotten Phyllis becomes Phil; Jacqueline, Jackie; and Martha, Marty. The reasoning goes that these women, having challenged society's basic and enduring values by parading around in men's (nick)names, are more likely to turn to crime and misdemeanor than those content with their pretty girls' names.

6   One 1992 study of names in television administered a questionnaire to about two hundred undergraduates at SUNY–Stony Brook. They were asked to match character traits with names of characters in soap operas that had been aired some years earlier (in order to reduce the possibility that memory would influence the answers). Here are two of the questions:

1. Which of the following is the most educated?
   a. Andrea Wolcot
   b. Kathy Brannon
   c. Ruby Daniel
   d. Elisa Asler

2. If you wanted to have a character who was a preppie, young, blond high school girl who was the only daughter of well-to-do parents and who was slightly spoiled, which of the following would you name her?
   a. Lillian McNeal
   b. Marina Sheldon
  —c. Kimberly Channing
   d. Karen Coleman

7   *The answers.* To the first question: Andrea Wolcot, doctor and radical feminist, was the most educated; Kathy and Elisa were waitresses; Ruby, a black jazz singer. To the second question: Kimberly Channing was the correct choice; Lillian was married to a New York cop; Marina was a gypsy con woman; while Karen was the widow of a rich pharmaceutical manufacturer. Among other television characters, those who have achieved financial success had fancy names like Avery, Bret, and Andrea. Bumblers and stumblers along life's pathways were apt to have cropped names like Ken, John, and Joe. Israel Sanchez (what do you get when you marry a Jew and a Latino?) turned up murdered. Stanley Nitski was a criminal, as was Clyde Regan. Jewish-sounding names were often given to people who commit crimes or are, at the very least, sleazy. Writers for television count on a basic transaction in which viewers pick up on such subliminal clues as the connection between "inappropriate" names and unacceptable behavior.

8   In 1965 an enterprising sorehead named Harvey Edwards somehow managed to organize 150 other Harveys to protest a series of television commercials featuring a klutz named Harvey who was always ankle deep in soapy water, having failed to operate the washing machine properly. These 150 Harveys hassled sponsors and advertising agencies into bagging the offensive commercials. The people who had given top billing to a loser named Harvey were at the very least subliminally aware that certain names give off a disagreeable odor, as if a cat had peed in the hallway. Harvey not only isn't as robust as, say, Robert, Sebastian, or William but brings to mind the mild-mannered rabbit—imaginary playmate to a hopeless drunk—in Mary C. Chase's 1944 play. It would probably take a famous Harvey with the personality of General George S. Patton, Jr., to alter the psychic image most of us form when we hear the name Harvey.

9   Some years ago researchers in Chicago discovered that about half the men in prison referred by the courts for psychiatric evaluation had peculiar names like Oder and Lethal. (Add to this list Sid Vicious of the Sex Pistols, the rocker who stabbed his female companion to death in Room 100 of New York's Chelsea Hotel.) Comparably, it's been argued that children with unpopular names turn out to be unpopular in school. It's reasonable to question, however, which first gave rise to the unpopularity—Bertha's name or her habit of wiping her runny nose on her sleeve, Homer's name or his tendency to snitch on his classmates. A group of grade school teachers, asked to grade essays turned out by students identified only by a first name, gave high marks to Karen, Lisa, David, and Michael (for almost the last fifty years the most popular boy's name in the United States, perhaps because "it goes with everything") and low marks to Elmer, Adele, Bertha, and Hubert, all of the latter deemed to be losers' names. But

what about the children with rare, strange, or funny names who were popular with their schoolmates, favored by their teachers, and went on to notable careers? What about Senator, Vice President, and presidential candidate Hubert Horatio Humphrey (whom Jimmy Carter once introduced as Hubert Horatio Hornblower, confusing him with C. S. Forester's fictional hero)? What about the Pulitzer Prize–winning playwright Elmer Rice (né Reizenstein) and other men and women with "funny" first names who became eminent citizens or at least made a pile of money?

10   If it were possible to leach all meaning from a name, you would be left with pure sound—the smile of the Cheshire Cat. Sounds can be soft or sharp, protracted or brusque. They can be equally or unequally stressed. They can roll along merrily or wobble like a flat tire. All of this feeds into the ear's reaction to a name, some of it conscious, the rest under water. Although the heroine of one of his major poems is "the lovely lady Christabel," Samuel Taylor Coleridge thought girls ought to be given two-syllable trochaic names, that is, accented on the first syllable, as in Laura, Doris, Emma (he named his only daughter Sara). Other name fanciers prefer the iamb, accented on the second syllable: Annette, Maureen. Then there are the advocates of the trisyllabic, with the accent on the first syllable, as in Abigail and Eleanor. Each kind of sound has its supporters, but it's silly to worry about a first name without considering what comes after it. Ideally, first and last names should meet and marry to create a strong, supple, melodic line. If your last name is a monosyllable like Jones and you can't do anything about it short of changing it, you probably ought to give your child a longer, more fluid first name, like Jeremy for a boy, Margaret or Elizabeth for a girl.

11   Fashions differ from region to region in the United States, but if one were to arrive at a national consensus (based on 1994–1995 figures) of the most popular boys' and girls' names for whites, blacks, Hispanics, and Asians together, it would read roughly like this, with the rankings varying somewhat by region:

Boys

Michael (number one since about 1960): Hebrew, "Who is like God?"

Kevin: Gaelic, diminutive of "comely, beloved." In 1994–1995 the most popular name for Hispanic boys in New York City and for Asian boys there and in San Francisco and Florida.

Christopher: Greek, "bearing Christ."

Joshua: Hebrew, "God is salvation."

Matthew: Hebrew, "gift of God."

Brandon: Old English, "gorse hill."

Andrew: Greek, after one of the twelve apostles.

Girls

Ashley: Old English, "ash" plus "wood." In 1994–1995 the most popular name for all girls in New York City, Texas, and Florida.

Stephanie: French, feminine form of Stephen.

Brittany: Latin, "Britain."

Jessica: Hebrew, "Iscah" (Abraham's niece).

Amanda: Latin, "worthy of being loved."

Sarah: Hebrew, "princess."

Emily: Latin, probably from *aemulus*, "rival."

Over the past twenty-five years, Jeffrey and Jennifer have suffered the steepest declines in popularity.

12   A patient of Dr. Oliver Sacks, Carl Bennett, suffered from Tourette's syndrome, a condition in which the victim is compelled, through some neurological anomaly, to repeat words (often obscene or offensive) over and over again, to his or her public embarrassment. Bennett craved new sounds to sing out, especially names, the way a child craves sweets, and he called his list of more than two hundred real names of real people "candy for the mind." Among the earliest entries were Oginga Odinga and Slavek J. Hurka. He insisted that the names he repeated in his fits of echolalia were meaningless; he was attracted to them only for their sound: Boris Blank, Floyd Flake, Morris Gook, Lubor J. Zink were among his short, staccato favorites. Yelberton A. Tittle and Babaloo Mandel were more complicated and, Sacks wrote, marked by "euphonious polysyllabic alliterations." Echolaling might not be a bad idea for parents trying out names for their offspring.

13   The comical name of Ima Hogg (1882–1975), philanthropist and community leader, has generated two virtually unkillable stories: one, that she had a sister, Ura (not true—she had no sister, and her brothers had ordinary names: William, Michael, Thomas); and two, that her father, Texas governor James Stephen Hogg, named her Ima Hogg so she wouldn't be vain about her looks (also not true: Ima was the heroine of an epic poem written by one of her uncles). Ima and Ura Hogg, meanwhile, continue to keep company with Ophelia Butt, I. Seymour Hare, I. P. Daly, Claude Balls, and such jokey phantoms.

14   Some parents, like Ima Hogg's father, are oblivious to secondary meanings or simply have tin ears and can't tell the difference between sounds that sing and those that squeak like chalk on a blackboard or thud like a ripe tomato landing on the kitchen floor: Stanley Conley and Martin Hensen, for example, are like dissonances in music or bad off-rhymes. The ear tends to be vexed but also captivated by names composed of two monosyllables. Sean Penn, James Joyce, Hale Boggs, James Bond, John Wayne—these work quite well, but possibly the best-worst name ever in this category is Shane Stant; he was the youth hired by the husband of skater Tanya Harding to break the kneecap of her rival on ice, Nancy Kerrigan.

Irony?

15   Before you name your child, it's a good idea to view your options from implausible as well as expected angles. Will his or her initials create a funny acronym, like Francis Albert Gilman's? As soon as his classmates learn to read, they'll figure it out and know what to call him. Or Barbara Upshaw Grasso? Once there was a young American boy whose first two names were John Thomas. When his family moved briefly to Australia, he came home from school every day in tears. What his parents

didn't know was that John Thomas is British and Australian slang for penis. Someone should have told them to read *Lady Chatterley's Lover* before they took off for down under.

<table>
<tr><td>

**Questions
on Content**

</td><td>

1. Discuss the appropriateness of the title of this selection. Where does the reader learn of its meaning?

2. The authors point out that "many people are convinced that first names send out fervid, compressed messages" (paragraph 5). Do you agree? Support your response with concrete examples.

3. Kaplan and Bernays assert that "Ideally, first and last names should meet and marry to create a strong, supple, melodic line" (paragraph 10). Explain. Use this assertion as a standard to evaluate your own name as well as selected names of friends and family members.

</td></tr>
</table>

Questions on Structure and Style

4. Do Kaplan and Bernays believe there is a "strange kind of magick bias" to names? Demonstrate how the authors do or do not reveal their bias.

5. The authors employ many concrete and diverse examples in this selection. Discuss the purpose and effectiveness of these examples.

6. Describe the structure of paragraph 12. What does this structure illustrate about paragraph development and coherence?

Assignments

1. Examine the two lists of names you prepared for the Journal Prompt. Assume the role of one of the authors, and write a letter to yourself in which you discuss and explain the names appearing on your lists.

2. Using examples of names with which you are familiar, write a response to one of the following:

    A. "The names we end up with are what we make of them and not the other way around" (paragraph 1).
    B. "Writers for television count on a basic transaction in which viewers pick up on such subliminal clues as the connection between 'inappropriate' names and unacceptable behavior" (paragraph 7).

C. "Echolaling might not be a bad idea for parents trying out names for their offspring" (paragraph 12).

3. To highlight the connotations certain names can carry for many people, match each name below with the "most appropriate" description.

Floyd	cheerleader
Emily	doctor
Florence	steelworker
Bobbi	accountant
Robert	child genius
Theodore	librarian
Bertha	farmer
Katherine	hairdresser
Bruno	overweight cook
Morris	nurse

Of course, there are no right or wrong answers, but compare your choices with those of your classmates. How much variation do you see?

from I Know Why the Caged Bird Sings

Maya Angelou

The power to name implies the power to control, but most of us have little firsthand experience with this aspect of names. In the following excerpt from the first volume of her autobiography, Maya Angelou details a clash of wills that centered on her name. As she reminds us, our names do not merely identify us; instead we believe they summarize who we are. We maintain our dignity in part by maintaining control over our own names. Angelou is a poet and actress who has been widely honored for her many accomplishments, including her contributions to the civil rights movement and her work as producer of a television series for Public Broadcasting.

■ **J O U R N A L   P R O M P T** *Think about the power of names. How much control comes with the power to name? How strong is the relationship between a person and his or her name? To what degree are we defined by our names?*

1   Recently a white woman from Texas, who would quickly describe herself as a liberal, asked me about my hometown. When I told her that in Stamps my grandmother had owned the only Negro general merchandise store since the turn of the century, she exclaimed, "Why, you were a debutante." Ridiculous and even ludicrous. But Negro girls in small Southern towns, whether poverty-stricken or just munching along on a few of life's necessities, were given as extensive and irrelevant preparations for adulthood as rich white girls shown in magazines. Admittedly the training was not the same. While white girls learned to waltz and sit gracefully with a tea cup balanced on their knees, we were lagging behind, learning the mid-Victorian values with very little money to indulge them. (Come and see Edna Lomax spending the money she made picking cotton on five balls of ecru tatting thread. Her fingers are bound to snag the work and she'll have to repeat the stitches time and time again. But she knows that when she buys the thread.)

2   We were required to embroider and I had trunkfuls of colorful dishtowels, pillowcases, runners and handkerchiefs to my credit. I mastered the art of crocheting and tatting, and there was a lifetime's supply of dainty doilies that would never be used in sacheted dresser drawers. It went without saying that all girls could iron and wash, but the finer touches around the home, like setting a table with real silver, baking roasts and cooking vegetables without meat, had to be learned elsewhere. Usually at the source of those habits. During my tenth year, a white woman's kitchen became my finishing school.

3   Mrs. Viola Cullinan was a plump woman who lived in a three-bedroom house somewhere behind the post office. She was singularly unattractive until she smiled,

and the lines around her eyes and mouth which made her look perpetually dirty disappeared, and her face looked like the mask of an impish elf. She usually rested her smile until late afternoon when her women friends dropped in and Miss Glory, the cook, served them cold drinks on the closed-in porch.

4   The exactness of her house was inhuman. This glass went here and only here. That cup had its place and it was an act of impudent rebellion to place it anywhere else. At twelve o'clock the table was set. At 12:15 Mrs. Cullinan sat down to dinner (whether her husband had arrived or not). At 12:16 Miss Glory brought out the food.

5   It took me a week to learn the difference between a salad plate, a bread plate and a dessert plate.

6   Mrs. Cullinan kept up the tradition of her wealthy parents. She was from Virginia. Miss Glory, who was a descendant of slaves that had worked for the Cullinans, told me her history. She had married beneath her (according to Miss Glory). Her husband's family hadn't had their money very long and what they had "didn't 'mount to much."

7   As ugly as she was, I thought privately, she was lucky to get a husband above or beneath her station. But Miss Glory wouldn't let me say a thing against her mistress. She was very patient with me, however, over the housework. She explained the dishware, silverware and servants' bells.

8   The large round bowl in which soup was served wasn't a soup bowl, it was a tureen. There were goblets, sherbet glasses, ice-cream glasses, wine glasses, green glass coffee cups with matching saucers, and water glasses. I had a glass to drink from, and it sat with Miss Glory's on a separate shelf from the others. Soup spoons, gravy boat, butter knives, salad forks and carving platter were additions to my vocabulary and in fact almost represented a new language. I was fascinated with the novelty, with the fluttering Mrs. Cullinan and her Alice-in-Wonderland house.

9   Her husband remains, in my memory, undefined. I lumped him with all the other white men that I had ever seen and tried not to see.

10   On our way home one evening, Miss Glory told me that Mrs. Cullinan couldn't have children. She said that she was too delicate-boned. It was hard to imagine bones at all under those layers of fat. Miss Glory went on to say that the doctor had taken out all her lady organs. I reasoned that a pig's organs included the lungs, heart and liver, so if Mrs. Cullinan was walking around without those essentials, it explained why she drank alcohol out of unmarked bottles. She was keeping herself embalmed.

11   When I spoke to Bailey about it, he agreed that I was right, but he also informed me that Mr. Cullinan had two daughters by a colored lady and that I knew them very well. He added that the girls were the spitting image of their father. I was unable to remember what he looked like, although I had just left him a few hours before, but I thought of the Coleman girls. They were very light-skinned and certainly didn't look very much like their mother (no one ever mentioned Mr. Coleman).

12   My pity for Mrs. Cullinan preceded me the next morning like the Cheshire cat's smile. Those girls, who could have been her daughters, were beautiful. They didn't have to straighten their hair. Even when they were caught in the rain, their braids still

hung down straight like tamed snakes. Their mouths were pouty little cupid's bows. Mrs. Cullinan didn't know what she missed. Or maybe she did. Poor Mrs. Cullinan.

13 For weeks after, I arrived early, left late and tried very hard to make up for her barrenness. If she had had her own children, she wouldn't have had to ask me to run a thousand errands from her back door to the back door of her friends. Poor old Mrs. Cullinan.

14 Then one evening Miss Glory told me to serve the ladies on the porch. After I set the tray down and turned toward the kitchen, one of the women asked, "What's your name, girl?" It was the speckled-faced one. Mrs. Cullinan said, "She doesn't talk much. Her name's Margaret."

15 "Is she dumb?"

16 "No. As I understand it, she can talk when she wants to but she's usually quiet as a little mouse. Aren't you, Margaret?"

17 I smiled at her. Poor thing. No organs and couldn't even pronounce my name correctly.

18 "She's a sweet little thing, though."

19 "Well, that may be, but the name's too long. I'd never bother myself. I'd call her Mary if I was you."

20 I fumed into the kitchen. That horrible woman would never have the chance to call me Mary because if I was starving I'd never work for her. I decided I wouldn't pee on her if her heart was on fire. Giggles drifted in off the porch and into Miss Glory's pots. I wondered what they could be laughing about.

21 Whitefolks were so strange. Could they be talking about me? Everybody knew that they stuck together better than the Negroes did. It was possible that Mrs. Cullinan had friends in St. Louis who heard about a girl from Stamps being in court and wrote to tell her. Maybe she knew about Mr. Freeman.

22 My lunch was in my mouth a second time and I went outside and relieved myself on the bed of four-o'clocks. Miss Glory thought I might be coming down with something and told me to go on home, that Momma would give me some herb tea, and she'd explain to her mistress.

23 I realized how foolish I was being before I reached the pond. Of course Mrs. Cullinan didn't know. Otherwise she wouldn't have given me the two nice dresses that Momma cut down, and she certainly wouldn't have called me a "sweet little thing." My stomach felt fine, and I didn't mention anything to Momma.

24 That evening I decided to write a poem on being white, fat, old and without children. It was going to be a tragic ballad. I would have to watch her carefully to capture the essence of her loneliness and pain.

25 The very next day, she called me by the wrong name. Miss Glory and I were washing up the lunch dishes when Mrs. Cullinan came to the doorway. "Mary?"

26 Miss Glory asked, "Who?"

27 Mrs. Cullinan, sagging a little, knew and I knew. "I want Mary to go down to Mrs. Randall's and take her some soup. She's not been feeling well for a few days."

28 Miss Glory's face was a wonder to see. "You mean Margaret, ma'am. Her name's Margaret."

29   "That's too long. She's Mary from now on. Heat that soup from last night and put it in the china tureen and, Mary, I want you to carry it carefully."

30   Every person I knew had a hellish horror of being "called out of his name." It was a dangerous practice to call a Negro anything that could be loosely construed as insulting because of the centuries of their having been called niggers, jigs, dinges, blackbirds, crows, boots and spooks.

31   Miss Glory had a fleeting second of feeling sorry for me. Then as she handed me the hot tureen she said, "Don't mind, don't pay that no mind. Sticks and stones may break your bones, but words . . . You know, I been working for her for twenty years."

32   She held the back door open for me. "Twenty years. I wasn't much older than you. My name used to be Hallelujah. That's what Ma named me, but my mistress give me 'Glory,' and it stuck. I likes it better too."

33   I was in the little path that ran behind the houses when Miss Glory shouted, "It's shorter too."

34   For a few seconds it was a tossup over whether I would laugh (imagine being named Hallelujah) or cry (imagine letting some white woman rename you for her convenience). My anger saved me from either outburst. I had to quit the job, but the problem was going to be how to do it. Momma wouldn't allow me to quit for just any reason.

35   "She's a peach. That woman is a real peach." Mrs. Randall's maid was talking as she took the soup from me, and I wondered what her name used to be and what she answered to now.

36   For a week I looked into Mrs. Cullinan's face as she called me Mary. She ignored my coming late and leaving early. Miss Glory was a little annoyed because I had begun to leave egg yolk on the dishes and wasn't putting much heart in polishing the silver. I hoped that she would complain to our boss, but she didn't.

37   Then Bailey solved my dilemma. He had me describe the contents of the cupboard and the particular plates she liked best. Her favorite piece was a casserole shaped like a fish and the green glass coffee cups. I kept his instructions in mind, so on the next day when Miss Glory was hanging out clothes and I had again been told to serve the old biddies on the porch, I dropped the empty serving tray. When I heard Mrs. Cullinan scream, "Mary!" I picked up the casserole and two of the green glass cups in readiness. As she rounded the kitchen door I let them fall on the tiled floor.

38   I could never absolutely describe to Bailey what happened next, because each time I got to the part where she fell on the floor and screwed up her ugly face to cry, we burst out laughing. She actually wobbled around on the floor and picked up shards of the cups and cried, "Oh, Momma. Oh, dear Gawd. It's Momma's china from Virginia. Oh, Momma, I sorry."

39   Miss Glory came running in from the yard and the women from the porch crowded around. Miss Glory was almost as broken up as her mistress. "You mean to say she broke our Virginia dishes? What we gone do?"

40   Mrs. Cullinan cried louder, "That clumsy nigger. Clumsy little black nigger."

41   Old speckled-face leaned down and asked, "Who did it, Viola? Was it Mary? Who did it?"

42   Everything was happening so fast I can't remember whether her action preceded her words, but I know that Mrs. Cullinan said, "Her name's Margaret, goddamn it, her name's Margaret!" And she threw a wedge of the broken plate at me. It could have been the hysteria which put her aim off, but the flying crockery caught Miss Glory right over her ear and she started screaming.

43   I left the front door wide open so all the neighbors could hear.

44   Mrs. Cullinan was right about one thing. My name wasn't Mary.

Questions on Content

1. Angelou says that Negro girls in small Southern towns were given "extensive and irrelevant preparations for adulthood" (paragraph 1). What does she mean?

2. Why does Angelou refer to Mrs. Cullinan's kitchen as her finishing school?

3. What is Miss Glory's relationship to Mrs. Cullinan? What does she tell Margaret about Mrs. Cullinan?

4. What is Miss Glory's given name? Compare her reaction to being renamed with Margaret's reaction. Why does Mrs. Cullinan decide to call Margaret Mary?

5. What information does Bailey share with his sister about Mrs. Cullinan? What does he suggest Margaret do to get even with her employer?

6. How well does Margaret know Mrs. Cullinan's husband?

7. Why does Mrs. Cullinan call Margaret by her correct name near the end of the selection?

Questions on Structure and Style

8. Angelou often uses the pronoun *we* rather than *I* at the opening of this autobiographical selection. What is her purpose in doing so?

9. Paragraphs 5 and 9 are among several unusually short paragraphs. What do the short paragraphs contribute to the author's purpose?

10. Although this selection is a chapter from Angelou's autobiographical book *I Know Why the Caged Bird Sings*, it reads like an independent and unified piece. Discuss how the structure of this selection helps to unify it.

Assignments   1. The concise yet vivid description of Mrs. Viola Cullinan in paragraph 3 leaves no doubt about the author's opinion. Examine Angelou's use of detail and tone, and then write a paragraph of your own in which you show (and don't merely tell about) strong feelings you have about an individual.

2. Margaret says, "Every person I knew had a hellish horror of being 'called out of his name' " (paragraph 30). Do you feel the same way? If so, what does this say about the importance of names? Write a short and concrete essay in response to Margaret's statement.

Just Call Me Mister

David Frum

In an era that glorifies informality, our first names have become public property, used by any stranger of any age when addressing us. What then does the world make of the resolutely "Mister" Frum, who believes that "it's not friendliness that drives first-namers; it's aggression"? As David Frum emphasizes, the way that we address others reflects relative power and status. The old rules favoring more reserved forms of address certainly do appear obsolete today, and Frum here speculates, with reasonable grumpiness, on why. Frum is law editor of *Forbes* magazine.

■ **JOURNAL PROMPT** *Describe the way that you address adults who are friends as well as adults who are strangers. What criteria do you use to determine whether to use first names or the more formal Mr., Mrs., Miss, or Ms.?*

1   On cold or wet days, middle-class Manhattanites take their children to Playspace, an old tenement building packed full of wonderful climbing and sliding contraptions. There's just one irritating detail: When you arrive at the wicket to pay your money, the girl pulls out a big felt marker and an adhesive lapel tag, and asks you your name.

2   "Frum," I say.

3   "No, your first name."

4   "What do you need my first name for?"

5   "I'm going to write it on the tag, so that if any of the other children or any of the staff members need to speak to you, they know what to call you."

6   "In that case, write 'Mr. Frum.'"

7   At which I am shot a look as if I had asked to be called the Duke of Plaza Toro.

8   In encouraging five-year-olds to address grown-ups by their first names, Playspace is only very slightly ahead of the times. As a journalist, I speak to dozens of total strangers on the telephone every day. I can faithfully report that the custom of addressing strangers formally is as dead as the carte de visite. There's hardly a secretary or receptionist left on the continent who does not reply when she's given a message for her boss, "I'll tell him you called, David," or a PR agent from Bangor to Bangkok who does not begin his telephonic spiel with a cheerful, "Hello David!"

9   This is true not only of telephone callers, but of letter writers too. Yesterday morning's mail brought a letter from a neighborhood chiropractor drumming up business. It begins, "Dear David . . ." . . . Here's a letter from the lady in charge of public relations at one of the largest banks in the United States. "Dear Dave," it starts. I like that even less.

10   You don't have to be a journalist to collect amazing first-name stories. Place a collect call, and the operator first-names you. A 78-year-old man who buys a hamburger at Lick's will be first-named by the teenager behind the counter.

11   Habitual first-namers claim they are motivated by nothing worse than uncontrollably exuberant friendliness. I don't believe it. If I asked the order-takers at Lick's to lend me $50, their friendliness would vanish in a whoosh. The PR-man drops all his cheerfulness the moment he hears I can't use his story idea. No, it's not friendliness that drives first-namers: it's aggression.

12   A little history. Until comparatively recently, the title "Mr." was reserved for people of a certain station in life. Think of Jane Austen's novels: the landlord is Mr. Knightley, but even the most prosperous of his tenant farmers was referred to by last name alone. Now think of a movie from the 1930s. *Everybody* is addressed as "Mr.," even the very poorest people—because everyone is entitled to be treated with respect.

13   Over the past two or three decades, we have reverted from the etiquette of the 1930s to that of the 18th century. The PR agents who call me "David" uninvited would never, if they could somehow get him on the phone, address Rupert Murdoch that way. The lady from the bank would never first-name the bank's chairman. Like the mock-cheery staff at Playspace, they are engaged in a smiley-faced act of belittlement, in an assertion of power disguised as bonhomie.

14   Precisely because it is disguised as bonhomie, though, most people have trouble objecting to first-naming, even when it bothers them. First-namers make it unmistakably clear they regard anyone who objects to the practice as unspeakably stuffy. And nobody wants to be thought stuffy.

15   But why not? Stuffiness is an excessive regard for one's dignity, and excess is relative. In a world where too many people behave with zero dignity, anyone who wants what would once have been considered a very ordinary ration will naturally seem stuffy in comparison. Oprah Winfrey thinks it's stuffy when politicians don't want to discuss their drinking problems on camera. *Playboy* thinks it's stuffy when an actress won't pose nude. At Playspace, they think it's stuffy of me not to want to be called "David" by my daughter's playmates. . . . To the boorish, self-respect will always seem stuffy. But why should the boors be permitted to make the rules?

**Questions
on Content**

1. Describe a few of the circumstances in which Frum objects to being called by his first name. Do you agree with his reasoning, or do you, in fact, feel his is "stuffy"?

2. Frum suggests that "first-namers" are driven by aggression, not friendliness, and a desire for power, not good cheer. Do you agree? Be prepared to defend your response.

**Questions
on Structure
and Style**

3. Discuss how Frum uses references to Playspace to provide structure as well as content in this selection.

4. Describe the tone of Frum's prose. Provide specific examples of diction and syntax that demonstrate his tone.

5. What is Frum's thesis? Is it implied or directly stated?

Assignments   1. Assume the role of a secretary who has called Mr. Frum by his first name. Also assume you read this selection after having called him David. Write a letter to Frum in which you justify being a "first-namer."

2. You have been selected to contribute to an etiquette manual designed to help individuals adjust to your culture. You are assigned to write the section on when to address adults and strangers by their first names and when to address them formally. Use concrete examples from this selection and from your personal experiences to justify your response.

Putting American English on the Map

W. F. Bolton

What happens when "a whole new nation . . . composed of literally millions of places—states, counties, cities and towns, rivers, mountains, even swamps—. . . [awaits] new names from its new inhabitants"? W. F. Bolton, a writer and philologist at Rutgers University, answers this question with wit and scholarship, concluding that place names are a major factor in defining the linguistic character of our nation. For Bolton, toponymics, the study of place names, is essential to a grasp of American English.

■ **JOURNAL PROMPT** *The history of a place or region can often be revealed by its place names. What do the place names in your neighborhood, room, or region reveal about its history?*

1   American English came of age in the nineteenth century when it accomplished the naming of places and naming of persons. For while the name for a native American plant or animal may be distinctive, it is usually no more so than its referent, and often rather less. The change of meaning for an ancient English word such as *robin*, for example, adds nothing to the resources of the vocabulary, although it does adjust them a trifle. Even the outright borrowing of a word like *boss* from a foreign language is only a minuscule addition. Most important of all, such adjustment or addition takes place unsystematically and anonymously.

2   But when a whole new nation, and a huge one at that, is composed of literally millions of places—states, counties, cities and towns, rivers, mountains, even swamps— all awaiting new names from its new inhabitants, then the consequence, whatever else it is, will be of equally huge importance in defining the linguistic character of the nation. So the study of toponymics—placenames—is essential to a grasp of American English.

3   When, furthermore, the nation's new inhabitants arrive in their millions from hundreds of other nations, and become parents in their new country to hundreds of millions more new inhabitants, then the patterns of personal name giving that they develop here are hundreds of millions of times more significant than the designation of an unfamiliar bird as a *robin*. So the study of onomastics—personal names—like the study of toponymics assumes an importance to be measured by nothing less than the nation into which America grew during the nineteenth century.

Names of Places

4   Twenty-seven of the fifty United States—over half—have names of native American origin. Eleven of the others have names that come from personal names; five are

29

named after other places; five are from common words in Spanish or French; and two are from common words in English. These five categories (native words, personal names, other placenames, common words in other European languages, and common words in English) account for most other American placenames as well, although not always in the same proportions.

5   The state names based on native words range from *Alabama* and *Alaska* to *Wisconsin* and *Wyoming*. They include the names of tribes (*Arkansas, Dakota*), descriptions (*Mississippi*, "big river"; *Alaska*, "mainland"), and words of long-lost meaning (*Hawaii, Idaho*). Many of them are now very far from the form they had in the native language, and some seem to be simply a mistake. The native *Mescousing* or *Mesconsing*, of uncertain meaning, was written *Ouisconsing* by the French who first heard it, and *Wisconsin* by the English. One map had the French form misspelled as *Ouariconsint* and broke the word before the last syllable, so a reader who did not notice the *sint* on the line below would take the name—here of the river—to be *Ouaricon*. At length, that became *Oregon*. The Spanish heard the Papago word *Arizonac* (little spring) as *Arizona*; Spanish and American alike now think it is from the Spanish for "arid zone."

6   The confusion is not surprising. The native Americans themselves often did not know what the placenames meant because the names had been around since time out of memory, perhaps given by a tribe that had long ago disappeared, taking its language and leaving the names. Many placenames were invented on the spot for the benefit of curious white settlers where the native Americans lacked a name; that was especially true of large features in the landscape like mountains. When a Choctaw chief was asked the name of his territory, he replied with the words for "red people"—*Oklahoma*. The names were transcribed in so many different forms that it is usually sheer accident, and often unhelpful, that one has survived as the "official" form rather than another. Delaware *Susquehanna* (a tribal name) became something quite indecipherable in Huron, from which the French got their version *Andastoei*; the English made this *Conestoga* (ultimate source of the name *Conestoga wagon*) and used the word to name a branch of the Susquehanna River, a toponymic variant of the "I'm my own grandpa" song. And careful study of native American languages did not begin until long after many of these names had become settled—indeed until many of the native speakers too had become settled in six feet of earth and were beyond unraveling the placename mysteries they had left behind. Maybe that is just as well, at least for delicate readers; native Americans had a vocabulary rich in abusive terms, and they were not above using them as a joke when a white inquired the name of a local river or neighboring tribe.

7   All that is true of state names from native sources is also true of other such placenames. *Chicago* appears to mean "the place of strong smells," but exactly *which* strong smells is not clear. *Mohawk* is a familiar name, but its derivation—apparently from the Iroquois for "bear"—is obscured by its early spellings in no fewer than 142 different forms, the most authentic seeming to be something like *mahaqua*. A single expedition might bring back many new names—the Frenchmen Joliet and Marquette, for example, brought back *Wisconsin, Peoria, Des Moines, Missouri, Osage, Omaha, Kansas, Iowa, Wabash*, and *Arkansas*. The story of *Des Moines* is

typical. The Frenchmen found a tribe, the Moingouena, who lived on a river. It was the explorers who named the river Rivière des Moinguoenas and later shortened it to Rivière des Moings. Now *moines* is "monks" in French, so by folk etymology *des Moings*, which is nothing in particular, became *des Moines*, which is at least something. But the French pronunciation /de mwan/ is far from what an American makes of the spelling *Des Moines*, and so we have /də mɔin/. It is a long way from the Moingouena tribe—too long for us to trace by the normal process of historical reconstruction back through Americanization, folk etymology, shortening, and the European transfer of a tribal name to a river, if we did not have the documents to help us. In most other cases, we do not have the documents, and the native names speak in a lost language.

8   Many of the earlier native placenames became disused among the descendants of the settlers who adopted them: *Powhatan's River* became the *James*, the *Agiochook Mountains* became the *White Mountains*. Fashion in these matters followed the fashion in the native Americans' prestige, some whites thinking them fine in an exotic and primitive way, others scorning them as crude and even barbaric. Frontier people were often among the latter, people in the settled regions among the former; but of course the frontier turned into the settled region, which sometimes brought about a return to a native name or the imposition of a new one. In New England, *Agawam* became *Ipswich* (after the English town), and later *Agawam* again. The names settlers chose were not always tribally appropriate; unlike the frontier people, settlers were insensitive to the differences among tribes about whom they knew next to nothing anyway, so that—for example—the name of a Florida chief would be given to some seventeen places, many of them far from his Florida habitat.

9   The vogue for native American placenames was supported by literary models like Longfellow's *Hiawatha*. But the native names did not always meet the demands of American literary taste or English poetic forms, and when they clashed it was the placenames that were reworked. As a result, the "beauty" of such names is sometimes in the pen of the poet and not on the lip of the native speaker. The same is true of translations: *Minnesota* is approximately "muddy river," but *muddy* could also be "cloudy," and skies are "cloudy" too. Clouds pass, skies remain, and what have you? *Minnesota* translated as "the sky-blue water." The nineteenth-century American fad for native placenames falsified the native American words in both form and meaning, and often imposed a native name where none had been before. Ironically, the travestied native name is often more recent than the English or other European placenames it replaced.

10   Native American names in their least native American form appear not only in places like *Indian Bottom, Indian Creek, Indian Harbour, Indian Head, Indian Lake, Indian Peak, Indian River*, but also *Cherokee River, Cherokee Strip, Chippewa River* (two), *Chippewa Village, Chippewa County* (three), *Chippewa Falls*, and *Chippewa Lake*.

Placenames from Personal Names and Other Words

11   The states named after persons stretch from *Pennsylvania* (after William Penn, the English Quaker who founded it) in the east to *Washington* (after George Washington) in the west. Three were named after one royal couple: Charles I named the two

Carolinas after himself (Latin *Carolus* means Charles), and *Maryland* after his wife, Queen Henrietta Maria. Queen Elizabeth I named *Virginia* both after herself (the virgin queen) and after the New World (the virgin land); *West Virginia* followed naturally. Other royal names remain in *Georgia* (King George II of England) and *Louisiana* (King Louis XIV of France). The governor, Lord de la Warr, supplied the name for *Delaware*. Just as *Arizona* seems to stem from the Spanish for "arid zone," so *California* seems to represent the Spanish for "hot oven." It figures. It figures, but it is wrong. When Cortés came to the place around 1530, he thought he had found a legendary land entirely peopled by women—his soldiers must have loved that—teeming in gold and jewels and ruled by the fabled Queen Calafia. He named it, accordingly, *California*, and California, accordingly, is a state named after a person.

12   The Americanization of placenames involves not only folk etymology, translation, and loan translation, but the distinctive rendition of words pronounced quite differently elsewhere. To English ears our pronunciation of *Birmingham* (Alabama) may or may not contain a giveaway /r/, depending on the regional dialect of the American who says it. If he is from the place itself, the /r/ will probably be absent, as it is in England. But almost any American will make the last syllable much more distinct than would an English resident of Birmingham (England), where the last three letters get no more than a syllabic [m]. This tendency is also observable in the local pronunciation of a place like *Norwich* (NJ), approximately "nor witch"; in England the place of the same name rhymes with "porridge." The tendency is not always present in common nouns, however; for example, the noun *record* is pronounced with two distinct syllables in Britain but not in America. The careful spelling-pronunciation seems to be a consistent Americanism only when it comes to placenames.

13   If the placename is not an English one, American pronunciation will vary even more. We have already seen that many native American placenames changed beyond all recognition in the white settlers' vocal apparatus. The same is often true of names from European languages other than English. *Los Angeles* is a notorious case—the common pronunciation contains several sounds not in Spanish, and the first word is liable to sound like *las* in Americanized form. But no matter; the city was not, in any case, named after the angels, but after the mother of Christ, "The Queen of the Angels."

Other Placenames

14   The five states that are named after other places show, in four of them, the origins of their settlers: *New Mexico* by Spanish explorers coming northward from "Old" Mexico; *New Hampshire, New Jersey*, and *New York* by Britons who remembered an English county, an island in the English Channel, and a northern English city, respectively. But *Rhode Island* is named after the Mediterranean island of Rhodes, where the famous Colossus once bestrode the entrance to the port, a statue of a man so huge that it gives us our adjective *colossal* today. Why the smallest state should struggle under a name associated with the largest statue is, all the same, a colossal mystery.

15   Spanish words for common things remain in the state names *Montana* (mountainous), *Colorado* ([colored] red), *Nevada* (snowed on), *Florida* (flowered, because it had many flowers, and because it was discovered a few days after Easter, called "the

Names of Discontinued Postal Units

Names Discontinued	Attached to	Mail to
Arapaho	Richardson	Richardson
Big Town	Mesquite	Mesquite
Blue Mound	Fort Worth	Fort Worth
Broadway	Mesquite	Mesquite
Camp San Saba		Brady
Canyon Creek Square	Richardson	Canyon Creek
Cedar Bayou	Baytown	Baytown
Cleo		Menard
Cottonwood	Baird	Baird
Dal-Rich	Richardson	Richardson
Easter	Hereford	Hereford
Edom	Brownsboro	Brownsboro
Field Creek		Pontotoc
Franklin	Houston	Houston
Freestone	Teague	Teague
Gay Hill		Brenham
Gilliland	Truscott	Truscott
Great SW Airport	Fort Worth	Fort Worth
Grit		Mason
Lake Air	Waco	Waco
Leary	Texarkana	Texarkana
McNair	Baytown	Baytown
Mount Sylvan	Lindale	Lindale
Oakalla		Killeen
Olmos Park	San Antonio	San Antonio
Pandale		Ozona
Patricia		Lamesa
Patroon		Shelbyville
Postoak		Bowie
Possum Kingdom	Graford	Graford
Raymond A. Stewart, Jr.	Galveston	Galveston
Richland Hills	Fort Worth	Greater Richlands Area
Sachse	Garland	Garland
Salt Gap		Lohn
Six Flags Over Texas	Arlington	Arlington
Slocum	Elkhart	Elkhart
Spring Hill	Longview	Longview
Stacy		Coleman
Startzville	New Braunfels	Canyon Lake
Sunnyvale	Mesquite	Mesquite

+---+
| **Names of Discontinued Postal Units (*Continued*)** |
+---+

Names Discontinued	*Attached to*	*Mail to*
Telico	Ennis	Ennis
Town Hall	Mesquite	Mesquite
Weldon		Lovelady
Woodlands	Spring	The Woodlands
Washburn	Claude	Claude

Ghost "Postal Units" in Texas.   The discontinued offices include native American names, Spanish names, British names, personal names, and still others for which there is no obvious category. Adapted from the *U.S. Directory of Post Offices* (1977). Copyright by the United States Postal Service.

Easter of flowers" in Spanish), and—in an unorthodox form—the French *Vermont* (green mountain). English common words remain in *Maine* (great or important, as in *mainland* or *main sea*, from which comes *the billowing main* or *the Spanish main*); and in *Indiana*, from the Indiana Company that was formed by land speculators to settle the former Indian Territory.

16   All these patterns, like the pattern of naming with native American words, are repeated in the patterns of naming places other than states. *Washington* names not only a state but, at one count, 32 counties; 121 cities, towns, and villages; 257 townships; 18 lakes and streams; 7 mountains; and no end of streets. Many saints' names appear in Spanish, French, and English placenames. With suitable suffixes on secular names we get *Pittsburgh, Jacksonville*, and many more. Common things remain in *Oil City* and in *Carbondale*, as well as in the rather less common Canadian *Moose Jaw* and *Medicine Hat*. Placenames are transferred from abroad—the English *Boston* supplied the name for the well-known city in Massachusetts and eighteen more *Bostons* and *New Bostons*—or from the east of the United States, reproducing *Princetons* (fifteen municipalities and, in Colorado, a peak) and *Philadelphias* across the American landscape with no more than a zip code of difference among them.

17   So what is true of the state names is true of other placenames. But the other placenames have a few features that, probably fortunately, never got put on the map in letters quite so large as those employed for states. Some of these are European words from languages other than the staple of Spanish, French, and English. Some are names from classical or biblical lore. Some describe the place or its animals or plants. And some seem to be inspired by nothing more serious than verbal playfulness, nothing more reverent than onomastic cussedness. Placenames such as these, especially the last category, have attracted the disproportionate attention of many otherwise judicious investigators of American English, and they have inspired poetic encomiums such as Stephen Vincent Benét's "American Names."* They are colorful, it is true, but you can scan the average gasoline company map for hours before you will find anything more than the usual, usually colorless, run of American placenames.

* Benét's poem is reprinted on pages 44 and 45.

18   Dutch names are among the most important following the native American, French, Spanish, and English. Like the others, the Dutch had a way with native names, and their way gave us *Hackensack* and *Hoboken* (the latter from *Hopoakanhacking*) and other names too. They named New World places after Old World places, like *New Amsterdam* and *Haarlem*; their *Bruekelyn* born anew on these shores became *Brooklyn*. They gave their personal names to places as well, so that Jonas Bronck (actually a Dane in a Dutch settlement) gave his to the *Bronx*, and Jonkheer (squire) Donck gave his title to *Yonkers*. And they gave the name of their language and culture to places like *Dutch Neck* (NJ). Many of the Dutch names did not survive the occupation of their settlements by the English—Nieuw Amsterdam became *New York*, for example—and in this as in the other Dutch placenames, only the language in question is different: the patterns of naming are the same as they were for the languages that named thousands of other places.

19   A somewhat more novel trait of American placenames is their reference to classical and biblical lore. *Philadelphia* may "mean" City of Brotherly Love, in approximate translation from the Greek, but it probably named (by William Penn) after an Asian city of the same name, with the additional warrant of the words of Saint Paul, "Be kindly affectionate one to another with brotherly love." Both the classical and the scriptural had singular importance in a country that, unlike Britain, had millions of new places awaiting names, places as often as not settled by those (again like Penn) whose wanderings had a religious impetus. When we today have a new product, we may invent a neoclassical name for it: *television* is the most common example. But when we want such a name, it is to the classical scholar that we turn. The early settlers likewise turned to the schoolteacher or to the minister who was, frequently, the same person. And they got just what they might have expected: in central New York there is a *Troy*, a *Utica*, a *Rome*, an *Ithaca*, and a *Syracuse*. (Troy was not the first name the place had; under the Dutch it had been *Vanderheyden* or *Vanderheyden's Ferry*.) State names like the *Carolinas* and *Virginia* took a Latin-like form, and when the Virginia town near the Alexander plantation got its name, it was more than a happy coincidence that it was called *Alexandria* after the great city of the ancient world. The practice is most notable in the east, but that has not stopped placenames farther west like *Cincinnati* (Ohio), *Cairo* (Illinois), *Tempe* and *Phoenix* (Arizona), and many others from achieving permanence.

20   The Bible too had an influence beyond the Philadelphia city limits. Mencken counted eleven *Beulahs*, nine *Canaans*, eleven *Jordans*, and twenty-one *Sharons*. The pattern is general: a preference for the Old Testament over the New as a toponymic source. Most of the American placenames with *St.-* are taken over from the French or the Spanish, as are the frequent placenames still untranslated from those languages: *Sacramento, San Francisco*, and so many more that Whitman grew angry at their number and demanded their renaming in secular terms. It didn't come about. Placenames very quickly lose their referential content beyond the place they name. They "mean" nothing more than the place, and so *Phoenix* (AZ), for example, becomes a different word from the phoenix that was a legendary bird. By the same process, *Sacramento* has no religious overtones for those who know it as a place, even though they may also know something of the sacrament it was originally meant to recall.

And folk etymology often made oblivion certain. The place the Spanish called *El Río de las Animas Predidas en Purgatorio* (River of the Souls Lost in Purgatory) was translated and shortened by the French into *Purgatoire*, and the Americans who followed them imitated this as *Picketwire*. Any resemblance between purgatory and picketwire is purely coincidental.

21   A name like the one the Spanish gave this river is a reference to something else not present, as is most naming for persons and places. But some placenames refer to the place itself by describing it: *Sugarloaf Mountain*, for example, which looked like a sugarloaf to those who had to name it, and *Cedar Mountain*, which was covered with trees. Nowadays no one knows what a sugarloaf looks like, so the name of the mountain is as abstract as if it had been Algonquian; and chances are the cedars have all been cut down as well to make shingles for houses where no sugarloaf will enter. No high school French course will enable the American pupil to see in the *Grand Teton* mountains the original comparison to "big breasts," which may be why the name has been left untranslated. Descriptive placenames have made a great comeback since World War II, for they appear to lend a quaint and historical air to new subdivision developments. *Oak Dell* certainly sounds worth a down payment, even if no oaks ever grew within miles of the spot and the terrain is perfectly flat; and *Miry Run* has the same reassuring sound, at least until the customer remembers what *miry* means.

22   The most colorful names are the rarest. They are found mostly in old accounts of the frontier and in books like this one. Many of the most colorful have been civilized out of existence: in Canada, *Rat Portage* became *Kenora*. But *King of Prussia* and *Intercourse* still survive in Pennsylvania, *Tombstone* in Arizona, and others elsewhere. Mencken claims that West Virginia is "full" of such placenames, giving as proof *Affinity, Bias, Big Chimney, Bulltown, Caress, Cinderella, Cowhide*, and *Czar*, just for the ABCs. But some of his examples are more madcap than others, and they do not really "fill" the state. *Truth or Consequences* (NM) is a recent alteration that needs no explanation. Almost self-explanatory are the portmanteau or blendword placenames such as *Calexico* (on the California side of the Mexican border; *Mexicali* is on the other side), *Penn Yan* (settled by Pennsylvanians and Yankees), *Delmarva* (a common though unofficial name for the peninsula that is partly in Delaware, partly in Maryland, partly in Virginia). The blend process is relatively common in all varieties of the English language, but as a source of placenames it seems to be distinctively American.

Questions on Content

1. Why is toponymics "essential to a grasp of American English" (paragraph 2)?

2. What five categories of U.S. place names does Bolton identify?

3. Explain the origins of the names *Wisconsin* and *Minnesota*.

4. Which states were named after famous persons?

5. Identify some U.S. place names that are Dutch in origin. What kinds of things are they named after?

6. Which source do you think accounts for the most colorful place names?

Questions on Structure and Style

7. Examine the relationship between paragraphs 1 and 2. What is the function of paragraph 2?

8. What kind of transitions are used in the first three paragraphs? Are the transitions in the rest of the selection similar?

9. We note Bolton's sense of humor in paragraph 6. Find other examples of his humor. What do they tell us about him and about his attitude toward his subject?

10. Are Bolton's examples appropriate? Does he include enough examples?

Assignments

1. Study Bolton's five categories for the names of the fifty states. Then write an essay classifying the place names in your region. (You may have to devise new categories.)

2. Write an essay discussing the history of your region as reflected in its place names.

Playing the Name Game by Other Rules

Chet Raymo

Biological naming takes two forms, scientific and common, so the butterfly categorized as *Cercyonis meadii* lives and delights human beings in flight as the Red-eyed Nymph. As scientist and author Chet Raymo makes vivid in the following essay, such strikingly different yet complementary names illustrate "a balance of the fluid and the firm," on which human creativity thrives. Naming and understanding are intimately connected, Raymo tells us, so the lepidopterist who named the Rainbow Skipper no doubt understood both butterflies and human beings, who need poetry and science both.

■ J O U R N A L   P R O M P T   *Before reading this selection, write one or two paragraphs in response to the following statement by Chet Raymo: "The mind is repelled by too much randomness, and stifled by too much order" (paragraph 18).*

1   Tradition has it that Adam was allowed by the Creator to name all the creatures of the Earth.

2   It must have been some task. According to biologists, there are between 10 and 100 million species of living organisms. That means if Adam thought up a name a minute for 16 hours a day (Sundays included), it would take him somewhere between 30 and 300 years to complete the job.

3   Still, it must have been fun coming up with names like "duck-billed platypus," "tufted titmouse" and "precious wentletrap" (a gastropod, or mollusk, of Southeast Asia). It was a mythic episode of creativity that makes the accomplishments of Newton and Mozart pale.

4   I was set to thinking about Adam's task when I came across a book called "The Common Names of North American Butterflies," compiled by zoologist Jacqueline Miller of the University of Florida. Her purpose was to bring some order to the jumble of names used by amateur and professional butterfly enthusiasts.

5   The book is sheer poetry.

6   Creamy Checkerspot. Buckwheat Blue. Hop-eating Hairstreak. A list of luscious language that would delight the soul of James Joyce or Vladimir Nabokov, those archmagicians of the English tongue.

7   Bloody Spot. Rainbow Skipper. Mad Flasher. Nabokov was himself a lepidopterist of note, and his name is recorded here too, as Nabokov's Blue and Nabokov's Fritillary. Joyce may never have netted a butterfly, but he would have appreciated the Redundant Swarthy Skipper and Mrs. Owen's Dusky Wing for their names alone.

8   The Parsnip Swallowtail is also called Parsleyworm, Celeryworm and Carawayworm, which suggests a certain catholicity of taste. The Flying Pansy is alternately

38

the California Dog Face, which suggests that one lepidopterist's beautiful is another's ugly. One wonders if the Lost-egg Skipper misses its progeny.

9   Certain professional (and even amateur) lepidopterists blanch at the very mention of common names and their attendant confusion. They plump for the use of scientific nomenclature exclusively—for clarity.

10   Adam, of course, was no scientist, so he went about his work with reckless disregard for nature's underlying order. One would never know from their common names that the Goggle Eye and the Red-eyed Nymph butterflies are first cousins.

11   Our system of scientific naming has a long history, going back to Aristotle, but owing most to the 18th-century Swedish botanist Karl von Linne, better known by his Latinized name, Linneaus. He proposed a two-name system, consisting of a genus designation for all species in a closely related group, followed by a species-specific modifier. Goggle Eye becomes *Cercyonis pegol* and Red eyed Nymph becomes *Cercyonis meadii,* with their kinship made manifest.

12   Many years ago I visited Linneaus' country house near Uppsala in Sweden. It was a charming place, filled and surrounded by nature's beauty. Butterflies flitted in the dooryard. The walls were papered with marvelous drawings of plants. In this Eden, Linneaus tossed out Adam's common names and proposed his system of Latin binomials.

13   He knew that nothing is well described unless well named, and that nothing is well named until well described. Naming and exact description go hand and hand, and, if carefully done, reveal the patterns of order implicit in nature itself.

14   This intimate connection between naming and understanding was an idea that was in the air in the 18th century. Not long after Linneaus proposed his nomenclature system for biology, Antoine Lavoisier set out to do much the same thing for chemistry. In the preface to his great work, "Elements of Chemistry," Lavoisier quotes the philosopher Condillac: "We think only through the medium of words. . . . The art of reasoning is nothing more than a language well arranged."

15   Lavoisier then goes on to tell us: "Thus, while I thought myself employed only in forming a nomenclature, and while I proposed to myself nothing more than to improve the chemical language, my work transformed itself by degrees, without my being able to prevent it, into a treatise upon the 'Elements of Chemistry.' "

16   Thus, too, did Linneaus' revision of biological nomenclature lead inexorably to the work of Charles Darwin and his revelation of nature's patterns of evolution.

17   The art of reasoning may be nothing more than well arranged language, but the lively chaos of common names has its own irreplaceable attraction. The Swallowtail butterfly may be *Papilio zelicaon* to the professional lepidopterist, but it will always be a Swallowtail to me. And a Sweetbriar rose called *Rosa eglanteria* truly doesn't smell as sweet.

18   The two systems of biological naming—common and scientific—are complementary and satisfy different parts of the human agenda, perhaps even different halves of the human brain. The mind is repelled by too much randomness, and stifled by too much order. Creativity thrives on a balance of the fluid and the firm.

19   Seeing the two lists of names side by side on the pages of Jacqueline Miller's book gives a powerful sense of the creative energy that flows back and forth between

them. Call them poetry and science, call them serendipity and logic. We are only partly ourselves without both.

Questions on Content

1. Return to the Journal Prompt, and discuss it now that you have read Raymo's essay.

2. Raymo discusses the processes that led to scientific as well as common names for butterflies. Which type of names does he prefer, or does he recognize the importance of each? Is he able to demonstrate that the two types of names complement one another?

3. Raymo implies there is an intimate connection between naming and understanding. Explain.

Questions on Structure and Style

4. Explain why Raymo, a scientist, begins with a look at Adam's task of naming all creatures on earth.

5. What is the function of the one-sentence paragraph: "The book is sheer poetry" (paragraph 5)?

6. Discuss Raymo's choice of verbs in paragraph 9.

Assignments

1. From his discussion of the common and scientific names of butterflies, Raymo, a scientist, emphasizes the importance of a balanced appreciation of science and art. In fact, he says, "We are only partly ourselves without both" (paragraph 19). Write an essay in which you discuss the importance of the well-rounded person's developing an appreciation for art and for science.

2. Choose three of the names that Raymo uses as examples in his essay, and in an essay of your own, explain why you especially like or dislike them.

Aesthetics

Felix Pollak

Is *salmonella* appetizing? It is if we remember that words are
simply sounds that have no true connection with the realities they
identify. The following poem by Felix Pollak reminds us that anyone
equipped with imagination (and a sense of humor) can find some
words surprisingly attractive.

■ **J O U R N A L   P R O M P T** *Make a list of words that please your ear and another
list of words that sound unpleasant. Are you able to separate the sound of a word from its
meaning? Felix Pollak, for example, hears beauty in* salmonella, glaucoma, *and* psoriasis *if he
hears only the sounds of the word and not its meaning.*

1
There are such beautiful
exotic
words in the dictionary,
euphonic songs that taste good
5
in the mouth—salmonella,
glaucoma, catatonia, ataxia,
words like the names of
legendary heroines or goddesses
—Acne, Hysterectomy,
10
Emphysema, Peritonitis, or thunderous
appellations reminiscent of old
warriors and lovers—Tetanus,
Staphylococcus, Stupor,
Cyanide, Carbuncle—

15
it is a joy like savoring the
hues & abstract shapes in
the medical atlas—those green
gangrenes and scarlet carcinomas,
the intricate pink & silver patterns of
20
psoriasis like islands on a yellow sea
of skin, Rubenesque hernias or the
Seurat-like pointillisms of atherosclerosis,
not to speak of the Japanese landscapes drawn by
cirrhosis of the liver, and the sculptures
25
created by certain amputations, rivalling even
the exquisite armstumps
of the Venus of Milo.

Questions on Content

1. What is the most significant point that Pollak makes about language in this poem?

2. How can *salmonella, glaucoma, catatonia*, and *ataxia* be "euphonic songs that taste good in the mouth" (lines 4–5)?

3. What do "Rubenesque hernias" (line 21) and the "armstumps of the Venus of Milo" (lines 26–27) have in common?

4. What does *euphonic* mean? What does euphony have to do with how this poem conveys its meaning?

Questions on Structure and Style

5. How does Pollak use irony in "Aesthetics"? In what ways is his diction ironic? His meaning?

6. How does Pollak manage to use sound so effectively in this poem? What is the relationship between sound and meaning? In what ways is this relationship incongruous?

Assignments

1. This poem is ironic because it demands that the reader respond on two levels: those of sound and meaning. Write a paragraph or two in which you illustrate how the poem sounds different to the reader who is familiar with the words that Pollak calls "euphonic" and the reader who is not.

2. In *Romeo and Juliet* Shakespeare says, "A rose by any other name would smell as sweet." Write a short essay on the relationship between Shakespeare's words and Pollak's poem.

ADDITIONAL ASSIGNMENTS AND RESEARCH TOPICS

1. Examine the following list of names of things, compiled by W. F. Bolton. (Bolton's overview of American place names, "Putting American English on the Map," appears earlier in this chapter.) Collecting place names is easy; any atlas or road map can supply interesting examples. Other types of proper names can prove just as entertaining, as is obvious to anyone who has examined carefully the yellow pages of a telephone directory. Below are a few categories of names, with examples in parentheses.

   Dishes and recipes (eggs Benedict, cherries jubilee)

   Sports teams (Philadelphia Flyers, Pittsburgh Penguins)

   State nicknames (Garden State, Blue Hen State)

   Street names (The Midway, Wall Street)

   Former telephone exchanges (now superseded by numbered exchanges)

   Apartment houses and housing developments (Olympic Towers, Co-Op City)

   Railroad cars, airplanes, naval and other ships (USS *Midway*)

   Houses of worship (St. Paul's, First Congregational, Temple Beth-El)

   Newspapers, magazines (*Town Topics, Road & Track*)

   Pets, race horses (Bowser, Court Fleet)

   Natural disasters (Hurricane Cora, the Hayward Fault)

   Novels, motion pictures (*Amok, The French Connection*)

   Consumer products (Vaseline, Touch and Go)

   Ailments (Legionnaires' disease, psoriasis, influenza)

   Garments (Fairisle sweater, miniskirt, Docksiders)

   Schools, colleges, universities (Arizona State, Oral Roberts)

   Car makes, models, names (Buick, Mustang, Draggin' Wagon)

   Government agencies (Small Business Administration)

   Charitable and nonprofit organizations (Nader's Raiders)

   Theaters and cinemas (Lyceum, Palace)

   Medicines (Kaopectate, aspirin)

   Plants and flowers (moneywort, mandrake, fuchsia)

   Weapons (bayonet, bazooka)

   Eras and generations (the age of anxiety, the "me" generation)

   Choose a category (such as names of professional baseball teams, street names, or names of automobiles), and write an essay in which you classify the names in the category and discuss what they reveal.

2. In an essay, respond to one or more of the following quotations:

   A. "For as his name is, so is he. . . ." 1 Samuel 25:25
   B. "A name is sound and smoke." Goethe
   C. "The renaming of things is the essence of conquest." William Broyles
   D. "A rose by any other name would smell as sweet." Shakespeare
   E. "A good name is better than riches." Cervantes
   F. "The beginning of wisdom is to call things by their right names." Chinese proverb

3. Many authors carefully select their characters' names to reflect the characters' personalities. Charles Dickens's Mr. Murdstone and Mr. Gradgrind and Ralph Ellison's Jim Trueblood and Dr. Bledsoe are examples. Think of novels or short stories you've read in which the authors send obvious messages with their characters' names, and in an essay, discuss the importance of these names.

4. The following is from the *Interpreter's Bible*: "In biblical thought a name is not a mere label of identification; it is an expression of the essential nature of the bearer. A man's name reveals his character. Adam was able to give names to beasts and birds because, as Milton says, he understood their nature."

   Write an essay explaining your own ideas about the importance of names. Consider the quotation from the *Interpreter's Bible*, and keep in mind the ideas presented in this chapter.

5. Write a research paper examining the meaning and importance of some type of name. You might, for example, write about U.S. place names or surnames. Be certain to narrow your topic carefully.

6. The American poet Stephen Vincent Benét was so consumed by the power of American names that he wrote the following poem about them.

AMERICAN NAMES

> I have fallen in love with American names,
> The sharp names that never get fat.
> The snakeskin-titles of mining claims.
> The plumed war-bonnet of Medicine Hat.
> Tucson and Deadwood and Lost Mule Flat.
>
> Seine and Piave are silver spoons,
> But the spoonbowl-metal is thin and worn,
> There are English counties like hunting-tunes
> Played on the keys of a postboy's horn.
> But I will remember where I was born.
>
> I will remember Carquinez Straits,
> Little French Lick and Lundy's Lane,
> The Yankee ships and the Yankee dates

And the bullet-towns of Calamity Jane,
I will remember Skunktown Plain.

. . . .

Rue des Martyrs and Bleeding-Heart-Yard,
Senlis, Pisa, and Blindman's Oast,
It is a magic ghost you guard
But I am sick for a newer ghost,
Harrisburg, Spartanburg, Painted Post.

Henry and John were never so
And Henry and John were always right?
Granted, but when it was time to go
And the tea and the laurels had stood all night,
Did they never watch for Nantucket Light?

I shall not rest quiet in Montparnasse.
I shall not lie easy at Winchelsea.
You may bury my body in Sussex grass,
You may bury my tongue at Champmedy.
I shall not be there. I shall rise and pass.
Bury my heart at Wounded Knee.

In an essay, compare your reaction to American names with Benét's reaction. Do you share his fascination? What names do you find most intriguing? Most revealing? Most meaningful?

7. Suppose that you had the power to choose for yourself three names: a formal name, to be used in all legal and public transactions during your lifetime; a social name, to be used informally with friends and family; and a name for eternity, to be used to identify you after your death and forever. What three names would you choose? Explain your choices in an essay.

CHAPTER TWO

Gender, Race, and Language Conflict

W̲e all belong to groups, sometimes by choice. When we attend school, we're "students." If we seek admission to a fraternity or sorority, we hope to become "brothers" or "sisters." A move to Texas makes us "Texans" or "Southerners." Often, however, we belong to groups because of qualities beyond our control: our sex, race, age, height, ethnic background, innate talents—the list is almost endless. Moreover, we are often *identified,* rightly or wrongly, by the qualities of the group, and one of the most important of these qualities is language. The use of language distinguishes human beings from other living creatures, but *which* language we use, and how we use it, distinguishes our group(s) from others.

This chapter examines the ways in which our language identifies us as members of certain groups: male or female, racial and ethnic. The chapter also looks at the relationship between language and discrimination, that is, at the ways that a group's language can be used to identify the group so as to set it apart unfairly from others.

As we discover in several of the readings in Chapter 5, Language and Cultural Diversity, language often identifies members of racial and ethnic groups. Language also reveals male or female identities, as well as attitudes toward men and women, and several of this chapter's readings examine the connection between language and sexual discrimination. In the first reading, "Sexism in English: A 1990s Update," Alleen Pace Nilsen provides an overview of the many ways that our language expresses sexist attitudes. Deborah Tannen then explores the question of why many people suspect that members of the opposite sex simply do not listen to them. In "'Put Down That Paper and Talk to Me!': Rapport-Talk and Report-Talk," we discover that because language can serve different purposes for men and women, each group often misinterprets and misrepresents the other.

The chapter offers two other voices that make obvious the complexity of the relationship between language and sexism. One voice offers a rebuttal to some of the views presented by Nilsen and Tannen. Eugene R. August believes that sexist language does not victimize women exclusively. In fact, and with abundant evidence, he argues that "Real Men Don't" favor sexist language, because such language victimizes men just as often as it does women. The highly personal "The Name Is Mine" then adds a very different perspective, as Anna Quindlen explores the powerful relationships among people that make last names a unifying force, not simply a form of personal property.

Other selections examine language as it affects, and is affected by, the African American experience. Geneva Smitherman traces the history of names for this group and explains why *African American* reflects only the latest stage in a process of self-identification marked by conflict and controversy. Black English, often now called Ebonics, has provoked its own controversy over cultural differences. Should black English be considered a dialect of standard English? Is it a dialect at all? What prompted its evolution? Why does the very existence of black English imply resistence to cultural diversity in our country? In his essay "On Black English," James Baldwin addresses these difficult questions.

Although our identity doesn't lie entirely in the language we use, our language does have immense power to declare who we are (and were, and sometimes who we want to be). Such declarations shouldn't work against us; that is, our language shouldn't be used against us. However, language is a convenient indicator for anyone who wants a simple way to include or exclude us from a group of job applicants, loan applicants, renters, candidates for promotion or public office, or any other group. Unfair efforts such as these will probably persist forever, but by understanding the power of our language to identify us, we can at least remain alert and ready to resist.

Sexism in English: A 1990s Update

Alleen Pace Nilsen

Sexist language expresses unfair assumptions about gender differences. It can be either explicit, as in the prejudicial use of male or female pronouns, or implicit. Using richly detailed historical evidence, Alleen Pace Nilsen reveals here how often English expresses sexist assumptions about differences between men and women. Nilsen is a writer and an administrator at Arizona State University.

■ **J O U R N A L   P R O M P T**   *Nilsen claims that "early in life, children are conditioned to the superiority of the masculine role." Among many language examples are the different messages that underlie "be a lady" and "be a man." Write about how language encourages unfair and untrue sexist attitudes.*

1   Twenty years ago I embarked on a study of the sexism inherent in American English. I had just returned to Ann Arbor, Michigan, after living for two years (1967–69) in Kabul, Afghanistan, where I had begun to look critically at the role society assigned to women. The Afghan version of the *chaderi* prescribed for Moslem women was particularly confining. Afghan jokes and folklore were blatantly sexist, such as this proverb: "If you see an old man, sit down and take a lesson; if you see an old woman, throw a stone."

2   But it wasn't only the native culture that made me question women's roles, it was also the American community.

3   Most of the American women were like myself—wives and mothers whose husbands were either career diplomats, employees of USAID, or college professors who had been recruited to work on various contract teams. We were suddenly bereft of our traditional roles: some of us became alcoholics, others got very good at bridge, while still others searched desperately for ways to contribute either to our families or to the Afghans. The local economy provided few jobs for women and certainly none for foreigners; we were isolated from former friends and the social goals we had grown up with.

4   When I returned in the fall of 1969 to the University of Michigan in Ann Arbor, I was surprised to find that many other women were also questioning the expectations they had grown up with. In the spring of 1970, a women's conference was announced. I hired a babysitter and attended, but I returned home more troubled than ever. The militancy of these women frightened me. Since I wasn't ready for a revolution, I decided I would have my own feminist movement. I would study the English language and see what it could tell me about sexism. I started reading a desk dictionary and making notecards on every entry that seemed to tell something about male and female. I soon had a dog-eared dictionary, along with a collection of notecards filling two shoe boxes.

5   Ironically, I started reading the dictionary because I wanted to avoid getting involved in social issues, but what happened was that my notecards brought me right back to looking at society. Language and society are as intertwined as a chicken and an egg. The language a culture uses is telltale evidence of the values and beliefs of that culture. And because there is a lag in how fast a language changes—new words can easily be introduced, but it takes a long time for old words and usages to disappear—a careful look at English will reveal the attitudes that our ancestors held and that we as a culture are therefore predisposed to hold. My notecards revealed three main points. Friends have offered the opinion that I didn't need to read the dictionary to learn such obvious facts. Nevertheless, it was interesting to have linguistic evidence of sociological observations.

Women Are Sexy; Men Are Successful

6   First, in American culture a woman is valued for the attractiveness and sexiness of her body, while a man is valued for his physical strength and accomplishments. A woman is sexy. A man is successful.

7   A persuasive piece of evidence supporting this view are the eponyms—words that have come from someone's name—found in English. I had a two-and-a-half-inch stack of cards taken from men's names but less than a half-inch stack from women's names, and most of those came from Greek mythology. In the words that came into American English since we separated from Britain, there are many eponyms based on the names of famous American men: *Bartlett pear, boysenberry, diesel engine, Franklin stove, ferris wheel, Gatling gun, mason jar, sideburns, sousaphone, Schick test,* and *Winchester rifle.* The only common eponyms taken from American women's names are *Alice blue* (after Alice Roosevelt Longworth), *bloomers* (after Amelia Jenks Bloomer), and *Mae West jacket* (after the buxom actress). Two out of the three feminine eponyms relate closely to a woman's physical anatomy, while the masculine eponyms (except for *sideburns* after General Burnsides) have nothing to do with the namesake's body but, instead, honor the man for an accomplishment of some kind.

8   Although in Greek mythology women played a bigger role than they did in the biblical stories of the Judeo-Christian cultures and so the names of goddesses are accepted parts of the language in such place names as Pomona from the goddess of fruit and Athens from Athena and in such common words as *cereal* from Ceres, *psychology* for Psyche, and *arachnoid* from Arachne, the same tendency to think of women in relation to sexuality is seen in the eponyms *aphrodisiac* from Aphrodite, the Greek name for the goddess of love and beauty, and *venereal disease* from Venus, the Roman name for Aphrodite.

9   Another interesting word from Greek mythology is *Amazon.* According to Greek folk etymology, the *a* means "without" as in *atypical* or *amoral,* while *mazon* comes from *mazos* meaning "breast" as still seen in *mastectomy.* In the Greek legend, Amazon women cut off their right breasts so that they could better shoot their bows. Apparently, the storytellers had a feeling that for women to play the active, "masculine" role the Amazons adopted for themselves, they had to trade in part of their femininity.

10   This preoccupation with women's breasts is not limited to ancient stories. As a volunteer for the University of Wisconsin's *Dictionary of American Regional English* (*DARE*), I read a western trapper's diary from the 1930s. I was to make notes of any unusual usages or language patterns. My most interesting finding was that the trapper referred to a range of mountains as *The Teats*, a metaphor based on the similarity between the shapes of the mountains and women's breasts. Because today we use the French wording, *The Grand Tetons*, the metaphor isn't as obvious, but I wrote to mapmakers and found the following listings: *Nippletop* and *Little Nipple Top* near Mount Marcy in the Adirondacks; *Nipple Mountain* in Archuleta County, Colorado; *Nipple Peak* in Coke County, Texas; *Nipple Butte* in Pennington, South Dakota; *Squaw Peak* in Placer County, California (and many other locations); *Maiden's Peak* and *Squaw Tit* (they're the same mountain) in the Cascade Range in Oregon; *Mary's Nipple* near Salt Lake City, Utah; and *Jane Russell Peaks* near Stark, New Hampshire.

11   Except for the movie star Jane Russell, the women being referred to are anonymous—it's only a sexual part of their body that is mentioned. When topographical features are named after men, it's probably not going to be to draw attention to a sexual part of their bodies but instead to honor individuals for an accomplishment. For example, no one thinks of a part of the male body when hearing a reference to Pike's Peak, Colorado, or Jackson Hole, Wyoming.

12   Going back to what I learned from my dictionary cards, I was surprised to realize how many pairs of words we have in which the feminine word has acquired sexual connotations while the masculine word retains a serious businesslike aura. For example, a *callboy* is the person who calls actors when it is time for them to go on stage, but a *call girl* is a prostitute. Compare *sir* and *madam*. *Sir* is a term of respect, while *madam* has acquired the specialized meaning of a brothel manager. Something similar has happened to *master* and *mistress*. Would you rather have a painting by an *old master* or an *old mistress*?

13   It's because the word *woman* had sexual connotations, as in "She's his woman," that people began avoiding its use, hence such terminology as *ladies' room, lady of the house*, and *girls' school* or *school for young ladies*. Feminists, who ask that people use the term *woman* rather than *girl* or *lady*, are rejecting the idea that *woman* is primarily a sexual term. They have been at least partially successful in that today *woman* is commonly used to communicate gender without intending implications about sexuality.

14   I found two hundred pairs of words with masculine and feminine forms, e.g., *heir-heiress, hero-heroine, steward-stewardess, usher-usherette*. In nearly all such pairs, the masculine word is considered the base, with some kind of a feminine suffix being added. The masculine form is the one from which compounds are made, e.g., from *king-queen* comes *kingdom* but not *queendom*, from *sportsman-sportslady* comes *sportsmanship* but not *sportsladyship*. There is one—and only one—semantic area in which the masculine word is not the base or more powerful word. This is in the area dealing with sex and marriage. When someone refers to a *virgin*, a listener will probably think of a female, unless the speaker specifies *male* or uses a masculine pronoun. The same is true for *prostitute*.

15   In relation to marriage, there is much linguistic evidence showing that weddings are more important to women than to men. A woman cherishes the wedding and is considered a bride for a whole year, but a man is referred to as a groom only on the day of the wedding. The word *bride* appears in *bridal attendant, bridal gown, bridesmaid, bridal shower*, and even *bridegroom. Groom* comes from the Middle English *grom*, meaning "man," and in the sense is seldom used outside of the wedding. With most pairs of male/female words, people habitually put the masculine word first, *Mr. and Mrs., his and hers, boys and girls, men and women, kings and queens, brothers and sisters, guys and dolls*, and *host and hostess*, but it is the *bride and groom* who are talked about, not the *groom and bride*.

16   The importance of marriage to a woman is also shown by the fact that when a marriage ends in death, the woman gets the title of *widow*. A man gets the derived title of *widower*. This term is not used in other phrases or contexts, but *widow* is seen in *widowhood, widow's peak*, and *widow's walk*. A *widow* in a card game is an extra hand of cards, while in typesetting it is an extra line of type.

17   How changing cultural ideas bring changes to language is clearly visible in this semantic area. The feminist movement has caused the differences between the sexes to be downplayed, and since I did my dictionary study two decades ago, the word *singles* has largely replaced such sex specific and value-laden terms as *bachelor, old maid, spinster, divorcée, widow*, and *widower*. And in 1970 I wrote that when a man is called a *professional* he is thought to be a doctor or a lawyer, but when people hear a woman referred to as *a professional* they are likely to think of a prostitute. That's not as true today because so many women have become doctors and lawyers that it's no longer incongruous to think of women in those professional roles.

18   Another change that has taken place is in wedding announcements. They used to be sent out from the bride's parents and did not even give the name of the groom's parents. Today, most couples choose to list either all or none of the parents' names. Also it is now much more likely that both the bride and groom's picture will be in the newspaper, while a decade ago only the bride's picture was published on the "Women's" or the "Society" page. Even the traditional wording of the wedding ceremony is being changed. Many officials now pronounce the couple "husband and wife" instead of the old "man and wife," and they ask the bride if she promises "to love, honor, and cherish," instead of "to love, honor, and obey."

Women Are Passive; Men Are Active

19   The wording of the wedding ceremony also relates to the second point that my cards showed, which is that women are expected to play a passive or weak role while men play an active or strong role. In the traditional ceremony, the official asks, "Who gives the bride away?" and the father answers, "I do." Some fathers answer, "Her mother and I do," but that doesn't solve the problem inherent in the question. The idea that a bride is something to be handed over from one man to another bothers people because it goes back to the days when a man's servants, his children, and his wife were all considered to be his property. They were known by his name because they belonged to him, and he was responsible for their actions and their debts.

20   The grammar used in talking or writing about weddings as well as other sexual relationships shows the expectation of men playing the active role. Men *wed* women while women *become* brides of men. A man *possesses* a woman; he *deflowers* her; he *performs*; he *scores*; he *takes away* her virginity. Although a woman can *seduce* a man, she cannot offer him her virginity. When talking about virginity, the only way to make the woman the actor in the sentence is to say that "She lost her virginity," but people lose things by accident rather than by purposeful actions, and so she's only the grammatical, not the real-life, actor.

21   The reason that women tried to bring the term *Ms.* into the language to replace *Miss* or *Mrs.* relates to this point. Married women resent being identified only under their husband's names. For example, when Susan Glascoe did something newsworthy, she would be identified in the newspaper only as Mrs. John Glascoe. The dictionary cards showed what appeared to be an attitude on the part of the editors that it was almost indecent to let a respectable woman's name march unaccompanied across the pages of a dictionary. Women were listed with male names whether or not the male contributed to the woman's reason for being in the dictionary or in his own right was as famous as the woman. For example, Charlotte Brontë was identified as Mrs. Arthur B. Nicholls, Amelia Earhart as Mrs. George Palmer Putnam, Helen Hayes as Mrs. Charles MacArthur, Jenny Lind as Mme. Otto Goldschmit, Cornelia Otis Skinner as the daughter of Otis, Harriet Beecher Stowe as the sister of Henry Ward Beecher, and Edith Sitwell as the sister of Osbert and Sacheverell. A very small number of women got into the dictionary without the benefit of a masculine escort. They were rebels and crusaders: temperance leaders Frances Elizabeth Caroline Willard and Carry Nation, women's rights leaders Carrie Chapman Catt and Elizabeth Cady Stanton, birth control educator Margaret Sanger, religious leader Mary Baker Eddy, and slaves Harriet Tubman and Phillis Wheatley.

22   Etiquette books used to teach that if a woman had *Mrs.* in front of her name, then the husband's name should follow because *Mrs.* is an abbreviated form of *Mistress* and a woman couldn't be a mistress of herself. As with many arguments about "correct" language usage, this isn't very logical because *Miss* is also an abbreviation of *Mistress*. Feminists hoped to simplify matters by introducing *Ms.* as an alternative to both *Mrs.* and *Miss*, but what happened is that *Ms.* largely replaced *Miss*, to become a catch-all business title for women. Many married women still prefer the title *Mrs.*, and some resent being addressed with the term *Ms.* As one frustrated newspaper reporter complained, "Before I can write about a woman, I have to know not only her marital status but also her political philosophy." The result of such complications may contribute to the demise of titles, which are already being ignored by many computer programmers who find it more efficient to simply use names, for example in a business letter: "Dear Joan Garcia," instead of "Dear Mrs. Joan Garcia," "Dear Ms. Garcia," or "Dear Mrs. Louis Garcia."

23   The titles given to royalty provide an example of how males can be disadvantaged by the assumption that they are always to play the more powerful role. In British royalty, when a male holds a title, his wife is automatically given the feminine equivalent. But the reverse is not true. For example, a *count* is a high political officer with a *countess* being his wife. The same is true for a *duke* and a *duchess* and a *king* and a

queen. But when a female holds the royal title, the man she marries does not automatically acquire the matching title. For example, Queen Elizabeth's husband has the title of *prince* rather than *king*, but if Prince Charles [had] become king while he [was] still married to Lady or Princess Diana, she [would have been] known as the queen. The reasoning appears to be that since masculine words are stronger, they are reserved for true heirs and withheld from males coming into the royal family by marriage. If Prince Philip were called *King Philip*, it would be much easier for British subjects to forget where the true power lies.

24   The names that people give their children show the hopes and dreams they have for them, and when we look at the differences between male and female names in a culture, we can see the cumulative expectations of that culture. In our culture girls often have names taken from small, aesthetically pleasing items, e.g., *Ruby, Jewel*, and *Pearl. Esther* and *Stella* mean "star," *Ada* means "ornament," and *Vanessa* means "butterfly." Boys are more likely to be given names with meanings of power and strength, e.g., *Neil* means "champion," *Martin* is from Mars, the God of War, *Raymond* means "wise protection," *Harold* means "chief of the army," *Ira* means "vigilant," *Rex* means "king," and *Richard* means "strong king."

25   We see similar differences in food metaphors. Food is a passive substance just sitting there waiting to be eaten. Many people have recognized this and so no longer feel comfortable describing women as "delectable morsels." However, when I was a teenager, it was considered a compliment to refer to a girl (we didn't call anyone a *woman* until she was middle-aged) as a *cute tomato,* a *peach,* a *dish,* a *cookie, honey, sugar,* or *sweetie-pie.* When being affectionate, women will occasionally call a man *honey* or *sweetie,* but in general, food metaphors are used much less often with men than with women. If a man is called a *fruit,* his masculinity is being questioned. But it's perfectly acceptable to use a food metaphor if the food is heavier and more substantive than that used for women. For example, pin-up pictures of women have long been known as *cheesecake,* but when Burt Reynolds posed for a nude centerfold the picture was immediately dubbed *beefcake,* cf. *a hunk of meat.* That such sexual references to men have come into the language is another reflection of how society is beginning to lessen the differences between their attitudes toward men and women.

26   Something similar to the *fruit* metaphor happens with references to plants. We insult a man by calling him a *pansy,* but it wasn't considered particularly insulting to talk about a girl being a *wallflower,* a *clinging vine,* or a *shrinking violet,* or to give girls such names as *Ivy, Rose, Lily, Iris, Daisy, Camellia, Heather*, and *Flora.* A plant metaphor can be used with a man if the plant is big and strong, for example, Andrew Jackson's nickname of *Old Hickory.* Also the phrases *blooming idiots* and *budding geniuses* can be used with either sex, but notice how they are based on the most active thing a plant can do which is to bloom or bud.

27   Animal metaphors also illustrate the different expectations for males and females. Men are referred to as *studs, bucks,* and *wolves* while women are referred to with such metaphors as *kitten, bunny, beaver, bird, chick,* and *lamb.* In the 1950s we said that boys went *tomcatting,* but today it's just *catting around* and both boys and girls do it.

When the term *foxy*, meaning that someone was sexy, first became popular it was used only for girls, but now someone of either sex can be described as a *fox*. Some animal metaphors that are used predominantly with men have negative connotations based on the size and/or strength of the animals, e.g., *beast, bull-headed, jackass, rat, loanshark*, and *vulture*. Negative metaphors used with women are based on smaller animals, e.g., *social butterfly, mousy, catty,* and *vixen*. The feminine terms connote action, but not the same kind of large scale action as with the masculine terms.

Women Are Connected with Negative Connotations; Men with Positive Connotations

28   The final point that my notecards illustrated was how many positive connotations are associated with the concept of masculine, while there are either trivial or negative connotations connected with the corresponding feminine concept. An example from the animal metaphors makes a good illustration. The word *shrew* taken from the name of a small but especially vicious animal was defined in my dictionary as "an ill-tempered scolding woman," but the word *shrewd* taken from the same root was defined as "marked by clever, discerning awareness" and was illustrated with the phrase "a shrewd businessman."

29   Early in life, children are conditioned to the superiority of the masculine role. As child psychologists point out, little girls have much more freedom to experiment with sex roles than do little boys. If a little girl acts like a *tomboy*, most parents have mixed feelings, being at least partially proud. But if their little boy acts like a *sissy* (derived from *sister*), they call a psychologist. It's perfectly acceptable for a little girl to sleep in the crib that was purchased for her brother, to wear his hand-me-down jeans and shirts, and to ride the bicycle that he has outgrown. But few parents would put a boy baby in a white and gold crib decorated with frills and lace, and virtually no parents would have their little boys wear his sister's hand-me-down dresses, nor would they have their son ride a girl's pink bicycle with a flower-bedecked basket. The proper names given to girls and boys show this same attitude. Girls can have "boy" names—*Chris, Craig, Jo, Kelly, Shawn, Teri, Toni,* and *Sam*— but it doesn't work the other way around. A couple of generations ago, *Beverly, Francis, Hazel, Marion,* and *Shirley* were common boys' names. As parents gave these names to more and more girls, they fell into disuse for males, and some older men who have these names prefer to go by their initials or by such abbreviated forms as *Haze* or *Shirl*.

30   When a little girl is told to *be a lady*, she is being told to sit with her knees together and to be quiet and dainty. But when a little boy is told to *be a man* he is being told to be noble, strong, and virtuous—to have all the qualities that the speaker looks on as desirable. The concept of manliness has such positive connotations that it used to be a compliment to call someone a *he-man*, to say that he was doubly a man. Today many people are more ambivalent about this term and respond to it much as they do to the word *macho*. But calling someone a *manly man* or a *virile man* is nearly always meant as a compliment. *Virile* comes from the Indo-European

vir meaning "man," which is also the basis of *virtuous*. Contrast the positive connotations of both *virile* and *virtuous* with the negative connotations of *hysterical*. The Greeks took this latter word from their name for *uterus* (as still seen in *hysterectomy*). They thought that women were the only ones who experienced uncontrolled emotional outbursts, and so the condition must have something to do with a part of the body that only women have.

31   Differences in the connotations between positive male and negative female connotations can be seen in several pairs of words that differ denotatively only in the matter of sex. *Bachelor* as compared to *spinster* or *old maid* has such positive connotations that women try to adopt them by using the term *bachelor-girl* or *bachelorette*. *Old maid* is so negative that it's the basis for metaphors: pretentious and fussy old men are called *old maids*, as are the leftover kernels of unpopped popcorn, and the last card in a popular children's game.

32   *Patron* and *matron* (Middle English for *father* and *mother*) have such different levels of prestige that women try to borrow the more positive masculine connotations with the word *patroness*, literally "female father." Such a peculiar term came about because of the high prestige attached to *patron* in such phrases as *a patron of the arts* or *a patron saint*. *Matron* is more apt to be used in talking about a woman in charge of a jail or a public restroom.

33   When men are doing jobs that women often do, we apparently try to pay the men extra by giving them fancy titles, for example, a male cook is more likely to be called a *chef* while a male seamstress will get the title of *tailor*. The armed forces have a special problem in that they recruit under such slogans as "The Marine Corps builds men!" and "Join the Army! Become a Man." Once the recruits are enlisted, they find themselves doing much of the work that has been traditionally thought of as "women's work." The solution to getting the work done and not insulting anyone's masculinity was to change the titles as shown below:

waitress	orderly
nurse	medic or corpsman
secretary	clerk-typist
assistant	adjutant
dishwasher or kitchen helper	KP (kitchen police)

34   Compare *brave* and *squaw*. Early settlers in America truly admired Indian men and hence named them with a word that carried connotations of youth, vigor, courage. But they used the Algonquin's name for "woman" and over the years it developed almost opposite connotations to those of *brave*. *Wizard* and *witch* contrast almost as much. The masculine *wizard* implies skill and wisdom combined with magic, while the feminine *witch* implies evil intentions combined with magic. Part of the unattractiveness of both *witch* and *squaw* is that they have been used so often to refer to old women, something with which our culture is particularly uncomfortable, just as the Afghans were. Imagine my surprise when I ran across the phrases

grandfatherly advice and *old wives' tales* and realized that the underlying implication is the same as the Afghan proverb about old men being worth listening to while old women talk only foolishness.

35   Other terms that show how negatively we view old women as compared to young women are *old nag* as compared to *filly, old crow* or *old bat* as compared to *bird*, and of being *catty* as compared to *kittenish*. There is no matching set of metaphors for men. The chicken metaphor tells the whole story of a woman's life. In her youth she is a *chick*. Then she marries and begins *feathering her nest*. Soon she begins feeling *cooped up*, so she goes to *hen parties* where she *cackles* with her friends. Then she has her *brood*, begins to *henpeck* her husband, and finally turns into an *old biddy*.

36   I embarked on my study of the dictionary not with the intention of prescribing language change but simply to see what the language would tell me about sexism. Nevertheless I have been both surprised and pleased as I've watched the changes that have occurred over the past two decades. I'm one of those linguists who believes that new language customs will cause a new generation of speakers to grow up with different expectations. This is why I'm happy about people's efforts to use inclusive language, to say *he or she* or *they* when speaking about individuals whose names they do not know. I'm glad that leading publishers have developed guidelines to help writers use language that is fair to both sexes, and I'm glad that most newspapers and magazines list women by their own names instead of only by their husbands' names and that educated and thoughtful people no longer begin their business letters with "Dear Sir" or "Gentlemen," but instead use a memo form to begin with such salutations as "Dear Colleagues," "Dear Reader," or "Dear Committee Members." I'm also glad that such words as *poetess, authoress, conductress*, and *aviatrix* now sound quaint and old-fashioned and that *chairman* is giving way to *chair* or *head, mailman* to *mail carrier, clergyman* to *clergy*, and *stewardess* to *flight attendant*. I was also pleased when the National Oceanic and Atmospheric Administration bowed to feminist complaints and in the late 1970s began to alternate men's and women's names for hurricanes. However, I wasn't so pleased to discover that the change did not immediately erase sexist thoughts from everyone's mind, as shown by a headline about Hurricane David in a 1979 New York tabloid, "David Rapes Virgin Islands." More recently a similar metaphor appeared in a headline in the *Arizona Republic* about Hurricane Charlie, "Charlie Quits Carolinas, Flirts with Virginia."

37   What these incidents show is that sexism is not something existing independently in American English or in the particular dictionary that I happened to read. Rather, it exists in people's minds. Language is like an X ray in providing visible evidence of invisible thoughts. The best thing about people being interested in and discussing sexist language is that as they make conscious decisions about what pronouns they will use, what jokes they will tell or laugh at, how they will write their names, or how they will begin their letters, they are forced to think about the underlying issue of sexism. This is good because as a problem that begins in people's assumptions and expectations, it's a problem that will be solved only when a great many people have given it a great deal of thought.

1. In paragraph 1, Nilsen cites an old Afghan proverb: "If you see an old man, sit down and take a lesson; if you see an old woman, throw a stone." She later suggests that the attitude underlying this proverb is still prevalent in the United States in the 1990s. Explain.

2. How does the author use eponyms to advance her thesis? How does she use Greek mythology to strengthen her argument?

3. Nilsen mentions many pairs of words in which the feminine word has acquired negative connotations while the masculine word has not. What are some of these pairs? Can you think of others?

4. In what ways does Nilsen use the wedding ceremony and its aftermath to support her argument?

5. What are some of the problems that *Ms.* has presented as a replacement for *Mrs.* and *Miss*?

6. How do food and animal metaphors help to illustrate the sexist nature of language?

7. Nilsen claims that the chicken metaphor tells the whole story of a woman's life. Explain her point.

8. Nilsen begins her essay with a personal anecdote about experiences she had in Afghanistan. How does the anecdote help introduce her thesis? What is her thesis?

9. Describe the organizational strategy that guides this essay.

10. Discuss Nilsen's use of parallel structure in paragraph 36. Why does she choose to use so noticeable a device at this point in her essay?

11. A good writer relies on concrete examples to make points and develop thoughts. However, a writer who uses too many examples risks losing readers in tedious detail. How do you evaluate Nilsen's use of concrete examples?

Assignment

Write an essay in response to one of the following quotations. (Use Nilsen's examples as well as your own to develop your argument.)

A. "Language and society are as intertwined as a chicken and an egg" (paragraph 5).
B. "Early in life, children are conditioned to the superiority of the masculine role" (paragraph 29).
C. "I'm one of those linguists who believes that new language customs will cause a new generation of speakers to grow up with different expectations" (paragraph 36).

"Put Down That Paper and Talk to Me!": Rapport-Talk and Report-Talk

Deborah Tannen

Deborah Tannen is a university professor and author of many books and articles that stress the power of language to reveal human relationships and to influence them, often with considerable force. In the following excerpt from her best-selling book *You Just Don't Understand: Women and Men in Conversation,* Tannen poses the question, "Who talks more, women or men?" The answer involves not simply counting words; instead, we must understand how often men and women use language to achieve different, sometimes conflicting, purposes.

■ **JOURNAL PROMPT** *Before reading this selection, think about the speaking habits of men and women. Make a list of differences you recall. Consider both private and group conversations as well as public occasions (meetings, classes, and so forth).*

1   I was sitting in a suburban living room, speaking to a women's group that had invited men to join them for the occasion of my talk about communication between women and men. During the discussion, one man was particularly talkative, full of lengthy comments and explanations. When I made the observation that women often complain that their husbands don't talk to them enough, this man volunteered that he heartily agreed. He gestured toward his wife, who had sat silently beside him on the couch throughout the evening, and said, "She's the talker in our family."

2   Everyone in the room burst into laughter. The man looked puzzled and hurt. "It's true," he explained. "When I come home from work, I usually have nothing to say, but she never runs out. If it weren't for her, we'd spend the whole evening in silence." Another woman expressed a similar paradox about her husband: "When we go out, he's the life of the party. If I happen to be in another room, I can always hear his voice above the others. But when we're home, he doesn't have that much to say. I do most of the talking."

3   Who talks more, women or men? According to the stereotype, women talk too much. Linguist Jennifer Coates notes some proverbs:

> A woman's tongue wags like a lamb's tail.
> Foxes are all tail and women are all tongue.

> The North Sea will sooner be found wanting in water than
> a woman be at a loss for a word.

Throughout history, women have been punished for talking too much or in the wrong way. Linguist Connie Eble lists a variety of physical punishments used in Colonial America: Women were strapped to ducking stools and held underwater until they nearly drowned, put into the stocks with signs pinned to them, gagged, and silenced by a cleft stick applied to their tongues.

4   Though such institutionalized corporal punishments have given way to informal, often psychological ones, modern stereotypes are not much different from those expressed in the old proverbs. Women are believed to talk too much. Yet study after study finds that it is men who talk more—at meetings, in mixed-group discussions, and in classrooms where girls or young women sit next to boys or young men. For example, communications researchers Barbara and Gene Eakins tape-recorded and studied seven university faculty meetings. They found that, with one exception, men spoke more often and, without exception, spoke for a longer time. The men's turns ranged from 10.66 to 17.07 seconds, while the women's turns ranged from 3 to 10 seconds. In other words, the women's longest turns were still shorter than the men's shortest turns.

5   When a public lecture is followed by questions from the floor, or a talk show host opens the phones, the first voice to be heard asking a question is almost always a man's. And when they ask questions or offer comments from the audience, men tend to talk longer. Linguist Marjorie Swacker recorded question-and-answer sessions at academic conferences. Women were highly visible as speakers at the conferences studied; they presented 40.7 percent of the papers at the conferences studied and made up 42 percent of the audiences. But when it came to volunteering and being called on to ask questions, women contributed only 27.4 percent. Furthermore, the women's questions, on the average, took less than half as much time as the men's. (The mean was 23.1 seconds for women, 52.7 for men.) This happened, Swacker shows, because men (but not women) tended to preface their questions with statements, ask more than one question, and follow up the speaker's answer with another question or comment.

6   I have observed this pattern at my own lectures, which concern issues of direct relevance to women. Regardless of the proportion of women and men in the audience, men almost invariably ask the first question, more questions, and longer questions. In these situations, women often feel that men are talking too much. I recall one discussion period following a lecture I gave to a group assembled in a bookstore. The group was composed mostly of women, but most of the discussion was being conducted by men in the audience. At one point, a man sitting in the middle was talking at such great length that several women in the front rows began shifting in their seats and rolling their eyes at me. Ironically, what he was going on about was how frustrated he feels when he has to listen to women going on and on about topics he finds boring and unimportant.

Rapport-Talk and Report-Talk

7   Who talks more, then, women or men? The seemingly contradictory evidence is reconciled by the difference between what I call *public* and *private speaking*. More

men feel comfortable doing "public speaking," while more women feel comfortable doing "private" speaking. Another way of capturing these differences is by using the terms *report-talk* and *rapport-talk*.

8   For most women, the language of conversation is primarily a language of rapport: a way of establishing connections and negotiating relationships. Emphasis is placed on displaying similarities and matching experiences. From childhood, girls criticize peers who try to stand out or appear better than others. People feel their closest connections at home, or in settings where they *feel* at home—with one or a few people they feel close to and comfortable with—in other words, during private speaking. But even the most public situations can be approached like private speaking.

9   For most men, talk is primarily a means to preserve independence and negotiate and maintain status in a hierarchical social order. This is done by exhibiting knowledge and skill, and by holding center stage through verbal performance such as storytelling, joking, or imparting information. From childhood, men learn to use talking as a way to get and keep attention. So they are more comfortable speaking in larger groups made up of people they know less well—in the broadest sense, "public speaking." But even the most private situations can be approached like public speaking, more like giving a report than establishing rapport.

Best Friends

10   Once again, the seeds of women's and men's styles are sown in the ways they learn to use language while growing up. In our culture, most people, but especially women, look to their closest relationships as havens in a hostile world. The center of a little girl's social life is her best friend. Girls' friendships are made and maintained by telling secrets. For grown women too, the essence of friendship is talk, telling each other what they're thinking and feeling, and what happened that day: who was at the bus stop, who called, what they said, how that made them feel. When asked who their best friends are, most women name other women they talk to regularly. When asked the same question, most men will say it's their wives. After that, many men name other men with whom they do things such as play tennis or baseball (but never just sit and talk) or a chum from high school whom they haven't spoken to in a year.

11   When Debbie Reynolds complained that Dick Van Dyke didn't tell her anything, and he protested that he did, both were right. She felt he didn't tell her anything because he didn't tell her the fleeting thoughts and feelings he experienced throughout the day—the kind of talk she would have with her best friend. He didn't tell her these things because to him they didn't seem like anything to tell. He told her anything that seemed important—anything he would tell his friends.

12   Men and women often have very different ideas of what's important—and at what point "important" topics should be raised. A woman told me, with lingering incredulity, of a conversation with her boyfriend. Knowing he had seen his friend Oliver, she asked, "What's new with Oliver?" He replied, "Nothing." But later in the conversation it came out that Oliver and his girlfriend had decided to get married. "That's nothing?" the woman gasped in frustration and disbelief.

13   For men, "Nothing" may be a ritual response at the start of a conversation. A college woman missed her brother but rarely called him because she found it difficult to get talk going. A typical conversation began with her asking, "What's up with you?" and his replying, "Nothing." Hearing his "Nothing" as meaning "There is nothing personal I want to talk about," she supplied talk by filling him in on her news and eventually hung up in frustration. But when she thought back, she remembered that later in the conversation he had mumbled, "Christie and I got into another fight." This came so late and so low that she didn't pick up on it. And he was probably equally frustrated that she didn't.

14   Many men honestly do not know what women want, and women honestly do not know why men find what they want so hard to comprehend and deliver.

Making Adjustments

15   Such impasses will perhaps never be settled to the complete satisfaction of both parties, but understanding the differing views can help detoxify the situation, and both can make adjustments. Realizing that men and women have different assumptions about the place of talk in relationships, a woman can observe a man's desire to read the morning paper at the breakfast table without interpreting it as a rejection of her or a failure of their relationship. And a man can understand a woman's desire for talk without interpreting it as an unreasonable demand or a manipulative attempt to prevent him from doing what he wants to do.

16   A woman who had heard my interpretations of these differences between women and men told me how these insights helped her. Early in a promising relationship, a man spent the night at her apartment. It was a weeknight, and they both had to go to work the next day, so she was delighted when he made the rash and romantic suggestion that they have breakfast together and report late for work. She happily prepared breakfast, looking forward to the scene shaped in her mind: They would sit facing each other across her small table, look into each other's eyes, and say how much they liked each other and how happy they were about their growing friendship. It was against the backdrop of this heady expectation that she confronted an entirely different scene: As she placed on the table an array of lovingly prepared eggs, toast, and coffee, the man sat across her small table—and opened the newspaper in front of his face. If suggesting they have breakfast together had seemed like an invitation to get closer, in her view (or obstructing her view) the newspaper was now erected as a paper-thin but nonetheless impenetrable barrier between them.

17   Had she known nothing of the gender differences I discuss, she would simply have felt hurt and dismissed this man as yet another clunker. She would have concluded that, having enjoyed the night with her, he was now availing himself of her further services as a short-order cook. Instead, she realized that, unlike her, he did not feel the need for talk to reinforce their intimacy. The companionability of her presence was all he needed, and that did not mean that he didn't cherish her presence. By the same token, had he understood the essential role played by talk in women's definition of intimacy, he could have put off reading the paper—and avoided putting her off.

The Comfort of Home

18   For everyone, home is a place to be offstage. But the comfort of home can have opposite and incompatible meanings for women and men. For many men, the comfort of home means freedom from having to prove themselves and impress through verbal display. At last, they are in a situation where talk is not required. They are free to remain silent. But for women, home is a place where they are free to talk, and where they feel the greatest need for talk, with those they are closest to. For them, the comfort of home means the freedom to talk without worrying about how their talk will be judged.

19   This view emerged in a study by linguist Alice Greenwood of the conversations that took place among her three preadolescent children and their friends. Her daughters and son gave different reasons for their preferences in dinner guests. Her daughter Stacy said she would not want to invite people she didn't know well because then she would have to be "polite and quiet" and put on good manners. Greenwood's other daughter, Denise, said she liked to have her friend Meryl over because she could act crazy with Meryl and didn't have to worry about her manners, as she would with certain other friends who "would go around talking to people probably." But Denise's twin brother, Dennis, said nothing about having to watch his manners or worry about how others would judge his behavior. He simply said that he liked to have over friends with whom he could joke and laugh a lot. The girls' comments show that for them being close means being able to talk freely. And being with relative strangers means having to watch what they say and do. This insight holds a clue to the riddle of who talks more, women or men.

Public Speaking: The Talkative Man and the Silent Woman

20   So far I have been discussing the private scenes in which many men are silent and many women are talkative. But there are other scenes in which the roles are reversed. Returning to Rebecca and Stuart [the imaginary couple introduced earlier as an example], we saw that when they are home alone, Rebecca's thoughts find their way into words effortlessly, whereas Stuart finds he can't come up with anything to say. The reverse happens when they are in other situations. For example, at a meeting of the neighborhood council or the parents' association at their children's school, it is Stuart who stands up and speaks. In that situation, it is Rebecca who is silent, her tongue tied by an acute awareness of all the negative reactions people could have to what she might say, all the mistakes she might make in trying to express her ideas. If she musters her courage and prepares to say something, she needs time to formulate it and then waits to be recognized by the chair. She cannot just jump up and start talking the way Stuart and some other men can.

21   Eleanor Smeal, president of the Fund for the Feminist Majority, was a guest on a call-in radio talk show, discussing abortion. No subject could be of more direct concern to women, yet during the hour-long show, all the callers except two were men.

Diane Rehm, host of a radio talk show, expresses puzzlement that although the audience for her show is evenly split between women and men, 90 percent of the callers to the show are men. I am convinced that the reason is not that women are uninterested in the subjects discussed on the show. I would wager that women listeners are bringing up the subjects they heard on *The Diane Rehm Show* to their friends and family over lunch, tea, and dinner. But fewer of them call in because to do so would be putting themselves on display, claiming public attention for what they have to say, catapulting themselves onto center stage.

22   I myself have been the guest on innumerable radio and television talk shows. Perhaps I am unusual in being completely at ease in this mode of display. But perhaps I am not unusual at all, because, although I am comfortable in the role of invited expert, I have never called in to a talk show I was listening to, although I have often had ideas to contribute. When I am the guest, my position of authority is granted before I begin to speak. Were I to call in, I would be claiming that right on my own. I would have to establish my credibility by explaining who I am, which might seem self-aggrandizing, or not explain who I am and risk having my comments ignored or not valued. For similar reasons, though I am comfortable lecturing to groups numbering in the thousands, I rarely ask questions following another lecturer's talk, unless I know both the subject and the group very well.

23   My own experience and that of talk show hosts seems to hold a clue to the difference in women's and men's attitudes toward talk: Many men are more comfortable than most women in using talk to claim attention. And this difference lies at the heart of the distinction between report-talk and rapport-talk.

Avoiding Mutual Blame

24   The difference between public and private speaking, or report-talk and rapport-talk, can be understood in terms of status and connections. It is not surprising that women are most comfortable talking when they feel safe and close, among friends and equals, whereas men feel comfortable talking when there is a need to establish and maintain their status in a group. But the situation is complex, because status and connection are bought with the same currency. What seems like a bid for status could be intended as a display of closeness, and what seems like distancing may have been intended to avoid the appearance of pulling rank. Hurtful and unjustified misinterpretations can be avoided by understanding the conversational styles of the other gender.

25   When men do all the talking at meetings, many women—including researchers—see them as "dominating" the meeting, intentionally preventing women from participating, publicly flexing their higher-status muscles. But the *result* that men do most of the talking does not necessarily mean that men *intend* to prevent women from speaking. Those who readily speak up assume that others are as free as they are to take the floor. In this sense, men's speaking out freely can be seen as evidence that they assume women are at the same level of status: "We are all equals," the meta-message of their behavior could be, "competing for the floor." If this is indeed the

intention (and I believe it often, though not always is), a woman can recognize women's lack of participation at meetings and take measures to redress the imbalance, without blaming men for intentionally locking them out.

26   The culprit, then, is not an individual man or even men's styles alone, but the difference between women's and men's styles. If that is the case, then both can make adjustments. A woman can push herself to speak up without being invited, or begin to speak without waiting for what seems a polite pause. But the adjustment should not be one-sided. A man can learn that a woman who is not accustomed to speaking up in groups is not as free as he is to do so. Someone who is waiting for a nice long pause before asking her question does not find the stage set for her appearance, as do those who are not awaiting a pause, the moment after (or before) another speaker stops talking. Someone who expects to be invited to speak ("You haven't said much, Millie. What do you think?") is not accustomed to leaping in and claiming the floor for herself. As in so many areas, being admitted as an equal is not in itself assurance of equal opportunity, if one is not accustomed to playing the game in the way it is being played. Being admitted to a dance does not ensure the participation of someone who has learned to dance to a different rhythm.

Questions on Content

1. Describe the differences Tannen mentions between the speech habits of men and women.

2. In your own words, describe the differences between rapport-talk and report-talk.

3. According to Tannen, how do women and men regard the notion of best friend? How are these differences consistent with Tannen's thesis?

4. Explain why Tannen suggests it is important for both men and women to understand differences in "gender-speak."

5. Discuss how differently men and women view home. Explain how these attitudes relate to speaking habits.

Questions on Structure and Style

6. Tannen begins her essay with an anecdote. Discuss the effectiveness of this opening technique. Suggest other opening techniques that might be appropriate for this essay.

7. Describe the tone of this essay. Is Tannen objective in her discussion of speech habits, or is she judgmental? Do you find humor in the essay?

8. Discuss the effectiveness of Tannen's final two sentences.

Assignments

1. Reflect on Tannen's essay as well as the list you compiled for the Journal Prompt. Write an essay in which you draw on personal experience and observation to illustrate the contrasting styles of speech of men and women. Use an anecdote to open your essay. Be certain to develop your essay with concrete illustrations.

2. Write an essay in which you describe the speech habits of a couple you know well. Does the couple correspond to the gender distinctions Tannen suggests?

3. On most dates, who talks more, men or women? On most dates, what do men talk about? And women? If they don't talk about the same things, why? Respond in an essay.

Real Men Don't: Anti-Male Bias in English

Eugene R. August

"Sexist language" usually connotes antifemale language. However, as university professor Eugene R. August illustrates with abundant specific evidence, antimale language permeates the English we use every day, and it warps both our expectations for men as well as their own codes of behavior. For August, just as bigotry victimizes both men and women, language can, and too often does, target either sex with equal efficiency.

■ **J O U R N A L   P R O M P T** *In the selection that follows, Eugene R. August asserts that men are as victimized by language as women. Before reading the essay, freewrite for ten or fifteen minutes on situations you have observed in which language victimizes both men and women.*

1 Despite numerous studies of sex bias in language during the past fifteen years, only rarely has anti-male bias been examined. In part, this neglect occurs because many of these studies have been based upon assumptions which are questionable at best and which at worst exhibit their own form of sex bias. Whether explicitly or implicitly, many of these studies reduce human history to a tale of male oppressors and female victims or rebels. In this view of things, all societies become *patriarchal societies*, a familiar term used to suggest that for centuries males have conspired to exploit and demean females. Accordingly, it is alleged in many of these studies that men control language and that they use it to define women and women's roles as inferior.

2 Despite the popularity of such a view, it has received scant support from leading social scientists, including one of the giants of modern anthropology, Margaret Mead. Anticipating current ideology, Mead in *Male and Female* firmly rejected the notion of a "male conspiracy to keep women in their place," arguing instead that

> the historical trend that listed women among the abused minorities . . . lingers on to obscure the issue and gives apparent point to the contention that this is a man-made world in which women have always been abused and must always fight for their rights.
>
> It takes considerable effort on the part of both men and women to reorient ourselves to thinking—when we think basically—that this is a world not made by men alone, in which women are unwilling and helpless dupes and fools or else powerful schemers hiding their power under their ruffled petticoats, but a world made by mankind for human beings of both sexes. (298, 299–300)

The model described by Mead and other social scientists shows a world in which women and men have lived together throughout history in a symbiotic relationship, often mutually agreeing upon the definition of gender roles and the distribution of various powers and duties.

3   More importantly for the subject of bias in speech and writing, women—as well as men—have shaped language. As Walter J. Ong reminds us,

> Women talk and think as much as men do, and with few exceptions we all . . . learn to talk and think in the first instance largely from women, usually and predominantly our mothers. Our first tongue is called our "mother tongue" in English and in many other languages. . . . There are no father tongues. . . . (36)

Feminists like Dorothy Dinnerstein agree: "There seems no reason to doubt that the baby-tending sex contributed at least equally with the history-making one to the most fundamental of all human inventions: language" (22). Because gender roles and language are shaped by society in general—that is, by both men and women— anti-male bias in language is as possible as anti-female bias.

4   To say this, however, is emphatically not to blame women alone, or even primarily, for anti-male usage. If guilt must be assigned, it would have to be placed upon sexist people, both male and female, who use language to manipulate gender role behavior and to create negative social attitudes towards males. But often it is difficult to point a finger of blame: except where prejudiced gender stereotypes are deliberately fostered, most people evidently use sex-biased terminology without clearly understanding its import. In the long run, it is wiser to concentrate not on fixing blame, but on heightening public awareness of anti-male language and on discouraging its use. In particular, teachers and writers need to become aware of and to question language which denigrates or stereotypes males.

5   In modern English, three kinds of anti-male usage are evident: first, gender-exclusive language which omits males from certain kinds of consideration; second, gender-restrictive language which attempts to restrict males to an accepted gender role, some aspects of which may be outmoded, burdensome, or destructive; and third, negative stereotypes of males which are insulting, dehumanizing, and potentially dangerous.

6   Although gender-exclusive language which excludes females has often been studied, few students of language have noted usage which excludes males. Those academics, for example, who have protested *alumnus* and *alumni* as gender-exclusive terms to describe a university's male and female graduates have failed to notice that, by the same logic, *alma mater* (nourishing mother) is an equally gender-exclusive term to describe the university itself. Those who have protested *man* and *mankind* as generic terms have not begun to question *mammal* as a term of biological classification, but by categorizing animals according to the female's ability to suckle the young through her mammary glands, *mammal* clearly omits the male of the species. Consequently, it is as suspect as generic *man*.

7   In general, gender-exclusive usage in English excludes males as parents and as victims. Until recently, the equating of *mother* with *parent* in the social sciences was notorious: a major sociological study published in 1958 with the title *The Changing American Parent* was based upon interviews with 582 mothers and no fathers (Roman and Haddad 87). Although no longer prevalent in the social sciences, the interchangeability of *mother* and *parent* is still common, except for *noncustodial parent* which is almost always a synonym for *father*. A recent ad for *Parents* magazine

begins: "To be the best mother you can be, you want practical, reliable answers to the questions a mother must face." Despite the large number of men now seen pushing shopping carts, advertisers still insist that "Choosy mothers choose Jif" and "My Mom's a Butternut Mom." Frequently, children are regarded as belonging solely to the mother, as in phrases like *women and their children*. The idea of the mother as primary parent can be glimpsed in such expressions as *mother tongue, mother wit, mother lode, mother of invention*, and *mothering* as a synonym for *parenting*.

8   The male as victim is ignored in such familiar expressions as *innocent women and children*. In June 1985, when President Reagan rejected a bombing strike to counter terrorist activities, newspapers reported that the decision had been made to prevent "the deaths of many innocent women and children in strife-torn Lebanon" (Glass). Presumably, strife-torn Lebanon contained no innocent men. Likewise, *rape victim* means females only, an assumption made explicit in the opening sentences of this newspaper article on rape: "Crime knows no gender. Yet, there is one offense that only women are prey to: rape" (Mougey). The thousands of males raped annually, in addition to the sexual assaults regularly inflicted upon males in prison, are here entirely overlooked. (That these males have been victimized mostly by other males does not disqualify them as victims of sexual violence, as some people assume.) Similarly, the term *wife and child abuse* conceals the existence of an estimated 282,000 husbands who are battered annually (O'Reilly et al. 23). According to many expressions in English, males are not parents and they are never victimized.

9   Unlike gender-exclusive language, gender-restrictive language is usually applied to males only, often to keep them within the confines of a socially prescribed gender role. When considering gender-restrictive language, one must keep in mind that—as Ruth E. Hartley has pointed out—the masculine gender role is enforced earlier and more harshly than the feminine role is (235). In addition, because the boy is often raised primarily by females in the virtual absence of close adult males, his grasp of what is required of him to *be a man* is often unsure. Likewise, prescriptions for male behavior are usually given in the negative, leading to the "Real Men Don't" syndrome, a process which further confuses the boy. Such circumstances leave many males extremely vulnerable to language which questions their sense of masculinity.

10   Furthermore, during the past twenty years an increasing number of men and women have been arguing that aspects of our society's masculine gender role are emotionally constrictive, unnecessarily stressful, and potentially lethal. Rejecting "the myth of masculine privilege," psychologist Herb Goldberg reports in *The Hazards of Being Male* that "every critical statistic in the area of [early death], disease, suicide, crime, accidents, childhood emotional disorders, alcoholism, and drug addiction shows a disproportionately higher male rate" (5). But changes in the masculine role are so disturbing to so many people that the male who attempts to break out of familiar gender patterns often finds himself facing hostile opposition which can be readily and powerfully expressed in a formidable array of sex-biased terms.

11   To see how the process works, let us begin early in the male life cycle. A boy quickly learns that, while it is usually acceptable for girls to be *tomboys*, God forbid that he should be a *sissy*. In *Sexual Signatures: On Being a Man or a Woman* John Money and Patricia Tucker note:

> The current feminine stereotype in our culture is flexible enough to let a girl behave "boyishly" if she wants to without bringing her femininity into question, but any boy who exhibits "girlish" behavior is promptly suspected of being queer. There isn't even a word corresponding to "tomboy" to describe such a boy. "Sissy" perhaps comes closest, or "artistic" and "sensitive," but unlike "tomboy," such terms are burdened with unfavorable connotations. (72)

Lacking a favorable or even neutral term to describe the boy who is quiet, gentle, and emotional, the English language has long had a rich vocabulary to insult and ridicule such boys—*mama's boy, molly-coddle, milksop, muff, twit, softy, creampuff, panty-waist, weenie, Miss Nancy*, and so on. Although sometimes used playfully, the currently popular *wimp* can be used to insult males from childhood right into adulthood.

12   Discussion of words like *sissy* as insults has been often one-sided: most commentators are content to argue that the female, not the male, is being insulted by such usage. "The implicit sexism" in such terms, writes one commentator, "disparages the woman, not the man" (Sorrels 87). Although the female is being slurred indirectly by these terms, a moment's reflection will show that the primary force of the insult is being directed against the male, specifically the male who cannot differentiate himself from the feminine. Ong argues in *Fighting for Life* that most societies place heavy pressure on males to differentiate themselves from females because the prevailing environment of human society is feminine (70–71). In English-speaking societies, terms like *sissy* and *weak sister*, which have been used by both females and males, are usually perceived not as insults to females but as ridicule of males who have allegedly failed to differentiate themselves from the feminine.

13   Being *all boy* carries penalties, however: for one thing, it means being less lovable. As the nursery rhyme tells children, little girls are made of "sugar and spice and all that's nice," while little boys are made of "frogs and snails and puppy-dogs' tails." Or, as an American version of the rhyme puts it:

> Girls are dandy
> Made of candy—
> That's what little girls are made of.
> Boys are rotten,
> Made of cotton—
> That's what little boys are made of.
>
> (Baring-Gould 176n116)

When not enjoined to *be all boy*, our young lad will be urged to *be a big boy, be a brave soldier*, and (the ultimate appeal) *be a man*. These expressions almost invariably mean that the boy is about to suffer something painful or humiliating. The variant—*take it like a man*—provides the clue. As Paul Theroux defines it, *be a man* means: "Be stupid, be unfeeling, obedient and soldierly, and stop thinking."

14   Following our boy further into the life cycle, we discover that in school he will find himself in a cruel bind: girls his age will be biologically and socially more mature than he is, at least until around age eighteen. Until then, any ineptness in his social role will be castigated by a host of terms which are reserved almost entirely for males.

"For all practical purposes," John Gordon remarks, "the word 'turkey' (or whatever the equivalent is now) can be translated as 'a boy spurned by influential girls'" (141). The equivalents of *turkey* are many: *jerk, nerd, clod, klutz, schmuck, dummy, goon, dork, square, dweeb, jackass, meathead, geek, zero, reject, goofball, drip*, and numerous others, including many obscene terms. Recently, a Michigan high school decided to do away with a scheduled "Nerd Day" after a fourteen-year-old male student, who apparently had been so harassed as a nerd by other students, committed suicide ("'Nerd' day"). In this case, the ability of language to devastate the emotionally vulnerable young male is powerfully and pathetically dramatized.

15   As our boy grows, he faces threats and taunts if he does not take risks or endure pain to prove his manhood. *Coward,* for example, is a word applied almost exclusively to males in our society, as are its numerous variants—*chicken, chickenshit, yellow, yellow-bellied, lily-livered, weak-kneed, spineless, squirrelly, fraidy cat, gutless wonder, weakling, butterfly, jellyfish*, and so on. If our young man walks away from a stupid quarrel or prefers to settle differences more rationally than with a swift jab to the jaw, the English language is richly supplied with these and other expressions to call his masculinity into question.

16   Chief among the other expressions that question masculinity is a lengthy list of homophobic terms such as *queer, pansy, fag, faggot, queen, queeny, pervert, bugger, deviant, fairy, tinkerbell, puss, priss, flamer, feller, sweet, precious, fruit, sodomite*, and numerous others, many obscene. For many people, *gay* is an all-purpose word of ridicule and condemnation. Once again, although homosexuals are being insulted by these terms, the primary target is more often the heterosexual male who fails or refuses to live up to someone else's idea of masculinity. In "Homophobia Among Men" Gregory Lehne explains, "Homophobia is used as a technique of social control . . . to enforce the norms of male sex-role behavior. . . . [H]omosexuality is not the real threat, the real threat is change in the male sex-role" (77).

17   Nowhere is this threat more apparent than in challenges to our society's male-only military obligation. When a young man and a young woman reach the age of eighteen, both may register to vote; only the young man is required by law to register for military service. For the next decade at least, he must stand ready to be called into military service and even into combat duty in wars, "police actions," "peacekeeping missions," and "rescue missions," often initiated by legally dubious means. Should he resist this obligation, he may be called a *draft dodger, deserter, peacenik, traitor, shirker, slacker, malingerer*, and similar terms. Should he declare himself a conscientious objector, he may be labeled a *conchy* or any of the variants of *coward.*

18   In his relationships with women, he will find that the age of equality has not yet arrived. Usually, he will be expected to take the initiative, do the driving, pick up the tab, and in general show a deferential respect for women that is a left-over from the chivalric code. Should he behave in an *ungentlemanly* fashion, a host of words— which are applied almost always to males alone—can be used to tell him so: *louse, rat, creep, sleaze, scum, stain, worm, fink, heel, stinker, animal, savage, bounder, cad, wolf, gigolo, womanizer, Don Juan, pig, rotter, boor*, and so on.

19   In sexual matters he will usually be expected to take the initiative and to *perform.* If he does not, he will be labeled *impotent.* This word, writes Goldberg, "is clearly

sexist because it implies a standard of acceptable masculine sexual performance that makes a man abnormal if he can't live up to it" (*New Male* 248). Metaphorically, *impotent* can be used to demean any male whose efforts in any area are deemed unacceptable. Even if our young man succeeds at his sexual performance, the sex manuals are ready to warn him that if he reaches orgasm before a specified time he is guilty of *premature ejaculation*.

[handwritten margin note: What this does to have to do w/ anything?]

20   When our young man marries, he will be required by law and social custom to support his wife and children. Should he not succeed as breadwinner or should he relax in his efforts, the language offers numerous terms to revile him: *loser, dead-beat, bum, freeloader, leech, parasite, goldbrick, sponge, mooch, ne'er-do-well, good for nothing*, and so on. If women in our society have been regarded as sex objects, men have been regarded as success objects, that is, judged by their ability to provide a standard of living. The title of a recent book—*How to Marry a Winner*—reveals immediately that the intended audience is female (Collier).

21   When he becomes a father, our young man will discover that he is a second-class parent, as the traditional interchangeability of *mother* and *parent* indicates. The law has been particularly obtuse in recognizing fathers as parents, as evidenced by the awarding of child custody to mothers in ninety percent of divorce cases. In 1975 a father's petition for custody of his four-year-old son was denied because, as the family court judge said, "Fathers don't make good mothers" (qtd. in Levine 21). The judge apparently never considered whether *fathers* made good *parents*.

22   And so it goes throughout our young man's life: if he deviates from society's gender role norm, he will be penalized and he will hear about it.

23   The final form of anti-male bias to be considered here is negative stereotyping. Sometimes this stereotyping is indirectly embedded in the language, sometimes it resides in people's assumptions about males and shapes their response to seemingly neutral words, and sometimes it is overtly created for political reasons. It is one thing to say that some aspects of the traditional masculine gender role are limiting and hurtful; it is quite another to gratuitously suspect males in general of being criminal and evil or to denounce them in wholesale fashion as oppressors, exploiters, and rapists. In *The New Male* Goldberg writes, "Men may very well be the last remaining subgroup in our society that can be blatantly, negatively and vilely stereotyped with little objection or resistance" (103). As our language demonstrates, such sexist stereotyping, whether unintentional or deliberate, is not only familiar but fashionable.

24   In English, crime and evil are usually attributed to the male. As an experiment I have compiled lists of nouns which I read to my composition students, asking them to check whether the words suggest "primarily females," "primarily males," or "could be either." Nearly all the words for law-breakers suggest males rather than females to most students. These words include *murderer, swindler, crook, criminal, burglar, thief, gangster, mobster, hood, hitman, killer, pickpocket, mugger*, and *terrorist*. Accounting for this phenomenon is not always easy. *Hitman* may obviously suggest "primarily males," and the *-er* in *murderer* may do the same, especially if it reminds students of the word's feminine form, *murderess*. Likewise, students may be aware that most murders are committed by males. Other words—like *criminal* and *thief*—are more clearly gender-neutral in form, and it is less clear why they should

be so closely linked with "primarily males." Although the dynamics of the association may be unclear, English usage somehow conveys a subtle suggestion that males
are to be regarded as guilty in matters of law-breaking.

25   This hint of male guilt extends to a term like *suspect*. When the person's gender
is unknown, the suspect is usually presumed to be a male. For example, even before
a definite suspect had been identified, the perpetrator of the 1980–1981 Atlanta child
murders was popularly known as *The Man*. When a male and female are suspected
of a crime, the male is usually presumed the guilty party. In a recent murder case,
when two suspects—Debra Brown and Alton Coleman—were apprehended, police
discovered *Brown's* fingerprint in a victim's car and interpreted this as evidence of
Coleman's guilt. As the Associated Press reported:

> Authorities say for the first time they have evidence linking Alton Coleman with the
> death of an Indianapolis man.
>   A fingerprint found in the car of Eugene Scott has been identified as that of Debra
> Brown, Coleman's traveling companion . . ." ("Police").

Nowhere does the article suggest that Brown's fingerprint found in the victim's car
linked Brown with the death: the male suspect was presumed the guilty party, while
the female was only a "traveling companion." Even after Brown had been convicted
of two murders, the Associated Press was still describing her as "the accused accom-
plice of convicted killer Alton Coleman" ("Indiana").

26   In some cases, this presumption of male guilt extends to crimes in which males
are not the principal offenders. As noted earlier, a term like *wife and child abuse*
ignores battered husbands, but it does more: it suggests that males alone abuse
children. In reality most child abuse is committed by mothers (Straus, Gelles,
Steinmetz 71). Despite this fact, a 1978 study of child abuse bears the title *Sins of
the Fathers* (Inglis).

27   The term *rape* creates special problems. While the majority of rapes are committed by males and the number of female rape victims outdistances the number of
male rape victims, it is widely assumed—as evidenced by the newspaper article cited
above—that rape is a crime committed only by males in which only females are
victims. Consequently, the word *rape* is often used as a brush to tar all males. In
Against Our Will Susan Brownmiller writes: "From prehistoric times to the present,
I believe, rape . . . is nothing more or less than a conscious process of intimidation
by which *all men* keep *all women* in a state of fear" (15; italics in original). Making
the point explicitly, Marilyn French states, "All men are rapists and that's all they
are" (qtd. in Jennes 33). Given this kind of smear tactic, *rape* can be used metaphorically to indict males alone and to exonerate females, as in this sentence: "The
rape of nature—and the ecological disaster it presages—is part and parcel of a dominating masculinity gone out of control" (Hoch 137). The statement neatly blames
males alone even when the damage to the environment has been caused in part by
females like Anne Gorsuch Burford and Rita Lavelle.

28   Not only crimes but vices of all sorts have been typically attributed to males.
As Muriel R. Schulz points out, "The synonyms for *inebriate* . . . seem to be coded

primarily 'male': for example, *boozer, drunkard, tippler, toper, swiller, tosspot, guzzler, barfly, drunk, lush, boozehound, souse, tank, stew, rummy*, and *bum*" (126). Likewise someone may be *drunk as a lord* but never *drunk as a lady*.

29   Sex bias or sexism itself is widely held to be a male-only fault. When *sexism* is defined as "contempt for women"—as if there were no such thing as contempt for men—the definition of *sexism* is itself sexist (Bardwick 34).

30   Part of the reason for this masculinization of evil may be that in the Western world the source of evil has long been depicted in male terms. In the Bible the Evil One is consistently referred to as *he*, whether the reference is to the serpent in the Garden of Eden, Satan as Adversary in Job, Lucifer and Beelzebub in the gospels, Jesus' tempter in the desert, or the dragon in Revelations. *Beelzebub*, incidentally, is often translated as *lord of the flies*, a term designating the demon as masculine. So masculine is the word *devil* that the female prefix is needed, as in *she-devil*, to make a feminine noun of it. The masculinization of evil is so unconsciously accepted that writers often attest to it even while attempting to deny it, as in this passage:

> From the very beginning, the Judeo-Christian tradition has linked women and evil. When second-century theologians struggled to explain the Devil's origins, they surmised that Satan and his various devils had once been angels.
>
>   (Gerzon 224)

If the Judeo-Christian tradition has linked women and evil so closely, why is the writer using the masculine pronoun *his* to refer to Satan, the source of evil according to that tradition? Critics of sex-bias in religious language seldom notice or mention its masculinization of evil: of those objecting to *God the Father* as sexist, no one—to my knowledge—has suggested that designating Satan as the *Father of Lies* is equally sexist. Few theologians talk about Satan and her legions.

31   The tendency to blame nearly everything on men has climaxed in recent times with the popularity of such terms as *patriarchy, patriarchal society*, and *male-dominated society*. More political than descriptive, these terms are rapidly becoming meaningless, used as all-purpose smear words to conjure up images of male oppressors and female victims. They are a linguistic sleight of hand which obscures the point that, as Mead has observed (299–300), societies are largely created by both sexes for both sexes. By using a swift reference to *patriarchal structures* or *patriarchal attitudes*, a writer can absolve females of all blame for society's flaws while fixing the onus solely on males. The give-away of this ploy can be detected when *patriarchy* and its related terms are never used in a positive or neutral context, but are always used to assign blame to males alone.

32   Wholesale denunciations of males as oppressors, exploiters, rapists, Nazis, and slave-drivers have become all too familiar during the past fifteen years. Too often the academic community, rather than opposing this sexism, has been encouraging it. All too many scholars and teachers have hopped on the male-bashing bandwagon to disseminate what John Gordon calls "the myth of the monstrous male." With increasing frequency, this academically fashionable sexism can also be heard echoing from our students. "A white upper-middle-class straight male should seriously consider another

college," declares a midwestern college student in *The New York Times Selective Guide to Colleges*. "You [the white male] are the bane of the world. . . . Ten generations of social ills can and will be strapped upon your shoulders" (qtd. in Fiske 12). It would be comforting to dismiss this student's compound of misinformation, sexism, racism, and self-righteousness as an extreme example, but similar yahooisms go unchallenged almost everywhere in modern academia.

33   Surely it is time for men and women of good will to reject and protest such bigotry. For teachers and writers, the first task is to recognize and condemn forms of anti-male bias in language, whether they are used to exclude males from equal consideration with females, to reinforce restrictive aspects of the masculine gender role, or to stereotype males callously. For whether males are told that *fathers don't make good mothers*, that *real men don't cry*, or that *all men are rapists*, the results are potentially dangerous: like any other group, males can be subtly shaped into what society keeps telling them they are. In *Why Men Are the Way They Are* Warren Farrell puts the matter succinctly: "The more we make men the enemy, the more they will have to behave like the enemy" (357).

Works Cited

Bardwick, Judith. *In Transition: How Feminism, Sexual Liberation, and the Search for Self-Fulfillment Have Altered Our Lives*. New York: Holt, 1979.

Baring-Gould, William S., and Ceil Baring-Gould. *The Annotated Mother Goose: Nursery Rhymes Old and New, Arranged and Explained*. New York: Clarkson N. Potter, 1962.

Brownmiller, Susan. *Against Our Will: Men, Women and Rape*. New York: Simon, 1975.

Collier, Phyllis K. *How to Marry a Winner*. Englewood Cliffs, NJ: Prentice, 1982.

Dinnerstein, Dorothy. *The Mermaid and the Minotaur: Sexual Arrangements and Human Malaise*. New York: Harper, 1976.

Farrell, Warren. *Why Men Are the Way They Are: The Male-Female Dynamic*. New York: McGraw-Hill, 1986.

Fiske, Edward B. *The New York Times Selective Guide to Colleges*. New York: Times Books, 1982.

Gerzon, Mark. *A Choice of Heroes: The Changing Faces of American Manhood*. Boston: Houghton, 1982.

Glass, Andrew J. "President wants to unleash military power, but cannot." *Dayton Daily News* 18 June 1985: 1.

Goldberg, Herb. *The Hazards of Being Male: Surviving the Myth of Masculine Privilege*. 1976. New York: NAL, 1977.

———. *The New Male: From Self-Destruction to Self-Care*. 1979. New York: NAL, 1980.

Gordon, John. *The Myth of the Monstrous Male, and Other Feminist Fables*. New York: Playboy P, 1982.

Hartley, Ruth E. "Sex-Role Pressures and the Socialization of the Male Child." *The Forty-Nine Percent Majority: The Male Sex Role*. Ed. Deborah S. David and Robert Brannon. Reading, MA: Addison-Wesley, 1976, 235–44.

Hoch, Paul. *White Hero, Black Beast: Racism, Sexism and the Mask of Masculinity*. London: Pluto P, 1979.

"Indiana jury finds Brown guilty of murder, molesting." *Dayton Daily News* 18 May 1986: 7A.

Inglis, Ruth. *Sins of the Fathers: A Study of the Physical and Emotional Abuse of Children*. New York: St. Martin's, 1978.

Jennes, Gail. "All Men Are Rapists." *People* 20 Feb. 1978: 33–34.

Lehne, Gregory. "Homophobia Among Men." *The Forty-Nine Percent Majority: The Male Sex Role*. Ed. Deborah S. David and Robert Brannon. Reading, MA: Addison-Wesley, 1976. 66–88.

Levine, James A. *Who Will Raise the Children? New Options for Fathers (and Mothers).* Philadelphia: Lippincott, 1976.

Mead, Margaret, *Male and Female: A Study of the Sexes in a Changing World.* New York: Morrow, 1949, 1967.

Money, John, and Patricia Tucker. *Sexual Signatures: On Being a Man or a Woman.* Boston: Little, 1975.

Mougey, Kate. "An act of confiscation: Rape." *Kettering-Oakwood* [OH] *Times* 4 Feb. 1981: 1b.

"'Nerd' day gets a boot after suicide." *Dayton Daily News* 24 Jan. 1986: 38.

Ong, Walter J. *Fighting for Life: Contest, Sexuality, and Consciousness.* Ithaca, New York: Cornell University Press, 1981.

O'Reilly, Jane, et al. "Wife-Beating: The Silent Crime." *Time* 5 Sept. 1983: 23–4, 26.

"Police: Print links Coleman, death." *Dayton Daily News* 31 Aug. 1984: 26.

Roman, Mel, and William Haddad. *The Disposable Parent: The Case for Joint Custody.* 1978. New York: Penguin, 1979.

Schulz, Muriel R. "Is the English Language Anybody's Enemy?" *Speaking of Words: A Language Reader.* Ed. James MacKillop and Donna Woolfolk Cross. 3rd ed. New York: Holt, 1986. 125–27.

Sorrels, Bobbye D. *The Nonsexist Communicator: Solving the Problems of Gender and Awkwardness in Modern English.* Englewood Cliffs, NJ: Prentice, 1983.

Straus, Murray A., Richard J. Gelles, and Suzanne K. Steinmetz. *Behind Closed Doors: Violence in the American Family.* 1980. Garden City, New York: Doubleday, 1981.

Theroux, Paul. "The Male Myth." *New York Times Magazine* 27 Nov. 1983: 116.

Questions on Content

1. Explain how August uses the authority of Margaret Mead in paragraph 2 to advance his essay.

2. Respond to the assertion that "anti-male bias in language is as possible as anti-female bias" (paragraph 3).

3. How does August use the word *mammal* to counter those who argue that the word *man* used generically is sexist?

4. What solution does August suggest for both anti-male and anti-female language?

5. August states that "if women in our society have been regarded as sex objects, men have been regarded as success objects" (paragraph 20). Explain.

6. Explain August's references to theology and the Bible as sources of antimale bias in language.

Questions on Structure and Style

7. Explain how August uses paragraph 5 to organize his essay. Describe his organizational and his developmental strategies.

8. Discuss the author's use of evidence for developmental as well as for persuasive purposes.

Assignments

1. Identify the three types of anti-male usage that August identifies. Write a short paragraph in which you explain each.

2. August cites the following passage from *The New Male*: "Men may very well be the last remaining subgroup in our society that can be blatantly, negatively, and vilely stereotyped with little objection or resistance." Discuss this notion with a small group of your male and female peers.

3. Write a letter to Mr. August in which you respond to his essay. Cite specific reasons that cause you to agree or disagree with him.

The Name Is Mine

Anna Quindlen

Names define relationships, making us part of groups or separating us from groups. As Anna Quindlen illustrates here, even though the choice of a married woman not to take her husband's name is settled, the virtue of independence sometimes seems less important when the group involved is a family. Quindlen, a novelist, has worked as a columnist and as an editor at the *New York Times*.

■ J O U R N A L   P R O M P T   *How does your name link you with others? Given the chance, how would you use your name to change those links?*

1   I am on the telephone to the emergency room of the local hospital. My elder son is getting stitches in his palm, and I have called to make myself feel better, because I am at home, waiting, and my husband is there, holding him. I am 34 years old, and I am crying like a child, making a slippery mess of my face. "Mrs. Krovatin?" says the nurse, and for the first time in my life I answer "Yes."

2   This is a story about a name. The name is mine. I was given it at birth, and I have never changed it, although I married. I could come up with lots of reasons why. It was a political decision, a simple statement that I was somebody and not an adjunct of anybody, especially a husband. As a friend of mine told her horrified mother, "He didn't adopt me, he married me."

3   It was a professional and a personal decision, too. I grew up with an ugly dog of a name, one I came to love because I thought it was weird and unlovable. Amid the Debbies and Kathys of my childhood, I had a first name only my grandmothers had and a last name that began with a strange letter. "Sorry, the letters I, O, Q, U, V, X, Y and Z are not available," the catalogues said about monogrammed key rings and cocktail napkins. Seeing my name in black on white at the top of a good story, suddenly it wasn't an ugly dog anymore.

4   But neither of these are honest reasons, because they assume rational consideration, and it so happens that when it came to changing my name, there was no consideration, rational or otherwise. It was mine. It belonged to me. I don't even share a checking account with my husband. Damned if I was going to be hidden beneath the umbrella of his identity.

5   It seemed like a simple decision. But nowadays I think the only simple decisions are whether to have grilled cheese or tuna fish for lunch. Last week, my older child wanted an explanation of why he, his dad and his brother have one name, and I have another.

6   My answer was long, philosophical and rambling—that is to say, unsatisfactory. What's in a name? I could have said disingenuously. But I was talking to a person who had just spent three torturous, exhilarating years learning names for things, and I wanted to communicate to him that mine meant something quite special to me, had

seemed as form-fitting as my skin, and as painful to remove. Personal identity and independence, however, were not what he was looking for; he just wanted to make sure I was one of them. And I am—and then again, I am not. When I made this decision, I was part of a couple. Now, there are two me's, the me who is the individual and the me who is part of a family of four, a family of four in which, in a small way, I am left out.

7   A wise friend who finds herself in the same fix says she never wants to change her name, only to have a slightly different identity as a family member, an identity for pediatricians' offices and parent-teacher conferences. She also says that the entire situation reminds her of the women's movement as a whole. We did these things as individuals, made these decisions about ourselves and what we wanted to be and do. And they were good decisions, the right decisions. But we based them on individual choice, not on group dynamics. We thought in terms of our sense of ourselves, not our relationships with others.

8   Some people found alternative solutions: hyphenated names, merged names, matriarchal names for the girls and patriarchal ones for the boys, one name at work and another at home. I did not like those choices; I thought they were middle grounds, and I didn't live much in the middle ground at the time. I was once slightly disdainful of women who went all the way and changed their names. But I now know too many smart, independent, terrific women who have the same last names as their husbands to be disdainful anymore. (Besides, if I made this decision as part of a feminist world view, it seems dishonest to turn around and trash other women for deciding as they did.)

9   I made my choice. I haven't changed my mind. I've just changed my life. Sometimes I feel like one of those worms I used to hear about in biology, the ones that, chopped in half, walked off in different directions. My name works fine for one half, not quite as well for the other. I would never give it up. Except for that one morning when I talked to the nurse at the hospital, I always answer the question "Mrs. Krovatin?" with "No, this is Mr. Krovatin's wife." It's just that I understand the down side now.

10   When I decided not to disappear beneath my husband's umbrella, it did not occur to me that I would be the only one left outside. It did not occur to me that I would ever care—not enough to change, just enough to think about the things we do on our own and what they mean when we aren't on our own anymore.

Questions on Content

1. When did Quindlen finally resolve that she liked her name, that it was no longer ugly? How do you feel about your own name?

2. What are some alternate solutions for changing a name at marriage? How does Quindlen regard such solutions? How do you feel about them?

3. In a discussion with her young son, how does Quindlen defend her choice of keeping her maiden name?

**Questions
on Structure
and Style**

4. Discuss the relationships among the opening three paragraphs. What is Quindlen's opening strategy?

5. Discuss the tone of this selection. Does Quindlen use humor? Is her tone consistently confident, or does she reveal some doubt?

6. In your opinion, does the final paragraph strengthen or weaken this essay?

Assignments

1. Write a letter to Anna Quindlen in response to her decision. Do you agree or disagree with her choice of keeping her name, or are your feelings mixed? Do you, for example, feel a less strident position might be more appropriate?

2. Write a short essay in which you discuss the ideas you explored in responding to the Journal Prompt. How does your name link you to others? As you write, you may certainly look beyond your immediate family.

From African to African American

Geneva Smitherman

"Names for the race have been a continuing issue," which Geneva
Smitherman recounts in the following excerpt from her book
Black Talk: Words and Phrases from the Hood to the Amen Corner.
African, Colored, Negro, Black—all these names and others have
served, well and poorly, at various times during nearly four centuries
in North America for the millions who trace their cultural origins to
Africa. *African American,* which is widely accepted today, reflects
the latest stage in a process of self-identification—and the naming
that inevitably accompanies it. (Smitherman here capitalizes words
and expressions that she believes originated in, or first achieved
popularity within, the African American community.)

■ **J O U R N A L   P R O M P T** *Consider the epithets* Colored, Negro, Black, *and*
African American. *Which do you feel is most appropriate for this important group of Americans? Write a paragraph or two in which you justify your choice.*

*Just as we were called colored, but were not that . . . and then Negro, but not that . . .
to be called Black is just as baseless. . . . Black tells you about skin color and what side
of town you live on. African American evokes discussion of the world.*

> *Reverend Jesse Jackson, quoted in Clarence Page, "African American
> or Black? It's Debatable," in the* Detroit Free Press, *January 1, 1989,
> and in Isabel Wilkerson, "Many Who Favor Black Favor New Term for
> Who They Are," in the* New York Times, *January 31, 1989.*

1   Names for the race have been a continuing issue since GIDDYUP, 1619, when the first
slave ship landed at Jamestown. From "AFRICAN" to "COLORED" to "negro" to
"NEGRO" (with the capital) to "BLACK" to "AFRICAN AMERICAN," with side trips to
"AFROAMERICAN," "AFRIAMERICAN," "AFRAAMERICAN," and "AFRIKAN"—what are
we Africans in America, today thirty-five million strong, "we people who are darker
than blue," as Curtis Mayfield once sang, to call ourselves?

2   Debates rage. The topic is discussed at conferences. Among leaders and intellectuals, as well as among everyday people, the issue is sometimes argued so hotly that
folk stop speaking to each other! In 1904, the *A.M.E. Church Review* sponsored a
symposium of Black leaders to debate whether the "n" of "negro" should be capital-
ized. However, participants at that symposium went beyond the mere question of capitalization to debate whether "negro" was the right name for the race in the first place.
In 1967, during the shift from "Negro" to "Black," and again in 1989, during the shift
from "Black" to "African American," *Ebony* magazine devoted several pages to the

question "What's in a Name?" And the beat goes on . . . because the status of Blacks remains unsettled. Name changes and debates over names reflect our uncertain status and come to the forefront during the crises and upheavals in the Black condition.

3   Although African Americans are linked to Africans on the Continent and in the DIASPORA, the Black American, as the late writer James Baldwin once put it, is a unique creation. For one thing, other Diasporic Africans claim citizenship in countries that are virtually all Black—Jamaicans, Bajans, Nigerians, Ghanaians, etc., are not minorities in their native lands. For another, not only are Blacks a distinct minority in America, but our status as first-class citizens is debatable, even at this late hour in U.S. history. As the SISTA said about Rodney King's beating in Los Angeles, the torching of a Black man by whites in Florida, and Malice Green's death in Detroit, "After all we done been through, here it is 1992, and we still ain free." Some activists and AFRICAN-CENTERED Blacks have coined the term NEO-SLAVERY to capture the view that the present Black condition, with whites still powerful and Blacks still powerless, is just enslavement in another form.

4   Blacks are a minority amidst a population who look distinctly different physically and who promote race supremacist standards of physical attractiveness. This state of affairs has created a set of negative attitudes about skin color, hair, and other physical features that are reflected in the Black Lexicon—terms such as GOOD HAIR, BAD HAIR, HIGH YELLUH, LIVER-LIPS. Because black skin color was so devalued at one time, to call an African person "black" was to CALL him or her OUTA THEY NAME. It was: "If you white, you all right, if you brown, stick around, if you Black, git back." Thus the necessity, during the Black Freedom Struggle of the 1960s and 1970s, of purging the racial label "Black" and adopting it as a name for the race in symbolic celebration of the changed status of Africans in America.

5   Back to the RIP. The British colonists, who would become Americans in 1776, called the Africans "free" (a few were, but most were not), "slave," or, following fifteenth century Portuguese slave traders, *negro* (a Portuguese adjective, meaning "black"). [*Negro* is also a Spanish adjective that means "black"; however, the Portuguese were the first to use the term in reference to Africans.] But the Africans called themselves "African" and so designated their churches and organizations—as in the names "African Educational and Benevolent Society," "African Episcopal Church," and "African Masonic Lodge No. 459." In those early years, the thought was Africa on my mind and in my MIND'S EYE. Enslaved Africans kept thinking and hoping, all the way up until the nineteenth century, that they would one day return to Mother Africa. Some hummed the tune "I'll Fly Away," believing that, like the legendary hero Solomon, they would be able to fly back to Africa. And especially after fighting at Lexington, Concord, and Bunker Hill in America's Revolutionary War, they just knew they would be free to return home. Instead, the thirteen British colonies that became the United States tightened the reins on their African slaves, passing laws abolishing temporary enslavement and indentured servitude for Africans and making them slaves for life.

6   By 1800, several generations of Africans had been born on American soil, thousands had been transported from Africa, and the Black population numbered over

one million. Both the vision and the possibility of returning to Africa had become impractical and remote. Further, a movement had begun to abolish slavery and to make the Africans citizens. And both free and enslaved Africans were becoming critically aware of their contributions to the development of American wealth. In light of this new reality and in preparation for citizenship and what-they thought would be opportunities to enjoy the national wealth they had helped create through two hundred years of free labor, enslaved Africans began to call themselves "Colored" (often spelled "coloured" in those days), and the designation "African" declined in use.

7   "Colored" was used throughout much of the nineteenth century, until the white backlash began. The year 1877 marked the end of Reconstruction and set the stage for "the Coloreds" to be put back in their "place." The political deal cut in D.C. led to the withdrawal of the Federal/Union troops that had been stationed in the South to ensure justice for the ex-enslaved Africans. Power and home rule were returned to the Old Confederacy. The "freedmen" (as they were called by the Federal Government and whites) lost the small gains in education, citizenship, and political power that the Civil War and the Emancipation Proclamation had made possible. New forms of repression and torture began—lynch mobs, the Ku Klux Klan, the loss of voting rights, and the beginning of separate but (UN)equal. By 1900, the quest was on for a new name to capture the new reality of being neither "slave nor free," as one ex-enslaved African put it.

8   Although some Colored had begun using and rallying for the label "negro," when the National Association for the Advancement of Colored People (NAACP) was founded in 1909, the COMMUNITY had not yet reached group consensus. The push for "negro" and for its capitalization hit its full stride during the period between the two World Wars. The vision was that with the U.S. campaign to "make the world safe for democracy," and with Colored soldiers shedding their blood for America, surely the yet-unsettled contradictory status of Africans in America would be resolved on the side of first-class citizenship and economic equity. Leaders such as Dr. W. E. B. DuBois, editor of the NAACP journal, *Crisis,* launched a massive nationwide effort to capitalize "negro" and to elevate the Portuguese-derived adjective "negro" to a level of dignity and respect. The NAACP mailed out over seven hundred letters to publishers and editors. Community newsletters addressed the issue, debates were held, and the name issue was addressed in talks and sermons in the Traditional Black Church. By 1930, the major European American media were using "Negro" and capitalizing it. (The two glaring exceptions were *Forum* magazine and the U.S. Government Printing Office.) The *New York Times* put it this way: "[This] is not merely a typographical change, it is an act in recognition of racial self-respect for those who have been for generations in the 'lower case'."

9   "Negro" was the name until the 1960s, when Africans in America struggled to throw off the shackles of Jim Crow and embraced Black Culture, the Black Experience—and black skin color. Again, conferences were held, many under the rubric of "Black Power," debates ensued, and yes, folk had hot arguments and FELL OUT with one another about abandoning the name "Negro" for "Black," which was "only an

adjective." However, the motion of history could not be stopped. The name change to "Black" and the profound significance of this change in the language and life of Blacks was captured in a 1968 hit song by James Brown: "Say it Loud (I'm Black, and I'm Proud)."

10   The final period in the name debate (for now at least) began in late 1988 with a proposal from Dr. Ramona Edelin, president of the National Urban Coalition, to call the upcoming 1989 summit the "African American," rather than the "Black," Summit. She asserted that this name change "would establish a cultural context for the new agenda." Her view was that present-day Africans in America were facing a new reality—the erosion of hard-won progress since the late 1970s, high unemployment, the rise of racism, the growth of urban youth violence, the proliferation of crack and other drugs, and the general deterioration of the community. The situation called for reassessment within the framework of a global identity linking Africans in North America with those on the Continent and throughout the Diaspora.

11   As in previous eras, the name issue, this time around being the shift from "Black" to "African American," has been debated at community forums and conferences. It has been the topic of conversation and heated arguments at the barber shop and the BEAUTY SHOP, at family reunions, social gatherings, and at Church events. The change has not been as cataclysmic, though, as the shift from "Negro" to "Black" was in the 1960s, since "African American" lacks the negative history of "Black." Further, "African American" returns us to the source—the "African" of early years, but with a significant dimension added: "American." This addition calls attention to four hundred years of building wealth in America and legitimates the demand for political and economic equity. This is what David Walker, one of the first RED, BLACK, AND GREEN DUDES, conveyed in his *Appeal, in four Articles: Together with a Preamble to the Coloured Citizens of the World, but in particular, and very Expressly, to those of the United States of America.* His *Appeal* was published in 1829 during the era of "Colored." Calling for open rebellion against enslavement, and opposing the American Colonization Society's plan to resettle enslaved Africans in parts of Africa, Walker wrote:

> Men who are resolved to keep us in eternal wretchedness are also bent on sending us to Liberia. . . . America is more our country than it is the whites—we have enriched it with our BLOOD AND TEARS.

12   To date, "African American" appears to have caught on throughout the community, although "Black" continues to be used also (and to a lesser extent, the name "African"/"Afrikan"). In opinion polls about the name issue, Black youth are the strongest supporters of "African American," which is not surprising, given the African-Centered consciousness emerging in HIP HOP Culture. However, there are those—generally the parents and older siblings of the youth—who still favor "Black" because this name generated an intense, long-overdue struggle over old, past scripts of racial self-hatred and because the eventual adoption of the name "Black" symbolized a victorious shift to the positive in the African American psyche.

Questions on Content	1. Explain what Smitherman means by the following: "Name changes and debates over names reflect our uncertain status."

Questions on Content

1. Explain what Smitherman means by the following: "Name changes and debates over names reflect our uncertain status."

2. Do you agree with the African-Centered Blacks who regard the present Black condition as neoslavery?

3. Explain the importance of adopting the racial label *black* as a name for African Americans during the 1960s and 1970s.

4. Discuss the origin of the epithets *negro, Negro, colored,* and *African American.*

5. Discuss the different connotative values of *Black* and *African American* among youths of today and their parents. Explain the differences.

Questions on Structure and Style

6. Identify Smitherman's audience. Discuss how her diction and tone are appropriate for this audience.

7. Does Smitherman take a position in the ongoing debate she describes? Consider her tone and use of authority.

Assignments

1. Assume that you are disturbed by epithets you have heard white students use to describe Americans of African decent. Assume further that you have decided, after reading Smitherman's selection, to write an editorial in your student newspaper on the appropriate name for this group of Americans. Write the editorial relying on Smitherman and your own experiences and observations.

2. Interview an African American or a member of another minority group. Discuss the issue of appropriate names for that particular group. Pay attention to the origin and the connotative value of the names. Write a concrete essay in which you discuss your findings.

On Black English

James Baldwin

James Baldwin, a distinguished novelist, essayist, and playwright,
devoted much of his public life to civil rights causes. In the following essay he presents his argument that black English is not simply a
dialect of standard English; it is, he maintains, a distinct language
created by people who, like many others, have found in language the
only unity and security available to them. If black English differs
from standard English, it is because the speakers of each "have very
different realities to articulate, or control."

■ **JOURNAL PROMPT** *Baldwin asserts that language "is the most vivid and
crucial key to identity." Discuss how your language enables you to connect with your language community. Does it ever enable you to disconnect intentionally from this community?*

1   The argument concerning the use, or the status, or the reality, of black English is
rooted in American history and has absolutely nothing to do with the question the
argument supposes itself to be posing. The argument has nothing to do with language itself but with the *role* of language. Language, incontestably, reveals the
speaker. Language, also, far more dubiously, is meant to define the other—and, in
this case, the other is refusing to be defined by a language that has never been able
to recognize him.

2   People evolve a language in order to describe and thus control their circumstances,
or in order not to be submerged by a reality that they cannot articulate. (And, if they
cannot articulate it, they *are* submerged.) A Frenchman living in Paris speaks a subtly
and crucially different language from that of the man living in Marseilles; neither
sounds very much like a man living in Quebec; and they would all have great difficulty in apprehending what the man from Guadeloupe, or Martinique, is saying, to
say nothing of the man from Senegal—although the "common" language of all these
areas is French. But each has paid, and is paying, a different price for this "common"
language, in which, as it turns out, they are not saying, and cannot be saying, the same
things: They each have very different realities to articulate, or control.

3   What joins all languages, and all men, is the necessity to confront life, in order,
not inconceivably, to outwit death: The price for this is the acceptance, and achievement, of one's temporal identity. So that, for example, though it is not taught in the
schools (and this has the potential of becoming a political issue) the south of France
still clings to its ancient and musical Provençal, which resists being described as a
"dialect." And much of the tension in the Basque countries, and in Wales, is due to
the Basque and Welsh determination not to allow their languages to be destroyed.
This determination also feeds the flames in Ireland for among the many indignities
the Irish have been forced to undergo at English hands is the English contempt for
their language.

4   It goes without saying, then, that language is also a political instrument, means, and proof of power. It is the most vivid and crucial key to identity: It reveals the private identity, and connects one with, or divorces one from, the larger, public, or communal identity. There have been, and are, times, and places, when to speak a certain language could be dangerous, even fatal. Or, one may speak the same language, but in such a way that one's antecedents are revealed, or (one hopes) hidden. This is true in France, and is absolutely true in England: The range (and reign) of accents on that damp little island make England coherent for the English and totally incomprehensible for everyone else. To open your mouth in England is (if I may use black English) to "put your business in the street": You have confessed your parents, your youth, your school, your salary, your self-esteem, and, alas, your future.

5   Now, I do not know what white Americans would sound like if there had never been any black people in the United States, but they would not sound the way they sound. *Jazz*, for example, is a very specific sexual term, as in *jazz me, baby*, but white people purified it into the Jazz Age. *Sock it to me*, which means, roughly, the same thing, has been adopted by Nathaniel Hawthorne's descendants with no qualms or hesitations at all, along with *let it all hang out* and *right on! Beat to his socks,* which was once the black's most total and despairing image of poverty, was transformed into a thing called the Beat Generation, which phenomenon was, largely, composed of *uptight*, middle-class white people, imitating poverty, trying to *get down*, to get *with it*, doing their *thing*, doing their despairing best to be *funky*, which we, the blacks, never dreamed of doing—we *were* funky, baby, like *funk* was going out of style.

6   Now, no one can eat his cake, and have it, too, and it is late in the day to attempt to penalize black people for having created a language that permits the nation its only glimpse of reality, a language without which the nation would be even more *whipped* than it is.

7   I say that this present skirmish is rooted in American history, and it is. Black English is the creation of the black diaspora. Blacks came to the United States chained to each other, but from different tribes: Neither could speak the other's language. If two black people, at that bitter hour of the world's history, had been able to speak to each other, the institution of chattel slavery could never have lasted as long as it did. Subsequently, the slave was given, under the eye, and the gun, of his master, Congo Square, and the Bible—or, in other words, and under these conditions, the slave began the formation of the black church, and it is within this unprecedented tabernacle that black English began to be formed. This was not, merely, as in the European example, the adoption of a foreign tongue, but an alchemy that transformed ancient elements into a new language: *A language comes into existence by means of brutal necessity, and the rules of the language are dictated by what the language must convey.*

8   There was a moment, in time, and in this place, when my brother, or my mother, or my father, or my sister, had to convey to me, for example, the danger in which I was standing from the white man standing just behind me, and to convey this with a speed, and in a language, that the white man could not possibly understand, and that, indeed, he cannot understand, until today. He cannot afford to understand it. This understanding would reveal to him too much about himself, and smash that mirror before which he has been frozen for so long.

9   Now, if this passion, this skill, this (to quote Toni Morrison) "sheer intelligence," this incredible music, the mighty achievement of having brought a people utterly unknown to, or despised by "history"—to have brought this people to their present, troubled, troubling, and unassailable and unanswerable place—if this absolutely unprecedented journey does not indicate that black English is a language, I am curious to know what definition of language is to be trusted.

10   A people at the center of the Western world, and in the midst of so hostile a population, has not endured and transcended by means of what is patronizingly called a "dialect." We, the blacks, are in trouble, certainly, but we are not doomed, and we are not inarticulate because we are not compelled to defend a morality that we know to be a lie.

11   The brutal truth is that the bulk of the white people in America never had any interest in educating black people, except as this could serve white purposes. It is not the black child's language that is in question, it is not his language that is despised: It is his experience. A child cannot be taught by anyone who despises him, and a child cannot afford to be fooled. A child cannot be taught by anyone whose demand, essentially, is that the child repudiate his experience, and all that gives him sustenance, and enter a limbo in which he will no longer be black, and in which he knows that he can never become white. Black people have lost too many black children that way.

12   And, after all, finally, in a country with standards so untrustworthy, a country that makes heroes of so many criminal mediocrities, a country unable to face why so many of the non-white are in prison, or on the needle, or standing, futureless, in the streets—it may very well be that both the child, and his elder, have concluded that they have nothing whatever to learn from the people of a country that has managed to learn so little.

Questions on Content

1. Identify "the other" referred to in paragraph 1. Why is this reference intentionally vague?

2. Explain the origin of the term *Beat Generation*.

3. According to Baldwin, what is the relationship between the black church and black English?

4. In paragraph 8 the author asserts that white Americans "cannot afford to understand" black English. What does he mean?

5. Why does Baldwin object to use of the term *dialect* to describe black English?

6. Why, according to Baldwin, are black children unable to learn from most white educators?

Questions on Structure and Style

7. As you read paragraph 1, what tone and audience do you think Baldwin has in mind? Does your perception of either alter as you read the rest of the essay?

8. Why does Baldwin bring up the varieties of French in paragraphs 2 and 3?

9. What effect does the author achieve by referring to white Americans as "Nathaniel Hawthorne's descendants" (paragraph 5)?

Assignments

1. Baldwin asserts that language is "the most vivid and crucial key to identity" (paragraph 4). In an essay, explain what he means, agree or disagree with his position, and provide examples that support your position.

2. The author states, "Black English is the creation of the black diaspora" (paragraph 7). What does he mean? Write a few paragraphs in which you hypothesize whether a similar statement would be true of any of the other minorities in the United States.

3. The author states, "To open your mouth in England is (if I may use black English) to 'put your business in the street'" (paragraph 4). In an essay based on your own experience and observation, discuss whether or not Americans "put their business in the street" when they speak.

ADDITIONAL ASSIGNMENTS AND RESEARCH TOPICS

1. Select an occupational group in which both men and women are well represented—health care workers or teachers, for example. Interview people of each sex in the same occupation, or just listen carefully to their use of language. What differences do you note in the ways in which the men and women speak? Report your findings, being sure to establish a consistent basis for your comparison.

2. In "Sexism in English: A 1990s Update," Alleen Pace Nilsen examines the sexist aspects of our language. Listen carefully to a local or network news program, paying attention to whether the broadcasters use sexually neutral language. Compare your findings with those of your classmates.

3. James Baldwin asserts that he does "not know what white Americans would sound like if there had never been any black people in the United States, but they would not sound the way they sound" (paragraph 5). To be sure, the African American influence on standard American English has been much more significant than most speakers realize. Do some investigating in your library, and prepare a documented essay on this topic. If your school has the film series *The Story of English*, the film "Black on White" would be a good place to begin your investigation, as would the corresponding chapter in the book that accompanies the film series, also called *The Story of English*, by McCrum, Cran, and MacNeil. Another of many possible sources is J. L. Dillard's *Black English*.

4. Common sense tells us that language often reflects what we feel. If we're hostile or fearful, our language reflects those feelings. Some of the authors in this chapter believe that the process can also work the other way: language itself can generate hostility and fear. They maintain that we could improve human relationships by correcting elements of language that cause discrimination. Does language cause bias, or does it merely reflect the biases that people already have? Respond to this question in an essay, using the reading selections in this chapter as source material.

CHAPTER THREE

Right Words, Wrong Words, My Words

When we're unsure about the spelling of a word, we look it up in a dictionary. We also look in dictionaries to verify the accepted meanings of words, and we look in handbooks for rules about using commas. So where do we find the correct language to use when we're asked, during a job interview, "Tell me a little about yourself"? Where do we look up the right way to speak at the breakfast table at home and later in the cafeteria at school or work?

Although we find some answers to questions about language usage in books, many times we rely on a variety of more appropriate language authorities. Our families, friends, employers, and even our culture can function as language authorities, identifying for us, explicitly or implicitly, the correct language to use. This chapter examines the role of various language authorities in guiding us toward language that's "right" for us.

The dictionary, the language authority we recognize most easily, provides guidance on the accepted spellings and meanings of words. In the chapter's first selection, Bill Bryson examines the role of dictionaries in establishing "Order Out of Chaos"—the process of standardizing English usage in which three famous lexicographers have figured prominently. Another language authority receives attention here, an authority quite different from the dictionary. As we listen to Robert Klose offer "A Rarity: Grammar Lessons from Dad," we hear grammatical rules being transformed into opportunities for memorable conversations between a father and his son.

Attention then turns to three examples of "wrong words," language that we're usually told to avoid. The first example centers on language considered obscene. Movies, books, and everyday conversations now seem regularly punctuated with such language, but despite its apparent acceptability, obscene language actually can work against us, as two of the chapter's authors show how. Barbara Lawrence examines the true implications of our vocabulary of strong words and concludes that "Four-Letter Words Can Hurt You." Wallace Stegner treats this vocabulary as a practical issue of resources conserved and wasted, and his own conclusion is to say "Good-bye to All T__t!" language.

The other quite different examples of "wrong" language—euphemisms and slang—actually aren't always wrong. Euphemism, that ever-evolving stockpile of words and expressions substituted for language considered too strong, often is dismissed as a vocabulary favored only by the cowardly or dishonest. However, "a day with the euphemism detector set on high" leaves author Cullen Murphy experiencing far more amusement than dread. Slang, which the chapter also addresses, usually is marked as an error when it appears in students' writings. The truth is that slang sometimes serves valuable purposes, a fact made clear in "Words with Attitude" by Gerald Parshall.

The chapter concludes with a comforting reminder from Robert MacNeil. In "English Belongs to Everybody," an excerpt from his book *Wordstruck*, MacNeil illustrates how inconsistent English language usage has always seemed. As MacNeil emphasizes, the speakers of English, including all of us today, always serve as the language authorities whose decisions eventually become final. Dictionaries and various other authorities offer us advice, often conflicting, about language usage, but the language authority that matters most actually rests with us.

Order Out of Chaos

Bill Bryson

Dictionaries, which today are inexpensive and readily available, serve as our most obvious language authority. Dictionaries, however, only *describe* how language is being used; they do not *prescribe* usage. Moreover, with a language as vast and complex as English, simply compiling descriptions of language usage has always proven a staggering task, even for the three famous lexicographers whose labors Bryson describes here. Bill Bryson is a journalist and author of several books, including *A Dictionary of Troublesome Words.*

■ **J O U R N A L   P R O M P T**   *If your task were to appoint a panel of people who would select the words to be included in every dictionary, as well as words to be excluded, whom would you appoint to this panel?*

1 How big is the English language? That's not an easy question. Samuel Johnson's dictionary contained 43,000 words. The unabridged *Random House* of 1987 has 315,000. *Webster's Third New International* of 1961 contains 450,000. And the revised *Oxford English Dictionary* of 1989 has 615,000 entries. But in fact this only begins to hint at the total.

2 For one thing, meanings in English are much more various than a bald count of entry words would indicate. The mouse that scurries across your kitchen floor and the mouse that activates your personal computer clearly are two quite separate entities. Shouldn't they then be counted as two words? And then what about related forms like *mousy, mouselike*, and *mice*? Shouldn't they also count as separate words? Surely there is a large difference between something that is a mouse and something that is merely mousy.

3 And then of course there are all the names of flora and fauna, medical conditions, chemical substances,* laws of physics, and all the other scientific and technical terms that don't make it into ordinary dictionaries. Of insects alone, there are 1.4 million named species. Total all these together and you have—well, no one knows. But certainly not less than three million.

4 So how many of these words do we know? Again, there is no simple answer. Many scholars have taken the trouble (or more probably compelled their graduate students to take the trouble) of counting the number of words used by various authors, on the assumption, one supposes, that that tells us something about human vocabulary. Mostly what it tells us is that academics aren't very good at counting. Shakespeare, according to Pei and McCrum, had a vocabulary of 30,000 words, though Pei

---

* One of which, incidentally, is said to be the longest word in the English language. It begins *methianyl-glutaminyl* and finishes 1,913 letters later as *alynalalanylthreonilarginylserase*. I don't know what it is used for, though I daresay it would take some rubbing to get it out of the carpet.

acknowledges seeing estimates putting the figure as low as 16,000. Lincoln Barnett puts it at 20,000 to 25,000. But most other authorities—Shipley, Baugh and Cable, Howard—put the number at a reassuringly precise 17,677. The King James Bible, according to Laird, contains 8,000 words, but Shipley puts the number at 7,000, while Barnett confidently zeroes in on a figure of 10,442. Who knows who's right?

5   One glaring problem with even the most scrupulous tabulation is that the total number of words used by an author doesn't begin to tell us the true size of his vocabulary. I know the meanings of *frangible, spiffing*, and *cutesy-poo*, but have never had occasion to write them before now. A man of Shakespeare's linguistic versatility must have possessed thousands of words that he never used because he didn't like or require them. Not once in his plays can you find the words *Bible, Trinity*, or *Holy Ghost*, and yet that is not to suggest that he was not familiar with them.

6   Estimates of the size of the average person's vocabulary are even more contentious. Max Müller, a leading German philologist at the turn of the century, thought the average farm laborer had an everyday vocabulary of no more than 300 words. Pei cites an English study of fruit pickers, which put the number at no more than 500, though he himself thought that the figure was probably closer to 30,000. Stuart Berg Flexner, the noted American lexicographer, suggests that the average well-read person has a vocabulary of about 20,000 words and probably uses about 1,500 to 2,000 in a normal week's conversation. McCrum puts an educated person's vocabulary at about 15,000.

7   There are endless difficulties attached to adjudging how many words a person knows. Consider just one. If I ask you what *incongruent* means and you say, "It means not congruent," you are correct. That is the first definition given in most dictionaries, but that isn't to say that you have the faintest idea what the word means. Every page of the dictionary contains words we may not have encountered before—*inflationist, forbiddance, moosewood, pulsative*—and yet whose meanings we could very probably guess.

8   At the same time there are many words that we use every day and clearly know and yet might have difficulty proving. How would you define *the* or *what* or *am* or *very*? Imagine trying to explain to a Martian in a concise way just what *is* is. And then what about all those words with a variety of meanings? Take *step*. The *American Heritage Dictionary* lists a dozen common meanings for the word, ranging from the act of putting one foot in front of the other to the name for part of a staircase. We all know all these meanings, yet if I gave you a pencil and a blank sheet of paper could you list them? Almost certainly not. The simple fact is that it is hard to remember what we remember, so to speak. Put another way, our memory is a highly fickle thing. Dr. Alan Baddeley, a British authority on memory, cites a study in which people were asked to name the capital cities of several countries. Most had trouble with the capitals of countries like Uruguay and Bulgaria, but when they were told the initial letter of the capital city, they often suddenly remembered and their success rate soared. In another study people were shown long lists of random words and then asked to write down as many of them as they could remember. A few hours later, without being shown the list again, they were asked to write down as many of the words as they could remember then. Almost always the number of

words would be nearly identical, but the actual words recalled from one test to another would vary by 50 percent or more. In other words, there is vastly more verbal information locked away in our craniums than we can get out at any one time. So the problem of trying to assess accurately just how much verbal material we possess in total is fraught with difficulties.

9   For this reason educational psychologists have tended to shy away from such studies, and such information as exists is often decades old. One of the most famous studies was conducted in 1940. In it, two American researchers, R. H. Seashore and L. D. Eckerson, selected a random word from each left-hand page of a Funk & Wagnalls standard desktop dictionary and asked a sampling of college students to define those words or use them in a sentence. By extrapolating those results onto the number of entries in the dictionary, they concluded that the average student had a vocabulary of about 150,000 words—obviously very much larger than previously supposed. A similar study carried out by K. C. Diller in 1978, cited by Aitchison in *Words in the Mind*, put the vocabulary level even higher—at about 250,000 words. On the other hand, Jespersen cites the case of a certain Professor E. S. Holden who early in the century laboriously tested himself on every single word in *Webster's Dictionary* and arrived at a total of just 33,456 known words. It is clearly unlikely that a university professor's vocabulary would be four to six times smaller than that of the average student. So such studies would seem to tell us more about the difficulties of framing tests than about the size of our vocabularies.

10   What is certain is that the number of words we use is very much smaller than the number of words we know. In 1923 a lexicographer named G. H. McKnight did a comprehensive study of how words are used and found that just forty-three words account for fully half of all the words in common use, and that just nine account for fully one quarter of all the words in almost any sample of written English. Those nine are: *and, be, have, it, of, the, to, will*, and *you*.

11   By virtue of their brevity, dictionary definitions often fail to convey the nuances of English. *Rank* and *rancid* mean roughly the same thing, but, as Aitchison notes, we would never talk about eating rank butter or wearing rancid socks. A dictionary will tell you that *tall* and *high* mean much the same thing, but it won't explain to you that while you can apply either term to a building you can apply only tall to a person. On the strength of dictionary definitions alone a foreign visitor to your home could be excused for telling you that you have an abnormal child, that your wife's cooking is exceedingly odorous, and that your speech at a recent sales conference was laughable, and intend nothing but the warmest praise.

12   The fact is that the real meanings are often far more complex than the simple dictionary definitions would lead us to suppose. In 1985, the department of English at the University of Birmingham in England ran a computer analysis of words as they are actually used in English and came up with some surprising results. The primary dictionary meaning of words was often far adrift from the sense in which they were actually used. *Keep*, for instance, is usually defined as to retain, but in fact the word is much more often employed in the sense of continuing, as in "keep cool" and "keep smiling." *See* is only rarely required in the sense of utilizing one's eyes, but much more often used to express the idea of knowing, as in "I see what you mean."

Give, even more interestingly, is most often used, to quote the researchers, as "mere verbal padding," as in "give it a look" or "give a report." [London Sunday *Times*, March 31, 1985]

13   In short, dictionaries may be said to contain a certain number of definitions, but the true number of meanings contained in those definitions will always be much higher. As the lexicographer J. Ayto put it: "The world's largest data bank of examples in context is dwarfed by the collection we all carry around subconsciously in our heads."

14   English is changing all the time and at an increasingly dizzy pace. At the turn of the century words were being added at the rate of about 1,000 a year. Now, according to a report in *The New York Times* [April 3, 1989], the increase is closer to 15,000 to 20,000 a year. In 1987, when Random House produced the second edition of its masterly twelve-pound unabridged dictionary, it included over 50,000 words that had not existed twenty-one years earlier and 75,000 new definitions of old words. Of its 315,000 entries, 210,000 had to be revised. That is a phenomenal amount of change in just two decades. The new entries included *preppy, quark, flextime, chairperson, sunblocker*, and the names of 800 foods that had not existed or been generally heard of in 1966—*tofu, piña colada, chapati, sushi*, and even *crêpes*.

15   Unabridged dictionaries have about them a stern, immutable air, as if here the language has been captured once and for all, and yet from the day of publication they are inescapably out of date. Samuel Johnson recognized this when he wrote: "No dictionary of a living tongue can ever be perfect, since while it is hastening to publication, some words are budding, and some are fading away." That, however, has never stopped anyone from trying, not least Johnson himself.

16   The English-speaking world has the finest dictionaries, a somewhat curious fact when you consider that we have never formalized the business of compiling them. From the seventeenth century when Cardinal Richelieu founded the Académie Française, dictionary making has been earnest work indeed. In the English-speaking world, the early dictionaries were almost always the work of one man rather than a ponderous committee of academics, as was the pattern on the Continent. In a kind of instinctive recognition of the mongrel, independent, idiosyncratic genius of the English tongue, these dictionaries were often entrusted to people bearing those very characteristics themselves. Nowhere was this more gloriously true than in the person of the greatest lexicographer of them all, Samuel Johnson.

17   Johnson, who lived from 1709 to 1784, was an odd candidate for genius. Blind in one eye, corpulent, incompletely educated, by all accounts coarse in manner, he was an obscure scribbler from an impoverished provincial background when he was given a contract by the London publisher Robert Dodsley to compile a dictionary of English.

18   Johnson's was by no means the first dictionary in English. From *Cawdrey's Table Alphabeticall* in 1604 to his opus a century and a half later there were at least a dozen popular dictionaries, though many of these were either highly specialized or slight (*Cawdrey's Table Alphabeticall* contained just 3,000 words and ran to barely a hundred pages). Many also had little claim to scholarship. *Cawdrey's*, for all the credit it gets as the first dictionary, was a fairly sloppy enterprise. It gave the definition of *aberration* twice and failed to alphabetize correctly on other words.

19   The first dictionary to aim for anything like comprehensiveness was the *Universal Etymological Dictionary* by Nathaniel Bailey, published in 1721, which anticipated Johnson's classic volume by thirty-four years and actually defined more words. So why is it that Johnson's dictionary is the one we remember? That's harder to answer than you might think.

20   His dictionary was full of shortcomings. He allowed many spelling inconsistencies to be perpetuated—*deceit* but *receipt, deign* but *disdain, hark* but *hearken, convey* but *inveigh, moveable* but *immovable*. He wrote *downhil* with one *l*, but *uphill* with two; *install* with two *l*'s, but *reinstal* with one; *fancy* with an *f*, but *phantom* with a *ph*. Generally he was aware of these inconsistencies, but felt that in many cases the inconsistent spellings were already too well established to tamper with. He did try to make spelling somewhat more sensible, institutionalizing the differences between *flower* and *flour* and between *metal* and *mettle*—but essentially he saw his job as recording English spelling as it stood in his day, not changing it. This was in sharp contrast to the attitude taken by the revisers of the Académie Française dictionary a decade or so later, who would revise almost a quarter of French spellings.

21   There were holes in Johnson's erudition. He professed a preference for what he conceived to be Saxon spellings for words like *music, critic*, and *prosaic*, and thus spelled them with a final *k*, when in fact they were all borrowed from Latin. He was given to flights of editorializing, as when he defined a *patron* as "one who supports with insolence, and is paid with flattery" or *oats* as a grain that sustained horses in England and people in Scotland. His etymologies, according to Baugh and Cable, were "often ludicrous" and his proofreading sometimes strikingly careless. He defined a *garret* as a "room on the highest floor in the house" and a *cockloft* as "the room over the garret." Elsewhere, he gave identical definitions to *leeward* and *windward*, even though they are quite obviously opposites.

22   Even allowing for the inflated prose of his day, he had a tendency to write passages of remarkable denseness, as here: "The proverbial oracles of our parsimonious ancestors have informed us, that the fatal waste of our fortune is by small expenses, by the profusion of sums too little singly to alarm our caution, and which we never suffer ourselves to consider together." *Too little singly?* I would wager good money that that sentence was as puzzling to his contemporaries as it is to us. And yet at least it has the virtue of relative brevity. Often Johnson constructed sentences that ran to 250 words or more, which sound today uncomfortably like the ramblings of a man who has sat up far too late and drunk rather too much port.

23   Yet for all that, his *Dictionary of the English Language*, published in two volumes in June 1755, is a masterpiece, one of the landmarks of English literature. Its definitions are supremely concise, its erudition magnificent, if not entirely flawless. Without a nearby library to draw on, and with appallingly little financial backing (his publisher paid him a grand total of just £1,575, less than £200 a year, from which he had to pay his assistants), Johnson worked from a garret room off Fleet Street, where he defined some 43,000 words, illustrated with more than 114,000 supporting quotations drawn from every area of literature. It is little wonder that he made some errors and occasionally indulged himself with barbed definitions.

24   He had achieved in under nine years what the forty members of the Académie Française could not do in less than forty. He captured the majesty of the English language and gave it a dignity that was long overdue. It was a monumental accomplishment and he well deserved his fame.

25   But its ambitious sweep was soon to be exceeded by a persnickety schoolteacher/lawyer half a world away in Connecticut. Noah Webster (1758–1843) was by all accounts a severe, correct, humorless, religious, temperate man who was not easy to like, even by other severe, religious, temperate, humorless people. A provincial schoolteacher and not-very-successful lawyer from Hartford, he was short, pale, smug, and boastful. (He held himself superior to Benjamin Franklin because he was a Yale man while Franklin was self-educated.) Where Samuel Johnson spent his free hours drinking and discoursing in the company of other great men, Webster was a charmless loner who criticized almost everyone but was himself not above stealing material from others, most notably from a spelling book called *Abysel-pha* by an Englishman named Thomas Dilworth. In the marvelously deadpan phrase of H. L. Mencken, Webster was "sufficiently convinced of its merits to imitate it, even to the extent of lifting whole passages." He credited himself with coining many words, among them *demoralize, appreciation, accompaniment, ascertainable*, and *expenditure*, which in fact had been in the language for centuries. He was also inclined to boast of learning that he simply did not possess. He claimed to have mastered twenty-three languages, including Latin, Greek, all the Romance languages, Anglo-Saxon, Persian, Hebrew, Arabic, Syriac, and a dozen more. Yet, as Thomas Pyles witheringly puts it, he showed "an ignorance of German which would disgrace a freshman," and his grasp of other languages was equally tenuous. According to Charlton Laird, he knew far less Anglo-Saxon than Thomas Jefferson, who never pretended to be an expert at it. Pyles calls his *Dissertations on the English Language* "a fascinating farago of the soundest linguistic common sense and the most egregious poppycock." It is hard to find anyone saying a good word about him.

26   Webster's first work, *A Grammatical Institute of the English Language*—consisting of three books: a grammar, a reader, and a speller—appeared between 1783 and 1785, but he didn't capture the public's attention until the publication in 1788 of *The American Spelling Book*. This volume (later called the *Elementary Spelling Book*) went through so many editions and sold so many copies that historians appear to have lost track. But it seems safe to say that there were at least 300 editions between 1788 and 1829 and that by the end of the nineteenth century it had sold more than sixty million copies—though some sources put the figure as high as a hundred million. In either case, with the possible exception of the Bible, it is probably the best-selling book in American history.

27   Webster is commonly credited with changing American spelling, but what is seldom realized is how wildly variable his own views on the matter were. Sometimes he was in favor of radical and far-reaching changes—insisting on such spellings as *soop, bred, wimmen, groop, definit, fether, fugitiv, tuf, thum, hed, bilt*, and *tung*—but at other times he acted the very soul of orthographic conservatism, going so far as to attack the useful American tendency to drop the *u* from *colour*,

humour, and the like. The main book with which he is associated in the popular mind, his massive *American Dictionary of the English Language* of 1828, actually said in the preface that it was "desirable to perpetuate the sameness" of American and British spellings and usages.

28   Many of the spellings that he insisted on in his *Compendious Dictionary of the English Language* (1806) and its later variants were simply ignored by his loyal readers. They overlooked them, as one might a tic or stammer, and continued to write *group* rather than *groop*, *crowd* rather than *croud*, *medicine* rather than *medicin*, *phantom* for *fantom*, and many hundreds of others. Such changes as Webster did manage to establish were relatively straightforward and often already well underway—for instance, the American tendency to transpose the British *re* in *theatre*, *centre*, and other such words. Yet even here Webster was by no means consistent. His dictionaries retained many irregular spellings, some of which have stuck in English to this day (*acre*, *glamour*) and some of which were corrected by the readers themselves (*frolick*, *wimmen*). Other of his ideas are of questionable benefit. His insistence on dropping one of the *l*'s in words such as *traveller* and *jeweller* (which way they are still spelled in England) was a useful shortcut, but it has left many of us unsure whether we should write *excelling* or *exceling*, or *fulfilled*, *fullfilled*, or *fulfiled*.

29   Webster was responsible also for the American *aluminum* in favor of the British *aluminium*. His choice has the fractional advantage of brevity, but defaults in terms of consistency. *Aluminium* at least follows the pattern set by other chemical elements—*potassium*, *radium*, and the like.

30   But for the most part the differences that distinguish American spelling from British spelling became common either late in his life or after his death, and would probably have happened anyway.

31   In terms of pronunciation he appears to have left us with our pronunciation of *schedule* rather than the English "shedjulle" and with our standard pronunciation of *lieutenant* which was then widely pronounced "lefftenant" in America, as it still is in England today. But just as he sometimes pressed for odd spellings, so he called for many irregular pronunciations: "deef" for *deaf*, "nater" for *nature*, "heerd" for *heard*, "booty" for *beauty*, "voloom" for *volume*, and others too numerous (and, I am tempted to add, too laughable) to dwell on. He insisted that *Greenwich* and *Thames* be pronounced as spelled and favored giving *quality* and *quantity* the short "â" of *hat*, while giving *advance*, *clasp*, and *grant* the broad "ah" sound of southern England. No less remarkably, Webster accepted a number of clearly ungrammatical usages, among them "it is me," "we was," and "them horses." It is a wonder that anyone paid any attention to him at all. Often they didn't.

32   Nonetheless his dictionary was the most complete of its age, with 70,000 words—far more than Johnson had covered—and its definitions were models of clarity and conciseness. It was an enormous achievement.

33   All Webster's work was informed by a passionate patriotism and the belief that American English was at least as good as British English. He worked tirelessly, churning out endless hectoring books and tracts, as well as working on the more

or less constant revisions of his spellers and dictionaries. In between time he wrote impassioned letters to congressmen, dabbled in politics, proffered unwanted advice to presidents, led his church choir, lectured to large audiences, helped found Amherst College, and produced a sanitized version of the Bible, in which Onan doesn't spill his seed but simply "frustrates his purpose," in which men don't have testicles but rather "peculiar members," and in which women don't have wombs (or evidently anything else with which to contribute to the reproductive process).

34   Like Samuel Johnson, he was a better lexicographer than a businessman. Instead of insisting on royalties he sold the rights outright and never gained the sort of wealth that his tireless labors merited. After Webster's death in 1843, two business-men from Springfield, Massachusetts, Charles and George Merriam, bought the rights to his dictionaries and employed his son-in-law, the rather jauntily named Chauncey A. Goodrich, to prepare a new volume (and, not incidentally, expunge many of the more ridiculous spellings and far-fetched etymologies). This volume, the first Merriam-Webster dictionary, appeared in 1847 and was an instant success. Soon almost every home had one. There is a certain neat irony in the thought that the book with which Noah Webster is now most closely associated wasn't really his work at all and certainly didn't adhere to many of his most cherished precepts.

35   In early February 1884, a slim paperback book bearing the title *The New English Dictionary on Historical Principles*, containing all the words in the language (ob-scenities apart) between *A* and *ant* was published in Britain at the steepish price of twelve shillings and six pence. This was the first of twelve volumes of the most masterly and ambitious philological exercise ever undertaken, eventually redubbed the *Oxford English Dictionary*. The intention was to record every word used in English since 1150 and to trace it back through all its shifting meanings, spellings, and uses to its earliest recorded appearance. There was to be at least one citation for each century of its existence and at least one for each slight change of meaning. To achieve this, almost every significant piece of English literature from the last 7½ centuries would have to be not so much read as scoured.

36   The man chosen to guide this enterprise was James Augustus Henry Murray (1837–1915), a Scottish-born bank clerk, schoolteacher, and self-taught philologist. He was an unlikely, and apparently somewhat reluctant, choice to take on such a daunting task. Murray, in the best tradition of British eccentrics, had a flowing white beard and liked to be photographed in a long black housecoat with a mortarboard on his head. He had eleven children, all of whom were, almost from the moment they learned the alphabet, roped into the endless business of helping to sift through and alphabetize the several million slips of paper on which were recorded every twitch and burble of the language over seven centuries.

37   The ambition of the project was so staggering that one can't help wondering if Murray really knew what he was taking on. In point of fact, it appears he didn't. He thought the whole business would take a dozen years at most and that it would fill half a dozen volumes covering some 6,400 pages. In the event, the project took more than four decades and sprawled across 15,000 densely printed pages.

language ('læŋgwɪdʒ), *sb.*[1] Forms: 3-6 langage, (3 langag, 4 longage, langwag, 5 langwache, langegage), 3, 5- language. [a. F. *langage* (recorded from 12th c.) = Pr. *leng(u)atge, lengage,* Sp. *lenguaje,* Pg. *linguage(m,* It. *linguaggio:*—pop.L. type **linguāticum,* f. *lingua* tongue, language (F. *langue*: see LANGUE).

The form with *u*, due to assimilation with the F. *langue,* occurs in A.F. writings of the 12th c., and in Eng. from about 1300.]

1. a. The whole body of words and of methods of combination of words used by a nation, people, or race; a 'tongue'. **dead language**: a language no longer in vernacular use. **first language**: one's native language. **second language**: a language spoken in addition to one's native language; the first foreign language one learns.

c **1290** *S.E. Leg.* I. 108/55 With men þat onder-stoden hire langage. **1297** R. GLOUC. (Rolls) 1569 Vor in þe langage of rome rane a frogge is. *a* **1300** *Cursor M.* 247 (Gött.) Seldom was for ani chance Englis tong preched in france, Gif we þaim ilkan þair language [*MS. Cott.* langage], And þan do we na vtetrage. *Ibid.,* 6384 (Gött.) þis mete.. þai called it in þair langag man. **1387** TREVISA *Higden* (Rolls) II. 157 Walsche men and Scottes, þat beeþ nouȝt i-medled wiþ oþer nacions, holdeþ wel nyh hir firste longage and speche. *c* **1400** *Apol. Loll.* 32 In a langwag vnknowun ilk man and womman mai rede. *c* **1449** PECOCK *Repr.* I. xii. 66 Thei.. han vsid the hool Bible.. in her modris langage. *c* **1450** *Mirour Saluacioun* 3650 Wymmen spak these diuerse langegages. **1588** SHAKS. *L.L.L.* v. i. 40 They haue beene at a great feast of Languages, and stolne the scraps. **1589** PUTTENHAM *Eng. Poesie* III. iv. (Arb.) 156 After a speach is fully fashioned to the common vnderstanding, and accepted by consent of a whole countrey and nation, it is called a language. **1699** BENTLEY *Phal.* xiii. 392 Every living Language.. is in perpetual motion and alteration. **1769** DE FOE'S *Tour Gt. Brit.* (ed. 7) IV. 303 It is called in the Irish Language, I-colm-kill; some call it Iona. **1779-81** JOHNSON *L.P., Addison* Wks. III. 44 A dead language, in which nothing is mean because nothing is familiar. **1823** DE QUINCEY *Lett. Yng. Man* Wks. 1860 XIV. 37 On this Babel of an earth.. there are said to be about three thousand languages and jargons. **1845** M. PATTISON *Ess.* (1889) I. 13 In fact, Bede is writing in a dead language, Gregory in a living. **1875** STUBBS *Const. Hist.* II. 414 The use of the English language in the Courts of law was ordered in 1362. **1875** W. D. WHITNEY *Life & Growth of Language* ii. 25 We realize better in the case of a second or 'foreign', than in that of a first or 'native' language, that the process of acquisition is a never-ending one. **1876** C. M. YONGE *Womankind* vi. 40 The second language has been really and grammatically learnt. **1943** I. A. RICHARDS *Basic Eng. & its Uses* 14 The history of the nationalist movement in India is an instructive instance. Its leaders and its chief supporters are speakers of English and sometimes use it rather as their first than as their second language. **1962** R. QUIRK *Use of English* i. 6 Something like 250 million people for whom English is the mother-tongue or 'first language'. **1971** *Guardian* 23 June 7/3 Indians and Pakistanis.. using a second language at school and their first language for many home activities.

fig. **1720** GAY *Prol. Dione* 4 Love, devoid of art, Spoke the consenting language of the heart. **1812** W. C. BRYANT *Thanatopsis* 3 To him who in the love of Nature holds Communion with her visible forms, she speaks A various language.

b. *transf.* Applied to methods of expressing the thoughts, feelings, wants, etc., otherwise than by words. **finger language** = DACTYLOLOGY. **language of flowers**: a method of expressing sentiments by means of flowers. .

1606 SHAKS. *Tr. & Cr.* IV. v. 55 Ther's a language in her eye, her cheeke, her lip. **1697** COLLIER *Ess. Mor. Subj.* II. 120 As the language of the Face is universal so 'tis very comprehensive. **1711** STEELE *Spect.* No. 66 ▶2 She is utterly a Foreigner in the Language of Looks and Glances. **1827** WHATELY *Logic* (1850) Introd. §6 A Deaf-mute, before he has been taught a Language, either the Finger-language, or Reading, cannot carry on a train of Reasoning. **1834** tr. *C. de la Tour's Lang. Flowers* 95 It is more especially by.. modifications that the Language of Flowers becomes the

interpretation of our thoughts. **1837** *Penny Cycl.* VIII. 282/2 Dactylology must not be confounded with the natural language of the deaf and dumb, which is purely a language of mimic signs. **1847** THACKERAY *Van. Fair* (1848) iv. 31 Perhaps she just looked first into the bouquet, to see whether there was a *billet-doux* hidden... 'Do they talk the language of flowers at Boggley Wollah, Sedley?' asked Osborne, laughing. **1876** MOZLEY *Univ. Serm.* vi. 134 All action is.. besides being action, language. **1880** *Times* 23 June 9/5 Teaching the deaf by signs and by finger language. **1894** H. DRUMMOND *Ascent Man* 212 A sign Language is of no use when one savage is at one end of a wood and his wife at the other. **1949** *Enquire within upon Everything* (ed. 122) 462 *Language of Flowers.* The symbolism of flowers has always possessed a certain fascination, especially for the young person of either sex.

c. *transf.* Applied to the inarticulate sounds used by the lower animals, birds, etc.

1601 SHAKS. *All's Well* IV. i. 22 Choughs language, gabble enough, and good enough. **1667** MILTON *P.L.* VIII. 373 Is not the Earth With various living creatures, and the Aire Replenisht,.. know'st thou not Thir language and thir wayes? **1797** BEWICK *Brit. Birds* (1847) I. p. xxvii, The notes, or as it may with more propriety be called, the language of birds.

d. *Computers.* Any of numerous systems of precisely defined symbols and rules for using them that have been devised for writing programs or representing instructions and data.

1959 E. M. GRABBE et al. *Handbk. Automation, Computation, & Control* II. ii. 186 The purpose of these activities has been to.. set up a class of languages that will be easily translatable by machine from one to another, and also easily recognizable to the ordinary human user... Such languages form the input to a class of automatic computer programs called translators, which perform a translation.. into a second or target language. The latter may be either (1) an assembly language such as SOAP, SAP, or MAGIC.., or (2) a straight machine language, in pure decimal, binary (or in some cases such as the Univac I and II), alphanumeric. **1961** LEEDS & WEINBERG *Computer Programming Fund.* ii. 46 The best way of writing down operations is to write them in alphabetical format. A format used for writing down these alphabetical instructions is called the programming language or paper language, to distinguish it from the machine language.. acceptable to the machine circuitry. **1964** F. L. WESTWATER *Electronic Computers* ix. 145 As the benefits of these codes were realised, each manufacturer produced different 'languages'. **1966** A. BATTERSBY *Math. in Managem.* viii. 206 If each manufacturer prepares a compiler routine which will translate instructions in some universal 'language' into a program in his own code, then programs written in the universal language can be run on any machine. **1967** A. HASSITT *Computer Programming* i. 1 An efficient way of learning to use a computing machine utilizes one of the problem oriented languages such as Fortran, Algol, or PL/1. **1970** A. CAMERON et al. *Computers & Old Eng. Concordances* 27 If we program in so-called higher-languages, like Fortran, conceivably PLI,.. I myself will be very surprised if the next generation of machines will not accept Fortran programming and probably Cobol, Algol, and PLI programming.

2. a. In generalized sense: Words and the methods of combining them for the expression of thought.

1599 SHAKS. *Much Ado* IV. i. 98 There is not chastitie enough in language, Without offence to vtter them. **1644** MILTON *Educ. Wks.* (1847) 98/2 Language is but the instrument conveying to us things useful to be known. **1781** COWPER *Conversat.* 15 So language in the mouths of the adult,.. Too often proves an implement of play. **1841** TRENCH *Parables* ii. (1877) 25 Language is ever needing to be recalled, minted and issued anew. **1862** J. MARTINEAU *Ess.* (1891) IV. 104 Language, that wonderful crystallization of the very flow and spray of thought. **1892** WESTCOTT *Gospel of Life* 186 Language must be to the last inadequate to express the results of perfect observation.

b. Power or faculty of speech; ability to speak a foreign tongue. Now *rare*.

1526 WOLSEY *Let. to Tayler* in Strype *Eccl. Mem.* I. v. 66 A gentleman.. who had knowledge of the country and good language to pass. **1601** SHAKS. *All's Well* IV. i. 77, I shall loose my life for want of language. If there be heere German or Dane, Low Dutch, Italian, or French, let him speake to me. **1610** —— *Temp.* II. ii. 86 Here is that which will giue language to you Cat; open your mouth. **1790** COWPER *Receipt Mother's Pict.* 1 Oh that those lips had language!

3. a. The form of words in which a person expresses himself; manner or style of expression. *bad language*: coarse or vulgar expressions. *strong language*: expressions indicative of violent or excited feeling.
1809-10 COLERIDGE *Friend* (1865) 135 These pretended constitutionalists recurred to the language of insult. **1849** MACAULAY *Hist. Eng.* vi. II. 118 He lived and died, in the significant language of one of his countrymen, a bad Christian, but a good Protestant. **1855** MOTLEY *Dutch Rep.* II. ii. (1856) 155 In all these interviews he had uniformly used one language: his future wife was to 'live as a Catholic'. *c* **1863** T. TAYLOR in M. R. Booth *Eng. Plays of 19th Cent.* (1969) II. 109 Come, cheeky! Don't you use bad language. **1875** JOWETT *Plato* (ed. 2) V. 348 The language used to a servant ought always to be that of a command. *a* **1910** 'MARK TWAIN' *Autobiogr.* (1924) II. 88 She made a guarded remark which censured strong language. **1934** R. MACAULAY *Milton* vi. 100 Milton's familiarity with the tradition [of scurrility] may account for much of his strong language, even when reviling in English.
b. The phraseology or terms of a science, art, profession, etc., or of a class of persons.
1502 *Ord. Crysten Men* (W. de W. 1506) Prol. 4 The swete and fayre langage of theyr phylosophy. **1596** SHAKS. *1 Hen. IV,* II. iv. 21, I can drinke with any Tinker in his owne Language. **1611** —— *Cymb.* III. iii. 74 This is not Hunters Language. **1651** HOBBES *Leviath.* III. xxxiv. 207 The words Body, and Spirit, which in the language of the Schools are termed Substances, Corporeall and Incorporeall. **1747** SPENCE *Polymetis* VIII. xv. 243 Those attributes of the Sword, Victory, and Globe, say very plainly (in the language of the statuaries) that [etc.]. **1841** J. R. YOUNG *Math. Dissert.* I. 10 Thus can be expressed in the language of algebra, not only distance but position. **1891** *Speaker* 2 May 532.1 In it metaphysics have again condescended to speak the language of polite letters.
c. The style (of a literary composition); also, the wording (of a document, statute, etc.).
1712 ADDISON *Spect.* No. 285 ¶6 It is not therefore sufficient that the Language of an Epic Poem be Perspicuous, unless it be also Sublime. **1781** COWPER *Conversat.* 236 A tale should be judicious, clear, succinct, The language plain. **1886** SIR J. STIRLING in *Law Times Rep.* LV. 283/2 There are two remarks which I desire to make on the language of the Act.
d. *long language*: †(a) verbosity (tr. Gr. μακρολογία; (b) language composed of words written in full, as opposed to cipher.
e. *vulgar.* Short for *bad language* (see above).
1860 DICKENS *Uncomm. Trav.* (1861) v 65 Mr Victualler's assurance that he 'never allowed any language, and never suffered any disturbance'. **1865** —— *Dr. Marigold's Prescriptions* i, in *All Year Round* Extra Christmas No., 7 Dec. 4/1 But have a temper in the cart, flinging language and the hardest goods in stock at you, and where are you then? **1886** BESANT *Childr. Gibeon* II. xxv, That rude eloquence which is known in Ivy Lane as 'language'. **1893** SELOUS *Trav. S.E. Africa* 3 The sailor had never ceased to pour out a continuous flood of 'language' all the time. **1929** C. C. MARTINDALE *Risen Sun* 173, I have heard more 'language' in a 'gentleman's' club in ten minutes than in all that evening in the Melbourne Stadium. **1974** 'M. INNES' *Mysterious Commission* vii. 75 'You behave like bloody fools.' 'Language, now, Mr Honeybath, language.'
f. *Phr. to speak (talk) someone's language, to speak (talk) the same language*: to have an understanding with someone through similarity of outlook and expression, to get on well with someone; *to speak a different language (from someone)*: to have little in common (with.
† 4. a. The act of speaking or talking; the use of speech. *by language*: so to speak. *in language with*: in conversation with. *without language*: not to make many words. *Obs.*

a **1400** *Cov. Myst.* iv. *Noah's Flood* ii, Afftyr Adam with-outyn langage, The secunde fadyr am I [Noe] in fay. *a* **1450** *Knt. de la Tour* (1868) 18 My fader sette me in langage with her. **1461** *Paston Lett.* No. 393 II. 17, I said I dwelled uppon the cost of the see here, and be langage hit were more necessare to with hold men here than take from hit. **1477** EARL RIVERS (Caxton) *Dictes* 57 One was surer in keping his tunge, than in moche speking, for in moche langage one may lightly erre. **1490** CAXTON *Eneydos* xxviii. 107 Wythout eny more langage dydo.. seased thenne the swerde. **1514** BARCLAY *Cyt. & Uplondyshm.* (Percy Soc.) p. xviii, To morowe of court we may have more language.
† b. That which is said, words, talk, report; *esp.* words expressive of censure or opprobrium. Also *pl.* reports, sayings. *to say language against*: to talk against, speak opprobriously of. *Obs.*
a **1450** *Knt. de la Tour* (1868) 2 And so thei dede bothe desciue ladies and gentilwomen, and bere forthe diuerse langages on hem. **1465** MARG. PASTON in *P. Lett.* No. 502 II. 188, I hyre moch langage of the demenyng betwene you and herre. **1467** *Mann. & Househ. Exp.* (Roxb.) 172 3e haue mekel on setenge langwache aȝenste me, were of 1 mervel gretely for I haue ȝeffen ȝowe no schwsche kawse. **1470-85** MALORY *Arthur* II. xl, Euery daye syre Palomydes brauled and sayd langage agrynst syr Tristram. **1636** SIR H. BLUNT *Voy. Levant* 33 A Turke.. gave such a Language of our Nation, and threatning to all whom they should light upon, as made me upon all demands professe my selfe a Scotchman.
5. a. A community of people having the same form of speech, a nation. *arch.* [A literalism of translation.]
1388 WYCLIF *Dan.* v. 19 Alle puplis, lynagis, and langagis [**1382** tungis]. **1611** BIBLE *Ibid* **1653** URQUHART *Rabelais* I. x, All people, and all languages and nations.
b. A national division or branch of a religious and military Order, *e.g.* of the Hospitallers.
1727-52 CHAMBERS *Cycl. Language* is also used, in the order of Malta, for *nation.* **1728** MORGAN *Algiers* I. v. 314 Don Raimond Perellos de Roccapoul, of the Language of Aragon, .. was elected Grand Master. **1885** *Catholic Dict.* (ed. 3) 413/2 The order [of Hospitallers] .. was divided into eight 'languages', Provence, Auvergne, France, Aragon, Castile, England, Germany, and Italy.
6. *attrib.* and *Comb.* **a.** simple attributive, as *language acquisition, -capacity, change, course, description, engineering, event, -family, -form, -group, -history, -pattern, sign, structure, -study, -system, -turn, -use.* **b.** objective, as *language-learner, -learning, -maker, -teacher, -teaching, -user, -using;* **language area,** (a) an area of the cerebral cortex regarded as especially concerned with the use of language; (b) a region where a particular language is spoken; **language barrier,** a barrier to communication between people which results from their speaking or writing different languages; **language-contact** *Linguistics* (see quot. 1964); **language-game** *Philos.*, a speech-activity or limited system of communication and action, complete in itself, which may or may not form a part of our existing use of language; **language laboratory** (*colloq.* **language lab**), a classroom, equipped with tape recorders, etc., where foreign languages are learnt by means of repeated oral practice; **language-master,** a teacher of language or languages; **language-particular** *a.*, = *language-specific* adj.; **language-specific** *a. Linguistics,* distinctive to a specified language.

38   Hundreds of volunteers helped with the research, sending in citations from all over the world. Many of them were, like Murray, amateur philologists and often they were as eccentric as he. One of the most prolific contributors was James Platt, who specialized in obscure words. He was said to speak a hundred languages and certainly knew as much about comparative linguistics as any man of his age, and yet he owned no books of his own. He worked for his father in the City of London and each lunchtime collected one book—never more—from the Reading Room of the British Museum, which he would take home, devour, and replace with another volume the next day. On weekends he haunted the opium dens and dockyards of Wapping and Whitechapel looking for native speakers of obscure tongues whom he would query on small points of semantics. He provided the histories of many thousands of words. But an even more prolific contributor was an American expatriate named Dr. W. C. Minor, a man of immense erudition who provided from his private library the etymologies of tens of thousands of words. When Murray invited him to a gathering of the dictionary's contributors, he learned, to his considerable surprise, that Dr. Minor could not attend for the unfortunate reason that he was an inmate at Broadmoor, a hospital for the criminally insane, and not sufficiently in possession of his faculties to be allowed out. It appears that during the U.S. Civil War, having suffered an attack of sunstroke, Dr. Minor developed a persecution mania, believing he was being pursued by Irishmen. After a stay in an asylum he was considered cured and undertook, in 1871, a visit to England. But one night while walking in London his mania returned and he shot dead an innocent stranger whose misfortune it was to have been walking behind the crazed American. Clearly Dr. Minor's madness was not incompatible with scholarship. In one year alone, he made 12,000 contributions to the *OED* from the private library he built up at Broadmoor.

39   Murray worked ceaselessly in his dictionary for thirty-six years, from his appointment to the editorship in 1879 to his death at the age of seventy-eight in 1915. (He was knighted in 1908.) He was working on the letter *u* when he died, but his assistants carried on for another thirteen years until in 1928 the final volume, Wise to Wyzen, was issued. (For some reason, volume 12, XYZ, had appeared earlier.) Five years later, a corrected and slightly updated version of the entire set was re-issued, under the name by which it has since been known: the *Oxford English Dictionary*. The completed dictionary contained 414,825 entries supported by 1,827,306 citations (out of 6 million collected) described in 44 million words of text spread over 15,487 pages. It is perhaps the greatest work of scholarship ever produced.

40   The *OED* confirmed a paradox that Webster had brought to light decades earlier—namely, that although readers will appear to treat a dictionary with the utmost respect, they will generally ignore anything in it that doesn't suit their tastes. The *OED*, for instance, has always insisted on *-ize* spellings for words such as *characterize, itemize*, and the like, and yet almost nowhere in England, apart from the pages of *The Times* newspaper (and not always there) are they observed. The British still spell almost all such words with *-ise* endings and thus enjoy a consistency with words such as *advertise, merchandise*, and *surprise* that we in America fail to achieve. But perhaps the most notable of all the *OED*'s minor quirks is its insistence that Shakespeare should be spelled Shakspere. After explaining at some length why this is the only

correct spelling, it grudgingly acknowledges that the commonest spelling "is perh. Shakespeare." (To which we might add, it cert. is.)

41   In the spring of 1989, a second edition of the dictionary was issued, containing certain modifications, such as the use of the International Phonetic Alphabet instead of Murray's own quirky system. It comprised the original twelve volumes, plus four vast supplements issued between 1972 and 1989. Now sprawling over twenty volumes, the updated dictionary is a third bigger than its predecessor, with 615,000 entries, 2,412,000 supporting quotations, almost 60 million words of exposition, and about 350 million keystrokes of text (or one for each native speaker of English in the world). No other language has anything even remotely approaching it in scope. Because of its existence, more is known about the history of English than any other language in the world.

Questions on Content

1. What did each of the following contribute to English lexicography?

Nathaniel Bailey	Charles and George Merriam
Robert Cawdrey	James Murray
Samuel Johnson	Noah Webster

2. Why is it so difficult to determine how many words are in the English language? In an individual's vocabulary?

3. What is the best-selling book in U.S. history? The next-best-selling book?

4. Who promoted the spelling *theater* in the United States?

5. How did Murray's purpose in compiling his *Oxford English Dictionary* differ from Johnson's purpose in compiling his dictionary? From Webster's purpose?

6. What paradox about dictionaries did Webster's work reveal? How did Murray's *Oxford English Dictionary* confirm it?

7. Why, according to Bryson, is more known about the history of English than that of any other language in the world?

Questions on Structure and Style

8. What is Bryson's purpose in this selection? Does he state it specifically in a thesis statement? If so, where?

9. Think about the tone and content of this essay, and try to define Bryson's audience.

10. Why does Bryson include descriptions of the physical appearance of Johnson, Webster, and Murray? What possible relevance could these descriptions have to his purpose?

11. Why does Bryson begin this selection with a sweeping question: "How big is the English language?" Is the use of *big* appropriate? Do you believe that *large* or *vast* would have been more or less appropriate? Explain.

Assignments

1. Because Bryson presents various lexicographers with such attention to their physical detail, careful readers should be able to formulate a physical description of each of them. Write a paragraph in which you describe the physical appearance of two of the following: Samuel Johnson, Noah Webster, James Murray.

2. Write an essay about one of the lexicographers—Johnson, Webster, or Murray—in which you include descriptions of his physical appearance, personality traits, and contributions to English lexicography.

A Rarity: Grammar Lessons from Dad

Robert Klose

What happens when a father compliments his son's vocabulary? In this case, one result is a painless introduction to adverbs for his son, but the incident also prompts biology teacher Robert Klose to offer this broader reflection. Many adults, including many employers, lament the language deficiencies of today's students, who too commonly receive almost no training in grammar and syntax. Klose places blame for this problem squarely on schools, where study of the "underpinnings of the language" is ignored and where many younger teachers are themselves ignorant of the mechanics of the language they speak.

■ **JOURNAL PROMPT** *Think about sources in your experience that have encouraged you to consider language correctness in your speaking and writing. Think, for example, about the roles of schools, parents, friends, and the media.*

1   If I am the only parent who still corrects his child's English, then perhaps my son is right: To him I am an oddity, a father making remarks about something that no longer seems to merit comment.

2   I think I got serious about this only recently, when I ran into one of my former students, fresh from two months in Europe. "How was it?" I asked, full of anticipation.

3   She nodded three or four times, searched the heavens for the right words, and then informed me, "It was, like, whoa."

4   And that was it. The glory of Greece and the grandeur of Rome summed up in a nonstatement. My student's "whoa" was exceeded only by my head-shaking woe.

5   As a biology teacher, perhaps I shouldn't be overly concerned with my students' English. After all, the traditional refuge of the science teacher is the hated multiple-choice exam, where students are asked to recognize, but not actually use, language. My English-teaching colleagues are, however, duty-bound to extract essays, compositions and position papers from their charges. These products, I am told, are becoming increasingly awful. I still harbor the image of an English-teacher colleague who burst into my office one day in a sweat of panic. "Quick!" she commanded. "A dictionary!"

6   She tore through the book. "Just as I thought!" she exclaimed, pinning the entry with her finger. "It is spelled r-e-c-e-i-v-e."

7   Her point, whether she knew it or not, was that students make the same mistakes repeatedly. As for their teachers, they must read hundreds and eventually thousands of errors, which in time become more familiar than the accepted forms, so that the instructors themselves become uncertain whether it's "recieve" or receive, "protien" or protein.

8   The one thing that stories about the demise of English in America have in common is that they're all true. And students usually bear the brunt of the infamy, because there is a sense that they should know better. The truth is that they are being misled everywhere they look and listen.

9   Supermarket aisles point them to the "stationary," even though the pads and notebooks are not nailed down; people "could care less," even when they couldn't; and, more and more, friends and loved ones announce that they've just "ate" when, in fact, they've eaten.

10   Blame must be laid (and lie, not lay, it does) somewhere, and I am happy to place it squarely on the schools, which should be safe harbors for the standards of the English language. Instead, they don't teach grammar at all. Or syntax or vocabulary. In fact, the younger teachers themselves have little knowledge of these underpinnings of the language, because they also went without exposure to them.

11   The schools having affirmed poor or sloppy speech habits through their lack of attention to them, I am obligated to do the dirty work of gently ushering my son onto the path of competent communication. But, as the Wicked Witch of the West said in one of her rhetorical musings, "These things must be handled delicately." (Alyosha's patience is limited when his dad behaves like a teacher.)

12   The other day, I was driving to a nearby town with my son. As we set out on our 5-mile trip, he noticed a bird in eccentric flight and said, "It's flying so raggedly." Impressed with his description, I remarked, "Good adverb!"

13   He asked me what an adverb was. I explained that it's a word that tells you something about a verb, which led to his asking me what a verb was. I explained that it's an action word, giving him an example: "Dad drives the truck. 'Drives' is the verb," I told him, "because it's the thing Dad is doing."

14   He became intrigued with the idea of action words. So we listed a few more. Fly, swim, dive, run. And then, having fallen prey to his own curiosity, he asked me if other words had names. This led to a discussion of nouns, adjectives and articles. The upshot of all this is that within the span of a 10-minute drive, he had learned—from scratch—to recognize the major parts of speech in a sentence.

15   It was painless and fun, but it's not being taught in the schools. There seems to be a sense that as long as a student is making himself understood, all is well. Sort of like driving a junker that blows smoke and has a flat tire. If it gets you there, what's the problem?

16   Perhaps, then, language should be looked upon as a possession: keeping it clean and in repair shows concern and effort. It demonstrates attentiveness to detail and the accomplishment of a goal—clear, accurate, descriptive speech.

17   Just this morning my son and I were eating breakfast when I attempted to add milk to my tea. "Dad," he cautioned, "if I were you, I wouldn't do that. It's sour."

18   "Alyosha," I said, swelling with pride, "that's a grammatically perfect sentence. You used 'were' instead of 'was.'"

19   "I know, I know," he said with a degree of weary irritation. "It's the subjunctive mood."

20   I was, like, whoa.

Questions on Content

1. Klose suggests that "language should be looked upon as a possession: keeping it clean and in repair shows concern and effort" (paragraph 16). Explain.

2. Does Klose blame poor language preparation on any source other than elementary and high school curricula?

Questions on Structure and Style

3. Discuss Klose's use of the anecdote that begins in paragraph 12.

4. Comment on the effectiveness of Klose's conclusion. What rhetorical technique does he employ?

5. Comment on the tone of this essay. Provide examples of Klose's language that illustrate his tone.

Assignments

1. Klose, a biology teacher, believes that university students typically do not use the English language correctly because elementary and high schools are not preparing them to do so. Write an essay in response to Klose's assertion. Employ concrete illustrations that reveal how language correctness has or has not been a part of your education. Try to use at least one anecdote to develop your essay.

2. You have been asked to write an essay in which you develop one or two specific episodes that reveal the character of a close relative. Assume that you are the son of Robert Klose. Write a concrete essay in which you describe your father's (Klose's) attitude about language correctness and his "grammar lessons."

Four-Letter Words Can Hurt You

Barbara Lawrence

Barbara Lawrence has worked as a magazine editor and college
instructor and as a writer of fiction, poetry, and criticism. The following well-known essay addresses the implications of using language
considered obscene. As Lawrence explains, sexual pejoratives victimize women just as brutally as racial and ethnic pejoratives victimize
their targets. The prevalence of such language today leads one to
question our values as a society.

■ **JOURNAL PROMPT** *Lawrence begins the selection with this question:
"Why should any words be called obscene?" Think about how you would answer the question before reading what the author says.*

1   Why should any words be called obscene? Don't they all describe natural human
functions? Am I trying to tell them, my students demand, that the "strong, earthy,
gut-honest"—or, if they are fans of Norman Mailer, the "rich, liberating, exis-
tential"—language they use to describe sexual activity isn't preferable to "phony-
sounding, middle-class words like 'intercourse' and 'copulate'?" "Cop You Late!"
they say with fancy inflections and gagging grimaces. "Now, what is *that* supposed
to mean?"

2   Well, what is it supposed to mean? And why indeed should one group of words
describing human functions and human organs be acceptable in ordinary conversation and another, describing presumably the same organs and functions, be
tabooed—so much so, in fact, that some of these words still cannot appear in print
in many parts of the English-speaking world?

3   The argument that these taboos exist only because of "sexual hangups" (middle-
class, middle-age, feminist), or even that they are a result of class oppression (the
contempt of the Norman conquerors for the language of their Anglo-Saxon serfs),
ignores a much more likely explanation, it seems to me, and that is the sources and
functions of the words themselves.

4   The best known of the tabooed sexual verbs, for example, comes from the
German *ficken*, meaning "to strike"; combined, according to Partridge's etymological dictionary *Origins*, with the Latin sexual verb *futuere*; associated in turn
with the Latin *fustis*, "a staff or cudgel"; the Celtic *buc*, "a point, hence to pierce";
the Irish *bot*, "the male member"; the Latin *battuere*, "to beat"; the Gaelic *batair*,
"a cudgeller"; the Early Irish *bualaim*, "I strike"; and so forth. It is one of what
etymologists sometimes call "the sadistic group of words for the man's part in
copulation."

5   The brutality of this word, then, and its equivalents ("screw," "bang," etc.), is not an illusion of the middle class or a crotchet of Women's Liberation. In their origins and imagery these words carry undeniably painful, if not sadistic, implications, the object of which is almost always female. Consider, for example, what a "screw" actually does to the wood it penetrates; what a painful, even mutilating, activity this kind of analogy suggests. "Screw" is particularly interesting in this context, since the noun, according to Partridge, comes from words meaning "groove," "nut," "ditch," "breeding sow," "scrofula" and "swelling," while the verb, besides its explicit imagery, has antecedent associations to "write on," "scratch," "scarify," and so forth—a revealing fusion of a mechanical or painful action with an obviously denigrated object.

6   Not all obscene words, of course, are as implicitly sadistic or denigrating to women as these, but all that I know seem to serve a similar purpose: to reduce the human organism (especially the female organism) and human functions (especially sexual and procreative) to their least organic, most mechanical dimension; to substitute a trivializing or deforming resemblance for the complex human reality of what is being described.

7   Tabooed male descriptives, when they are not openly denigrating to women, often serve to divorce a male organ or function from any significant interaction with the female. Take the word "testes," for example, suggesting "witnesses" (from the Latin *testis*) to the sexual and procreative strengths of the male organ; and the obscene counterpart of this word, which suggests little more than a mechanical shape. Or compare almost any of the "rich," "liberating" sexual verbs, so fashionable today among male writers, with that much-derided Latin word "copulate" ("to bind or join together") or even that Anglo-Saxon phrase (which seems to have had no trouble surviving the Norman Conquest) "make love."

8   How arrogantly self-involved the tabooed words seem in comparison to either of the other terms, and how contemptuous of the female partner. Understandably so, of course, if she is only a "skirt," a "broad," a "chick," a "pussycat" or a "piece." If she is, in other words, no more than her skirt, or what her skirt conceals; no more than a breeder, or the broadest part of her; no more than a piece of a human being or a "piece of tail."

9   The most severely tabooed of all the female descriptives, incidentally, are those like "a piece of tail," which suggest (either explicitly or through antecedents) that there is no significant difference between the female channel through which we are all conceived and born and the anal outlet common to both sexes—a distinction that pornographers have always enjoyed obscuring.

10   This effort to deny women their biological identity, their individuality, their humanness, is such an important aspect of obscene language that one can only marvel at how seldom, in an era preoccupied with definitions of obscenity, this fact is brought to our attention. One problem, of course, is that many of the people in the best position to do this (critics, teachers, writers) are so reluctant today to admit that they are angered or shocked by obscenity. Bored, maybe, unimpressed, aesthetically displeased, but—no matter how brutal or denigrating the material—never angered, never shocked.

11   And yet how eloquently angered, how piously shocked many of these same people become if denigrating language is used about any minority group other than women; if the obscenities are racial or ethnic, that is, rather than sexual. Words like "coon," "kike," "spic," "wop," after all, deform identity, deny individuality and humanness in almost exactly the same way that sexual vulgarisms and obscenities do.

12   No one that I know, least of all my students, would fail to question the values of a society whose literature and entertainment rested heavily on racial or ethnic pejoratives. Are the values of a society whose literature and entertainment rest as heavily as ours on sexual pejoratives any less questionable?

Questions on Content

1. Do you agree with those who suggest that sexual-language taboos exist only because of sexual hang-ups? How does Lawrence respond to this argument?

2. Lawrence contends that obscenities "reduce the human organism (especially the female organism) and human functions (especially sexual and procreative) to their least organic, most mechanical dimension" (paragraph 6). Explain.

3. Lawrence argues that sexual taboos deny women their biological identity, their humanness. Explain what she means. Does this phenomenon affect only women?

4. In what ways, according to Lawrence, are tabooed male descriptives different from tabooed female descriptives?

Questions on Structure and Style

5. Lawrence begins her essay with a volley of questions, and she concludes with a question. How does this strategy serve her purpose and her audience?

6. What does Lawrence gain with the lengthy etymology she offers in the fourth paragraph?

7. Each of the first three paragraphs has a specific function as Lawrence introduces her essay. Identify the function of each.

Assignments

1. Do you agree that people today tend to be more "put off" by racial and ethnic pejoratives than by sexual obscenities—

that, in effect, the former are more obscene than the latter? Interview your peers on this issue, and discuss your findings in an essay.

2. Summarize Lawrence's essay in a paragraph that clearly states her thesis.

Good-bye to All T__t!

Wallace Stegner

Can taboo language be used responsibly? Wallace Stegner asserts that it can and explains in the following argument the link between restraint and emphasis in the use of language. If used properly, taboo language has power. Stegner, a novelist as well as a teacher, believes that this power evaporates with the "impropriety" of using "a loaded word in the wrong place or in the wrong quantity." Any fault lies not in taboo language but in its misuse.

■ **JOURNAL PROMPT** *Think about situations that have prompted you to use obscene language. In retrospect, do you feel such use of taboos was always inappropriate? Is it possible for obscene language to be appropriate, even "correct"?*

1   Not everyone who laments what contemporary novelists have done to the sex act objects to the act itself, or to its mention. Some want it valued higher than fiction seems to value it; they want the word "climax" to retain some of its literary meaning. Likewise, not everyone who has come to doubt the contemporary freedom of language objects to strong language in itself. Some of us object precisely because we value it.

2   I acknowledge that I have used four-letter words familiarly all my life, and have put them into books with some sense that I was insisting on the proper freedom of the artist. I have applauded the extinction of those d—d emasculations of the Genteel Tradition and the intrusion into serious fiction of honest words with honest meanings and emphasis. I have wished, with D. H. Lawrence, for the courage to say shit before a lady, and have sometimes had my wish.

3   Words are not obscene: naming things is a legitimate verbal act. And "frank" does not mean "vulgar," any more than "improper" means "dirty." What vulgar does mean is "common"; what improper means is "unsuitable." Under the right circumstances, any word is proper. But when any sort of word, especially a word hitherto taboo and therefore noticeable, is scattered across a page like chocolate chips through a tollhouse cookie, a real impropriety occurs. The sin is not the use of an "obscene" word; it is the use of a loaded word in the wrong place or in the wrong quantity. It is the sin of false emphasis, which is not a moral but a literary lapse, related to sentimentality. It is the sin of advertisers who so plaster a highway with neon signs that you can't find the bar or liquor store you're looking for. Like any excess, it quickly becomes comic.

4   If I habitually say shit before a lady, what do I say before a flat tire at the rush hour in Times Square or on the San Francisco Bay Bridge? What do I say before a revelation of the inequity of the universe? And what if the lady takes the bit in her teeth and says shit before *me*?

5   I have been a teacher of writing for many years and have watched this problem since it was no bigger than a man's hand. It used to be that with some Howellsian

114

notion of the young-girl audience, one tried to protect tender female members of a mixed class from the coarse language of males trying to show off. Some years ago Frank O'Connor and I agreed on a system. Since we had no intention whatever of restricting students' choice of subject or language, and no desire to expurgate or bowdlerize while reading their stuff aloud for discussion, but at the same time had to deal with these young girls of an age our daughters might have been, we announced that any stuff so strong that it would embarrass us to read it aloud could be read by its own author.

6   It was no deterrent at all, but an invitation, and not only to coarse males. For clinical sexual observation, for full acceptance of the natural functions, for discrimination in the selection of graffiti, for boldness in the use of words that it should take courage to say before a lady, give me a sophomore girl every time. Her strength is as the strength of ten, for she assumes that if one shocker out of her pretty mouth is piquant, fifty will be literature. And so do a lot of her literary idols.

7   Some acts, like some words, were never meant to be casual. That is why houses contain bedrooms and bathrooms. Profanity and so-called obscenities are literary resources, verbal ways of rendering strong emotion. They are not meant to occur every ten seconds, any more than—Normal Mailer to the contrary not withstanding—orgasms are.

8   So I am not going to say shit before any more ladies. I am going to hunt words that have not lost their sting, and it may be I shall have to go back to gentility to find them. Pleasant though it is to know that finally a writer can make use of any word that fits his occasion, I am going to investigate the possibilities latent in restraint.

9   I remember my uncle, a farmer who had used four-letter words ten to the sentence ever since he learned to talk. One day he came too near the circular saw and cut half his fingers off. While we stared in horror, he stood watching the bright arterial blood pump from his ruined hand. Then he spoke, and he did not speak loud. "Aw, the dickens," he said.

10   I think he understood, better than some sophomore girls and better than some novelists, the nature of emphasis.

Questions on Content

1. Stegner deals with the use of taboo language in general and his own use of it in particular. What central point does he make about each use?

2. In paragraph 3 Stegner says, "Naming things is a legitimate verbal act." Why does he use the word *legitimate*? What other adjectives could he have used?

3. The author refers to "the sin of false emphasis" and cites the example of "advertisers who . . . plaster a highway with neon signs" (paragraph 3). Have you yourself encountered similar examples of false emphasis? What were they?

4. Stegner calls taboo expressions "literary resources" (paragraph 7). What does he mean? What other resources might he name?

5. Stegner often refers to his own life as a writer. If we consider this essay an argument, how do these references strengthen Stegner's position?

Questions on Structure and Style

6. Identify the topic sentences of paragraphs 6, 7, and 8.

7. In a periodic sentence, the speaker's meaning is not fully revealed until the end of the sentence. Identify the periodic sentence in paragraph 6.

8. Mark at least three places in which Stegner uses parallel construction. What effects does he create at these places?

9. Does paragraph 10 serve well as a conclusion? Why or why not?

10. Describe Stegner's tone. Where does he establish it? Does he maintain it consistently?

11. Stegner often shifts his focus from one paragraph to the next, yet he seldom uses stock transitional words and expressions (*also, however, therefore*). What effect does he achieve by avoiding these standard devices?

Assignments

1. Stegner claims that "under the right circumstances, any word is proper" (paragraph 3). Do you agree? Respond in a paragraph.

2. "Words are not obscene" (paragraph 3), according to Stegner. If you agree that words can never be obscene, what can be? Write a paragraph or essay in which you define the word *obscene* and provide specific examples.

3. Stegner argues for restraint in the use of language. Think of a specific incident you witnessed in which someone failed to exercise restraint in the use of language. Write an essay describing the event and explaining why restraint would have been wiser. Be sure not to confuse lack of restraint with anger.

The E Word

Cullen Murphy

Euphemisms, words substituted for language considered too harsh, sometimes signal respect for other people's feelings. Sometimes, though, less honorable motives are at work. So what do we make of an era such as ours, when euphemism has become "the characteristic literary device of our time"? Cullen Murphy states here his reassuring belief that any euphemism actually draws attention to the truth, and his extensive catalog of euphemisms offers more cause for amusement than anxiety. Murphy, essayist and managing editor of the *Atlantic,* also writes the comic strip *Prince Valiant.*

■ **J O U R N A L   P R O M P T** *Look up the word* euphemism *in a dictionary, and then comment on the following statement by lexicographer Robert Burchfield: "A language without euphemisms would be a defective instrument of communication" (paragraph 4).*

1   Driving along a highway in southern New Mexico not long ago, I came within the gravitational pull of a truck stop, and was ineluctably drawn in. This was not one of those mom-and-pop "truck stops," so prevalent in the East, where cars outnumber semis and the restaurant has a children's menu. This was the real thing, lit up in the desert darkness like an outpost in *Mad Max,* visible from six counties. Cars in the parking lot looked like Piper Cubs at O'Hare. It was the kind of place where tough men sit at the counter and call the waitress "doll," which she likes, and order flesh and starch while they smoke, leaning over the counter, a crescent of lower back visible between pants and shirt. Outside, their mounts hungrily lap up petrochemicals.

2   In a truck stop such as this the aesthetic pinnacle is typically reached in the design of the men's-room condom dispenser, and here I was not disappointed. Taking up nearly one full wall was a kind of Ghent Altarpiece of prophylaxis, each glass panel displaying its own delicately crafted vignette: a yellow sunset through palm trees, a couple strolling lazily along a beach, a herd of galloping white stallions, a flaxen-haired succubus in gauzy silhouette—exquisite examples of late-*novecento* venereal iconography.

3   Above it hung a sign saying FAMILY PLANNING CENTER.

4   Robert Burchfield, for many years the editor of *The Oxford English Dictionary,* once observed that "a language without euphemisms would be a defective instrument of communication." By this criterion, at least, contemporary American English cannot be judged defective. All epochs, of course, have employed euphemisms both to downplay and to amplify: to camouflage the forbidden, to dress up the unseemly and the unpleasant, and, like Chaucer's Wife of Bath, to find genteel expression for some earthy fun. Some periods have specialized. The eighteenth century is famous as a time of inventive sexual innuendo and political circumlocution (consult almost any

passage in *Gulliver's Travels*). The Victorians were linguistically circumspect not only about sex and the human body but also about money and death. But in the late twentieth century euphemism has achieved what it never achieved before: it has become a fit medium for the expression of just about everything. Putty as it is in the hands of its employer, bereft (unlike irony) of any solid core, euphemism can take on almost any task at all. It is the characteristic literary device of our time—as much a hallmark of the era as were inflated honorifics in fifth-century Rome.

5   The one thing that all euphemisms have in common is their willingness to show themselves in public—sometimes with audacity. A press release arrived recently from the Fur Information Council of America, and it contained this sentence: "Twice as many animals are killed each year in animal shelters and pounds as are used by the fur industry." The word "partition" was politically unacceptable in the Dayton Agreement, signed by the warring parties in the former Yugoslavia, and so the agreement does not employ it; but what might the term "inter-entity boundary" mean? A spokesperson for the United Nations, asked to explain the routine disappearance of millions of dollars' worth of computers, vehicles, and cash whenever UN forces withdraw from a locale, blamed a phenomenon she called "end-of-mission *tristesse*."

6   Most euphemisms, though, do not call such attention to themselves; we slide right over them. Some weeks ago I decided to spend a day with the euphemism detector set on high, just to see what kinds of things turned up in newspapers and magazines, on radio and television, and in ordinary conversation. Here is part of the harvest: "deer management" for the enlistment of paid sharpshooters; "remedial college skills" for reading; "traffic-calming measures" for speed bumps; "comparative ads" for attack ads; "legacy device" for an obsolete computer; "assistance devices" for hearing aids; "firm," in the parlance of produce merchants, for underripe; "hand-check," in the parlance of basketball players, for shove; "peace enforcement" for combat; "hard to place" for disturbed; "growth going backwards" for recession (itself a euphemism); "post-verdict response" for riot; "cult favorite" for low-rated; and "gated community" for affluent residential compound with private security. (Imagine a sign outside Windsor Castle 500 years ago: A GATED COMMUNITY.) This is but a modest sample, and I have not included any euphemisms ending with "syndrome" or "challenged."

7   The newest category of euphemism—which takes the idea into unexplored metaphysical territory—is one in which a euphemistic term is invented for a word or idea that actually requires none, the euphemism thereby implicitly back-tainting the original word or idea itself. In its most widespread manifestation this kind of euphemizing takes its form from such locutions for unutterables as "the F word" and, in a racial context, "the N word." Thus, during his race for the presidency against Michael Dukakis, George Bush castigated his opponent for being a liberal by bringing up what he called "the L word." Since then we have had "the O word," referring to orphanages (or, at the other demographic extreme, to old age); "the T word," referring to taxes; "the U word" (unions); "the V word" (vouchers); and "the W word" (welfare). William Safire, who briefly took note of this phenomenon in its infancy, during the 1988 campaign, predicted that it would "probably peter out in a few years, after we go through the alphabet and begin to get confused about what a given letter is supposed to signify." In fact the euphemistic abecedarium is now both

complete and several meanings deep, and seems to be evincing considerable staying power. The cheap mass production of E words has apparently proved irresistible.

8   On balance, are euphemisms bad for us? One school of thought holds that a truly healthy, stable, psychologically mature society would have no need for euphemisms. Those who subscribe to this school would hold further, with George Orwell, that political euphemism "is designed to make lies sound truthful and murder respectable, and to give an appearance of solidity to pure wind." They might add that the emergence of the new genre of faux euphemism is particularly insidious, in that it implies a kind of equivalence among the concepts or terminology represented by letters of the alphabet—as if "the L word" and "the T word" really did belong in the same category as "the N word." There is something to be said for all these points, the last one in particular. I'm surely not alone in observing that the phrase "the N word" has lately come into the mainstream, as the N word itself never could again.

9   A second school of though about euphemisms might be called the white-blood-cell school; it holds that yes, an elevated count might well be a sign of mild or serious pathology—but it's also a sign that a natural defense mechanism has kicked in. By and large my sympathies lie with the white-blood-cell school. Although euphemism sets some to spluttering about its deceitfulness, I suspect that few people are really deceived—that, indeed, the transparent motives and awkward semantics only undermine the euphemist's intention. When a nuclear warhead is referred to as "the physics package," when genocide is referred to as "ethnic cleansing," when wife-beating is referred to as "getting physical"—in all these cases the terminology trains a spotlight on the truth.

10   Philosophers and linguists will argue the matter for years to come. In the meantime, though, it might be useful to begin acquiring a database of euphemisms by monitoring their prevalence in our national life. The model would be the Consumer Price Index.

11   The Consumer Price Index does not, of course, keep track of inflation by watching trends in the prices of everything. It focuses on a "basket" of major economic goods and services: food, clothing, rent, oil and gas, interest rates, and so on. With euphemisms, too, a handful of big items account for a disproportionate share of all euphemistic activity. Thus we might devise a preliminary formula with a basket of concepts including sex, God, money, politics, social pathology, bodily functions, disease, and death (along with, perhaps, a few minor bellwether indicators such as euphemisms for criminal behavior by juveniles and for lack of achievement in school). Logoplasticians, as those who study euphemisms might be called, would follow the emergence of promising synonyms in all these areas, producing at regular intervals a Semantic Engineering Index, or SEI.

12   Some might anticipate that in a society like ours the SEI would show gains quarter after quarter. I am not sure that this would happen in the aggregate: a macro-euphemistic view of history shows significant ups and downs over time. But in any event internal shifts would be abundant and revealing. Euphemisms are fragile organisms, surprisingly sensitive to the outside environment. Frequently they come to embody so fully the thing being euphemized that they themselves demand

replacement. H. W. Fowler's *Modern English Usage* (Second Edition) shows how "toilet" is but the latest in a series of progressively superseded euphemisms—"water-closet," "latrine," "privy," "jakes"—going back many centuries. (Last year a Methodist singles group, recognizing the danger of euphemistic succession and hoping to stave it off, held a retreat with the theme "Intimacy Is Not a Euphemism for Sex." Good luck.) Some euphemisms eventually attract such knowing derision that their useful life is abbreviated. This was the case, for instance, with the term "revenue enhancement" as a stealthy substitute for "higher taxes." Other euphemisms, such as "custodial engineer" and "sandwich technician," pass from the moment of coinage into a state of ironic suspension without ever experiencing an intermediate condition of utility.

13   Given the avidity with which professional lexicographers today comb through books and periodicals for evidence of emerging and fading terminology, compiling a Semantic Engineering Index would no doubt be quite simple. And popular acceptance of the idea of "leading euphemistic indicators" would come easily. "The SEI rose three tenths of a point this month, paced by a rise in the T word and public jitters about peace enforcement." I see a cult favorite already.

Questions on Content

1. Discuss the meaning of each of the following:

   A. "But in the late twentieth century euphemism has achieved what it never achieved before: it has become a fit medium for the expression of just about everything" (paragraph 4).
   B. "The one thing that all euphemisms have in common is their willingness to show themselves in public—sometimes with audacity" (paragraph 5).
   C. "Although euphemism sets some to splattering about its deceitfulness, I suspect that few people are really deceived" (paragraph 9).

2. Explain what Murphy means by a Semantic Engineering Index.

3. Murphy begins paragraph 8 with a question: "On balance, are euphemisms bad for us?" How do you feel the author would respond to his own question?

Questions on Structure and Style

4. Comment on Murphy's diction in the first three paragraphs. What is the tone and purpose of these paragraphs?

5. Discuss the organization of Murphy's essay. What is the relationship between his organizational strategy and his content?

Assignments

1. Write an essay in which you demonstrate how euphemisms affect the way you communicate with others. Do you rely more heavily on euphemisms in some groups than in others in which you communicate? What role do euphemisms play in your communication with family members, friends, and employers, for example?

2. Euphemisms might seem valuable or humorous, but they also can be incongruous, ridiculous, or immoral. Choose five euphemisms from the list below. Identify the people most likely to employ each euphemism, and explain what motives these people might have for using the euphemism.

friendly fire	civil servant
nuclear exchange	persona non grata
terminal illness	adult reading material
special needs child	irregularity
golden agers	facial blemishes
security system	water closet
the economically disadvantaged	the departed
revenue enhancement	put to sleep
authoritarian government	fib
incarcerated offender	downsize

3. From the list of euphemisms in question 2, choose three that you consider acceptable and three that you disapprove of, and write a short essay explaining the reasons for your reactions.

Words with Attitude

Gerald Parshall

> Depending on its use, *slang* might imply "proletarian poetry" or, as one nineteenth-century wit labeled it, "the grunt of the human hog." For students, slang usually constitutes a writing error noted by instructors whose message is clear: Don't use it. The truth about slang is more complicated, however, and in the following review of the first volume of *Random House Dictionary of American Slang,* Gerald Parshall dispels many of the mistaken notions about this colorful, and sometimes uniquely serviceable, variety of language.

■ **JOURNAL PROMPT** *In his essay Parshall says, "Misconceptions abound even about what slang is" (paragraph 10). Make a list of slang words and expressions that you use in your speech. Classify the examples in a two- or three-paragraph definition of slang.*

1 Allen Walker Read, a distinguished professor at the University of Chicago, sat down to write a scholarly article about "the most disreputable of all English words." It was 1934, and bluenoses lurked behind every pillar in academia. Not to worry. Read would fox them with a fine batch of pedagogic fudge. In the American Dialect Society journal, *American Speech,* he urged respectable folk to make "unostentatious" use of the obscenity lest its avoidance abet a silly taboo. But not once in his 15-page discourse did Read himself actually use what he called "our word."

2 The new Random House Historical Dictionary of American Slang [1994] suffers no such reticence. Crack open Volume I at letter F, and our word leaps out 1,117 times. Defined for 12 pages and illustrated with historical examples as verb, noun, adjective, adverb, interjection, prefix and suffix, the dark jewel in America's lexical underbelly stands revealed in all its scapegrace vigor and variety.

3 So, too, the rest of American slang, as never before. Volume I of the Random House Historical Dictionary of American Slang, now arriving in bookstores, offers 20,000 entries, A through G. Volume II will follow in 1996 with letters H through R, Volume III in 1997 with S through Z. The HDAS (as it will come to be known) is doing for slang what the OED (Oxford English Dictionary) did for standard English in 1928, supplying a record of each word's development from its earliest known use in print. John Simpson, chief editor of the Oxford English Dictionary, calls the new slang opus "one of those rare books which prompts the realization that you have never seen the subject in sharp focus before."

Great Divide

4 Historically, intellectuals spit into two camps on slang. One camp classed it as offal—"the grunt of the human hog," Ambrose Bierce wrote in his dictionary. The other saw proletarian poetry—a product of "the work, needs, ties, joys, affections, tastes, of long

generations of humanity," wrote Walt Whitman. Both sides will find support in the 1,006 pages of HDAS I. Uncut diamonds glisten amid the forests of sexual metaphor and bogs of scatology, refracting light back into ages gone by.

5   Readers who time-travel through the word *apple,* for example, will find that it can mean a horse dropping (1800), or a person (1887), or a saddle horn (1915), or a grenade (1918), or a baseball (1919), or a football (1974), or a basketball (1980), or the Adam's apple (1922), or a woman's breast (1942), or a weakly or inaccurately bowled ball (1966), or a soft, billed cap (1966), or a barrack ship (1971) or an American Indian who has adopted the values of white American society (1980).

Big Deal

6   In letter B, the browser enters a cultural highway of sinewy and sensuous "big" entries that stretches from New York, *Big Apple* (1909), to Chicago, *Big Wind* (1944), with 138 stops along the way, among them *Big Blue* (1984—IBM), *Big Board* (1934—New York Stock Exchange), *Big Chill* (1984—"an unfortunate or depressing state of affairs; death," from 1983 movie title), *Big D* (1930 Dallas), *Big Ditch* (1825—the Erie Canal), *Big Easy* (1970—New Orleans), *big hair* (1988—long hair worn teased and sprayed), *big house* (1913—a prison), *big nickel* (1929—$500 or $5,000), *big pond* (1833—the Atlantic), *Big Red Machine* (1989—the Cincinnati Reds baseball team), *big sleep* (1938—death, from title of Raymond Chandler novel), *big-ticket* (1945—high-priced). "Big" words meaning "an important person" include *bigwig* (1703), *big-bug* (1817), *big gun* (1834), *big fish* (1836), *big toad* (1846), *big potato* (1884), *big casino* (1893), *big Ike* (1902), *big stick* (1908), *big stuff* (1911), *big cheese* (1914), *big boy* (1924), *big shot* (1927), *big wheel* (1927), *big rod* (1929), *big number* (1942), *big daddy* (1948), *big hat* (1952), *big boot* (1969), *big enchilada* (1973) and *big banana* (1984).

7   Slang supplies more than 10 percent of the words the average American knows. Yet it has been so neglected by scholars that all of the country's experts on the subject could ride to an American Dialect Society convention in a single taxi—and still have room for all 20 volumes of the OED jostling on the seat beside them. Part of the *hang-up* (1952) is the mistaken belief that slang words have shorter life spans than June bugs (even the Random House Webster's College Dictionary says slang is "more ephemeral than ordinary language"). "People say, 'Oh, slang. There is no point in collecting it. It is out of date as soon as it exists,'" says Jesse Sheidlower, Random House project editor for the HDAS. "Which is manifestly untrue."

8   HDAS research shows that many slang words are older than most people would guess. *Groovy,* for instance, dates not from the 1960s but from the 1930s. *Wimp* wasn't originated by Reaganites *badmouthing* (1941) George Bush; it's been around since the 1920s. *Out of sight* (the height of excellence) goes back to the 1890s; *sweat it out* to the 1860s. The slang use of *man* ("Hey, man, this is the '60s!") is found in Shakespeare. The word *gay* (the sense that means male homosexual) is not a 1950s coinage, as most dictionaries indicate. The HDAS traces it to the 1930s.

9   The HDAS will also help to *deep six* (1949) another widespread notion about slang: that a great many words now regarded as standard English started out as slang.

Some slang terms have achieved acceptance in formal English—*bamboozle* (1703), *flabbergast* (1772), *blizzard* (1859), *guy* (1875) and *GI* (1939) are a few examples. Yet most slang remains slang, no matter how widely used. And some words start out as standard English only to sink into the linguistic demimonde. In the Middle Ages, when more polite synonyms were scarce, the commonest four-letter word for excrement was standard English. It was banished to the barnyard as refinement flowered (*excrement* is Latin. Ergo, it is refined).

10   Misconceptions abound even about what slang is. "The general public uses the word for anything an English teacher might oppose—anything new or odd," says J. E. Lighter, the chief editor of the HDAS and almost a one-man band in bringing it about. . . . Lighter defines slang by the motives behind its creation: "It is very unusual for a standard English word to have a powerful anti-Establishment atmosphere around it. But that is the essence of slang." Slang has an *in-your-face!* (1976) quality ranging from the satirical to the cynical. It strips the world to its *skivvies* (1918), laying bare humanity's knobby knees and fallen arches. Freighted with nuance, it is language with an *attitude* (1962). At its worst, it is "stupidly coarse and provocative," as Lighter concedes. At its best, it makes standard English seem pallid in its play-it-safe neutrality—"standard English" being what teachers, editors, writers and other Establishment figures deem proper for formal use. Standard English calls military leaders *officers,* slang calls them *brass* (1864). Standard English speaks of the *country,* slang of *the sticks* (1905). In standard English, people *go to bed, sleep* or *snore;* in slang, they *hit the sack* (1942) or *saw wood* (1855).

11   The term *slang* itself came along in the 18th century from unknown origins. Samuel Johnson, who believed the English language to be "perfect," did not deign even to list the word in his famous 1755 dictionary. Noah Webster included it in his in 1828, but defined it unsympathetically as "low, vulgar unmeaning language." The concept of slang predates the word by 200 years. In the 16th century, the London literati found that beggars, cut-purses and other members of the underworld had created their own idiom. That tiny rivulet of words (an estimated 200) has since grown into a vast river of perhaps 100,000 words worldwide. A great many of those words have been spawned by subcultures—the military, high school and college kids, sportswriters and athletes, musicians, African-Americans, factory workers, drug users.

A Social Signal

12   For these and a couple dozen other subcultures, the creation and use of slang is a solidarity ritual. The new soldier, the new kid on campus, the new assembly-line worker—all learn the lingo of their new domain to show that they fit in, while old-timers revel in talking the talk because it buttresses their sense of self and demarcates their status. "One of the things you are saying when you use a lot of slang," says Lighter, "is that your perception of the world is rather different from someone else's, from your parents or those outside your group, or whoever, and you like this. You want to enjoy this difference.

13   Even outside the subcultures, many people use slang to advertise an anti-Establishment stance that suits their temperament. They may see it as a "truer" form

of communication than standard English. Its arsenal of insult can vent anger with merciless economy. One other thing: It is fun. John Algeo, a longtime professor of English at the University of Georgia and perhaps America's leading expert on new words, says language was "probably humanity's first play toy. Slang is a form of popular play. Anybody can do it, and I think a great many people do."

14   Only a few slang terms have been traced to individuals. Columnist Walter Winchell was credited with *making whoopee* (1929), the staff of *Variety* with *disk jockey, turkey, flack, lay an egg* and *nabe* and Tom Wolfe with *flak-catcher* (1970). The overwhelming majority of slang words sprout unseen, like toadstools after a rain, pushed up into general usage by anonymous creators. Algeo believes ordinary people make words all the time—a tiny fraction of which take root. "Often a family will invent or evolve new words, sometimes mistakes of children, sometimes some kind of in-joke. That is not different in principle from the invention of any other kind of new word where the motive is not that you need a name for something which has no name but that you want a name which will somehow express your attitude toward the thing or toward the people you're using it with or toward yourself."

15   Slang has spiced American life ever since colonial times, when you could go to a grogshop and get *stew'd,* or *boozy,* or *cock-ey'd.* Or whatever was your pleasure— there were 200 slang terms for drunkenness (the full list was printed by Ben Franklin in the *Pennsylvania Gazette* in 1737). The spread of slang was handicapped in the 18th and 19th centuries by editors and literary lions who condemned it as a corrupting influence on civilization by swarms of schoolmarms who ratified the malediction and by the slowness of communications.

16   These restraints dissolved early in the 20th century. America was soon turning into the great factory of slang it is today. Romanticism gave way to realism in literature, flooding the country with novels and short stories crammed with true-to-life dialogue (although printing four-letter words would remain *verboten* until after World War II). Hollywood was feeding slangy chitchat to enraptured millions even before the movies and Garbo learned to talk. Newspapers and magazines cast off their high-button-shoe starchiness and adopted breezier styles, receptive to the slang of each era.

Gangland Gab

17   In the 1920s, Prohibition glamorized gangsters, teaching underworld slang to the law abiding—*fence* (1698), *gun moll* (1908), *flatfoot* (1912), etc. In the 1930s, words from black English moved into the mainstream as African-Americans migrated out of the South and swing bands heated up the nightclubs. (Contrary to common belief, however, *dig* and *cat,* in the senses popularized by the jazz giant Louis Armstrong, did not appear in earlier black English, according to HDAS. Satchmo was a creative cat, you dig?) In later decades, hippies, homosexuals, CB-radio users and other subgroups with their own pungent lingos seized the media's interest at one time or another.

18   The two world wars and lesser conflicts, meanwhile, were inoculating much of the male population with the hard-boiled slang of the soldier, the sailor and the *flyboy* (1937). World War I popularized *bump off, leatherneck, foxhole* and many, many other

words; World War II spread an even larger lexicon, much of which remains in widespread use today including *boondocks, snafu, goof up, foul up, buy it* and *pissed off.* Vietnam yielded an especially ugly crop of coinages and rediscoveries, matching the mood of the *grunts* (1961). Among favorites were *zap, waste* and *gook* (the last a gross insult in use in the services at least since 1920).

Doing His Thing

19   For much of U.S. history, indeed, slang has been largely a male thing. In 1868, a women's magazine, the *Ladies' Repository,* voiced a common view: "If it were not for our women there would be danger of having our English smothered in slang. They seldom use it—a well-bred woman never uses it." Little wonder. All those words for tippling and coupling, for the private regions of the female form, all those metaphors like *cookie* and *tart* equating women with food, usually oversweet baked goods.

20   Nowadays, however, increasing numbers of women sling slang without compunction. Ask a Valley girl. Or ask Connie Eble, professor of English at the University of North Carolina at Chapel Hill. Eble has collected slang for many years from the largely female classes she teaches, made up of future English teachers. Slang terms fall easily from her students' young lips. Sorority slang includes: *to suicide* (for a rushee to write down only one sorority when stating her preferences); *ax-queen* (a sorority member who dislikes all prospective pledges); *VNB* (short for a rushee who is "very nice but" we don't want her); *diamond in the rough* (a rushee no member knows). The emergence of women in varsity athletics, Eble says, is exposing them to locker-room slang, and they are using it. In his introduction to HDAS, Lighter declares that in the past three decades "college women—no longer so middle class as in previous generations—almost certainly have begun to affect a more 'masculine,' scatological speech style."

21   So has the whole society, of course. A quarter century of R-rated films and raunchy lyrics intent on showing how people really talk has affected the way people really talk. For the worse. In the 19th century, it was customary to resort to blasphemy when you truly wanted to shock. Between World War I and World War II, blasphemy faded and obscenity became the mode of choice for giving grievous offense. Now, obscenity is losing its potency and ethnic epithets, which could be used rather openly into the 1950s, are the new thermonuclear taboos. Lighter believes that if any controversy flares over the content of HDAS, it will not be over its four-letter words but over its many ethnic epithets. Professor Eble says that if she used "the F word" to tell her students that they had messed up on a test, "my class would not bat an eye." If she used a racial epithet in any context, however, "I'd never be forgiven." At the University of Michigan, someone stole a computer password and sent a racial diatribe onto Internet under school's logo, causing a furor. Richard Bailey, Michigan professor of English and author of *Images of English,* a history of attitudes toward the language, cites the incident as evidence of the eternal impulse that much slang embodies, the impulse to hurl a horse apple "in the punch bowl. . . . It seems we need *something* to shake the pillars of civilization."

Questions on Content

1. Parshall states that the HDAS is doing for slang what the *OED* (*Oxford English Dictionary*) did for standard English. Explain.

2. Parshall describes slang as "language with an *attitude*" (paragraph 10). Explain.

3. In paragraph 12 Parshall addresses the issue of why people use slang. Paraphrase the paragraph. Do you agree? Be prepared to discuss why you use slang.

4. When the author suggests that "slang is a form of popular play" (paragraph 13), what does he mean?

5. Richard Bailey, Michigan professor of English, suggests that much slang "embodies . . . the impulse to hurl a horse apple 'in the punch bowl. . . .'" (paragraph 18). Explain.

Questions on Structure and Style

6. The closing sentences in paragraphs 2 and 4 are examples of Parshall's use of metaphoric language. Find other such examples. How do such passages contribute to tone and attitude?

7. Parshall employs many concrete examples of slang in his essay. How do such abundant examples affect the author's purpose?

Assignments

1. In paragraph 4 Parshall notes that "historically, intellectuals split into two camps on slang." Write an essay in which you align with one of the two positions. Give concrete reasons and illustrations to support your position.

2. Parshall notes that often families "invent or evolve new words, sometimes mistakes of children, sometimes some kind of in-joke" (paragraph 14). In effect, families often develop their own slang language habits. Write an essay in which you discuss your family's language, including its slang. Be certain to provide specific examples and explain how the examples evolved.

English Belongs to Everybody

Robert MacNeil

Language "authorities"—grammarians, teachers, writers, and others—regularly decry the creeping illiteracy they perceive among Americans. Perhaps, though, such authorities have forgotten how unruly the English language has always been. In the following excerpt from his collection of autobiographical reflections, Robert MacNeil reminds us that seemingly chaotic changes in our language indicate its vitality, not its decay, and the authorities in charge of "proper" English include every one of us. MacNeil, a journalist, became well known as cohost of the *MacNeil/Lehrer NewsHour*.

■ **JOURNAL PROMPT** *MacNeil is fascinated with "how differently we all speak in different circumstances." He says, "We have levels of formality, as in our clothing." Describe the levels of formality in your speech, and write about circumstances that require you to shift from one level to another.*

1   This is a time of widespread anxiety about the language. Some Americans fear that English will be engulfed or diluted by Spanish and want to make it the official language. There is anxiety about a crisis of illiteracy, or a crisis of semiliteracy among high school, even college, graduates.

2   Anxiety, however, may have a perverse side effect: experts who wish to "save" the language may only discourage pleasure in it. Some are good-humored and tolerant of change, others intolerant and snobbish. Language reinforces feelings of social superiority or inferiority; it creates insiders and outsiders; it is a prop to vanity or a source of anxiety, and on both emotions the language snobs play. Yet the changes and the errors that irritate them are no different in kind from those which have shaped our language for centuries. As Hugh Kenner wrote of certain British critics in *The Sinking Island*, "They took note of language only when it annoyed them." Such people are killjoys: they turn others away from an interest in the language, inhibit their use of it, and turn pleasure off.

3   Change is inevitable in a living language and is responsible for much of the vitality of English; it has prospered and grown because it was able to accept and absorb change.

4   As people evolve and do new things, their language will evolve too. They will find ways to describe the new things and their changed perspective will give them new ways of talking about the old things. For example, electric light switches created a brilliant metaphor for the oldest of human experiences, being *turned on* or *turned off*. To language conservatives those expressions still have a slangy, low ring to them; to others they are vivid, fresh-minted currency, very spendable, very "with it."

5   That tolerance for change represents not only the dynamism of the English-speaking peoples since the Elizabethans, but their deeply rooted ideas of freedom as well. This was the idea of the Danish scholar Otto Jespersen, one of the great authorities on English. Writing in 1905, Jespersen said in his *Growth and Structure of the English Language*:

> The French language is like the stiff French garden of Louis XIV, while the English is like an English park, which is laid out seemingly without any definite plan, and in which you are allowed to walk everywhere according to your own fancy without having to fear a stern keeper enforcing rigorous regulations. The English language would not have been what it is if the English had not been for centuries great respecters of the liberties of each individual and if everybody had not been free to strike out new paths for himself.

6   I like that idea and do not think it just coincidence. Consider that the same cultural soil, the Celtic-Roman-Saxon-Danish-Norman amalgam, which produced the English language also nourished the great principles of freedom and rights of man in the modern world. The first shoots sprang up in England and they grew stronger in America. Churchill called them "the joint inheritance of the English-speaking world." At the very core of those principles are popular consent and resistance to arbitrary authority; both are fundamental characteristics of our language. The English-speaking peoples have defeated all efforts to build fences around their language, to defer to an academy on what was permissible English and what not. They'll decide for themselves, thanks just the same.

7   Nothing better expresses resistance to arbitrary authority than the persistence of what grammarians have denounced for centuries as "errors." In the common speech of English-speaking peoples—Americans, Englishmen, Canadians, Australians, New Zealanders, and others—these usages persist, despite rising literacy and wider education. We hear them every day:

Double negative: "I don't want none of that."

Double comparative: "Don't make that any more heavier!"

Wrong verb: "Will you learn me to read?"

8   These "errors" have been with us for at least four hundred years, because you can find each of them in Shakespeare.

Double negative: In *Hamlet*, the King says:

> Nor what he spake, though it lack'd form a little,
> Was not like madness.

Double comparative: In *Othello*, the Duke says:

> Yet opinion . . . throws a more safer voice on you.

Wrong verb: In *Othello*, Desdemona says:

> My life and education both do learn me how to respect you.

9   I find it very interesting that these forms will not go away and lie down. They were vigorous and acceptable in Shakespeare's time; they are far more vigorous today, although not acceptable as standard English. Regarded as error by grammarians, they are nevertheless in daily use all over the world by a hundred times the number of people who lived in Shakespeare's England.

10   It fascinates me that *axe*, meaning "ask," so common in black American English, is standard in Chaucer in all forms—*axe, axen, axed*: "and *axed* him if Troilus were there." Was that transmitted across six hundred years or simply reinvented?

11   English grew without a formal grammar. After the enormous creativity of Shakespeare and the other Elizabethans, seventeenth- and eighteenth-century critics thought the language was a mess, like an overgrown garden. They weeded it by imposing grammatical rules derived from tidier languages, chiefly Latin, whose precision and predictability they trusted. For three centuries, with some slippage here and there, their rules have held. Educators taught them and written English conformed. Today, English-language newspapers, magazines, and books everywhere broadly agree that correct English obeys these rules. Yet the wild varieties continue to threaten the garden of cultivated English and, by their numbers, actually dominate everyday usage.

12   Nonstandard English formerly knew its place in the social order. Characters in fiction were allowed to speak it occasionally. Hemingway believed that American literature really did not begin until Mark Twain, who outraged critics by reproducing the vernacular of characters like Huck Finn. Newspapers still clean up the grammar when they quote the ungrammatical, including politicians. The printed word, like Victorian morality, has often constituted a conspiracy of respectability.

13   People who spoke grammatically could be excused the illusion that their writ held sway, perhaps the way the Normans thought that French had conquered the language of the vanquished Anglo-Saxons. A generation ago, people who considered themselves educated and well-spoken might have had only glancing contact with nonstandard English, usually in a well-understood class, regional, or rural context.

14   It fascinates me how differently we all speak in different circumstances. We have levels of formality, as in our clothing. There are very formal occasions, often requiring written English: the job application or the letter to the editor—the dark-suit, serious-tie language, with everything pressed and the lint brushed off. There is our less formal out-in-the-world language—a more comfortable suit, but still respectable. There is language for close friends in the evenings, on weekends—blue-jeans-and-sweat-shirt language, when it's good to get the tie off. There is family language, even more relaxed, full of grammatical short cuts, family slang, echoes of old jokes that have become intimate shorthand—the language of pajamas and uncombed hair. Finally, there is the language with no clothes on; the talk of couples—murmurs, sighs, grunts—language at its least self-conscious, open, vulnerable, and primitive.

15   Broadcasting has democratized the publication of language, often at its most informal, even undressed. Now the ears of the educated cannot escape the language of the masses. It surrounds them on the news, weather, sports, commercials, and the ever-proliferating talk and call-in shows.

16   This wider dissemination of popular speech may easily give purists the idea that the language is suddenly going to hell in this generation, and may explain the new paranoia about it.

17   It might also be argued that more Americans hear more correct, even beautiful, English on television than was ever heard before. Through television more models of good usage reach more American homes than was ever possible in other times. Television gives them lots of colloquial English, too, some awful, some creative, but that is not new.

18   Hidden in this is a simple fact: our language is not the special private property of the language police, or grammarians, or teachers, or even great writers. The genius of English is that it has always been the tongue of the common people, literate or not.

19   English belongs to everybody: the funny turn of phrase that pops into the mind of a farmer telling a story; or the traveling salesman's dirty joke; or the teenager saying, "Gag me with a spoon"; or the pop lyric—all contribute, are all as valid as the tortured image of the academic, or the line the poet sweats over for a week.

20   Through our collective language sense, some may be thought beautiful and some ugly, some may live and some may die; but it is all English and it belongs to everyone—to those of us who wish to be careful with it and those who don't care.

Questions on Content

1. MacNeil suggests that anxiety about language "may have a perverse side effect" (paragraph 2). What does he mean?

2. What does the quotation from Otto Jespersen contribute to the content of this essay?

3. The author suggests that grammatical errors such as use of the double negative, the double comparative, and the wrong verb contribute to the development of English in a positive way. Explain.

4. MacNeil points out that "English grew without a formal grammar" (paragraph 11). How did this happen?

5. How, according to MacNeil, has broadcasting "democratized the . . . language" (paragraph 15)?

Questions on Structure and Style

6. Apart from its content, how does the quotation from Jespersen in paragraph 5 contribute to the unity of the essay? (Look at MacNeil's simile in paragraph 11.)

7. Discuss the clothing simile in paragraph 14. What does the simile contribute to MacNeil's tone? To his purpose?

8. Most frequently the thesis statement appears early in an essay, often in the opening paragraph. Is this true of Mac-Neil's essay? What is his thesis?

Assignments

1. Examine your own language closely, and write an essay in which you classify the levels of formality of your speech. Give examples of the language MacNeil identifies in paragraph 14 as "the dark-suit, serious-tie language," "out-in-the-world language," "blue-jeans-and-sweat-shirt language," the "language of pajamas and uncombed hair," and the "language with no clothes on."

2. In a paragraph, define the level of formality of MacNeil's language in this essay. Is it consistent throughout the essay? Quote carefully from the essay to substantiate your answer.

3. MacNeil believes "that more Americans might hear more correct, even beautiful, English on television than was ever heard before" (paragraph 17). Collect examples of such language that you hear on television. How different are these examples from the language you hear in everyday conversation? Respond in an essay.

ADDITIONAL ASSIGNMENTS AND RESEARCH TOPICS

1. As Bill Bryson points out in "Order Out of Chaos," "the real meanings [of words] are often far more complex than the simple dictionary definitions would lead us to suppose" (paragraph 12). Turn to the front pages of your desk dictionary, and make a list of the usage labels that the dictionary employs, along with their meanings. There are, for example, seven usage labels in *Webster's New World Dictionary*: colloquial, slang, obsolete, archaic, poetic, dialect, and British (or Canadian, Scottish, and so forth). Then look through your dictionary to find three entries exemplifying each of the usages. As you consider the usage issue, think about what is meant by the term *standard American English*.

2. Suppose that certain members of Congress hope to pass a law saying, in effect, that meanings of words should be fixed to eliminate confusion.

   A. Take a stand in favor of the proposed law, and write a letter to your representative in Congress giving reasons for permanently standardizing the meanings of words.
   B. Take a stand against the proposed law, and write a letter to your representative in Congress urging opposition to any such measure. Give specific reasons why such a law would be dangerous.

3. In the *Dictionary of American Slang* (1975), Harold Wentworth and Stuart Berg Flexner state, "The concept having the most slang synonyms is *drunk*" (page 652). They then provide a long list of these synonyms (pages 653–655), many of which are included in the dictionary itself. Use the *Dictionary of American Slang* to demonstrate the wide variety of origins of these synonyms. Consider both where the terms originated and when.

4. British lexicographer Eric Partridge says that slang and colloquial speech is "more than mere self-expression. It connotes personality, a method of distinguishing ourselves by virtue of our linguistic virtuosity." Write an essay in which you demonstrate how Gerald Parshall and Robert MacNeil would respond to Partridge.

5. Robert MacNeil suggests that "broadcasting has democratized the publication of language, often at its most informal, even undressed" (paragraph 15). He goes on to point out how the media allow no one to escape hearing the language of the masses. Spend time listening to the language of television and radio. Pay particular attention to popular talk shows and situation comedies. Collect examples of informal and "undressed" language, and write an essay in which you verify MacNeil's assertion.

6. Slang always reflects the lifestyle of the group that employs it. Make a list of slang expressions currently popular with teenagers. In a short essay, explain what this slang vocabulary reveals about the lifestyles of teenagers.

CHAPTER FOUR

Language Development: Personal and Social

Just what *is* language?

Briefly stated, language is a set of agreements we make. We agree that certain symbols (letters, numbers, words, and other less obvious symbols) will, at a given time, mean certain things to us. Any short definition like this one, however, can never reveal how important—how profoundly human—language is. The best way to approach that deeper significance is to answer two questions: Why did language develop? How does it go on developing even today? The selections in this chapter seek answers to these fundamental, yet highly revealing, questions.

Language developed not merely so that humans could communicate with each other. Grunting and pointing constitute communication, too, but they restrict "speakers" to the here and now. Language, however, frees us from place and time, and in this liberation we have the true purpose of language. The first selection in this chapter, an excerpt from the autobiography of Helen Keller, reminds us of this most important purpose for language. Deaf and blind from the age of nineteen months, Keller acquired language at the age of six years. In the selection here titled "Everything Had a Name," Keller describes how words freed her from isolation and made possible the links with other people that most of us take for granted.

When not seriously disrupted, as happened in Keller's case, the process through which a human acquires language passes through clearly defined, well-studied stages. The earliest stages, from birth through the age of three, become vivid for us in Steven Pinker's "Baby Born Talking—Describes Heaven," a richly detailed excerpt from his book *The Language Instinct*. Neil Postman then looks at definitions, questions, metaphors, technology, and much else in his reflection on the ways that we all use language, not simply to describe our relationships with the world and other people but to create those relationships.

Development implies change, and three readings in this chapter examine how a language, in this case English, can change and be changed by those using it. In his well-known historical sketch "A Brief History of English," Paul Roberts explores reasons why the English we use today seems so different from that of the people who first used "English." In "Old World, New World," Bill Bryson examines the growth of American English, a language whose rapid evolution has been guided by forces uniquely American. Not all change constitutes progress, however, as Leslie Savan illustrates in a vigorous protest aimed at the belligerent "Yadda, Yadda, Yadda" of many of today's favorite catch phrases.

Rounding out the chapter is "The Story of Writing" in which C. M. Millward traces the evolution of written language, whose development differed greatly from that of spoken language. Millward reaffirms, as do all of this chapter's authors, the fundamental fact that language is integral to what we are as humans. It's an energy running throughout humanity. If our relationship to language is difficult to appreciate and easy to underestimate, it's only because that relationship is so intense and compelling.

Everything Had a Name

Helen Keller

Most of us acquire language too early to appreciate the freedom it
gives us from the here and now. Helen Keller (1880–1968), deaf and
blind from the age of nineteen months, began acquiring language at the
age of six years. In the following excerpt from *The Story of My Life*,
Keller recalls her joyous reactions to a world rendered infinitely bigger
by language, which finally made links with other people possible.

■ J O U R N A L   P R O M P T   *Think of how you could describe colors to a friend
who is blind or how you could describe music to a deaf friend.*

1   The most important day I remember in all my life is the one on which my teacher,
Anne Mansfield Sullivan, came to me. I am filled with wonder when I consider the
immeasurable contrasts between the two lives which it connects. It was the third of
March, 1887, three months before I was seven years old.

2   On the afternoon of that eventful day, I stood on the porch, dumb, expectant. I
guessed vaguely from my mother's signs and from the hurrying to and fro in the
house that something unusual was about to happen, so I went to the door and waited
on the steps. The afternoon sun penetrated the mass of honeysuckle that covered
the porch, and fell on my upturned face. My fingers lingered almost unconsciously
on the familiar leaves and blossoms which had just come forth to greet the sweet
southern spring. I did not know what the future held of marvel or surprise for me.
Anger and bitterness had preyed upon me continually for weeks and a deep languor
had succeeded this passionate struggle.

3   Have you ever been at sea in a dense fog, when it seemed as if a tangible white
darkness shut you in, and the great ship, tense and anxious, groped her way toward
the shore with plummet and sounding-line, and you waited with beating heart for
something to happen? I was like that ship before my education began, only I was
without compass or sounding-line, and had no way of knowing how near the harbour
was. "Light! give me light!" was the wordless cry of my soul, and the light of love
shone on me in that very hour.

4   I felt approaching footsteps. I stretched out my hand as I supposed to my mother.
Some one took it, and I was caught up and held close in the arms of her who had
come to reveal all things to me, and, more than all things else, to love me.

5   The morning after my teacher came she led me into her room and gave me a doll.
The little blind children at the Perkins Institution had sent it and Laura Bridgman had
dressed it; but I did not know this until afterward. When I had played with it a little
while, Miss Sullivan slowly spelled into my hand the word "d-o-l-l." I was at once
interested in this finger play and tried to imitate it. When I finally succeeded in
making the letters correctly I was flushed with childish pleasure and pride. Running
downstairs to my mother I held up my hand and made the letters for doll. I did not

know that I was spelling a word or even that words existed; I was simply making my fingers go in monkey-like imitation. In the days that followed I learned to spell in this uncomprehending way a great many words, among them *pin*, *hat*, *cup* and a few verbs like *sit*, *stand* and *walk*. But my teacher had been with me several weeks before I understood that everything has a name.

6   One day, while I was playing with my new doll, Miss Sullivan put my big rag doll into my lap also, spelled "d-o-l-l" and tried to make me understand that "d-o-l-l" applied to both. Earlier in the day we had had a tussle over the words "m-u-g" and "w-a-t-e-r." Miss Sullivan had tried to impress it upon me that "m-u-g" is *mug* and that "w-a-t-e-r" is *water*, but I persisted in confounding the two. In despair she had dropped the subject for the time, only to renew it at the first opportunity. I became impatient at her repeated attempts and, seizing the new doll, I dashed it upon the floor. I was keenly delighted when I felt the fragments of the broken doll at my feet. Neither sorrow nor regret followed my passionate outburst. I had not loved the doll. In the still, dark world in which I lived there was no strong sentiment or tenderness. I felt my teacher sweep the fragments to one side of the hearth, and I had a sense of satisfaction that the cause of my discomfort was removed. She brought me my hat, and I knew I was going out into the warm sunshine. This thought, if a wordless sensation may be called a thought, made me hop and skip with pleasure.

7   We walked down the path to the well-house, attracted by the fragrance of the honeysuckle with which it was covered. Some one was drawing water and my teacher placed my hand under the spout. As the cool stream gushed over one hand she spelled into the other the word *water*, first slowly, then rapidly. I stood still, my whole attention fixed upon the motions of her fingers. Suddenly I felt a misty consciousness as of something forgotten—a thrill of returning thought; and somehow the mystery of language was revealed to me. I knew then that "w-a-t-e-r" meant the wonderful cool something that was flowing over my hand. That living word awakened my soul, gave it light, hope, joy, set it free! There were barriers still, it is true, but barriers that could in time be swept away.

8   I left the well-house eager to learn. Everything had a name and each name gave birth to a new thought. As we returned to the house every object which I touched seemed to quiver with life. That was because I saw everything with the strange, new sight that had come to me. On entering the door I remembered the doll I had broken. I felt my way to the hearth and picked up the pieces. I tried vainly to put them together. Then my eyes filled with tears; for I realized what I had done, and for the first time I felt repentance and sorrow.

9   I learned a great many new words that day. I do not remember what they all were; but I do know that *mother, father, sister, teacher* were among them—words that were to make the world blossom for me, "like Aaron's rod, with flowers." It would have been difficult to find a happier child than I was as I lay in my crib at the close of that eventful day and lived over the joys it had brought me, and for the first time longed for a new day to come.

10   I had now the key to all language, and I was eager to learn to use it. Children who hear acquire language without any particular effort; the words that fall from others'

lips they catch on the wing, as it were, delightedly, while the little deaf child must trap them by a slow and often painful process. But whatever the process, the result is wonderful. Gradually, from naming an object we advance step by step until we have traversed the vast distance between our first stammered syllable and the sweep of thought in a line of Shakespeare.

11   At first, when my teacher told me about a new thing I asked very few questions. My ideas were vague, and my vocabulary was inadequate; but as my knowledge of things grew, and I learned more and more words, my field of inquiry broadened, and I would return again and again to the same subject, eager for further information. Sometimes a new word revived an image that some earlier experience had engraved on my brain.

12   I remember the morning that I first asked the meaning of the word "love." This was before I knew many words. I had found a few early violets in the garden and brought them to my teacher. She tried to kiss me; but at that time I did not like to have any one kiss me except my mother. Miss Sullivan put her arm gently round me and spelled into my hand, "I love Helen."

13   "What is love?" I asked.

14   She drew me closer to her and said, "It is here," pointing to my heart, whose beats I was conscious of for the first time. Her words puzzled me very much because I did not then understand anything unless I touched it.

15   I smelt the violets in her hand and asked, half in words, half in signs, a question which meant, "Is love the sweetness of flowers?"

16   "No," said my teacher.

17   Again I thought. The warm sun was shining on us.

18   "Is this not love?" I asked, pointing in the direction from which the heat came, "Is this not love?"

19   It seemed to me that there could be nothing more beautiful than the sun, whose warmth makes all things grow. But Miss Sullivan shook her head, and I was greatly puzzled and disappointed. I thought it strange that my teacher could not show me love.

20   A day or two afterward I was stringing beads of different sizes in symmetrical groups—two large beads, three small ones, and so on. I had made many mistakes, and Miss Sullivan had pointed them out again and again with gentle patience. Finally I noticed a very obvious error in the sequence and for an instant I concentrated my attention on the lesson and tried to think how I should have arranged the beads. Miss Sullivan touched my forehead and spelled with decided emphasis, "Think."

21   In a flash I knew that the word was the name of the process that was going on in my head. This was my first conscious perception of an abstract idea.

22   For a long time I was still—I was not thinking of the beads in my lap, but trying to find a meaning for "love" in the light of this new idea. The sun had been under a cloud all day, and there had been brief showers; but suddenly the sun broke forth in all its southern splendour.

23   Again I asked my teacher, "Is this not love?"

24   "Love is something like the clouds that were in the sky before the sun came out," she replied. Then in simpler words than these, which at that time I could not have

understood, she explained: "You cannot touch the clouds, you know; but you feel the rain and know how glad the flowers and the thirsty earth are to have it after a hot day. You cannot touch love either; but you feel the sweetness that it pours into everything. Without love you would not be happy or want to play."

25   The beautiful truth burst upon my mind—I felt that there were invisible lines stretched between my spirit and the spirits of others.

26   From the beginning of my education Miss Sullivan made it a practice to speak to me as she would speak to any hearing child; the only difference was that she spelled the sentences into my hand instead of speaking them. If I did not know the words and idioms necessary to express my thoughts she supplied them, even suggesting conversation when I was unable to keep up my end of the dialogue.

27   This process was continued for several years; for the deaf child does not learn in a month, or even in two or three years, the numberless idioms and expressions used in the simplest daily intercourse. The little hearing child learns these from constant repetition and imitation. The conversation he hears in his home stimulates his mind and suggests topics and calls forth the spontaneous expression of his own thoughts. This natural exchange of ideas is denied to the deaf child. My teacher, realizing this, determined to supply the kinds of stimulus I lacked. This she did by repeating to me as far as possible, verbatim, what she heard, and by showing me how I could take part in the conversation. But it was a long time before I ventured to take the initiative, and still longer before I could find something appropriate to say at the right time.

28   The deaf and the blind find it very difficult to acquire the amenities of conversation. How much more this difficulty must be augmented in the case of those who are both deaf and blind! They cannot distinguish the tone of the voice or, without assistance, go up and down the gamut of tones that give significance to words; nor can they watch the expression of the speaker's face, and a look is often the very soul of what one says.

Questions on Content

1. How old was Helen Keller when she began her experience with Anne Sullivan? How might the experience have been different had she been younger? Older?

2. What was it that finally awakened Keller to the connection between a group of letters and what the group of letters represented?

3. Describing her state of mind when she broke her doll in a moment of anger, Keller says, "Neither sorrow nor regret followed my passionate outburst." She goes on to say, "In the still, dark world in which I lived there was no strong sentiment or tenderness" (paragraph 6). Explain the relationship between this lack of emotional response and a lack of language.

4. What was Keller's first conscious perception of an abstraction? Explain how her teacher inspired the perception.

5. Keller concluded this selection with these words: "A look is often the very soul of what one says." Explain.

Questions on Structure and Style

6. This selection is filled with examples of description that do not refer to the senses of hearing and sight. Paragraph 2 provides one example. Discuss the sensory detail in it, and try to find other examples of such description.

7. Do you notice a change in the descriptive passages as Keller acquires language? Give specific examples.

8. Discuss the simile in paragraph 3. Can you find other examples of figurative language? What do such passages contribute to the tone of the essay?

9. Discuss the tone of Keller's memoir. What audience did she have in mind?

Assignments

1. Assume that you are Anne Sullivan, Helen Keller's teacher. Write a letter to a friend and colleague in which you describe Keller's progress in language acquisition.

2. Write an essay about how Keller shows that language "awakened [her] soul, gave it light, hope, joy, set it free!" (paragraph 7).

3. Describe in a paragraph how Keller felt about her world and how she responded to it in her prelanguage existence.

Baby Born Talking— Describes Heaven

Steven Pinker

Tabloids might require such headlines as "Baby Born Talking—
Describes Heaven" to hook gullible readers, but truth in this case
proves equally amazing. With only rare exceptions, according to
Steven Pinker, "all languages are acquired, with equal ease, before
the child turns four." This rapid, complex process actually begins
before birth and passes through stages that can be described in surprising detail, a fact Pinker demonstrates in this always accessible
excerpt from his book *The Language Instinct*.

■ **J O U R N A L   P R O M P T**   *Just how children acquire language is a controversial
topic among linguists and developmental psychologists. Before reading Pinker's theories, write
a brief essay in which you describe how you imagine children learn to speak and understand
language.*

1   On May 21, 1985, a periodical called the *Sun* ran these intriguing headlines:

> John Wayne Liked to Play with Dolls
>
> Prince Charles' Blood Is Sold for $10,000
> by Dishonest Docs
>
> Family Haunted by Ghost of Turkey
> They Ate for Christmas
>
> BABY BORN TALKING—DESCRIBES HEAVEN
> Incredible proof of reincarnation

The last headline caught my eye—it seemed like the ultimate demonstration that
language is innate. According to the article,

> Life in heaven is grand, a baby told an astounded obstetrical team seconds after birth.
> Tiny Naomi Montefusco literally came into the world singing the praises of God's
> firmament. The miracle so shocked the delivery room team, one nurse ran screaming
> down the hall. "Heaven is a beautiful place, so warm and so serene," Naomi said. "Why
> did you bring me here?" Among the witnesses was mother Theresa Montefusco, 18,
> who delivered the child under local anesthetic . . . "I distinctly heard her describe
> heaven as a place where no one has to work, eat, worry about clothing, or do anything
> but sing God's praises. I tried to get off the delivery table to kneel down and pray, but
> the nurses wouldn't let me."

Scientists, of course, cannot take such reports at face value; any important finding
must be replicated. A replication of the Corsican miracle, this time from Taranto,

Italy, occurred on October 31, 1989, when the *Sun* (a strong believer in recycling) ran the headline "BABY BORN TALKING—DESCRIBES HEAVEN. Infant's words prove reincarnation exists." A related discovery was reported on May 29, 1990: "BABY SPEAKS AND SAYS: I'M THE REINCARNATION OF NATALIE WOOD." Then, on September 29, 1992, a second replication, reported in the same words as the original. And on June 8, 1993, the clincher: "AMAZING 2-HEADED BABY IS PROOF OF REINCARNATION. ONE HEAD SPEAKS ENGLISH— THE OTHER ANCIENT LATIN."

2   Why do stories like Naomi's occur only in fiction, never in fact? Most children do not begin to talk until they are a year old, do not combine words until they are one and a half, and do not converse in fluent grammatical sentences until they are two or three. What is going on in those years? Should we ask why it takes children so long? Or is a three-year-old's ability to describe earth as miraculous as a newborn's ability to describe heaven?

3   All infants come into the world with linguistic skills. We know this because of the ingenious experimental technique . . . in which a baby is presented with one signal over and over to the point of boredom, and then the signal is changed; if the baby perks up, he or she must be able to tell the difference. Since ears don't move the way eyes do, the psychologists Peter Eimas and Peter Jusczyk devised a different way to see what a one-month-old finds interesting. They put a switch inside a rubber nipple and hooked up the switch to a tape recorder, so that when the baby sucked, the tape played. As the tape droned on with *ba ba ba ba* . . . , the infants showed their boredom by sucking more slowly. But when the syllables changed to *pa pa pa* . . . , the infants began to suck more vigorously, to hear more syllables. Moreover, they were using the sixth sense, speech perception, rather than just hearing the syllables as raw sound: two *ba*'s that differed acoustically from each other as much as a *ba* differs from a *pa,* but that are both heard as *ba* by adults, did not revive the infants' interest. And infants must be recovering phonemes, like *b,* from the syllables they are smeared across. Like adults, they hear the same stretch of sound as a *b* if it appears in a short syllable and as a *w* if it appears in a long syllable.

4   Infants come equipped with these skills; they do not learn them by listening to their parents' speech. Kikuyu and Spanish infants discriminate English *ba*'s and *pa*'s which are not used in Kikuyu or Spanish and which their parents cannot tell apart. English-learning infants under the age of six months distinguish phonemes used in Czech, Hindi, and Inslekampx (a Native American language), but English-speaking adults cannot, even with five hundred trials of training or a year of university coursework. Adult ears can tell the sounds apart, though, when the consonants are stripped from the syllables and presented alone as chirpy sounds; they just cannot tell them apart *as phonemes*.

5   The *Sun* article is a bit sketchy on the details, but we can surmise that because Naomi was understood, she must have spoken in Italian, not Proto-World or Ancient Latin. Other infants may enter the world with some knowledge of their mother's language, too. The psychologists Jacques Mehler and Peter Jusczyk have shown that four-day-old French babies such harder to hear French than Russian, and pick up their sucking more when a tape changes from Russian to French than from French to

Russian. This is not an incredible proof of reincarnation; the melody of mothers' speech carries through their bodies and is audible in the womb. The babies still prefer French when the speech is electronically filtered so that the consonant and vowel sounds are muffled and only the melody comes through. But they are indifferent when the tapes are played backwards, which preserves the vowels and some of the consonants but distorts the melody. Nor does the effect prove the inherent beauty of the French language: non-French infants do not prefer French, and French infants do not distinguish Italian from English. The infants must have learned something about the prosody of French (its melody, stress, and timing) in the womb, or in their first days out of it.

6   Babies continue to learn the sounds of their language throughout the first year. By six months, they are beginning to lump together the distinct sounds that their language collapses into a single phoneme, while continuing to discriminate equivalently distinct ones that their language keeps separate. By ten months they are no longer universal phoneticians but have turned into their parents; they do not distinguish Czech or Inslekampx phonemes unless they are Czech or Inslekampx babies. Babies make this transition before they produce or understand words, so their learning cannot depend on correlating sound with meaning. That is, they cannot be listening for the difference in sound between a word they think means *bit* and a word they think means *beet,* because they have learned neither word. They must be sorting the sounds directly, somehow tuning their speech analysis module to deliver the phonemes used in their language. The module can then serve as the front end of the system that learns words and grammar.

7   During the first year, babies also get their speech production systems geared up. First, ontogeny recapitulates phylogeny. A newborn has a vocal tract like a non-human mammal. The larynx comes up like a periscope and engages the nasal passage, forcing the infant to breathe through the nose and making it anatomically possible to drink and breathe at the same time. By three months the larynx has descended deep into the throat, opening up the cavity behind the tongue (the pharynx) that allows the tongue to move forwards and backwards and produce the variety of vowel sounds used by adults.

8   Not much of linguistic interest happens during the first two months, when babies produce the cries, grunts, sighs, clicks, stops, and pops associated with breathing, feeding, and fussing, or even during the next three, when coos and laughs are added. Between five and seven months babies begin to play with sounds, rather than using them to express their physical and emotional states, and their sequences of clicks, hums, glides, trills, hisses, and smacks begin to sound like consonants and vowels. Between seven and eight months they suddenly begin to babble in real syllables like *ba-ba-ba, neh-neh-neh,* and *dee-dee-dee.* The sounds are the same in all languages, and consist of the phonemes and syllable patterns that are most common across languages. By the end of the first year, babies vary their syllables, like *neh-nee, da-dee,* and *meh-neh,* and produce that really cute sentencelike gibberish.

9   In recent years pediatricians have saved the lives of many babies with breathing abnormalities by inserting a tube into their tracheas (the pediatricians are trained on cats, whose airways are similar), or by surgically opening a hole in their trachea below the larynx. The infants are then unable to make voiced sounds during the normal

period of babbling. When the normal airway is restored in the second year of life, those infants are seriously retarded in speech development, though they eventually catch up, with no permanent problems. Deaf children's babbling is later and simpler—though if their parents use sign language, they babble, on schedule, with their hands!

10   Why is babbling so important? The infant is like a person who has been given a complicated piece of audio equipment bristling with unlabeled knobs and switches but missing the instruction manual. In such situations people resort to what hackers call frobbing—fiddling aimlessly with the controls to see what happens. The infant has been given a set of neural commands that can move the articulators every which way, with wildly varying effects on the sound. By listening to their own babbling, babies in effect write their own instruction manual; they learn how much to move which muscle in which way to make which change in the sound. This is a prerequisite to duplicating the speech of their parents. Some computer scientists, inspired by the infant, believe that a good robot should learn an internal software model of its articulators by observing the consequences of its own babbling and flailing.

11   Shortly before their first birthday, babies begin to understand words, and around that birthday, they start to produce them. Words are usually produced in isolation; this one-word stage can last from two months to a year. For over a century, and all over the globe, scientists have kept diaries of their infants' first words, and the lists are almost identical. About half the words are for objects: food (*juice, cookie*), body parts (*eye, nose*), clothing (*diaper, sock*), vehicles (*car, boat*), toys (*doll, block*), household items (*bottle, light*), animals (*dog, kitty*), and people (*dada, baby*). (My nephew Eric's first word was *Batman.*) There are words for actions, motions, and routines, like *up, off, open, peekaboo, eat,* and *go,* and modifiers, like *hot, allgone, more, dirty,* and *cold.* Finally, there are routines used in social interaction, like *yes, no, want, bye-bye,* and *hi*—a few of which, like *look at that* and *what is that,* are words in the sense of listemes (memorized chunks), but not, at least for the adult, words in the sense of morphological products and syntactic atoms. Children differ in how much they name objects or engage in social interaction using memorized routines. Psychologists have spent a lot of time speculating about the causes of those differences (sex, age, birth order, and socioeconomic status have all been examined), but the most plausible to my mind is that babies are people, only smaller. Some are interested in objects, others like to shmooze.

12   Since word boundaries do not physically exist, it is remarkable that children are so good at finding them. A baby is like the dog being yelled at in the two-panel cartoon by Gary Larson:

WHAT WE SAY TO DOGS: "Okay, Ginger! I've had it! You stay out of the garbage! Understand, Ginger? Stay out of the garbage, or else!"

WHAT THEY HEAR: "Blah blah GINGER blah blah blah blah blah blah blah blah GINGER blah blah blah blah blah."

Presumably children record some words parents use in isolation, or in stressed final positions, like *Look-at-the BOTTLE.* Then they look for matches to these words in longer stretches of speech, and find other words by extracting the residues in between the matched portions. Occasionally there are near misses, providing great entertainment to family members:

I don't want to go to your ami. [from *Miami*]

I am heyv! [from *Behave!*]

Daddy, when you go tinkle you're an eight, and when I go tinkle I'm an eight, right? [from *urinate*]

I know I sound like Larry, but who's Gitis? [from *laryngitis*]

Daddy, why do you call your character Sam Alone? [from *Sam Malone,* the bartender in *Cheers*]

The ants are my friends, they're blowing in the wind. [from *The answer, my friend, is blowing in the wind*]

But these errors are surprisingly rare, and of course adults occasionally make them too, as in . . . Pullet Surprise and doggy-dog world. . . . In an episode of the television show *Hill Street Blues,* police officer JD Larue began to flirt with a pretty high school student. His partner, Neal Washington, said, "I have only three words to say to you, JD. Statue. Tory. Rape."

13   Around eighteen months, language takes off. Vocabulary growth jumps to the new-word-every-two-hours minimum rate that the child will maintain through adolescence. And syntax begins, with strings of the minimum length that allows it: two. Here are some examples:

All dry.	All messy.	All wet.
I sit.	I shut.	No bed.
No pee.	See baby.	See pretty.
More cereal.	More hot.	Hi Calico.
Other pocket.	Boot off.	Siren by.
Mail come.	Airplane allgone.	Bye-bye car.
Our car.	Papa away.	Dry pants.

Children's two-word combinations are so similar in meaning the world over that they read as translations of one another. Children announce when objects appear, disappear, and move about, point out their properties and owners, comment on people doing things and seeing things, reject and request objects and activities, and ask about who, what, and where. These microsentences already reflect the language being acquired: in ninety-five percent of them, the words are properly ordered.

14   There is more going on in children's minds than in what comes out of their mouths. Even before they put two words together, babies can comprehend a sentence using its syntax. For example, in one experiment, babies who spoke only in single words were seated in front of two television screens, each of which featured a pair of

adults improbably dressed up as Cookie Monster and Big Bird from *Sesame Street*. One screen showed Cookie Monster tickling Big Bird; the other showed Big Bird tickling Cookie Monster. A voiceover said, "OH LOOK!!! BIG BIRD IS TICKLING COOKIE MONSTER!! FIND BIG BIRD TICKLING COOKIE MONSTER!!" (or vice versa). The children must have understood the meaning of the ordering of subject, verb, and object—they looked more at the screen that depicted the sentence in the voiceover.

15   When children do put words together, the words seem to meet up with a bottleneck at the output end. Children's two- and three-word utterances look like samples drawn from longer potential sentences expressing a complete and more complicated idea. For example, the psychologist Roger Brown noted that although the children he studied never produced a sentence as complicated as *Mother gave John lunch in the kitchen*, they did produce strings containing all of its components, and in the correct order:

Agent	Action	Recipient	Object	Location
(Mother	gave	John	lunch	in the kitchen.)
Mommy	fix.			
Mommy			pumpkin.	
Baby				table.
Give		doggie.		
	Put		light.	
	Put			floor.
I	ride		horsie.	
Tractor	go			floor.
	Give	doggie	paper.	
	Put		truck	window.
Adam	put		it	box.

16   If we divide language development into somewhat arbitrary stages, like Syllable Babbling, Gibberish Babbling, One-Word Utterances, and Two-Word Strings, the next stage would have to be called All Hell Breaks Loose. Between the late twos and the mid-threes, children's language blooms into fluent grammatical conversation so rapidly that it overwhelms the researchers who study it, and no one has worked out the exact sequence. Sentence length increases steadily, and because grammar is a discrete combinatorial system, the number of syntactic types increases exponentially, doubling every month, reaching the thousands before the third birthday. You can get a feel for this explosion by seeing how the speech of a little boy called Adam grows in sophistication over the period of a year, starting with his early word combinations at the age of two years and three months ("2;3"):

2;3:   Play checkers. Big drum. I got horn. A bunny-rabbit walk.

2;4:   See marching bear go? Screw part machine. That busy bulldozer truck.

2;5:   Now put boots on. Where wrench go? Mommy talking bout lady. What that paper clip doing?

2;6:   Write a piece a paper. What that egg doing? I lost a shoe. No, I don't want to sit seat.

2;7:   Where piece a paper go? Ursula has a boot on. Going to see kitten. Put the cigarette down. Dropped a rubber band. Shadow has hat just like that. Rintintin don't fly, Mommy.

2;8:   Let me get down with the boots on. Don't be afraid a horses. How tiger be so healthy and fly like kite? Joshua throw a penguin.

2;9:   Where Mommy keep her pocket book? Show you something funny. Just like turtle make mud pie.

2;10: Look at that train Ursula brought. I simply don't want put in chair. You don't have paper. Do you want little bit, Cromer? I can't wear it tomorrow.

2;11: That birdie hopping by Missouri in bag. Do want some pie on your face? Why you mixing baby chocolate? I finish drinking all up down my throat. I said why not you coming in? Look at that piece a paper and tell it. Do you want me tie that round? We going turn light on so you can't see.

3;0:   I going come in fourteen minutes. I going wear that to wedding. I see what happens. I have to save them now. Those are not strong mens. They are going sleep in wintertime. You dress me up like a baby elephant.

3;1:   I like to play with something else. You know how to put it back together. I gon' make it like a rocket to blast off with. I put another one on the floor. You went to Boston University? You want to give me some carrots and some beans? Press the button and catch it, sir. I want some other peanuts. Why you put the pacifier in his mouth? Doggies like to climb up.

3;2:   So it can't be cleaned? I broke my racing car. Do you know the light wents off? What happened to the bridge? When it's got a flat tire it's need a go to the station. I dream sometimes. I'm gong to mail this so the letter can't come off. I want to have some espresso. The sun is not too bright. Can I have some sugar? Can I put my head in the mailbox so the mailman can know where I are and put me in the mailbox? Can I keep the screwdriver just like a carpenter keep the screwdriver?

17   Normal children can differ by a year or more in their rate of language development, though the stages they pass through are generally the same regardless of how stretched out or compressed. I choose to show you Adam's speech because his language development is rather *slow* compared with other children's. Eve, another child Brown studied, was speaking in sentences like this before she was two:

I got peanut butter on the paddle.

I sit in my high chair yesterday.

Fraser, the doll's not in your briefcase.

Fix it with the scissor.

Sue making more coffee for Fraser.

Her stages of language development were telescoped into just a few months.

18   Many things are going on during this explosion. Children's sentences are getting not only longer but more complex, with deeper, bushier trees, because the children can embed one constituent inside another. Whereas before they might have said *Give doggie paper* (a three-branch verb phrase) and *Big doggie* (a two-branch noun phrase), they now say *Give big doggie paper,* with the two-branch NP embedded inside the middle branch of three-branch VP. The earlier sentences resembled telegrams, missing unstressed function words like *of, the, on,* and *does,* as well as inflections like *-ed, -ing,* and *-s*. By the threes, children are using these function words more often than they omit them, many in more than ninety percent of the sentences that require them. A full range of sentence types flower—questions with words like *who, what,* and *where,* relative clauses, comparatives, negations, complements, conjunctions, and passives.

19   Though many—perhaps even most—of the young three-year-old's sentences are ungrammatical for one reason or another, we should not judge them too harshly, because there are many things that can go wrong in any single sentence. When researchers focus on one grammatical rule and count how often a child obeys it and how often he or she flouts it, the results are astonishing: for any rule you choose, three-year-olds obey it most of the time. As we have seen, children rarely scramble word order and, by the age of three, come to supply most inflections and function words in sentences that require them. Though our ears perk up when we hear errors like *mens, wents, Can you broke those?, What he can ride in?, That's a furniture, Button me the rest,* and *Going to see kitten,* the errors occur in only 0.1% to 8% of the opportunities for making them; more than 90% of the time, the child is on target. The psychologist Karin Stromswold analyzed sentences containing auxiliaries from the speech of thirteen preschoolers. The auxiliary system in English (including words like *can, should, must, be, have,* and *do*) is notorious among grammarians for its complexity. There are about twenty-four billion billion logically possible combinations of auxiliaries (for instance, *He have might eat; He did be eating*), of which only a hundred are grammatical (*He might have eaten; He has been eating*). Stromswold wanted to count how many times children were seduced by several dozen kinds of tempting errors in the auxiliary system—that is, errors that would be natural generalizations of the sentence patterns children heard from their parents:

Pattern in Adult English	*Error That Might Tempt a Child*
He seems happy. → Does he seem happy?	He is smiling. → Does he be smiling?
	She could go. → Does she could go?
He did eat. → He didn't eat.	He did a few things. → He didn't a few things.

He did eat. → Did he eat?

I like going. → He likes going.

They want to sleep. → They wanted to sleep.

He is happy. → He is not happy.

He is happy. → Is he happy?

He did a few things. → Did he a few things?

I can go. → He cans go.

I am going. → He ams (*or* be's) going.

They are sleeping. → They are'd (*or* be'd) sleeping.

He ate something. → He ate not something.

He ate something. → Ate he something?

For virtually all of these patterns, she found *no* errors among the 66,000 sentences in which they could have occurred.

20   The three-year-old child is grammatically correct in quality, not just quantity. In earlier chapters we learned of experiments showing that children's movement rules are structure-dependent ("Ask Jabba if the boy who is unhappy is watching Mickey Mouse") and showing that their morphological systems are organized into layers of roots, stems, and inflections ("This monster likes to eat rats; what do you call him?"). Children also seem fully prepared for the Babel of languages they may face: they swiftly acquire free word order, SOV and VSO orders, rich systems of case and agreement, strings of agglutinated suffixes, ergative case marking, or whatever else their language throws at them, with no lag relative to their English-speaking counterparts. Languages with grammatical gender like French and German are the bane of the Berlitz student. In his essay "The Horrors of the German Language," Mark Twain noted that "a tree is male, its buds are female, its leaves are neuter; horses are sexless, dogs are male, cats are female—tomcats included." He translated a conversation in a German Sunday school book as follows:

Gretchen: Wilhelm, where is the turnip?

Wilhelm: She has gone to the kitchen.

Gretchen: Where is the accomplished and beautiful English maiden?

Wilhelm: It has gone to the opera.

But little children learning German (and other languages with gender) are not horrified; they acquire gender marking quickly, make few errors, and never use the association with maleness and femaleness as a false criterion. It is safe to say that except for constructions that are rare, used predominantly in written language, or mentally taxing even to an adult (like *The horse that the elephant tickled kissed the pig*), all languages are acquired, with equal ease, before the child turns four.

21   The errors children do make are rarely random garbage. Often the errors follow the logic of grammar so beautifully that the puzzle is not why the children make the errors, but why they sound like errors to adult ears at all. Let me give you two examples that I have studied in great detail.

22   Perhaps the most conspicuous childhood error is to overgeneralize—the child puts a regular suffix, like the plural *-s* or the past tense *-ed*, onto a word that forms its plural or its past tense in an irregular way. Thus the child says *tooths* and *mouses* and comes up with verb forms like these:

My teacher holded the baby rabbits and we patted them.

Hey, Horton heared a Who.

I finded Renée.

I love cut-upped egg.

Once upon a time a alligator was eating a dinosaur and the dinosaur was eating the alligator and the dinosaur was eaten by the alligator and the alligator goed kerplunk.

These forms sound wrong to use because English contains about 180 irregular verbs like *held, heard, cut,* and *went*—many inherited from Proto-Indo-European!—whose past-tense forms cannot be predicted by rule but have to be memorized by rote. Morphology is organized so that whenever a verb has an idiosyncratic form listed in the mental dictionary, the regular *-ed* rule is blocked: *goed* sounds ungrammatical because it is blocked by *went*. Elsewhere, the regular rule applies freely.

23   So why do children make this kind of error? There is a simple explanation. Since irregular forms have to be memorized and memory is fallible, any time the child tries to use a sentence in the past tense with an irregular verb but cannot summon its past-tense form from memory, the regular rule fills the vacuum. If the child wants to use the past tense of *hold* but cannot dredge up *held,* the regular rule, applying by default, marks it as *holded.* We know fallible memory is the cause of these errors because the irregular verbs that are used the least often by parents (*drank* and *knew,* for instance) are the ones their children err on the most; for the more common verbs, children are correct most of the time. The same thing happens to adults: lower-frequency, less-well-remembered irregular forms like *trod, strove, dwelt, rent, slew,* and *smote* sound odd to modern American ears and are likely to be regularized to *treaded, strived, dwelled, rended, slayed,* and *smited.* Since it's we grownups who are forgetting the irregular past, we get to declare that the forms with *-ed* are not errors! Indeed, over the centuries many of these conversions have become permanent. Old English and Middle English had about twice as many irregular verbs as Modern English; if Chaucer were here today, he would tell you that the past tenses of *to chide, to geld, to abide,* and *to cleave* are *chid, gelt, abode,* and *clove.* As time passes, verbs can wane in popularity, and one can imagine a time when, say, the verb *to geld* had slipped so far that a majority of adults could have lived their lives seldom having heard its past-tense form *gelt.* When pressed, they would have used *gelded;* the verb had become regular for them and all subsequent generations. The psychological process is no different from what happens when a young child has lived his or her brief life seldom having heard the past-tense form *built* and, when pressed, comes up with *builded.* The only difference is that the child is surrounded by grownups who are still using *built.* As the child lives longer and hears *built* more and more times, the

mental dictionary entry for *built* becomes stronger and it comes to mind more and more readily, turning off the "add -*ed*" rule each time it does.

24   Here is another lovely set of examples of childhood grammatical logic, discovered by the psychologist Melissa Bowerman:

Go me to the bathroom before you go to bed.

The tiger will come and eat David and then he will be died and I won't have a little brother any more.

I want you to take me a camel ride over your shoulders into my room.

Be a hand up your nose.

Don't giggle me!

Yawny Baby—you can push her mouth open to drink her.

These are examples of the causative rule, found in English and many other languages, which takes an intransitive verb meaning "to do something" and converts it to a transitive verb meaning "to cause to do something":

The butter melted. → Sally melted the butter.

The ball bounced. → Hiram bounced the ball.

The horse raced past the barn. → The jockey raced the horse past the barn.

The causative rule can apply to some verbs but not others; occasionally children apply it too zealously. But it is not easy, even for a linguist, to say why a ball can bounce or be bounced, and a horse can race or be raced, but a brother can only die, not be died, and a girl can only giggle, not be giggled. Only a few kinds of verbs can easily undergo the rule: verbs referring to a change of the physical state of an object, like *melt* and *break,* verbs referring to a manner of motion, like *bounce* and *slide,* and verbs referring to an accompanied locomotion, like *race* and *dance.* Other verbs, like *go* and *die,* refuse to undergo the rule in English, and verbs involving fully voluntary actions, like *cook* and *play,* refuse to undergo the rule in almost every language (and children rarely err on them). Most of children's errors in English, in fact, would be grammatical in other languages. English-speaking adults, like their children, occasionally stretch the envelope of the rule:

In 1976 the Parti Québecois began to deteriorate the health care system.

Sparkle your table with Cape Cod classic glass-ware.

Well, that decided me.

This new golf ball could obsolete many golf courses.

If she subscribes us up, she'll get a bonus.

Sunbeam whips out the holes where staling air can hide.

So both children and adults stretch the language a bit to express causation; adults are just a tiny bit more fastidious in which verbs they stretch.

Questions on Content

1. Early in this essay Pinker demonstrates why he believes "all infants come into the world with linguistic skills" (paragraph 3). Discuss how he uses speech perception to explain this claim.

2. Pinker argues that infants' recognition of sounds has nothing to do with a correlation between sound and meaning. Explain.

3. Define *infant babbling*. Why is it so important to language acquisition?

4. Define the following: *word boundaries, telegraphic speech, syntax,* and *overgeneralization.*

5. What point does Pinker affirm by describing how German children acquire gender marking?

6. Explain why a child might make the following errors: "She holded the kitty when she goed to her room."

Questions on Structure and Style

7. Explain what Pinker accomplishes rhetorically in his first two paragraphs. Why, for example, does he quote from the *Sun?* Why does he employ so many rhetorical questions? Why is the final sentence in paragraph 2 so important?

8. Discuss the organizational and developmental strategies Pinker employs in this selection.

9. Pinker's final sentence in paragraph 11 is one of many examples of his use of humor. Find other such examples of humor, and discuss their rhetorical effectiveness.

Assignments

1. Clearly Pinker believes that children are prewired to speak and understand language. In this selection he provides many examples of experiments and instances of children speaking that support his hypothesis. If possible, spend some time observing a child under the age of three and perhaps interviewing the caregivers. Write an essay in which you describe the process of language acquisition as you observed and noted it. Discuss how your evidence is or is not consistent with Pinker's theory.

2. Isolate one of the developmental stages Pinker describes, such as recognition of word boundaries, development of syntax, or telegraphic speech. Write a summary of what the author says about the stage and why it is so important to the acquisition of language.

The Word Weavers/
The World Makers

Neil Postman

"The ways in which language creates a worldview" forms Neil
Postman's subject in the following selection from Postman's book
The End of Education. Postman concentrates on definitions, questions, and metaphors, which for him determine the nature of the
relationship we develop with others, and he suggests ways to correct
the chronic mishandling of these elements in schools. Technology
also receives prominent attention in this reflection on our mapping
of the world through language—an analysis as far reaching as it is
thoughtful and well informed. Neil Postman, a professor at New
York University, is well known for his books on popular culture,
language, technology, and education.

■ **J O U R N A L   P R O M P T**   *Before reading this selection, write 3 one-paragraph
definitions of language. Each of the following sentences should begin one of the paragraphs:*

Language is like a tree.

Language is like a river.

Language is like a building.

1   In an effort to clear up confusion (or ignorance) about the meaning of a word, does
anyone ask, What is *a* definition of this word? Just about always, the way of putting
the question is, What is *the* definition of this word? The difference between *a* and *the*
in this context is vast, and I have no choice but to blame the schools for the mischief
created by an inadequate understanding of what a definition is. From the earliest
grades through graduate school, students are given definitions and, with few exceptions, are not told whose definitions they are, for what purposes they were invented,
and what alternative definitions might serve equally as well. The result is that students come to believe that definitions are *not* invented; that they are not even human
creations; that, in fact, they are—how shall I say it?—part of the natural world, like
clouds, trees, and stars.

2   In a thousand examinations on scores of subjects, students are asked to give definitions of hundreds of things, words, concepts, procedures. It is to be doubted that
there are more than a few classrooms in which there has been any discussion of what
a definition is. How is that possible?

3   Let us take the equally strange case of questions. There will be no disagreement,
I think, to my saying that all the answers given to students are the end products of
questions. Everything we know has its origin in questions. Questions, we might say,
are the principal intellectual instruments available to human beings. Then how is it

154

possible that no more than one in one hundred students has ever been exposed to an extended and systematic study of the art and science of question-asking? How come Alan Bloom didn't mention this, or E. D. Hirsch, Jr., or so many others who have written books on how to improve our schools? Did they simply fail to notice that *the principal intellectual instrument available to human beings is not examined in school*?

4 We are beginning to border on absurdity here. And we cross the line when we consider what happens in most schools on the subject of metaphor. Metaphor does, in fact, come up in school, usually introduced by an English teacher wanting to show how it is employed by poets. The result is that most students come to believe metaphor has a decorative function and only a decorative function. It gives color and texture to poetry, as jewelry does to clothing. The poet wants us to see, smell, hear, or feel something concretely, and so resorts to metaphor. I remember a discussion, when I was in college, of Robert Burns's lines: "O, my love is like a red, red rose / That's newly sprung in June. / O my love is like the melodie / That's sweetly play'd in tune."

5 The first questions on the test were: "Is Burns using metaphors or similes? Define each term. Why did Burns choose to use metaphors instead of similes, or similes instead of metaphors?"

6 I didn't object to these questions at the time except for the last one, to which I gave a defiant but honest answer: How the hell should I know? I have the same answer today. But today, I have some other things to say on the matter. Yes, poets use metaphors to help us see and feel. But so do biologists, physicists, historians, linguists, and everyone else who is trying to say something about the world. A metaphor is not an ornament. It is an organ of perception. Through metaphors, we see the world as one thing or another. Is light a wave or a particle? Are molecules like billiard balls or force fields? Is history unfolding according to some instructions of nature or a divine plan? Are our genes like information codes? Is a literary work like an architect's blueprint or a mystery to be solved?

7 Questions like these preoccupy scholars in every field. Do I exaggerate in saying that a student cannot understand what a subject is about without some understanding of the metaphors that are its foundation? I don't think so. In fact, it has always astonished me that those who write about the subject of education do not pay sufficient attention to the role of metaphor in giving form to the subject. In failing to do so, they deprive those studying the subject of the opportunity to confront its basic assumptions. Is the human mind, for example, like a dark cavern (needing illumination)? A muscle (needing exercise)? A vessel (needing filling)? A lump of clay (needing shaping)? A garden (needing cultivation)? Or, as so many say today, is it like a computer that processes data? And what of students? Are they patients to be cared for? Troops to be disciplined? Sons and daughters to be nurtured? Personnel to be trained? Resources to be developed?

8 There was a time when those who wrote on the subject of education, such as Plato, Comenius, Locke, and Rousseau, made their metaphors explicit and in doing so revealed how their metaphors controlled their thinking. "Plants are improved by cultivation," Rousseau wrote in *Emile,* "and man by education." And his entire philosophy rests upon this comparison of plants and children. Even in such ancient texts as the Mishnah, we find that there are four kinds of students: the sponge, the funnel, the

strainer, and the sieve. It will surprise you to know which one is preferred. The sponge, we are told, absorbs all; the funnel receives at one end and spills out at the other; the strainer lets the wine drain through it and retains the dregs; but the sieve—that is the best, for it lets out the flour dust and retains the fine flour. The difference in educational philosophy between Rousseau and the compilers of the Mishnah is precisely reflected in the difference between a wild plant and a sieve.

9   Definitions, questions, metaphors—these are three of the most potent elements with which human language constructs a worldview. And in urging, as I do, that the study of these elements be given the highest priority in school, I am suggesting that world making through language is a narrative of power, durability, and inspiration. It is the story of how we make the world known to ourselves, and how we make ourselves known to the world. It is different from other narratives because it is about nouns and verbs, about grammar and inferences, about metaphors and definitions, but it is a story of creation, nonetheless. Even further, it is a story that plays a role in all other narratives. For whatever we believe in, or don't believe in, is to a considerable extent a function of how our language addresses the world. Here is a small example:

10   Let us suppose you have just finished being examined by a doctor. In pronouncing his verdict, he says somewhat accusingly, "Well, you've done a very nice case of arthritis here." You would undoubtedly think this is a strange diagnosis, or more likely, a strange doctor. People do not "do" arthritis. They "have" it, or "get" it, and it is a little insulting for the doctor to imply that you have produced or manufactured an illness of this kind, especially since arthritis will release you from certain obligations and, at the same time, elicit sympathy from other people. It is also painful. So the idea that you have done arthritis to yourself suggests a kind of self-serving masochism.

11   Now, let us suppose a judge is about to pass sentence on a man convicted of robbing three banks. The judge advises him to go to a hospital for treatment, saying with an air of resignation, "You certainly have a bad case of criminality." On the face of it, this is another strange remark. People do not "have" criminality. They "do" crimes, and we are usually outraged, not saddened, by their doings. At least that is the way we are accustomed to thinking about the matter.

12   The point I am trying to make is that such simple verbs as *is* or *does* are, in fact, powerful metaphors that express some of our most fundamental conceptions of the way things are. We believe there are certain things people "have," certain things people "do," even certain things people "are." These beliefs do not necessarily reflect the structure of reality. They simply reflect an habitual way of talking about reality. In his book *Erewhon*, Samuel Butler depicted a society that lives according to the metaphors of my strange doctor and strange judge. There, illness is something people "do" and therefore have moral responsibility for; criminality is something you "have" and therefore is quite beyond your control. Every legal system and every moral code is based on a set of assumptions about what people are, have, or do. And, I might add, any significant changes in law or morality are preceded by a reordering of how such metaphors are employed.

13   I am not, incidentally, recommending the culture of the people of Erewhon. I am trying to highlight the fact that our language habits are at the core of how we imagine

the world. And to the degree that we are unaware of how our ways of talking put such ideas in our heads, we are not in full control of our situation. It needs hardly to be said that one of the purposes of an education is to give us greater control of our situation.

14   School does not always help. In schools, for instance, we find that tests are given to determine how smart someone *is* or, more precisely, how much smartness someone *has*. If, on an IQ test, one child scores a 138 and another a 106, the first is thought to *have* more smartness than the other. But this seems to me a strange conception—every bit as strange as "doing" arthritis or "having" criminality. I do not know anyone who *has* smartness. The people I know sometimes *do* smart things (as far as I can judge) and sometimes *do* dumb things—depending on what circumstances they are in, how much they know about a situation, and how interested they are. Smartness, so it seems to me, is a specific performance, done in a particular set of circumstances. It is not something you *are* or *have* in measurable quantities. In fact, the assumption that smartness is something you *have* has led to such nonsensical terms as *over-* and *underachievers.* As I understand it, an overachiever is someone who doesn't *have* much smartness but does a lot of smart things. An underachiever is someone who *has* a lot of smartness but does a lot of dumb things.

15   The ways in which language creates a worldview are not usually part of the schooling of our young. There are several reasons for this. Chief among them is that in the education of teachers, the subject is not usually brought up, and if it is, it is introduced in a cavalier and fragmentary fashion. Another reason is that it is generally believed that the subject is too complex for schoolchildren to understand, with the unfortunate result that language education is mostly confined to the study of rules governing grammar, punctuation, and usage. A third reason is that the study of language as "world-maker" is, inescapably, of an interdisciplinary nature, so that teachers are not clear about which subject ought to undertake it.

16   As to the first reason, I have no good idea why prospective teachers are denied knowledge of this matter. (Actually, I have *some* ideas, but a few of them are snotty and all are unkind.) But if it were up to me, the study of the subject would be at the center of teachers' professional education and would remain there until they were done—that is, until they retire. This would require that they become well acquainted with the writings of Aristotle and Plato (among the ancients), Locke and Kant (among recent "ancients"), and (among the moderns) I. A. Richards, Benjamin Lee Whorf, and, especially, Alfred Korzybski.

17   A few paragraphs about Korzybski are in order here, since his work offers the most systematic means of introducing the subject, deepening it, and staying with it. Another reason that academics at the university level either do not know about Korzybski's work or, if they do, do not understand it (which does not mean, by the way, that fifth graders cannot). If they do understand it, they hate it. The result is that an exceedingly valuable means of exploring the relationship between language and reality goes unused.

18   Korzybski was born in Poland in 1879. He claimed to be of royal ancestry, referring to himself as Count Alfred Korzybski—another reason why academics have kept him at arm's length. He was trained in mathematics and engineering, and served as an artillery officer in World War I. The carnage and horror he witnessed left him

haunted by a question of singular importance. He wondered why scientists could have such astonishing successes in discovering the mysteries of nature while, at the same time, the nonscientific community experienced appalling failure in its efforts to solve psychological, social, and political problems. Scientists signify their triumphs by almost daily announcements of new theories, new discoveries, new pathways to knowledge. The rest of us announce our failures by warring against ourselves and others. Korzybski began to publish his answer to this enigma in 1921 in his book *Manhood of Humanity: The Science and Art of Human Engineering.* This was followed in 1926 by *Time-Binding: The General Theory,* and finally by his magnum opus, *Science and Sanity,* in 1933.

19   In formulating his answer, Korzybski was at all times concerned that his ideas should have practical applications. He conceived of himself as an educator who would offer to humanity both a theory and a method by which it might find some release from the poignant yet catastrophic ignorance whose consequences were to be witnessed in all the historic forms of human degradation. This, too, was held against him by many academics, who accused him of grandiosity and hubris. Perhaps if Korzybski had thought *smaller,* his name would now appear more frequently in university catalogues.

20   Korzybski began his quest to discover the roots of human achievement and failure by identifying a critical functional difference between humans and other forms of life. We are, to use his phrase, "time-binders," while plants are "chemistry-binders," and animals are "space-binders." Chemistry-binding is the capacity to transform sunlight into organic chemical energy; space-binding, the capacity to move about and control a physical environment. Humans have these capacities, too, but are unique in their ability to transport their experience through time. As time-binders, we can accumulate knowledge from the past and communicate what we know to the future. Science-fiction writers need not strain invention in their search for interesting time-transporting machinery: *We* are the universe's time machines.

21   Our principal means of accomplishing the binding of time is the symbol. But our capacity to symbolize is dependent upon and integral to another process, which Korzybski called "abstract." Abstracting is the continuous activity of selecting, omitting, and organizing the details of reality so that we experience the world as patterned and coherent. Korzybski shared with Heraclitus the assumption that the world is undergoing continuous change and that no two events are identical. We give stability to our world only through our capacity to re-create it by ignoring differences and attending to similarities. Although we know that we cannot step into the "same" river twice, abstracting allows us to act as if we can. We abstract at the neurological level, at the physiological level, at the perceptual level, at the verbal level; all of our systems of interaction with the world are engaged in selecting data from the world, organizing data, generalizing data. An abstraction, to put it simply, is a kind of summary of what the world is like, a generalization about its structure.

22   Korzybski might explain the process in the following way: Let us suppose we are confronted by the phenomenon we call a "cup." We must understand, first of all, that a cup is not a thing, but an event; modern physics tells us that a cup is made of billions of electrons in constant movement, undergoing continuous change. Although

none of this activity is perceptible to us, it is important to acknowledge it, because by so doing, we may grasp the idea that *the world is not the way we see it*. What we see is a summary—an abstraction, if you will—of electronic activity. But even what we *can* see is not what we *do* see. No one has ever seen a cup in its entirety, all at once in space-time. We see only parts of wholes. But usually we see enough to allow us to reconstruct the whole and to act as if we know what we are dealing with. Sometimes, such a reconstruction betrays us, as when we lift a cup to sip our coffee and find that the coffee has settled in our lap rather than on our palate. But most of the time, our assumptions about a cup will work, and we carry those assumptions forward in a useful way by the act of naming. Thus we are assisted immeasurably in our evaluations of the world by our language, which provides us with names for the events that confront us and, by our naming them, tells us what to expect and how to prepare ourselves for action.

23   The naming of things, of course, is an abstraction of a very high order and of crucial importance. By naming an event and categorizing it as a "thing," we create a vivid and more or less permanent map of what the world is like. But it is a curious map indeed. The word *cup*, for example, *does not in fact denote anything that actually exists in the world*. It is a concept, a summary of millions of particular things that have a similar look and function. The word *tableware* is at a still higher level of abstraction, since it includes not only all the things we normally call cups but also millions of things that look nothing like cups but have a vaguely similar function.

24   The critical pint about our mapping of the world through language is that the symbols we use, whether *patriotism* and *love* or *cups* and *spoons*, are always at a considerable remove from the reality of the world itself. Although these symbols become part of ourselves—Korzybski believed they become imbedded in our neurological and perceptual systems—we must never take them completely for granted. As Korzybski once remarked, "Whatever we say something *is*, it is not."

25   Thus, we may conclude that humans live in two worlds—the world of events and things, and the world of *words* about events and things. In considering the relationship between these two worlds, we must keep in mind that language does much more than construct concepts about the events and things in the world; it tells us what sorts of concepts we ought to construct. For we do not have a name for everything that occurs in the world. Languages differ not only in their names for things but in what things they choose to name. Each language, as Edward Sapir observed, constructs reality differently from all the others.

26   This, then, is what Korzybski meant by what he called general semantics: the study of the relationship between the world of words and the world of "not words," the study of the territory we call reality and how, through abstracting and symbolizing, we map the territory. In focusing on this process, Korzybski believed he had discovered why scientists are more effective than the rest of us in solving problems. Scientists tend to be more conscious of the abstracting process; more aware of the distortions in their verbal maps; more flexible in altering their symbolic maps to fit the world. His main educational objective was to foster the idea that by making our ordinary uses of language more like the scientific uses of language, we may avoid misunderstanding, superstition, prejudice, and just plain nonsense. Some of his

followers, S. I. Hayakawa, Irving Lee, and Wendell Johnson, wrote readable texts for use in schools, but their material is not much in fashion these days. I wrote some texts along these lines myself, mostly to find out if these ideas are suitable for younger students, and discovered that they are. (I remember with delight the easy success we had with them in Arlington, Virginia, at the Fort Myer Elementary School.) But, of course, not all of the ideas are useful, and not all of them are good. General semantics, like any other system, has to be applied with a considerable degree of selectivity. Assuming teachers know something about the subject, they will discover what works and what doesn't. It is, in any case, a mistake to assume that profound ideas about language, from general semantics or any other place, cannot be introduced until graduate school.

27 Of course, there are plenty of "other places" from which profound ideas about language may come. The work of I. A. Richards (generally) and what he says, specifically, on definition and metaphor are good introductions to language as world-maker. On definition (from his *Interpretation in Teaching*):

> I have said something at several places . . . about the peculiar paralysis which the mention of definitions and, still more, the discussion of them induces. It can be prevented, I believe, by stressing the purposive aspect of definitions. We want to do something and a definition is a means of doing it. If we want certain results, then we must use certain meanings (or definitions). But no definition has any authority apart from a purpose, or to bar us from other purposes. And yet they endlessly do so. Who can doubt that we are often deprived of very useful thoughts merely because the words which might express them are being temporarily preempted by other meanings? Or that a development is often frustrated merely because we are sticking to a former definition of no service to the new purpose?

28 What Richards is talking about here is how to free our minds from the tyranny of definitions, and I can think of no better way of doing this than to provide students, as a matter of course, with alternative definitions of the important concepts with which they must deal in a subject. Whether it be molecule, fact, law, art, wealth, genes, or whatever, it is essential that students understand that definitions are instruments designed to achieve certain purposes, that the fundamental question to ask of them is not, Is this the real definition? or Is this the correct definition? but What purpose does the definition serve? That is, Who made it up and why?

29 I have had some great fun, and so have students, considering the question of definition in a curious federal law. I refer to what you may not say when being frisked or otherwise examined before boarding an airplane. You may not, of course, give false or misleading information about yourself. But beyond that, you are also expressly forbidden to joke about any of the procedures being used. This is the only case I know of where a joke is prohibited by law (although there are many situations in which it is prohibited by custom).

30 Why joking is illegal when you are being searched is not entirely clear to me, but that is only one of several mysteries surrounding this law. Does the law distinguish, for example, between good jokes and bad jokes? (Six months for a good one, two years for a bad one?) I don't know. But even more important, how would one know when something is a joke at all? Is there a legal definition of a joke? Suppose, while

being searched, I mention that my middle name is Milton (which it is) and that I come from Flushing (which I do). I can tell you from experience that people of questionable intelligence sometimes find those names extremely funny, and it is not impossible that a few of them are airport employees. If that were the case, what would be my legal status? I have said something that has induced laughter in another. Have I, therefore, told a joke? Or look at it from the opposite view: Suppose that, upon being searched, I launched into a story about a funny thing that happened to me while boarding a plane in Chicago, concluding by saying, "And then the pilot said, 'That was no stewardess. That was my wife.'" Being of questionable intelligence myself, I think it is a hilarious story, but the guard does not. If he does not laugh, have I told a joke? Can a joke be a story that does *not* make people laugh?

31   It can, of course, if someone of authority says so. For the point is that in every situation, including this one, someone (or some group) has a decisive power of definition. In fact, to have power means to be able to define and to make it stick. As between the guard at the airport and me, he will have the power, not me, to define what a joke is. If his definition places me in jeopardy, I can, of course, argue my case at a trial, at which either a judge or a jury will then have the decisive authority to define whether or not my words qualified as a joke. But it is also worth noting that even if I confine my joke-telling to dinner parties, I do not escape the authority of definition. For at parties, popular opinion will decide whether or not my jokes are good ones, or even jokes at all. If opinion runs against me, the penalty is that I am not invited to many parties. There is, in short, no escaping the jurisdiction of definitions. Social order requires that there be authoritative definitions, and though you may search from now to doomsday, you will find no system without official definitions and authoritative sources to enforce them. And so we must add to the questions we ask of definition, What is the source of power that enforces the definition? And we may add further the question of what happens when those with the power to enforce definitions go mad. Here is an example that came from the Prague government several years ago. I have not made this up and produce it without further comment:

> Because Christmas Eve falls on a Thursday, the day has been designated a Saturday for work purposes. Factories will close all day, with stores open a half day only. Friday, December 25, has been designated a Sunday, with both factories and stores open all day. Monday, December 28, will be a Wednesday for work purposes. Wednesday, December 30, will be a business Friday. Saturday, January 2, will be a Sunday, and Sunday, January 3, will be a Monday.

32   As for metaphor, I pass along a small assignment which I. A. Richards used on an occasion when I attended a seminar he conducted. (It is but one of a hundred ways to introduce the subject.) Richards divided the class into three groups. Each group was asked to write a paragraph describing language. However, Richards provided each group with its first sentence. Group A had to begin with "Language is like a tree"; Group B with "Language is like a river"; Group C with "Language is like a building." You can imagine, I'm sure, what happened. The paragraphs were strikingly different, with one group writing of roots and branches and organic growth; another of tributaries, streams, and even floods; another of foundations, rooms, and

sturdy structures. In the subsequent discussion, we did not bother with the question, Which is the "correct" description? Our discussion centered on how metaphors control what we say, and to what extent what we say controls what we see.

33   As I have said there are hundreds of ways to study the relationship between language and reality, and I could go on at interminable length with ideas on how to get into it. Instead, I will confine myself to three further suggestions. The first is, simply, that the best book I know for arousing interest in the subject is Helen Keller's *The Story of My Life*. It is certainly the best account we have—from the inside, as it were—of how symbols and the abstracting process work to create a world.

34   Second, I would propose that in every subject—from history to biology to mathematics—students be taught, explicitly and systematically, the universe of discourse that comprises the subject. Each teacher would deal with the structure of questions, the process of definition, and the role of metaphor as these matters are relevant to his or her particular subject. Here I mean, of course, not merely what are the questions, definitions, and metaphors of a subject but also *how* these are formed and how they have been formed in the past.

35   Of special importance are the ways in which the forms of questions have changed over time and how these forms vary from subject to subject. The idea is for students to learn that the terminology of a question determines the terminology of its answer; that a question cannot be answered unless there are procedures by which reliable answers can be obtained; and that the value of a question is determined not only by the specificity and richness of the answers it produces but also by the quantity and quality of the new questions it raises.

36   Once this topic is opened, it follows that some attention must be given to how such terms as *right, wrong, truth,* and *falsehood* are used in a subject, as well as what assumptions they are based upon. This is particularly important, since words of this type cause far more trouble in students' attempts to understand a field of knowledge than do highly technical words. It is peculiar, I think, that of all the examinations I have ever seen, I have never come across one in which students were asked to say what is the basis of "correctness" or "falsehood" in a particular subject. Perhaps this is because teachers believe the issue is too obvious for discussion or testing. If so, they are wrong. I have found that students at all levels rarely have thought about the meaning of such terms in relation to a subject they are studying. They simply do not know in what sense an historical fact is different from a biological fact, or a mathematical "truth" is different from the "truth" of a literary work. Equally astonishing is that students, particularly those in elementary and secondary schools, rarely can express an intelligible sentence on the uses of the word *theory.* Since most subjects studied in school consist largely of theories, it is difficult to imagine exactly what students are in fact studying when they do their history, biology, economics, physics, or whatever. It is obvious, then, that language education must include not only the serious study of what truth and falsehood mean in the context of a subject but also what is meant by a theory, a fact, an inference, an assumption, a judgment, a generalization.

37   In addition, some attention must obviously be given to the style and tone of the language in a given subject. Each subject is a manner of speaking and writing. There is a rhetoric of knowledge, a characteristic way in which arguments, proofs, speculations,

experiments, polemics, even humor, are expressed. One might even say that speaking or writing a subject is a performing art, and each subject requires a somewhat different kind of performance from every other. Historians, for example, do not speak or write the way biologists do. The differences have much to do with the kind of material they are dealing with, the degree of precision their generalizations permit, the type of facts they marshal, the traditions of their subject, the type of training they receive, and the purposes for which they are making their inquiries. The rhetoric of knowledge is not an easy matter to go into, but it is worth remembering that some scholars—one thinks of Veblen in sociology, Freud in psychology, Galbraith in economics—have exerted influence as much through their manner as their matter. The point is that knowledge is a form of literature, and the various styles of knowledge ought to be studied and discussed.

38   What we are after here is to tell the story of language as an act of creation. This is what Socrates meant when he said, "When the mind is thinking, it is talking to itself." Twenty-five hundred years later, the great German philologist Max Müller said the same: ". . . thought cannot exist without signs, and our most important signs are words." In between, Hobbes, Locke, and Kant said the same thing. So did Bertrand Russell, Werner Heisenberg, Benjamin Lee Whorf, I. A. Richards, Alfred Korzybski, and everyone else who has thought about the matter, including Marshall McLuhan.

39   McLuhan comes up here because he is associated with the phrase "the extensions of man." And my third and final suggestion has to do with inquiries into the ways in which humans have extended their capacities to "bind" time and control space. I am referring to what may be called "technology education." It is somewhat embarrassing that this needs to be proposed as an innovation in schools, since Americans never tire of telling themselves that they have created a technological society. They even seem to be delighted about this and many of them believe that the pathway to a fulfilling life is through continuous technological change. One would expect then that technology education would be a familiar subject in American schools. But it is not. Technology may have entered the schools but *not* technology education. Those who doubt my contention might ask themselves the following questions: Does the average high school or college graduate know where the alphabet comes from, something of its development, and *anything* about its psychic and social effects? Does he or she know anything about illuminated manuscripts, about the origin of the printing press and its role in reshaping Western culture, about the origins of newspapers and magazines? Do our students know where clocks, telescopes, microscopes, X rays, and computers come from? Do they have any idea about how such technologies have changed the economic, social, and political life of Western culture? Could they say who Morse, Daguerre, Bell, Edison, Marconi, De Forest, Zworykin, Pulitzer, Hearst, Eisenstein, and Von Neumann were? After all, we might say these men invented the technological society. Is it too much to expect that those who live in such a society will know about them and what they thought they were creating?

40   I realize I am beginning to sound like E. D. Hirsch, Jr.,* but I find it truly astonishing that the great story of humanity's perilous and exciting romance with technology

---

* Author of the controversial 1987 book *Cultural Literacy: What Every American Needs to Know.*

is not told in our schools. There is certainly no shortage of writers on the subject. McLuhan, while an important contributor, was neither the first nor necessarily the best who has addressed the issue of how we become what we make. One thinks, for example, of Martin Heidegger, Lewis Mumford, Jacques Ellul, Paul Goodman, Walter Ong, Walter Benjamin, Elizabeth Eisenstein, Alvin Toffler, Theodore Roszak, Norbert Wiener, Sherry Turkle, Joseph Weizenbaum, Seymour Papert, and Herbert Schiller. One may also find ideas about the subject in the "science fiction" writers I have previously alluded to—Huxley, Orwell, and Bradbury, for example. It would seem that everywhere one turns these days, there are books, articles, films, and television shows on the subject of how our technology has remade the world, and continues to remake it. It is among the leading topics of everyday conversation, especially among academics. There is, for example, hardly a school superintendent anywhere, or a college dean, who cannot give us a ready-made sermon on how we now live in an "information age." Then why do we not have a subject in which students address such questions as these: How does information differ in symbolic form? How are ideographs different from letters? How are images different from words? Paintings from photographs? Speech from writing? Television from books? Radio from television? Information comes in many forms, and at different velocities and in different quantities. Do the differences matter? Do the differences have varying psychic and social effects? The questions are almost endless. This is a serious subject.

41   I do not know the reasons why there is no such subject in most schools, although I have one suspect under surveillance. It is that educators confuse the teaching of how to use technology with technology education. No objection can be raised against students' learning how to use television and movie cameras, Xerox machines, and computers. (I most certainly believe students ought to be taught how to use the alphabet.) I have no intention of quarrelling with Seymour Papert, Bill Gross, or Alan Kay about the possibility that the intelligent use of computer technology can increase students' competence in mathematics or stimulate their interest in other subjects. And I endorse those attempts (for example, in New Mexico) to have students make their own television programs so that they will gain insights into the technical problems involved. These are not trivial matters, but they are only a small part of the way in which I define technology education. As I see it, the subject is mainly about how television and movie cameras, Xerox machines, and computers recorder our psychic habits, our social relations, our political ideas, and our moral sensibilities. It is about how the meanings of information and education change as new technologies intrude upon a culture, how the meanings of truth, law, and intelligence differ among oral cultures, writing cultures, printing cultures, electronic cultures. Technology education is not a technical subject. It is a branch of the humanities. Technical knowledge can be useful, but one does not need to know the physics of television to study the social and political effects of television. One may not own an automobile, or even know how to drive one, but this is no obstacle to observing what the automobile has done to American culture.

42   It should also be said that technology education does not imply a negative attitude toward technology. It does imply a critical attitude. To be "against technology" makes no more sense than to be "against food." We can't live without either. But to

observe that it is dangerous to eat too much food, or to eat food that has no nutritional value, is not to be "antifood." It is to suggest what may be the best uses of food. Technology education aims at students' learning about what technology helps us to do and what it hinders us from doing; it is about how technology uses us, for good or ill, and about how it has used people in the past, for good or ill. It is about how technology creates new worlds, for good or ill.

43   But let us assume that we may overcome any obstacles to making the story of technology a core subject in schools. What is it we would want students to know? Well, for one thing, we would want them to know the answers to all the questions I have cited. But in addition, I would include the following ten principles.

1. All technological change is a Faustian bargain. For every advantage a new technology offers, there is always a corresponding disadvantage.
2. The advantages and disadvantages of new technologies are never distributed evenly among the population. This means that every new technology benefits some and harms others.
3. Embedded in every technology there is a powerful idea, sometimes two or three powerful ideas. Like language itself, a technology predisposes us to favor and value certain perspectives and accomplishments and to subordinate others. Every technology has a philosophy, which is given expression in how the technology makes people use their minds, in what it makes us do with our bodies, in how it codifies the world, in which of our senses it amplifies, in which of our emotional and intellectual tendencies it disregards.
4. A new technology usually makes war against an old technology. It competes with it for time, attention, money, prestige, and a "worldview."
5. Technological change is not additive; it is ecological. A new technology does not merely add something; it changes everything.
6. Because of the symbolic forms in which information is encoded, different technologies have different *intellectual* and *emotional* biases.
7. Because of the accessibility and speed of their information, different technologies have different *political* biases.
8. Because of their physical form, different technologies have different *sensory* biases.
9. Because of the conditions in which we attend to them, different technologies have different *social* biases.
10. Because of their technical and economic structure, different technologies have different *content* biases.

44   All of these principles being deeply, continuously, and historically investigated by students, I would then propose the following final examination, which is in two parts.

45   Part I: Choose one pre–twentieth century technology—for example, the alphabet, the printing press, the telegraph, the factory—and indicate what were the main intellectual, social, political, and economic advantages of the technology, and why. Then indicate what were the main intellectual, social, political, and economic disadvantages of the technology, and why.

46   Part II: Indicate, first, what you believe are or will be the main advantages of computer technology, and why; second, indicate what are or will be the main disadvantages of computer technology, and why.

47   Any student who can pass this examination will, I believe, know something worthwhile. He or she will also have a sense of how the world was made and how it is being remade, and may even have some ideas on how it *should* be remade.

Questions on Content

1. Postman states that students come to believe that definitions are "part of the natural world, like clouds, trees, and stars" (paragraph 1). Later he states teachers should help free students' minds from the "tyranny of definitions" (paragraph 28). Explain.

2. What does the author believe is the principal intellectual instrument available to human beings?

3. In paragraphs 10 and 11 Postman illustrates the power of such simple verbs as *have* and *do*. Explain what he means, and provide similar illustrations of your own.

4. Why does Postman object to traditional IQ tests?

5. Explain why Postman feels the writings of Alfred Korzybski are so important. Why does Korzybski describe human beings as "time-binders"? Explain why language is so important to the notion of human beings as time-binders.

6. The author argues that human beings live in two worlds. What are they?

7. In paragraph 37 Postman states that "speaking or writing a subject is a performing art, and each subject requires a somewhat different kind of performance from every other." Discuss this statement in the context of courses you are presently taking.

Questions on Structure and Style

8. Discuss the structure and development of paragraph 7. Describe the transition between paragraphs 7 and 8, and discuss the relationships between the paragraphs. Now describe how paragraphs 1–9 work together.

9. Discuss whether or not you believe paragraph 13 is where Postman formally presents his thesis.

10. What is the purpose of Postman's discussion of jokes in paragraph 30?

11. Discuss the significance and appropriateness of the selection's title.

Assignments

1. Discuss the three definitions of language that you prepared in the Journal Prompt. How do the definitions illustrate an important point that Postman makes in this selection? (Pay attention to the author's definition of *metaphor* in paragraph 6.)

2. In the closing paragraphs Postman discusses what he refers to as "technology education" (paragraph 39). He states that technology education is not a technical subject; rather, "it is a branch of the humanities" (paragraph 41). Explain what he means by *technology education,* and write an essay that describes some of the changes that might be made in your school to move the curriculum in the direction that Postman advocates.

A Brief History of English

Paul Roberts

This well-known essay by Paul Roberts makes it clear that language
development is determined by historical change. What people do
contributes to the language they speak. Thus, to understand English,
we must understand English history, and Roberts approaches his
subject with history in mind. The resulting essay, remarkable for its
brevity, takes a complex subject and makes it accessible—and
engaging, thanks to Roberts's skill at storytelling.

■ JOURNAL PROMPT *Prior to reading Roberts's selection, consider how the
English language you speak has been influenced by other languages. Consider, among other
areas, vocabulary, pronunciation, and place names.*

1   No understanding of the English language can be very satisfactory without a notion
of the history of the language. But we shall have to make do with just a notion. The
history of English is long and complicated, and we can only hit the high spots.

2   The history of our language begins a little after A.D. 600. Everything before that is
pre-history, which means that we can guess at it but can't prove much. For a thousand
years or so before the birth of Christ our linguistic ancestors were savages wandering
through the forests of northern Europe. Their language was a part of the Germanic
branch of the Indo-European family.

3   At the time of the Roman Empire—say, from the beginning of the Christian Era to
around A.D. 400—the speakers of what was to become English were scattered along
the northern coast of Europe. They spoke a dialect of Low German. More exactly, they
spoke several different dialects, since they were several different tribes. The names
given to the tribes who got to England are *Angles, Saxons*, and *Jutes*. For convenience,
we can refer to them all as Anglo-Saxons.

4   Their first contact with civilization was a rather thin acquaintance with the Roman
Empire on whose borders they lived. Probably some of the Anglo-Saxons wandered
into the Empire occasionally, and certainly Roman merchants and traders traveled
among the tribes. At any rate, this period saw the first of our many borrowings from
Latin. Such words as *kettle, wine, cheese, butter, cheap, plum, gem, bishop, church*
were borrowed at this time. They show something of the relationship of the Anglo-
Saxons with the Romans. The Anglo-Saxons were learning, getting their first taste
of civilization.

5   They still had a long way to go, however, and their first step was to help smash the
civilization they were learning from. In the fourth century the Roman power weakened badly. While the Goths were pounding away at the Romans in the Mediterranean
countries, their relatives, the Anglo-Saxons, began to attack Britain.

168

6   The Romans had been the ruling power in Britain since A.D. 43. They had sub-
jugated the Celts whom they found living there and had succeeded in setting up a
Roman administration. The Roman influence did not extend to the outlying parts of
the British Isles. In Scotland, Wales, and Ireland the Celts remained free and wild, and
they made periodic forays against the Romans in England. Among other defense
measures, the Romans built the famous Roman Wall to ward off the tribes in the north.

7   Even in England the Roman power was thin. Latin did not become the language
of the country as it did in Gaul and Spain. The mass of people continued to speak
Celtic, with Latin and the Roman civilization it contained in use as a top dressing.

8   In the fourth century, troubles multiplied for the Romans in Britain. Not only did
the untamed tribes of Scotland and Wales grow more and more restive, but the
Anglo-Saxons began to make pirate raids on the eastern coast. Furthermore, there
was growing difficulty everywhere in the Empire, and the legions in Britain were
siphoned off to fight elsewhere. Finally, in A.D. 410, the last Roman ruler in England,
bent on becoming emperor, left the islands and took the last of the legions with him.
The Celts were left in possession of Britain but almost defenseless against the im-
pending Anglo-Saxon attack.

9   Not much is surely known about the arrival of the Anglo-Saxons in England.
According to the best early source, the eighth-century historian Bede, the Jutes came
in 449 in response to a plea from the Celtic king, Vortigern, who wanted their help
against the Picts attacking from the north. The Jutes subdued the Picts but then quar-
reled and fought with Vortigern, and, with reinforcements from the Continent, settled
permanently in Kent. Somewhat later the Angles established themselves in eastern
England and the Saxons in the south and west. Bede's account is plausible enough,
and these were probably the main lines of the invasion.

10   We do know, however, that the Angles, Saxons, and Jutes were a long time secur-
ing themselves in England. Fighting went on for as long as a hundred years before the
Celts in England were all killed, driven into Wales, or reduced to slavery. This is the
period of King Arthur, who was not entirely mythological. He was a Romanized Celt,
a general, though probably not a king. He had some success against the Anglo-
Saxons, but it was only temporary. By 550 or so the Anglo-Saxons were firmly established. English was in England.

11   All this is pre-history, so far as the language is concerned. We have no record of
the English language until after 600, when the Anglo-Saxons were converted to
Christianity and learned the Latin alphabet. The conversion began, to be precise, in
the year 597 and was accomplished within thirty or forty years. The conversion was
a great advance for the Anglo-Saxons, not only because of the spiritual benefits but
because it reestablished contact with what remained of Roman civilization. This civilization didn't amount to much in the year 600, but it was certainly superior to anything in England up to that time.

12   It is customary to divide the history of the English language into three periods: Old
English, Middle English, and Modern English. Old English runs from the earliest
records—i.e., seventh century—to about 1100; Middle English from 1100 to 1450 or
1500; Modern English from 1500 to the present day. Sometimes Modern English is
further divided into Early Modern, 1500–1700, and Late Modern, 1700 to the present.

13   When England came into history, it was divided into several more or less autonomous kingdoms, some of which at times exercised a certain amount of control
over the others. In the century after the conversion the most advanced kingdom
was Northumbria, the area between the Humber River and the Scottish border. By
A.D. 700 the Northumbrians had developed a respectable civilization, the finest in
Europe. It is sometimes called the Northumbrian Renaissance, and it was the first of
the several renaissances through which Europe struggled upward out of the ruins of
the Roman Empire. It was in this period that the best of the Old English literature
was written, including the epic poem *Beowulf.*

14   In the eighth century, Northumbrian power declined, and the center of influence
moved southward to Mercia, the kingdom of the Midlands. A century later the center
shifted again, and Wessex, the country of the West Saxons, became the leading power.
The most famous king of the West Saxons was Alfred the Great, who reigned in the
second half of the ninth century, dying in 901. He was famous not only as a military
man and administrator but also as a champion of learning. He founded and supported
schools and translated or caused to be translated many books from Latin into English.
At this time also much of the Northumbrian literature of two centuries earlier was
copied in West Saxon. Indeed, the great bulk of Old English writing which has come
down to us is in the West Saxon dialect of 900 or later.

15   In the military sphere, Alfred's great accomplishment was his successful opposition to the Viking invasions. In the ninth and tenth centuries, the Norsemen emerged
in their ships from their homelands in Denmark and the Scandinavian peninsula.
They traveled far and attacked and plundered at will and almost with impunity. They
ravaged Italy and Greece, settled in France, Russia and Ireland, colonized Iceland
and Greenland, and discovered America several centuries before Columbus. Nor did
they overlook England.

16   After many years of hit-and-run raids, the Norsemen landed an army on the east
coast of England in the year 866. There was nothing much to oppose them except
the Wessex power led by Alfred. The long struggle ended in 877 with a treaty by
which a line was drawn roughly from the northwest of England to the southeast. On
the eastern side of the line Norse rule was to prevail. This was called the Danelaw.
The western side was to be governed by Wessex.

17   The linguistic result of all this was a considerable injection of Norse into the
English language. Norse was at this time not so different from English as Norwegian or Danish is now. Probably speakers of English could understand, more or less,
the language of the newcomers who had moved into eastern England. At any rate,
there was considerable interchange and word borrowing. Examples of Norse words
in the English language are *sky, give, law, egg, outlaw, leg, ugly, scant, sly, crawl,
scowl, take, thrust.* There are hundreds more. We have even borrowed some pronouns from Norse—*they, their,* and *them.* These words were borrowed first by the
eastern and northern dialects and then in the course of hundreds of years made their
way into English generally.

18   It is supposed also—indeed, it must be true—that the Norsemen influenced the
sound structure and the grammar of English. But this is hard to demonstrate in detail.

19   We may now have an example of Old English. The favorite illustration is the Lord's Prayer, since it needs no translation. This has come to us in several different versions. Here is one:

> Fæder ure þuðe eart on heofonum si þin nama gehalgod. Tobecume þin rice. Gewurðe þin willa on eorðan swa swa on heofonum. Urne gedæghwamlican hlaf syle us to dæg. And forgyf us ure gyltas swa swa we forgyfaþ urum gyltendum. And ne gelæd þu us on costnunge ac alys us of yfele. Soðlice.

20   Some of the differences between this and Modern English are merely differences in orthography. For instance, the sign æ is what Old English writers use for a vowel sound like that in modern *hat* or *and*. The *th* sounds of modern *thin* or *then* are represented in Old English by þ or ð. But of course there are many differences in sound too. *Ure* is the ancestor of modern *our*, but the first vowel was like that in *too* or *ooze*. *Hlaf* is modern *loaf;* we have dropped the *h* sound and changed the vowel, which in *hlaf* was pronounced something like the vowel in *father*. Old English had some sounds which we do not have. The sound represented by *y* does not occur in Modern English. If you pronounce the vowel in *bit* with your lips rounded, you may approach it.

21   In grammar, Old English was much more highly inflected than Modern English is. That is, there were more case endings for nouns, more person and number endings for verbs, a more complicated pronoun system, various endings for adjectives, and so on. Old English nouns had four cases—nominative, genitive, dative, accusative. Adjectives had five—all these and an instrumental case besides. Present-day English has only two cases for nouns—common case and possessive case. Adjectives now have no case system at all. On the other hand, we now use a more rigid word order and more structure words (prepositions, auxiliaries, and the like) to express relationships than Old English did.

22   Some of this grammar we can see in the Lord's Prayer. *Heofonum,* for instance, is a dative plural; the nominative singular was *heofon. Urne* is an accusative singular; the nominative is *ure*. In *urum gyltendum* both words are dative plural. *Forgyfaþ* is the third person plural form of the verb. Word order is different: "urne gedæghwamlican hlaf syle us" in place of "Give us our daily bread." And so on.

23   In vocabulary Old English is quite different from Modern English. Most of the Old English words are what we may call native English: that is, words which have not been borrowed from other languages but which have been a part of English ever since English was a part of Indo-European. Old English did certainly contain borrowed words. We have seen that many borrowings were coming in from Norse. Rather large numbers had been borrowed from Latin, too. Some of these were taken while the Anglo-Saxons were still on the Continent (*cheese, butter, bishop, kettle,* etc.); a large number came into English after Conversion (*angel, candle, priest, martyr, radish, oyster, purple, school, spend,* etc.). But the great majority of Old English words were native English.

24   Now, on the contrary, the majority of words in English are borrowed, taken mostly from Latin and French. Of the words in *The American College Dictionary* only about

14 percent are native. Most of these, to be sure, are common, high-frequency words—*the, of, I, and, because, man, mother, road,* etc.; of the thousand most common words in English, some 62 percent are native English. Even so, the modern vocabulary is very much Latinized and Frenchified. The Old English vocabulary was not.

25   Sometime between the year 1000 and 1200 various important changes took place in the structure of English, and Old English became Middle English. The political event which facilitated these changes was the Norman Conquest. The Normans, as the name shows, came originally from Scandinavia. In the early tenth century they established themselves in northern France, adopted the French language, and developed a vigorous kingdom and a very passable civilization. In the year 1066, led by Duke William, they crossed the Channel and made themselves masters of England. For the next several hundred years, England was ruled by kings whose first language was French.

26   One might wonder why, after the Norman Conquest, French did not become the national language, replacing English entirely. The reason is that the Conquest was not a national migration, as the earlier Anglo-Saxon invasion had been. Great numbers of Normans came to England, but they came as rulers and landlords. French became the language of the court, the language of the nobility, the language of polite society, the language of literature. But it did not replace English as the language of the people. There must always have been hundreds of towns and villages in which French was never heard except when visitors of high station passed through.

27   But English, though it survived as the national language, was profoundly changed after the Norman Conquest. Some of the changes—in sound structure and grammar—would no doubt have taken place whether there had been a Conquest or not. Even before 1066 the case system of English nouns and adjectives was becoming simplified; people came to rely more on word order and prepositions than on inflectional endings to communicate their meanings. The process was speeded up by sound changes which caused many of the endings to sound alike. But no doubt the Conquest facilitated the change. German, which didn't experience a Norman Conquest, is today rather highly inflected compared to its cousin English.

28   But it is in vocabulary that the effects of the Conquest are most obvious. French ceased, after a hundred years or so, to be the native language of very many people in England, but it continued—and continues still—to be a zealously cultivated second language, the mirror of elegance and civilization. When one spoke English, one introduced not only French ideas and French things but also their French names. This was not only easy but socially useful. To pepper one's conversation with French expressions was to show that one was well-bred, elegant, *au courant.* The last sentence shows that the process is not yet dead. By using *au courant* instead of, say *abreast of things,* the writer indicates that he is no dull clod who knows only English but an elegant person aware of how things are done in *le haut monde.*

29   Thus French words came into English, all sorts of them. There were words to do with government: *parliament, majesty, treaty, alliance, tax, government;* church words: *parson, sermon, baptism, incense, crucifix, religion;* words for foods: *veal, beef, mutton, bacon, jelly, peach, lemon, cream, biscuit;* colors: *blue, scarlet, vermilion;* household words: *curtain, chair, lamp, towel, blanket, parlor;* play words: *dance,*

chess, music, leisure, conversation; literary words: *story, romance, poet, literary;* learned words: *study, logic, grammar, noun, surgeon, anatomy, stomach;* just ordinary words of all sorts: *nice, second, very, age, bucket, gentle, final, fault, flower, cry, count, sure, move, surprise, plain.*

30   All these and thousands more poured into the English vocabulary between 1100 and 1500, until at the end of that time many people must have had more French words than English at their command. This is not to say that English became French. English remained English in sound structure and in grammar, though these also felt the ripples of French influence. The very heart of the vocabulary, too, remained English. Most of the high-frequency words—the pronouns, the prepositions, the conjunctions, the auxiliaries, as well as a great many ordinary nouns and verbs and adjectives—were not replaced by borrowings.

31   Middle English, then, was still a Germanic language, but it differed from Old English in many ways. The sound system and the grammar changed a good deal. Speakers made less use of case systems and other inflectional devices and relied more on word order and structure words to express their meanings. This is often said to be a simplification, but it isn't really. Languages don't become simpler; they merely exchange one kind of complexity for another. Modern English is not a simple language, as any foreign speaker who tries to learn it will hasten to tell you.

32   For us Middle English is simpler than Old English just because it is closer to Modern English. It takes three or four months at least to learn to read Old English prose and more than that for poetry. But a week of good study should put one in touch with the Middle English poet Chaucer. Indeed, you may be able to make some sense of Chaucer straight off, though you would need instruction in pronunciation to make it sound like poetry. Here is a famous passage from the *General Prologue to the Canterbury Tales,* fourteenth century:

> Ther was also a nonne, a Prioresse,
> That of hir smyling was ful symple and coy,
> Hir gretteste oath was but by Seinte Loy,
> And she was cleped Madam Eglentyne.
> Ful wel she song the service dyvyne,
> Entuned in hir nose ful semely.
> And Frenshe she spak ful faire and fetisly,
> After the scole of Stratford-atte-Bowe,
> For Frenshe of Parys was to hir unknowe.

33   Sometime between 1400 and 1600 English underwent a couple of sound changes which made the language of Shakespeare quite different from that of Chaucer. Incidentally, these changes contributed much to the chaos in which English spelling now finds itself.

34   One change was the elimination of a vowel sound in certain unstressed positions at the end of words. For instance, the words *name, stone wine, dance* were pronounced as two syllables by Chaucer but as just one by Shakespeare. The *e* in these words became, as we say, "silent." But it wasn't silent for Chaucer; it represented a vowel

sound. So also the words *laughed, seemed, stored* would have been pronounced by Chaucer as two-syllable words. The change was an important one because it affected thousands of words and gave a different aspect to the whole language.

35 The other change is what is called the Great Vowel Shift. This was a systematic shifting of half a dozen vowels and diphthongs in stressed syllables. For instance, the word *name* had in Middle English a vowel something like that in the modern word *father; wine* had the vowel of modern *mean; he* was pronounced something like modern *hey; mouse* sounded like *moose; moon* had the vowel of *moan.* Again the shift was thoroughgoing and affected all the words in which these vowel sounds occurred. Since we still keep the Middle English system of spelling these words, the differences between Modern English and Middle English are often more real than apparent.

36 The vowel shift has meant also that we have come to use an entirely different set of symbols for representing vowel sounds than is used by writers of such languages as French, Italian, or Spanish, in which no such vowel shift occurred. If you come across a strange word—say, *bine*—in an English book, you will pronounce it according to the English system, with the vowel of *wine* or *dine.* But if you read *bine* in a French, Italian, or Spanish book, you will pronounce it with the vowel of *mean* or *seen.*

37 These two changes, then, produced the basic differences between Middle English and Modern English. But there were several other developments that had an effect upon the language. One was the invention of printing, an invention introduced into England by William Caxton in the year 1475. Where before books had been rare and costly, they suddenly became cheap and common. More and more people learned to read and write. This was the first of many advances in communication which have worked to unify languages and to arrest the development of dialect differences, though of course printing affects writing principally rather than speech. Among other things it hastened the standardization of spelling.

38 The period of Early Modern English—that is, the sixteenth and seventeenth centuries—was also the period of the English Renaissance, when people developed, on the one hand, a keen interest in the past and, on the other, a more daring and imaginative view of the future. New ideas multiplied, and new ideas meant new language. Englishmen had grown accustomed to borrowing words from French as a result of the Norman Conquest; now they borrowed from Latin and Greek. As we have seen, English had been raiding Latin from Old English times and before, but now the floodgates really opened, and thousands of words from the classical languages poured in. *Pedestrian, bonus, anatomy, contradict, climax, dictionary, benefit, multiply, exist, paragraph, initiate, scene, inspire* are random examples. Probably the average educated American today has more words from French in his vocabulary than from native English sources, and more from Latin than from French.

39 The greatest writer of the Early Modern English period is of course Shakespeare, and the best-known book is the King James Version of the Bible, published in 1611. The Bible (if not Shakespeare) has made many features of Early Modern English perfectly familiar to many people down to present times, even though we do not use

these features in present-day speech and writing. For instance, the old pronouns *thou* and *thee* have dropped out of use now, together with their verb forms, but they are still familiar to us in prayer and in Biblical quotation: "Whither thou goest, I will go." Such forms as *hath* and *doth* have been replaced by *has* and *does*; "Goes he hence tonight?" would now be "Is he going away tonight?"; Shakespeare's "Fie on't, sirrah" would be "Nuts to that, Mac." Still, all these expressions linger with us because of the power of the works in which they occur.

40   It is not always realized, however, that considerable sound changes have taken place between Early Modern English and the English of the present day. Shakespearean actors putting on a play speak the words, properly enough, in their modern pronunciation. But it is very doubtful that this pronunciation would be understood at all by Shakespeare. In Shakespeare's time, the word *reason* was pronounced like modern *raisin; face* had the sound of modern *glass;* the *l* in *would, should, palm* was pronounced. In these points and a great many others the English language has moved a long way from what it was in 1600.

41   The history of English since 1700 is filled with many movements and counter-movements, of which we can notice only a couple. One of these is the vigorous attempt made in the eighteenth century, and the rather half-hearted attempts made since, to regulate and control the English language. Many people of the eighteenth century, not understanding very well the forces which govern language, proposed to polish and prune and restrict English, which they felt was proliferating too wildly. There was much talk of an academy which would rule on what people could and could not say and write. The academy never came into being, but the eighteenth century did succeed in establishing certain attitudes which, though they haven't had much effect on the development of the language itself, have certainly changed the native speaker's feeling about the language.

42   In part a product of the wish to fix and establish the language was the development of the dictionary. The first English dictionary was published in 1603; it was a list of 2500 words briefly defined. Many others were published with gradual improvements until Samuel Johnson published his *English Dictionary* in 1755. This, steadily revised, dominated the field in England for nearly a hundred years. Meanwhile in America, Noah Webster published his dictionary in 1828, and before long dictionary publishing was a big business in this country. The last century has seen the publication of one great dictionary: the twelve-volume *Oxford English Dictionary,* compiled in the course of seventy-five years through the labors of many scholars. We have also, of course, numerous commercial dictionaries which are as good as the public wants them to be if not, indeed, rather better.

43   Another product of the eighteenth century was the invention of "English grammar." As English came to replace Latin as the language of scholarship it was felt that one should also be able to control and dissect it, parse and analyze it, as one could Latin. What happened in practice was that the grammatical description that applied to Latin was removed and superimposed on English. This was silly, because English is an entirely different kind of language, with its own forms and signals and ways of producing meaning. Nevertheless, English grammars on the Latin model were

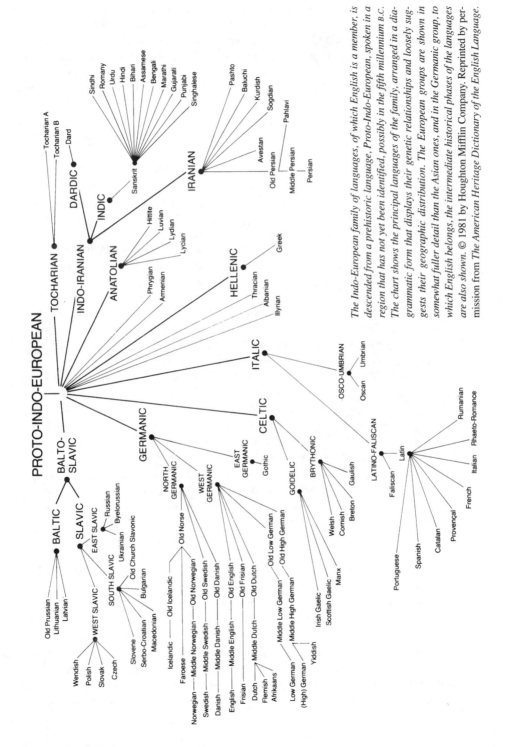

The Indo-European family of languages, of which English is a member, is descended from a prehistoric language, Proto-Indo-European, spoken in a region that has not yet been identified, possibly in the fifth millennium B.C. The chart shows the principal languages of the family, arranged in a diagrammatic form that displays their genetic relationships and loosely suggests their geographic distribution. The European groups are shown in somewhat fuller detail than the Asian ones, and in the Germanic group, to which English belongs, the intermediate historical phases of the languages are also shown. © 1981 by Houghton Mifflin Company. Reprinted by permission from The American Heritage Dictionary of the English Language.

worked out and taught in the schools. In many schools they are still being taught. This activity is not often popular with school children, but it is sometimes an interesting and instructive exercise in logic. The principal harm in it is that it has tended to keep people from being interested in English and has obscured the real features of English structure.

44   But probably the most important force in the development of English in the modern period has been the tremendous expansion of English-speaking peoples. In 1500 English was a minor language, spoken by a few people on a small island. Now it is perhaps the greatest language of the world, spoken natively by over a quarter of a billion people and as a second language by many millions more. When we speak of English now, we must specify whether we mean American English, British English, Australian English, Indian English, or what, since the differences are considerable. The American cannot go to England or the Englishman to America confident that he will always understand and be understood. The Alabaman in Iowa or the Iowan in Alabama shows himself a foreigner every time he speaks. It is only because communication has become fast and easy that English in this period of its expansion has not broken into a dozen mutually unintelligible languages.

Questions on Content

1. What is the significance of each of the following in the development of the English language?

Alfred the Great	William Caxton
Norman Conquest	English Renaissance
Great Vowel Shift	

2. What are the three major periods in the history of the English language? What does Roberts suggest were the major characteristics of the language during each period?

3. What does Roberts mean when he calls Old English a more inflected language than Modern English?

4. Are structure words more important in Old English or Modern English? Why?

5. What are some of the problems with the system of grammar that was imposed on the English language in the eighteenth century?

6. Why is the vocabulary of Modern English so different from that of Old English?

7. Why was the printing press so important to the development of English?

8. What audience does Roberts have in mind for this essay? Identify three paragraphs that clearly show this audience.

9. Where does Roberts state the thesis of his essay?

10. How does Roberts organize his material? Is this method effective? What other methods might he have used?

11. There are forty-four relatively short paragraphs in this selection. Obviously, Roberts has to be conscious of transitions. Discuss his use of transitions in one section of the essay.

Assignments

1. Choose a short passage of modern prose written for a general audience. Look up in a dictionary at least ten of the words in the passage. Do your findings substantiate some of the major points that Roberts makes about the development of English?

2. List five words that have recently become part of the English lexicon. (You might look in the field of technology to find such words or look for slang terms or foreign influences.)

3. Study some of the place names in your geographic area. What do they tell you about the language history of your region?

4. Roberts feels that "no understanding of the English language can be very satisfactory without a notion of the history of the language" (paragraph 1). Write an essay explaining why Roberts says this and why you agree or disagree.

5. Each family has its own language and/or dialect history. Look back two or three generations in your own family, and discuss the personal linguistic history of your ancestors (both immediate and distant).

Old World, New World

Bill Bryson

The United States, a nation of immigrants, enjoys a language that also has arrived here, piece by piece, from many places. In this delightfully detailed overview, Bill Bryson, an American journalist living in England, examines the process that turned the English of the Pilgrims into American English. He shows how many clamorous influences from around the world have created a variety of English uniquely American (and not always appreciated by the British).

■ **J O U R N A L   P R O M P T**   *One of the points Bryson makes in the following selection is that differences between American and British English were more significant fifty years ago than they are today. How can this be possible? What do you imagine when you think of British English?*

1 The first American pilgrims happened to live in the midst of perhaps the most exciting period in the history of the English language—a time when 12,000 words were being added to the language and revolutionary activities were taking place in almost every realm of human endeavor. It was also a time of considerable change in the structure of the language. The 104 pilgrims who sailed from Plymouth in 1620 were among the first generation of people to use the *s* form on verbs, saying *has* rather than *hath*, *runs* rather than *runneth*. Similarly, *thee* and *thou* pronoun forms were dying out. Had the pilgrims come a quarter of a century earlier, we might well have preserved those forms, as we preserved other archaisms such as *gotten*.

2 The new settlers in America obviously had to come up with new words to describe their New World, and this necessity naturally increased as they moved inland. Partly this was achieved by borrowing from others who inhabited or explored the untamed continent. From the Dutch we took *landscape*, *cookie*, and *caboose*. We may also have taken *Yankee*, as a corruption of the Dutch Jan Kees ("John Cheese"). The suggestion is that Jan Kees was a nonce name for a Dutchman in America, rather like John Bull for an Englishman, but the historical evidence is slight. Often the new immigrants borrowed Indian terms, though these could take some swallowing since the Indian languages, particularly those of the eastern part of the continent, were inordinately agglomerative. As Mary Helen Dohan notes in her excellent book on the rise of American English, *Our Own Words*, an early translator of the Bible into Iroquoian had to devise the word *kummogkodonattootummooetiteaonganunnonash* for the phrase "our question." In Massachusetts there was a lake that the Indians called Chargoggagomanchaugagochaubunagungamaug, which is said to translate as "You fish on that side, we'll fish on this side, and nobody will fish in the middle." Not surprisingly, such words were usually shortened and modified. The English-sounding *hickory* was whittled out of the Indian *pawcohiccora*. *Raugraoughcun* was hacked into *raccoon* and *isquonterquashes* into *squash*. *Hoochinoo*, the name of an Indian

tribe noted for its homemade liquor, produced *hooch*. Some idea of the bewilderments of Indian orthography are indicated by the fact that Chippewa and Ojibway are different names for the same tribe as interpreted by different people at different times. Sometimes words went through many transformations before they sat comfortably on the English-speaking tongue. *Manhattan* has been variously recorded as *Manhates, Manthanes, Manhatones, Manhatesen, Manhattae*, and at least half a dozen others. Even the simple word *Iowa*, according to Dohan, has been recorded with sixty-four spellings. Despite the difficulties of rendering them into English, Indian names were borrowed for the names of more than half our states and for countless thousands of rivers, lakes, and towns. Yet we borrowed no more than three or four dozen Indian words for everyday objects—among them *canoe, raccoon, hammock*, and *tobacco*.

3   From the early Spanish settlers, by contrast, we took more than 500 words—though many of these, it must be said, were Indian terms adopted by the Spaniards. Among them: *rodeo, bronco, buffalo, avocado, mustang, burro, fiesta, coyote, mesquite, canyon*, and *buckaroo. Buckaroo* was directly adapted from the Spanish *vaquero* (a cowboy) and thus must originally have been pronounced with the accent on the second syllable. Many borrowings are more accurately described as Mexican than Spanish since they did not exist in Spain, among them *stampede, hoosegow*, and *cafeteria. Hoosegow* and *jug* (for jail) were both taken from the Mexican-Spanish *juzgado*, which, despite the spelling, was pronounced more or less as "hoosegow." Sometimes it took a while for the pronunciation to catch up with the spelling. *Rancher*, a term borrowed from the Spanish *rancho*, was originally pronounced in the Mexican fashion, which made it something much closer to "ranker."

4   From the French, too, we borrowed liberally, taking the names for Indian tribes, territories, rivers, and other geographical features, sometimes preserving the pronunciation (Sioux, Mackinac) and sometimes not (Illinois, Detroit, Des Plaines, Beloit). We took other words from the French, but often knocked them about in a way that made them look distinctively American, as when we turned *gaufre* into *gopher* and *chaudière* into *chowder*. Other New World words borrowed from the French were *prairie* and *dime*.

5   Oftentimes words reach us by the most improbable and circuitous routes. The word for the American currency, *dollar*, is a corruption of *Joachimsthaler*, named for a sixteenth-century silver mine in Joachimsthal, Germany. The first recorded use of the word in English was in 1553, spelled *daler*, and for the next two centuries it was applied by the English to various continental currencies. Its first use in America was not recorded until 1782, when Thomas Jefferson, in *Notes on a Money Unit for the United States*, plumped for *dollar* as the name of the national currency on the ground that "the [Spanish] dollar is a known coin and the most familiar of all to the mind of the people." That may be its first recorded appearance, but clearly if it was known to the people the term had already been in use for some time. At all events, Jefferson had his way: In 1785 the dollar was adopted as America's currency, though it was not until 1794 that the first dollars rolled off the presses. That much we know, but what we don't know is where the dollar sign ($) comes from. "The most plausible account," according to Mario Pei, "is that it represents the first and last letters of

the Spanish pesos, written one over the other." It is an attractive theory but for the one obvious deficiency that the dollar sign doesn't look anything like a *p* superimposed on an *s*.

6   Perhaps even more improbable is how America came to be named in the first place. The name is taken from Americus Vespucius, a Latinized form of Amerigo Vespucci. A semiobscure Italian navigator who lived from 1454 to 1512, Vespucci made four voyages to the New World though without ever once seeing North America. A contemporary mapmaker wrongly thought Vespucci discovered the whole of the continent and, in the most literal way, put his name on the map. When he learned of his error, the mapmaker, one Martin Waldesmüller, took the name off, but by then it had stuck. Vespucci himself preferred the name Mundus Novus, "New World."

7   In addition to borrowing hundreds of words, the Mundus Novians (far better word!) devised many hundreds of their own. The pattern was to take two already existing English words and combine them in new ways: *bullfrog, eggplant, grasshopper, rattlesnake, mockingbird, catfish*. Sometimes, however, words from the Old World were employed to describe different but similar articles in the New. So *beech, walnut, laurel, partridge, robin, oriole, hemlock* and even *pond* (which in England is an artificial lake) all describe different things in the two continents.

8   Settlers moving west not only had to find new expressions to describe features of their new outsized continent—*mesa, butte, bluff*, and so on—but also outsized words that reflected their zestful, virile, wildcat-wrassling, hell-for-leather approach to life. These expressions were, to put it mildly, often colorful, and a surprising number of them have survived: *hornswoggle, cattywampus, rambunctious, absquatulate, to move like greased lightning, to kick the bucket, to be in cahoots with, to root hog or die*. Others have faded away: *monstracious, teetotaciously, helliferocious, conbobberation, obflisticate*, and many others of equal exuberance.

9   Of all the new words to issue from the New World, the quintessential Americanism without any doubt was *O.K.* Arguably America's single greatest gift to international discourse, *O.K.* is the most grammatically versatile of words, able to serve as an adjective ("Lunch was O.K."), verb ("Can you O.K. this for me?"), noun ("I need your O.K. on this"), interjection ("O.K., I hear you"), and adverb ("We did O.K."). It can carry shades of meaning that range from casual assent ("Shall we go?" "O.K."), to great enthusiasm ("O.K.!"), to lukewarm endorsement ("The party was O.K."), to a more or less meaningless filler of space ("O.K., may I have your attention please?").

10   It is a curious fact that the most successful and widespread of all English words, naturalized as an affirmation into almost every language in the world, from Serbo-Croatian to Tagalog, is one that has no correct agreed spelling (it can be O.K., OK, or okay) and one whose origins are so obscure that it has been a matter of heated dispute almost since it first appeared. The many theories break down into three main camps:

1. It comes from someone's or something's initials—a Sac Indian chief called Old Keokuk, or a shipping agent named Obadiah Kelly, or from President Martin Van Buren's nickname, Old Kinderhook, or from Orrins-Kendall crackers, which were popular in the nineteenth century. In each of these theories the

initials were stamped or scribbled on documents or crates and gradually came to be synonymous with quality or reliability.

2. It is adapted from some foreign or English dialect word or place name, such as the Finnish *oikea,* the Haitian *Aux Cayes* (the source of a particularly prized brand of rum), or the Choctaw *okeh*. President Woodrow Wilson apparently so liked the Choctaw theory that he insisted on spelling the word *okeh*.

3. It is a contraction of the expression "oll korrect," often said to be the spelling used by the semiliterate seventh President, Andrew Jackson.

11   This third theory, seemingly the most implausible, is in fact very possibly the correct one—though without involving Andrew Jackson and with a bit of theory one thrown in for good measure. According to Allen Walker Read of Columbia University, who spent years tracking down the derivation of O.K., a fashion developed among young wits of Boston and New York in 1838 of writing abbreviations based on intentional illiteracies. They thought it highly comical to write O.W. for "oll wright," O.K. for "oll korrect," K.Y. for "know yuse," and so on. O.K. first appeared in print on March 23, 1839, in the *Boston Morning Post*. Had that been it, the expression would no doubt have died an early death, but coincidentally in 1840 Martin Van Buren, known as Old Kinderhook from his hometown in upstate New York, was running for reelection as president, and an organization founded to help his campaign was given the name the Democratic O.K. Club. O.K. became a rallying cry throughout the campaign and with great haste established itself as a word throughout the country. This may have been small comfort to Van Buren, who lost the election to William Henry Harrison, who had the no-less-snappy slogan "Tippecanoe and Tyler Too."

12   Although the residents of the New World began perforce to use new words almost from the first day they stepped ashore, it isn't at all clear when they began pronouncing them in a distinctively American way. No one can say when the American accent first arose—or why it evolved quite as it did. As early as 1791, Dr. David Ramsay, one of the first American historians, noted in his *History of the American Revolution* that Americans had a particular purity of speech, which he attributed to the fact that people from all over Britain were thrown together in America where they "dropped the peculiarities of their several provincial idioms, retaining only what was fundamental and common to them all."

13   But that is not to suggest that they sounded very much like Americans of today. According to Robert Burchfield, George Washington probably sounded as British as Lord North. On the other hand, Lord North probably sounded more American than would any British minister today. North would, for instance, have given *necessary* its full value. He would have pronounced *path* and *bath* in the American way. He would have given *r*'s their full value in words like *cart* and *horse*. And he would have used many words that later fell out of use in England but were preserved in the New World.

14   The same would be true of the soldiers on the battlefield, who would, according to Burchfield, have spoken identically "except in minor particularities." [*The English Language*, page 36] Soldiers from both sides would have tended not to say *join* and

poison as we do today, but something closer to "jine" and "pison." *Speak* and *tea* would have sounded to modern ears more like "spake" and "tay," *certain* and *merchant* more like "sartin" and "marchant."

15   It has been said many times that hostility towards Britain at the end of the Revolutionary War was such that America seriously considered adopting another language. The story has been repeated many times, even by as eminent an authority as Professor Randolph Quirk of Oxford,* but it appears to be without foundation. Someone *may* have made such a proposal. At this remove we cannot be certain. But what we can say with confidence is that if such a proposal was made it appears not to have stimulated any widespread public debate, which would seem distinctly odd in a matter of such moment. We also know that the Founding Fathers were so little exercised by the question of an official language for the United States that they made not one mention of it in the Constitution. So it seems evident that such a proposal was not treated seriously, if indeed it ever existed.

16   What is certain is that many people, including both Thomas Jefferson and Noah Webster, expected American English to evolve into a separate language over time. Benjamin Franklin, casting an uneasy eye at the Germans in his native Pennsylvania, feared that America would fragment into a variety of speech communities. But neither of these things happened. It is worth looking at why they did not.

17   Until about 1840 America received no more than about 20,000 immigrants a year, mostly from two places: Africa in the form of slaves and the British Isles. Total immigration between 1607 and 1840 was no more than one million. Then suddenly, thanks to a famine in Ireland in 1845 and immense political upheaval elsewhere, America's immigration became a flood. In the second half of the nineteenth century, thirty million people poured into the country, and the pace quickened further in the early years of the twentieth century. In just four years at its peak, between 1901 and 1905, America absorbed a million Italians, a million Austro-Hungarians, and half a million Russians, plus tens of thousands of other people from scores of other places.

18   At the turn of the century, New York had more speakers of German than anywhere in the world except Vienna and Berlin, more Irish than anywhere but Dublin, more Russians than in Kiev, more Italians than in Milan or Naples. In 1890 the United States had 800 German newspapers and as late as the outbreak of World War I Baltimore alone had four elementary schools teaching in German only.

19   Often, naturally, these people settled in enclaves. John Russell Bartlett noted that it was possible to cross Oneida County, New York, and hear nothing but Welsh. Probably the most famous of these enclaves—certainly the most enduring—was that of the Amish who settled primarily in and around Lancaster County in southern Pennsylvania and spoke a dialect that came to be known, misleadingly, as Pennsylvania Dutch. (The name is a corruption of Deutsch, or German.) Some 300,000 people in America still use Pennsylvania Dutch as their first language, and perhaps twice as many more can speak it. The large number is accounted for no doubt by the extraordinary

---

* "At the time when the United States split off from Britain, for example, there were proposals that independence should be linguistically acknowledged by the use of a different language from that of Britain." [*The Use of English*, page 3]

insularity of most Amish, many of whom even now shun cars, tractors, electricity, and the other refinements of modern life. Pennsylvania Dutch is a kind of institutionalized broken English, arising from adapting English words to German syntax and idiom. Probably the best known of their expressions is "Outen the light" for put out the light. Among others:

Nice day, say not?	—Nice day, isn't it?
What's the matter of him?	—What's the matter with him?
It's going to give rain.	—It's going to rain.
Come in and eat yourself.	—Come and have something to eat.
It wonders me where it could be.	—I wonder where it could be.

20   Pennsylvania Dutch speakers also have a tendency to speak with semi-Germanic accents—saying "chorge" for *George*, "britches" for *bridges*, and "tolt" for *told*. Remarkably, many of them still have trouble, despite more than two centuries in America, with "v" and "th" sounds, saying "wisit" for *visit* and "ziss" for *this*. But two things should be borne in mind. First, Pennsylvania Dutch is an anomaly, nurtured by the extreme isolation from modern life of its speakers. And second, it is an *English* dialect. That is significant.

21   Throughout the last century, and often into this one, it was easy to find isolated speech communities throughout much of America: Norwegians in Minnesota and the Dakotas, Swedes in Nebraska, Germans in Wisconsin and Indiana, and many others. It was natural to suppose that the existence of these linguistic pockets would lead the United States to deteriorate into a variety of regional tongues, rather as in Europe, or at the very least result in widely divergent dialects of English, each heavily influenced by its prevailing immigrant group. But of course nothing of the sort happened. In fact, the very opposite was the case. Instead of becoming more divergent, people over the bulk of the American mainland continued to evince a more or less uniform speech. Why should that be?

22   There were three main reasons. First, the continuous movement of people back and forth across the continent militated against the formation of permanent regionalisms. Americans enjoyed social mobility long before sociologists thought up the term. Second, the intermingling of people from diverse backgrounds worked in favor of homogeneity. Third, and above all, social pressures and the desire for a common national identity encouraged people to settle on a single way of speaking.

23   People who didn't blend in risked being made to feel like outsiders. They were given names that denigrated their backgrounds: *wop* from the Italian *guappo* (a strutting fellow), *kraut* (from the supposed German fondness for sauerkraut), *yid* (for Yiddish speakers), *dago* from the Spanish *Diego*, *kike* (from the *-ki* and *-ky* endings on many Jewish names), *bohunk* from Bohemian-Hungarian, *micks* and *paddies* for the Irish. . . . The usual pattern was for the offspring of immigrants to become completely assimilated—to the point of being unable to speak their parents' language.

24   Occasionally physical isolation, as with the Cajuns in Louisiana or the Gullah speakers on the Sea Islands off the East Coast, enabled people to be more resistant

to change. It has often been said that if you want to hear what the speech of Elizabethan England sounded like, you should go to the hills of Appalachia or the Ozarks,
where you can find isolated communities of people still speaking the English of
Shakespeare. To be sure, many of the words and expressions that we think of today
as "hillbilly" words—*afeared, tetchy, consarn it, yourn* (for *yours*), *hisn* (for *his*), *et*
(for *ate*), *sassy* (for *saucy*), *jined* (for *joined*), and scores of others—do indeed reflect
the speech of Elizabethan London. But much the same claim could be made for the
modern-day speech of Boston or Charleston or indeed almost anywhere else. After
all, every person in American uses a great many expressions and pronunciations
familiar to Shakespeare but which have since died out in England—*gotten, fall* (for
the season), the short *a* of *bath* and *path*, and so on. The mountain regions may
possess a somewhat greater abundance of archaic expressions and pronunciations
because of their relative isolation, but to imply that the speech there is a near replica
of the speech of Elizabethan England is taking it too far. Apart from anything else,
most of the mountain areas weren't settled for a century or more after Elizabeth's
death. H. L. Mencken traced this belief to an early authority, one A. J. Ellis, and then
plunged the dagger in with the conclusion that "Ellis was densely ignorant of the history of the English settlements in America, and ascribed to them a cultural isolation
that never existed." Still, it is easy to find the belief, or something very like it,
repeated in many books.

25   It is certainly true to say that America in general preserved many dozens of words
that would otherwise almost certainly have been lost to English. The best noted, perhaps, is *gotten*, which to most Britons is the quaintest of Americanisms. It is now so
unused in Britain that many Britons have to have the distinction between *got* and
gotten explained to them—they use *got* for both—even though they make exactly the
same distinction with *forgot* and *forgotten*. *Gotten* also survives in England in one or
two phrases, notably "ill-gotten gains." *Sick* likewise underwent a profound change
of sense in Britain that was not carried over to America. Shakespeare uses it in
the modern American sense in *Henry V* ("He is very sick, and would to bed"), but
in Britain the word has come to take on the much more specific sense of being nau-
seated. Even so, the broader original sense survives in a large number of expressions
in Britain, such as *sick bay, sick note, in sickness and in health, to be off sick* (that
is, to stay at home from work or school because of illness), *sickbed, homesick*, and
lovesick. Conversely, the British often use *ill* where Americans would only use
injured, as in newspaper accounts describing the victim of a train crash as being
"seriously ill in hospital."

26   Other words and expressions that were common in Elizabethan England that died
in England were *fall* as a synonym for autumn, *mad* for angry, *progress* as a verb,
platter for a large dish, *assignment* in the sense of a job or task (it survived in
England only as a legal expression), *deck of cards* (the English now say pack), *slim*
in the sense of small (as in slim chance), *mean* in the sense of unpleasant instead of
stingy, *trash* for rubbish (used by Shakespeare), *hog* as a synonym for pig, *mayhem,
magnetic, chore, skillet, ragamuffin, homespun*, and the expression *I guess*. Many of
these words have reestablished themselves in England, so much so that most Britons
would be astonished to learn that they had ever fallen out of use there. *Maybe* was

described in the original *Oxford English Dictionary* in this century as "archaic and dialectal." *Quit* in the sense of resigning had similarly died out in Britain. To *leaf through* a book was first recorded in Britain in 1613, but then fell out of use there and was reintroduced from America, as was *frame-up*, which the *Oxford English Dictionary* in 1901 termed obsolete, little realizing that it would soon be reintroduced to its native land in a thousand gangster movies.

27   America also introduced many words and expressions that never existed in Britain but which have for the most part settled comfortably into domestic life there. Among these words and phrases are—and this really is a bare sampling—*commuter, bedrock, snag, striptease, cold spell, gimmick, baby-sitter, lengthy, sag, soggy, teenager, telephone, typewriter, radio, to cut no ice, to butt in, to side-track, hangover, to make good* (to be successful), *fudge, publicity, joyride, bucket shop, blizzard, stunt, law-abiding, department store, notify, advocate* (as a verb), *currency* (for money), *to park, to rattle* (in the sense of to unnerve or unsettle), *hindsight, beeline, raincoat, scrawny, take a backseat, cloudburst, graveyard, know-how, to register* (as in a hotel), *to shut down, to fill the bill, to hold down* (as in keep), *to hold up* (as in rob), *to bank on, to stay put, to be stung* (cheated), and even *stiff upper lip.* In a rather more roundabout way, so to speak, the word *roundabout,* their term for traffic circles, is of American origin. More precisely, it was a term invented by Logan Pearsall Smith, an American living in England, who was one of the members in the 1920s of the BBC Advisory Committee on Spoken English. This lofty panel had the job of deciding questions of pronunciation, usage, and even vocabulary for the BBC. Before Smith came along, traffic circles in Britain were called gyratory circuses.*

28   Of course, the traffic has not been entirely one way. Apart from the several thousand words that the British endowed Americans with in the first place, they have since the colonial exodus also given the world *smog, weekend, gadget, miniskirt, radar, brain drain,* and *gay* in the sense of homosexual. Even so, there is no denying that the great bulk of words introduced into the English language over the last two centuries has traveled from west to east. And precious little thanks we get. Almost from the beginning of the colonial experience it has been a common assumption in Britain that a word or turn of phrase is inferior simply by dint of its being American-bred. In dismissing the "vile and barbarous word *talented*," Samuel Taylor Coleridge observed that "most of these pieces of slang come from America." That clearly was ground enough to detest them. In point of fact, I am very pleased to tell you, *talented* was a British coinage, first used in 1422. Something of the spirit of the age was captured in Samuel Johnson's observation in 1769 that Americans were "a race of convicts and ought to be thankful for any thing we allow them short of hanging." [Quoted by Pyles, in *Words and Ways of American English*, page 106] A reviewer of Thomas Jefferson's *Notes on the State of Virginia* (1787) entreated Jefferson to say what he would about the British character, but "O spare, we beseech you, our mother-tongue." Another, noting his use of the word *belittle,* remarked: "It may be an elegant [word] in Virginia, and even perfectly intelligible; but for our part

---

* Smith also wanted traffic lights to be called stop-and-goes and brainwave to be replaced by mindfall, among many other equally fanciful neologisms, but these never caught on.

all we can do is to guess at its meaning. For shame, Mr. Jefferson!" [Quoted by Pyles, *Words and Ways of American English*, page 17] Jefferson also coined the word *Anglophobia*; little wonder.

29   As often as not, these sneerers showed themselves to be not only gratuitously offensive but also etymologically underinformed because the objects of their animus were invariably British in origin. Johnson disparaged *glee, jeopardy*, and *smolder*, little realizing that they had existed in England for centuries. *To antagonize*, coined by John Quincy Adams, was strenuously attacked. So was *progress* as a verb, even though it had been used by both Bacon and Shakespeare. *Scientist* was called "an ignoble Americanism" and "a cheap and vulgar product of trans-Atlantic slang."

30   Americans, alas, were often somewhat sniveling cohorts in this caviling—perhaps most surprisingly Benjamin Franklin. When the Scottish philosopher David Hume criticized some of his Americanisms, Franklin meekly replied: "I thank you for your friendly admonition relating to some unusual words in the pamphlet. It will be of service to me. The *pejorate* and the *colonize* . . . I give up as bad; for certainly in writings intended for persuasion and for general information, one cannot be too clear; and every expression in the least obscure is a fault; The *unshakable* too, tho clear, I give up as rather low. The introducing new words, where we are already possessed of old ones sufficiently expressive, I confess must be generally wrong. . . . I hope with you, that we shall always in America make the best English of this island our standard, and I believe it will be so." And yet he went right on introducing words: *eventuate, demoralize, constitutionality*. This servility persisted for a long time among some people. William Cullen Bryant, the editor of the New York *Evening Post* and one of the leading journalists of the nineteenth century in America, refused to allow such useful words as *lengthy* and *presidential* into his paper simply because they had been dismissed as Americanisms a century earlier. Jefferson, more heroically, lamented the British tendency to raise "a hue and cry at every word he [Samuel Johnson] has not licensed."

31   The position has little improved with time. To this day you can find authorities in Britain attacking such vile "Americanisms" as *maximize, minimize*, and *input*, quite unaware that the first two were coined by Jeremy Bentham more than a century ago and the last appeared more than 600 years ago in Wycliffe's translation of the Bible. *Loan* as a verb (rather than *lend*) is often criticized as an Americanism, when in fact it was first used in England a full eight centuries ago. The stylebook of the *Times* of London sniffily instructs its staff members that "normalcy should be left to the Americans who coined it. *The English* [italics mine] is normality." In point of fact *normalcy* is a British coinage. As Baugh and Cable put it, "The English attitude toward Americanisms is still quite frankly hostile."

32   Indeed, it occasionally touches new peaks of smugness. In 1930, a Conservative member of Parliament, calling for a quota on the number of American films allowed into Britain, said: "The words and accent are perfectly disgusting, and there can be no doubt that such films are an evil influence on our language." [Quoted by Norman Moss in *What's the Difference*, page 12] More recently, during a debate in the House of Lords in 1978 one of the members said: "If there is a more hideous language on the face of the earth than the American form of English, I should like to know what

is." (We should perhaps bear in mind that the House of Lords is a largely powerless, nonelective institution. It is an arresting fact of British political life that a Briton can enjoy a national platform and exalted status simply because he is the residue of an illicit coupling 300 years before between a monarch and an orange seller.)

33   Even when they have not been actively hostile, the British have often struck an aloof, not to say fantastical, attitude to the adoption of American words. In *The King's English* (1931), the Fowler brothers, usually paragons of common sense in matters linguistic, take the curious and decidedly patronizing view that although there is nothing wrong with American English, and that it is even capable of evincing occasional flashes of genius, it is nonetheless a foreign tongue and should be treated as such. "The English and the American language and literature are both good things; but they are better apart than mixed." They particularly cautioned against using three vulgar Americanisms: *placate, transpire*, and *antagonize*.

34   Putting aside the consideration that without America's contribution English today would enjoy a global importance about on a par with Portuguese, it is not too much to say that this attitude is unworthy of the British. It is at any rate an arresting irony that the more dismissive they grow of American usages, the more lavishly they borrow them—to the extent of taking phrases that have no literal meaning in British English. People in Britain talk about doing something on a shoestring even though the word there is *shoelace*. They talk about the 64,000-dollar question, looking like a million bucks, having a megabucks salary, stepping on the gas (when they fuel their cars with petrol), and taking a raincheck even though probably not one Briton in a hundred knows what a raincheck is. They have even quietly modified their grammar and idiom to fit the American model. Ernest Gowers, in the revised edition of *A Dictionary of Modern English Usage*, noted that under the influence of American usage the British had begun to change *aim at doing* into *aim to do, haven't got* to *don't have*, begun using *in* instead of *for* in phrases like "the first time in years," and started for the first time using *begin to* with a negative, as in "This doesn't begin to make sense." And these changes go on. Just in the last decade or so, *truck* has begun driving out *lorry. Airplane* is more and more replacing *aeroplane*. The American sense of billion (1,000,000,000) has almost completely routed the British sense (1,000,000,000,000).

35   American spelling, too, has had more influence on the British than they might think. *Jail* instead of *gaol, burden* rather than *burthen, clue* rather than *clew, wagon* rather than *waggon, today* and *tomorrow* rather than *to-day* and *to-morrow, mask* rather than *masque, reflection* rather than *reflexion*, and *forever* and *onto* as single words rather than two have all been nudged on their way towards acceptance by American influence. For most senses of the word *program*, the British still use *programme*, but when the context is of computers they write *program*. A similar distinction is increasingly made with *disc* (the usual British spelling) and *disk* for the thing you slot into your home computer.

36   Although the English kept the *u* in many words like *humour, honour*, and *colour*, they gave it up in several, such as *terrour, horrour*, and *governour*, helped at least in part by the influence of American books and journals. Confusingly, they retained it in some forms but abandoned it in others, so that in England you write *honour* and

honourable but *honorary* and *honorarium; colour* and *colouring* but *coloration; humour* but *humorist; labour* and *labourer* but *laborious.* There is no logic to it, and no telling why some words gave up the *u* and others didn't. For a time it was fashionable to drop the *u* from honor and humor—Coleridge for one did it—but it didn't catch on.

37   People don't often appreciate just how much movies and television have smoothed the differences between British and American English, but half a century ago the gap was very much wider. In 1922, when Sinclair Lewis's novel *Babbitt* was published in Britain it contained a glossary. Words that are commonplace in Britain now were quite unknown until the advent of talking pictures—among them *grape-vine, fan* (in the sense of a sports enthusiast), *gimmick* and *phoney.* As late as 1955, a writer in the *Spectator* could misapprehend the expression *turn of the century,* and take it to mean midcentury, when the first half turns into the second. In 1939, the preface to *An Anglo-American Interpreter* suggested that "an American, if taken suddenly ill while on a visit to London, might die in the street through being unable to make himself understood." [Quoted in *Our Language,* page 169] That may be arrant hyperbole, designed to boost sales, but it is probably true that the period up to the Second World War marked the age of the greatest divergence between the two main branches of English.

38   Even now, there remains great scope for confusion, as evidenced by the true story of an American lady, newly arrived in London, who opened her front door to find three burly men on the steps informing her that they were her dustmen. "Oh," she blurted, "but I do my own dusting." It can take years for an American to master the intricacies of British idiom, and vice versa. In Britain *homely* is a flattering expression (equivalent to *homey*); in America it means "ugly." In Britain *upstairs* is the first floor; in America it is the second. . . . *Presently* means "now" in America; in Britain it means "in a little while." Sometimes these can cause considerable embarrassment, most famously with the British expression "I'll knock you up in the morning," which means "I'll knock on your door in the morning." *To keep your pecker up* is an innocuous expression in Britain (even though, curiously, *pecker* has the same slang meaning there), but *to be stuffed* is distinctly rude, so that if you say at a dinner party, "I couldn't eat another thing; I'm stuffed," an embarrassing silence will fall over the table. (You may recognize the voice of experience in this.) Such too will be your fate if you innocently refer to someone's fanny; in England it means a woman's pudenda.

39   Other terms are less graphic, but no less confusing. English people bathe wounds but not their babies; they *bath* their babies. Whereas an American wishing to get clean would bathe in a bathtub, an English person would bath in a bath. English people do bathe, but what they mean by that is to go for a swim in the sea. Unless, of course, the water is too cold (as it always is in Britain) in which case they stand in water up to their knees. This is called having a paddle, even though their hands may never touch the water.

40   Sometimes these differences in meaning take on a kind of bewildering circularity. A tramp in Britain is a bum in America, while a bum in Britain is a fanny in America, while a fanny in Britain is—well, we've covered that. To a foreigner it must seem sometimes as if we are being intentionally contrary. Consider that in Britain the Royal

Mail delivers the post, not the mail, while in America the Postal Service delivers the mail, not the post. These ambiguities can affect scientists as much as tourists. The British billion, as we have already seen, has surrendered to the American billion, but for other numbers agreement has yet to be reached. A decillion in America is a one plus thirty-three zeros. In Britain it is a one plus sixty zeros. Needless to say, that can make a difference.

41   In common speech, some 4,000 words are used differently in one country from the other. That's a very large number indeed. Some are well known on both sides of the Atlantic—*lift/elevator, dustbin/garbage can, biscuit/cookie*—but many hundreds of others are still liable to befuddle the hapless traveler. Try covering up the right-hand column below and seeing how many of the British terms in the left-hand column you can identify. If you get more than half you either know the country well or have been reading too many English murder mysteries.

British	*American*
cot	baby's crib
cotton (for sewing)	thread
courgette	zucchini
to skive	to loaf
candy floss	cotton candy
full stop (punctuation)	period
inverted commas	quotation marks
berk	idiot, boor
joiner	skilled carpenter
knackered	worn out
numbered plate	license plate
Old Bill	policeman
scarper	run away
to chivvy	to hurry along
subway	pedestrian underpass
pantechnicon	furniture removal truck
flyover	vehicle overpass
leading article	newspaper editorial
fruit machine	one-armed bandit
smalls	ladies' underwear
coach	long-distance bus
spiv	petty thief
to grizzle	to whine
to hump	to carry a heavy load

Questions on Content

1. Explain the origins of the following Americanisms:

buckaroo	kike
chowder	kraut
gopher	mick
hickory	Pennsylvania Dutch
hooch	wop
hornswoggle	Yankee

2. Explain the different meanings of *sick* in America and in England.

3. How might American English be different if the Pilgrims had arrived twenty-five years earlier?

4. What was the first recorded use of the word *dollar*? When was it first used in America? How does linguist Mario Pei explain where the dollar sign ($) came from?

5. Explain how America might well have been named Mundus Novus.

6. Bryson suggests that the eighteenth-century English noble Lord North probably sounded more American than does any British noble today. Why?

7. Benjamin Franklin feared that America could become fragmented into a variety of speech communities. Explain Franklin's concern.

8. Why did Jefferson coin the word *Anglophobia*?

Questions on Structure and Style

9. Bryson uses the second person plural *we* frequently in this selection. Why does he make this unusual choice of pronoun? What effect does the choice have on the tone of the selection?

10. Which paragraph contains what you consider to be the thesis of this selection?

11. The use of "by contrast" in the first sentence of paragraph 3 is one of many examples of effective paragraph transitions. Discuss the many types of transitions Bryson employs.

12. Why does the author devote so much space to the origin of
    O.K.?

13. Paragraph 32 contains one of many examples of parenthetic
    remarks. Find other examples, and discuss their purpose
    and effectiveness.

14. Although scholarly and serious in its message, Bryson's
    essay is not without humor. Find examples of his use of
    humor.

Assignments

1. *The Dictionary of American English* and *The Dictionary of
   Americanisms* are full of words that are uniquely American.
   Use one of these dictionaries to locate the origins of the fol-
   lowing terms:

blue laws	dicker
carpet bagger	dude
clambake	ranch
conniption	sidewinder

   Browse in a dictionary to find ten other examples of Americanisms that reveal our special history, culture, prejudices,
   and values.

2. Write a summary of Bryson's account of the origin of *O.K.*

3. Outline "Old World, New World" by topic, and discuss
   Bryson's organizational strategy. Is it, for example, strictly
   chronological?

Yadda, Yadda, Yadda

Leslie Savan

Popular entertainment, which seldom draws praise for its originality, here faces another charge. As essayist Leslie Savan illustrates with abundant examples, today's popular movies and television shows generate clichés that have "a faintly combative edge," thereby setting themselves apart from yesterday's Hollywood-inspired substitutes for wit, which seemed equally dreary but benign in comparison. Moreover, today's "media-marinated catchphrases" encourage not thinking at all.

■ **J O U R N A L   P R O M P T** *Compile a list of "trendy" phrases that have been made popular by television characters. Examples of such phrases might be "I love you, man," "What part of* no *don't you understand?" and "I don't* think *so." In the selection that follows, Savan objects to such phrases. Write a paragraph or two in which you anticipate her objections.*

1   During the fall [1996] campaign, Bob Dole said on TV that General Motors has been replaced as the nation's largest employer by a temp agency, and he asked, "That's a good economy? I don't *think* so." You don't have to be running for President to be fond of tossing off that pat rejoinder. The police in Madison, Wisconsin, for example, reported that when they ordered a young scofflaw to approach their squad car, he replied, "I don't *think* so," and tried to run. (The cops caught him by his fanny pack.)

2   If pols and petty criminals use the same buzzphrases these days, they probably get them from TV, like everyone else. One week on *Friends,* when David Schwimmer's all-thumbs buddies offered to baby-sit his infant son, he said, "I don't *think* so"; an hour later, Jerry Seinfeld told an unctuous magician who asked to borrow him for a trick, "I don't *think* so."

3   *Oh, pulleeze. Don't even think about telling me. I hate when that happens. Get over it. These phrases from hell are history. I'll be their worst nightmare. Yeah, right. As if. Hel-lo-oh!*

4   Every day, Americans are belting out more of these ready-made, media-marinated catchphrases, usually of the in-your-face (to use another) variety. Conversations, movies, E-mail, ads, lovers' quarrels, punditry and stand-up comedy can barely be conducted without resort to an annoyingly popular riposte. A random gleaning, from just one *Cybill* episode on CBS, produced: *Hel-lo-oh!; Oh, pulleeze; Get a life; Yadda yadda; Yesss!* and *Haven't we had enough fun yet?*

5   These pop phrases are not just clichés. They're more like a bad case of television-ary Tourette's—snappy, canned punch lines that bring the rhythms of sitcom patter into everyday experience. Whether originating from Valley Girls, drag queens or CEOs, these phrases, once they're disseminated by the media, become part of our

shared response to the little frustrations of modern life. More and more, that response tends to be a dismissive pique, as these buzzbarbs—expressed with just the right inflections—verbally roll up the window on any nuisance that might come tapping at the tinted glass.

6   TV and movies have catapulted catchphrases before—*Get Smart* launched *Would you believe . . . ?* and *Sorry about that* into nationwide use in the 1970s—but this newer slang is different. It is supposed to confer upon its users an edge, sometimes a comedic but always a faintly combative edge. The era of *Saturday Night Live* that dished out Dennis Miller's "I'm outta here" and Dana Carvey's "Isn't that special?" fed a hunger for a renewable supply of ironic put-downs. But what may have started as a boomer/Xer shtick has now become a reflex common to all ages, from Bob Dole to Macaulay Culkin (who gave *I don't think so* its big push by uttering it twice in the top box-office hit of 1990, *Home Alone*). The militia code name for a possible counter-attack on the feds? "Project Worst Nightmare." The would-be zinger in the G.O.P.'s last-minute ads warning against Democratic control of both Congress and the White House? "Been there, done that."

7   A whole nation barking Hollywood retorts—creepy but all too useful. In the daily battlefield of misunderstandings and impatient busyness, such locutions as *Don't go there, In your dreams* and *What part of no don't you understand?* are Nerf-like weaponry: When you're blind with anger or exasperation, you grab the nearest item of modular meanness. Of course, not all coolster coinages are overtly fightin' words. Indeed, some affect affectlessness: *Same old, same old; Blah blah blah; Yadda yadda yadda.* But given the right nuances, indifference can pack a wallop: *Yadda* will out-snide *blah,* for instance but wither before the passive-aggressive champ (and Bob Dole favorite), *Whatever.*

8   Even if these phrases were the nastiest bomb mots on earth, who'd want a civilization without frequent hits of wicked wit? The real reason modular meanness grates isn't the meanness—it's the modularness.

9   Whether biting or benign, what these supposedly trenchant comebacks have in common is the roar of a phantom crowd; they always speak of other people having spoken them. It's as if they come with a built-in laugh track. And keeping us on track, they provoke in us click responses, the sort of electronic-entertainment reaction we twitch and jerk to more often lately. We hear *Not even close, He's history* or *What's wrong with this picture?*, and we immediately sense the power structure of the moment. In fact, we may subconsciously applaud such speakers because they've hypertexted our little lives right into *Friends, Seinfeld* or the "I love you, man" ads, and for a moment, at least, we know perfectly how to relate to people, deal with conflict and banish discomfort. Not being in control—that's our real worst nightmare.

10   Think about it. For all the references to thinking—*I don't* think *so, no-brainer, clueless,* all the brain surgeons and rocket scientists you don't have to be, and the injunction on some New York City street signs, "Don't even think of parking here"—isn't the real message of these phrases simply, Don't even think?

11   Duh.

Questions on Content

1. In this selection Savan responds to pop phrases that we pick up from the media. She refers to such phrases as "Isn't that special" and "Get a life" as modular meanness (paragraph 8). Explain what modular meanness is and why what grates "isn't the meanness—it's the modularness."

2. Explain the significance of the title, "Yadda, Yadda, Yadda." Is it appropriate?

3. Savan describes media-induced pop phrases as "Nerf-like weaponry" (paragraph 7). Explain.

4. The author suggests that we use such pop phrases as "I don't *think* so" and "I love you, man" to alleviate our worst nightmare—not being in control. Explain what she means.

Questions on Structure and Style

5. Describe Savan's attitude toward pop phrases. At what point does the reader first learn of this attitude? How does she sustain it?

6. Discuss the effectiveness of the closing paragraphs.

Assignments

1. Identify a social fad. (Trends in fashion, diet, or automobiles are likely examples.) Write an essay in which you reveal your attitude toward the trend. Make a conscious effort to imitate Savan's techniques.

2. Write a letter to Leslie Savan in which you argue that in her essay she is too harsh in her judgment of television and the effect it has on our language habits. Point out ways that television enhances language development and correctness. Be specific.

The Story of Writing

C. M. Millward

As student writers discover, something we say aloud may serve poorly or not at all if simply transcribed onto paper. Spoken and written language are different partly because they were invented to serve different purposes. In the following excerpt from her book *The Biography of the English Language*, language scholar and teacher C. M. Millward explains why writing was invented and how writing systems evolve. As she explains in prose notable for its clarity and voice, "Civilization as we know it depends on the written word," even though written words once seemed more like magic than like language.

■ **J O U R N A L P R O M P T** *Frequently, things we say aloud lose their meaning when we write them on paper. Think about the primary functions of oral and written language. How do they differ, and how do they complement one another?*

To be a well-favoured man is the gift of fortune; but to write and read comes by nature.
William Shakespeare

1   Speech is of course primary to language. People were speaking for hundreds of thousands—perhaps millions—of years before writing was invented. Human beings speak before they learn to read and write; even today, many people never learn to read and write, and there are still languages with no writing systems. People learn how to speak without formal training, but most have to be taught how to read and write. Further, all forms of writing are ultimately based on spoken language. In other words, writing is a derivative of speech; it is a secondary form of language. Speech is, quite properly, the focus of most linguistic study.

2   Nonetheless, we should not underestimate the importance of writing. Civilization as we know it depends on the written word. We study speech by means of writing and we use writing to represent the phonetics of speech. Most of our information about language, and certainly all of our information about the history of languages, is in writing.

3   Writing has become so important that, for the educated person, it can become almost totally independent of speech. Most of us know many words that we can read, understand, and even write but that we would hesitate to try to pronounce. For example, I think of the word *gneiss*. I know that it is a kind of rock, that it is usually metamorphic in origin, and that (to my untrained eye) it looks somewhat like granite. Yet I do not normally speak this word and I have to refer to a dictionary—another written source—to discover that *gneiss* is pronounced /nɑis/ and not /nis/ or /gnɑis/ or /nɪs/. We also use words and grammatical constructions in writing that we rarely if ever spontaneously produce in speech. Who uses the subordinating conjunction *lest* in a casual conversation? What does a paragraph sound like? Many people read and

sometimes even write fluently in languages that they cannot speak. Skilled readers take in and mentally process written texts at a rate so rapid that the words cannot possibly have been silently articulated and "listened to"; clearly, for such readers, writing has become a form of language virtually independent of speech. Finally, there is even physiological evidence that writing is more than simply a secondary form of speech: Some brain-damaged people are competent in reading and writing but are unable to speak or understand speech.

The Effects of Writing on Speech

4   Writing has numerous effects on the spoken language, and the more literate a culture is, the greater these effects are. Because of the prestige, the conservatism, and the permanency of writing, it tends to act as a brake on changes in the spoken language. Conversely, writing tends to spread changes from one area or group of speakers to another; this is especially true of vocabulary items. Most of us can recall new words that we first encountered in a written text and only later—or perhaps never—heard spoken. Writing also preserves archaisms that have been lost in the spoken language and sometimes even revives words that have become obsolete in the spoken language. For example, Edmund Spenser probably reintroduced *rampant* in the meaning of "fierce" through his writings; the OED's last citation in this meaning prior to Spenser is nearly two hundred years earlier.

5   Writing and literacy give rise to spelling pronunciations, that is, the pronunciation of words as they are spelled. These may take the form of the reinsertion of lost sounds or the insertion of unhistorical sounds. Many people today pronounce the word *often* as [oftən], even though the [t] dropped out of the spoken language centuries ago, and even though they do not pronounce a [t] in such parallel words as *soften* or *listen*. Similarly, because English readers associate the letter sequence ⟨th⟩* with the sounds [θ] and [ð], words spelled with that sequence that historically were pronounced with [t] have come to be pronounced with [θ]. Examples include the given names *Katherine* and *Arthur* (compare the short forms *Art* and *Kate* that retain the [t]). The river *Thames* is pronounced [tɛmz] in Britain, but [θemz] in Connecticut because the influence of the spelling proved stronger than earlier oral tradition.

6   Conventional spellings for vocal gestures involving noises outside the English phonemic system may also lead to a literal pronunciation. Examples include the vocal gesture for disapproval or commiseration, an alveolar click. Because this sound is written *tsk-tsk*, it is occasionally pronounced [tɪsk tɪsk]. Even more familiar are the pronunciations [bər:] for ⟨brrr⟩, a spelling originally intended to represent a voiced bilabial trill, and [i:k] for *eek*, a spelling intended to represent a high-pitched scream.

7   Literacy and our alphabet so permeate our culture that even our vocabulary is affected. The widespread use of acronyms presupposes speakers who are familiar with the letters with which words begin. We even use letter shapes as analogies to

---

* When it is necessary to distinguish graphemic forms from phonological representations, angled brackets (⟨⟩) are used for the graphemes.

describe objects: The words *T square, U-turn, ell* (as a wing of a building), *S-curve,* and *V-neck* are all derived from the names of alphabetic characters.

8   In sum, writing has been such an integral part of English for the past thirteen hundred years or so that it is impossible to imagine what the spoken language would be like today if English had never been committed to writing. Indeed, without writing, English probably would have split up into numerous mutually unintelligible dialects long ago.

Why Was Writing Invented?

9   Efficient as speech is, it is severely limited in both time and space. Once an utterance has been made, it is gone forever, and the preservation of its contents is dependent on human memory. Writing is as permanent as the materials used in producing it; readers can return to a written record as often as or after as long a period of time as they like. Further, speech is much more limited in space than is writing. Until the recent developments of electronic media—all of which require supplementary apparatus in the form of transmitters and receivers—speech was spatially limited to the range of the unamplified human voice. Writing can be done on portable materials and carried wherever people can go.

A POOR DEVIL

Slips of the tongue and pen have always been a part of natural language, but perhaps only medieval monks would invent a patron demon for them. Titivillus, as he was named, collected fragments of mispronounced, mumbled, or skipped words in the divine services. He put them all into a sack and carried them to his master in hell, where they were registered against the offender.

Later Titivillus' jurisdiction was extended to orthographic and printing errors. He never lacked for material to put in his sack. For instance, when Pope Sixtus V (1585–1590) authorized the printing of a new edition of the Vulgate Bible, he decided to insure against printing errors by automatically excommunicating ahead of time any printer who altered the text in any way. Furthermore, he himself proofread every page as it came off the press. Nonetheless, the final text was so full of errors that the Pope finally had to recall every copy for destruction.

Titivillus was well enough known, both in England and on the Continent, to appear as a character in medieval mystery plays and other literature. Hence his introduction in *Myroure of Oure Ladye*, an anonymous fifteenth-century devotional treatise:

I am a poure dyuel, and my name ys Tytyuyllus . . . I muste eche day . . . brynge my master a thousande pokes full of faylynges, and of neglygences in syllables and wordes.

Myroure of Oure Ladye I.xx.54

10   Although it would perhaps be esthetically comforting to think that the first writing systems were created to preserve literary works, all the evidence indicates that the first true writing was used for far more mundane purposes. Although "creative" literature arose long before the invention of writing, it was orally transmitted, with devices such as alliteration, repetition, and regular meter being used as aids to memory. Writing was invented for the same practical purpose to which, in terms of sheer bulk, most writing today is dedicated, commercial recordkeeping—the number of lambs born in a season, the number of pots of oil shipped to a customer, the wages paid to laborers. A second important early use of writing was to preserve the exact wording of sacred texts that would otherwise be corrupted by imperfect memories and changes in the spoken language. For most of the history of writing, literacy has been restricted to a small elite of bookkeepers and priests; often, the two occupations were combined in one scribe. To the illiterate, writing would have seemed a form of magic, an impression that was not discouraged by those who understood its mysteries.

Types of Writing Systems

11   If we can judge by the delight a child takes in its own footprints or scribbles made with any implement on any surface, human beings have always been fascinated by drawing. The urge to create pictures is revealed by the primitive drawings—early forms of graffiti—found in caves and on rocks all over the world. But pictures as such are not writing, although it is not always easy to distinguish pictures from writing. If we define writing as human communication by means of a system of conventional visible marks,* then, in many cases, we do not know whether the marks are systematic because we do not have a large enough sample. Nor do we know if the marks were intended to communicate a message. For example, Figure 1 is an American Indian **petroglyph** (a drawing or carving on rock) from Cottonwood Canyon, Utah.

Figure 1. American Indian Petroglyph†

---

* The definition is adapted from I. J. Gelb, A *Study of Writing*, rev. ed. (Chicago: University of Chicago Press, 1963), p. 12.

† Drawing adapted from Roland Siegrist, ed., *Prehistoric Petroglyphs and Pictographs in Utah* (Salt Lake City: Utah State Historical Society, 1972), p. 62. Reproduced with permission of the Utah State Historical Society.

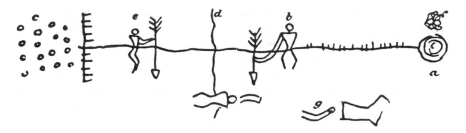

Figure 2. American Indian Picture Story

Conceivably, the dotted lines, wavy lines, spiral, and semicircle had some conventional meaning that could be interpreted by a viewer familiar with the conventions. If so, the petroglyph might be called prewriting, but not actual writing.

Pictographs and Ideograms

12   More clearly related to writing are the picture stories of American Indians. Like the modern cartoon strip without words, these **pictographs** communicate a message. Further, they often include conventional symbols. Figure 2 is from a birch-bark record made by Shahâsh'king (b), the leader of a group of Mîlle Lacs Ojibwas (a) who undertook a military expedition against Shákopi (e). Shákopi's camp of Sioux (c) was on the St. Peter's River (d). The Ojibwas under Shahâsh'king lost one man (f) at the St. Peter's River, and they got only one arm of an Indian (g).*

13   Although such pictographs do communicate a message, they are not a direct sequential representation of speech. They may include **ideographic** symbols, symbols that represent ideas or concepts but do not stand for specific sounds, syllables, or words. In Figure 2, the drawing at (f) means that the Ojibwas lost one man, but it does not represent a unique series of sounds or words. It could be translated as "We lost one man" or "The Sioux killed a warrior" or "Little Fox died on this expedition" or "One man fell by the river." To take a more familiar example, the picture ☞ is an **ideogram**; it does not represent a sequence of sounds, but rather a concept that can be expressed in English in various ways: "go that way" or "in this direction" or "over there" or, combined with words or other ideograms, such notions as "the stairs are to the right" or "pick up your luggage at that place." Ideograms are not necessarily pictures of objects; the arithmetic "minus sign" is an ideogram that depicts not an object, but a concept that can be translated as "minus" or "subtract the following from the preceding" or "negative."

Logograms

14   Ideograms are not writing, but they are the ancestors of writing. If a particular ideogram is always translated by the same spoken word, it can come to stand for that word and that word alone. At this point, **logograms**, or symbols representing a single

---

* Adapted from Garrick Mallery, "Picture-Writing of the American Indians," in *Tenth Annual Report of the Bureau of Ethnology* (Washington, D.C.: Government Printing Office, 1893), pp. 559–60.

word, have been invented, and true writing has begun. Indeed, an entire writing system may be based on the logographic principle. This is the case with Chinese, in which each character stands for a word or part of a compound word. In their purest forms, logographic symbols have no relationship to individual sounds, but only to entire words. For example, the Chinese character 吊 stands for a verb meaning "to hang, to suspend"; it is pronounced roughly as [diɑu] in Standard Chinese, but no particular part of the character represents [d] or [i] or [ɑ] or [u]. By itself, the top part of the character, 口, is pronounced [kou], and the bottom part, 巾, is pronounced [ĭin]. The character 钓 is pronounced in exactly the same way as 吊, but 钓 means "to fish with a hook and line." Like all writing systems actually used for natural languages, Chinese is less than totally pure; many characters contain both ideographic and phonetic components. Still, the Chinese system is basically logographic in that each character stands for an entire word or morpheme, and one cannot determine the pronunciation of an unfamiliar character from its components.

15   The distinction between ideograms and logograms is somewhat arbitrary. If, within a given language, a symbol is always interpreted as representing one word and one word alone, it is a logogram for that language. However, if it has the same meaning but is represented by different words in other languages, it is, strictly speaking, an ideogram. An example would be the symbol &, which stands only for the word *and* in English, but for *agus* in Irish, *et* in French, *och* in Swedish, *u* in Russian, *na* in Swahili, and so forth. It is a logogram within a given language, but an ideogram across languages.

Syllabaries

16   Logographic systems are inefficient for most languages because, if every single word in the language is to be represented by a different symbol, an astronomical number of complex symbols is required. Therefore, while the writing is still at the ideographic-logographic stage, scribes may begin to use symbols to represent sounds instead of concepts. They probably begin by punning on existing logograms. For example, assume that English used the logogram ◁●▷ to stand for the word *eye*. Noting that, in speech, the word *eye* sounds like the word *I*, a clever scribe might decide to use ◁●▷ to mean *I* in writing too. If the logogram for *scream* were (ⴲ) then *ice cream* could be written ◁●▷ (ⴲ) . Symbols would now represent sound sequences or syllables instead of entire words.

17   When this kind of punning becomes widely used, the writing system is turning into a **syllabary**, or a system in which each symbol stands for a syllable. Over time, the sound values of symbols become predominant and their picture values less important. As scribes simplify the symbols to save time and space, the original pictures often become unrecognizable. To use our hypothetical example from English again, the logogram for *eye* might change from ◁●▷ to ◁○▷ to ◁Ⅰ▷ to ⅅ as a syllabic writing system evolved.

18   Old Persian cuneiform provides an example of a syllabic writing system that lost its pictorial qualities completely. The symbols in Figure 3 are not alphabetic because one cannot separate the consonant portions from the vowel portions. That is, there is

Figure 3. Old Persian Cuneiform

no particular part of ⳅ⩔⩔ [ta] that represents either [t] or [a]; the sign stands only for the syllable as a whole.*

19   The first syllabaries were developed among the Semites of the Middle East, perhaps as long ago as seven or eight thousand years, and the concept of the syllabary rapidly spread over the entire area. Although, strictly speaking, a syllabary represents vowel differences as well as consonant differences among syllables, most of the Semitic syllabaries indicated only consonants. That is, while [ba], [ma], and [ka] were represented by distinct symbols, [ba], [be], and [bi] were all written the same way.

20   For languages with very simple syllable structures, such as Japanese or Chinese, a syllabary provides an efficient writing system because relatively few symbols are needed to represent every possible syllable in the language. Modern Japanese has two syllabaries, the *katakana* and the *hiragana*. The simpler of these, the *katakana*, consists of only 47 basic signs, plus a few diacritical marks. Although the syllabaries are completely adequate for writing anything in Japanese, the prestige of Chinese logograms is so great that contemporary Japanese continues to use a mixture of Chinese characters and *kana* syllabic signs—illustrating how cultural factors may outweigh logic and efficiency in determining the written form of a language.

Alphabets

21   The final step in the phonemicization of writing is the **alphabet**, in which each symbol represents a separate phoneme, not an entire syllable. So far as we know, the alphabet has been invented only once. The Greeks borrowed the Semitic syllabary and, probably over a fairly long period of time, began using unneeded characters to represent vowels separately from consonants. Once there were separate characters for vowels, the originally syllabic characters could always be used for consonants alone, and the alphabet had been invented.

22   The precise form of the Greek letters, or **graphemes**, changed somewhat over time, and the Romans introduced still further changes when they borrowed the Greek

---

* Although the signs illustrated in Figure 3 are purely syllabic, the Old Persian system also retained four logograms and even included alphabetic features. Real writing systems are never as tidy as theoretical ones.

WORDS FROM MISTAKES

New words can originate in many different ways. One entertaining kind of origin is simple misreading due to confusion of similar letter forms. For example, the English word *gravy* comes from Old French *grave*, but the original French form was probably *grane*; the letters *n* and *v* (*u*) looked much alike in medieval handwriting. The word *sneeze* is apparently the result of misreading an *f* for an *s*; its Old English ancestor was *fneosan* (*f* and *s* were formed in much the same way in Old English times). In some instances, both the correct and the erroneous form have survived, with differentiation of meaning. Hence we have both the original Greek form *acme* and the misread form *acne*.

---

alphabet to write Latin, partly because the sound system of Latin differed in a number of important ways from that of Greek. The Romans did not adopt the Greek letters Θ Ξ Φ Ψ or Ω at all. They modified the most common forms or orientations of Greek Γ Δ Λ Σ to C, D, L, and S, respectively, and then added a tail to C to form G. The archaic Greek letter F had represented [w], but the Romans used it for [f] instead. In Greek, H is a vowel symbol, but it became a consonant symbol in Latin. The grapheme P represents [r] in Greek, but, because the Romans used P for [p], they had to modify it to R to represent [r]. The Romans adopted the obsolete Greek character Q to represent [k] before [w], as in Latin *quo*. Because Latin used three symbols, C, Q, and K (though K was rarely used) to represent [k], the Latin alphabet almost from the beginning violated the principle of an ideal alphabet, a one-to-one correspondence between phoneme and grapheme.

23   Primarily through the spread of Christianity from Rome, the Latin version of the alphabet was eventually adopted in all of Western Europe. Because Russia was Christianized by the Eastern Church, whose official language was Greek, its alphabet (the Cyrillic alphabet) was borrowed independently from Greek; in many ways it is closer to the classical Greek alphabet than the Latin alphabet is. For example, its forms Γ Д Л Н П Р Ф Х for [g d l n p r f x], respectively, are similar to their Greek originals. However, the Cyrillic alphabet uses В for [v], and Б, a modified form of B, for [b]. С represents [s], and у represents [u]. З, a modified form of Greek Z, is used for [z]. Because Russian is much richer in fricatives and affricates than Greek, new symbols were devised to represent them: Ж, Ц, Ч, Ш, Щ stand for [ž, ts, č, š, šč], respectively. The Cyrillic characters И, Ы, Э, Ю, Я represent the vowels or diphthongs [i y ɛ ju ja], respectively. Finally, Russian also uses two graphemes as diacritics; they represent no sound of their own, but indicate that a preceding consonant is palatalized (Ь) or not palatalized (Ъ).

24   English has had two different alphabets. Prior to the Christianization of England, the little writing that was done in English was in an alphabet called the **futhorc** or **runic alphabet**. The futhorc was originally developed by Germanic tribes on the Continent and probably was based on Etruscan or early Italic versions of the Greek alphabet. Its association with magic is suggested by its name, the runic alphabet, and

the term used to designate a character or letter, **rune**. In Old English, the word *rūn* meant not only "runic character," but also "mystery, secret." The related verb, *rūnian*, meant "to whisper, talk secrets, conspire." . . .

25   As a by-product of the Christianization of England in the sixth and seventh centuries, the English received the Latin alphabet. Although it has been modified somewhat over the centuries, the alphabet we use today is essentially the one adopted in the late sixth century. However, its fit to the sound system is much less accurate than at the time of its adoption because many phonological changes have not been reflected in the writing system.

26   An ideal alphabet contains one symbol for each phoneme, and represents each phoneme by one and only one symbol. In practice, few alphabets are perfect. Even if they are a good match to the sound system when they are first adopted (not always the case), subsequent sound changes destroy the fit. Writing is always much more conservative than speech, and, as the years go by, the fit between phoneme and grapheme becomes worse and worse unless there is regular spelling and even alphabet reform. Such reform has taken place in a number of countries; regular reform is even required by law in Finland. Major reform in the Soviet Union occurred after the 1917 revolution. In 1928, Turkey under Kemal Atatürk switched from the Arabic writing system to the Latin alphabet. However, as the history of Russian and Turkish suggests, resistance to reform is usually so strong that it takes a cataclysmic event like a revolution to achieve it. In general, reform is easier in small countries that do not use a language of worldwide distribution and prestige. Even under these circumstances, resistance to reform will be fierce if the country has a long tradition of literacy and literature. Icelandic, for instance, is spoken by fewer than a quarter of a million people, a large proportion of whom are bilingual or trilingual in other European languages. However, pride in their long native literary traditions has to date prevented any significant spelling reform. A person reasonably skilled in Old Norse (c. A.D. 900–c. A.D. 1350) can read modern Icelandic without much difficulty even though the spoken language has undergone vast changes since Old Norse times and even though the present match between grapheme and phoneme is poor indeed. Clearly, people become as emotionally entangled with their writing systems as with their spoken languages.

Questions on Content

1. Explain why writing is a secondary form of language.

2. Was writing invented to preserve literary works, or was it invented for more mundane purposes?

3. Define the following:

   ideogram

   logogram

   petroglyph

   pictograph

   syllabary

4. Explain why logographic systems are inefficient for most languages.

5. Millward points out that an alphabet was invented only once. Who invented it, and what is an alphabet?

6. What is the Cyrillic alphabet? How is it related to ours?

7. In her closing paragraph, Millward points out that "in practice, few alphabets are perfect." What does she mean? What are some imperfections in our alphabet?

8. What kind of writing system underlies such mathematical symbols as +, −, and ×?

Questions on Structure and Style

9. Look at Millward's use of transitions. Comment on transitions in the first eight paragraphs in particular.

10. Comment on the structure and organization of this selection. Does it follow a predictable pattern of organization?

11. Discuss the development and coherence of paragraph 10.

Assignments

1. Determine what Millward means by "spelling pronunciation" (paragraph 5). Make a list of words with spelling pronunciations in your own dialect. Are there other dialects of English in which these words do not have spelling pronunciations?

2. Explain in a few paragraphs how syllabic writing systems may have evolved from a system of logograms.

3. Write a pictographic message that you feel can be decoded by your classmates. Exchange your messages, and discuss some of your discoveries about writing systems.

4. Look for examples of pictographic and ideographic writing on road and traffic signs as well as on maps. Write a brief essay in which you discuss your findings.

ADDITIONAL ASSIGNMENTS AND RESEARCH TOPICS

1. If you're interested in or speak another language, write an essay examining the ways in which that language has influenced English. How has knowing English helped you learn the other language? How has being a speaker of English presented problems in learning another language?

2. The best-known ancient theory on the origin of the world's different languages is the story of the Tower of Babel in Genesis 11: 1–9. Read this passage in the 1611 King James version of the Bible and in a modern translation, such as *The Way*. Write an essay discussing some of the differences in the English language as reflected in the two translations of this passage.

3. Write an essay explaining your personal language history. What languages did your ancestors speak? Try to show how these languages have affected English. If your own family tree is difficult to trace, interview a non-native speaker, and write a paper describing his or her language history.

4. Choose one of the following, and write a research paper explaining why this person or event was important to the development of English:

   Alfred the Great

   Norman Conquest

   William Caxton

   William the Conqueror

5. Most communities have their own language histories, language features that make the community different from a community of similar size in a neighboring state. Write a paper exploring the language history of your community. A good way to begin is by examining geographic place names in your region and interviewing long-time residents of your community.

6. The Indo-Europeans were the speakers of the original language from which most of the languages of Europe and Asia were derived. Evidence suggests that the speakers of this language began in a compact homeland and then migrated. Over the centuries, distances separated the immigrants, and new languages evolved. Where do you think the homeland might have been, and why do you think so? (To answer this question, you'll need to study the chart on page 176 to determine where the languages are spoken today, if they are.)

7. Interview several parents of young children. Focus your interview on how their children acquired language. In an essay, reveal your results. Mention whether you discovered more differences or similarities among the children you discussed. Based on your information, do you feel biology or environment ("nature or nurture") is more important in a child's acquisition of language?

8. If you've spent extended periods of time in more than one area of the country, you've surely noticed regional differences in the way people speak. For example, the American English of eastern Massachusetts is not the same as that in Georgia (or in Oklahoma or on Long Island). The differences involve pronunciation, vocabulary, and sometimes sentence cadence. Write an essay comparing two regional dialects. Be specific. (One way to structure the essay might be to describe a single typical experience you had in each place, perhaps grocery shopping or attending school. This way you have a consistent basis for comparing the dialects.)

9. Think about the different ways in which animals communicate. Observe, if possible, parrots, mynah birds, chimpanzees, your own pets, or even the dancing of bees. Drawing freely from research in this area, write an essay discussing the differences among these types of communication.

CHAPTER FIVE

Language and Cultural Diversity

Language is the cultural difference that we notice most easily, and as such it often invites us to learn more about other cultures. Sometimes, though, language differences invite judgments about groups, judgments based primarily on how closely those groups resemble, or do not resemble, the prevailing cultural standards. The readings in this chapter examine the link between language and culture, as well as what happens as people react to language differences.

First, David Crystal raises the neglected issue of language extinction, whose pace has accelerated in modern times. As Crystal makes clear, the disappearance of specific languages should matter to all humans for reasons that illuminate many facets of the cultural diversity embodied in languages worldwide. Next, Robert D. King reacts strongly to the "English only" movement and its desire to make English the "official" language of the United States. King's review of such efforts elsewhere in the world creates an illuminating picture of political wrangling and, just as important, of human nature itself.

Bilingual education has generated another prominent language controversy, and Richard Rodriguez addresses this politically charged issue in "Aria: A Memoir of a Bilingual Childhood." For Rodriguez, growing up and adapting to adult society and to its culture should mean acquiring a public identity, and language plays a role in this process of becoming "different" through growing up. Following Rodriguez we find another author who presents a highly personal reaction to language diversity. Rose Del Castillo Guilbault's "Americanization Is Tough on 'Macho'" explains why this word, as it is incorporated into the English vocabulary of many people, actually reflects cultural biases instead of the admirable qualities implied by *macho* in Spanish.

The chapter concludes with two selections that look at cultural differences from very different perspectives. In "Names in the Melting Pot," Justin Kaplan and Anne Bernays reveal some surprising facts about the cultural mix reflected in, and sometimes distorted by, the last names of people who live in the United States. In an article specially written for this edition of *About Language*, Tara Elyssa catalogs the perplexing messiness of English for those attempting to learn it as a second language. After reading "Learning English Good," no native speaker of English will likely hear the language in quite the same way again.

As the American language now encounters powerful new cultural influences, tolerating differences and change seems more complicated than ever, a fact made clear by this chapter's readings.

Vanishing Languages

David Crystal

Should anyone care that the Welsh language is dying? or that Red
Cloud Thunder, last-known fluent speaker of the Siouan language
Catawba, has died? David Crystal here offers startling evidence of
the continuing decline in the number of languages worldwide.
Because language embodies culture, when a language dies, a culture
dies as well. But what should be done, if anything, to preserve the
world's endangered languages, including those whose extinction con-
stitutes a deliberate goal in a broader policy of political repression?
David Crystal, who lives in Wales, is a linguist and author of *The
Cambridge Encyclopedia of the English Language.*

■ J O U R N A L   P R O M P T   *In his opening paragraph Crystal cites an old Welsh
proverb:* Cenedl heb iaith, cenedl heb galon *("A nation without a language [is] a nation without a heart"). Comment on the importance of this sentiment before reading Crystal's essay.*

1   There's a Welsh proverb I've known for as long as I can remember: *"Cenedl heb iaith,
cenedl heb galon."* It means, "A nation without a language [is] a nation without a heart,"
and it's become more poignant over the years as more and more families who live
around me in North Wales speak in English instead of Welsh across the dinner table.

2   Welsh, the direct descendant of the Celtic language that was spoken throughout
most of Britain when the Anglo-Saxons invaded, has long been under threat from
English. England's economic and technological dominance has made English the language of choice, causing a decline in the number of Welsh speakers. And although the
decline has steadied in the past 15 years, less than 20 percent of the population of
Wales today can speak Welsh in addition to English.

3   The Welsh language is clearly in trouble. Someday, it may even join the rapidly
growing list of extinct languages, which includes Gothic and Hittite, Manx and
Cornish, Powhatan and Piscataway. If present trends continue, four of the world's
languages will die between the publication of this issue of CIVILIZATION and the
next. Eighteen more will be gone by the end of 1997. A century from now, one-half
of the world's 6,000 or more languages may be extinct.

4   The decline is evident the world over. Consider the case of Sene: In 1978 there
were fewer than 10 elderly speakers remaining in the Morobe province of Papua
New Guinea. Or Ngarla: In 1981 there were just two speakers of the Aboriginal language still alive in northwest Western Australia. And in 1982 there were 10 surviving
speakers of Achumawi out of a tribal population of 800 in northeastern California.
Does it matter? When the last representatives of these peoples die, they take with them
their oral history and culture, though their passing is rarely noticed. Sometimes, years
later, we find hints of a culture's existence, in the form of inscriptions or fragments of
text, but many of these—the Linear A inscriptions from ancient Crete, for example—
remain undeciphered to this day.

5   There is some controversy over exactly how to count the number of languages in the world. A great deal depends on whether the speech patterns of different communities are viewed as dialects of a single language or as separate languages. The eight main varieties of spoken Chinese, for example, are as mutually unintelligible as, say, French and Spanish—which suggests that they are different languages. On the other hand, they share a writing system, and so perhaps are best described as dialects of the same language. If you opt for the first solution, you will add eight to your tally of the world's languages. If you opt for the second, you will add just one.

6   Taking a conservative estimate of 6,000 languages worldwide, one fact becomes immediately clear: Languages reveal enormous differences in populations. At one extreme, there is English, spoken by more people globally than any other language in history, probably by a third of the world's population as a first, second or foreign language. At the other extreme is Ngarla (and most of the other languages of the native peoples of Australia, Canada and the United States) whose total population of speakers may amount to just one or two. And then there are closely related groups of languages like the Maric family in Queensland, Australia, which consists of 12 languages. When it was surveyed in 1981, only one of these, Bidyara, had as many as 20 speakers. Most had fewer than five. Five of them had only one speaker each.

7   The loss of languages may have accelerated recently, but it is hardly a new problem. In the 19th century, there were more than 1,000 Indian languages in Brazil, many spoken in small, isolated villages in the rain forest; today there are a mere 200, most of which have never been written down or recorded. In North America, the 300 or more indigenous languages spoken in the past have been halved.

8   People sometimes talk of the "beauty of Italian" or of "German's authority," as if such characteristics might make a language more or less influential. But there is no internal mechanism in a language that settles its fate. Languages are not, in themselves, more or less powerful. People don't adopt them because they are more precise. They gain ascendancy when their speakers gain power, and they die out when people die out or disperse. It's as simple as that.

9   A dramatic illustration of how a language disappears took place in Venezuela in the 1960s. As part of the drive to tap the vast resources of the Amazonian rain forests, a group of Western explorers passed through a small village on the banks of the Coluene River. Unfortunately, they brought with them the influenza virus, and the villagers, who lacked any immunity, were immediately susceptible to the disease. Fewer than 10 people survived. A human tragedy, it was a linguistic tragedy too, for this village contained the only speakers of the Trumai language. And with so few people left to pass it on, the language was doomed.

10   Other languages—such as Welsh and Scottish Gaelic—have been threatened when indigenous populations have moved or been split up. Brighter economic prospects tempt young members of the community away from their villages. And even if they choose to stay, it doesn't take much exposure to a dominant culture to motivate ambitious young people to replace their mother tongue with a language that gives them better access to education, jobs and new technology.

11   A language's fortunes are tied to its culture's. Just as one language holds sway over others when its speakers gain power—politically, economically or technologically—

it diminishes, and may even die, when they lose that prominence. Latin, now used almost exclusively in its written form, had its day as a world language because of the power of Rome. English, once promoted by the British Empire, is thriving today chiefly because of the prominence of the U.S.A., but it was once an endangered language, threatened by the Norman invaders of Britain in the 11th century, who brought with them a multitude of French words. In South America, Spanish and Portuguese, the languages of colonialists, have replaced many of the indigenous Indian tongues.

12　　The death of languages is most noticeable in parts of the world where large numbers of languages are concentrated in a few small geographical regions. Travel to the tropical forests of the Morobe province in Papua New Guinea and you'll find five isolated villages in a mountain valley where fewer than 1,000 people speak the Kapin language. They support themselves by agriculture and have little contact with outsiders. Other tiny communities, speaking completely different languages, live in neighboring valleys. Linguists estimate that in the country as a whole there is approximately one language for every 200 people. Indeed, three countries, which together amount to less than 2 percent of the earth's land area, support 1,700—or a quarter—of the world's living languages: Papua New Guinea has 862; Indonesia, 701; and Malaysia, 140. These countries' isolation and physical geography account in large part for the existence of such concentrations, and it is hardly surprising to find that, as remote areas of the globe have opened up for trade or tourism, there have been a dramatic increase in the rate of language death. Valuable reserves of gold, silver and timber in Papua New Guinea, for example, are bringing speculators to the islands—and with them their languages.

13　　There has been little research into exactly what happens when a language begins to die. The process depends on how long there has been contact between the users of the minority language and their more powerful neighbors. If the contact has been minimal, as in the case of Trumai in the Amazon, the minority language might remain almost unchanged until the last of its speakers dies. But if two languages have been in contact for generations, the dominant language will slowly erode the pronunciation, vocabulary and grammar of the minority language. Take the Celtic languages of northwest Europe. Following the death of the last mother-tongue speakers of Cornish (spoken in Cornwall until the 19th century) and Manx (spoken in the Isle of Man until the 1940s), the only remaining Celtic languages are Breton (in northwest France), Irish and Scottish Gaelic, and Welsh. All have been in steady decline during the 20th century. Equally, all have been the focus of strenuous efforts to revive their fortunes (or, in the case of Cornish and Manx, to resurrect a new first-language base). But the effects of four centuries of domination by English are evident everywhere.

14　　Walk into the stores in the strongly Welsh-speaking areas of North Wales, as I regularly do, and you will hear the Welsh language widely used—and apparently in good health. But there is also a great deal of recognizable English vocabulary scattered throughout the speech. Of course, all languages have what linguists refer to as "loan words"—words taken from other languages to supplement the vocabulary. English itself has tens of thousands of words borrowed from French, Spanish, Latin and other languages. But there is an important difference between traditional vocabulary borrowing and what takes place in an endangered language. When *arsenic, lettuce* and *attorney* came into English in the Middle Ages, it was because these items did not exist in the English-speaking community: The nouns were introduced to describe new objects, and so to supplement the existing vocabulary. But in the case of an endangered language, the loan words tend to replace words that already exist. And as the decline continues, even quite basic words in the language are replaced.

15   I meet this phenomenon every day on the Welsh island of Anglesey, where I live. It's become quite unusual to hear locals referring to large sums of money in anything other than English. In a Holyhead butcher's shop recently, I overheard someone say *"Mae'n twelve fifty"* (It's twelve fifty), where the first part of the sentence is colloquial Welsh and the second part is colloquial English. As I waited for a train at the station the same day, I heard a porter calling out to disgruntled passengers *"Mae'n late"* (It's late). And I later overheard a group of people using the English word *injection* as they stood in a street describing in Welsh someone's visit to a doctor's clinic. In all these cases, perfectly good Welsh words already exist, but the speakers did not use them. Why they chose not to is not at all clear. Maybe they did not know the Welsh words, or maybe it is a sign of status or education to use the English equivalents. But when something as basic as its number system is affected, a language is clearly in danger.

16   Mixed languages are an inevitable result of language contact, and they exist all over the world, often given a dismissive label by more educated speakers: Wenglish, Franglais, Spanglish. Such mixed varieties often become complex systems of communication in their own right—and may even result in brand-new languages, or pidgins such as Tok Pisin, which is now spoken by more than 1 million people in Papua New Guinea. But when one of the languages in question has no independent existence elsewhere in the world, as in the case of Welsh, mixed languages are a symptom of linguistic decline.

17   In the West, when a population fears that its language is threatened, speakers often react defensively, establishing a committee or board to oversee and coordinate political policy and to plan dictionaries, grammars and local broadcasting. The best-known example is France, home of the Académie Française, where there is now a law banning the use of English words—such as *le week-end* and *le computeur*—in official publications if a native French term already exists (in these cases, *la fin de semaine* and *l'ordinateur*). Often two levels of language ability emerge as a consequence. There is an educated standard, used as a norm in education and the media. And there is a colloquial standard, used by the majority of the population (including many educated users, who thereby become bilingual—more technically, bidialectal—in their own language). It is the usage of the elite minority that is called by the majority the "proper" or "correct" language, even though it often represents a far more artificial style of speech than the language of the streets.

18   The plight of the indigenous languages of America was made vivid by James Fenimore Cooper as long ago as 1826, when the Indian chief Tamenund lamented that "before the night has come, have I lived to see the last warrior of the wise race of the Mohicans." There are 200 North American Indian languages, but only about 50 have more than 1,000 speakers, and only a handful have more than 50,000. Just over a year ago, Red Thunder Cloud, the last known fluent speaker of the Siouan language Catawba, died. The only surviving fluent speaker of Quileute is 80-year-old Lillian Pullen, of La Push, Washington. But at least the decline of American Indian languages

has begun to attract widespread attention from politicians and the media—sources of support that are unlikely to help such equally threatened but less well known cases as Usku in Irian Jaya or Pipil in El Salvador.

19   In Europe, public attention is regularly focused on language rights by the European Bureau of Lesser Used Languages, headquartered in Brussels. A recent book, *A Week in Europe,* edited by the Welsh magazine editor Dylan Iorwerth, offers a glimpse of Western European life by journalists writing in minority languages. Some of these are minority uses of major languages, such as German in Denmark, Swedish in Finland, and Croatian in Italy; but in most cases the entire language-using community is found in a single region, such as Scottish Gaelic, Galician, Alsatian, Welsh, Catalan, Asturian, Breton, Friulian, Basque, Sorbian, Occitan, Provençal, Frisian and Irish. Political concern over the status of minority languages is regularly voiced by the European Parliament, and occasionally words are backed up with financial commitment—to local newspapers and broadcasting, literary festivals and teaching programs.

20   When an endangered language (such as Gaelic) is spoken in a culture whose historical significance is widely appreciated—perhaps because it is associated with prowess in arts and crafts, or because it is known for its literary achievements—it may provoke widespread concern. And sometimes endangered languages that have suffered as a result of colonial expansion win support from speakers of the dominant language, who wish to distance themselves from the aggression of their ancestors. But in most cases, anxiety, like charity, begins at home. In the 1970s, Gwynfor Evans held a hunger strike as part of his (successful) campaign for a Welsh-language TV channel. And in 1952 in Madras, India, Potti Sriramulu died following a hunger strike in support of the Telugu language. Language, as that Welsh proverb reminds us, is truly at the heart of a culture. It is a matter of identity, of nationhood.

21   With enough personal effort, time and money, and a sympathetic political climate, it is possible to reverse the fortunes of an endangered language. Catalan, spoken in northeast Spain, was allocated the status of an official regional language, and it now has more native speakers than it did 30 years ago. And the Hocąk, or Winnebago, tribe in Wisconsin is hoping to develop a full Hocąk-speaking school system. In an effort funded entirely by profits from the tribe's casinos, schoolchildren use interactive multimedia computer programs to gain familiarity with a language that was traditionally passed down orally from parent to child. Such advances generally depend upon collaboration between minority groups, such as those who united to form the European Bureau for Lesser Used Languages. Together they have a realistic chance of influencing international policies, without overlooking the vast differences between the political and cultural situations of minority languages: Welsh, Gaelic, Maori, Quechua and Navajo demand very different solutions.

22   Welsh, strongly supported by Welsh-language broadcasting and Welsh-medium schools, is alone among the Celtic languages in stopping its decline. The census figures for the last 20 years show a leveling out, and even some increase in usage among certain age groups, especially young children. A similar vigorous concern seems to be stimulating Navajo and several other American languages, as well as some minority languages in continental Europe. But it is quite clear that most of the endangered languages of the

world are beyond practical help, in the face of economic colonialism, the growth of urbanization and the development of global communication systems. And, given the difficulty there has been in achieving language rights for such well-known communities as the Navajo or the Welsh, the likelihood of attracting world interest in the hundreds of languages of Papua New Guinea, each of which has only a few speakers left, is remote. Clearly, with some 3,000 languages at risk, the cost of supporting them on a worldwide scale would be immense. Can, or should, anything be done?

23   On an intellectual level, the implications are clear enough: To lose a language is to lose a unique insight into the human condition. Each language presents a view of the world that is shared by no other. Each has its own figures of speech, its own narrative style, its own proverbs, its own oral or written literatures. Preserving a language may also be instructive; we can learn from the way in which different languages structure reality, as has been demonstrated countless times in the study of comparative literature. And there is no reason to believe that the differing accounts of the human condition presented by the peoples of, say, Irian Jaya will be any less insightful than those presented by writers in French, English, Russian and Sanskrit. Moreover, the loss of a language means a loss of inherited knowledge that extends over hundreds or thousands of years. As human beings have spread around the globe, adapting to different environments, the distilled experiences of generations have been retained chiefly through the medium of language. At least when a dying language has been written down, as in the case of Latin or Classical Greek, we can usually still read its messages. But when a language without a writing system disappears, its speakers' experience is lost forever. The Bithynian, Cappadocian and Cataonian cultures are known today only from passing references in Greek literature. Language loss is knowledge loss, and it is irretrievable.

24   Such intellectual arguments may persuade the dispassionate observer, but most arguments in favor of language preservation are quite the opposite: They are particular, political and extremely passionate. Language is more than a shared code of symbols for communication. People do not fight and die, as they have done in India, to preserve a set of symbols. They do so because they feel that their identity is at stake—that language preservation is a question of human rights, community status and nationhood. This profoundly emotional reaction is often expressed in metaphors. Language nationalists see their language as a treasure house, as a repository of memories, as a gift to their children, as a birthright. And it is this conviction that has generated manifestoes and marches in Melbourne in support of Aboriginal languages; referendums, rioting and the defacing of public signs in Montreal on behalf of French; civil disobedience in India and Pakistan, in Belgium and in Spain.

25   Such demonstrations stand in stark contrast to places where cultural and linguistic pluralism works successfully, as in Switzerland and Sweden, where the dominant culture respects the identities and rights of its linguistic minorities, and provides educational opportunities for speakers. Successful multilingual communities such as Sweden's serve as examples for the United Nations, UNESCO, the Council of Europe, and the European Parliament as they act to preserve minority language use.

26   Conversely, several countries have actively repressed minority languages, such as Basque by the Spanish fascists, or Sorbian (a Slavic language spoken in southern

Germany) by the Nazis. And laws forbidding the use of minority languages have been commonplace; children have been punished for using a minority language in school; street signs in a minority language have been outlawed; the publication of books in the language has been banned; people's names have been forcibly changed to their equivalents in the language of the dominant power. Whole communities, such as several in the Basque-speaking parts of northern Spain, have had their linguistic identity deliberately eliminated.

27   Political arguments for and against preservation have been expressed with such vehemence that they tend to dominate any discussion of minority languages. Does the loss of linguistic diversity present civilization with a problem analogous to the loss of species in biology? Not entirely. A world containing only one species is impossible. But a world containing only one language is by no means impossible, and may not be so very far away. Indeed, some argue strongly in favor of it. The possibility of creating a unilingual world has motivated artificial-language movements (such as Esperanto) since the 16th century, and there are many who currently see the remarkable progress of English as a promising step toward global communication. They argue that mutual intelligibility is desirable and should be encouraged: Misunderstandings will decrease; individuals and countries will negotiate more easily; and the world will be more peaceful.

28   This kind of idealism wins little sympathy from language nationalists, who point out that the use of a single language by a community is no guarantee of civil peace—as is currently evident in the states of the former Yugoslavia or in Northern Ireland. But language nationalists are faced with major practical concerns: How can one possibly evaluate the competing claims of thousands of endangered languages? Is it sensible to try to preserve a language (or culture) when its recent history suggests that it is heading for extinction? In the next few years, international organizations may have to decide, on chiefly economic grounds, which languages should be kept alive and which allowed to die.

29   The publication in the early 1990s of major surveys of the world's languages has brought some of these issues before the public. UNESCO's Endangered Languages Project, the Foundation for Endangered Languages (established in the U.K. in 1995) and the Linguistic Society of America's Committee on Endangered Languages and their Preservation are fostering research into the status of minority languages. Information is gradually becoming available on the Internet—such as through the World Wide Web site of the Summer Institute of Linguistics. And a clearinghouse for the world's endangered languages was established in 1995, by request of UNESCO, at the University of Tokyo.

30   But after the fact-finding, the really hard work consists of tape-recording and transcribing the endangered languages before they die. The fieldwork procedures are well established among a small number of dedicated linguists, who assess the urgency of the need, document what is already known about the languages, extend that knowledge as much as possible, and thus help preserve languages, if only in archive form.

31   The concept of a language as a "national treasure" still takes many people by surprise—and even English has no international conservation archive. It is hard to imagine the long hours and energy needed to document something as complex as a

language—and it's often a race against time. Thirty years ago, when anthropologist J. V. Powell began working with the Quileute Indians in Washington state, 70 members of the tribe were fluent speakers. Around that time the tribal elders decided to try to revitalize the language, writing dictionaries and grammars, and imagining a day when their children would sit around chatting in Quileute. "But," says Powell, "their prayers haven't been answered." Now they've scaled back to a more modest goal: basic familiarity rather than fluency. Powell recognizes that they will not save Quileute, but it will be preserved in recordings for future scholars—and will serve as a symbol of the tribe's group identity. That may seem like a small success, but it's a far better fate than the one facing most endangered languages.

Questions on Content

1. Explain why the Welsh language has long been threatened by English.

2. Explain the nature of the controversy over exactly how to count the number of living languages in the world.

3. Crystal says that "a language's fortunes are tied to its culture's" (paragraph 11). Explain what he means.

4. Explain the difference between traditional vocabulary borrowing and that which takes place in an endangered language.

Questions on Structure and Style

5. David Crystal lives on the small Welsh island of Anglesey. How does he use that fact to strengthen his essay?

6. What point does Crystal make about the Quileute language in his final paragraph? Explain why this is an appropriate conclusion for this essay.

7. Crystal ends paragraph 22 with a question. Explain why this question is important to the essay's structure and why its answer is important to the content.

Assignments

1. Assume that you live in a society in which your language is threatened by a dominant language. Write an essay in which you describe measures that might help to preserve your language and why you feel such preservation is important. (You may refer freely to Crystal's selection as you develop your essay.)

2. Crystal suggests that a unilingual world (a world with one language) is by no means impossible to imagine. Write an essay in which you argue for or against such a development.

Should English Be the Law?

Robert D. King

"Language riot? It sounds like a joke." However, in some countries,
governmental policies intended to regulate the language that people
use have indeed sparked militant protest. Could similar protests
occur in the United States, where efforts to make English the
"official" language already have generated heated discussion?
Using richly varied examples and surprising historical evidence,
Robert D. King here warns Americans that "Benign neglect is a
good policy for any country when it comes to language." King
teaches at the University of Texas at Austin.

■ **JOURNAL PROMPT** *Assume that the U.S. Senate has just passed a law
making English the only official and legally recognized language in the United States. Try to
imagine public response across the nation to such a governmental action. Make a list of the
positive and negative responses you would expect to hear.*

1   We have known race riots, draft riots, labor violence, secession, anti-war protests,
and a whiskey rebellion, but one kind of trouble we've never had: a language riot.
Language riot? It sounds like a joke. The very idea of language as a political force—
as something that might threaten to split a country wide apart—is alien to our way
of thinking and to our cultural traditions.

2   This may be changing. On August 1 of last year the U.S. House of Representatives
approved a bill that would make English the official language of the United States. The
vote was 259 to 169, with 223 Republicans and thirty-six Democrats voting in favor
and eight Republicans, 160 Democrats, and one independent voting against. The debate was intense, acrid, and partisan. On March 25 of last year the Supreme Court
agreed to review a case involving an Arizona law that would require public employees
to conduct government business only in English. Arizona is one of several states that
have passed "Official English" or "English Only" laws. The appeal to the Supreme
Court followed a 6-to-5 ruling, in October of 1995, by a federal appeals court striking
down the Arizona law. These events suggest how divisive a public issue language
could become in America—even if it has until now scarcely been taken seriously.

3   Traditionally, the American way has been to make English the national language—but to do so quietly, locally, without fuss. The Constitution is silent on
language: the Founding Fathers had no need to legislate that English be the official
language of the country. It has always been taken for granted that English *is* the national language, and that one must learn English in order to make it in America.

4   To say that language has never been a major force in American history or politics,
however, is not to say that politicians have always resisted linguistic jingoism. In 1753
Benjamin Franklin voiced his concern that German immigrants were not learning

218

English: "Those [Germans] who come hither are generally the most ignorant Stupid Sort of their own Nation. . . . they will soon so out number us, that all the advantages we have will not, in My Opinion, be able to preserve our language, and even our government will become precarious." Theodore Roosevelt articulated the unspoken American linguistic-melting-pot theory when he boomed, "We have room for but one language here, and that is the English language, for we intended to see that the crucible turns our people out as Americans, of American nationality, and not as dwellers in a polyglot boarding house." And: "We must have but one flag. We must also have but one language. That must be the language of the Declaration of Independence, of Washington's Farewell address, of Lincoln's Gettysburg speech and second inaugural."

Official English

5   TR's linguistic tub-thumping long typified the tradition of American politics. That tradition began to change in the wake of the anything-goes attitudes and the celebration of cultural differences arising in the 1960s. A 1975 amendment to the Voting Rights Action of 1965 mandated the "bilingual ballot" under certain circumstances, notably when the voters of selected language groups reached five percent or more in a voting district. Bilingual education became a byword of educational thinking during the 1960s. By the 1970s linguists had demonstrated convincingly—at least to other academics—that black English (today called African-American vernacular English or Ebonics) was not "bad" English but a different kind of authentic English with its own rules. Predictably, there have been scattered demands that black English be included in bilingual-education programs.

6   It was against this background that the movement to make English the official language of the country arose. In 1981 Senator S. I. Hayakawa, long a leading critic of bilingual education and bilingual ballots, introduced in the U.S. Senate a constitutional amendment that not only would have made English the official language but would have prohibited federal and state laws and regulations requiring the use of other languages. His English Language Amendment died in the Ninety-seventh Congress.

7   In 1983 the organization called U.S. English was founded by Hayakawa and John Tanton, a Michigan ophthalmologist. The primary purpose of the organization was to promote English as the official language of the United States. (The best background readings on America's "neolinguisticism" are the books *Hold Your Tongue,* by James Crawford, and *Language Loyalties,* edited by Crawford, both published in 1992.) Official English initiatives were passed by California in 1986, by Arkansas, Mississippi, North Carolina, North Dakota, and South Carolina in 1987, by Colorado, Florida, and Arizona in 1988, and by Alabama in 1990. The majorities voting for these initiatives were generally not insubstantial: California's, for example, passed by 73 percent.

8   It was probably inevitable that the Official English (or English Only—the two names are used almost interchangeably) movement would acquire a conservative, almost reactionary undertone in the 1990s. Official English is politically very incorrect. But its cofounder John Tanton brought with him strong liberal credentials. He had been active in the Sierra Club and Planned Parenthood, and in the 1970s served as the national president of Zero Population Growth. Early advisers of U.S. English

resist ideological pigeonholding: they included Walter Annenberg, Jacques Barzun, Bruno Bettelheim, Alistair Cooke, Denton Cooley, Walter Cronkite, Angier Biddle Duke, George Gilder, Sidney Hook, Norman Podhoretz, Arnold Schwarzenegger, and Karl Shapiro. In 1987 U.S. English installed as its president Linda Chávez, a Hispanic who had been prominent in the Reagan Administration. A year later she resigned her position, citing "repugnant" and "anti-Hispanic" overtones in an internal memorandum written by Tanton. Tanton, too, resigned, and Walter Cronkite, describing the affair as "embarrassing," left the advisory board. One board member, Norman Cousins, defected in 1986, alluding to the "negative symbolic significance" of California's Official English initiative, Proposition 63. The current chairman of the board and CEO of U.S. English is Mauro E. Mujica, who claims that the organization has 650,000 members.

9   The popular wisdom is that conservatives are pro and liberals con. True, conservatives such as George Will and William F. Buckley Jr. have written columns supporting Official English. But would anyone characterize as conservatives the present and past U.S. English board members Alistair Cooke, Walter Cronkite, and Norman Cousins? One of the strongest opponents of bilingual education is the Mexican-American writer Richard Rodríguez, best known for his eloquent autobiography, *Hunger of Memory* (1982). There is a strain of American liberalism that defines itself in nostalgic devotion to the melting pot.

10   For several years relevant bills awaited consideration in the U.S. House of Representatives. The Emerson Bill (H.R. 123), passed by the House last August, specifies English as the official language of government, and requires that the government "preserve and enhance" the official status of English. Exceptions are made for the teaching of foreign languages; for actions necessary for public health, international relations, foreign trade, and the protection of the rights of criminal defendants; and for the use of "terms of art" from languages other than English. It would, for example, stop the Internal Revenue Service from sending out income-tax forms and instructions in languages other than English, but it would not ban the use of foreign languages in census materials or documents dealing with national security. "*E Pluribus Unum*" can still appear on American money. U.S. English supports the bill.

11   What are the chances that some version of Official English will become federal law? Any language bill will face tough odds in the Senate, because some western senators have opposed English Only measures in the past for various reasons, among them a desire by Republicans not to alienate the growing number of Hispanic Republicans, most of whom are uncomfortable with mandated monolingualism. Texas Governor George W. Bush, too, has forthrightly said that he would oppose any English Only proposals in his state. Several of the Republican candidates for President in 1996 (an interesting exception is Phil Gramm) endorsed versions of Official English, as has Newt Gingrich. While governor of Arkansas, Bill Clinton signed into law an English Only bill. As President, he has described his earlier action as a mistake.

12   Many issues intersect in the controversy over Official English: immigration (above all), the rights of minorities (Spanish-speaking minorities in particular), the pros and cons of bilingual education, tolerance, how best to educate the children of immigrants, and the place of cultural diversity in school curricula and in American society

in general. The question that lies at the root of most of the uneasiness is this: Is America threatened by the preservation of languages other than English? Will America, if it continues on its traditional path of benign linguistic neglect, go the way of Belgium, Canada, and Sri Lanka—three countries among many whose unity is gravely imperiled by language and ethnic conflicts?

Language and Nationality

13   Language and nationalism were not always so intimately intertwined. Never in the heyday of rule by sovereign was it a condition of employment that the King be able to speak the language of his subjects. George I spoke no English and spent much of his time away from England, attempting to use the power of his kingship to shore up his German possessions. In the Middle Ages nationalism was not even part of the picture: one owed loyalty to a lord, a prince, a ruler, a family, a tribe, a church, a piece of land, but not to a nation and least of all to a nation as a language unit. The capital city of the Austrian Hapsburg empire was Vienna, its ruler a monarch with effective control of peoples of the most varied and incompatible ethnicities, and languages, throughout Central and Eastern Europe. The official language, and the lingua franca as well, was German. While it stood—and it stood for hundreds of years—the empire was an anachronistic relic of what for most of human history had been the normal relationship between country and language: none.

14   The marriage of language and nationalism goes back at least to Romanticism and specifically to Rousseau, who argued in his *Essay on the Origin of Languages* that language must develop before politics is possible and that language originally distinguished nations from one another. A little-remembered aim of the French Revolution—itself the legacy of Rousseau—was to impose a national language on France, where regional languages such as Provençal, Breton, and Basque were still strong competitors against standard French, the French of the Ile de France. As late as 1789, when the Revolution began, half the population of the south of France, which spoke Provençal, did not understand French. A century earlier the playwright Racine said that he had had to resort to Spanish and Italian to make himself understood in the southern French town of Uzès. After the Revolution nationhood itself became aligned with language.

15   In 1846 Jacob Grimm, one of the Brothers Grimm of fairy-tale fame but better known in the linguistic establishment as a forerunner of modern comparative and historical linguists, said that "a nation is the totality of people who speak the same language." After midcentury, language was invoked more than any other single criterion to define nationality. Language as a political force helped to bring about the unification of Italy and of Germany and the secession of Norway from its union with Sweden in 1905. Arnold Toynbee observed—unhappily—soon after the First World War that "the growing consciousness of Nationality had attached itself neither to traditional frontiers nor to new geographical associations but almost exclusively to mother tongues."

16   The crowning triumph of the new desideratum was the Treaty of Versailles, in 1919, when the allied victors of the First World War began redrawing the map of Central and Eastern Europe according to nationality as best they could. The magic

word was "self-determination," and none of Woodrow Wilson's Fourteen Points mentioned the word "language" at all. Self-determination was thought of as being related to "nationality," which today we would be more likely to call "ethnicity"; but language was simpler to identify than nationality or ethnicity. When it came to drawing the boundary lines of various countries—Czechoslovakia, Yugoslavia, Romania, Hungary, Albania, Bulgaria, Poland—it was principally language that guided the draftsman's hand. (The main exceptions were Alsace-Lorraine, South Tyrol, and the German-speaking parts of Bohemia and Moravia.) Almost by default language became the defining characteristic of nationality.

17   And so it remains today. In much of the world, ethnic unity and cultural identification are routinely defined by language. To be Arab is to speak Arabic. Bengali identity is based on language in spite of the division of Bengali-speakers between Hindu India and Muslim Bangladesh. When eastern Pakistan seceded from greater Pakistan in 1971, it named itself Bangladesh: *desa* means "country"; *bangla* means not the Bengali people or the Bengali territory but the Bengali language.

18   Scratch most nationalist movements and you find a linguistic grievance. The demands for independence of the Baltic states (Latvia, Lithuania, and Estonia) were intimately bound up with fears for the loss of their respective languages and cultures in a sea of Russianness. In Belgium the war between French and Flemish threatens an already weakly fused country. The present atmosphere of Belgium is dark and anxious, costive; the metaphor of divorce is a staple of private and public discourse. The lines of terrorism in Sri Lanka are drawn between Tamil Hindus and Sinhalese Buddhists—and also between the Tamil and Sinhalese languages. Worship of the French language fortifies the movement for an independent Quebec. Whether a united Canada will survive into the twenty-first century is a question too close to call. Much of the anxiety about language in the United States is probably fueled by the "Quebec problem": unlike Belgium, which is a small European country, or Sri Lanka, which is halfway around the world, Canada is our close neighbor.

19   Language is a convenient surrogate for nonlinguistic claims that are often awkward to articulate, for they amount to a demand for more political and economic power. Militant Sikhs in India call for a state of their own: Khalistan ("Land of the Pure" in Punjabi). They frequently couch this as a demand for a linguistic state, which has a certain simplicity about it, a clarity of motive—justice, even, because states in India are normally linguistic states. But the Sikh demands blend religion, economics, language, and retribution for sins both punished and unpunished in a country where old sins cast long shadows.

20   Language is an explosive issue in the countries of the former Soviet Union. The language conflict in Estonia has been especially bitter. Ethnic Russians make up almost a third of Estonia's population, and most of them do not speak or read Estonian, although Russians have lived in Estonia for more than a generation. Estonia has passed legislation requiring knowledge of the Estonian language as a condition of citizenship. Nationalist groups in independent Lithuania sought restrictions on the use of Polish—again, old sins, long shadows.

21   In 1995 protests erupted in Moldova, formerly the Moldavian Soviet Socialist Republic, over language and the teaching of Moldovan history. Was Moldovan history a

part of Romanian history or of Soviet history? Was Moldova's language Romanian? Moldovan—earlier called Moldavian—*is* Romanian, just as American English and British English are both English. But in the days of the Moldavian SSR, Moscow insisted that the two languages were different, and in a piece of linguistic nonsense required Moldavian to be written in the Cyrillic alphabet to strengthen the case that it was not Romanian.

22   The official language of Yugoslavia was Serbo-Croatian, which was never so much a language as a political accommodation. The Serbian and Croatian languages are mutually intelligible. Serbian is written in the Cyrillic alphabet, is identified with the Eastern Orthodox branch of the Catholic Church, and borrows its high-culture words from the east—from Russian and Old Church Slavic. Croatian is written in the Roman alphabet, is identified with Roman Catholicism, and borrows its high-culture words from the west—from German, for example, and Latin. One of the first things the newly autonomous Republic of Serbia did, in 1991, was to pass a law decreeing Serbian in the Cyrillic alphabet the official language of the country. With Croatia divorced from Serbia, the Croatian and Serbian languages are diverging more and more. Serbo-Croatian has now passed into history, a language-museum relic from the brief period when Serbs and Croats called themselves Yugoslavs and pretended to like each other.

23   Slovakia, relieved now of the need to accommodate to Czech cosmopolitan sensibilities, has passed a law making Slovak its official language. (Czech is to Slovak pretty much as Croatian is to Serbian.) Doctors in state hospitals must speak to patients in Slovak, even if another language would aid diagnosis and treatment. Some 600,000 Slovaks—more than 10 percent of the population—are ethnically Hungarian. Even staff meetings in Hungarian-language schools must be in Slovak. (The government dropped a stipulation that church weddings be conducted in Slovak after heavy opposition from the Roman Catholic Church.) Language inspectors are told to weed out "all sins perpetrated on the regular Slovak language." Tensions between Slovaks and Hungarians, who had been getting along, have begun to arise.

24   The twentieth century is ending as it began—with trouble in the Balkans and with nationalist tensions flaring up in other parts of the globe. (Toward the end of his life Bismarck predicted that "some damn fool thing in the Balkans" would ignite the next war.) Language isn't always part of the problem. But it usually is.

Unique Otherness

25   Is there no hope for language tolerance? Some countries manage to maintain their unity in the face of multilingualism. Examples are Finland, with a Swedish minority, and a number of African and Southeast Asian countries. Two others could not be more unlike as countries go: Switzerland and India.

26   German, French, Italian, and Romansh are the languages of Switzerland. The first three can be and are used for official purposes; all four are designated "national" languages. Switzerland is politically almost hyperstable. It has language problems (Romansh is losing ground), but they are not major, and they are never allowed to threaten national unity.

27   Contrary to public perception, India gets along pretty well with a host of different languages. The Indian constitution officially recognizes nineteen languages,
English among them. Hindi is specified in the constitution as the national language
of India, but that is a pious postcolonial fiction: outside the Hindi-speaking northern
heartland of India, people don't want to learn it. English functions more nearly than
Hindi as India's lingua franca.

28   From 1947, when India obtained its independence from the British, until the 1960s
blood ran in the streets and people died because of language. Hindi absolutists wanted
to force Hindi on the entire country, which would have split India between north and
south and opened up other fracture lines as well. For as long as possible Jawaharlal
Nehru, independent India's first Prime Minister, resisted nationalist demands to redraw
the capricious state boundaries of British India according to language. By the time he
capitulated, the country had gained a precious decade to prove its viability as a union.

29   Why is it that India preserves its unity with not just two languages to contend
with, as Belgium, Canada, and Sri Lanka have, but nineteen? The answer is that
India, like Switzerland, has a strong national identity. The two countries share something big and almost mystical that holds each together in a union transcending language. That something I call "unique otherness."

30   The Swiss have what the political scientist Karl Deutsch called "learned habits,
preferences, symbols, memories, and patterns of landholding": customs, cultural traditions, and political institutions that bind them closer to one another than to people
of France, Germany, or Italy living just across the border and speaking the same language. There is Switzerland's traditional neutrality, its system of universal military
training (the "citizen army"), its consensual allegiance to a strong Swiss franc—and
fondue, yodeling, skiing, and mountains. Set against all this, the fact that Switzerland has four languages doesn't even approach the threshold of becoming a threat.

31   As for India, what Vincent Smith, in the *Oxford History of India,* calls its "deep
underlying fundamental unity" resides in institutions and beliefs such as caste, cow
worship, sacred places, and much more. Consider *dharma, karma,* and *maya,* the
three root convictions of Hinduism; India's historical epics; Gandhi; *ahimsa* (non-
violence); vegetarianism; a distinctive cuisine and way of eating; marriage customs;
a shared past; and what the Indologist Ainslie Embree calls "Brahmanical ideology."
In other words, "We are Indian; we are different."

32   Belgium and Canada have never managed to forge a stable national identity;
Czechoslovakia and Yugoslavia never did either. Unique otherness immunizes countries against linguistic destabilization. Even Switzerland and especially India have
problems; in any country with as many different languages as India has, language
will never *not* be a problem. However, it is one thing to have a major illness with a
bleak prognosis; it is another to have a condition that is irritating and occasionally
painful but not life-threatening.

33   History teaches a plain lesson about language and governments: there is almost
nothing the government of a free country can do to change language usage and practice significantly, to force its citizens to use certain languages in preference to others,
and to discourage people from speaking a language they wish to continue to speak.
(The rebirth of Hebrew in Palestine and Israel's successful mandate that Hebrew be

spoken and written by Israelis is a unique event in the annals of language history.) Quebec has since the 1970s passed an array of laws giving French a virtual monopoly in the province. One consequence—unintended, one wishes to believe—of these laws is that last year kosher products imported for Passover were kept off the shelves, because the packages were not labeled in French. Wise governments keep their hands off language to the extent that it is politically possible to do so.

34   We like to believe that to pass a law is to change behavior; but passing laws about language, in a free society, almost never changes attitudes or behavior. Gaelic (Irish) is living out a slow, inexorable decline in Ireland despite enormous government support of every possible kind since Ireland gained its independence from Britain. The Welsh language, in contrast, is alive today in Wales in spite of heavy discrimination during its history. Three out of four people in the northern and western countries of Gwynedd and Dyfed speak Welsh.

35   I said earlier that language is a convenient surrogate for other national problems. Official English obviously has a lot to do with concern about immigration, perhaps especially Hispanic immigration. America may be threatened by immigration; I don't know. But America is not threatened by language.

36   The usual arguments made by academics against Official English are commonsensical. Who needs a law when, according to the 1990 census, 94 percent of American residents speak English anyway? (Mauro E. Mujica, the chairman of U.S. English, cites a higher figure: 97 percent.) Not many of today's immigrants will see their first language survive into the second generation. This is in fact the common lament of first-generation immigrants: their children are not learning their language and are losing the culture of their parents. Spanish is hardly a threat to English, in spite of isolated (and easily visible) cases such as Miami, New York City, and pockets of the Southwest and southern California. The everyday language of south Texas is Spanish, and yet south Texas is not about to secede from America.

37   But empirical, calm arguments don't engage the real issue: language is a symbol, an icon. Nobody who favors a constitutional ban against flag burning will ever be persuaded by the argument that the flag is, after all, just a "piece of cloth." A draft card in the 1960s was never merely a piece of paper. Neither is a marriage license.

38   Language, as one linguist has said, is "not primarily a means of communication but a means of communion." Romanticism exalted language, made it mystical, sublime—a bond of national identity. At the same time, Romanticism created a monster: it made of language a means for destroying a country.

39   America has that unique otherness of which I spoke. In spite of all our racial divisions and economic unfairness, we have the frontier tradition, respect for the individual, and opportunity; we have our love affair with the automobile; we have in our history a civil war that freed the slaves and was fought with valor; and we have sports, hot dogs, hamburgers, and milk shakes—things big and small, noble and petty, important and trifling. "We are Americans; we are different."

40   If I'm wrong, then the great American experiment will fail—not because of language but because it no longer means anything to be an American; because we have forfeited that "willingness of the heart" that F. Scott Fitzgerald wrote was America; because we are no longer joined by Lincoln's "mystic chords of memory."

41   We are not even close to the danger point. I suggest that we relax and luxuriate in our linguistic richness and our traditional tolerance of language differences. Language does not threaten American unity. Benign neglect is a good policy for any country when it comes to language, and it's a good policy for America.

Questions on Content	1. Is there anything in the U.S. Constitution that could serve as a guide on the "Official English" question? Explain.

2. King suggests that today "Official English is politically very incorrect" (paragraph 8). Explain what he means.

3. King believes that any language bill is likely to have tough odds in the U.S. Senate. Summarize his reasoning.

4. How did language issues affect the treaty written at the end of World War I (the Treaty of Versailles) in 1919?

5. Language tolerance is a way of life in such diverse cultures as India and Switzerland. King argues that such tolerance exists because each country is united by what he calls "unique otherness" (paragraph 29). Explain what he means. Is the United States united by unique otherness?

Questions on Structure and Style	6. What is King's personal position on such movements as English Only? Is his essay an objective analysis of the issues and their history, or is he writing to persuade an audience?

7. Discuss the effectiveness of the illness metaphor the author employs in paragraph 32.

Assignments	1. Assume that an English Only referendum is to appear on a ballot in a forthcoming statewide election. Write a letter to a relative or friend in which you urge this person how to vote. You may appeal emotionally, but you should also use objective information based on King's essay.

2. Read the next selection, Richard Rodriguez's "Aria: A Memoir of a Bilingual Childhood." Assume the role of Rodriguez, and write a letter to King in response to this essay.

3. In paragraph 12 King lists six issues that "intersect in the controversy over Official English." Write an essay in which you present and discuss these six issues.

Aria: A Memoir of a Bilingual Childhood

Richard Rodriguez

Growing up usually means growing away—away from childhood, away from home, and sometimes away from family. Language plays a role in this growth. In this selection from *Hunger of Memory*, his collection of autobiographical essays, Richard Rodriguez explains how having different languages at home and at school intensified his own "growing away" and how, in his opinion, those who advocate bilingual education in schools "equate mere separateness with individuality." Bilingualists "simplistically scorn the value and necessity of assimilation" into public society, but for the author, assimilation is part of growth, and public language should be part of our inescapable public identity.

■ J O U R N A L   P R O M P T   *Most of us use different languages for private and public situations. For example, your private language that you share with your family is quite different from your public language. Comment on some of the differences you can observe between your public and private languages.*

1   I remember to start with that day in Sacramento—a California now nearly thirty years past—when I first entered a classroom, able to understand some fifty stray English words.

2   The third of four children, I had been preceded to a neighborhood Roman Catholic school by an older brother and sister. But neither of them had revealed very much about their classroom experiences. Each afternoon they returned, as they left in the morning, always together, speaking in Spanish as they climbed the five steps of the porch. And their mysterious books, wrapped in shopping-bag paper, remained on the table next to the door, closed firmly behind them.

3   An accident of geography sent me to a school where all my classmates were white, many the children of doctors and lawyers and business executives. All my classmates certainly must have been uneasy on that first day of school—as most children are uneasy—to find themselves apart from their families in the first institution of their lives. But I was astonished.

4   The nun said, in a friendly but oddly impersonal voice, "Boys and girls, this is Richard Rodriguez." (I heard her sound out: *Rich-heard Road-ree-guess.*) It was the first time I had heard anyone name me in English. "Richard," the nun repeated more slowly, writing my name down in her black leather book. Quickly I turned to see my mother's face dissolve in a watery blur behind the pebbled glass door.

5   Many years later there is something called bilingual education—a scheme proposed in the late 1960s by Hispanic-American social activists, later endorsed by a congressional vote. It is a program that seeks to permit non-English-speaking children,

many from lower-class homes, to use their family language as the language of school. (Such is the goal its supporters announce.) I hear them and am forced to say no: It is not possible for a child—any child—ever to use his family's language in school. Not to understand this is to misunderstand the public uses of schooling and to trivialize the nature of intimate life—a family's "language."

6   Memory teaches me what I know of these matters; the boy reminds the adult. I was a bilingual child, a certain kind—socially disadvantaged—the son of working-class parents, both Mexican immigrants.

7   In the early years of my boyhood, my parents coped very well in America. My father had steady work. My mother managed at home. They were nobody's victims. Optimism and ambition led them to a house (our home) many blocks from the Mexican south side of town. We lived among *gringos* and only a block from the biggest, whitest houses. It never occurred to my parents that they couldn't live wherever they chose. Nor was the Sacramento of the fifties bent on teaching them a contrary lesson. My mother and father were more annoyed than intimidated by those two or three neighbors who tried initially to make us unwelcome. ("Keep your brats away from my sidewalk!") But despite all they achieved, perhaps because they had so much to achieve, any deep feeling of ease, the confidence of "belonging" in public was withheld from them both. They regarded the people at work, the faces in crowds, as very distant from us. They were the others, *los gringos*. That term was interchangeable in their speech with another, even more telling, *los americanos*.

8   I grew up in a house where the only regular guests were my relations. For one day, enormous families of relatives would visit and there would be so many people that the noise and the bodies would spill out to the backyard and front porch. Then, for weeks, no one came by. (It was usually a salesman who rang the doorbell.) Our house stood apart. A gaudy yellow in a row of white bungalows. We were the people with the noisy dog. The people who raised pigeons and chickens. We were the foreigners on the block. A few neighbors smiled and waved. We waved back. But no one in the family knew the names of the old couple who lived next door; until I was seven years old, I did not know the names of the kids who lived across the street.

9   In public, my father and mother spoke a hesitant, accented, not always grammatical English. And they would have to strain—their bodies tense—to catch the sense of what was rapidly said by *los gringos*. At home they spoke Spanish. The language of their Mexican past sounded in counterpoint to the English of public society. The words would come quickly, with ease. Conveyed through those sounds was the pleasing, soothing, consoling reminder of being at home.

10   During those years when I was first conscious of hearing, my mother and father addressed me only in Spanish; in Spanish I learned to reply. By contrast, English (*inglés*), rarely heard in the house, was the language I came to associate with *gringos*. I learned my first words of English overhearing my parents speak to strangers. At five years of age, I knew just enough English for my mother to trust me on errands to stores one block away. No more.

11   I was a listening child, careful to hear the very different sounds of Spanish and English. Wide-eyed with hearing, I'd listen to sounds more than words. First, there were English (*gringo*) sounds. So many words were still unknown that when the

butcher or the lady at the drugstore said something to me, exotic polysyllabic sounds would bloom in the midst of their sentences. Often, the speech of people in public seemed to me very loud, booming with confidence. The man behind the counter would literally ask, "What can I do for you?" But by being so firm and so clear, the sound of his voice said that he was a *gringo*; he belonged in public society.

12   I would also hear then the high nasal notes of middle-class American speech. The air stirred with sound. Sometimes, even now, when I have been traveling abroad for several weeks, I will hear what I heard as a boy. In hotel lobbies or airports, in Turkey or Brazil, some Americans will pass, and suddenly I will hear it again—the high sound of American voices. For a few seconds I will hear it with pleasure, for it is now the sound of *my* society—a reminder of home. But inevitably—already on the flight headed for home—the sound fades with repetition. I will be unable to hear it anymore.

13   When I was a boy, things were different. The accent of *los gringos* was never pleasing nor was it hard to hear. Crowds at Safeway or at bus stops would be noisy with sound. And I would be forced to edge away from the chirping chatter above me.

14   I was unable to hear my own sounds, but I knew very well that I spoke English poorly. My words could not stretch far enough to form complete thoughts. And the words I did speak I didn't know well enough to make into distinct sounds. (Listeners would usually lower their heads, better to hear what I was trying to say.) But it was one thing for *me* to speak English with difficulty. It was more troubling for me to hear my parents speak in public: their high-whining vowels and guttural consonants; their sentences that got stuck with 'eh' and 'ah' sounds; the confused syntax; the hesitant rhythm of sounds so different from the way *gringos* spoke. I'd notice, moreover, that my parents' voices were softer than those of *gringos* we'd meet.

15   I am tempted now to say that none of this mattered. In adulthood I am embarrassed by childhood fears. And, in a way, it didn't matter very much that my parents could not speak English with ease. Their linguistic difficulties had no serious consequences. My mother and father made themselves understood at the county hospital clinic and at government offices. And yet, in another way, it mattered very much—it was unsettling to hear my parents struggle with English. Hearing them, I'd grow nervous, my clutching trust in their protection and power weakened.

16   There were many times like the night at a brightly lit gasoline station (a blaring white memory) when I stood uneasily, hearing my father. He was talking to a teen-aged attendant. I do not recall what they were saying, but I cannot forget the sounds my father made as he spoke. At one point his words slid together to form one word— sounds as confused as the threads of blue and green oil in the puddle next to my shoes. His voice rushed through what he had left to say. And, toward the end, reached falsetto notes, appealing to his listener's understanding. I looked away to the lights of passing automobiles. I tried not to hear anymore. But I heard only too well the calm, easy tones in the attendant's reply. Shortly afterward, walking toward home with my father, I shivered when he put his hand on my shoulder. The very first chance that I got, I evaded his grasp and ran on ahead into the dark, skipping with feigned boyish exuberance.

17   But then there was Spanish. *Español*: my family's language. *Español*: the language that seemed to me a private language. I'd hear strangers on the radio and in

the Mexican Catholic church across town speaking in Spanish, but I couldn't really believe that Spanish was a public language, like English. Spanish speakers, rather, seemed related to me, for I sensed that we shared—through our language—the experience of feeling apart from *los gringos*. It was thus a ghetto Spanish that I heard and I spoke. Like those whose lives are bound by a barrio, I was reminded by Spanish of my separateness from *los otros, los gringos* in power. But more intensely than for most barrio children—because I did not live in a barrio—Spanish seemed to me the language of home. (Most days it was only at home that I'd hear it.) It became the language of joyful return.

18   A family member would say something to me and I would feel myself specially recognized. My parents would say something to me and I would feel embraced by the sounds of their words. Those sounds said: *I am speaking with ease in Spanish. I am addressing you in words I never use with* los gringos. *I recognize you as someone special, close, like no one outside. You belong with us. In the family.*

19   (*Ricardo*)

20   At the age of five, six, well past the time when most other children no longer easily notice the difference between sounds uttered at home and words spoken in public, I had a different experience. I lived in a world magically compounded of sounds. I remained a child longer than most; I lingered too long, poised at the edge of language—often frightened by the sounds of *los gringos*, delighted by the sounds of Spanish at home. I shared with my family a language that was startlingly different from that used in the great city around us.

21   For me there were none of the gradations between public and private society so normal to a maturing child. Outside the house was public society; inside the house was private. Just opening or closing the screen door behind me was an important experience. I'd rarely leave home all alone or without reluctance. Walking down the sidewalk, under the canopy of tall trees, I'd warily notice the—suddenly—silent neighborhood kids who stood warily watching me. Nervously, I'd arrive at the grocery store to hear there the sounds of the *gringo*—foreign to me—reminding me that in this world so big, I was a foreigner. But then I'd return. Walking back toward our house, climbing the steps from the sidewalk, when the front door was open in summer, I'd hear voices beyond the screen door talking in Spanish. For a second or two, I'd stay, linger there, listening. Smiling, I'd hear my mother call out, saying in Spanish (words): "Is that you, Richard?" All the while her sounds would assure me: *You are home now; come closer; inside. With us.*

22   "*Sí*," I'd reply.

23   Once more inside the house I would resume (assume) my place in the family. The sounds would dim, grow harder to hear. Once more at home, I would grow less aware of that fact. It required, however, no more than the blurt of the doorbell to alert me to listen to sounds all over again. The house would turn instantly still while my mother went to the door. I'd hear her hard English sounds. I'd wait to hear her voice return to soft-sounding Spanish, which assured me, as surely as did the clicking tongue of the lock on the door, that the stranger was gone.

24   Plainly, it is not healthy to hear such sounds so often. It is not healthy to distinguish public words from private sounds so easily. I remained cloistered by sounds,

timid and shy in public, too dependent on voices at home. And yet it needs to be emphasized: I was an extremely happy child at home. I remember many nights when my father would come back from work, and I'd hear him call out to my mother in Spanish, sounding relieved. In Spanish, he'd sound light and free notes he never could manage in English. Some nights I'd jump up just at hearing his voice. With *mis hermanos* I would come running into the room where he was with my mother. Our laughing (so deep was the pleasure!) became screaming. Like others who know the pain of public alienation, we transformed the knowledge of our public separateness and made it consoling—the reminder of intimacy. Excited, we joined our voices in a celebration of sounds. *We are speaking now the way we never speak out in public. We are alone—together*, voices sounded, surrounded to tell me. Some nights, no one seemed willing to loosen the hold sounds had on us. At dinner, we invented new words. (Ours sounded Spanish, but made sense only to us.) We pieced together new words by taking, say, an English verb and giving it Spanish endings. My mother's instructions at bedtime would be lacquered with mock-urgent tones. Or a word like *sí* would become, in several notes, able to convey added measures of feeling. Tongues explored the edges of words, especially the fat vowels. And we happily sounded that military drum roll, the twirling roar of the Spanish *r*. Family language: my family's sounds. The voices of my parents and sisters and brother. Their voices insisting: *You belong here. We are family members. Related. Special to one another. Listen!* Voices singing and sighing, rising, straining, then surging, teeming with pleasure that burst syllables into fragments of laughter. At times it seemed there was steady quiet only when, from another room, the rustling whispers of my parents faded and I moved closer to sleep.

25   Supporters of bilingual education today imply that students like me miss a great deal by not being taught in their family's language. What they seem not to recognize is that, as a socially disadvantaged child, I considered Spanish to be a private language. What I needed to learn in school was that I had the right—and the obligation—to speak the public language of *los gringos*. The odd truth is that my first-grade classmates could have become bilingual, in the conventional sense of that word, more easily than I. Had they been taught (as upper-middle-class children are often taught early) a second language like Spanish or French, they could have regarded it simply as that: another public language. In my case such bilingualism could not have been so quickly achieved. What I did not believe was that I could speak a single public language.

26   Without question, it would have pleased me to hear my teachers address me in Spanish when I entered the classroom. I would have felt much less afraid. I would have trusted them and responded with ease. But I would have delayed—for how long postponed?—having to learn the language of public society. I would have evaded—and for how long could I have afforded to delay?—learning the great lesson of school, that I had a public identity.

27   Fortunately, my teachers were unsentimental about their responsibility. What they understood was that I needed to speak a public language. So their voices would search me out, asking me questions. Each time I'd hear them, I'd look up in surprise to see a nun's face frowning at me. I'd mumble, not really meaning to answer. The

nun would persist, "Richard, stand up. Don't look at the floor. Speak up. Speak to the entire class, not just to me!" But I couldn't believe that the English language was mine to use. (In part, I did not want to believe it.) I continued to mumble. I resisted the teacher's demands. (Did I somehow suspect that once I learned public language my pleasing family life would be changed?) Silent, waiting for the bell to sound, I remained dazed, diffident, afraid.

28   Because I wrongly imagined that English was intrinsically a public language and Spanish an intrinsically private one, I easily noted the difference between classroom language and the language of home. At school, words were directed to a general audience of listeners. ("Boys and girls.") Words were meaningfully ordered. And the point was not self-expression alone but to make oneself understood by many others. The teacher quizzed: "Boys and girls, why do we use that word in this sentence? Could we think of a better word to use there? Would the sentence change its meaning if the words were differently arranged? And wasn't there a better way of saying much the same thing?" (I couldn't say. I wouldn't try to say.)

29   Three months. Five. Half a year passed. Unsmiling, ever watchful, my teachers noted my silence. They began to connect my behavior with the difficult progress my older sister and brother were making. Until one Saturday morning three nuns arrived at the house to talk to our parents. Stiffly, they sat on the blue living room sofa. From the doorway of another room, spying the visitors, I noted the incongruity—the clash of two worlds, the faces and voices of school intruding upon the familiar setting of home. I overheard one voice gently wondering, "Do your children speak only Spanish at home, Mrs. Rodriguez?" While another voice added, "That Richard especially seems so timid and shy."

30   *That Rich-heard!*

31   With great tact the visitors continued, "Is it possible for you and your husband to encourage your children to practice their English when they are home?" Of course, my parents complied. What would they not do for their children's well-being? And how could they have questioned the Church's authority which those women represented? In an instant, they agreed to give up the language (the sounds) that had revealed and accentuated our family's closeness. The moment after the visitors left, the change was observed. "*Ahora*, speak to us *en inglés*," my father and mother united to tell us.

32   At first, it seemed a kind of game. After dinner each night, the family gathered to practice "our" English. (It was still then *inglés*, a language foreign to us, so we felt drawn as strangers to it.) Laughing, we would try to define words we could not pronounce. We played with strange English sounds, often over-anglicizing our pronunciations. And we filled the smiling gaps of our sentences with familiar Spanish sounds. But that was cheating, somebody shouted. Everyone laughed. In school, meanwhile, like my brother and sister, I was required to attend a daily tutoring session. I needed a full year of special attention. I also needed my teachers to keep my attention from straying in class by calling out, *Rich-heard*—their English voices slowly prying loose my ties to my other name, its three notes, *Ri-car-do*. Most of all I needed to hear my mother and father speak to me in a moment of seriousness in broken—suddenly heartbreaking—English. The scene was inevitable: One Saturday

morning I entered the kitchen where my parents were talking in Spanish. I did not realize that they were talking in Spanish however until, at the moment they saw me, I heard their voices change to speak English. Those *gringo* sounds they uttered startled me. Pushed me away. In that moment of trivial misunderstanding and profound insight, I felt my throat twisted by unsounded grief. I turned quickly and left the room. But I had no place to escape to with Spanish. (The spell was broken.) My brother and sisters were speaking English in another part of the house.

33   Again and again in the days following, increasingly angry, I was obliged to hear my mother and father: "Speak to us *en inglés*." (*Speak.*) Only then did I determine to learn classroom English. Weeks after, it happened: One day in school I raised my hand to volunteer an answer. I spoke out in a loud voice. And I did not think it remarkable when the entire class understood. That day, I moved very far from the disadvantaged child I had been only days earlier. The belief, the calming assurance that I belonged in pubic, had at last taken hold.

34   Shortly after, I stopped hearing the high and loud sounds of *los gringos*. A more and more confident speaker of English, I didn't trouble to listen to *how* strangers sounded, speaking to me. And there simply were too many English-speaking people in my day for me to hear American accents anymore. Conversations quickened. Listening to persons who sounded eccentrically pitched voices, I usually noted their sounds for an initial few seconds before I concentrated on *what* they were saying. Conversations became content-full. Transparent. Hearing someone's *tone* of voice—angry or questioning or sarcastic or happy or sad—I didn't distinguish it from the words it expressed. Sound and word were thus tightly wedded. At the end of a day, I was often bemused, always relieved, to realize how "silent," though crowded with words, my day in public had been. (This public silence measured and quickened the change in my life.)

35   At last, seven years old, I came to believe what had been technically true since my birth: I was an American citizen.

36   But the special feeling of closeness at home was diminished by then. Gone was the desperate, urgent, intense feeling of being at home; rare was the experience of feeling myself individualized by family intimates. We remained a loving family, but one greatly changed. No longer so close; no longer bound tight by the pleasing and troubling knowledge of our public separateness. Neither my older brother nor sister rushed home after school anymore. Nor did I. When I arrived home there would often be neighborhood kids in the house. Or the house would be empty of sounds.

37   Following the dramatic Americanization of their children, even my parents grew more publicly confident. Especially my mother. She learned the names of all the people on our block. And she decided we needed to have a telephone installed in the house. My father continued to use the word *gringo*. But it was no longer charged with the old bitterness or distrust. (Stripped of any emotional content, the word simply became a name for those Americans not of Hispanic descent.) Hearing him, sometimes, I wasn't sure if he was pronouncing the Spanish word *gringo* or saying gringo in English.

38   Matching the silence I started hearing in public was a new quiet at home. The family's quiet was partly due to the fact that, as we children learned more and more

English, we shared fewer and fewer words with our parents. Sentences needed to be spoken slowly when a child addressed his mother or father. (Often the parent wouldn't understand.) The child would need to repeat himself. (Still the parent misunderstood.) The young voice, frustrated, would end up saying, "Never mind"—the subject was closed. Dinners would be noisy with the clinking of knives and forks against dishes. My mother would smile softly between her remarks; my father at the other end of the table would chew and chew at his food, while he stared over the heads of his children.

39   My *mother*! My *father*! After English became my primary language, I no longer knew what words to use in addressing my parents. The old Spanish words (those tender accents of sound) I had used earlier—*mamá* and *papá*—I couldn't use anymore. They would have been too painful reminders of how much had changed in my life. On the other hand, the words I heard neighborhood kids call *their* parents seemed equally unsatisfactory. *Mother* and *Father*; *Ma, Papa, Pa, Dad, Pop* (how I hated the all-American sound of that last word especially)—all these terms I felt were unsuitable, not really terms of address for *my* parents. As a result, I never used them at home. Whenever I'd speak to my parents, I would try to get their attention with eye contact alone. In public conversations, I'd refer to "my parents" or "my mother and father."

40   My mother and father, for their part, responded differently, as their children spoke to them less. She grew restless, seemed troubled and anxious at the scarcity of words exchanged in the house. It was she who would question me about my day when I came home from school. She smiled at small talk. She pried at the edges of my sentences to get me to say something more. (What?) She'd join conversations she overheard, but her intrusions often stopped her children's talking. By contrast, my father seemed reconciled to the new quiet. Though his English improved somewhat, he retired into silence. At dinner he spoke very little. One night his children and even his wife helplessly giggled at his garbled English pronunciation of the Catholic Grace before Meals. Thereafter he made his wife recite the prayer at the start of each meal, even on formal occasions, when there were guests in the house. Hers became the public voice of the family. On official business, it was she, not my father, one would usually hear on the phone or in stores, talking to strangers. His children grew so accustomed to his silence that, years later, they would speak routinely of his shyness. (My mother would often try to explain: Both his parents died when he was eight. He was raised by an uncle who treated him like little more than a menial servant. He was never encouraged to speak. He grew up alone. A man of few words.) But my father was not shy, I realized, when I'd watch him speaking Spanish with relatives. Using Spanish, he was quickly effusive. Especially when talking with other men, his voice would spark, flicker, flare alive with sounds. In Spanish, he expressed ideas and feelings he rarely revealed in English. With firm Spanish sounds, he conveyed confidence and authority English would never allow him.

41   The silence at home, however, was finally more than a literal silence. Fewer words passed between parent and child, but more profound was the silence that resulted from my inattention to sounds. At about the time I no longer bothered to listen with care to the sounds of English in public, I grew careless about listening to

the sounds family members made when they spoke. Most of the time I heard someone speaking at home and didn't distinguish his sounds from the words people
uttered in public. I didn't even pay much attention to my parents' accented and ungrammatical speech. At least not at home. Only when I was with them in public
would I grow alert to their accents. Though, even then, their sounds caused me less
and less concern. For I was increasingly confident of my own public identity.

42   I would have been happier about my public address had I not sometimes recalled
what it had been like earlier, when my family had conveyed its intimacy through a
set of conveniently private sounds. Sometimes in public, hearing a stranger, I'd hark
back to my past. A Mexican farmworker approached me downtown to ask directions
to somewhere. "¿*Hijito* . . . ?" he said. And his voice summoned deep longing. Another time, standing beside my mother in the visiting room of a Carmelite convent,
before the dense screen which rendered the nuns shadowy figures, I heard several
Spanish-speaking nuns—their busy, singsong overlapping voices—assure us that
yes, yes, we were remembered, all our family was remembered in their prayers.
(Their voices echoed faraway family sounds.) Another day, a dark-faced old
woman—her hand light on my shoulder—steadied herself against me as she boarded
a bus. She murmured something I couldn't quite comprehend. Her Spanish voice
came near, like the face of a never-before-seen relative in the instant before I was
kissed. Her voice, like so many of the Spanish voices I'd hear in public, recalled the
golden age of my youth. Hearing Spanish then, I continued to be a careful, if sad,
listener to sounds. Hearing a Spanish-speaking family walking behind me, I turned
to look. I smiled for an instant, before my glance found the Hispanic-looking faces
of strangers in the crowd going by.

43   Today I hear bilingual educators say that children lose a degree of "individuality" by
becoming assimilated into public society. (Bilingual schooling was popularized in
the seventies, that decade when middle-class ethnics began to resist the process of
assimilation—the American melting pot.) But the bilingualists simplistically scorn
the value and necessity of assimilation. They do not seem to realize that there are
two ways a person is individualized. So they do not realize that while one suffers
a diminished sense of *private* individuality by becoming assimilated into public
society, such assimilation makes possible the achievement of *public* individuality.

44   The bilingualists insist that a student should be reminded of his difference from
others in mass society, his heritage. But they equate mere separateness with individuality. The fact is that only in private—with intimates—is separateness from the
crowd a prerequisite for individuality. (An intimate draws me apart, tells me that I
am unique, unlike all others.) In public, by contrast, full individuality is achieved,
paradoxically, by those who are able to consider themselves members of the crowd.
Thus it happened for me: Only when I was able to think of myself as an American,
no longer an alien in *gringo* society, could I seek the rights and opportunities necessary for full public individuality. The social and political advantages I enjoy as a man
result from the day that I came to believe that my name, indeed, is *Rich-heard Road-
ree-guess.* It is true that my public society today is often impersonal. (My public society is usually mass society.) Yet despite the anonymity of the crowd and despite the

fact that the individuality I achieve in public is often tenuous—because it depends on my being one in a crowd—I celebrate the day I acquired my new name. Those middle-class ethnics who scorn assimilation seem to me filled with decadent self-pity, obsessed by the burden of public life. Dangerously, they romanticize public separateness and they trivialize the dilemma of the socially disadvantaged.

45   My awkward childhood does not prove the necessity of bilingual education. My story discloses instead an essential myth of childhood—inevitable pain. If I rehearse here the changes in my private life after my Americanization, it is finally to emphasize the public gain. The loss implies the gain: The house I returned to each afternoon was quiet. Intimate sounds no longer rushed to the door to greet me. There were other noises inside. The telephone rang. Neighborhood kids ran past the door of the bedroom where I was reading my schoolbooks—covered with shopping-bag paper. Once I learned public language, it would never again be easy for me to hear intimate family voices. More and more of my day was spent hearing words. But that may only be a way of saying that the day I raised my hand in class and spoke loudly to an entire roomful of faces, my childhood started to end.

Questions on Content

1. In paragraph 4 Rodriguez says of his teacher, "I heard her sound out: *Rich-heard Road-ree-guess*." Why is this memory so strong for him?

2. What important distinction does Rodriguez make between public and private language?

3. When did the author stop concentrating on how *los gringos* sounded and begin concentrating on what they were saying?

4. How did knowing English affect the author's family life? Did this Americanization affect all members of his family similarly? Explain.

5. Rodriguez still has difficulty using the words *Mother* and *Father*. Why?

Questions on Structure and Style

6. This essay is both an argument and a memoir, and its tone shifts as the author moves between the two rhetorical methods. Where is the first shift? Is there a thesis to the argument? Is it directly stated or implied?

7. Characterize the tone of the memoir and that of the argument. Do the two complement each other?

8. Rodriguez's use of italics, parentheses, and extremely short paragraphs (sometimes single words) is characteristic of his

style and consistent throughout the essay. Why does he use these devices? Are they merely ways to be different, or are they systematic, serving identifiable purposes?

9. How effective is the concluding paragraph? Does it clearly relate to the opening? If so, how? Does it pull the argument and the memoir together?

10. In paragraph 16 Rodriguez uses a simile: "At one point his words slid together to form one word—sounds as confused as the threads of blue and green oil in the puddle next to my shoes." Find other examples of figurative language in the essay. What does the figurative language contribute to Rodriguez's presentation?

11. Rodriguez describes bilingual education as a "scheme" (paragraph 5). What effect does the word *scheme* create? What other terms could he have used, and what effects would they create?

Assignments

1. Later in *Hunger of Memory*, Rodriguez again discusses his childhood and says, "The great change in my life was not linguistic but social." Using "Aria" as evidence, write an essay explaining this assertion.

2. Many people, even native speakers, have had to change their language habits. Write an account of such a change that you or someone close to you made. Explain both what changed and why it had to change.

3. Rodriguez focuses on public language and its effect on private language, which in this case could be called family language. Think of how the language you use with your family differs from your public language—the language you use at school, at work, and with strangers. Write an essay describing the differences and explaining why they exist.

Americanization Is Tough on "Macho"

Rose Del Castillo Guilbault

Many speakers of American English possess a Spanish vocabulary that consists only of *si, adios,* and *macho,* with this last word possessing uniformly ugly connotations in English. However, in the following reflection on language, culture, and her own father, Rose Del Castillo Guilbault makes clear that the word *macho* in Spanish implies only admiration and respect. The distortion of *macho* as it passed into everyday English thus serves as one more example of how cultural misunderstandings can create language which then reinforces those misunderstandings. The author writes a column for the *San Francisco Chronicle*, from which this essay is taken.

■ **JOURNAL PROMPT** *Near the conclusion of this essay Del Castillo Guilbault says, "It's [macho] become an accepted stereotype of the Latin male. And like all stereotypes, it distorts truth" (paragraph 17). Make a list of other terms and labels we use in stereotyping gender, ethnic, and social groups.*

1   What is *macho*? That depends which side of the border you come from.

2   Although it's not unusual for words and expressions to lose their subtlety in translation, the negative connotations of *macho* in this country are troublesome to Hispanics.

3   Take the newspaper descriptions of alleged mass murderer Ramon Salcido. That an insensitive, insanely jealous, hard-drinking, violent Latin male is referred to as *macho* makes Hispanics cringe.

4   *"Es muy macho,"* the women in my family nod approvingly, describing a man they respect. But in the United States, when women say, "He's so macho," it's with disdain.

5   The Hispanic *macho* is manly, responsible, hardworking, a man in charge, a patriarch. A man who expresses strength through silence. What the Yiddish language would call a *mensch*.

6   The American *macho* is a chauvinist, a brute, uncouth, selfish, loud, abrasive, capable of inflicting pain, and sexually promiscuous.

7   Quintessential *macho* models in this country are Sylvester Stallone, Arnold Schwarzenegger and Charles Bronson. In their movies, they exude toughness, independence, masculinity. But a closer look reveals their machismo is really violence masquerading as courage, sullenness disguised as silence and irresponsibility camouflaged as independence.

8   If the Hispanic ideal of *macho* were translated to American screen roles, they might be Jimmy Stewart, Sean Connery and Laurence Olivier.

9   In Spanish, *macho* ennobles Latin males. In English it devalues them. This pattern seems consistent with the conflicts ethnic minority males experience in this country.

Typically the cultural traits other societies value don't translate as desirable characteristics in America.

10   I watched my own father struggle with these cultural ambiguities. He worked on a farm for twenty years. He laid down miles of irrigation pipe, carefully plowed long, neat rows in fields, hacked away at recalcitrant weeds and drove tractors through whirlpools of dust. He stoically worked twenty-hour days during harvest season, accepting the long hours as part of agricultural work. When the boss complained or upbraided him for minor mistakes, he kept quiet, even when it was obvious the boss had erred.

11   He handled the most menial tasks with pride. At home he was a good provider, helped out my mother's family in Mexico without complaint, and was indulgent with me. Arguments between my mother and him generally had to do with money, or with his stubborn reluctance to share his troubles. He tried to work them out in his own silence. He didn't want to trouble my mother—a course that backfired, because the imagined is always worse than the reality.

12   Americans regarded my father as decidedly un-*macho*. His character was interpreted as nonassertive, his loyalty non-ambition, and his quietness, ignorance. I once overheard the boss's son blame him for plowing crooked rows in a field. My father merely smiled at the lie, knowing the boy had done it, but didn't refute it, confident his good work was well known. But the boss instead ridiculed him for being "stupid" and letting a kid get away with a lie. Seeing my embarrassment, my father dismissed the incident, saying "They're the dumb ones. Imagine, me fighting with a kid."

13   I tried not to look at him with American eyes because sometimes the reflection hurt.

14   Listening to my aunts' clucks of approval, my vision focused on the qualities America overlooked. "He's such a hard worker. So serious, so responsible." My aunts would secretly compliment my mother. The unspoken comparison was that he was not like some of their husbands, who drank and womanized. My uncles represented the darker side of *macho*.

15   In a partiarchal society, few challenge their roles. If men drink, it's because it's the manly thing to do. If they gamble, it's because it's how men relax. And if they fool around, well, it's because a man simply can't hold back so much man! My aunts didn't exactly meekly sit back, but they put up with these transgressions because Mexican society dictated this was their lot in life.

16   In the United States, I believe it was the feminist movement of the early '70s that changed *macho*'s meaning. Perhaps my generation of Latin women was in part responsible. I recall Chicanas complaining about the chauvinistic nature of Latin men and the notion they wanted their women barefoot, pregnant and in the kitchen. The generalization that Latin men embodied chauvinistic traits led to this interesting twist of semantics. Suddenly a word that represented something positive in one culture became a negative prototype in another.

17   The problem with the use of *macho* today is that it's become an accepted stereotype of the Latin male. And like all stereotypes, it distorts truth.

18   The impact of language in our society is undeniable. And the misuse of *macho* hints at a deeper cultural misunderstanding that extends beyond mere word definitions.

Questions on Content

1. Summarize the different connotations of the word *macho* for Hispanic and non-Hispanic Americans.

2. What does the author believe are the origins of the two meanings for *macho* mentioned in question 1 above?

3. About her father, Del Castillo Guilbault states, "I tried not to look at him with American eyes because sometimes the reflection hurt" (paragraph 13). Explain.

Questions on Structure and Style

4. Does the author explicitly state her thesis in her opening paragraphs?

5. Del Castillo Guilbault's father's struggle with cultural ambiguity is central to this selection. Discuss the purpose and effect of this important section.

Assignments

1. Del Castillo Guilbault closes paragraph 9 with this sentence: "Typically the cultural traits other societies value don't translate as desirable characteristics in America." Interview a member of another ethnic group, and write a concrete essay in which you describe how cultural traits don't translate well into this culture. (If you are a member of such a group, feel free to write from personal experience.)

2. Choose one of the terms you listed in the Journal Prompt. Write an essay in which you discuss the stereotype and how it distorts truth.

Names in the Melting Pot

Justin Kaplan and Anne Bernays

If we take pride in being "a nation of immigrants," we also should know why our last names often do not identify our racial, ethnic, or cultural background as accurately as we sometimes assume they do. In the following excerpt from their book *The Language of Names,* Justin Kaplan and Anne Bernays examine the unexpected, sometimes unintended transformation of surnames that occurred as millions of immigrants arrived in the United States at the turn of this century.

■ **J O U R N A L   P R O M P T**   *In the selection that follows Kaplan and Bernays state, "If first names whisper, surnames shout, and they often give misleading messages" (paragraph 16). Write a paragraph in response before reading the selection.*

1 "All of our people, except the pure-blooded Indians," President Franklin Delano Roosevelt said in a 1944 campaign speech, "are immigrants or descendants of immigrants, including even those who came over the *Mayflower.*" Echoed by countless other public figures, John F. Kennedy among them, declarations like this, once considered incendiary by the Daughter of the American Revolution, are now part of the conventional wisdom and as ritualized as Lincoln's Gettysburg Address. It's probable, however, that even "the pure-blooded Indians"—often called First Americans, Native Americans, or Amerinds—were immigrants themselves, having long ago migrated east to Alaska by way of the Bering Strait land bridge. Following "the hyphenate craze," the late William A. Henry III remarked, perhaps they should be called Siberian-Americans.

2 Roosevelt's paternal ancestor, Claes Martenzen van Rosenvelt (meaning, roughly, "open land overgrown with roses") was a Dutchman who arrived in New Amsterdam around 1644. The Delanos, on FDR's mother's side, descended from Philippe de la Noye, a Luxembourger who landed in Plymouth in 1621 with the Pilgrims. Apollos De Revoire, a silversmith of French Huguenot descent, came over from the Isle of Guernsey, set up shop in Boston, and to lubricate his business dealings with "the Bumpkins" there, anglicized Revoire to Revere. Apollos's son Paul learned the trade and in time gave his name to a classic design of silver bowls and a famous horseback ride to Lexington.

3 Voluntarily or not, the Roosevelts, the Delanos, the Reveres, and other by now unarguably American founding families had all been exposed to a common action, described by a student of surnames, Howard F. Barker, as "the abrasion" and "heavy grinding of common speech." Syllables and letters disappear along with foreign identifying marks; names become shorter, and easier to spell and pronounce; and as

Barker noted in 1932, "common names gain in usage because rarer ones are compared unfavorably with them."

4   Since then, administrative mechanisms such as the draft, automobile registration, Social Security, the Internal Revenue Service, credit card networks, and data processing in general have speeded up the standardizing of last names. Still, a 1984 tabulation ranks 8,414 surnames that appear five thousand or more times in the roughly 350 million individual records kept by the Social Security Administration since its inception in 1936. The top five are Smith (with 3,376,494 entries), Johnson, Williams, Brown, and Jones (with 1,930,318). Cohen, the commonest Jewish surname, ranks 243 (with 147,864 entries). Going alphabetically, Aaron (with 19,166 entries) ranks 2,367 in frequency; Zuniga (with 20,846 entries), 2,201. The 1984 tabulation yielded 1.7 million different names. Discounting the many minor variants in form and spelling, the gross figure suggests that there are roughly 25,000 unique surnames borne by a nation of immigrants who represent every language and ethnicity in the world. In contrast, China, with a population of more than a billion, four and a half times that of the United States, has a pool of only about 150 to 400 basic surnames (or about 3,000, including regional variants), even though the Chinese have had hereditary names a thousand years longer than any other culture.

5   Like stones at the seashore, foreign and difficult names yield their roughness and irregularity to the tidal wash of American convenience and usage: Pfoersching turns into Pershing; Huber, Hoover; Roggenfelder, Rockefeller; Kouwenhoven, Conover; L'Archeveque, Larch; Bjorkegren, Burke. Smith is the ultimate catchall for linguistic naturalization: it takes in Schmidt, Schmitt, Schmitz, Smed, Szmyt, Schmieder, Smidnovic, Seppanen, Fevre, Kalvaitis, Kovars, Haddad, McGowan, and other variants that in their original language mean someone who works with metal. Comedian Ernie Kovacs, Simon Kuznets (winner of the Nobel Prize in Economics), and Stanley Kowalski of Tennessee Williams's *A Streetcar Named Desire* are all Smith brothers under the skin. Johnson is a similar linguistic melting pot, its original imported ingredients ranging from Johansson to McShane.

6   The inexorable Americanization of foreign names was "a mass movement as great in its way as the settlement of the West," Barker wrote—and, he might have added, the tide of immigration from southern and eastern Europe. Mounting in volume from the late 1840s, the influx from abroad reached a high point between 1903 and 1908, when a nation of about 80 million absorbed nearly 6 million foreigners. By 1910 the New York that expatriate novelist Henry James recalled from his childhood in Manhattan as a "small warm dusky homogeneous" island community had become the largest Italian city and the largest Jewish city in the world. Three quarters of its 6 million inhabitants were either foreign-born or first-generation Americans.

7   Visiting Ellis Island in 1904, James compared "this visible act of ingurgitation on the part of our body politic" to a circus performer eating fire or swallowing a sword. James was only a second-generation American (Scotch Irish on his father's side), but in a country as young as the United States, this gave him almost the status of an original settler. What he saw at Ellis Island left him with a "sense of dispossession." At the same time he acknowledged that alienness was a condition that all Americans shared,

whatever their origin or date of arrival or degree of concern over "race-suicide" and "mongrelization" of the native blood stock. "Who and what is an alien," he asked, "in a country peopled from the first under the jealous eye of history?—peopled, that is, by migrations at once recent, perfectly traceable and urgently required."

8   A dialogue from a Jewish vaudeville skit a few decades earlier confronted the matter of alienness on a homelier level.

9   "Are you a foreigner?"

10   "No," says the greenhorn, "I'm an American from de oder side."

11   Over the three centuries since the Dutch settled in New York, Ellis Island was drastically enlarged, with landfill adding twenty-four acres to the original three. It changed in function, from oystering ground to gallows, fort, POW camp, convalescent hospital, and munitions depot. "No one wanted the island for anything," the novelist Mary Gordon wrote. "It was the perfect place to build an immigration center." After closing as a receiving station in 1954, Ellis Island became a Coast Guard training facility, a derelict property abandoned by the federal government, and finally a historic site that now draws a reverse traffic, this one of native tourists. It also went through the same naming and renaming cycle as many of the immigrants who passed through it. Ellis Island was Gull Island when the Dutch bought it from the Mohegan Indians; then Oyster Island, Dyre's Island, Bucking Island, and Anderson's (or Gibbet) Island, for a pirate who was hanged there in 1765; finally Samuel Ellis, a butcher, bought the place and left it to his heirs. Between 1892, when it opened for business and admitted Annie Moore, a fifteen-year-old from County Cork, and 1924, when Congress curtailed mass immigration, more than 12 million foreigners passed through Ellis Island—a record 12 thousand on one day alone in 1907—and saw their names placed in its registers. Today at Ellis Island a circular wall of names commemorates half a million immigrant families, with a new section scheduled to be added in 1998.

12   "The immigrant's arrival in his new home is like a second birth to him," journalist and novelist Abraham Cahan wrote. "Imagine a new born babe in possession of a fully developed intellect. Would it ever forget its entry into the world?" The immigrant's first experience of officialdom on passing from the confinement of steerage reenacted a rite of birth: He was named, and the name that he took or was given often differed from the one he had carried in the old country, but this was not a time for sentiment and retrospection. In order to pass through the golden door, his first concern then was to be certified physically and mentally intact—free of loathsome, contagious, or incurable disease (trachoma in particular) and unlikely to be a public charge.

13   The recording of names at Ellis Island, at Castle Garden (its predecessor in New York harbor), and at about seventy other receiving stations in the United States generated colorful changes. Enhanced by anecdote, invention, and family transmission, they have become part of American folklore, along with the generally accepted belief, as the columnist Ellen Goodman wrote, that

> immigration officials at Ellis Island christened more Americans than any church in the Northern Hemisphere. One of my own grandfathers had a name twice as long as the one he was left by some efficient or harassed bureaucrat. Another relative nervously

repeated the word spoken by the man in front of him in line. He assumed that "Goodman" was a password to get into the country.

14   Weary immigration officers whose only language was English processed foreigners from a dozen and more language cultures as different as Arabic and Polish, Turkish and Italian, Finnish and Greek. Even with the help of interpreters, they could hardly help making goulash, baba ghanouj, or tzimmes of names they could neither pronounce nor spell. However, at least as much linguistic maceration and random christening had already taken place in passenger manifests drawn up on the other side of the ocean. According to the historian Robert M. Rennick,

> The belief that most "foreign" names were mutilated by ignorant or indifferent officials at the ports of debarkation in this country, at least after the Federal Government assumed jurisdiction over immigration in 1882, seems to have little basis in fact. Under the provisions of the Act of 1891, whatever name was given on the immigrant's manifest, made out for him at the port of embarkation in Europe or on board the vessel taking him to America, was the name recorded at the place of entry. It was in the preparation of manifests and passenger lists that most of the name errors probably occurred until 1924, when immigrants were required to present visas for admission.

15   Yitzchak sailed from Bremen and landed on the American shore as Hitchcock; Yankele (little Jacob) as John Kelly, who went on to run a saloon; Harlampoulas as Harris; Rabinowitz as Robbins; Cheskel as Elwell; Ilyan as Williams; Levy as Lamar; Warschawsky as Ward; Katz as Feline and thence Filene, or so the story goes. According to another family tale, four Mikeloshansky brothers from the same Polish shtetl passed through separate immigration gates and emerged Finberg, Friedman, Reddinov, and Rubenstein. One Russian immigrant protested, *"Ne ponemya"* (I don't understand), and, according to legend, was admitted as Panama. In another familiar story the man who said *"Schon vergessen"* (I've already forgotten) in answer to a question he didn't understand became Shane Ferguson. A more likely explanation is that this Ferguson, if he ever existed, was originally a Feygelson. Often all that survived of a surname was its initial letter.

16   If first names whisper, surnames shout, and they often give misleading messages. "In daily life," Mary Waters, a sociologist, reported, "Americans routinely use surnames to guess one another's ethnic origins," but the conclusions they reach, based on folk knowledge of what is a typical Irish, Italian, or Dutch name, deal only with the father's ethnicity, ignore the mother's, and disregard mixed marriages, mixed ancestries, and earlier name changes. Even so, beginning with the first tidal waves of immigration, a surname could cut you off from employment and social acceptance as effectively as a criminal record. If it was O'Reilly or Epstein or Bertucci, your destiny was shaped in the cradle. Some people with undesirable names went the pragmatic route and changed them. Others, who couldn't tolerate the psychic wrench of a name change, did not and often paid for their refusal in reduced earning power and career advancement, although they may have slept better at night than the name changers.

Questions on Content

1. In paragraph 4 the authors turn to a brief discussion of the relatively small number of surnames in China. Why?

2. What was novelist Henry James's attitude about the immigration patterns in the early years of this century?

3. Kaplan and Bernays point out that "a surname could cut you off from employment and social acceptance as effectively as a criminal record" (paragraph 16). Do such prejudicial attitudes still exist?

Questions on Structure and Style

4. Kaplan and Bernays begin this selection with a discussion of the following names: Roosevelt, Delano, and Revere. Explain the purpose and effect of these choices.

5. Discuss the effectiveness of the simile that opens paragraph 5. Where do the authors echo this simile later in the selection?

Assignments

1. Examine surnames (paternal and maternal) in your family going back several generations. Write an essay in which you describe what these surnames reveal about your ethnicity.

2. Interview an acquaintance, and write an essay similar to the one described in assignment 1.

Learning English Good

Tara Elyssa

Native English speakers seldom notice the confusing messiness of
English grammar and pronunciation. However, for the increasing
number of English second language (ESL) students worldwide,
English presents a formidable challenge. The experiences of these
students reveal much about English, its evolution, all languages, and
human nature, too. In the following essay, written especially for
About Language, Tara Elyssa reveals what it's like to study a new
language and discover that thinking systematically and logically
doesn't help very much. Elyssa, born and raised in Zimbabwe, has
spent twenty-five years teaching English and French. She also has
established and coordinated ESL and multicultural programs in
Namibia, Zimbabwe, and the United States.

■ **J O U R N A L   P R O M P T**   *If you speak a second language, or if you have ever
tried to learn another language, think about features of the new language that were most difficult for you. Were the difficulties caused because the features were not similar to the grammar
or pronunciation systems of English?*

1   "Between, between and drink a chair," I am greeted as I enter the dorm room of my
ESL students. Only their warm smiles and gesturing toward an armchair convey the
meaning of these perfectly good English words. The mystery unravels later when my
English-Spanish dictionary reveals that the command form *entre* (for "come in")
corresponds to *between*, the Spanish *tome* can mean "take" or "drink" in English,
and *silla* translates as "seat" or "chair." In other words, "Come in, come in, and take
a seat." Now I understand the bewildered reactions I get when I try to compose
Spanish sentences by directly translating from a dictionary.

2   Whether the new language is English or any other language, the most intelligent
of learners struggles with the many complex tasks of transition between languages.
It's so much more complicated than learning a new vocabulary. Perhaps only those
of you native English speakers who have studied a foreign language in the classroom
for four or five years, and then found yourselves helpless on the streets of that foreign country, can understand the complexities facing the growing number of English
Second Language (ESL) speakers in the United States and around the world. Even
if you did succeed in memorizing the dictionary vocabulary of a new language such
as English, how would you know which meanings were appropriate in which situations, how the words were pronounced and delivered in an authentic way, or the way
to combine words into accurate grammatical structures using a system very different
from that of your first language? Alternatively, imagine you had been speaking
English for years and then entered an English-speaking university—only to discover
that what you had learned from TV and your peers was considered incorrect and had
to be relearned.

3   These struggles by so many people to learn correct English reveal fascinating and humorous characteristics of language itself. The following examples of ESL speakers' experiences help us discover, first, more about the nature of English, and second, curious relationships among the new universal youth jargon, English sub-dialects, and ESL.

4   One such struggle is learning *how* to say something in English—the delivery. Many native English speakers don't realize that in addition to developing English vocabulary and pronunciation, they have also acquired a complicated system of juncture (where to separate and join the word sounds) and stress (where to place emphasis within a group of words). One day one of my ESL students, who could surpass any of the native English speakers in the class on grammar or spelling tests, asked me why the American students were always shouting "Jedoo" and "Djee che?" at him after a test. I had to follow him outside one evening to discover that they were actually asking him "How did you do?" (on the test) and "Did you eat yet?" English words such as *did you* are often joined into one syllable (*djoo*), and words ending in a consonant such as *t* are often broken before the consonant, which is then joined to the next word (*ea—tyet*). ESL learners expect the sound breaks to exist at the same places as the spelling breaks and are naturally confused by such utterances.

5   For people who know the system for speaking English, other important indicators of meaning include raising or lowering the tone of voice and placing emphasis on certain syllables. These techniques show whether we are asking a question or stating a fact, whether the speaker is sincere or being sarcastic, and a host of other important aspects of communication. Try reading this next sentence aloud—first as a sincere fact, then as a question, then in a sarcastic tone:

> They broke up again.

If you're a native or advanced English speaker, raising, lowering, pausing, and stressing your voice to change the meaning of the sentence came easily, but these techniques are completely lost on those who have not learned the same system and perhaps learned a very different system for their first language. In the "Jedoo" situation previously mentioned, the misunderstanding between the students after class was compounded because the ESL student did not recognize that the English speakers, through their tone, were asking questions. Further confusion resulted from the raised volume and changing tone as the American students repeated their questions. The Americans were attempting to make the communication clearer and friendlier, but their tone was interpreted by the foreign speaker as angry and hostile.

6   In addition to the challenges of vocabulary, juncture, and stress, structural difficulties are common for ESL learners. We often hear incorrect utterances such as the following two, but have you ever wondered *why* ESL speakers consistently make such mistakes?

> My roommate last night me help.
>
> I hope making a decisions tomorrow.

An analysis of why these errors are common reveals interesting aspects of English.

7   Linguists and classroom practitioners often analyze errors using the scientific techniques of contrastive analysis (contrasting language systems to find out their points of greatest difference and therefore points of greatest difficulty for learners who are making the transition between languages) and error analysis (analyzing common errors made by speakers of various first languages who are learning a second language to discover particularly weak or difficult aspects of the second language). When these two scientific techniques are applied to the learning of English, differences among languages become clearer, and we can understand what leads ESL learners to make the two incorrect utterances in the previous paragraph. These differences involve word order, tenses or time markers, singular and plural concepts, and gerund-infinitive requirements.

8   The first incorrect utterance, "My roommate last night me help," reminds us that not all languages use the same word order. For English speakers it is important to indicate immediately the doer of the action (subject), followed by the action itself (verb), followed by the receiver of the action (object)—SVO. In other languages, German, for example, the action word often comes at the end of the sentence—SOV. For speakers who consider the action to be most important, the verb is placed first with the doer and receiver following. If you've perceived action-doer relationships this way since infancy, the normal English word order sounds very awkward to you. You tend to translate your thoughts into English using the word order from your first language.

9   Next time you're on campus, in a restaurant, or in any casual U.S. environment, listen for the most common word order. Frequently, you will hear American English speakers begin their sentences with *I* followed by the verb and object. Then imagine what this sounds like to speakers of other languages who find it culturally inappropriate, even conceited, to put themselves first in an utterance. For them, composing many common English utterances feels awkward and maybe even rude.

10   Another difficulty with the first incorrect utterance is time confusion. For English speakers, even if they have indicated a specific time such as *last night*, they also must add a tense or time marker to the verb (for example, "My roommate helpED me"). Therefore, when an ESL speaker doesn't use a time marker on the verb, the statement sounds odd to native English speakers. However, consider the awkwardness of the English system. We have to conjugate or transform verbs to show several different kinds of present and future tenses, as well as a multitude of past tenses. We have to use auxiliary verbs and past participle forms, which even TV announcers can't use correctly and sometimes even university professors can't spell. One of my ESL classes actually burst into laughter when I told them that English needs *four* words to explain some time periods (for example, "will have been eating").

11   With such an unwieldy system for showing time or tense, it is not surprising that in a recent project to create a universal computer language, experimenters tried to show tense by adding, to any pure verb form, one simple word to convey past and another simple word for future. The absence of either of these two time words would signify about the same as the simple present tense in English. If these modern experimenters studied some of the oldest languages still used by the largest populations on earth (Asian and African languages), they would find a similarly simple, yet

refined, time-marking system. For example, in Bantu languages common throughout southern Africa, one simple syllable is inserted into the subject-verb phrase to indicate past and another to indicate future, without ever changing the pure form of the verb. Knowing this, we can understand how strange it is for many others to hear and create English verb tenses.

12   Let's see what more we can learn from the second incorrect ESL utterance: "I hope making a decisions tomorrow." First of all, how many decisions is the speaker hoping to make? English grammar books clearly explain that any noun that can be counted is singular when preceded by *a* and made plural by adding *s*. So why, many English teachers moan, can't the ESL learners just study that? Once again we must remember that the differences among language systems are very complicated, and we can learn fascinating facts about how different cultural groups think by analyzing how people talk. For English speakers, dogs or books or boys or decisions can be counted easily, and therefore can be made singular or plural with the rule above. However, for speakers of Chinese and many other languages, nouns such as *dogs* and the rest fall into different categories, and only certain categories can be made singular or plural. English speakers would have to learn the appropriate categories before knowing how to apply the very sophisticated rules for singular and plural in Chinese, and Chinese people often transfer their own concepts of singular and plural when speaking English.

13   For ESL students from areas such as India, Russia, and Turkey, even if a noun were considered singular (*dog*, for example), no need exists to indicate this yet again by adding an article such as *a* in front of it. It sounds less redundant, and therefore better, to such speakers to leave out *a.* To complicate matters further, even when two languages have the same system for making nouns plural or singular, disagreement exists about how to treat certain nouns. For example, in English the nouns *garbage, advice, information,* and *news* are considered singular; however, in Spanish they are plural. So, native Spanish-language speakers naturally would say, "We need some advices." They are shocked that English speakers consider such concepts to be singular. Perhaps you can understand this shock better if you are an English speaker who has studied French or Spanish. You discovered that in these languages nouns are male and female, and you have to memorize the category for each noun. No wonder learning any language takes so long.

14   Now we understand why the ESL speaker would say, "a decisions," but how do we explain the "I hope making" error? Consider other errors of this type, which violate gerund/infinitive requirements. For example:

> I enjoy to play sports.
>
> He promises helping me with my computer project.

You probably could not explain the problems with these English sentences. People subconsciously internalize the rules of a language, especially the first language they learn as children. Therefore, when others learning our language break the rules, we may know something sounds wrong without knowing why or which rule has been broken.

15   ESL learners, however, need a conscious awareness of the English rule (for example, for gerund/infinitive requirements) and why their utterance is flawed. They likely make the error because they apply to English the rules of their own languages, which they, too, subconsciously internalized. They then have the difficult task of consciously learning which English verbs must be followed by gerunds (*ing* words such as *helping*), which English verbs require infinitives (*to* words such as *to help*), and which verbs can be followed by either gerunds or infinitives. For example, in English we say, "I like *to play* soccer" or "I like *playing* soccer." However, instead of "I enjoy *to play* soccer," we must say "I enjoy *playing* soccer." We say, "She wants *to be* an astronaut" but not "She wants *being* an astronaut." (These idiosyncrasies of English inspire all teachers' dreams of the perfect universal language.)

· · ·

16   Analyzing the ESL struggle as we did through common errors is an important step to understanding the English language system. However, ESL experiences also raise some questions about how our language is changing (for example, through the new youth jargon and widespread subdialects) and how we might improve our communication abilities.

17   As hinted previously, ESL errors can be viewed in two different ways:

1. These deviations are "wrong" and are caused by incomplete knowledge of the English system; therefore, such speakers must be corrected until they perform with "standard" English usage.
2. These deviations indicate important differences between English and other languages, and when performed widely and in obvious patterns by both native English and ESL speakers, they indicate the legitimate needs of the speakers as well as weaknesses in English, which could be corrected.

18   Consider, for example, some common errors made frequently by both ESL and native English speakers:

> There's so many reasons why I don't want to go.
>
> One of the reasons for her problems have to be drugs.

Guardians of the English language are appalled when subjects and verbs do not agree in number, as happens in these two sentences. However, ask a hundred native English speakers how the plural is made in English. The answer most often will be "Add *s*" when, in fact, that rule works only for the noun. To make verbs plural, we actually *drop* the *s* and say, "One boy walk*s*" but "Two boy*s* walk." Whenever grammar rules become this complicated, perhaps even contradictory and with the logic so vague, few people can internalize the rules whether they are learning a first or a second language. Only if you were raised in an environment in which such rules constantly were followed correctly could you use them consistently and naturally.

19   Could this be the reason why the English rules for subject-verb agreement are so frequently reversed, not only by ESL speakers but also in the common English subdialect used on TV, in the streets, by famous athletes, and even in many classrooms?

Should this widespread phenomenon among English-speaking groups around the world be considered an ESL error or an unacceptable subdialect usage even when it is now commonplace on the evening news? Furthermore, why is this particular error so persistent despite the combined efforts of English grammar texts and teachers from England to Africa to India to the United States to New Zealand?

20   Some linguists theorize that the growing number of ESL speakers in the world, particularly within the U.S. population, is weakening the English language in such areas as subject-verb agreement. Others suggest that a weak and illogical rule in English is finally reversing, and the pressure from other language groups is improving English by making it more flexible.

21   Other curious language trends reveal a strong new influence on standard English. Consider the possibility that this influence is coming from the growing number of ESL speakers who use and perpetuate a simplified form of English that could be considered a subdialect in itself. Evidence of this new subdialect comes through common new expressions such as *seemli* (pronounced "seem la-ee"). "Seemli gonna rain today" can be translated into standard English as "It seems as if it's going to rain today." Another explanation is that the widening acceptability of the common English subdialect (sometimes referred to as Black English Vernacular) is easier for ESL students to learn and identify with culturally, and therefore they are joining the large number of speakers in this group. In any case, many of the language characteristics of these two groups (ESL and Black English speakers) are identical, including reversal of subject-verb agreement rules, almost exclusive use of the simple present tense (or complete omission of the verb), use of adjectives for adverbs, and use of the simple present tense verb for the past participle or adjective form. (For example, the utterance "They's real surprise" substitutes for "They're really surprised.")

22   Consider also the relationship among the ESL substandard dialect, Black English, and the current jargon or speech style of English-speaking youth universally. Language features once considered substandard English, and now described as Black English Vernacular, have become part of a new youth jargon. In all three cases the main tense is simple present and subject-verb agreement rules are reversed; verbs can be dropped completely; a limited set of vocabulary words typically describes things or feelings vaguely or in extremes; adjectives can be used as adverbs; verbs can be used as adjectives; and degrees of meaning or qualifications are expressed only with disqualifiers. For example, "It's like, so sad, or whatever, that he come to her and he's like, this a suck relationship."

23   So, are ESL speakers influencing other subdialect groups or vice versa, or is there something about the nature of English that causes different groups to arrive at the same simplifications in adopting a sort of universal shorthand English? Regardless of where the influences originate, this widespread subdialect poses a dilemma for ESL students. Imagine the confusion of a Chinese student with perfectly accurate English grammar who was welcomed by an American native English speaker, "You sure learning English good!" Imagine students in English classes, where we constantly insist that they "Report something that happened before now in *past* tenses," walking out of the classroom and being barraged by their peers, TV heroes, news reporters, politicians, and even other university professors narrating all past events

in the simple present tense with no qualms whatsoever. Any progress ESL students may have made in the classroom toward mastering standard English is undermined by this more "real" communication style. The dilemma is obvious in the question of one frustrated Hispanic student who asked me, "Why don't you just teach us English the way people use it?"

24   A clue to the answer to this student's question lies in the ESL errors we examined earlier. Using contrastive analysis and error analysis helps us to determine whether common difficulties for ESL students result from major points of difference between their first language and English or whether the difficulties arise from some inefficient or ineffective aspect in the English system, which therefore needs improvement. However, improvement must mean a refinement or expansion in the language system that enhances, and does not limit, our ability to communicate. Improvement in our communication abilities must mean we can express our thoughts, arguments, and sentiments, and the relationships among them, more accurately.

25   Why is it so easy for ESL learners from all language backgrounds around the world to pick up expressions such as *awesome, gross,* and *like* and to use them with completely authentic pronunciation, juncture, stress, and grammatical consistency? This, while it is so difficult for them to acquire English phrases that express subtler shades of meaning, more precise thoughts, or relationships among ideas? Apparently, this shorthand is a style or subdialect of English arrived at by ESL speakers as well as others partly through the urgent necessity to communicate orally, without the encumbrances of language structures that could add depths and shades of meaning but are too difficult or take too long to use. This need naturally results in a reduced basic vocabulary and a system that ignores such refinements as tense markers. The subject-verb agreement rules of this system are more logical. (For instance, *s* consistently is added to both subjects and verbs to make them plural.) Furthermore, the system avoids redundancy in the same way that many respected languages of the world do. (For example, if you say, "two apple," the word *two* is sufficient to show plural, so there is no need to add an *s* to the noun.)

26   If this subdialect system is so logical and functional for so many English-speaking groups, what should be our attitude toward it? Can such trends in language be allowed to develop naturally, or will they contaminate the standard English needed for academic pursuits and deeper levels of expression? When answering, we cannot ignore the simple practicality of this shorthand system, and we cannot ignore the cultural and psychological reasons why so many ESL speakers, other ethnic groups, and young people relate to this style of speech. Therefore, our answer must be that the questions themselves are pointless. This subdialect exists and serves a need by speeding up transmission of basic information for those who do not have or do not wish to use more sophisticated language features and by helping those who wish to identify with a cultural style or attitude.

27   When responding to the Hispanic student's question ("Why don't you just teach us English the way people use it?"), our challenge is multifaceted. However, we must not assume that limited-English speakers have limited abilities to learn. To become fully functioning members of society, ESL learners, just as native English-language speakers, need to understand and express themselves using the casual communication

style of their peers as well as the standard English necessary for academic and professional performance and situations that call for more advanced expression. To expect ESL learners to perform at only one of these levels seriously limits their potential and participation in society. Providing them with chances to explore various levels of language provides all of us with fascinating opportunities to discover language phenomena from a cross-cultural perspective.

28   In spite of all its complexities and oddities, the strength of the English language lies in its multicultural, multilingual heritage. English is a system of expression that has grown out of a multiplicity of peoples and situations around the world and through time. Through speakers of English as a Second Language, English continues to develop and function as a most efficient and expressive tool for communication worldwide.

Questions on Content

1. Elyssa points out that there is more to learning a language than just learning grammar, vocabulary, and pronunciation. What are some of the other language elements that must be learned?

2. Summarize Elyssa's explanation for the following errors:

   My roommate last night help me.
   I hope making a decisions tomorrow.

3. Explain why some non-English speakers have difficulty with the fact that so many English speakers begin sentences with *I*.

4. Define *contrastive analysis* and *error analysis*.

5. Explain the differences between natural gender and grammatical gender.

6. Explain why so many native and non-native speakers of English have difficulties with subject and verb agreement.

7. Elyssa begins paragraph 25 with a question. What is her answer?

Questions on Structure and Style

8. Consider Elyssa's opening paragraph. Describe the rhetorical technique she employs. Is it effective? Consider also what you learn about her voice and audience.

9. What is the rhetorical function of paragraph 3? Discuss how the transition works in paragraph 16.

Assignments

1. Interview an acquaintance for whom English is not the first language. Determine what features of English are most and least difficult. Attempt to account for some of the responses by asking questions about the first language. Do you feel that error analysis and contrastive analysis might account for some of your findings? Write an essay in which you discuss your interview.

2. Write a summary of the major points Elyssa makes in paragraphs 16–23.

3. Arrange to interview an ESL teacher or perhaps observe an ESL class. Write an essay in which you describe what you observed. Did you see or hear anything that was consistent with Elyssa's remarks? What did you learn about the difficulties in learning English?

ADDITIONAL ASSIGNMENTS AND RESEARCH TOPICS

1. Richard Rodriguez (in "Aria") addresses tensions experienced by elementary school children from families whose primary language is not English.

   A. In an essay, describe the ways in which Rodriguez discusses these tensions.
   B. If you grew up in a home where English was not the primary language, write an essay comparing your experiences with those of Rodriguez.

2. Write a letter to the U.S. English organization in which you assume the role of Robert D. King. Respond to the organization's position as you believe he would.

3. Some of the authors in this chapter point out that in the United States languages other than English have achieved a noticeable, sometimes startling public presence. Take a walking tour of any city. Note the use of languages other than English on signs, advertisements, product packaging, newspapers and other publications, and elsewhere. Report your findings in an essay or in an oral presentation, and comment on the implications of these findings.

4. Richard Rodriguez discusses how an individual's response to the world is determined by the language he or she uses. He suggests that, at least in part, the Sapir-Whorf hypothesis may be correct. This hypothesis states that how one functions in the world probably depends a great deal on the language used. Interview an international student or an immigrant who now knows English well. Focus your discussion on how that person's ability to function in this culture changed as he or she learned the language. Try to lead the discussion toward specific anecdotal experiences. Write an essay in which you summarize and discuss your findings.

5. Take another look at King's "Should English Be the Law" and Crystal's "Vanishing Languages." Write an essay in which you discuss the value of linguistic diversity in the United States. Be certain to include your own opinions as well as those of the two authors.

6. (A) If you could acquire fluency in another language by listening only once to a thirty-minute tape, which language would you choose and why? Explain your choice in a paragraph. (B) Collect the responses of everyone in your class. Examine the results. Do patterns exist either in the choices of languages or reasons for choosing them? (C) If such patterns exist, explain in an essay both the possible causes for them and whether similar patterns likely would exist in other geographic locations or in other eras.

CHAPTER SIX

The Language of Politics and Advertising

Consider the stereotypical image of a politician, the one so dear to cartoonists. The politician stands before a crowd, sleeves rolled to the elbows, arms in the air, and—always—mouth wide open. This popular image reminds us how automatically we associate politicians with words. Consider, too, how another term, *salesman,* so easily predicts a smooth talker, someone for whom words are the favorite sales tool. We make assumptions such as these because we understand, as politicians and advertisers do, that language has immense power to inspire and reassure, to prompt action and deceive—that is, to persuade. Any study of language must eventually look at the ways that politicians and advertisers use language to persuade, and this chapter's reading selections do just that.

Advertisers know well our needs and weaknesses and how effectively words can influence behavior, and they've always manipulated language to manipulate us. The history of American advertising forms part of Daniel Boorstin's subject in "The Rhetoric of Democracy." Boorstin emphasizes the central role of advertising in American folk culture, and he analyzes, with clarity and precision, advertising's six rhetorical qualities. The resulting essay is a model of skillful exposition.

The chapter then moves in for a closer examination of common persuasive tactics employed by advertisers. William Lutz cautions us about "Empty Eggs: The Doublespeak of Weasel Words" that "help" persuade us to do whatever advertisers want us to do. In "Things Go Better with Quark?" journalist Chris Reidy reveals the methodical, expensive process by which product names can be custom created for manufacturers today. Then, to provide everyone with some territory to explore, three advertisements are presented for analysis.

Politicians, like skillful advertisers, usually want something from us, and they, too, rely on an extensive repertoire of persuasive tactics. Exceptions, which are rare, oftentimes actually prove the rule. Ellen Goodman reacts to one such "violation" of accepted political practice in which a governmental official engaged in "Unprotected Sex Talk" and other politically unwise public discussion—and lost an important job as a result.

Political language often expresses a truth in ways that generate action, but *how* we express a truth can sometimes distort it. "Types of Propaganda" reviews common techniques for bending the truth for political (and other) purposes. All political speechmakers are then satirized in E. E. Cummings's poem "next to of course god america i." The chapter concludes with two representative, historically noteworthy examples of political language: John F. Kennedy's inaugural address and Ronald Reagan's first inaugural address.

Taken together, the selections in this chapter form a warning. Every news broadcast and newspaper presents us with the words of politicians. Advertisers also address us so regularly that the average American encounters about 1,600 commercials every day—*every day.* In short, politicians and advertisers are almost inescapable.

And the warning is this: Political rhetoric and advertising are not information; they're tools of persuasion. Whenever we ignore this fact, the choices we make actually aren't choices at all.

The Rhetoric of Democracy

Daniel J. Boorstin

We've all heard the cliché "as American as apple pie and motherhood."
A more accurate short list of things quintessentially American would
include advertising. As Daniel J. Boorstin explains in this chapter from
his book *Democracy and Its Discontents*, advertising is at the heart of
our culture, a phenomenon uniquely American. With notable clarity,
Boorstin analyzes the historical reasons for this phenomenon, the
qualities of our advertising, and the implications of these qualities.
Boorstin is well qualified to speak on the American character. One
of our country's best-respected historians, he has written more than
fifteen books on U.S. history and has served as senior historian of the
Smithsonian Institution and as director of the Library of Congress.

■ **J O U R N A L   P R O M P T**   *Write about the effects of advertisements on you as a
consumer. What qualities do most advertisements have in common? Do advertisements always
emphasize persuasion at the expense of knowledge, as Boorstin suggests?*

1   Advertising, of course, has been part of the mainstream of American civilization, although you might not know it if you read the most respectable surveys of American
history. It has been one of the enticements to the settlement of this New World, it has
been a producer of the peopling of the United States, and in its modern form, in its
world-wide reach, it has been one of our most characteristic products.

2   Never was there a more outrageous or more unscrupulous or more ill-informed
advertising campaign than that by which the promoters for the American colonies
brought settlers here. Brochures published in England in the seventeenth century,
some even earlier, were full of hopeful overstatements, half-truths, and downright
lies, along with some facts which nowadays surely would be the basis for a restrain-
ing order from the Federal Trade Commission. Gold and Silver, fountains of youth,
plenty of fish, venison without limit, all these were promised, and of course some of
them were found. It would be interesting to speculate on how long it might have taken
to settle this continent if there had not been such promotion by enterprising advertisers. How has American civilization been shaped by the fact that there was a kind of
natural selection here of those people who were willing to believe advertising?

3   Advertising has taken the lead in promising and exploiting the new. This was a
new world, and one of the advertisements for it appears on the dollar bill on the Great
Seal of the United States, which reads *novus ordo seclorum*, one of the most effective
advertising slogans to come out of this country. "A new order of the centuries"—
belief in novelty and in the desirability of opening novelty to everybody has been
important in our lives throughout our history and especially in this century. Again and

258

again advertising has been an agency for inducing Americans to try anything and everything—from the continent itself to a new brand of soap. As one of the more literate and poetic of the advertising copywriters, James Kenneth Frazier, a Cornell graduate, wrote in 1900 in "The Doctor's Lament":

> This lean M.D. is Dr. Brown
> Who fares but ill in Spotless Town.
> The town is so confounded clean,
> It is no wonder he is lean,
> He's lost all patients now, you know,
> Because they use *Sapolio*.

4   The same literary talent that once was used to retail Sapolio was later used to induce people to try the Edsel or the Mustang, to experiment with Lifebuoy or Body-All, to drink Pepsi-Cola or Royal Crown Cola, or to shave with a Trac II razor.

5   And as expansion and novelty have become essential to our economy, advertising has played an ever-larger role: in the settling of the continent, in the expansion of the economy, and in the building of an American standard of living. Advertising has expressed the optimism, the hyperbole, and the sense of community, the sense of reaching which has been so important a feature of our civilization.

6   Here I wish to explore the significance of advertising, not as a force in the economy or in shaping an American standard of living, but rather as a touchstone of the ways in which we Americans have learned about all sorts of things.

7   The problems of advertising are of course not peculiar to advertising, for they are just one aspect of the problems of democracy. They reflect the rise of what I have called Consumption Communities and Statistical Communities, and many of the special problems of advertising have arisen from our continuously energetic effort to give everybody everything.

8   If we consider democracy not just as a political system, but as a set of institutions which do aim to make everything available to everybody, it would not be an overstatement to describe advertising as the characteristic rhetoric of democracy. One of the tendencies of democracy, which Plato and other antidemocrats warned against a long time ago, was the danger that rhetoric would displace or at least overshadow epistemology; that is, *the temptation to allow the problem of persuasion to overshadow the problem of knowledge*. Democratic societies tend to become more concerned with what people believe than with what is true, to become more concerned with credibility than with truth. All these problems become accentuated in a large-scale democracy like ours, which possesses all the apparatus of modern industry. And the problems are accentuated still further by universal literacy, by instantaneous communication, and by the daily plague of words and images.

9   In the early days it was common for advertising men to define advertisements as a kind of news. The best admen, like the best journalists, were supposed to be those who were able to make their news the most interesting and readable. This was natural enough, since the verb to "advertise" originally meant, intransitively, to take note or to consider. For a person to "advertise" meant originally, in the fourteenth and

fifteenth centuries, to reflect on something, to think about something. Then it came to mean, transitively, to call the attention of another to something, to give him notice, to notify, admonish, warn or inform in a formal or impressive manner. And then, by the sixteenth century, it came to mean: to give notice of anything, to make generally known. It was not until the late eighteenth century that the word "advertising" in English came to have a specifically "advertising" connotation as we might say today, and not until the late nineteenth century that it began to have a specifically commercial connotation. By 1879 someone was saying, "Don't advertise unless you have something worth advertising." But even into the present century, newspapers continued to call themselves by the title "Advertiser"—for example, the Boston *Daily Advertiser*, which was a newspaper of long tradition and one of the most dignified papers in Boston until William Randolph Hearst took it over in 1917. Newspapers carried "Advertiser" on their mastheads, not because they sold advertisements but because they brought news.

10   Now, the main role of advertising in American civilization came increasingly to be that of persuading and appealing rather than that of educating and informing. By 1921, for instance, one of the more popular textbooks, Blanchard's *Essentials of Advertising*, began: "Anything employed to influence people favorably is advertising. The mission of advertising is to persuade men and women to act in a way that will be of advantage to the advertiser." This development—in a country where a shared, a rising, and a democratized standard of living was the national pride and the national hallmark—meant that advertising had become the rhetoric of democracy.

11   What, then, were some of the main features of modern American advertising—if we consider it as a form of rhetoric? First, and perhaps most obvious is *repetition*. It is hard for us to realize that the use of repetition in advertising is not an ancient device but a modern one, which actually did not come into common use in American journalism until just past the middle of the nineteenth century.

12   The development of what came to be called "iteration copy" was a result of a struggle by a courageous man of letters and advertising pioneer, Robert Bonner, who bought the old New York *Merchant's Ledger* in 1851 and turned it into a popular journal. He then had the temerity to try to change the ways of James Gordon Bennett, who of course was one of the most successful of the American newspaper pioneers, and who was both a sensationalist and at the same time an extremely stuffy man when it came to things that he did not consider to be news. Bonner was determined to use advertisements in Bennett's wide-circulating New York *Herald* to sell his own literary product, but he found it difficult to persuade Bennett to allow him to use any but agate type in his advertising. (Agate was the smallest type used by newspapers in that day, only barely legible to the naked eye.) Bennett would not allow advertisers to use larger type, nor would he allow them to use illustrations except stock cuts, because he thought it was undignified. He said, too, that to allow a variation in the format of ads would be undemocratic. He insisted that all advertisers use the same size type so that no one would be allowed to prevail over another simply by presenting his message in a larger, more clever, or more attention-getting form.

13   Finally Bonner managed to overcome Bennett's rigidity by leasing whole pages of the paper and using the tiny agate type to form larger letters across the top of the

page. In this way he produced a message such as "Bring home the New York Ledger tonight." His were unimaginative messages, and when repeated all across the page they technically did not violate Bennett's agate rule. But they opened a new era and presaged a new freedom for advertisers in their use of the newspaper page. Iteration copy—the practice of presenting prosaic content in ingenious, repetitive form— became common, and nowadays of course is commonplace.

14   A second characteristic of American advertising which is not unrelated to this is the development of *an advertising style*. We have histories of most other kinds of style—including the style of many unread writers who are remembered today only because they have been forgotten—but we have very few accounts of the history of advertising style, which of course is one of the most important forms of our language and one of the most widely influential.

15   The development of advertising style was the convergence of several very respectable American traditions. One of these was the tradition of the "plain style," which the Puritans made so much of and which accounts for so much of the strength of the Puritan literature. The "plain style" was of course much influenced by the Bible and found its way into the rhetoric of American writers and speakers of great power like Abraham Lincoln. When advertising began to be self-conscious in the early years of this century, the pioneers urged copywriters not to be too clever, and especially not to be fancy. One of the pioneers of the advertising copywriters, John Powers, said, for example, "The commonplace is the proper level for writing in business; where the first virtue is plainness, 'fine writing' is not only intellectual, it is offensive." George P. Rowell, another advertising pioneer, said, "You must write your advertisement to catch damned fools—not college professors." He was a very tactful person. And he added, "And you'll catch just as many college professors as you will of any other sort." In the 1920's, when advertising was beginning to come into its own, Claude Hopkins, whose name is known to all in the trade, said, "Brilliant writing has no place in advertising. A unique style takes attention from the subject. Any apparent effort to sell creates corresponding resistance. . . . One should be natural and simple. His language should not be conspicuous. In fishing for buyers, as in fishing for bass, one should not reveal the hook." So there developed a characteristic advertising style in which plainness, the phrase that anyone could understand, was a distinguishing mark.

16   At the same time, the American advertising style drew on another, and what might seem an antithetic, tradition—the tradition of hyperbole in tall talk, the language of Davy Crockett and Mike Fink. While advertising could think of itself as 99.44 percent pure, it used the language of "Toronado" and "Cutlass." As I listen to the radio in Washington, I hear a celebration of heroic qualities which would make the characteristics of Mike Fink and Davy Crockett pale, only to discover at the end of the paean that what I have been hearing is a description of the Ford dealers in the District of Columbia neighborhood. And along with the folk tradition of hyperbole and tall talk comes the rhythm of folk music. We hear that Pepsi-Cola hits the spot, that it's for the young generation—and we hear other products celebrated in music which we cannot forget and sometimes don't want to remember.

17   There grew somehow out of all these contradictory tendencies—combining the commonsense language of the "plain style," and the fantasy language of "tall talk"—

an advertising style. This characteristic way of talking about things was especially designed to reach and catch the millions. It created a whole new world of myth. A myth, the dictionary tells us, is a notion based more on tradition or convenience than on facts; it is a received idea. Myth is not just fantasy and not just fact but exists in a limbo, in the world of the "Will to Believe," which William James has written about so eloquently and so perceptively. This is the world of the neither true nor false—of the statement that 60 percent of the physicians who expressed a choice said that our brand of aspirin would be more effective in curing a simple headache than any other leading brand.

18   That kind of statement exists in a penumbra. I would call this the "advertising penumbra." It is not untrue, and yet, in its connotation it is not exactly true.

19   Now, there is still another characteristic of advertising so obvious that we are inclined perhaps to overlook it. I call that *ubiquity*. Advertising abhors a vacuum and we discover new vacuums every day. The parable, of course, is the story of the man who thought of putting the advertisement on the other side of the cigarette package. Until then, that was wasted space and a society which aims at a democratic standard of living, at extending the benefits of consumption and all sorts of things and services to everybody, must miss no chance to reach people. The highway billboard and other outdoor advertising, bus and streetcar and subway advertising, and skywriting, radio and TV commercials—all these are of course obvious evidence that advertising abhors a vacuum.

20   We might reverse the old mousetrap slogan and say that anyone who can devise another place to put another mousetrap to catch a consumer will find people beating a path to his door. "Avoiding advertising will become a little harder next January," the *Wall Street Journal* reported on May 17, 1973, "when a Studio City, California, company launches a venture called StoreVision. Its product is a system of billboards that move on a track across supermarket ceilings. Some 650 supermarkets so far are set to have the system." All of which helps us understand the observation attributed to a French man of letters during his recent visit to Times Square. "What a beautiful place, if only one could not read!" Everywhere is a place to be filled, as we discover in a recent *Publishers Weekly* description of one advertising program: "The $1.95 paperback edition of Dr. Thomas A. Harris' million-copy best seller 'I'm O.K., You're O.K.' is in for full-scale promotion in July by its publisher, Avon Books. Plans range from bumper stickers to airplane streamers, from planes flying above Fire Island, the Hamptons and Malibu. In addition, the $100,000 promotion budget calls for 200,000 bookmarks, plus brochures, buttons, lipcards, floor and counter displays, and advertising in magazines and TV."

21   The ubiquity of advertising is of course just another effect of our uninhibited efforts to use all the media to get all sorts of information to everybody everywhere. Since the places to be filled are everywhere, the amount of advertising is not determined by the *needs* of advertising, but by the *opportunities* for advertising which become unlimited.

22   But the most effective advertising, in an energetic, novelty-ridden society like ours, tends to be "self-liquidating." To create a cliché you must offer something which everybody accepts. The most successful advertising therefore self-destructs

because it becomes cliché. Examples of this are found in the tendency for copyrighted names of trademarks to enter the vernacular—for the proper names of products which have been made familiar by costly advertising to become common nouns, and so to apply to anybody's products. Kodak becomes a synonym for camera. Kleenex a synonym for facial tissue, when both begin with a small *k*, and Xerox (now, too, with a small *x*) is used to describe all processes of copying, and so on. These are prototypes of the problem. If you are successful enough, then you will defeat your purpose in the long run—by making the name and the message so familiar that people won't notice them, and then people will cease to distinguish your product from everybody else's.

23   In a sense, of course, as we will see, the whole of American civilization is an example. When this was a "new" world, if people succeeded in building a civilization here, the New World would survive and would reach the time—in our age—when it would cease to be new. And now we have the oldest written Constitution in use in the world. This is only a parable of which there are many more examples.

24   The advertising man who is successful in marketing any particular product, then—in our high-technology, well-to-do democratic society, which aims to get everything to everybody—is apt to be diluting the demand for his particular product in the very act of satisfying it. But luckily for him, he is at the very same time creating a fresh demand for his services as advertiser.

25   And as a consequence, there is yet another role which is assigned to American advertising. This is what I call "erasure." Insofar as advertising is competitive or innovation is widespread, erasure is required in order to persuade consumers that this year's model is superior to last year's. In fact, we consumers learn that we might be risking our lives if we go out on the highway with those very devices that were last year's lifesavers but without whatever special kind of brakes or wipers or seat belt is on this year's model. This is what I mean by "erasure"—and we see it on our advertising pages or our television screen every day. We read in the *New York Times* (May 20, 1973), for example, that "For the price of something small and ugly, you can drive something small and beautiful"—an advertisement for the Fiat 250 Spider. Or another, perhaps more subtle example is the advertisement for shirts under a picture of Oliver Drab: "Oliver Drab. A name to remember in fine designer shirts? No kidding. . . . Because you pay extra money for Oliver Drab. And for all the other superstars of the fashion world. Golden Vee [the name of the brand that is advertised] does not have a designer's label. But we do have designers. . . . By keeping their names *off* our label and simply saying Golden Vee, we can afford to sell our $7 to $12 shirts for just $7 to $12, which should make Golden Vee a name to remember. Golden Vee, you only pay for the shirt."

26   Having mentioned two special characteristics—the self-liquidating tendency and the need for erasure—which arise from the dynamism of the American economy, I would like to try to place advertising in a larger perspective. The special role of advertising in our life gives a clue to a pervasive oddity in American civilization. A leading feature of past cultures, as anthropologists have explained, is the tendency to distinguish between "high" culture and "low" culture—between the culture of the literate and the learned on the one hand and that of the populace on the other. In other

words, between the language of literature and the language of the vernacular. Some of the most useful statements of this distinction have been made by social scientists at the University of Chicago—first by the late Robert Redfield in his several pioneering books on peasant society, and then by Milton Singer in his remarkable study of Indian civilization, *When a Great Tradition Modernizes* (1972). This distinction between the great tradition and the little tradition, between the high culture and the folk culture, has begun to become a commonplace of modern anthropology.

27   Some of the obvious features of advertising in modern America offer us an opportunity to note the significance or insignificance of that distinction for us. Elsewhere I have tried to point out some of the peculiarities of the American attitude toward the *high* culture. There is something distinctive about the place of thought in American life, which I think is not quite what it has been in certain Old World cultures.

28   But what about distinctive American attitudes to *popular* culture? What is our analogue to the folk culture of other peoples? Advertising gives us some clues—to a characteristically American democratic folk culture. Folk culture is a name for the culture which ordinary people everywhere lean on. It is not the writings of Dante and Chaucer and Shakespeare and Milton, the teachings of Machiavelli and Descartes, Locke or Marx. It is, rather, the pattern of slogans, local traditions, tales, songs, dances, and ditties. And of course holiday observances. Popular culture in other civilizations has been for the most part both an area of continuity with the past, a way in which people reach back into the past and out to their community, and at the same time an area of local variations. An area of individual and amateur expression in which a person has his own way of saying, or notes his mother's way of saying or singing, or his own way of dancing, his own view of folk wisdom and the cliché.

29   And here is an interesting point of contrast. In other societies outside the United States, it is the *high* culture that has generally been an area of centralized, organized control. In Western Europe, for example, universities and churches have tended to be closely allied to the government. The institutions of higher learning have had a relatively limited access to the people as a whole. This was inevitable, of course, in most parts of the world, because there were so few universities. In England, for example, there were only two universities until the early nineteenth century. And there was central control over the printed matter that was used in universities or in the liturgy. The government tended to be close to the high culture, and that was easy because the high culture itself was so centralized and because literacy was relatively limited.

30   In our society, however, we seem to have turned all of this around. Our high culture is one of the least centralized areas of our culture. And our universities express the atomistic, diffused, chaotic, and individualistic aspect of our life. We have in this country more than twenty-five hundred colleges and universities, institutions of so-called higher learning. We have a vast population in these institutions, somewhere over seven million students.

31   But when we turn to our popular culture, what do we find? We find that in our nation of Consumption Communities and emphasis on Gross National Product (GNP) and growth rates, advertising has become the heart of the folk culture and even its very prototype. And as we have seen, American advertising shows many characteristics

of the folk culture of other societies: repetition, a plain style, hyperbole and tall talk, folk verse, and folk music. Folk culture, wherever it has flourished, has tended to thrive in a limbo between fact and fantasy, and of course, depending on the spoken word and the oral tradition, it spreads easily and tends to be ubiquitous. These are all familiar characteristics of folk culture and they are ways of describing our folk culture, but how do the expressions of our peculiar folk culture come to *us*?

32   They no longer sprout from the earth, from the village, from the farm, or even from the neighborhood or the city. They come to us primarily from enormous centralized self-consciously *creative* (an overused word, for the overuse of which advertising agencies are in no small part responsible) organizations. They come from advertising agencies, from networks of newspapers, radio, and television, from outdoor-advertising agencies, from the copywriters for ads in the largest-circulation magazines, and so on. These "creators" of folk culture—or pseudo-folk culture—aim at the widest intelligibility and charm and appeal.

33   But in the United States, we must recall, the advertising folk culture (like all advertising) is also confronted with the problems of self-liquidation and erasure. These are by-products of the expansive, energetic character of our economy. And they, too, distinguish American folk culture from folk cultures elsewhere.

34   Our folk culture is distinguished from others by being discontinuous, ephemeral, and self-destructive. Where does this leave the common citizen? All of us are qualified to answer.

35   In our society, then, those who cannot lean on the world of learning, on the high culture of the classics, on the elaborated wisdom of the books, have a new problem. The University of Chicago, for example, in the 1930's and 1940's was the center of a quest for a "common discourse." The champions of that quest, which became a kind of crusade, believed that such a discourse could be found through familiarity with the classics of great literature—and especially of Western European literature. I think they were misled; such works were not, nor are they apt to become, the common discourse of our society. Most people, even in a democracy, and a rich democracy like ours, live in a world of popular culture, our special kind of popular culture.

36   The characteristic folk culture of our society is a creature of advertising, and in a sense it *is* advertising. But advertising, our own popular culture, is harder to make into a source of continuity than the received wisdom and common sense slogans and catchy songs of the vivid vernacular. The popular culture of advertising attenuates and is always dissolving before our very eyes. Among the charms, challenges, and tribulations of modern life, we must count this peculiar fluidity, this ephemeral character of that very kind of culture on which other peoples have been able to lean, the kind of culture to which they have looked for the continuity of their traditions, for their ties with the past and with the future.

37   We are perhaps the first people in history to have a centrally organized mass-produced folk culture. Our kind of popular culture is here today and gone tomorrow—or the day after tomorrow. Or whenever the next semiannual model appears. And insofar as folk culture becomes advertising, and advertising becomes centralized, it becomes a way of depriving people of their opportunities for individual and small-

community expression. Our technology and our economy and our democratic ideals have all helped make that possible. Here we have a new test of the problem that is at least as old as Heraclitus—an everyday test of man's ability to find continuity in his experience. And here democratic man has a new opportunity to accommodate himself, if he can, to the unknown.

Questions on Content

1. Why does Boorstin use the term *natural selection* in discussing the settling of America (paragraph 2)?

2. Explain the historical link between advertising and news. Why is this important to an understanding of what advertising is today?

3. Boorstin titles his essay "The Rhetoric of Democracy"; he uses the term *rhetoric* again in paragraph 10. Define this term as Boorstin uses it.

4. Boorstin states in paragraph 14 that "many unread writers . . . are remembered today only because they have been forgotten." What does he mean?

5. Why is plainness traditional in American advertising language?

6. Why does Boorstin use the word *parable* in paragraph 23? Is he using the word conventionally, or does he have a special meaning for it?

7. What is folk culture? How does American folk culture differ from that found in Western Europe? Why is folk culture so important to Boorstin's analysis?

Questions on Structure and Style

8. Where does Boorstin state his thesis? Why doesn't he state it immediately?

9. Explain how paragraphs 14 through 18 are related. Why do they function as a short essay in themselves?

10. Boorstin is always careful to provide smooth, strong transitions. Circle the transitions in paragraphs 14 through 18.

11. Describe Boorstin's tone. How does this tone affect our impression of him as an authority on his subject?

Assignments

1. Boorstin's essay is a model of careful structure. Outline the essay, revealing its parts and their relationships.

2. Boorstin identifies six qualities of American advertising. List these qualities, and then cite two or three specific examples of each. (Finding examples is easy—as Boorstin points out, one quality of American advertising is ubiquity.) An effective way to conduct research is to work in groups, perhaps having each person search for examples of one or two specific qualities.

3. According to Boorstin, American folk culture originates in advertising, and this fact separates us from other societies. What constitutes the folk culture of your own life? (Review Boorstin's analysis of this term before answering.) Do the elements of your personal folk culture originate in advertising, as Boorstin claims? Respond in an essay.

Empty Eggs: The Doublespeak of Weasel Words

William Lutz

William Lutz, chair of the Committee on Public Doublespeak of the National Council of Teachers of English, also teaches at Rutgers University. In the following selection Lutz targets weasel words, an immediately recognizable vocabulary that advertisers employ when making claims empty enough to mean almost anything. As the author makes clear, when "new and improved" products "work like" magic to "help" us, the language of such claims actually means nothing except increased profits.

■ **J O U R N A L   P R O M P T**   *In this selection Lutz contends that advertisers try to wrap their claims in language that sounds concrete, specific, and objective, when in fact the language of advertising is anything but. Think about ads you hear or see or read frequently. How is the language of the ads misleading? As you prepare your response, focus on words such as* help, virtually, new, improved, *and* like.

1   One problem advertisers have when they try to convince you that the product they are pushing is really different from other, similar products is that their claims are subject to some laws. Not a lot of laws, but there are some designed to prevent fraudulent or untruthful claims in advertising. Even during the happy years of non-regulation under President Ronald Reagan, the FTC did crack down on the more blatant abuses in advertising claims. Generally speaking, advertisers have to be careful in what they say in their ads, in the claims they make for the products they advertise. Parity claims are safe because they are legal and supported by a number of court decisions. But beyond parity claims there are weasel words.

2   Advertisers use weasel words to appear to be making a claim for a product when in fact they are making no claim at all. Weasel words get their name from the way weasels eat the eggs they find in the nests of other animals. A weasel will make a small hole in the egg, suck out the insides, then place the egg back in the nest. Only when the egg is examined closely is it found to be hollow. That's the way it is with weasel words in advertising: Examine weasel words closely and you'll find that they're as hollow as any egg sucked by a weasel. Weasel words appear to say one thing when in fact they say the opposite, or nothing at all.

"Help"—The Number One Weasel Word

3   The biggest weasel word used in advertising doublespeak is "help." Now "help" only means to aid or assist, nothing more. It does not mean to conquer, stop, eliminate,

end, solve, heal, cure, or anything else. But once the ad says "help," it can say just about anything after that because "help" qualifies everything coming after it. The trick is that the claim that comes after the weasel word is usually so strong and so dramatic that you forget the word "help" and concentrate only on the dramatic claim. You read into the ad a message that the ad does not contain. More importantly, the advertiser is not responsible for the claim that you read into the ad, even though the advertiser wrote the ad so you would read that claim into it.

4   The next time you see an ad for a cold medicine that promises that it "helps relieve cold symptoms fast," don't rush out to buy it. Ask yourself what this claim is really saying. Remember, "helps" means only that the medicine will aid or assist. What will it aid or assist in doing? Why, "relieve" your cold "symptoms." "Relieve" only means to ease, alleviate, or mitigate, not to stop, end, or cure. Nor does the claim say how much relieving this medicine will do. Nowhere does this ad claim it will cure anything. In fact, the ad doesn't even claim it will *do* anything at all. The ad only claims that it will aid in relieving (not curing) your cold symptoms, which are probably a runny nose, watery eyes, and a headache. In other words, this medicine probably contains a standard decongestant and some aspirin. By the way, what does "fast" mean? Ten minutes, one hour, one day? What is fast to one person can be very slow to another. Fast is another weasel word.

5   Ad claims using "help" are among the most popular ads. One says, "Helps keep you young looking," but then a lot of things will help keep you young looking, including exercise, rest, good nutrition, and a facelift. More importantly, this ad doesn't say the product will keep you young, only "young *looking*." Someone may look young to one person and old to another.

6   A toothpaste ad says, "Helps prevent cavities," but it doesn't say it will actually prevent cavities. Brushing your teeth regularly, avoiding sugars in food, and flossing daily will also help prevent cavities. A liquid cleaner ad says, "Helps keep your home germ free," but it doesn't say it actually kills germs, nor does it even specify which germs it might kill.

7   "Help" is such a useful weasel word that it is often combined with other action-verb weasel words such as "fight" and "control." Consider the claim, "Helps control dandruff symptoms with regular use." What does it really say? It will assist in controlling (not eliminating, stopping, ending, or curing) the *symptoms* of dandruff, not the cause of dandruff nor the dandruff itself. What are the symptoms of dandruff? The ad deliberately leaves that undefined, but assume that the symptoms referred to in the ad are the flaking and itching commonly associated with dandruff. But just shampooing with *any* shampoo will temporarily eliminate these symptoms, so this shampoo isn't any different from any other. Finally, in order to benefit from this product, you must use it regularly. What is "regular use"—daily, weekly, hourly? Using another shampoo "regularly" will have the same effect. Nowhere does this advertising claim say this particular shampoo stops, eliminates, or cures dandruff. In fact, this claim says nothing at all, thanks to all the weasel words.

8   Look at ads in magazines and newspapers, listen to ads on radio and television, and you'll find the word "help" in ads for all kinds of products. How often do you read or hear such phrases as "helps stop . . . ," "helps overcome . . . ," "helps eliminate . . . ,"

"helps you feel . . . ," or "helps you look . . ."? If you start looking for this weasel word in advertising, you'll be amazed at how often it occurs. Analyze the claims in the ads using "help," and you will discover that these ads are really saying nothing.

9   There are plenty of other weasel words used in advertising. In fact, there are so many that to list them all would fill the rest of this book. But, in order to identify the doublespeak of advertising and understand the real meaning of an ad, you have to be aware of the most popular weasel words in advertising today.

Virtually Spotless

10   One of the most powerful weasel words is "virtually," a word so innocent that most people don't pay any attention to it when it is used in an advertising claim. But watch out. "Virtually" is used in advertising claims that appear to make specific, definite promises when there is no promise. After all, what does "virtually" mean? It means "in essence or effect, although not in fact." Look at that definition again. "Virtually" means *not in fact*. It does *not* mean "almost" or "just about the same as," or anything else. And before you dismiss all this concern over such a small word, remember that small words can have big consequences.

11   In 1971 a federal court rendered its decision on a case brought by a woman who became pregnant while taking birth control pills. She sued the manufacturer, Eli Lilly and Company, for breach of warranty. The woman lost her case. Basing its ruling on a statement in the pamphlet accompanying the pills, which stated that, "When taken as directed, the tablets offer virtually 100% protection," the court ruled that there was no warranty, expressed or implied, that the pills were absolutely effective. In its ruling, the court pointed out that, according to *Webster's Third New International Dictionary*, "virtually" means "almost entirely" and clearly does not mean "absolute" (*Whitting-ton* v. *Eli Lilly and Company*, 333 F. Supp. 98). In other words, the Eli Lilly company was really saying that its birth control pill, even when taken as directed, *did not in fact* provide 100 percent protection against pregnancy. But Eli Lilly didn't want to put it that way because then many women might not have bought Lilly's birth control pills.

12   The next time you see the ad that says that this dishwasher detergent "leaves dishes virtually spotless," just remember how advertisers twist the meaning of the weasel word "virtually." You can have lots of spots on your dishes after using this detergent and the ad claim will still be true, because what this claim really means is that this detergent does not *in fact* leave your dishes spotless. Whenever you see or hear an ad claim that uses the word "virtually," just translate that claim into its real meaning. So the television set that is "virtually trouble free" becomes the television set that is not in fact trouble free, the "virtually foolproof operation" of any appliance becomes an operation that is in fact not foolproof, and the product that "virtually never needs service" becomes the product that is not in fact service free.

New and Improved

13   If "new" is the most frequently used word on a product package, "improved" is the second most frequent. In fact, the two words are almost always used together. It

seems just about everything sold these days is "new and improved." The next time you're in the supermarket, try counting the number of times you see these words on products. But you'd better do it while you're walking down just one aisle, otherwise you'll need a calculator to keep track of your counting.

14   Just what do these words mean? The use of the word "new" is restricted by regulations, so an advertiser can't just use the word on a product or in an ad without meeting certain requirements. For example, a product is considered new for about six months during a national advertising campaign. If the product is being advertised only in a limited test market area, the word can be used longer, and in some instances has been used for as long as two years.

15   What makes a product "new"? Some products have been around for a long time, yet every once in a while you discover that they are being advertised as "new." Well, an advertiser can call a product new if there has been "a material functional change," in the product. What is "a material functional change," you ask? Good question. In fact it's such a good question it's being asked all the time. It's up to the manufacturer to prove that the product has undergone such a change. And if the manufacturer isn't challenged on the claim, then there's no one to stop it. Moreover, the change does not have to be an improvement in the product. One manufacturer added an artificial lemon scent to a cleaning product and called it "new and improved," even though the product did not clean any better than without the lemon scent. The manufacturer defended the use of the word "new" on the grounds that the artificial scent changed the chemical formula of the product and therefore constituted "a material functional change."

16   Which brings up the word "improved." When used in advertising, "improved" does not mean "made better." It only means "changed" or "different from before." So, if the detergent maker puts a plastic pour spout on the box of detergent, the product has been "improved," and away we go with a whole new advertising campaign. Or, if the cereal maker adds more fruit or a different kind of fruit to the cereal, there's an improved product. Now you know why manufacturers are constantly making little changes in their products. Whole new advertising campaigns, designed to convince you that the product has been changed for the better, are based on small changes in superficial aspects of a product. The next time you see an ad for an "improved" product, ask yourself what was wrong with the old one. Ask yourself just how "improved" the product is. Finally, you might check to see whether the "improved" version costs more than the unimproved one. After all, someone has to pay for the millions of dollars spent advertising the improved product.

17   Of course, advertisers really like to run ads that claim a product is "new and improved." While what constitutes a "new" product may be subject to some regulation, "improved" is a subjective judgment. A manufacturer changes the shape of its stick deodorant, but the shape doesn't improve the function of the deodorant. That is, changing the shape doesn't affect the deodorizing ability of the deodorant, so the manufacturer calls it "improved." Another manufacturer adds ammonia to its liquid cleaner and calls it "new and improved." Since adding ammonia does affect the cleaning ability of the product, there has been a "material functional change" in the product, and the manufacturer can now call its cleaner "new," and "improved" as well. Now the weasel words "new and improved" are plastered all over the package

and are the basis for a multimillion-dollar ad campaign. But after six months the word "new" will have to go, until someone can dream up another change in the product. Perhaps it will be adding color to the liquid, or changing the shape of the package, or maybe adding a new dripless pour spout, or perhaps a———. The "improvements" are endless, and so are the new advertising claims and campaigns.

18   "New" is just too useful and powerful a word in advertising for advertisers to pass it up easily. So they use weasel words that say "new" without really saying it. One of their favorites is "introducing," as in, "Introducing improved Tide," or "Introducing the stain remover." The first is simply saying, here's our improved soap; the second, here's our new advertising campaign for our detergent. Another favorite is "now," as in, "Now there's Sinex," which simply means that Sinex is available. Then there are phrases like "Today's Chevrolet," "Presenting Dristan," and "A fresh way to start the day." The list is really endless because advertisers are always finding new ways to say "new" without really saying it. If there is a second edition of this book, I'll just call it the "new and improved" edition. Wouldn't you really rather have a "new and improved" edition of this book rather than a "second" edition?

Acts Fast

19   "Acts" and "works" are two popular weasel words in advertising because they bring action to the product and to the advertising claim. When you see the ad for the cough syrup that "Acts on the cough control center," ask yourself what this cough syrup is claiming to do. Well, it's just claiming to "act," to do something, to perform an action. What is it that the cough syrup does? The ad doesn't say. It only claims to perform an action or do something on your "cough control center." By the way, what and where is your "cough control center"? I don't remember learning about that part of the body in human biology class.

20   Ads that use such phrases as "acts fast," "acts against," "acts to prevent," and the like are saying essentially nothing, because "act" is a word empty of any specific meaning. The ads are always careful not to specify exactly what "act" the product performs. Just because a brand of aspirin claims to "act fast" for headache relief doesn't mean this aspirin is any better than any other aspirin. What is the "act" that this aspirin performs? You're never told. Maybe it just dissolves quickly. Since aspirin is a parity product, all aspirin is the same and therefore functions the same.

Works Like Anything Else

21   If you don't find the word "acts" in an ad, you will probably find the weasel word "works." In fact, the two words are almost interchangeable in advertising. Watch out for ads that say a product "works against," "works like," "works for," or "works longer." As with "acts," "works" is the same meaningless verb used to make you think that this product really does something, and maybe even something special or unique. But "works," like "acts," is basically a word empty of any specific meaning.

Like Magic

22   Whenever advertisers want you to stop thinking about the product and to start thinking about something bigger, better, or more attractive than the product, they use that very popular weasel word, "like." The word "like" is the advertiser's equivalent of a magician's use of misdirection. "Like" gets you to ignore the product and concentrate on the claim the advertiser is making about it. "For skin like peaches and cream" claims the ad for a skin cream. What is this ad really claiming? It doesn't say this cream will give you peaches-and-cream skin. There is no verb in this claim, so it doesn't even mention using the product. How is skin ever like "peaches and cream"? Remember, ads must be read literally and exactly, according to the dictionary definition of words. (Remember "virtually" in the Eli Lilly case.) The ad is making absolutely no promise or claim whatsoever for this skin cream. If you think this cream will give you soft, smooth, youthful-looking skin, you are the one who has read that meaning into the ad.

23   The wine that claims "It's like taking a trip to France" wants you to think about a romantic evening in Paris as you walk along the boulevard after a wonderful meal in an intimate little bistro. Of course, you don't really believe that a wine can take you to France, but the goal of the ad is to get you to think pleasant, romantic thoughts about France and not about how the wine tastes or how expensive it may be. That little word "like" has taken you away from crushed grapes into a world of your own imaginative making. Who knows, maybe the next time you buy wine, you'll think those pleasant thoughts when you see this brand of wine, and you'll buy it. Or, maybe you weren't even thinking about buying wine at all, but now you just might pick up a bottle the next time you're shopping. Ah, the power of "like" in advertising.

24   How about the most famous "like" claim of all, "Winston tastes good like a cigarette should"? Ignoring the grammatical error here, you might want to know what this claim is saying. Whether a cigarette tastes good or bad is a subjective judgment because what tastes good to one person may well taste horrible to another. Not everyone likes fried snails, even if they are called escargot. (*De gustibus non est disputandum*, which was probably the Roman rule for advertising as well as for defending the games in the Colosseum.) There are many people who say all cigarettes taste terrible, other people who say only some cigarettes taste all right, and still others who say all cigarettes taste good. Who's right? Everyone, because taste is a matter of personal judgment.

25   Moreover, note the use of the conditional, "should." The complete claim is, "Winston tastes good like a cigarette should taste." But should cigarettes taste good? Again, this is a matter of personal judgment and probably depends most on one's experiences with smoking. So, the Winston ad is simply saying that Winston cigarettes are just like any other cigarette: Some people like them and some people don't. On that statement R. J. Reynolds conducted a very successful multimillion-dollar advertising campaign that helped keep Winston the number-two-selling cigarette in the United States, close behind number one, Marlboro.

Can It Be Up to the Claim?

26   Analyzing ads for doublespeak requires that you pay attention to every word in the ad and determine what each word really means. Advertisers try to wrap their claims in language that sounds concrete, specific, and objective, when in fact the language of advertising is anything but. Your job is to read carefully and listen critically so that when the announcer says that "Crest can be of significant value . . ." you know immediately that this claim says absolutely nothing. Where is the doublespeak in this ad? Start with the second word.

27   Once again, you have to look at what words really mean, not what you think they mean or what the advertiser wants you to think they mean. The ad for Crest only says that using Crest "can be" of "significant value." What really throws you off in this ad is the brilliant use of "significant." It draws your attention to the word "value" and makes you forget that the ad only claims that Crest "can be." The ad doesn't say that Crest *is* of value, only that it is "able" or "possible" to be of value, because that's all that "can" means.

28   It's so easy to miss the importance of those little words, "can be." Almost as easy as missing the importance of the words "up to" in an ad. These words are very popular in sale ads. You know, the ones that say, "Up to 50% Off!" Now, what does that claim mean? Not much, because the store or manufacturer has to reduce the price of only a few items by 50 percent. Everything else can be reduced a lot less, or not even reduced. Moreover, don't you want to know 50 percent off of what? Is it 50 percent off the "manufacturer's suggested list price," which is the highest possible price? Was the price artificially inflated and then reduced? In other ads, "up to" expresses an ideal situation. The medicine that works "up to ten times faster," the battery that lasts "up to twice as long," and the soap that gets you "up to twice as clean" all are based on ideal situations for using those products, situations in which you can be sure you will never find yourself.

Unfinished Words

29   Unfinished words are a kind of "up to" claim in advertising. The claim that a battery lasts "up to twice as long" usually doesn't finish the comparison—twice as long as what? A birthday candle? A tank of gas? A cheap battery made in a country not noted for its technological achievements? The implication is that the battery lasts twice as long as batteries made by other battery makers, or twice as long as earlier model batteries made by the advertiser, but the ad doesn't really make these claims. You read these claims into the ad, aided by the visual images the advertiser so carefully provides.

30   Unfinished words depend on you to finish them, to provide the words the advertisers so thoughtfully left out of the ad. Pall Mall cigarettes were once advertised as "A longer finer and milder smoke." The question is, longer, finer, and milder than what? The aspirin that claims it contains "Twice as much of the pain reliever doctors recommend most" doesn't tell you what pain reliever it contains twice as much of. (By the way, it's aspirin. That's right; it just contains twice the amount of aspirin.

And how much is twice the amount? Twice of what amount?) Panadol boasts that "nobody reduces fever faster," but, since Panadol is a parity product, this claim simply means that Panadol isn't any better than any other product in its parity class. "You can be sure if it's Westinghouse," you're told, but just exactly what it is you can be sure of is never mentioned. "Magnavox gives you more" doesn't tell you what you get more of. More value? More television? More than they gave you before? It sounds nice, but it means nothing, until you fill in the claim with your own words, the words the advertiser didn't use. Since each of us fills in the claim differently, the ad and the product can become all things to all people, and not promise a single thing.

31   Unfinished words abound in advertising because they appear to promise so much. More importantly, they can be joined with powerful visual images on television to appear to be making significant promises about a product's effectiveness without really making any promises. In a television ad, the aspirin product that claims fast relief can show a person with a headache taking the product and then, in what appears to be a matter of minutes, claiming complete relief. This visual image is far more powerful than any claim made in unfinished words. Indeed, the visual image completes the unfinished words for you, filling in with pictures what the words leave out. And you thought that ads didn't affect you. What brand of aspirin do you use?

32   Some years ago, Ford's advertisements proclaimed "Ford LTD—700% quieter." Now, what do you think Ford was claiming with these unfinished words? What was the Ford LTD quieter than? A Cadillac? A Mercedes-Benz? A BMW? Well, when the FTC asked Ford to substantiate this unfinished claim, Ford replied that it meant that the inside of the LTD was 700% quieter than the outside. How did you finish those unfinished words when you first read them? Did you even come close to Ford's meaning?

Combining Weasel Words

33   A lot of ads don't fall neatly into one category or another because they use a variety of different devices and words. Different weasel words are often combined to make an ad claim. The claim, "Coffee-mate gives coffee more body, more flavor," uses Unfinished Words ("more" than what?) and also uses words that have no specific meaning ("body" and "flavor"). Along with "taste" (remember the Winston ad and its claim to taste good), "body" and "flavor" mean nothing because their meaning is entirely subjective. To you, "body" in coffee might mean thick, black, almost bitter coffee, while I might take it to mean a light brown, delicate coffee. Now, if you think you understood that last sentence, read it again, because it said nothing of objective value; it was filled with weasel words of no specific meaning: "thick," "black," "bitter," "light brown," and "delicate." Each of those words has no specific, objective meaning, because each of us can interpret them differently.

34   Try this slogan: "Looks, smells, tastes like ground-roast coffee." So, are you now going to buy Taster's Choice instant coffee because of this ad? "Looks," "smells," and "tastes" are all words with no specific meaning and depend on your interpretation of

them for any meaning. Then there's that great weasel word "like," which simply suggests a comparison but does not make the actual connection between the product and the quality. Besides, do you know what "ground-roast" coffee is? I don't, but it sure sounds good. So, out of seven words in this ad, four are definite weasel words, two are quite meaningless, and only one has any clear meaning.

35   Remember the Anacin ad—"Twice as much of the pain reliever doctors recommend most"? There's a whole lot of weaseling going on in this ad. First, what's the pain reliever they're talking about in this ad? Aspirin, of course. In fact, any time you see or hear an ad using those words "pain reliever," you can automatically substitute the word "aspirin" for them. (Makers of acetaminophen and ibuprofen pain relievers are careful in their advertising to identify their products as nonaspirin products.) So, now we know that Anacin has aspirin in it. Moreover, we know that Anacin has twice as much aspirin in it, but we don't know twice as much as what. Does it have twice as much aspirin as an ordinary aspirin tablet? If so, what is an ordinary aspirin tablet, and how much aspirin does it contain? Twice as much as Excedrin or Bufferin? Twice as much as a chocolate chip cookie? Remember those Unfinished Words and how they lead you on without saying anything.

36   Finally, what about those doctors who are doing all that recommending? Who are they? How many of them are there? What kind of doctors are they? What are their qualifications? Who asked them about recommending pain relievers? What other pain relievers did they recommend? And there are a whole lot more questions about this "poll" of doctors to which I'd like to know the answers, but you get the point. Sometimes, when I call my doctor, she tells me to take two aspirin and call her office in the morning. Is that where Anacin got this ad?

Questions on Content

1. Explain what weasel words are, and describe how they became so named.

2. Why are *virtually* and *help* such effective weasel words?

3. What does the Eli Lilly court case tell us about the effectiveness of weasel words?

4. What does *new* really tell us when it appears on a product label? What is the effect when *new* is preceded by *improved*?

5. Define "unfinished words" and discuss how advertisers use them.

Questions on Structure and Style

6. Comment on Lutz's use of concrete illustrations. How does he use them to help organize as well as to develop the selection?

7. Lutz frequently uses the pronoun *you*. Why does he employ this technique? How does it contribute to his tone and his purpose?

Assignments

1. Collect examples of weasel words from advertisements in magazines, in newspapers, and on television. Discuss the use of these weasel words with a small group of peers.

2. Write an essay in which you classify weasel words by type, much as Lutz does. Develop your essay with the concrete examples that you are able to find.

Things Go Better with Quark?

Chris Reidy

Batteries called "Duracell" might sound reliable in the United States, but not in France—and for a reason that no businessperson would care to explain. Blunders such as this one have become so costly today that many goods and services, from cars to banking, are sold under names that are themselves manufactured by companies that invent product names for a fee. These companies supposedly apply a process of painstaking research to identify appealing names while screening out potential troublemakers. The following newspaper article by Chris Reidy details some notable product-naming successes and failures. The article, with its short paragraphs and weak transitions, also nicely illustrates the journalistic style of writing.

■ **JOURNAL PROMPT** *In the selection that follows, Chris Reidy states that the most important aspect of marketing a new product is creating its name. Think about names in a product line that interests you (cars or cosmetics, for example). What is the marketing appeal of the names? What do the names say about the product? What consumer groups will the names likely attract?*

1   As Reebok International Ltd. found out last week [mid-February 1997], coming up with a good name for a new product isn't always easy.

2   "The most important piece of marketing is naming," claims Sam Birger, a co-founder of Whatchamacallit Inc., a small naming firm with offices in Cambridge and Mill Valley, Calif. "It's the handshake, the first impression."

3   Reebok made a bad impression with a shoe it called the Incubus. According to the dictionary, an incubus is an evil spirit who has sex with women while they sleep.

4   Embarrassed, the Stoughton-based footwear giant said it plans to implement new guidelines for checking product names.

5   The art of naming a product or a company is increasingly big business—whether it's done within a company's marketing department or whether outside forces are brought in to help. Finding an appropriate, nonoffensive name, say companies, can have a direct effect on sales, and in some cases can mean success or failure.

6   Because so many different methods are used, it's hard to say how much US companies spend on naming new products. Some companies sponsor in-house competitions. Others seek help from their ad agencies and design firms. And still others use naming consultants who can charge anywhere from $20,000 to $250,000 for their services.

7   In return for such fees, these consultants often agree to remain anonymous. Just as some politicians don't like it to be known that their principles were shaped by

278

public opinion polls, many corporations don't like to admit that they needed outside help to come up with a new name.

8   Cadillac used a variety of sources to name its new Catera. A search begun in 1993 reviewed more than a thousand options, including Pegasus, Helios and Ascent, Cadillac said. After winnowing the list several times, eight names were submitted to focus group in "three US cities as well as Paris, Dusseldorf and the Far East," Cadillac said.

9   In part, Catera was chosen for its European flavor and also because the name is inoffensive in a variety of languages, an important consideration in a global economy.

10   Indeed, names that are perfectly serviceable in English can suffer in translation. Could Duracell's name be a factor in why its European battery sales have not always met expectations?

11   Duracell sounds suspiciously like a French phrase that means "difficult to defecate" or "hard stool," said Robert Sprung, chairman of Harvard Translations, a Boston-based foreign language consulting firm with revenues of about $3 million.

12   (Duracell disputes Sprung's interpretation.)

13   Elinor Selame, president of a Newton, [Massachusetts]-based firm called Brandequity International, noted that using a name that makes customers uneasy can cost a company millions of dollars.

14   As an example, she cited the Harlem Savings Bank, which bought another bank in the mid-1980s. When Harlem Savings put its name on some of its newly acquired suburban branches, "deposits walked out the door," Selame recalled.

15   The bank found that the word Harlem evoked negative connotations for many suburbanites, and it hired Selame's firm to find an agreeable new name. Rechristened the Apple Bank for Savings, the bank quickly gained new customers, Selame said, adding that Brandequity doesn't simply choose a name; it seeks to integrate a name with a corporate logo and marketing plan.

16   "Verbal and visual should work hand in hand," she said. "You have to consider how a name will look on signs and business cards and how it will be used in advertising.

17   In the case of the Harlem bank, Selame's company showed it's client a color scheme, a lettering typeface and an advertising tagline: "Apple Bank. We're good for you."

18   "If we had just showed them a name—Apple Bank—they probably would have turned us down," she said.

19   Because new products constantly flood the market, it's hard to find clever names that someone else isn't already using.

20   And, as Avon Products Inc. found out earlier this month, using someone else's name can have unfortunate results.

21   A recent Avon catalog made numerous mentions of the word "Maxx," prompting a lawsuit by the TJX Cos. of Framingham, which operates the T.J. Maxx chain of offprice apparel stores.

22   To avoid lawsuits, naming consultants often turn to made-up words, and searches for made-up words frequently begin with lists of morphemes. A morpheme, according to linguists, is the smallest fragment of language that conveys meaning.

23   Car companies are especially keen on morpheme-derived names.

24   Using morphemes, a San Francisco firm called Namelab Inc. came up with Acura for the line of luxury cars that Honda introduced in the United States several years ago.

25   The morpheme "acu" connotes precision and care in several languages, said Ira Bachrach, president of Namelab, a company with about $1.5 million in annual revenues.

26   According to Bachrach, the made-up word—Acura—helped exorcise the impression that Japanese companies could make only economy cars that did not deserve to be mentioned in the same breath as Mercedes and BMW.

27   Catera is also supposed to suggest a European commitment to luxury and engineering. Focus groups told Cadillac they thought of a "cat or a fast-moving, agile object" when they heard the word Catera.

28   Lawsuits aren't the only reason to prefer made-up names to real words. In the mid 1980s, a company toyed with calling a computer printer "the Shuttle," but when the space shuttle Challenger blew up, the company became afraid customers would associate the name with a disaster, said linguist Sprung.

29   To generate lists of morpheme-based names, some consultants use computers, but not Namelab, which relies on linguists.

30   "We've wasted a couple of hundred thousand bucks trying to come up with software" to help choose names, Bachrach said.

31   "Intellectually, it's a far more arduous process than you might think," Bachrach said of matching a name to a product.

32   Whether real or made up, names should be "short, memorable, relevant" and immune to lawsuit, said Whatchamacallit's Birger.

33   It also helps if a name is easy to pronounce in many languages.

34   By Bachrach's lights, the name Coca-Cola represents a perfect marketing haiku. Like a Byronic scholar scanning a poem for rhyme and meter, Bachrach noted that Coca-Cola is not only short and visually memorable, but it also pleases the ear by being "alliterative, assonant, repetitive and iambic."

35   Most consultants agree that a great name won't sell a bad product, but opinions can very about the effect of an unfortunate name on the sales of a good product.

36   In Europe, a US company has had success with a desktop publishing tool called Quark Express even though Quark sounds like a German word for cottage cheese, Sprung said.

37   However, in "The Reckoning," a book about the auto industry, author David Halberstam noted that the habit of giving cars lame names was one of several reasons why Datsun and Toyota had trouble cracking the US market in the early 1960s.

38   Americans were not enamored of cars with names such as Bluebonnett and Cedric. And a car that Datsun planned to market as the Fair Lady seemed destined to do little better.

39   Then, at the last minute, the name was changed to the 240-Z, and a sports car was on its way to becoming a legend.

Questions on Content

1. Explain the evolution of the name of Cadillac's new model, *Catera*.

2. Discuss the advantages of morpheme-derived names. Can you think of examples other than the ones that Reidy offers?

Questions on Structure and Style

3. This selection, written for a large urban newspaper, demonstrates many principles of journalistic writing. Discuss how this type of writing differs from the essay writing with which you are more familiar.

4. How do Reidy's last three paragraphs build to an effective conclusion?

Assignments

1. Think once again about your response in the Journal Prompt. Write an essay in which you discuss names in a particular product group such as cosmetics, automobiles, or toys. Be concrete as you pay attention to audience and marketing strategy.

2. Pretend you have been asked to develop a morpheme-based name for a new lipstick or sports utility vehicle. Write an essay in which you describe the process of discovering the name and discuss marketing strategy and appeal.

Three Advertisements for Analysis

The following ads represent automobiles that appeal to a variety of audiences. The ads are as different in some ways as the cars themselves; in other ways they follow well-established advertising practice and were no doubt designed by professionals skilled by attracting customers. Ads such as these are expensive to produce, and the magazines paying for them naturally believe the ads will work. As you examine them, consider what the ads assume about their audiences, and look for both differences and similarities in their use of language as a marketing tool.

IT'S COLD, WINDY, AND THE FISH DIDN'T HIT. STILL, YOU DRIVE HOME WITH A SMILE ON YOUR FACE.

THE NEW JEEP GRAND CHEROKEE ORVIS® EDITION

Were you blessed with a sunny disposition? Or could it be the overwhelming feeling of contentment you get sitting in the new Jeep Grand Cherokee Orvis Edition?

Imagine. A rich saddle and moss green leather-trimmed interior; heated front seats with individual heat settings and 10-way power adjusters, including power lumbar and recline. Plus, an available power sunroof. (Do we detect a slight grin?)

Designed in cooperation with Orvis, the premier manufacturer of outdoor sporting and fly-fishing equipment, the Orvis Edition also includes over 40 other major advancements. Dual air bags,† a quieter 4.0 litre I-6 engine, enhanced Quadra-Trac® all-the-time four-wheel drive system, and standard Up Country suspension takes you wherever the fish are hitting. Or not hitting.

The Jeep Grand Cherokee Orvis Edition. It's bound to make you feel better on the inside.

Jeep
THERE'S ONLY ONE

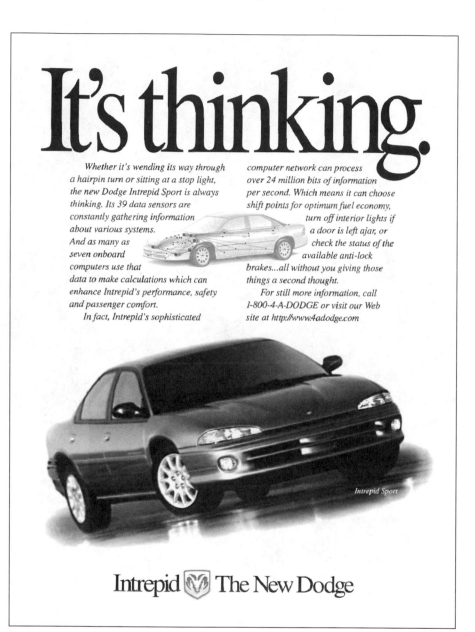

It's thinking.

Whether it's wending its way through a hairpin turn or sitting at a stop light, the new Dodge Intrepid Sport is always thinking. Its 39 data sensors are constantly gathering information about various systems. And as many as seven onboard computers use that data to make calculations which can enhance Intrepid's performance, safety and passenger comfort.

In fact, Intrepid's sophisticated computer network can process over 24 million bits of information per second. Which means it can choose shift points for optimum fuel economy, turn off interior lights if a door is left ajar, or check the status of the available anti-lock brakes...all without you giving those things a second thought.

For still more information, call 1-800-4-A-DODGE or visit our Web site at http://www.4adodge.com

Intrepid Sport

Intrepid 🐏 The New Dodge

"I'm getting a lot more car than what I'm writing a check for."
Steve Schlief
Former Acura Owner

"It's fun to drive."
Julia Maynard
Former Accord Owner

"It handles extremely well."
Kenneth Wilburn
Former Saturn Owner

EXCELLENT HANDLING. GREAT RESPONSE.

STARTING AT
$18,545*

FORD TAURUS
THE BEST-SELLING CAR IN AMERICA.

• 24-VALVE, DOHC DURATEC V-6 ENGINE** • SPEED-SENSITIVE POWER STEERING • QUADRALINK REAR SUSPENSION • STANDARD DUAL AIR BAGS (ALWAYS WEAR YOUR SAFETY BELT) • SAFETY CELL CONSTRUCTION • AVAILABLE SIX-PASSENGER SEATING • www.ford.com

*'97 Taurus G MSRP; LX shown w/PEP 210A MSRP $23,870. Tax, title extra. **LX model only.

HAVE YOU DRIVEN A FORD LATELY? *Ford*

Questions on Content

1. In each ad, what words or expressions appear repeatedly? What words or expressions are actually synonymous and represent an effort to say the same thing in different words?

2. The selling idea of an ad usually is found in the single line that succinctly sums up the major theme or idea of the ad. What is the selling idea of each ad reprinted here? What words or expressions are used to capture that idea, perhaps becoming each ad's slogan (a phrase emphasized through repetition or some other tactic and designed to hook into the audience's consciousness)?

3. Modifiers are vital in advertising language. What modifiers appear in the three automobile ads? What purposes are they designed to serve?

4. In "Types of Propaganda" (pages 291–295), the authors list seven devices often used to sway political opinion: name calling, glittering generalities, transfer, testimonial, plain folks, card stacking, and band wagon. These devices also serve advertisers, who are certainly concerned with influencing the public. Identify any examples of propaganda devices in the magazine ads.

5. To what audience is each ad appealing?

6. What does each ad assume about its audience's tastes, habits, aspirations, weaknesses, and fears?

Questions on Structure and Style

7. In most ads an invisible person is speaking to us. Listen carefully to the ads, and describe, in as much detail as possible, the voice you hear and the person you imagine behind it.

8. Examine the visual elements of each ad. What links exist between the copy (text) and the visual elements? Generally, how do these elements relate to each other?

9. Ad language sounds distinct from the language we normally use in day-to-day life. In what ways are we hearing ad language in the magazine ad, language we don't hear from our family, friends, instructors, and other "real-life" sources?

Assignments

1. In an essay, explain which of the three ads you believe will prove most successful. Be sure to define "most successful" according to the standard of success you believe should apply.

2. Assume you've been hired to write the copy for an advertisement soliciting subscriptions to a new magazine. The magazine is aimed at college students and includes articles on academic life nationwide, popular culture (particularly music, movies, and books), and fashion. Write the ad, using any advertising technique (or trick) you believe might help.

Unprotected Sex Talk

Ellen Goodman

As surgeon general, appointed by President Clinton in 1993, Joycelyn Elders spoke openly about many controversial issues, such as condom distribution in schools and the medicinal use of marijuana. In politically sensitive positions, being outspoken usually serves poorly, and it made Elders such a political liability that fifteen months after her appointment she lost her job. The reasons why Elders's public utterances seemed so indiscreet to so many Americans form the subject of the following reaction by Pulitzer Prize–winning newspaper columnist Ellen Goodman.

■ **J O U R N A L   P R O M P T**   *In the following selection Ellen Goodman has this to say about public people and free speech: "The higher you rise, the smaller the zone of privacy. Private talk is often reduced to pillow talk" (paragraph 11). Write a response that explains what you imagine Goodman's comment means. Before reading the selection, try to think of specific examples of public people who have encountered difficulties with this "zone of privacy."*

1   Leave it to Joycelyn Elders to force the country into one final sex lesson on her way out the door. This many people haven't stuttered over a word since the network anchors choked on "tampon" while describing toxic shock syndrome.

2   When it was first proclaimed that the surgeon general had advocated masturbation lessons in sex education classes, even her admirers threw up their hands. What would the kids do for a final exam? Achieve orgasm?

3   Then slowly the facts began filtering through the flak. She wasn't signing up school children for how-to classes. In her answer to a rambling question at an AIDS conference, the surgeon general reflected on her opinion that masturbation was a natural part of human sexuality and perhaps educators could say so.

4   But by the time the text and the context of her remarks had gone public, Elders was gone altogether. She was fired for again crossing the invisible, shifting line between being outspoken and loose-lipped. As in loose lips sink ships.

5   Bill Clinton had protected Elders when she was charged—unfairly—with favoring the legalization of drugs. He stood by her when she said that pro-lifers had to get over their "love affair with the fetus." But by the time the M-word came into play, it was three, four, five strikes and you're out.

6   Didn't anybody ever teach Elders not to have unprotected sex talks with strangers in public places?

7   The White House inner circle determined they had enough trouble fighting Newt Gingrich and his orphanages without worrying that Joycelyn Elders was talking about masturbation. She was the sacrificial lamb who carried the knife around in her own shoot-from-the-hip pocket.

8   The common and conflicted wisdom about Joycelyn Elders is that she may have been right but she didn't have the right to say it. Or at least she didn't have the right way to say it.

9   Before she came to Washington, Elders admitted/bragged: "I never learned to tone it down." She leaves Washington with that reputation intact. She has become the profile of an impolitic woman in a political job.

10   And so she also leaves behind a question about what exactly you can say in public life. Are you responsible for what you mean and for how you're understood? For your own words and the opposition spin?

11   One of the things that public people learn, often to their chagrin, is that the mike is always open. The higher you rise, the smaller the zone of privacy. Private talk is often reduced to pillow talk.

12   Sooner or later, most people who are funny, colorful, outrageous—the exciting people who like to float ideas just to see where they'll go—learn to check their mouths at the government door. Or they get into trouble.

13   The freedom of speech that can be exercised with intellectual or even mischievous abandon in academic papers, think-tank circles, talk shows, newspapers, street corners, is virtually forbidden to the politically ambitious. Their views can end up as unnuanced nuggets of outrage at confirmation hearings, in attack ads or editorials.

14   It's a rare idea-monger, like Lani Guinier,* who gets a second chance to be heard. It's a rare outspoken soul, like Elders' predecessor C. Everett Koop, who keeps the individuality in the uniform. (Could Koop, with his patriarchal beard and clinical manner have gotten away with Elders' words? Maybe.)

15   The truly dumbing variety of political correctness is not the inhibition from the right or the left. It's the political correctness of politics itself, the narrow constraints of permissible speech.

16   Somewhere, most politicians learn protective linguistics. They adopt a doublespeak, a drearily responsible way to respond, a vocabulary that carefully avoids tripping the startle reflex. They become predictable purveyors of words.

17   The irony is that the public is turned off by such deadening political speech, by such dull caution. We yearn, or so we say, for honesty and integrity, for colorful, real people, individuals who speak out. Yet we accept the speech code against those who violate its rules.

18   In Arkansas, one of Elders' most fervent opponents said to her, "Joycelyn, you're shaking us out of our comfort zone." Not any more. This outspoken woman is out, guilty of the one unforgivable political act. Joycelyn Elders practiced unsafe speech.

---

* Nominated by President Clinton in 1993 to head the Justice Department's Civil Rights Division. Her published writings on various politically sensitive issues made her a controversial choice, and Clinton withdrew the nomination. Guinier later spoke publicly of the issues raised by her difficulties as a nominee.

Questions on Content

1. Why was Joycelyn Elders asked to resign as surgeon general of the United States? Are the private reasons the same as the public ones?

2. Explain the meaning of the final sentence of paragraph 7: "She was the sacrificial lamb who carried the knife around in her own shoot-from-the-hip pocket." What does this statement reveal about Elders and about Goodman?

Questions on Structure and Style

3. Consider the tone of the first two paragraphs. Is Goodman's attitude clear? If not, where does it become clear? How does paragraph 3 relate to paragraphs 1 and 2?

4. In paragraph 10 Goodman asks two rhetorical questions. How would Goodman and Elders answer them?

Assignments

1. Goodman asserts, "We yearn, or so we say, for honesty and integrity, for colorful, real people, individuals who speak out. Yet we accept the speech code against those who violate its rules" (paragraph 17). Write an essay in which you respond to this passage. Be concrete as you develop your answer.

2. Assume the role of Dr. Joycelyn Elders, and write a letter to Goodman in response to this selection.

Types of Propaganda

Institute for Propaganda Analysis

Many terms are tossed about carelessly in political discourse, and *propaganda* is one of them. The word is valuable, however, because it focuses attention on the many tactics of politicians (and others) who use language to deceive. These tactics are detailed in the following extended definition. The essay, written in 1937, refers to people and places that have faded from newspaper headlines, but its message remains pertinent. Headlines change, but propaganda endures.

■ **J O U R N A L   P R O M P T**   *Today, propaganda tends to have a negative connotation. Can you think of any positive and useful functions of propaganda?*

1   If American citizens are to have clear understanding of present-day conditions and what to do about them, they must be able to recognize propaganda, to analyze it, and to appraise it.

2   But what is propaganda?

3   As generally understood, *propaganda is expression of opinion or action by individuals or groups deliberately designed to influence opinions or actions of other individuals or groups with reference to predetermined ends.* Thus propaganda differs from scientific analysis. The propagandist is trying to "put something across," good or bad, whereas the scientist is trying to discover truth and fact. Often the propagandist does not want careful scrutiny and criticism; he wants to bring about a specific action. Because the action may be socially beneficial or socially harmful to millions of people, it is necessary to focus upon the propagandist and his activities the searchlight of scientific scrutiny. Socially desirable propaganda will not suffer from such examination, but the opposite type will be detected and revealed for what it is.

4   We are fooled by propaganda chiefly because we don't recognize it when we see it. It may be fun to be fooled but, as the cigarette ads used to say, it is more fun to know. We can more easily recognize propaganda when we see it if we are familiar with the seven common propaganda devices. These are:

1. The Name Calling Device
2. The Glittering Generalities Device
3. The Transfer Device
4. The Testimonial Device
5. The Plain Folks Device
6. The Card Stacking Device
7. The Band Wagon Device

5   Why are we fooled by these devices? Because they appeal to our emotions rather than to our reason. They make us believe and do something we would not believe or do if we thought about it calmly, dispassionately. In examining these devices, note

that they work most effectively at those times when we are too lazy to think for ourselves; also, they tie into emotions which sway us to be "for" or "against" nations, races, religions, ideals, economic and political policies and practices, and so on through automobiles, cigarettes, radios, toothpastes, presidents, and wars. With our emotions stirred, it may be fun to be fooled by these propaganda devices, but it is more fun and infinitely more to our own interests to know how they work.

6   Lincoln must have had in mind citizens who could balance their emotions with intelligence when he made his remark: ". . . but you can't fool all of the people all of the time."

Name Calling

7   "Name Calling" is a device to make us form a judgment without examining the evidence on which it should be based. Here the propagandist appeals to our hate and fear. He does this by giving "bad names" to those individuals, groups, nations, races, policies, practices, beliefs, and ideals which he would have us condemn and reject. For centuries the name "heretic" was bad. Thousands were oppressed, tortured, or put to death as heretics. Anybody who dissented from popular or group belief or practice was in danger of being called a heretic. In the light of today's knowledge, some heresies were bad and some were good. Many of the pioneers of modern science were called heretics; witness the cases of Copernicus, Galileo, Bruno. Today's bad names include: Fascist, demagogue, dictator, Red, financial oligarchy, Communist, muckraker, alien, outside agitator, economic royalist, Utopian, rabble-rouser, troublemaker, Tory, Constitution wrecker.

8   "Al" Smith called Roosevelt a Communist by implication when he said in his Liberty League speech, "There can be only one capital, Washington or Moscow." When "Al" Smith was running for the presidency many called him a tool of the Pope, saying in effect, "We must choose between Washington and Rome." That implied that Mr. Smith, if elected President, would take his orders from the Pope. Likewise Mr. Justice Hugo Black has been associated with a bad name, Ku Klux Klan. In these cases some propagandists have tried to make us form judgments without examining essential evidence and implications. "Al Smith is a Catholic. He must never be President." "Roosevelt is a Red. Defeat his program." "Hugo Black is or was a Klansman. Take him out of the Supreme Court."

9   Use of "bad names" without presentation of their essential meaning, without all their pertinent implications, comprises perhaps the most common of all propaganda devices. Those who want to *maintain* the status quo apply bad names to those who would change it. . . . Those who want to *change* the status quo apply bad names to those who would maintain it. For example, the *Daily Worker* and the *American Guardian* apply bad names to conservative Republicans and Democrats.

Glittering Generalities

10   "Glittering Generalities" is a device by which the propagandist identifies his program with virtue by use of "virtue words." Here he appeals to our emotions of love, generosity, and brotherhood. He uses words like truth, freedom, honor, liberty, social

justice, public service, the right to work, loyalty, progress, democracy, the American way, Constitution defender. These words suggest shining ideals. All persons of good will believe in these ideals. Hence the propagandist, by identifying his individual group, nation, race, policy, practice, or belief with such ideals, seeks to win us to his cause. As Name Calling is a device to make us form a judgment to *reject and condemn*, without examining the evidence, Glittering Generalities is a device to make us *accept and approve*, without examining the evidence.

11   For example, use of the phrases "the right to work" and "social justice" may be a device to make us accept programs for meeting labor-capital problems, which, if we examined them critically, we would not accept at all.

12   In the Name Calling and Glittering Generalities devices, words are used to stir up our emotions and to befog our thinking. In one device "bad words" are used to make us mad; in the other "good words" are used to make us glad.

13   The propagandist is most effective in the use of these devices when his words make us create devils to fight or gods to adore. By his use of the "bad words," we personify as a "devil" some nation, race, group, individual, policy, practice, or ideal; we are made fighting mad to destroy it. By use of "good words," we personify as a godlike idol some nation, race, group, etc. Words which are "bad" to some are "good" to others, or may be made so. Thus, to some the New Deal is "a prophecy of social salvation" while to others it is "an omen of social disaster."

14   From consideration of names, "bad" and "good," we pass to institutions and symbols, also "bad" and "good." We see these in the next device.

Transfer

15   "Transfer" is a device by which the propagandist carries over the authority, sanction, and prestige of something we respect and revere to something he would have us accept. For example, most of us respect and revere our church and our nation. If the propagandist succeeds in getting church or nation to approve a campaign in behalf of some program, he thereby transfers its authority, sanction, and prestige to that program. Thus we may accept something which otherwise we might reject.

16   In the Transfer device, symbols are constantly used. The cross represents the Christian Church. The flag represents the nation. Cartoons like Uncle Sam represent a consensus of public opinion. Those symbols stir emotions. At their very sight, with the speed of light, is aroused the whole complex of feelings we have with respect to church or nation. A cartoonist by having Uncle Sam disapprove a budget for unemployment relief would have us feel that the whole United States disapproves relief costs. By drawing an Uncle Sam who approves the same budget, the cartoonist would have us feel that the American people approve it. Thus the Transfer device is used both for and against causes and ideas.

Testimonial

17   The "Testimonial" is a device to make us accept anything from a patent medicine or a cigarette to a program of national policy. In this device the propagandist makes use

of testimonials. "When I feel tired, I smoke a Camel and get the grandest 'lift.'" "We believe the John L. Lewis plan of labor organization is splendid; C.I.O. should be supported." This device works in reverse also; counter-testimonials may be employed. Seldom are these used against commercial products like patent medicines and cigarettes, but they are constantly employed in social, economic, and political issues. "We believe that the John L. Lewis plan of labor organization is bad; C.I.O. should not be supported."

Plain Folks

18 "Plain Folks" is a device used by politicians, labor leaders, businessmen, and even by ministers and educators to win our confidence by appearing to be people like ourselves—"just plain folks among the neighbors." In election years especially do candidates show their devotion to little children and the common, homey things of life. They have front porch campaigns. For the newspapermen they raid the kitchen cupboard, finding there some of the good wife's apple pie. They go to country picnics; they attend service at the old frame church; they pitch hay and go fishing; they show their belief in home and mother. In short, they would win our votes by showing that they're just as common as the rest of us—"just plain folks"—and, therefore, wise and good. Businessmen often are "plain folks" with the factory hands. Even distillers use the device. "It's our family's whiskey, neighbor; and neighbor, it's your price."

Card Stacking

19 "Card Stacking" is a device in which the propagandist employs all the arts of deception to win our support for himself, his group, nation, race, policy, practice, belief, or ideal. He stacks the cards against the truth. He uses under-emphasis and over-emphasis to dodge issues and evade facts. He resorts to lies, censorship, and distortion. He omits facts. He offers false testimony. He creates a smoke screen of clamor by raising a new issue when he wants an embarrassing matter forgotten. He draws a red herring across the trail to confuse and divert those in quest of facts he does not want revealed. He makes the unreal appear real and the real appear unreal. He lets half-truth masquerade as truth. By the Card Stacking device, a mediocre candidate, through the "build-up," is made to appear an intellectual titan; an ordinary prize fighter, a probable world champion; a worthless patent medicine, a beneficent cure. By means of this device propagandists would convince us that a ruthless war of aggression is a crusade for righteousness. Some member nations of the Non-Intervention Committee send their troops to intervene in Spain. Card Stacking employs sham, hypocrisy, effrontery.

The Band Wagon

20 The "Band Wagon" is a device to make us follow the crowd, to accept the propagandist's program en masse. Here his theme is: "Everybody's doing it." His techniques range from those of medicine show to dramatic spectacle. He hires a hall, fills a great stadium, marches a million men in parade. He employs symbols, colors, music,

movement, all the dramatic arts. He appeals to the desire, common to most of us, to "follow the crowd." Because he wants us to "follow the crowd" in masses, he directs his appeal to groups held together by common ties of nationality, religion, race, environment, sex, vocation. Thus propagandists campaigning for or against a program will appeal to us as Catholics, Protestants, or Jews; as members of the Nordic race or as Negroes; as farmers or as school teachers; as housewives or as miners. All the artifices of flattery are used to harness the fears and hatreds, prejudices and biases, convictions and ideals common to the group; thus emotion is made to push and pull the group onto the Band Wagon. In newspaper articles and in the spoken word this device is also found. "Don't throw your vote away. Vote for our candidate. He's sure to win." Nearly every candidate wins in every election—before the votes are in.

Propaganda and Emotion

21 Observe that in all these devices our emotion is the stuff with which propagandists work. Without it they are helpless; with it, harnessing it to their purposes, they can make us glow with pride or burn with hatred, they can make us zealots in behalf of the program they espouse. As we said at the beginning, propaganda as generally understood is expression of opinion or action by individuals or groups with reference to predetermined ends. Without the appeal to our emotion—to our fears and to our courage, to our selfishness and unselfishness, to our loves and to our hates—propagandists would influence few opinions and few actions.

22 To say this is not to condemn emotion, an essential part of life, or to assert that all predetermined ends of propagandists are "bad." What we mean is that the intelligent citizen does not want propagandists to utilize his emotions, even to the attainment of "good" ends, without knowing what is going on. He does not want to be "used" in the attainment of ends he may later consider "bad." He does not want to be gullible. He does not want to be fooled. He does not want to be duped, even in a "good" cause. He wants to know the facts and among these is included the fact of the utilization of his emotions.

23 Keeping in mind the seven common propaganda devices, turn to today's newspapers and almost immediately you can spot examples of them all. At election time or during any campaign, Plain Folks and Band Wagon are common. Card Stacking is hardest to detect because it is adroitly executed or because we lack the information necessary to nail the lie. A little practice with the daily newspapers in detecting these propaganda devices soon enables us to detect them elsewhere—in radio, newsreel, books, magazines, and in expressions of labor unions, business groups, churches, schools, political parties.

Questions on Content

1. Briefly explain the "present-day conditions" mentioned in paragraph 1.

2. Explain the difference between propaganda and scientific analysis.

3. What is the difference between the devices of name calling and glittering generalities?

4. Explain the devices of transfer and card stacking.

5. The essay asserts that "our emotion is the stuff with which propagandists work" (paragraph 21). Explain.

6. What response do the authors of this essay want from their audience?

7. This essay, written in the 1930s, refers to specific people and events. Many of the references are dated. What present-day people and events would be appropriate replacements for those named at the end of paragraph 7 ("Today's bad names include . . .")?

Questions on Structure and Style

8. Where is the thesis? Is it fully developed in the essay?

9. Classification is the rhetorical device used to organize this essay, but definition as well as comparison and contrast are also important. Find examples of these rhetorical devices.

10. What is the function of paragraph 4?

11. How effective is the conclusion of this essay?

12. No single author is named for this essay, but does the essay sound impersonal or "bureaucratic"? Why or why not?

Assignments

1. Using dictionaries and encyclopedias, determine the etymology of the word *propaganda*. Then, in a paragraph, explain how the etymology is related to today's customary use of the word.

2. *Propaganda* tends to have a negative connotation. In an essay, discuss the positive and useful functions of propaganda. Before starting, reread the definition of propaganda given in paragraph 3. Be sure to provide concrete examples that you considered in the Journal Prompt.

3. Select one of the seven propaganda devices, and see how many television or radio commercials you can find that rely

on that device. Present your findings to your class, and compare your observations with those of your classmates.

4. This essay was written prior to the television era. Do you think the American public, thanks to television, is more or less able to recognize propaganda today? Respond in a paragraph or an essay.

next to of course god america i

E. E. Cummings

Political voices are often unmistakable. Here, E. E. Cummings
presents his version of one such voice—or perhaps all of them.
In his familiar style, the poet satirizes politicians through their
language, achieving a ghastly accurate rendering of political speech
at its worst.

■ J O U R N A L   P R O M P T   *Write down what comes to your mind when you con-*
sider the language of politicians.

> "next to of course god america i
> love you land of the pilgrims' and so forth oh
> say can you see by the dawn's early my
> country 'tis of centuries come and go
> and are no more what of it we should worry
> in every language even deafanddumb
> thy sons acclaim your glorious name by gorry
> by jingo by gee by gosh by gum
> why talk of beauty what could be more beaut-
> iful than these heroic happy dead
> who rushed like lions to the roaring slaughter
> they did not stop to think they died instead
> then shall the voices of liberty be mute?"
>
> He spoke. and drank rapidly a glass of water

4

8

12

Questions on Content

1. The poem contains two voices. Where does the second
   voice enter, and what is its function?

2. What is the poem's theme?

3. Describe Cummings's attitude toward the political voice he
   captures.

4. Does Cummings want only to make us laugh? What other
   reaction is he hoping for, if any?

Questions on Structure and Style

5. List five of the many clichés in the poem. What effect does Cummings achieve by running them together?

6. What is the effect of "by gorry/by jingo by gee by gosh by gum" (lines 7–8)?

7. Punctuation and capitalization are more regular in the last line. Why does the poem become more conventional here? Why does Cummings leave out the final period?

Assignments

1. To determine what any poem means, we need to examine its structure and language. In an essay, discuss the content of Cummings's sonnet in light of its structure and language. In other words, discuss *what* the poem says by examining *how* it says it.

2. This poem by E. E. Cummings is a good example of satire. In a paragraph, explain the value of a satire such as this one. What can satire do that can't be done through some other approach? Use the poem as an example to illustrate your ideas.

3. Write your own satire (essay or poem) on language and behavior. Possible subjects include your friends, family, or public figures, such as religious leaders or Hollywood celebrities. Remember that satire involves ridicule (usually through exaggeration) and reveals the author's beliefs about the subject of the satire.

Two Presidential Speeches

Presidents' inaugural addresses are composed with great deliberation on the part of the presidents themselves, their advisers, and/or professional speechwriters. These addresses are intended to inspire, reassure, and establish a tone as well as to articulate political philosophy and priorities. The following two speeches are examples of the language two presidents chose as befitting a historic occasion.

■ J O U R N A L P R O M P T *Here are two memorable passages from the inaugural addresses of Presidents Kennedy and Reagan:*

"Ask not what your country can do for you—ask what you can do for your country."

"Government is not the solution to our problem; government is the problem."

Based on the two passages, think about what you expect to be the theme and tone of the inaugural addresses that follow.

John F. Kennedy's Inaugural Address (1961)

Vice President Johnson, Mr. Speaker, Mr. Chief Justice, President Eisenhower, Vice President Nixon, President Truman, Reverend Clergy, fellow citizens:

1   We observe today not a victory of party but a celebration of freedom—symbolizing an end as well as a beginning—signifying renewal as well as change. For I have sworn before you and Almighty God the same solemn oath our forebears prescribed nearly a century and three quarters ago.

2   The world is very different now. For man holds in his mortal hands the power to abolish all forms of human poverty and all forms of human life. And yet the same revolutionary beliefs for which our forebears fought are still at issue around the globe—the belief that the rights of man come not from the generosity of the state but from the hand of God.

3   We dare not forget today that we are the heirs of that first revolution. Let the word go forth from this time and place, to friend and foe alike, that the torch has been passed to a new generation of Americans—born in this century, tempered by war, disciplined by a hard and bitter peace, proud of our ancient heritage—and unwilling to witness or permit the slow undoing of those human rights to which this nation has always been committed, and to which we are committed today at home and around the world.

4   Let every nation know, whether it wishes us well or ill, that we shall pay any price, bear any burden, meet any hardship, support any friend, oppose any foe to assure the survival and the success of liberty.

5   This much we pledge—and more.

6　　To those old allies whose cultural and spiritual origins we share, we pledge the loyalty of faithful friends. United, there is little we cannot do in a host of cooperative ventures. Divided, there is little we can do—for we dare not meet a powerful challenge at odds and split asunder.

7　　To those new states whom we welcome to the ranks of the free, we pledge our word that one form of colonial control shall not have passed away merely to be replaced by a far more iron tyranny. We shall not always expect to find them supporting our view. But we shall always hope to find them strongly supporting their own freedom—and to remember that, in the past, those who foolishly sought power by riding the back of the tiger ended up inside.

8　　To those people in the huts and villages of half the globe struggling to break the bonds of mass misery, we pledge our best efforts to help them help themselves, for whatever period is required—not because the communists may be doing it, not because we seek their votes, but because it is right. If a free society cannot help the many who are poor, it cannot save the few who are rich.

9　　To our sister republics south of the border, we offer a special pledge—to convert our good words into good deeds—in a new alliance for progress—to assist free men and free governments in casting off the chains of poverty. But this peaceful revolution of hope cannot become the prey of hostile powers. Let all our neighbors know that we shall join with them to oppose aggression or subversion anywhere in the Americas. And let every other power know that this Hemisphere intends to remain the master of its own house.

10　　To that world assembly of sovereign states, the United Nations, our last best hope in an age where the instruments of war have far outpaced the instruments of peace, we renew our pledge of support—to prevent it from becoming merely a forum for invective—to strengthen its shield of the new and the weak—and to enlarge the area in which its writ may run.

11　　Finally, to those nations who would make themselves our adversary, we offer not a pledge but a request: that both sides begin anew the quest for peace, before the dark powers of destruction unleashed by science engulf all humanity in planned or accidental self-destruction.

12　　We dare not tempt them with weakness. For only when our arms are sufficient beyond doubt can we be certain beyond doubt that they will never be employed.

13　　But neither can two great and powerful groups of nations take comfort from our present course—both sides overburdened by the cost of modern weapons, both rightly alarmed by the steady spread of the deadly atom, yet both racing to alter that uncertain balance of terror that stays the hand of mankind's final war.

14　　So let us begin anew—remembering on both sides that civility is not a sign of weakness, and sincerity is always subject to proof. Let us never negotiate out of fear. But let us never fear to negotiate.

15　　Let both sides explore what problems unite us instead of belaboring those problems which divide us.

16　　Let both sides, for the first time, formulate serious and precise proposals for the inspection and control of arms—and bring the absolute power to destroy other nations under the absolute control of all nations.

17   Let both sides seek to invoke the wonders of science instead of its terrors. Together let us explore the stars, conquer the deserts, eradicate disease, tap the ocean depths and encourage the arts and commerce.

18   Let both sides unite to heed in all corners of the earth the command of Isaiah— to "undo the heavy burdens . . . (and) let the oppressed go free."

19   And if a beach-head of cooperation may push back the jungle of suspicion, let both sides join in creating a new endeavor, not a new balance of power, but a new world of law, where the strong are just and the weak secure and the peace preserved.

20   All this will not be finished in the first one hundred days. Nor will it be finished in the first one thousand days, nor in the life of this Administration, nor even perhaps in our lifetime on this planet. But let us begin.

21   In your hands, my fellow citizens, more than mine, will rest the final success or failure of our course. Since this country was founded, each generation of Americans has been summoned to give testimony to its national loyalty. The graves of young Americans who answered the call to service surround the globe.

22   Now the trumpet summons us again—not as a call to bear arms, though arms we need—not as a call to battle, though embattled we are—but a call to bear the burden of a long twilight struggle, year in and year out, "rejoicing in hope, patient in tribulation"—a struggle against the common enemies of man: tyranny, poverty, disease and war itself.

23   Can we forge against these enemies a grand and global alliance, North and South, East and West, that can assure a more fruitful life for all mankind? Will you join in that historic effort?

24   In the long history of the world, only a few generations have been granted the role of defending freedom in its hour of maximum danger. I do not shrink from this responsibility—I welcome it. I do not believe that any of us would exchange places with any other people or any other generation. The energy, the faith, the devotion which we bring to this endeavor will light our country and all who serve it—and the glow from that fire can truly light the world.

25   And so, my fellow Americans: ask not what your country can do for you—ask what you can do for your country.

26   My fellow citizens of the world: ask not what America will do for you, but what together we can do for the freedom of man.

27   Finally, whether you are citizens of America or citizens of the world, ask of us here the same high standards of strength and sacrifice which we ask of you. With a good conscience our only sure reward, with history the final judge of our deeds, let us go forth to lead the land we love, asking His blessing and His help, but knowing that here on earth God's work must truly be our own.

**Questions
on Content**

1. In paragraph 2, Kennedy asserts that his world is different from and, at the same time, similar to the world of "our forebears" (paragraph 1). What does he mean?

2. Describe Kennedy's attitude toward the United Nations.

3. What is Kennedy's attitude toward our adversaries?

4. What does Kennedy imply is a major goal of his administration?

Questions on Structure and Style

5. Most paragraphs in this address are brief—one is as short as six words. Why does Kennedy favor this form? How does it contribute to his speaking style?

6. Paragraph 23 consists of two questions. What rhetorical strategy is Kennedy using here?

7. Kennedy often uses figurative language, such as "beachhead of cooperation" and "jungle of suspicion" (paragraph 19). Find three other examples of figurative language, and explain how they contribute to the address.

8. This speech is filled with the rhetorical devices of balance, parallel structure, and repetition. Find three examples of each device. What effect does each device create?

9. Kennedy's address contains many phrases that are carefully designed to be memorable. List three that seem particularly well crafted. Why do they stand out?

10. Overall, what effect does Kennedy hope to create with the ideas and language of this speech? How does he himself wish to appear to his audience?

Assignments

1. Looking back, we can see how this speech was an integral part of the 1960s, when John F. Kennedy's youth and enthusiasm inspired a generation of Americans. Write an essay discussing how an audience of the 1990s would respond to the tone, style, and content of this speech.

2. In an essay, describe and evaluate Kennedy's expression in this address. Pay attention to the rhetorical devices of balance, parallel structure, repetition, and figurative language, and consider the effects these devices create.

3. Write your own address, focusing on three key issues that affect college students of your generation.

Ronald Reagan's First Inaugural Address (1981)

1   To a few of us here today this is a solemn and most momentous occasion. And, yet, in the history of our Nation it is a commonplace occurrence. The orderly transfer of authority as called for in the Constitution routinely takes place, as it has for almost two centuries, and few of us stop to think how unique we really are. In the eyes of many in the world, this every-4-year ceremony we accept as normal is nothing less than a miracle.

2   Mr. President, I want our fellow citizens to know how much you did to carry on this tradition. By your gracious cooperation in the transition process you have shown a watching world that we are a united people pledged to maintaining a political system which guarantees individual liberty to a greater degree than any other, and I thank you and your people for all your help in maintaining the continuity which is the bulwark of our Republic.

3   The business of our Nation goes forward. These United States are confronted with an economic affliction of great proportions. We suffer from the longest and one of the worst sustained inflations in our national history. It distorts our economic decisions, penalizes thrift, and crushes the struggling young and the fixed-income elderly alike. It threatens to shatter the lives of millions of our people.

4   Idle industries have cast workers into unemployment, human misery, and personal indignity. Those who do work are denied a fair return for their labor by a tax system which penalizes successful achievement and keeps us from maintaining full productivity.

5   But great as our tax burden is, it has not kept pace with public spending. For decades we have piled deficit upon deficit, mortgaging our future and our children's future for the temporary convenience of the present. To continue this long trend is to guarantee tremendous social, cultural, political, and economic upheavals.

6   You and I, as individuals, can, by borrowing, live beyond our means, but for only a limited period of time. Why, then, should we think that collectively, as a nation, we're not bound by that same limitation? We must act today in order to preserve tomorrow. And let there be no misunderstanding—we are going to begin to act, beginning today.

7   The economic ills we suffer have come upon us over several decades. They will not go away in days, weeks, or months, but they will go away. They will go away because we as Americans have the capacity now, as we've had in the past, to do whatever needs to be done to preserve this last and greatest bastion of freedom.

8   In this present crisis, government is not the solution to our problem; government is the problem. From time to time we've been tempted to believe that society has become too complex to be managed by self-rule, that government by an elite group is superior to government for, by, and of the people. Well, if no one among us is capable of governing himself, then who among us has the capacity to govern someone else? All of us together—in and out of government—must bear the burden. The solutions we seek must be equitable with no one group singled out to pay a higher price.

9   We hear much of special interest groups. Well, our concern must be for a special interest group that has been too long neglected. It knows no sectional boundaries or

ethnic and racial divisions, and it crosses political party lines. It is made up of men and women who raise our food, patrol our streets, man our mines and factories, teach our children, keep our homes, and heal us when we're sick—professionals, industrialists, shopkeepers, clerks, cabbies, and truckdrivers. They are, in short, "We the people," this breed called Americans.

10   Well, this administration's objective will be a healthy, vigorous, growing economy that provides equal opportunities for all Americans with no barriers born of bigotry or discrimination. Putting America back to work means putting all Americans back to work. Ending inflation means freeing all Americans from the terror of runaway living costs. All must share in the productive work of this "new beginning," and all must share in the bounty of a revived economy. With the idealism and fair play which are the core of our system and our strength, we can have a strong and prosperous America, at peace with itself and the world.

11   So, as we begin, let us take inventory. We are a nation that has a government— not the other way around. And this makes us special among the nations of the Earth. Our government has no power except that granted it by the people. It is time to check and reverse the growth of government which shows signs of having grown beyond the consent of the governed.

12   It is my intention to curb the size and influence of the Federal establishment and to demand recognition of the distinction between the powers granted to the Federal Government and those reserved to the States or to the people. All of us need to be reminded that the Federal Government did not create the States; the States created the Federal Government.

13   Now, so there will be no misunderstanding, it's not my intention to do away with government. It is rather to make it work—work with us, not over us; to stand by our side, not ride on our back. Government can and must provide opportunity, not smother it; foster productivity, not stifle it.

14   If we look to the answer as to why for so many years we achieved so much, prospered as no other people on Earth, it was because here in this land we unleashed the energy and individual genius of man to a greater extent than has ever been done before. Freedom and the dignity of the individual have been more available and assured here than in any other place on Earth. The price for this freedom at times has been high. But we have never been unwilling to pay that price.

15   It is no coincidence that our present troubles parallel and are proportionate to the intervention and intrusion in our lives that result from unnecessary and excessive growth of government. It is time for us to realize that we're too great a nation to limit ourselves to small dreams. We're not, as some would have us believe, doomed to an inevitable decline. I do not believe in a fate that will fall on us no matter what we do. I do believe in a fate that will fall on us if we do nothing. So, with all the creative energy at our command, let us begin an era of national renewal. Let us renew our determination, our courage, and our strength. And let us renew our faith and our hope.

16   We have every right to dream heroic dreams. Those who say that we're in a time when there are no heroes, they just don't know where to look. You can see heroes every day going in and out of factory gates. Others, a handful in number, produce

enough food to feed all of us and then the world beyond. You meet heroes across a counter. And they're on both sides of that counter. There are entrepreneurs with faith in themselves and faith in an idea who create new jobs, new wealth and opportunity. They're individuals and families whose taxes support the government and whose voluntary gifts support church, charity, culture, art, and education. Their patriotism is quiet but deep. Their values sustain our national life.

17   Now, I have used the words "they" and "their" in speaking of these heroes. I could say "you" and "your," because I'm addressing the heroes of whom I speak—you, the citizens of this blessed land. Your dreams, your hopes, your goals are going to be the dreams, the hopes, and the goals of this administration, so help me God.

18   We shall reflect the compassion that is so much a part of your makeup. How can we love our country and not love our countrymen; and loving them, reach out a hand when they fall, heal them when they're sick, and provide opportunity to make them self-sufficient so they will be equal in fact and not just in theory?

19   Can we solve the problems confronting us? Well, the answer is an unequivocal and emphatic "yes." To paraphrase Winston Churchill, I did not take the oath I've just taken with the intention of presiding over the dissolution of the world's strongest economy.

20   In the days ahead I will propose removing the roadblocks that have slowed our economy and reduced productivity. Steps will be taken aimed at restoring the balance between the various levels of government. Progress may be slow, measured in inches and feet, not miles, but we will progress. It is time to reawaken this industrial giant, to get government back within its means, and to lighten our punitive tax burden. And these will be our first priorities, and on these principles there will be no compromise.

21   On the eve of our struggle for independence a man who might have been one of the greatest among the Founding Fathers, Dr. Joseph Warren, president of the Massachusetts Congress, said to his fellow Americans, "Our country is in danger, but not to be despaired of. . . . On you depend the fortunes of America. You are to decide the important question upon which rests the happiness and the liberty of millions yet unborn. Act worthy of yourselves."

22   Well, I believe we, the Americans of today, are ready to act worthy of ourselves, ready to do what must be done to ensure happiness and liberty for ourselves, our children, and our children's children. And as we renew ourselves here in our own land, we will be seen as having greater strength throughout the world. We will again be the exemplar of freedom and a beacon of hope for those who do not now have freedom.

23   To those neighbors and allies who share our freedom, we will strengthen our historic ties and assure them of our support and firm commitment. We will match loyalty with loyalty. We will strive for mutually beneficial relations. We will not use our friendship to impose on their sovereignty, for our own sovereignty is not for sale.

24   As for the enemies of freedom, those who are potential adversaries, they will be reminded that peace is the highest aspiration of the American people. We will negotiate for it, sacrifice for it; we will not surrender for it now or ever.

25   Our forbearance should never be misunderstood. Our reluctance for conflict should not be misjudged as a failure of will. When action is required to preserve our national

security, we will act. We will maintain sufficient strength to prevail if need be, knowing that if we do so we have the best chance of never having to use that strength.

26   Above all we must realize that no arsenal or no weapon in the arsenals of the world is so formidable as the will and moral courage of free men and women. It is a weapon our adversaries in today's world do not have. It is a weapon that we as Americans do have. Let that be understood by those who practice terrorism and prey upon their neighbors.

27   I'm told that tens of thousands of prayer meetings are being held on this day, and for that I'm deeply grateful. We are a nation under God, and I believe God intended for us to be free. It would be fitting and good, I think, if on each Inaugural Day in future years it should be declared a day of prayer.

28   This is the first time in our history that this ceremony has been held, as you've been told, on this West Front of the Capitol. Standing here, one faces a magnificent vista, opening up on this city's special beauty and history. At the end of this open mall are those shrines to the giants on whose shoulders we stand.

29   Directly in front of me, the monument to a monumental man, George Washington, father of our country. A man of humility who came to greatness reluctantly. He led America out of revolutionary victory into infant nationhood. Off to one side, the stately memorial to Thomas Jefferson. The Declaration of Independence flames with his eloquence. And then, beyond the Reflecting Pool, the dignified columns of the Lincoln Memorial. Whoever would understand in his heart the meaning of America will find it in the life of Abraham Lincoln.

30   Beyond those monuments to heroism is the Potomac River, and on the far shore the sloping hills of Arlington National Cemetery, with its row upon row of simple white markers bearing crosses or Stars of David. They add up to only a tiny fraction of the price that has been paid for our freedom.

31   Each one of those markers is a monument to the kind of hero I spoke of earlier. Their lives ended in places called Belleau Wood, The Argonne, Omaha Beach, Salerno, and halfway around the world on Guadalcanal, Tarawa, Pork Chop Hill, the Chosin Reservoir, and in a hundred rice paddies and jungles of a place called Vietnam.

32   Under one such marker lies a young man, Martin Treptow, who left his job in a small town barbershop in 1917 to go to France with the famed Rainbow Division. There, on the western front, he was killed trying to carry a message between battalions under heavy artillery fire.

33   We're told that on his body was found a diary. On the flyleaf under the heading, "My Pledge," he had written these words: "America must win this war. Therefore I will work, I will save, I will sacrifice, I will endure, I will fight cheerfully and do my utmost, as if the issue of the whole struggle depended on me alone."

34   The crisis we are facing today does not require of us the kind of sacrifice that Martin Treptow and so many thousands of others were called upon to make. It does require, however, our best effort and our willingness to believe in ourselves and to believe in our capacity to perform great deeds, to believe that together with God's help we can and will resolve the problems which now confront us.

35   And after all, why shouldn't we believe that? We are Americans.

36   God bless you, and thank you.

1. What "special interest group" is Reagan most interested in serving?

2. What does Reagan believe is the most important issue facing his administration?

3. Explain the following: "The Federal Government did not create the States; the States created the Federal Government" (paragraph 12).

4. Why does Reagan paraphrase Winston Churchill in paragraph 19? What parallel is he attempting to draw?

5. Why is Martin Treptow (paragraphs 32–34) important to Reagan's address?

6. Reagan refers to Dr. Joseph Warren (paragraph 21) and Martin Treptow (paragraphs 32–34), yet most of his audience has probably never heard these names before. Why does he mention them? How do these references contribute to Reagan's style in this address?

7. What is the tone of this speech?

8. Overall, what effect does Reagan hope to create with the ideas and language of this speech? Moreover, how does he himself wish to appear to his audience?

1. In this speech Reagan makes certain assumptions about the American people, assumptions that we can infer from his ideas and language. Are these assumptions different from those Kennedy makes in his inaugural address? Respond in an essay.

2. Write an essay comparing the language of Reagan's first inaugural address with that of Kennedy's 1961 inaugural address. Examine the level of diction, tone, and rhetorical devices each president used.

ADDITIONAL ASSIGNMENTS AND RESEARCH TOPICS

1. Assume you've been elected president of the student government, and you have chosen, as your first task, to defeat a proposed 10 percent increase in tuition. Prepare two speeches, one for the monthly Board of Trustees meeting and the other for an informal noontime rally of students. Each speech should last two minutes, be designed specifically for its audience, and be convincing. Read the speeches to your class.

2. Choose a controversial contemporary topic such as animal rights, militant environmentalism, or abortion. Find articles addressing the topic in two or three of the following periodicals: *American Opinion, National Review, Newsweek*, and *The New Republic*. Then, in an essay, describe the language used to discuss the topic, and explain the effects this language has on its audience. Remember that your essay should not debate the topic itself; it should *analyze the language* used in the periodicals you've examined.

3. Many colleges produce pamphlets highlighting their virtues as educational institutions. These pamphlets review educational philosophy, academic resources, and campus life—all for the purpose of attracting new students or financial contributions. Locate several of these pamphlets from various colleges and universities, and examine them as examples of advertising. How do they use language as a sales tool? What is each selling? What does their language reveal about their intended audiences? Discuss your findings in an essay.

4. The form letter shown on page 311, which seeks subscribers to *Esquire* magazine, was included in an advertising mailing sent to thousands of people. Write an analysis of this ad, using the following points to help you structure your essay.

   A. The words listed below seem common, but examine their meanings within the context of the ad. Be alert for *ad language*, which is different from the language we normally hear from our family, friends, teachers, and others with whom we interact on a day-to-day basis.

benefit	friend
extraordinary	success, successful
free	

   B. In advertising jargon, the *selling idea* of an ad is the single line that sums up the major theme, or idea, of the ad. What is the selling idea of the ad reprinted here? What words or expressions are used to capture that idea, perhaps becoming the ad's *slogan*—the phrase repeated or emphasized throughout the ad and meant to plant itself in the reader's mind?

C. Modifiers are often vital in advertising language. A car isn't simply new; it's "brand new" or "refreshingly new." A soap gives more than moisture; it gives "precious moisture." Beef isn't just beef; it's "tender, juicy beef." What modifiers are used in this ad? What purposes do they serve?

D. In "Types of Propaganda" (beginning on page 291), the authors list seven devices often used to sway political opinion: name calling, glittering generalities, transfer, testimonial, plain folks, card stacking, and band wagon. These devices also serve advertisers, who are equally concerned with influencing the public. Find any examples of these propaganda devices in the ad.

E. What does the ad assume about its audience's tastes, habits, aspirations, weaknesses, and fears?

F. Visualize the person speaking in the ad. What does this person look like? What is this person wearing? Create a clear mental picture of the speaker, and then describe the speaker's tone. *How* does the person utter the words we hear?

5. Select another ad, and in an essay, analyze it either by itself or in comparison to the *Esquire* ad.

You're invited to try a complimentary copy of ESQUIRE --
FREE of cost or obligation.

If, after receiving your FREE issue, you decide to
continue your subscription, you'll get a special discount
of 67% off the regular cover price. Yes, 67% off.

Now...let me tell you about ESQUIRE. The magazine for
today's successful man.

Dear Reader,

    Are you headed for success? Are you aiming for it?

    Will you know it when you find it? Could you use a good
"road map"?

    Rest assured, there is a road map to success. A timely,
witty, entertaining, and relevant guide for today's successful
man. Of course, I'm referring to ESQUIRE magazine.

    Every month, ESQUIRE brings you the latest information on
the subjects essential to achieving (and maintaining) your
success: Getting exactly what you want (and then some!) from
your career...Making the most of your finances (someone's going
to make money in the eighties -- why shouldn't it be you)...
your health (it's never too late to give yourself the body,
stamina and total fitness you deserve)...your relationships
(with family, friends, colleagues and lovers)...where to have
the vacation of a lifetime (or simply a great weekend getaway)
...how to dress for success (at work and at play)...and more.

    ESQUIRE talks to you as no other magazine can. As a
humorous, savvy, sophisticated, loyal, fun-loving yet knowledge-
able friend. One that will never let you down.

    And now you're invited to try the latest issue of ESQUIRE.
Free of cost, with absolutely no obligation to continue Simply
return your R.S.V.P. card in the envelope we've provided. We'll
even pay the postage.

    It's this simple: we believe someone with your drive, your
ambition, your determination for success should be reading --
and can benefit from reading -- ESQUIRE. To prove it, we're
betting nothing less than a FREE issue of our magazine. And,
should you choose to continue, we're backing that up with a
tremendous discount, plus an ironclad refund guarantee.

    Why such an irresistible invitation to such an extraordinary
magazine? Because, quite frankly, we're as committed to success
as you are!

                                        Sincerely,

W.H. Jordan

                                        W.H. Jordan
                                        General Manager

P.S. Return the R.S.V.P. card now, so that we can send your
      FREE issue of ESQUIRE by return mail. Thanks.

CHAPTER SEVEN

Technology and Language

Most students today take the computer for granted—as a writing tool, as the most visible aspect of many career paths, as a means of communication, and as a source of entertainment. Even the now-standard computer printout of grades has made the term *report card* sound like a quaint language inheritance from previous generations. This pervasive presence of computers in modern life evokes various responses. Some people embrace computers and all the technology they represent, claiming they simplify work and relieve us of drudgery. Others agree with Max Frisch, Swiss novelist and playwright, when he defines technology as "the knack of so arranging the world that we don't have to experience it." Regardless of whether we accept or reject the value of technology, we live almost everywhere with its effects, and so does our language. The readings in this chapter offer a small sampling of opinion on the many effects of technology as it shapes the ways that we use, record, and react to language.

Because of its speed, electronic mail has made everyone seem more accessible. Such rapid communication has affected some people by encouraging nasty behavior almost unheard of previously. In the chapter's first selection, Doug Stewart reacts to these "Flame Throwers" and the spectacles they create. On-line chat sessions form another facet of today's electronic communications. In this case as well, the apparent accessibility of others can create tensions. Nathan Cobb looks at these "Gender Wars in Cyberspace!" as men and women communicate, often anonymously, and always in very different ways, through electronic distances.

Next, machines themselves and those who create them become the focus. In "Getting Close to the Machine," Ellen Ullman describes the programmers who create today's computer software. In her unflattering description, products they design reflect both their skill and their contempt for computer users. John Yemma then reviews efforts to design machines that would translate human languages. Although their successes remain limited, the linguists, engineers, and scientists pursuing this dream have added much to our understanding of language itself. The chapter concludes with a look at high technology and its "Techniques of Coinage" in which language elements, in this case nouns and verbs, are manipulated in new, often bewildering ways.

Computers aren't the first invention to affect language; television and the telephone have left their marks, too, but the computer is the most recent, and thus most visible, technological force stretching and molding language. Regardless of its shape, however, language itself will survive as long as we do. Technology may change it, but language comes with a better guarantee than any machine: It won't become obsolete.

Flame Throwers

Doug Stewart

Computers are impersonal, emotionless, inflexible—utterly non-human. As a result, there's much irony in their ability to prompt such messy, very human behavior from us, especially as we communicate through them. Doug Stewart reacts here to "Flame Throwers," otherwise reasonable people who make embarrassing spectacles of themselves when they generate that emotionally overheated variety of electronic mail.

■ J O U R N A L   P R O M P T   *If you communicate with a computer (E-mail, networking, on-line), think about how that level of communication differs from face-to-face communication or even telephone communication. Think about how your writing style (and content) differs between E-mail and longhand letter and memo writing.*

1   "You are a thin-skinned reactionary jerk," begins the computer message sent from one highly educated professional to another. "I will tell you this, buster. If you were close enough and you called me that, you'd be picking up your teeth in a heartbeat." There follows an obscene three-word suggestion in screaming capital letters.

2   The writer of the above message, sent over the Byte Information Exchange, was apparently enraged after a sarcasm he'd sent earlier was misinterpreted as racist. In the argot of computers, his response was a "flame"—a rabid, abusive, or otherwise overexuberant outburst sent via computer. In networking's early days, its advocates promised a wonderful new world of pure mind-to-mind, speed-of-light electronic conversation. What networkers today often find instead are brusque put-downs, off-color puns, and screenfuls of anonymous gripes. The computer seems to be acting as a collective Rorschach test. In the privacy of their cubicles office workers are firing off spontaneous salvos of overheated prose.

3   Sara Kiesler, a social psychologist at Carnegie Mellon University, and Lee Sproull, a Boston University sociologist, have observed that networking can make otherwise reasonable people act brash. In studies originally designed to judge the efficiency of computerized decision making, they gave small groups of students a deadline to solve a problem. Groups either talked together in a room or communicated via isolated computer terminals. The face-to-face groups reported no undue friction. The computerized sessions frequently broke down into bickering and name-calling. In one case, invective escalated into physical threats. "We had to stop the experiment and escort the students out of the building separately," Kiesler recalls. Kiesler and Sproull documented a tendency toward flaming on corporate electronic-mail systems as well. At one large company, employees cited an average of 33 flames a month over the E-mail system; comparable outbursts in face-to-face meetings occurred about four times a month.

4   Kiesler and Sproull attribute the phenomenon largely to the absence of cues normally guiding a conversation—a listener's nod or raised eyebrows. "With a computer,"

Kiesler says, "there's nothing to remind you there are real humans on the other end of the wire." Messages become overemphatic—all caps to signify a shout; "(smile)" or "(-:", a sideways happy face, to mean "I'm kidding." Anonymity makes flaming worse, she says, by creating the electronic equivalent of "a tribe of masked and robed individuals."

5   In real life, what we say is tempered by when and where we say it. A remark where lights are low and colleagues tipsy might not be phrased the same under fluorescent light on Monday morning. But computerized messages may be read days later and by hundreds or thousands of readers. Flaming's ornery side is only half the picture, says Sproull, who coauthored *Connections: New Ways of Working in the Networked Organization* with Kiesler. "People on networks feel freer to express more enthusiasm and positive excitement as well as socially undesirable behavior," she says. Sproull finds it ironic that computers are viewed as symbols of cool, impersonal efficiency. "What's fascinating is the extent to which they elicit deeply emotional behaviors. We're not talking about zeros and ones. People reveal their innermost souls or type obscenities about the boss." What, she asks, could be more human?

Questions on Content

1. Explain what a "flame" is in the argot of computer users.

2. Discuss what Stewart means when he says "the computer seems to be acting as a collective Rorschach test" (paragraph 2).

3. The author maintains that anonymity affects how we communicate electronically. Explain.

Questions on Structure and Style

4. Consider the effectiveness of Stewart's opening paragraph.

5. Explain the quotation and the irony in the closing paragraph. Explain how such a conclusion is appropriate to Stewart's audience and purpose.

Assignments

1. Stewart points out that "in real life, what we say is tempered by when and where we say it" (paragraph 5). Write an essay in response to Stewart's assertion. How is your own communication different in such different contexts as face to face, networking, E-mail, telephone, and longhand? Be certain to consider such factors as conversational cues and anonymity.

2. Assume you have been asked to write a set of instructions for manners on the Internet. Meet with a group of students in class, discuss what should be included in these instructions, and report your findings in an essay.

Gender Wars in Cyberspace!

Nathan Cobb

If "walking into a real bad '70s disco" doesn't sound appealing, why do so many people choose to communicate on-line today? Journalist Nathan Cobb offers a few possibilities as he examines the clearly delineated, strongly contrasting male/female approaches to on-line communication. Its participants often reveal far more about themselves than they realize.

■ **JOURNAL PROMPT** *If you have had experience with chat rooms on electronic on-line services, think about whether or not you noted gender-related differences in language and attitudes. If you have not had such an experience, try to imagine how gender-related differences might become apparent in cyberspace.*

1 Consider the Yo alert.

2 Yo?

3 Yo. Subscribers to ECHO, a small online service based in Manhattan, use the greeting to signify important messages when they converse with one another via computer. But there's a difference between those who Yo and those who don't.

4 "What we've found is that men tend to 'Yo' a lot more than women," says Stacy Horn, who founded ECHO five years ago. "And they're much more likely to 'Yo' strangers. Women simply do not 'Yo' strangers."

5 But wait. Isn't cyberspace supposed to be gender neutral, a place where women can feel empowered and men don't think they have to flex their pecs? Aren't the Internet and its commercial online siblings supposed to go beyond the notion that men are men and women are women, washing away this pre-Infobahn concept with rivers of sexless text? "Online, we don't know gender," declares Newton-based Internet analyst Daniel Dern.

6 A growing group of people beg to differ, no small number of them women. They contend not only that there are differences between male and female 'Netiquette— a k a online manners—but also differences in the overall conversational styles used by men and women who "talk" via computer.

7 "Although a lot of people have said that online communication removes cues about gender, age and background, that's not true," argues Laurel Sutton, a graduate student in linguistics at the University of California at Berkeley who has studied on-line discourse. "Everything that you communicate about yourself when you communicate face-to-face comes through when you communicate online. So men talk like men and women talk like women."

Still a Man's Cyberworld

8   Statistically speaking, of course, it's still a man's cyberworld out there. Among the major online services, CompuServe estimates that 83 percent of its users are men, while America Online pegs its male subscribers at 84 percent. Prodigy claims a 60/40 male/female ratio among users. Nobody keeps figures for the Internet, the vast web of interconnected computer networks that is owned and operated by no single entity, but estimates of female participation run from 10 to 35 percent. Indeed, most of the computer culture is male-dominated.

9   If you don't think there's a shortage of women online, listen to the dialogue one recent evening inside an America Online "chat" room known as the Romance Connection, a kind of digital dating bar. When the lone female in the room departed—assuming she really was female—after entertaining the other 22 members of the group with a bit of soft-core titillation, there was an awkward pause.

10   "What are we going to do now?" one participant typed.

11   "Who wants to play the naked female?" someone else asked.

12   "Not me," came a response.

13   "Not me, either," came another.

14   "Well, if you can't fake it, don't volunteer," offered the first.

15   Most women who go online quickly learn that many such chat areas and certain Internet newsgroups—places where cyberians sharing similar interests can post messages to one another—are spots where testosterone-based lifeforms are likely to harass them, inquiring about their measurements and sexual preferences as if they've phoned 1-900-DIALSEX. "It's like walking into a real bad '70s disco," says David Fox, the author of "Love Bytes," a new book about online dating. "The fact that people can be anonymous is a major factor. I mean, a 13-year-old can go around living his teen-age fantasy of picking up women."

16   As a result, many women adopt gender-neutral screen names, switching from, say, Victoria to VBG, Nova to Vanity, and Marcia to Just Being Me. "This way, if some jerk comes along you can always say you're a man," says Pleiades (real name: Phyllis), whose screen handle refers to the seven daughters of Atlas and Pleione but is apparently enough to throw off pursuers.

17   Almost everyone also agrees that men "flame" more than women, meaning they are more prone to firing off missives that are intended as insults or provocations. "For men, the ideal of the Internet is that it should be this exchange of conflicting views," says Susan Herring, a linguistics professor at University of Texas at Arlington who has written extensively about women's participation on computer networks. "But women are made uncomfortable by flaming. As little girls, women are taught to be nice. Little boys are taught to disagree and argue and even fight."

18   A recent case in point: Entering a debate on smoking in restaurants that was taking place in a newsgroup on the Internet, a user named Colleen politely staked out her position as a question. "Why is it necessary to smoke inside a restaurant?" she asked. In reply, a user named Peter instantly flamed. He announced he would not

pay good money to eat if he couldn't smoke at the same time. "You people are complete and utter morons!" he declared.

19   "Women come online more to build relationships, to talk about issues," contends Susan William DeFife, the founding partner of Women's Leadership Connection (WLC), an online service linked to Prodigy.

20   Ask Rebecca Shnur of Easton, Pa., a WLC subscriber who effusively likens being online to an "all-night college bull session. It's been a long time since I've talked like this with women," she says.

21   Men tend to be less concerned about making permanent connections. "I think they're much more willing to just jump online and see where it goes," says DeFife. "And, of course, to flame."

22   If men tend to be flamers, do women tend to be flamees? Nancy Tamosaitis, a New York author who has written several books about the online world, thinks they do. "By expressing any kind of strong opinion, women tend to get flamed a lot more than men do," Tamosaitis says. "There's a real strong culture on Internet. Men feel they own it. It's like an old boys' club. They don't want women or newcomers, especially female newcomers."

23   When Tamosaitis is flamed, she points out, it's almost always by a man. "I can count the flames I've gotten from women on the fingers of both hands," she says. "And men seem to bring it to a personal level. A woman will say, 'You're out of place!' A man will say, 'You're ugly!'"

Confrontation Works

24   But women who seek a softer, gentler information superhighway may find themselves sending messages into the wind. Says Sherry Terkle, an MIT professor and an authoritative voice on the subject of sociology and technology: "If you send out an online message that's inclusive, that includes many points of view, or that's conciliatory, you may get no response. And women are more likely to make that kind of communication, whereupon no message comes back.

25   "But if you make a controversial statement, maybe even an exaggeration, you're more likely to get responses. So the medium pushes people toward a controversial style. It rewards the quick jab. It encourages a kind of confrontational style, which men are more comfortable with."

26   When Susan Herring, the University of Texas linguist, disseminated an electronic questionnaire on 'Netiquette, even some of the online comments about the survey itself took on male/female styles. "I hope this doesn't sound terribly rude, but a survey is one of the last things I want to see in my mailbox," apologized one woman in declining to respond. A man who also had better things to do was less polite. "What bothers me most," he declared, "are abuses of networking such as yours: unsolicited, lengthy and intrusive postings designed to further others' research by wasting my time."

Women Are 'Lurkers'

27   Meanwhile, research shows that women who go online tend to send fewer messages per capita than do men and that their messages are shorter. There is also a widespread belief that their messages are shorter. There is also a widespread belief that more

women than men are "lurkers": people who go online to read other people's messages rather than to participate. "It's the same way you find many women sitting in physics class and acting like wallpaper," Terkle says, referring to male-dominated science classrooms. "They're just not comfortable because it matters who's in charge. It matters who seems to be in a position of power."

28   Even Michael O'Brien, an Internet magazine columnist who is by no means convinced that there is much difference between the online sexes ("I see fewer differences on the Internet than in everyday life"), allows that women "usually come across as the voice of reason. You almost never see a female counterflame. Men flame back and forth. Usually women just shut up and go away."

29   In her best-selling 1990 book, "You Just Don't Understand: Women & Men in Conversation," Georgetown University linguist Deborah Tannen described men as being comfortable with the language of confrontation and women comfortable with consensus. A self-described e-mail junkie, Tannen sees much of the same behavior online. "Actually, I would say that the differences that typify men's and women's [offline] style actually get *exaggerated* online," she says. "I subscribe to very few universals, but one I believe in is that men are more likely to use opposition, or fighting, or even warlike images. Women are not as likely to do that. They're more likely to take things as a nasty attack."

30   Tannen recalls coming across a seemingly angry online message written by a male graduate student that concluded with the command to "get your hands off my Cyberspace!"

31   "I had an exchange with the fellow about it because it struck me, a woman, as being fairly hostile and inappropriate," Tannen recalls. "But then I realized I was overinterpreting the hostility of what to him was a fairly ritualized and almost playful statement."

32   Nancy Rhine wishes more women would adopt this type of playfulness in cyberspace. Slightly more than a year ago, Rhine founded Women's Wire, a minuscule online service (1,500 subscribers compared to, say, America Online's 2 million), because she believed women weren't participating enough online. Between 90 and 95 percent of her subscribers are female, she says, and she contends that Women's Wire is a more polite and less flame-filled place than other services.

33   "But there's a pro and con to that," she concedes. "On the one hand, this is a very comfortable environment. On the other hand, I sometimes wish there were more characters posting things that were thought-provoking and stimulating.

34   "Women are conditioned to be nice, to be the caretakers, and that's the way it feels online here," Rhine says. "But I'd like to see us take more risks. I'd like to see women be more outrageous online."

Questions on Content

1. Do you believe on-line communication removes all cues about gender, age, and race? Does Cobb?

2. Susan Herring, a linguistics professor, believes "women are made uncomfortable by flaming" (paragraph 17). Explain her reasoning.

3. Some experts suggest women get flamed much more than men. Can you account for this?

4. Do you agree with professor Sherry Terkle that "the medium pushes people toward a controversial style" (paragraph 25)?

Questions on Structure and Style

5. Does Cobb believe that gender-specific behavior in on-line language is a problem? Is his purpose to describe the issue or to suggest a solution? Use his tone and diction to support your answer.

6. Discuss tone and diction in Cobb's selection. What do they tell us about purpose and audience?

Assignments

1. If you have on-line experience, write an essay in which you discuss how communicating on-line alters your behavior and your use of language.

2. Assume you have a sister who is preparing to subscribe to an on-line service. Write a letter in which you give advice on "'Netiquette," gender, and on-line styles. Draw from Cobb's selection and from your own experience.

Getting Close to the Machine

Ellen Ullman

Programmers today write computer software that we all depend on, directly or indirectly. The programmer's life and its relationship to our own form the subject of Ellen Ullman's not very reassuring view of computers and what they demand of us as we use them. For Ullman, the computer "is supposed to replace the rewards of fumbling for meaning with a mature human being, in the confusion of natural language." Moreover, "the computer's pretty, helpful face" actually expresses contempt for us, contempt that originates with those responsible for designing that face. Ullman, a consultant and editor, also has much experience as a computer programmer.

■ **J O U R N A L P R O M P T** *Before reading this essay, think about the effect computers have on socialization. What do you anticipate Ullman means by her title, "Getting Close to the Machine"?*

1   People imagine that computer programming is logical, a process like fixing a clock. Nothing could be further from the truth. Programming is more like an illness, a fever, an obsession. It's like riding a train and never being able to get off.

2   The problem with programming is not that the computer is illogical—the computer is terribly logical, relentlessly literal. It demands that the programmer explain the world on its terms; that is, as an algorithm that must be written down in order, in a specific syntax, in a strange language that is only partially readable by regular human beings. To program is to translate between the chaos of human life and the rational, line-by-line world of computer language.

3   When you program, reality presents itself as thousands of details, millions of bits of knowledge. This knowledge comes at you from one perspective and then another, then comes a random thought, then you remember something else important, then you reconsider that idea with a what-if attached. For example, try to think of everything you know about something as simple as an invoice. Now try to tell an idiot how to prepare one. That is programming.

4   I used to have dreams in which I was overhearing conversations I had to program. Once I dreamed I had to program two people making love. In my dream they sweated and tumbled while I sat looking for the algorithm. The couple went from gentle caresses to ever-deepening passion, and I tried desperately to find a way to express the act of love in the C computer language.

5   When you are programming, you must not let your mind wander. As the human-world knowledge tumbles about in your head, you must keep typing, typing. You must not be interrupted. Any break in your concentration causes you to lose a line

here or there. Some bit comes, then—oh no, it's leaving, please come back. But it may not come back. You may lose it. You will create a bug and there's nothing you can do about it.

6   People imagine that programmers don't like to talk because they prefer machines to people. This is not completely true. Programmers don't talk because they must not be interrupted.

7   This need to be uninterrupted leads to a life is strangely asynchronous to the one lived by other human beings. It's better to send e-mail to a programmer than to call. It's better to leave a note on the chair than to expect the programmer to come to a meeting. This is because the programmer must work in mind time while the phone rings and the meetings happen in real time. It's not just ego that prevents programmers from working in groups—it's the synchronicity problem. Synchronizing with other people (or their representations in telephones, buzzers, and doorbells) can only mean interrupting the thought train. Interruptions mean bugs. You must not get off the train.

8   I once had a job in which I didn't talk to anyone for two years. Here was the arrangement: I was the first engineer to be hired by a start-up software company. In exchange for large quantities of stock that might be worth something someday, I was supposed to give up my life.

9   I sat in a large room with two other engineers and three workstations. The fans in the machines whirred, the keys on the keyboard clicked. Occasionally one of us would grunt or mutter. Otherwise we did not speak. Now and then I would have an outburst in which I pounded the keyboard with my fists, setting off a barrage of beeps. My colleagues might have looked up, but they never said anything.

10   Real time was no longer compelling to me. Days, weeks, months, and years came and went without much change in my surroundings. Surely I was aging. My hair must have grown, I must have cut it, it must have slowly become grayer. Gravity must have been working on my late-thirties body, but I didn't pay attention.

11   What was compelling was the software. I was making something out of nothing, I thought, and I admit that the software had more life for me during those years than a brief love affair, my friends, my cat, my house, or my neighbor who was stabbed and nearly killed by her husband. One day I sat in a room by myself, surrounded by computer monitors. I remember looking at the screens and saying, "Speak to me."

12   I was creating something called a device-independent interface library. ("Creating"—that is the word we used, each of us a genius in the attic.) I completed the library in two years and left the company. Five years later, the company's stock went public, and the original arrangement was made good: the engineers who stayed—the ones who had given seven years of their lives to the machine—became very, very wealthy.

13   If you want money and prestige, you need to write code that only machines or other programmers understand. Such code is called "low." In regular life, "low" usually signifies something bad. In programming, "low" is good. Low means that you are close to the machine.

14   If the code creates programs that do useful work for regular human beings, it is called "high." Higher-level programs are called "applications." Applications are things

that people use. Although it would seem that usefulness is a good thing, direct people-use is bad from a programmer's point of view. If regular people, called "users," can understand the task accomplished by your program, you will be paid less and held in lower esteem.

15 A real programmer wants to stay close to the machine. The machine means midnight dinners of Diet Coke. It means unwashed clothes and bare feet on the desk. It means anxious rides through mind time that have nothing to do with the clock. To work on things used only by machines or other programmers—that's the key. Programmers and machines don't care how you live. They don't care when you live. You can stay, come, go, sleep—or not. At the end of the project looms a deadline, the terrible place where you must get off the train. But in between, for years at a stretch, you are free: free from the obligations of time.

16 I once designed a graphical user interface with a man who wouldn't speak to me. My boss hired him without letting anyone else sit in on the interview. My boss lived to regret it.

17 I was asked to brief my new colleague with the help of the third member of our team. We went into a conference room, where my coworker and I filled two white boards with lines, boxes, circles, and arrows while the new hire watched. After about a half hour, I noticed that he had become very agitated.

18 "Are we going too fast?" I asked him.

19 "Too much for the first day?" asked my colleague.

20 "No," said our new man, "I just can't do it like this."

21 "Do what?" I asked. "Like what?"

22 His hands were deep in his pockets. He gestured with his elbows. "Like this," he said.

23 "You mean design?" I asked.

24 "You mean in a meeting?" asked my colleague.

25 No answer from the new guy. A shrug. Another elbow motion.

26 Something terrible was beginning to occur to me. "You mean talking?" I asked.

27 "Yeah, talking," he said. "I can't do it by talking."

28 By this time in my career, I had met many strange software engineers. But here was the first one who wouldn't talk at all. We had a lot of design work to do. No talking was certainly going to make things difficult.

29 "So how *can* you do it?" I asked.

30 "Mail," he said. "Send me e-mail."

31 Given no choice, we designed a graphical user interface by e-mail. Corporations across North America and Europe are still using a system designed by three people in the same office who communicated via computer, one of whom barely spoke at all.

32 Pretty graphical interfaces are commonly called "user-friendly." But they are not really your friends. Underlying every user-friendly interface is terrific contempt for the humans who will use it.

33 The basic idea of a graphical interface is that it will not allow anything alarming to happen. You can pound on the mouse button, your cat can run across it, your baby can punch it, but the system should not crash.

34   To build a crash-proof system, the designer must be able to imagine—and disallow—the dumbest action possible. He or she has to think of every single stupid thing a human being could do. Gradually, over months and years, the designer's mind creates a construct of the user as an imbecile. This image is necessary. No crash-proof system can be built unless it is made for an idiot.

35   The designer's contempt for your intelligence is mostly hidden deep in the code. But now and then the disdain surfaces. Here's a small example: You're trying to do something simple such as copying files onto a diskette on your Mac. The program proceeds for a while, then encounters an error. Your disk is defective, says a message, and below the message is a single button. You absolutely must click this button. If you don't click it, the program will hang there indefinitely. Your disk is defective, your files may be bollixed up, but the designer leaves you only one possible reply. You must say, "OK."

36   The prettier the user interface, and the fewer replies the system allows you to make, the dumber you once appeared in the mind of the designer. Soon, everywhere we look, we will see pretty, idiot-proof interfaces designed to make us say, "OK." Telephones, televisions, sales kiosks will all be wired for "interactive," on-demand services. What power—demand! See a movie, order seats to a basketball game, make hotel reservations, send a card to mother—all of these services will be waiting for us on our televisions or computers whenever we want them, midnight, dawn, or day. Sleep or order a pizza: it no longer matters exactly what we do when. We don't need to involve anyone else in the satisfaction of our needs. We don't even have to talk. We get our services when we want them, free from the obligations of regularly scheduled time. We can all live, like programmers, close to the machine. "Interactivity" is misnamed. It should be called "asynchrony": the engineering culture come to everyday life.

37   The very word "interactivity" implies something good and wonderful. Surely a response, a reply, an answer is a positive thing. Surely it signifies an advance over something else, something bad, something that doesn't respond. There is only one problem: what we will be interacting with is a machine. We will be "talking" to programs that are beginning to look surprisingly alike; each has little animated pictures we are supposed to choose from, like push buttons on a toddler's toy. The toy is meant to please us. Somehow it is supposed to replace the rewards of fumbling for meaning with a mature human being, in the confusion of a natural language, together, in a room, within touching distance.

38   As the computer's pretty, helpful face (and contemptuous underlying code) penetrates deeper into daily life, the cult of the engineer comes with it. The engineer's assumptions and presumptions are in the code. That's the purpose of the program, after all: to sum up the intelligence and intentions of all the engineers who worked on the system over time—tens and hundreds of people who have learned an odd and highly specific way of doing things. The system reproduces and re-enacts life as engineers know it: alone, out of time, disdainful of anyone far from the machine.

Questions on Content

1. Explain the differences between mind time and real time and between low code and high code.

2. Ullman suggests that programmers don't talk because they must not be interrupted. Explain. She goes on to describe code, the language of computer programmers. How does this language differ from ordinary human discourse?

3. Explain why Ullman suggests computer programmers develop contempt for the people who will eventually use their programs.

Questions on Structure and Style

4. Ullman provides many personal anecdotes to illustrate her life as a computer programmer. One such anecdote begins with paragraph 16. Find other examples. What is the effect of these anecdotes?

5. Explain the purpose of the figurative language the author employs in her opening paragraph. Find other examples, and discuss their effectiveness.

6. Identify Ullman's audience and purpose. Use her content and style to support your answer.

Assignments

1. In paragraph 3 Ullman employs an analogy to help clarify what computer programming is. Think about a task you have been confronted with in the workplace. Develop an analogy to illustrate the task.

2. Write a one- or two-paragraph summary of Ullman's essay. Be certain to emphasize her central message.

3. Write an essay in which you discuss the effects of the computer on human discourse and socialization. Use anecdotes from personal experience.

C'est What?

John Yemma

Journalist John Yemma reviews the current state of efforts to create
translating machines, devices that would translate reliably from one
human language to another and would be worth huge sums to many
businesses worldwide. So far only human beings translate languages
reliably because only humans understand the cultural contexts in
which languages evolve. Attempts at designing machines with
similar understanding, or at least some useful approximation, thus
far have produced many failures, a few limited successes, and an
increased understanding of language itself.

■ J O U R N A L   P R O M P T   *In the selection that follows, John Yemma discusses
possibilities for computerized translation. He points out that "converting literal meaning
from words on a printed page is fairly easy for machines" (paragraph 6). Before reading this
essay, make a list of other aspects of human language that might not be so easy for machine
translation.*

1   Even an accomplished polylinguist has translation needs now and then. Learn Italian,
and you'll get offered a job in Tokyo. Drill in Arabic, and you'll fall in love with a
Thai. Study Swahili, and, sure, you'll use it in east Africa, but what about west Africa?

2   With world travel cheap and easy, and with perhaps 5,000 languages in the world
(242 spoken by a million or more people), your Berlitz library will never be able to
keep up.

3   But the great promise of our age is the computer, with its accelerating processing
speeds, steadily increasing memory, and ever more clever software. Surely, we are
only one or two more Pentium chips and Brookstone catalogs away from a "universal translator"— a device able to convert a line like "If it doesn't fit, you must acquit"
into meaningful Mandarin, Quechuan, or Farsi.

4   We are getting closer. A number of scientists are working toward such a machine.
And a number of businesses know that there is great market potential in fast, proficient,
automated translation. One study has estimated the size of the business-translation
market alone at $20 billion a year.

5   The Boston-Cambridge [Massachusetts] area is a world leader in machine-assisted
translation, with companies doing a brisk business in software packages that can deal
with tens of thousands of translation jobs. But it is slow going. Even with the fastest
computers and the best software boffins, undoing the damage done at Babel is going
to take time.

6   Imagine some of the problems. Converting literal meaning from words on a
printed page is fairly easy for machines. Current software can do a passable job of
it, though most programs still require a human editor to clean up messes. Take a look
at this dog's breakfast featured in "Computergram Internationals" newsletter. It's a
computer-generated French-to-English translation of a business letter:

7　　"We are a company of manufacture and distrution of pret has to carry feminin average, top-of-the-range. . . . Our manufacture in circuit short 100% Frenchwoman an a reassort permanent east ensures." The letter signed off with a jaunty: "Sincere greetings with the leisure of reading you."

8　　Not exactly *magnifique*. And that was a written translation. Imagine a chatty sales rep making the same pitch over the phone and relying on a voice-recognition system to translate. If any sense were conveyed at all, it might be an invitation to walk on the wild side with a short, 100 percent French woman.

9　　For, once you factor in idioms, irony, neologisms, nonsense, tonal differences, accents, body language, literary references, malapropisms, slang, mumbling, lisps, speed differences, and, most important of all, context—all of which humans can analyze almost instantaneously—you see what a marvel a skilled translator is.

10　　The smarter the human, the better the translation. High intelligence enables a good translator to deduce meaning. But why? Is it because a linguist has learned a secret code? Or because he or she has amassed a huge store of vocabulary and grammar?

11　　"When a human being translates something," says Robert Beard, a professor of modern languages at Bucknell University, in Pennsylvania, "he or she puts to use not only linguistic knowledge that he or she has, but all the general knowledge about how the world works in general, as well as how the cultures surrounding the two languages work. In order for a computer to ever successfully translate, it must have all this information, too."

12　　This is where the world of machine translation splits into two distinct camps. One is the artificial-intelligence camp. Its thesis is that there are patterns in intelligence. Get the patterns right, feed them to a machine, and you'll have a translator that figures out the right words. The other camp promotes brute-force computing. It says forget the formulas, just go for the biggest possible RAM cache and the highest processing speeds. Eventually, you'll get enough information into the brain of this super-fast machine—from the Hindu *Rig-Veda* to Shakespeare's sonnets to last week's episode of *Seinfeld*—that it will have every verbal and contextual angle covered.

13　　Artificial intelligence is more or less stalled. Brute force is the growth area. But some combination of the two might be the way forward, says Kenneth N. Stevens, a professor of electrical engineering at the Massachusetts Institute of Technology. Stevens has spent 45 years studying language. He specializes in breaking apart the spoken word so that the sound can be analyzed. In his lab, he and his students have cataloged thousands of sounds and arranged them into categories, much like the periodic table of the elements. These include click sounds from Bushman languages, Indian consonants, and the subtle differences in the way "B" sounds in "beat" and "bought."

14　　"The very first stage in a translation," Stevens says, "is trying to figure out from the acoustic wave what sounds a person is making." He recognizes that a massive database of sounds and words goes a long way to achieving speech recognition. That argues for the brute-force approach. But he points out that there must be some innate human capability that artificial intelligence can emulate. After all, until the age of 3 or 4, all children have inborn ability to master at least two languages. That can't be sheer brute force.

15 The closest anyone has yet gotten to a *Star Trek*-type universal translator is the work done by Jaime Carbonelle, who heads the Center for Machine Translation at Carnegie Mellon University, in Pittsburgh. He calls his device a Continuous Speech Recognizer.

16 It is still too big and clumsy to fit in a shirt pocket. Among other things, it requires the users to be equipped with microphones, which tend to get in the way of trash talking and breeze shooting. But it has demonstrated modest competence in controlled lab tests. It has succeeded, for instance, in setting up business meetings for speakers of English, Japanese, German, and Korean. By limiting the verbal palette to specific functions—meetings, business negotiations, medical applications, travel, meal ordering—Carbonelle thinks it won't be long before the Continuous Speech Recognizer is widely available.

17 "I've dedicated my research life to this," Carbonelle says. "It is one of the greatest challenges to address. We are living in a globalized society, and I think automation has to be the way to overcome language differences."

18 Everyone who has labored in the torture chamber of a language lab will want to join me in offering Dr. Carbonelle a hearty and sincere thank you, "with the leisure of reading you."

Questions on Content

1. Explain the meaning of the Babel allusion in paragraph 5.

2. In paragraph 9 the author provides a catalog of reasons that demonstrate what a marvel a skilled translator is. If necessary, use a dictionary to help you explain his reasons.

3. Describe the two camps into which the world of machine translation has split. Which of the two appears to be the more promising? Explain why.

4. Explain the meaning of Yemma's concluding words, "with the leisure of reading you" (paragraph 18).

Questions on Structure and Style

5. Analyze the rhetorical effect of the first three paragraphs. What do you notice about tone and attitude? Where does Yemma present his thesis, and why does he present it as he does?

6. In paragraph 16 Yemma uses such colloquial phrases as "trash talking" and "breeze shooting." Think about his language in this essay. What does it tell you about his audience and purpose?

Assignments

1. In paragraph 10 Yemma asks the question, "But why?" Write a few paragraphs in which you provide an answer to Yemma's question.

2. Yemma concludes paragraph 14 with these words: "That can't be sheer brute force." Think about what the sentence means, and write an essay on differences between human and machine language. You may find it helpful to refer to Steven Pinker's selection beginning on page 141.

Techniques of Coinage

John A. Barry

Engineering or business skill sometimes guarantees nothing when the product is language. For the computer industry, which seems every second to offer us some new invention or refinement, inventing new language for new things has produced a huge vocabulary noted mainly for the confusion it's created and for its plain ugliness. In the following excerpt from his book *Technobabble*, John A. Barry reviews what happens to nouns and verbs when the unimaginative and verbally challenged take charge of the dictionary. Barry has written many books and has worked as an editor in the computer-related publishing industry.

■ **JOURNAL PROMPT** *Make a list of words in your language that result directly from computer jargon.* Interface *and* access *are two examples. You may find that nouns have been changed to verbs (for example,* to mouse*) or that verbs have been changed to nouns (for example,* the install*). In addition, you will likely discover new words and acronyms.*

1 The computer industry moves fast. Many of its frantic denizens are "high energy" types. They have to think fast—although not necessarily coherently—to keep up. This sort of environment is conducive to hasty, reflexive coinages of terms.

2   The coinages may be reflexive, but most of the mechanisms are now well established in the computer industry. The rule of thumb is that nearly anything goes. Coin a word to fit a singular occasion, and then discard it. Turn practically any part of speech, acronym, name, or process into a noun or verb. Add various suffixes to just about any word to come up with a variant of that word. To paraphrase an industry buzzphrase, "The coinage possibilities are limited only by your imagination."

Verbs into Nouns

3 As its name suggests, the verbs-into-nouns technique involves changing verbs (usually transitive) into nouns. In this technique, the root meaning of the new noun stays the same. Take, for example, the "noun" *install,* as in the "the install usually takes two hours." *Install* is representative of the verb/noun in that a pseudonoun is created when a true noun is pared down to its verbal root. Thus, the noun *installation* becomes "the install." This technique also produces *the announce* in lieu of *the announcement, the disconnect* for *the disconnection, the interconnect* for *the interconnection,* and *the create* for *the creation.* Most of these verb/nouns substitute the verb form of a noun ending in *-tion* for the actual noun.

4   Documentation and other technical writing is replete with nouns *né* verbs such as *the acquire, the compile,* and *the connect.* Often the technique involves use of the auxiliary verb *to do*—as in "He did a compile." In addition to the verb/nouns listed above,

the following "nouns" are among those favored by high-tech types: *the attach, the concatenate, the interrupt, the configure, the evaluate, the debug,* and *the migrate.*

5   The last term in this list is interesting for a couple of reasons. Whereas the four "nouns" that precede *the debug* are the verb forms of *-tion* nouns, the noun that would correspond to *the debug* would be the gerund *debugging*—as in "The system needs debugging."

6   Sometimes when a verb becomes a noun, as in *the confirm,* an accent shift occurs. The verb *confirm* is accented on the second syllable; however, the neonoun *the confirm* receives an accent on the first syllable.

7   The verbs-into-nouns technique probably derives from industry conventions— once again, illustrating that terminology is a reflection of technology. Many nouns that become verbs do so because they are based on software commands or actions— for example, *install* and *compile.* In formal computer writing, such as a system-setup manual, verb-nouns are generally set in a different typeface (often Courier or some other monospaced font) to differentiate them from surrounding text and to signify that the verb-noun means to use the command on which it is based to perform the desired action: "The `install` is straightforward."

8   What has increasingly happened, however, is that such typographic distinctions have disappeared in a lot of writing about computers, especially in brochures and other "collateral": "The install is straightforward." This development is ironic because, presumably, people reading collateral, or "high level," material are not as familiar with technobabble conventions as are people who read manuals, so it would seem that more conventional English usages would be in order.

9   A variation on the verbs-into-nouns technique is verbs-into-adjectives. A couple of examples come from the world of computer graphics. Two types of software for artists are so-called paint and draw programs. Names of modes are frequently verbs employed as adjectives: "read mode," "write mode."

Nouns into Verbs

10   The obverse visage of verbs into nouns is nouns into verbs. PR specialist Doc Searls suggests that nouns used as verbs be called "nerbs." This technique turns nouns into transitive verbs. Again, this technique is not new; many of the verbs we use routinely started out as nouns. The verb *to contact,* for example, began life as a noun; it gained widespread use as a verb in spite of the apocryphal thundering of a New York publisher: "In this house, *contact* is not a verb!"

11   Despite the protestations of critics, nouns are constantly becoming verbs. "Any noun can be 'verbed,'" asserts author David Roth. And high-technology mavens are not the only group "verbifying" nouns. "Miss Watson," a fat-cat politician commands his secretary in the comic strip "Fran and Ernest," "turn some of these nouns into verbs for me. I want this [a sheaf of papers he holds up] to sound important." The implication here is that, at least in government circles, turning nouns into verbs inflates the perceived importance of an otherwise mundane pronouncement.

12   The reasons for verbifying nouns in the computer industry are sometimes more prosaic, often prompted by the need for a shorthand method of explaining an action

based on a new technology. When the computer mouse, for example, became a commercial product in the early 1980s, *Info World* columnist Doug Clapp needed a way
to describe the use of the device, so he wrote, "I predict that executives will never
learn to type properly or even to 'mouse' properly."

13   Clapp, an industry wag, probably had his tongue so far into his cheek that he
looked like a food-stuffed rodent, but the technique is illustrative of the need to come
up with verbs to explain or talk about phenomena that might otherwise require a
small dissertation. Another computer magazine that got in on the nouns-into-verbs
act was *MacUser,* with "Versionary lets you specify which applications of folders it
should 'version.'" On the other hand, sometimes the need, or desire, to sound important is the sole motivation for transforming nouns into spurious verbs.

14   Consider the verbal behavior of Steven P. Jobs, cofounder of Apple Computer and
a natural master of the nouns-into-verbs technique. In January 1983, Jobs addressed
about 2,000 Apple shareholders in an auditorium in Cupertino, California. The purpose of this business-cum-revival meeting was to introduce the company's new Lisa
computer, which, rumor had it, had been named after a person. The breathless prose
in the Lisa press kit, however, explained that Lisa was an acronym, standing for
Locally Integrated Software Architecture. The glossy press kit neglected to explain
exactly what "Locally Integrated Software Architecture" meant. Jobs was ebullient
when he proclaimed, "With Lisa, Apple has 'architected' a new standard." He was not
the first to "architect" this verb out of a noun, but in the years since he used the term,
it has continued to gain currency among computer people as part of the growing list
of nouns becoming verbs. Another young industry cheerleader, Scott McNealy of Sun
Microsystems, managed to use the neoverb "architect" twice—as well as the nominal
form once—in as many sentences in a 1989 interview.

15   The nouns-into-verbs technique has two variations. The first, as in "to mouse"
and "to database," turns nouns that have no acknowledged verbal meanings into
verbs. The second, as in "to tempest" . . . uses nouns that do have verbal forms but
employs them in a nonstandard context. The verb *to tempest* has a legitimate lexical
meaning, "to raise a tempest in and around," that dates from the fourteenth century.
The computerese verb *to tempest,* however, has nothing to do with this meaning.

16   Many nouns made the transition to verbs in the mid-1960s—a fecund period
for the acceptance by dictionary publishers of these verbs-once-nouns. *To interface, to access, to keyboard,* and *to format* all became verbs in the mid-1960s. The
latter verb took 124 years to make the transition; *format* entered English as a noun
in 1840.

**Questions
on Content**

1. Explain why the environment of the computer industry
   makes it ripe for the hasty coinage of new terms.

2. Explain what Barry means by this statement: "Terminology
   is a reflection of technology" (paragraph 7). Choose some
   examples of "technobabble" that illustrate this principle.

3. What is ironic about the disappearance of typographic distinctions in collateral material such as brochures about computers?

Questions on Structure and Style

4. Is Barry's objective to present an objective discussion of new coinages within the computer industry? If you think not, show how he reveals his attitude.

5. Discuss the effect of the simile with which Barry begins paragraph 13.

Assignments

1. Within all industries those who invent new things also invent new names. List steps in the procedure you believe should be followed when a business sets out to name new technology that it hopes to sell to the general public. Remember that the product is not simply a variation on something that already exists; the product consists of technology that's unfamiliar to the people to whom it will be offered.

2. Have you ever been confused by the language associated with technology? Have you ever witnessed someone else's confusion? In an essay, explain the possible long-term effects of this common phenomenon on a society such as ours.

ADDITIONAL ASSIGNMENTS AND RESEARCH TOPICS

1. Leaders in education and industry commonly insist that being computer literate is just as important for college and perhaps even high school graduates as being literate in English and math. However, others argue that computers, as mere tools, don't deserve special attention in anyone's schooling. In effect, we should "Teach carpentry, not hammers" because teaching tools, any tools, actually limit ability and therefore potential. Write an essay responding to either position by examining the importance of computer literacy for your generation.

2. This chapter's introduction quotes Max Frisch's definition of technology: "the knack of so arranging the world that we don't have to experience it." In an essay, respond to this definition, paying particular attention to technology's effects on our use of language.

3. The following poem was written by a computer programmed to produce syntactically correct sentences and parallel stanzas. In an essay, analyze the poem. Why was a computer able to produce it?

> A lustful twig can twiddle up to the tenderness of a spoon
> And can kill the motion of wisdom.
> But the brain beside gay power heals the action of earth
> While the tenderness of a spoon heals the lustful twig.
>
> A happy muffin shall bask under earth of night
> And can ensnare the pond up charity of earth.
> But the activity of charity strengthens sorrowful faith
> While the earth of night beseeches the happy muffin.
>
> A wanton gate may gurgle under the gate of the age of a star
> and should worship a gay shovel.
> But frail wisdom ensnares the endurance of night
> While the gate of the age of a star pursues the wanton gate.
>
> A moody cloud shall ponder over the motion of a shovel
> And should beseech the goodness of beauty.
> But war over nature worships a wanton goat
> While the motion of a shovel strengthens the mood cloud.

4. Elsewhere in *Technobabble,* John A. Barry offers the following lighthearted project:

Mix and Match

Stumped for a name for your company? Just select one item each from columns A, B, and C. In some cases, you could combine parts of words from the first and second columns (e.g., Intertech Solutions).

A	B	C
International	Technology	Corporation
Integrated	Software	Associates
Parallel	Development	Partners
Innovative	Hardware	Solutions
First	Generation	Systems
Worldwide	Enterprise	Configuration
Digital	Functions	Group

Using Barry's format as a guide, construct your own Mix and Match resource for naming a new product, perhaps a breakfast cereal or an exercise machine. Be sure to make the A-B-C categories systematic and the items representative of the language we regularly hear in advertising.

CHAPTER EIGHT

Writers and the Writing Process

Now here's your dream, one of the good ones. You write well, and your essays come back from the writing instructor with comments such as these: "convincing content . . . efficient structure . . . good use of evidence." No more comments such as "focus unclear . . . confusing structure . . . lacks fresh ideas."

Another dream. Three days before the assignment is due, you sit down and write, write, write. Words stream onto your paper, so many words that the hardest part of writing involves cutting out what's no good. Gone are those confrontations with an intimidating empty page, and laboring through every sentence, worrying that "cutting out what's no good" probably would mean cutting all of it.

Gone, too, is the comforting belief, however mistaken, that good writers are born, not made, and you simply lost the genetic lottery. Other people won the writer's genes. And that paper is still due next Monday.

The truth about writing is this: Good *writing* is not born; it's made. "Making" good writing is every writer's true job, and in this chapter professional writers and teachers offer advice, none of it dreamlike and all of it useful, on various aspects of the writing process.

Often we are not supplied with ready-made writing topics, and one popular tactic can make the blank page less intimidating. In "Freewriting" Chris Anderson explains this tactic through detailed illustrations from student writers and their experiences with freewriting. In a selection from *Bird by Bird: Some Reflections on Writing and Life,* novelist Anne Lamott reassures us that most first drafts, although flawed, constitute only one step in a process. Detailed writing advice is offered by Maxine C. Hairston in her recommendations for "Holding Your Reader" by creating the clarity and precision that banish any reader's boredom.

The next selection addresses revision, the aspect of writing that most students understand least. The title of Donald M. Murray's article neatly summarizes his fresh, practical approach: "Writing Is Revising." Joseph M. Williams stresses the need for "Concision," that is, for efficiency in prose that's possible only through cutting all words that are not doing useful work. The chapter concludes with "Computers and Writing." Here Sharon Cogdill examines why word processing can either help or hinder writers and why this technology sometimes affects writing in surprising ways.

One idea runs through all the selections in this chapter: Good writing is neither magic nor the product of dreaming. It results from experimentation and reflection, from careful thought and work. Through a highly personal process, and through sensitivity to language and meaning at every step of the process, we make good writing.

Freewriting

Chris Anderson

Freewriting: "a language-spinning machine . . . a kind of spigot you can turn on." Such a definition, intentionally unscholarly and deliciously metaphoric, introduces Chris Anderson's discussion of freewriting as a practical method for generating ideas and keeping them alive. Anderson also addresses "the paradox of the audience" for whom our writing is intended. As he points out, thinking too much too soon about audience will kill good writing. Anderson teaches writing at Oregon State University and has widely published scholarly work, nonfiction, and poetry.

■ **J O U R N A L   P R O M P T**   *Describe your writing process. Discuss, in particular, what you do from the time you receive an assignment until you complete an early draft.*

. . . On Freewriting

1   Freewriting is a brainstorming technique made famous by Peter Elbow in two very fine books, *Writing Without Teachers* and *Writing with Power*. It's a language-spinning machine that you can point at lots of different kinds of writing—a kind of spigot you can turn on to tap into some of your ideas and feelings.

2   If you're sitting at a computer screen with something to say, just start writing. Don't think about how to *introduce* your idea with some snappy opening or what the first point might be and the transition into the second. Don't think too much about the writing at all. Think about the thinking. Just start writing and don't stop for say ten minutes, or until you're done with this little piece. Write at a comfortable pace. Don't go too fast. Freewriting is a little like running, and you'll lose energy if you start out too fast. But don't go too slow, either, or you'll lose the energy of the words tumbling out and the momentum that builds. If you don't know what to say, write, "I don't know what to say," or repeat the last word you wrote ("wrote wrote wrote wrote") until you come up with something to say. The main thing is not to reread what you've written but to plunge ahead. That's surprisingly hard for most of us since we've been trained by years of school to be proper and not make a mess, especially in writing. But resist those impulses. Turn off the light on the screen and even write blind if you have to, just don't worry about grammar and punctuation and eloquence or anything else. Let the words flow out. Don't let your fingers leave the keys. Don't correct.

3   No one will ever look at this unless you want them to, so be brave. Take advantage. Try to write while ignoring the reader who might eventually get this (though this is finally impossible, it's a good mental exercise). Say what you really think and to hell with the consequences. (You can tone things down later if you have to. You can revise all of this later.) Imagine that the words are transparent, not there at all, and your raw thinking is showing through.

4   You can do the same thing with handwriting, too, though the experience is different in interesting ways. Don't let your pen leave the page. Keep up the pace.

5   Freewriting works best for producing an actual draft of something when you've already done some thinking about the subject. You've gotten all your research and material together. You've mulled over your main argument until you have a tentative focus to start with. Outlining is good, as long as you don't feel bound by it. Sketch out some ideas formally or informally, in a notebook or on a napkin or on a walk, and then freewrite each point, forcing yourself to stay on the subject as much as you can. The order will probably change as you go, and you'll probably come up with new ideas you hadn't planned. That's good. You can reorganize the points later, and besides, freewriting sometimes produces more natural transitions, subtler blends and combinations of ideas, than you can sketch out in advance.

6   If you haven't had time to incubate, or you're confused, or you only have a very vague idea, start freewriting to generate some possibilities. Use the writing to think about what you want to say. See what comes up. Just don't stop writing.

7   Here's an example of what you might produce this way, an entry from my current freewriting journal about a walk I take near my house. Notice that the sentences are a little jumbled and fragmentary but that they basically make sense:

```
I seem to need to do things over and over again, repeat
myself, circle round and round the same thing, in order to
feel comfortable with it and with myself in relation to it.
Which is a definition of habits. Of routine. I think I'd
rather take the same trail a hundred times than hike a
hundred trails. This time I found myself seeing things things
things I hadn't seen before in the other three walks. Was
getting general impressions (I guess)--impressions--better
term?--feelings and atmospheres and the general zones. Now I
was resolving things. Details resolving themselves. The
picture was focusing, zooming in. No, it was as if the things
in the woods were for a moment in boldface, or louder, or
clearer against the field of the other green. Ferns--two
kinds, one delicate, the other plainer and almost artificial
looking. The spruce--I think--that have been planted on the
clear cut. The honey-suckle--I think--among the undergrowth.
And the vine maples--are they?--their stems lifting up the
broad leaves (broad leaf maples?) like upturned palms and
they seem to levitate there, flattened out in midair,
hovering. I noticed it's Adair Village you can see from the
cut through the power lines by the forestry cabin. I noticed
```

```
that the forest isn't as deep as it seems. It's fragile.
It's a fringe and I can see through it really. The heavy wall
of green is dissolving and there are degrees and layers and
shades of green and light shining through and balder, barer
spots than first seemed, and the bands of trees shallower.
```

I freewrite at my computer, not worrying about spelling (I've corrected the mistakes here) or even about the rhythm of my sentences. I'm trying to record as clearly and immediately as I can what's going through my mind at the moment of the writing. I want the thinking and the writing to be simultaneous. There's a sense in this entry of my thinking aloud about the writing as I write. I try out different versions of phrases and descriptions as I go. I allow myself to comment on what I've just written, question it. I tread water sometimes, simply repeating the last word I wrote.

How to Use Freewriting for Style: Why It Helps

8   Most beginning and inexperienced writers overtranslate their own original language into some other language they think is more acceptable or formal or proper and in the process lose the force of their own voice. It's as if they have good, clean words inside them, or the potential for good, clean words, but then they panic—this all happens instantaneously, as they write—and instead of saying directly what they think, start trying to fancy it up. They go to a thesaurus. They say "obtain" instead of "get" and "proceed" instead of "go," as if they've gotten all dressed up in a business suit. Instead of saying, "I think we should," they say, "One might imagine the solution could be . . ." or some other language like that. And pretty soon the sentences are vague and lifeless, or even full of grammatical errors and usage problems, because these writers are using a voice they can't control.

9   But if you're freewriting, you don't have time to go to a thesaurus and look up a substitute for what you really have to say. If you're freewriting—going at a good pace, warmed up and relaxed—you don't have time to think enough about the elegance and sound of your words to start backing into sentences. You tend to use concrete subjects and concrete verbs. You tend to say things more directly. You tend to say what's really on your mind, or start discovering what's really on your mind. The writing sounds more like "you" and makes more sense, even if there are digressions and problems in it that have to be revised.

10   Freewriting makes a mess, but in that mess is the material you need to make a good paper or memo or report. You need the mess to get the usable material. The point is that you don't know which is the mess and which is the material when you're writing anyway, so let it all out. You're postponing the critic, the censor, entirely so that everything can get on the table. *Then* the critic can get to work, selecting and choosing from what's in front of you.

11   There's a parable about this process in Matthew. A man sowed good seed in his field and then his enemies came and sowed weeds among the wheat. When the weeds started growing the servants wanted to pull them up then and there, but the

householder wisely ordered that the weeds be left until harvest, "lest in gathering the weeds you root up the wheat along with them." The good and the bad sentences, the good and the bad ideas, are so bound up with each other that they can't be separated until they're all written down and available to intuition. You lose the good when you try to weed out the bad too early.

12   To put it another way, writing well is like all learning, all education. Education depends on *educing*, on bringing out what's inside to begin with—bringing it out and then improving it, clarifying it, adding to it, putting it in broader contexts. But you have to begin with what's there, take what's inside and use it. Otherwise learning is just affectation. It's something you pretend but don't feel or control because it's not connected to who you are or have become.

13   Central to this process is the paradox of audience. On the one hand audience is everything, structuring all that you say, determining what you leave out and what order you present things in. To be responsible, to belong to communities, you always need to be imagining what the audience wants and needs. And yet on the other hand, the demands of audience can be tyrannizing, especially in the early stages of writing. You can't write well in the beginning, or get the words out, say what you really mean, if you're trying to second-guess what your audience wants. Thinking about audience too much can lead to pandering and tailoring and even to Madison Avenue opinion sampling—to writing simply to please and impress—which is the source of all the things wrong in writing. The irony is that audiences are most moved by writing that doesn't seem to be a deliberate attempt to impress them.

14   Maybe it's more accurate to say that in freewriting we're not forgetting audience but holding it at bay, bracketing it. Or maybe it's that we temporarily imagine writing to a safer and more enabling audience, some internalized reader that we can do our best work for, someone we feel free to be ourselves around—knowing that later we can make whatever changes we want to make for the more threatening real-life reader. It's like having a late night conversation with an old friend, or a chat over coffee or beer somewhere. It often happens in real life that we're struggling with what to say for an important presentation or a paper and we turn to a friend or spouse and start trying to explain what we mean, what we're trying to get at, and suddenly it all comes tumbling out, in order, clear and usable.

15   That's the dynamic. Only by giving yourself permission to generate material that isn't going to be usable in the end can you get the usable material. The provisional *is* the usable, far more often than you think.

Some Examples

16   A typical paragraph from an essay written by one of my freshmen:

> This ritual of parading women before a panel of judges helps determine the goals that our culture pursues. If, in fact, an individual is only as valuable as the appeal of her or his appearance, that individual will seek those things that can enhance that appearance. One's outlook then becomes skewed, a self-centered fixation on the cosmetic. This perspective has blossomed (as a weed) into a multi-million dollar industry. One of the most incredible concepts born out of this idea is that of the tanning salon. Here one

can lay down good money to change the hue of the skin while fully conscious of the dangers involved and of the price that skin will have to pay further down the road.

There aren't any grammatical problems here. The passage is just boring and tedious, like the whole paper. I sigh as I pick it up: more going-to-college language, more trying-to-sound-like-you're-writing-an-English-paper language. The diction is inflated, the sentence structure unnecessarily indirect and complicated, none of the subjects direct.

17   In the original freewrite all the ideas are there but the language is much less forced. I get the sense of the writer thinking about his thinking and not about the writing. He's not trying to impress, and that, ironically, is what impresses me:

> Those beautiful women paraded before a panel of judges! What that says about our culture. If you're only as valuable as the appeal of your looks—if you're only valuable if you're beautiful—then no wonder women work so hard with makeup and clothes. And that's what the beauty pageants represent. Everybody's outlook is skewed, self-centered. Fixations on the cosmetic, and then this of course creates a multi-million dollar industry. Or what about the tanning salon? You lay down good money to get a tan, even though doctors are telling you all the time that the tanning machines are bad for you, that you'll get cancer.

The freewriting needs to be revised. Punctuation needs to be worked out, some sentences blended, others deleted. All I want to point out now is that the freewriting is better than the revision—more interesting, more readable—and that the writer has translated this nice directness into a papery, schoolish language no one really likes to read. The original has a voice, an energy, a movement. I'd rather read the freewrite, even though I also know that it's not quite acceptable as finished writing yet.

18   Or consider these two versions of a paragraph, the first from the paper the writer submitted for the grade and the second from the original ungraded freewriting she used as a base:

Finished:

> She was beautiful. And I watched her. I watched her lean her curvaceous, cheer-leader body against her locker, her weight slightly shifted to one delicate foot, as she stared up with her clear, untroubled baby blues into the eyes of her football player boyfriend. Her long blonde hair curved into a perfect crescent moon on her back, catching all the available light and male attention. Did she always wear her cheerleading outfit, skirt hem dancing on the edge of obscenity, and did he always wear his football jersey, shining with unscored touchdowns? They couldn't have and yet I don't remember ever seeing them any other way.

Freewriting:

> I hate being here. I never wanted to move here. My mom and dad divorce, my mom moves to California and I have to go with her. I hate it. I left my boyfriend Dan, someone who loves me and makes me feel special, to come to this hick school.
>
> In McMinnville I was one of the popular kids. I didn't yet cheerlead in ninth grade but my friends did and they were on the homecoming court. My boyfriend was a football player, a good one. He went to the shrine game. People knew who I was, I was included.

Now I eat lunch by myself. I'm never without a book because I'm alone so much. During the 15 minute brunch break, the worst because I won't even have eating lunch to occupy me, I stand by the wall and try not to look alone.

I watch the cheerleader with the long blonde perfectly curved hair. Her boyfriend is a football player. She seems so much a part of the fabric of this life.

I hate her.

I want to be like her.

What does she do, what does she say that gets her her place?

The polished, translated version seems too writerly or papery to me—canned, staged, played for effect, artificial, too smooth. It's "good" writing in the sense that it's syntactically sophisticated, the diction polished. But I get the feeling that the writer is performing for my benefit, striking up the band so that I will notice what a good writer she is. The freewrite is more interesting for me because it doesn't seem directed *to* me. The writer is inside the experience, recreating it as if it is happening now, on the page. The shorter, more emphatic sentences correspond more to the shape of the time and place they describe, are the kind of statements the writer actually would have made at that time and in that place, not the kind she would deliberately put in a paper. The effect is to suggest that she is thinking about the experience, not about the writing, that she isn't worrying about how she sounds, and *that*—again the irony—is what makes the writing itself more powerful and effective for me. Just on the level of sentence structure I find the rougher, less predictable rhythms of the freewriting more pleasing to the ear than the familiar, symmetrical phrasings of the translation.

Some Clarifications

19   Each burst of freewriting isn't magically natural and authentic. Often what comes up is too unfocused and rambling to be of any use, just talking to yourself or looking out the window, a record of the buzzing in your head. When you lower the barriers, all kinds of convoluted and pompous and ineffective voices can and do emerge, all the voices you have inside you and that you keep absorbing from TV and classes and the culture.

20   If a page or two of freewriting turns out to be awful, throw it away and go on, glad to get that language out of your system. Think of the writing as a warm-up for whatever conventional writing you have to do that day. In fact, it's a mistake to aim for a good or workable freewrite each time you sit down at the screen. That attitude only reproduces the kinds of pressures freewriting is trying to subvert, making you second-guess yourself that way.

21   The effect is cumulative. You have to do freewriting over time to get the benefits, and you have to be willing to put up with the messiness of your own thinking along the way. It's only if you keep freewriting and letting go of what doesn't work, keep freewriting regularly and in volume, just as a runner keeps running each day until she gets in shape, that you eventually seem to slip into a groove, some of the time, and your own natural rhythms and ways of speaking emerge.

Questions on Content

1. Anderson asks you to imagine that your "words are transparent . . . and your raw thinking is showing through" (paragraph 3). Explain what he means.

2. What does Anderson mean by the word *incubate* in paragraph 6? Why is it an effective word choice?

3. Anderson says that "writing well is like all learning, all education" (paragraph 12). Explain what he means.

4. What does Anderson mean by "the paradox of audience" (paragraph 13)? What central irony does he associate with audiences?

Questions on Structure and Style

5. Since you have been Anderson's audience for a few paragraphs, describe the relationship he has established with you. What techniques did he use to achieve this relationship?

6. What effect does Anderson achieve by including an example of his own freewriting in paragraph 7?

7. In paragraph 11 Anderson refers to a parable in the Gospel of Matthew. Describe the effectiveness and the purpose of such a reference.

Assignments

1. Write a dialogue between Anne Lamott (see page 345) and Chris Anderson. Assume they are discussing what you and your classmates can do to prepare for a writing assignment.

2. Assume the role of Maxine Hairston (see page 349), and write a letter to a freshman on the importance of a strong opening. In the letter be certain to suggest different approaches to openings.

from Bird by Bird: Some Instructions on Writing and Life

Anne Lamott

A step beyond freewriting lies the first draft, but as Anne Lamott declares in this vividly detailed prescription for peace of mind, "Almost all good writing begins with terrible first efforts." So accept the inevitable. A first draft is "the child's draft, where you let it all pour out and then let it romp all over the place, knowing that no one is going to see it and that you can shape it later." Lamott, the author of several highly praised novels, also has worked as a critic, columnist, and writing instructor.

■ **J O U R N A L   P R O M P T** *In the selection that follows, Lamott describes the suffering and anguish most writers (including herself) experience as they write a first draft. Describe in a paragraph or so what you do or feel when you begin writing a first draft.*

1 Now, practically even better news than that of short assignments is the idea of shitty first drafts. All good writers write them. This is how they end up with good second drafts and terrific third drafts. People tend to look at successful writers, writers who are getting their books published and maybe even doing well financially, and think that they sit down at their desks every morning feeling like a million dollars, feeling great about who they are and how much talent they have and what a great story they have to tell; that they take in a few deep breaths, push back their sleeves, roll their necks a few times to get all the cricks out, and dive in, typing fully formed passages as fast as a court reporter. But this is just the fantasy of the uninitiated. I know some very great writers, writers you love who write beautifully and have made a great deal of money, and not *one* of them sits down routinely feeling wildly enthusiastic and confident. Not one of them writes elegant first drafts. All right, one of them does, but we do not like her very much. We do not think that she has a rich inner life or that God likes her or can even stand her. (Although when I mentioned this to my priest friend Tom, he said you can safely assume you've created God in your own image when it turns out that God hates all the same people you do.)

2 Very few writers really know what they are doing until they've done it. Nor do they go about their business feeling dewy and thrilled. They do not type a few stiff warm-up sentences and then find themselves bounding along like huskies across the snow. One writer I know tells me that he sits down every morning and says to himself nicely, "It's not like you don't have a choice, because you do—you can either type or kill yourself." We all often feel like we are pulling teeth, even those writers whose prose ends up being the most natural and fluid. The right words and sentences just do not

345

come pouring out like ticker tape most of the time. Now, Muriel Spark is said to have felt that she was taking dictation from God every morning—sitting there, one supposes, plugged into a Dictaphone, typing away, humming. But this is a very hostile and aggressive position. One might hope for bad things to rain down on a person like this.

3   For me and most of the other writers I know, writing is not rapturous. In fact, the only way I can get anything written at all is to write really, really shitty first drafts.

4   The first draft is the child's draft, where you let it all pour out and then let it romp all over the place, knowing that no one is going to see it and that you can shape it later. You just let this childlike part of you channel whatever voices and visions come through and onto the page. If one of the characters wants to say, "Well, so what, Mr. Poopy Pants?," you let her. No one is going to see it. If the kid wants to get into really sentimental, weepy, emotional territory, you let him. Just get it all down on paper, because there may be something great in those six crazy pages that you would never have gotten to by more rational, grown-up means. There may be something in the very last line of the very last paragraph on page six that you just love, that is so beautiful or wild that you now know what you're supposed to be writing about, more or less, or in what direction you might go—but there was no way to get to this without first getting through the first five and a half pages.

5   I used to write food reviews for *California* magazine before it folded. (My writing food reviews had nothing to do with the magazine folding, although every single review did cause a couple of canceled subscriptions. Some readers took umbrage at my comparing mounds of vegetable puree with various ex-presidents' brains.) These reviews always took two days to write. First I'd go to a restaurant several times with a few opinionated, articulate friends in tow. I'd sit there writing down everything anyone said that was at all interesting or funny. Then on the following Monday I'd sit down at my desk with my notes, and try to write the review. Even after I'd been doing this for years, panic would set it. I'd try to write a lead, but instead I'd write a couple of dreadful sentences, xx them out, try again, xx everything out, and then feel despair and worry settle on my chest like an x-ray apron. It's over, I'd think, calmly. I'm not going to be able to get the magic to work this time. I'm ruined. I'm through. I'm toast. Maybe, I'd think, I can get my old job back as a clerk-typist. But probably not. I'd get up and study my teeth in the mirror for a while. Then I'd stop, remember to breathe, make a few phone calls, hit the kitchen and chow down. Eventually I'd go back and sit down at my desk, and sigh for the next ten minutes. Finally I would pick up my one-inch picture frame, stare into it as if for the answer, and every time the answer would come: all I had to do was to write a really shitty first draft of, say, the opening paragraph. And no one was going to see it.

6   So I'd start writing without reining myself in. It was almost just typing, just making my fingers move. And the writing would be *terrible*. I'd write a lead paragraph that was a whole page, even though the entire review could only be three pages long, and then I'd start writing up descriptions of the food, one dish at a time, bird by bird, and the critics would be sitting on my shoulders, commenting like cartoon characters. They'd be pretending to snore, or rolling their eyes at my overwrought descriptions, no matter how hard I tried to tone those descriptions down, no matter

how conscious I was of what a friend said to me gently in my early days of restaurant reviewing. "Annie," she said, "it is just a piece of *chick*en. It is just a bit of *cake.*"

7   But because by then I had been writing for so long, I would eventually let myself trust the process—sort of, more or less. I'd write a first draft that was maybe twice as long as it should be, with a self-indulgent and boring beginning, stupefying descriptions of the meal, lots of quotes from my black-humored friends that made them sound more like the Manson girls than food lovers, and no ending to speak of. The whole thing would be so long and incoherent and hideous that for the rest of the day I'd obsess about getting creamed by a car before I could write a decent second draft. I'd worry that people would read what I'd written and believe that the accident had really been a suicide, that I had panicked because my talent was waning and my mind was shot.

8   The next day, though, I'd sit down, go through it all with a colored pen, take out everything I possibly could, find a new lead somewhere on the second page, figure out a kicky place to end it, and then write a second draft. It always turned out fine, sometimes even funny and weird and helpful. I'd go over it one more time and mail it in.

9   Then, a month later, when it was time for another review, the whole process would start again, complete with the fears that people would find my first draft before I could rewrite it.

10   Almost all good writing begins with terrible first efforts. You need to start somewhere. Start by getting something—anything—down on paper. A friend of mine says that the first draft is the down draft—you just get it down. The second draft is the up draft—you fix it up. You try to say what you have to say more accurately. And the third draft is the dental draft, where you check every tooth, to see if it's loose or cramped or decayed, or even, God help us, healthy.

11   What I've learned to do when I sit down to work on a shitty first draft is to quiet the voices in my head. First there's the vinegar-lipped Reader Lady, who says primly, "Well, *that's* not very interesting, is it?" And there's the emaciated German male who writes these Orwellian memos detailing your thought crimes. And there are your parents, agonizing over your lack of loyalty and discretion; and there's William Burroughs, dozing off or shooting up because he finds you as bold and articulate as a houseplant; and so on. And there are also the dogs: let's not forget the dogs, the dogs in their pen who will surely hurtle and snarl their way out if you ever *stop* writing, because writing is, for some of us, the latch that keeps the door of the pen closed, keeps those crazy ravenous dogs contained.

12   Quieting these voices is at least half the battle I fight daily. But this is better than it used to be. It used to be 87 percent. Left to its own devices, my mind spends much of its time having conversations with people who aren't there. I walk along defending myself to people, or exchanging repartee with them, or rationalizing my behavior, or seducing them with gossip, or pretending I'm on their TV talk show or whatever. I speed or run an aging yellow light or don't come to a full stop, and one nanosecond later am explaining to imaginary cops exactly why I had to do what I did, or insisting that I did not in fact do it.

13   I happened to mention this to a hypnotist I saw many years ago, and he looked at me very nicely. At first I thought he was feeling around on the floor for the silent alarm button, but then he gave me the following exercise, which I still use to this day.

14   Close your eyes and get quiet for a minute, until the chatter starts up. Then isolate one of the voices and imagine the person speaking as a mouse. Pick it up by the tail and drop it into a mason jar. Then isolate another voice, pick it up by the tail, drop it in the jar. And so on. Drop in any high-maintenance parental units, drop in any contractors, lawyers, colleagues, children, anyone who is whining in your head. Then put the lid on, and watch all these mouse people clawing at the glass, jabbering away, trying to make you feel like shit because you won't do what they want—won't give them more money, won't be more successful, won't see them more often. Then imagine that there is a volume-control button on the bottle. Turn it all the way up for a minute, and listen to the stream of angry, neglected, guilt-mongering voices. Then turn it all the way down and watch the frantic mice lunge at the glass, trying to get to you. Leave it down, and get back to your shitty first draft.

15   A writer friend of mine suggests opening the jar and shooting them all in the head. But I think he's a little angry, and I'm sure nothing like this would ever occur to you.

Questions on Content

1. Explain why Lamott refers to the first draft as the "child's draft" (paragraph 4). Do you share her feelings?

2. Describe the frustrations and the process Lamott experiences writing first drafts.

3. A friend of the author's refers to the first draft as the "down draft" and the second draft as the "up draft" (paragraph 10). Explain.

4. Lamott states, "Almost all good writing begins with terrible first efforts" (paragraph 10). Does your experience with early drafts lead you to a similar conclusion?

Questions on Structure and Style

5. Lamott writes with an informal, chatty voice as she describes her efforts at first drafts. Discuss the effect this voice likely has on interested readers.

6. Does the fact that Lamott shares personal writing frustrations with her readers help them as writers?

Assignments

1. If you have saved early drafts of some of your own essays, use them to assist you in describing your own experience with first drafts. Your journal prompt may help you prepare for this assignment.

2. Write an essay in which you compare Lamott's experience with first drafts with your own.

Holding Your Reader

Maxine C. Hairston

"Readers, like tourists, are capricious and impatient, and they will
go off and do something else if they get confused, bored, or led off
on a detour that seems pointless to them." So how do you keep your
readers reading? In the following chapter from *Successful Writing*,
Maxine C. Hairston offers abundant guidance on issues ranging from
titles and good openings to sentence structure and transitions. The
best antidote to confusion and boredom is clarity—a quality that
Hairston's own prose nicely illustrates. Hairston taught at the
University of Texas at Austin for many years.

■ **J O U R N A L   P R O M P T** *Make a list of strategies a writer might employ to
hold the attention of readers.*

1   One writing teacher compares the task of a writer to that of a tour director escorting
a group of sightseers who do not have to pay their fares until they arrive at their des-
tination and get off the bus. The job of both author and tour director requires that they
keep their audiences so interested in what is going on that they will stay until the end
of the journey. Readers, like tourists, are capricious and impatient, and they will go
off and do something else if they get confused, bored, or led off on a detour that seems
pointless to them. When you write, you may find it helpful to keep this analogy in
mind and from time to time ask yourself, "Are my readers liable to get off the bus
here?" And writers, like tour directors, must keep their audiences oriented. If there is
any way for readers to get lost, they will!

2   All writers need to keep this caution in mind as they write (especially their second
or third drafts) and to work consciously to help their readers stay on track as they are
reading. Once they stray, they are hard to recapture. For that reason, a writer needs to
have some specific strategies for holding readers.

3   But you should also remember that the most important way of holding your readers involves a principle, not a strategy. That principle is that *most readers will stay
with you as long as they are learning something.* As long as you can give them
information that interests or entertains them, teach them something they didn't know
before, you are likely to keep them reading.

Choosing a Good Title

4   Titles play a crucial part in getting off to a good start with your readers. In fact, your
prospective readers will often decide whether or not to read what you write primarily
on the information you give them in the title. That's why it's so important that your
title be clear, accurate, and, if possible, interesting. It should also perform some very
specific functions.

5   First, a good title should *predict* the contents of the paper accurately enough for the reader to decide if he or she wants to read it. Titles like "The Roots of Country Music" or "How to Get the Most Car Stereo for Your Money" are direct and accurate enough to immediately attract readers who are interested in those subjects. Good titles also influence your course instructors, because they can signal whether you have chosen a manageable topic, and they help prepare your readers to concentrate on what you've written. A title like "Irony in Shakespeare's Histories" is so broad it would immediately trigger an instructor's skeptical instincts; one like "Richard's Manipulation of Women in *Richard III*" would probably make a better impression because it looks more specific and manageable.

6   An effective title *limits* the topic and *focuses* it for the readers; it helps point them in the right direction. It also prepares them to process the writer's message and thus makes it more likely that they will understand it. On complex issues, the writer can give the reader even more help by adding a more specific subtitle. For example, "Excellence or Elitism: Which Do Ivy League Colleges Promote?" or "The Cycle of Starvation in Africa: What Lies Ahead?"

7   A good title *identifies* and *categorizes* so that someone who is doing research can immediately tell whether an article relates to his or her topic. That may seem like a remote concern when you're writing for college courses, but it's a good idea to get in the habit of writing a title that won't allow your article to get lost. Some day you may turn something you have written into a publishable article, particularly if you go on to graduate work. So when you choose a title, imagine the cataloger or file clerk who may some day have to classify your paper but doesn't have time to read it. Will he or she be able to decide easily where it should be filed?

8   You can make your work easy to classify by using key words in your title that serve as "descriptors" for the computer. For example, an article on ways to start a small business while you are in college should have the words *small business* and *college* in it—perhaps "How to Work Your Way Through College by Starting a Small Business." That does everything a good title should do. If, however, you titled such an article "A Profit on Your Own Campus," would-be future readers would have no way to locate the article. In general, it's a good idea to get in the habit of testing your titles with the question, "Could this be misconstrued?" If it can be, you need to change it.

9   Finally, in most instances you should resist the impulse to give your writing cute, facetious, or deliberately ambiguous titles. They're tempting particularly if you like jokes, but they're risky. You may mislead your readers or annoy them because they don't share your sense of humor, and, of course, such titles are the ones most likely to be misclassified.

Writing Strong Leads

10   The lead of any piece of writing is critically important. In those first paragraphs and pages, you can make or break yourself with your reader. One well-known author and editor, William Zinsser, puts it this way:

> The most important sentence in any article is the first one. If it doesn't induce the reader to proceed to the second sentence, your article is dead. And if the second

sentence doesn't induce him to continue to the third sentence, it's equally dead. Of such a progression of sentences, each tugging the reader forward until he is safely hooked, a writer constructs that fateful unit: the "lead."

—William Zinsser, *On Writing Well,* 4th ed. (New York: HarperCollins, 1990), 65.

Even if you're not competing for that fickle audience of magazine readers, you still risk losing your readers' attention if you write weak openers. Readers like editors, vice-presidents, or members of admission committees are busy and impatient folks. Asked how long it takes them to make preliminary decisions about the manuscripts, reports, or personal statements that come across their desks, most would respond, "A minute or two. I read the first page or two and usually I can tell if it's worth my time to go on."

11   Harsh? Yes, indeed. But realistic too. If you want to hold your readers, you have about ninety seconds to convince them that what you are going to say will be interesting or informative or useful to them. "But," you say, "that's not really true of professors. They have to read what I write." Well, yes and no. Professors are busy and impatient too, and although they may have to read your papers, they don't have to like them or take much interest in them. If your writing begins with a long dull paragraph or you fail to make your main point clear, you stand to lose your reader—even when it's your instructor. I have known a professor who would draw a line and write, "I stopped reading here," if she couldn't grasp a student's main idea by the middle of the second page.

12   So openings are crucial, and you need to think carefully about how you handle those first few paragraphs. You don't necessarily have to come up with a startling or gimmicky opening to catch your reader; in fact, in many writing situations, such an opening would be so inappropriate it could do more harm than good. But for any opening, keep this in mind: *Good openings let the reader know what to expect.* In your opening section, you make a promise, or *commitment,* to your reader and raise his or her expectations. . . . Then you must go on to fulfill that promise and meet that commitment, or you will quickly lose your reader.

13   Writers use many kinds of opening commitments; two of the most common are those that promise *to intrigue* and those that promise *to inform.* The writer who wants to intrigue can do so with an anecdote, a quotation, an analogy, or an allusion of some kind. For instance, for a magazine article about the savings and loan debacle of the late 1980s, an author begins with this elegant first paragraph.

> Ever since the first Florentine loaned his first ducat to his first Medici, it has been one of the most shopworn clichés of the financial industry that the best way to rob a bank is to own one. This maxim, like all maxims, is rooted in a basic truth about human nature: to wit, if criminals are given easy access to large sums of money, they will steal, and under such tempting circumstances, even honest men may be corrupted. To forget this is to invite madness and ruin. In our time, such madness and ruin has visited in the form of the savings and loan scandal.
>
> —L. J. Davis, "Chronicle of a Debacle Foretold: How Deregulation Begat the S&L Scandal," *Harper's Magazine,* September 1990, 50.

Davis has intrigued his readers with a promise to tell them about the circumstances that led to the savings and loan crisis.

14   The management consultants Thomas Peters and Robert Waterman begin one of the chapters in their book *In Search of Excellence* with this intriguing quotation: "'The Navy,' says ex-Chief of Naval Operations Elmo Zumwalt, 'assumes that everyone below the rank of commander is immature.'" Having raised their readers' curiosity about how such a statement is related to business management, the authors go on to explain.

15   Here is a promise-to-inform opening from a *Smithsonian* article on astronomy:

> Ever since the human mind first grasped the immensity and complexity of the Universe, Man has tried to explain how it could have come into being.

The article goes on to explain the Big Bang theory of the origin of the universe and the formation of galaxies.

16   Which kind of opening is better? There is no easy answer; each time you write you have to decide according to what you perceive as your readers' expectations and according to your purpose in writing. Intriguing openers can capture fickle readers and persuade them to go on reading, but they can also annoy readers if they delay too long in getting to the point. Although the straight informative opening may not seem as interesting, often it is safer, particularly for documents in business or industry, because readers there generally want to go straight to the point. You will have to decide.

What First Paragraphs Do

17   You make your strongest commitment to your reader in your opening paragraph, giving strong signals and setting the tone for the rest of your paper or article. An opening paragraph should do these things.

- Engage the reader's attention.
- Predict content.
- Give readers a reason to continue reading.
- Set the tone of the writing.

Another way to put it is that the opening paragraph lays down the tracks for both writer and reader. It draws the readers in with a promise, it gives them signals about what lies ahead, it creates a link with the next paragraphs, and it establishes the writer's tone and stance by using certain kinds of language and structure.

Different Kinds of Opening Paragraphs

18   I can't give you clear-cut formulas for opening paragraphs because different kinds of writing tasks call for different kinds of openings. Sometimes—when you're writing technical reports or case studies for example—you'll have definite specifications about how your opening paragraphs should look and what they should cover. For other kinds of writing, there may be traditional patterns you should follow. If you think that might be the case, ask for specific directions so you won't be penalized for failing to conform with the approved model.

19   In other, more diverse kinds of writing, however—travel articles, informative essays, book or movie reviews, persuasive articles, to name just a few—you may use many kinds of opening paragraphs, all of them effective in different situations. Choose your introductory paragraph according to your writing situation, taking into account your goal and the kind of audience you envision yourself writing for. Here are several possibilities.

20   ***Straightforward Announcements.***   In many instances, you will do best to begin with a direct, clear, and economical statement. Certainly this guideline applies to writing whose main purpose is to convey factual information to a busy reader; for instance, market reports, case studies, summaries of action, or requests for information. In this kind of writing, the reader wants key information as quickly as possible—no anecdotes or ceremonial preliminaries. For example,

> Set in the heart of Athens, a splendid neoclassical villa holds some of Greece's most extraordinary art and artifacts. The Benaki Museum, founded in 1930 by Hellenophile and collector Anthony Benaki, is one of the world's most captivating treasure houses.
>
> —Kathleen Burke, "Golden Ornament from Greece,"
> *Smithsonian,* November 1990, 202.

21   Direct openings that announce your thesis also work well for academic research papers. For instance, here is the opening paragraph of a paper done for a course in international business:

> Lockheed Aircraft and Gulf Oil were recently prosecuted by the federal government for giving bribes to foreign businessmen in order to make their products more attractive to those potential clients. During indictment proceedings both corporations contended that their cash payments were both necessary and common among international businesses. The question then is how common is bribery in foreign nations and whether the United States should prevent our corporations from offering bribes even when doing so is a common and accepted practice.

22   Straight-to-the-point opening paragraphs also work well when you are writing a request. Although many of us are reluctant to be blunt when we have to ask people for time or money or favors, most readers prefer a straightforward request to a preliminary buildup that wastes their time. When you have a legitimate and reasonable request to make, state it quickly and clearly so you don't waste your readers' time.

23   ***Opening Anecdotes or Narratives.***   In other writing situations, you must find a way to entice your audience with the promise of something interesting to come. When you have only those first two minutes to catch the attention of a reader with no obligation to read what you write, you need to make that opening paragraph particularly provocative. Experienced free-lance writers know a multitude of ways to meet this challenge, but one of the most common is the description or anecdote that lures the reader into the world the author is going to write about. Here are two examples:

> A wiry young climber slips spider-like up an outward-angled rock face, clipping a nylon rope into carabiners attached to bolted anchors as she goes. Though the moves are finger-wrenching, she breezes through them: Earlier in the day, while hanging by

top-rope and drilling holes for the bolts needed to secure her in case of a fall, she had scrutinized every fingernail-width handhold and foothold on the face. Now, after dipping her fingers into a brightly colored bed of sweat-absorbing chalk, she lunges for the last hand-hold and pulls herself over the top of the cliff.

—Ed Webster, "To Bolt or Not to Bolt," *Sierra,* November–December 1990, 30.

"Please don't call me a guru," Dr. Dean Ornish asks. The voice is softly nasal but insistent, and its request ignores the fact the Ornish has posed for both the *Houston Post* and *People* magazine meditating in the lotus position. But Ornish, 37, has no problem with contradictions. These days, he finds himself preaching that a person can reverse coronary disease and find inner peace by opening his heart according to the Ornish plan—"a different type of 'open-heart' procedure, one based on love, knowledge, and compassion rather than just drugs and surgery"—while the demands of celebrity have turned him into a whirling dervish. Curls lapping at his receding hairline, blue eyes doleful, mustache adroop, he spread his message from his Sausalito, California, office, spinning from the VCR . . . to the fax . . . to the copy machine . . . with enviable deftness. Just this brief exposure to Ornish reveals one essential truth: Unlike the people who have committed to the restrictive diet and coronary-care regimen that has made him famous, Dean Ornish intends to have his cake and eat it too.

—Mimi Swartz, "The Ornish Treatment," *Texas Monthly,* March 1991, 104–105.

These are straigthforward but vivid openings that catch the readers' attention, give them strong clues about what to expect from the articles, and stimulate enough interest to make them want to go on reading.

24   *Questions.*   Questions often serve as excellent openers. They pique the readers' curiosity and focus their attention directly on the issue. You can use one question or several in a paragraph. For example,

I've always wondered about dog food. Is a Gaines-burger really like a hamburger? Can you fry it? Does dog food "cheese" taste like real cheese? Does Gravy Train actually make gravy in the dog's bowl, or is that brown liquid just dissolved crumbs? And exactly what *are* by-products?

—Ann Hodgman, "No Wonder They Call Me a Bitch," reprinted in *The Best American Essays of 1990,* ed. Justin Kaplan (New York: Ticknor & Fields, 1990), 112. This essay originally appeared in *Spy.*

Solving the Opening Paragraph Dilemma

25   Even experienced writers often find themselves caught in the opening paragraph dilemma. On one hand, they're hyperconscious that they must have a strong first paragraph to capture their readers and set them moving in the right direction. On the other hand, they know they can't afford to spend hours experimenting with different approaches and tinkering with first lines, or they'll never get to writing. They're caught between their high standards and their deadlines. That can be an agonizing experience, one you may have been through yourself more than once.

26   The best solution to this dilemma is to remember the advice on getting started. . . . In order to get started writing, get down on paper—or on screen—anything that seems

at all relevant: a statement of the problem you want to solve, a question you intend to answer, an anecdote that relates to your topic, even one of those tired openings "In this paper I intend to . . ." Even if you write a first paragraph that is obvious and dull, just getting it on paper will help you push off and get moving. Remind yourself that whatever you write, even though you love it, you may have to discard it later when you're revising. Right now you need to get on with your writing and produce a first draft.

27   You don't even need to come up with a wonderful first paragraph for your first revision. For that draft you may be narrowing your idea and rearranging some of your supporting points. With the second revision, you can start thinking seriously about crafting a good lead paragraph that draws on the ideas you've generated and reflects a sense of your audience. As you work on your opener, think about the four things it is supposed to do: catch the reader, predict content, stimulate further reading, and set the tone.

Tightening Your Writing

28   Writing that is highly readable has a quality called *linearity;* that is, the reader can move steadily through it in a straight line without having to stop to puzzle about what the writer means or double back to reread. Achieving this quality in your writing isn't easy, but it's a goal worth striving for if you want to hold your readers. Think how often you have bogged down in dense, difficult writing or found yourself hydroplaning across the surface, only to realize you were going to have to stop and go back. If you could quit reading, you probably did. If you couldn't, you plowed on but groaned and cursed the writer who was making life so difficult for you. None of us want our readers to feel that way about our writing, particularly not readers who are in a position to penalize us for giving them so much trouble.

29   There are a number of strategies you can use to keep your readers on track. They range from mastering transition devices to improving the body language of your writing.

Hooks and Nudges

30   Readers can lose their way or get bogged down in writing for a variety of reasons, of course, not all of them the writer's responsibility. But it is the writer's responsibility to provide hooks—*links* that hold writing together by showing connections— and *nudges,* words that give readers a little push from one point to another. You need a stock of such terms at your fingertips to draw on.

Hooks	*Nudges*
also	this
moreover	then
for example	first
in addition	consequently
however	next
in spite of	

For instance, here is a student paragraph with both hooks and nudges italicized.

> Like a rat that avoids electric shock, a child avoids contact with those who *hurt* him. *So* avoiding *punishment,* except as a last resort, is advisable. *Punishment* instills hate and fear and soon becomes an "aversive stimulus." *Also,* because the only real effect of *it* is to suppress a response temporarily, no permanent weakening of the unwanted behavior takes place. *And* as soon as the effect, or the sting of the *spanking,* wears off, the child repeats *it.*

31   It is important to realize, however, that the best source of unity in writing comes from the *inside,* from the underlying pattern or internal structure of a piece of writing, not from transitional words tacked on from the outside. Words like *moreover* and *nevertheless* should reflect organization, not impose it, and readers are most likely to feel that a piece of writing is tight and coherent if they sense that it follows one of the common thought patterns. . . . For example, here is a student paragraph that is held together by its narrative pattern, not by transitional devices:

> Just before noon under imposing dark storm clouds in the southern suburbs of Beirut, lunch was being served. It was an austere, poorly lit concrete house recently rebuilt from the rubble which still covered much of the suburb of Burj Al Barajinah, then the headquarters of the Shiite Muslim militia. The wife, clothed in the traditional long black robe of the local Shiite women, served coffee, small oranges and unleavened bread to be dipped in a lentil stew. She spoke with her husband and son with a boldness which custom would not permit out of doors. Friends came and went. One stayed for lunch, a tall man in new fatigues who laid his automatic rifle by the couch and began to eat. The young son, three or four by the looks of him, with chubby cheeks and a healthy pink glow showing through his olive skin, was exchanging playful banter with his mother. After the meal and conversation, the father's and soldier's attention turned to the boy. The father stood up, the boy hugged his father's leg playfully. The father kicked the boy to the ground, and as he was falling the playful smile turned to fear and tears of pain. After the boy stopped crying, the father turned to the visitor with a smile of pride and said, "He too will learn to fight."

Directional Signals

32   Often you need to add words that will act as *directional signals* to help your reader follow the thought pattern you are using. Some words and phrases act as *pointers* that tell the reader to keep moving forward. For example,

it follows that

then

another

for example

hence

(Notice that the categories of pointers and nudging words overlap.) Other kinds of pointers show causality.

as a result

therefore

consequently

because

since

All of them move the reader forward.

33   A different kind of transitional words and phrases acts as Slow or Caution signals to readers, warning them to slow down because they are going to run into some qualification or exception to a point that has just been made. Typical signals of this kind are

however

but

nevertheless

in spite of

on the other hand

instead

not only

These words warn readers to expect a contrasting example and prepare them to adjust their thinking to handle that exception. Thus it's important that when you use this kind of word, you really do follow it with a contrasting example. Otherwise you will confuse your readers and possibly lose them.

Repeating Words

34   Repeating keywords, phrases, or stylistic patterns in a piece of writing can help to focus your readers' attention on points you want to emphasize. A repeated word can also serve as an effective hook between paragraphs or between sections, providing the link that keeps readers from feeling a gap as they move from one section to another. This student paragraph furnishes a good example of using repetition as links within a paragraph. (I have added italics in the following selections.)

> Walt Disney's monumental idea for creating an *amusement park* began when he took his young daughters to an *amusement park* in Los Angeles. The girls were entertained while riding on the merry-go-round, but Walt was bored sitting on a bench eating peanuts. He realized the need for a place where children and their parents could have fun together. Impetus for his new *park* came from his own hobby, constructing his own backyard railroad. Trains were his boyhood passion . . . and he began to talk about building a railroad that would link the Burbank studios, then linked this idea to his conception of a new kind of *amusement park*. He realized that transportation and nostalgia were the key factors in making his *park* different. In July 1955, his dream became a reality with the opening of Disneyland.

35   Here is a passage in which one word, purposefully repeated in a parallel pattern, repeats the writer's central thesis:

> We believe public radio and public television *can* lead the way. Intelligently organized and adequately funded public broadcasting *can* help the creative spirit to flourish. It *can* reveal how we are different and what we share in common. It *can* illuminate the dark corners of the world and the dark corners of the mind. It *can* offer forums to a multitude of voices. It *can* reveal wisdom and understanding—and foolishness too. It *can* delight us. It *can* entertain us. It *can* inform us. Above all, it *can* add to our understanding of our own inner workings and of one another. In the conviction that it *can* be so, we make these recommendations.
>
> —From the report of the Carnegie Commission on the Future of Public Broadcasting, in *The Chronicle of Higher Education,* 5 February 1979, 9.

36   These writers value repetition as a simple and useful way of keeping their readers on the track.

Using Conjunctions at the Beginning of Sentences

37   The prejudice that many writers have against beginning a sentence with *and* or *but* seems to have grown out of the notion that because these words are called "conjunctions," they must always appear between two other words. Not necessarily. They are also strong signal words that tell readers what to expect next. For that reason they work particularly well when you want to stress the relationship of a sentence to the previous one. Notice how the following writers have used *and* and *but* for this purpose. (Again, italics have been added.)

> *Harvard Business Review* subscribers . . . recently rated "the ability to communicate" as the prime requisite of a promotable executive. *And,* of all the aspects of communication, the written form is the most trouble-some.
>
> —John S. Fielden, "What Do You Mean I Can't Write?" in *The Practical Craft,* ed. Keith Sparrow and Donald Cunningham (Boston: Houghton Mifflin, 1978), 47. This article originally appeared in the *Harvard Business Review,* May–June 1964.

> If we hear a well-constructed grammatical sentence, the ideas fall easily and quickly into the slots of our consciousness. *But,* if we hear a conglomerate, ungrammatical hodge-podge, we have to sort it out at an expenditure of time and effort.
>
> —Everett C. Smith, "Industry Views the Teaching of English," in *The Practical Craft,* ed. K. Sparrow and D. Cunningham (Boston: Houghton Mifflin, 1978). This article originally appeared in *English Journal,* March 1956.

38   *But* works especially well as the opening word of a paragraph that you want to highlight because it states an important qualification or contrast to the content of the previous paragraph. Notice the effect in these examples:

> . . . For the most part, readers are assumed to be ideal readers, fully prepared to relate to the fiction or poetry on the author's terms. This expectation is as it should be; it is appropriate for what we regard as creative writing.

But a different expectation exists in business and technical writing where readers are busy executives who want the important findings up front, or are privates last-class who need information at a level they can understand, or somewhere in the bewildering range between.

> —Keith Sparrow and Donald Cunningham, "What Are Some Important Writing Strategies," in *The Practical Craft,* ed. K. Sparrow and D. Cunningham (Boston: Houghton Mifflin, 1978), 114.

. . . As my students argue when I correct them . . . : "You got the meaning, didn't you?" Yes, I did, and so do we all get the meaning when a newspaper, a magazine, a set of directions stammers out its message. And I suppose, too, we could travel by ox-cart, or dress in burlap, or drive around with rattling fenders, and still get through a day.

But technical writing in this age can no more afford widespread sloppiness of expression, confusion of meaning, rattle-trap construction than a supersonic missile can afford to be made of the wrong materials, or be put together haphazardly with screws jutting out here and there, or have wiring circuits that may go off any way at all. . . .

> —Morris Freedman, "The Seven Sins of Technical Writing," in *The Practical Craft,* ed. K. Sparrow and D. Cunningham (Boston: Houghton Mifflin, 1978), 82. This article originally appeared in *College Composition and Communication,* February 1958.

These examples, deliberately selected from a collection of articles on business and technical writing, should convince you that it is not a sin, or even a grammatical lapse, to start a sentence with *and* or *but.* If you need additional proof, check the articles in any widely read magazine. You will find an abundance of corroborating evidence.

Other Aids to the Reader

Frequent Closure Within Sentences

39   By giving readers links and signals to keep them moving in the right direction, you meet one of an expository writer's main responsibilities: helping his or her audience to process information as quickly and efficiently as possible. You are trying to keep them from having to reread all or part of what you have written in order to get your meaning.

40   One way to help your readers is not to make them wait too long to discover meaning. If you can construct your sentences out of phrases and clauses that make sense by themselves, your readers can process meaning as they read rather than having to hold all the content in their minds until they get to the end of a sentence. For instance, here is a confusing sentence from a student paper:

> Furthermore, *that the United States has the best medical technology in the world, yet ranks sixteenth among countries in successful births per pregnancy* results because impossible medical costs force many people to go through childbirth at home.

The strung-out twenty-two-word subject in this sentence keeps readers in suspense for so long that they miss the verb, "results," on the first reading. If the writer had rearranged his ideas into manageable units, readers would not get lost. Here is a rewritten version with the units of thought marked off:

> Even though the United States has the best medical technology in the world, / it ranks below fifteen other countries in successful births per pregnancy / because impossible medical costs force many people to have their children at home.

41   The revised sentence is easier to read than the original because the words are arranged into segments that make sense by themselves. When we read, we make *closure* when we come to the point in a sentence where our minds make sense of a group of words; at that point, we can rest for a split second before going on to process the next segment. In the revised version, we can pause twice; in the original, we cannot pause at all until we get to the end of the sentence.

42   Because readers can assimilate information more efficiently when it is divided into small units, in most situations you should not let long, complicated sentences predominate. Frequently, just their appearance on the page frightens off readers. But long sentences in themselves do not necessarily cause reading problems; if closure occurs frequently, a sentence of 50 or 60 words or more can be read easily. Marking off the units of closure in this 108-word sentence from Tom Wolfe's *The Right Stuff* shows this:

> A career in flying was like climbing one of those ancient Babylonian pyramids / made up of a dizzy progression of steps and ledges, / a ziggurat, / a pyramid extraordinarily high and steep, / and the idea was to prove at every foot of the way up that pyramid / that you were one of the elected and anointed ones who had *the right stuff* / and could move higher and higher and even / —ultimately, God willing, one day— / that you might be able to join that special few at the very top, / that elite who had the capacity to bring tears to men's eyes, / the very Brotherhood of the Right Stuff itself.
>
> —Tom Wolfe, *The Right Stuff* (New York: Farrar, Straus, & Giroux, 1979), 24.

Chunking to Avoid Reader Overload

43   Another way of segmenting your writing to make it easier for your readers to follow is called *chunking;* that is, breaking up long units of writing into parts so that they will be easier to process. If you include too much information in one sentence or one paragraph, you risk overloading the mental circuits by which readers process information, and your readers either give up or have to go back to reread the material two or three times to absorb it.

44   *Chunking* is the principle behind grouping the digits in telephone numbers and social security numbers. Would you ever remember your sister's telephone number if it were written 2143889697? Or your social security number if it were written 328939775? If, however, the numbers are split into groups, they are fairly easy to process and remember.

214-388-9697   328-93-9775

When numbers are written like this, you process each unit separately and put it into short-term memory before you come to the next unit—that's the secret of memorization.

45   You can use chunking in your writing to break up long sentences that are overstuffed with information or paragraphs that include so many items that the reader gets

lost. One way to do that is to break long sentences into shorter ones. For instance, here is a sentence so overstuffed that it's almost impossible to follow.

> With the tension in Iraq cutting off substantial oil imports and its announced intention to last out the boycott however long it takes, the worldwide increase in oil prices and the probable effect of armed conflict on new exploration, and the ongoing determination of both auto manufacturers and several branches of government to resist any real efforts to move toward substantial conservation measures, an energy crisis of some magnitude seems imminent.

However, if we cut up the sentence and reorganize it into manageable chunks, it becomes easy to follow.

> For at least three reasons, an energy crisis seems imminent. First, the tension in Iraq is cutting off imports and its government says it will hold out against the boycott. Second, oil prices have increased worldwide and the prospect of armed conflict discourages new exploration. Third, U.S. auto manufacturers and several branches of government seem determined to resist any real efforts to push oil conservation.

46   Another excellent way to chunk an overloaded sentence or paragraph is to break the information into lists. For example, here's a sentence so overloaded that a reader would get lost halfway through.

> The factors that keep individuals interested in their jobs are interesting responsibilities, wide range of responsibilities, challenge, stimulation, recognition, impact on the organization, status, relationship with others, being one's own boss, freedom to act, quality of the organization, and compensation.

Impossible! Now let's redo it into a list.

> The factors that keep individuals interested in their jobs are these:

interesting responsibilities	recognition	being one's own boss
wide range of responsibilities	impact on the organization	freedom to act
challenge	status	quality of the organization
stimulation	relationships with others	compensation

You have to wonder whatever made the writer try to jam all that together in the first place. Whenever you find that you're loading a sentence or paragraph with more than three or four points of information, consider breaking it out into a list. (Notice how often I have done that in this text.) Such rearrangement can make a great difference in how your reader will respond to your writing.

Avoid Antagonizing Your Readers

47   My last suggestion on ways to hold your readers is psychological rather than editorial: Remember you will lose readers if you make them uncomfortable or angry. Most people are not willing to read or listen to someone who is attacking them or criticizing their beliefs. If you really want your audience to read what you are writing, you need to consider their emotions as well as their strictly intellectual reactions.

48   Sometimes, to be sure, you are writing for two sets of readers, particularly when you're writing an argument. The opposition—that group of readers whose position

you're criticizing—aren't likely to change their minds. You shouldn't worry too much about making them angry—it's probably inevitable. You should, however, take pains not to anger the other group—those readers who are undecided on the issue and whom you hope to influence. It's important to distinguish between these two segments of an audience when you're constructing your argument.

49   To avoid threatening readers whom you want to influence, keep these principles in mind.

- *Respect your audience.* From the beginning, assume that your readers are intelligent and rational people of goodwill and that they will respond to reason. Rather than attacking their positions, try to discover what common interests or common goals you may have and work from there. Give your readers the same kind of treatment you like to get when you read.

- *Use objective language.* Strong, biased words such as *disgraceful, vicious,* and *intolerable* are likely to trigger defensive reactions from readers who do not already agree with you. Their first response will be to argue rather than to pay attention to your point of view. If, however, you state your ideas in neutral language, they are likely to continue reading to learn more.

- *Learn to write provisionally, not dogmatically.* Learn to use the *subjunctive mood,* a much neglected but extremely useful verb form that allows you to speculate, hypothesize, or wish, and to express a courteous and inquiring attitude in your writing. Although fewer and fewer people seem to bother with using the subjunctive form of verbs in their writing, careful writers should at least know what the subjunctive forms are and when they should be used. They are used when one wants to express a point conditionally or to express wishes. For example,

    If Castle *were* in charge, he *would handle* the protester well.

    I wish I *were* not *involved* in that proposal.

    If that *should* happen, the admiral *would want* us to know.

    You *would be* a great help if you *were to join* us.

Occasionally *had* is combined with a subjunctive verb to talk about events that didn't take place. For example,

    Had I thought of it, I *would have written.*

    Had he *known* what he was getting into, he *would have been appalled.*

The subjunctive form of a verb should be used in clauses beginning with *that* when the main verb expresses desires, orders, or suggestions. For example,

    The lawyer requested that her client *be given* a new trial.

    We suggest that there *be* a recount of the votes.

50   If you use these words in phrases like "If I were," "It might be that," and "We could consider," you create an atmosphere of cooperation and courtesy in which your readers can pay attention to what you are proposing because they are not forced to defend themselves.

Questions on Content

1. Describe the characteristics of an effective title.

2. Hairston suggests writers should resist the impulse to give readers cute, ambiguous titles. Why?

3. Hairston mentions several opening strategies. What are they? What determines what strategy writers choose?

4. Hairston points out that good writing has a quality called linearity. Explain.

5. Hairston mentions *closure* and *chunking* as sentence-level reader aids. Define each.

Questions on Structure and Style

6. Discuss the effect of the tour director analogy with which Hairston begins this selection. Does she refer to the analogy later in the selection? Discuss this rhetorical technique.

7. This selection is from a successful writing textbook. What instructional and rhetorical strategies does Hairston employ that make her presentation effective?

Assignments

1. Examine titles of selections in this anthology and in some of your own essays. Select several you feel are particularly good, and be prepared to discuss reasons for their effectiveness.

2. Working with a group of peers, draft titles for the following topics. (Follow Hairston's advice for writing effective titles.)

   A. Radio talk shows
   B. Language in automobile advertisements
   C. Working women
   D. Television news

3. Choose an essay that you have written. Tighten the essay, paying attention to what Hairston says about hooks and nudges, directional signals, and repeating words.

4. Hairston lists three principles to avoid antagonizing your readers (paragraph 49). Write an essay in which you intentionally ignore these principles. Write on a needed change on your campus, and try to antagonize readers. Be prepared to discuss what you could do to avoid the antagonistic effect.

Writing Is Rewriting

Donald M. Murray

Donald M. Murray is a writer and teacher who has published much
on the subject of writing. He also writes a regular newspaper column.
In the following selection Murray the writer tells his own story of
how he came to accept, and benefit from, the fact that "revision is a
normal and essential part" of the work all writers do. "I wanted to
eat," he tells us, so he learned the process that he describes in the
following personal, vividly detailed account.

■ **J O U R N A L   P R O M P T**   *Prepare an honest description of what you do when
you revise one of your own papers. Do you believe there is a difference between revising and
editing?*

The myth: The writer sits down, turns on the faucet, and writing pours out—clean,
graceful, correct, ready for the printer.

The reality: The writer gets something—anything—down on paper, reads it, tries it
again, rereads, rewrites, again and again.

1   For years I denied the reality. I held firm to three beliefs:

- First draft was best. Good writing was spontaneous writing.
- Rewriting was punishment for failure. The editor or teacher who required revision
  was a bad reader who had no respect for my spontaneous writing.
- Revision was a matter of superficial correction that forced my natural style to conform to an old-fashioned, inferior style.

2   No one challenged my literary theology; editors simply didn't publish my writing. And I needed to get published. I wanted to eat.

3   Bob Johnson of the *Saturday Evening Post*, then the leading free-lance market,
liked what was in an article of mine. He said they would hire a writer to fix it up.

4   "I'm a writer," I said confidently.

5   "Well," he said doubtfully.

6   "I want to write it myself," I pleaded. "Please," I begged.

7   He sent me a single-spaced letter of criticism that was longer than the article I
had submitted. I rewrote, and then rewrote what I rewrote. He traveled from Philadelphia to Boston to go over my revision word-by-word, line-by-line. Again I
rewrote—and rewrote.

8   The article was published and editors on other magazines spent time teaching me
the craft of revision despite the guerrilla war of resistance I fought line-by-line.

9   I rewrote. I wanted to be published; I needed to eat. I still felt, however, that I
failed when I had to revise my first draft. I thought real writers had that faucet they
could turn on. I thought I was a poor writer who had to rewrite to be published.

10   Then I began to listen to what my editors and the publishing writers I met told me: Revision is a normal and essential part of the editorial process. I started to pay attention to—and be comforted by—the testimony of hundreds of the best writers of past and present:

> *Because the best part of all, the absolutely most delicious part, is finishing it and then doing it over . . . I rewrite a lot, over and over again, so that it looks like I never did.*
>
> *Toni Morrison*

> *I've done as many as twenty or thirty drafts of a story. Never less than ten or twelve drafts.*
>
> *Raymond Carver*

> *My writing is a process of rewriting, of going back and changing and filling in.*
>
> *Joan Didion*

> *When I see a paragraph shrinking under my eyes like a strip of bacon in a skillet, I know I'm on the right track.*
>
> *Peter DeVries*

> *What makes me happy is rewriting.*
>
> *Ellen Goodman*

> *Rewriting is when playwriting really gets to be fun. In baseball you only get three swings and you're out. In rewriting, you get almost as many swings as you want and you know, sooner or later, you'll hit the ball.*
>
> *Neil Simon*

> *I love the flowers of afterthought.*
>
> *Bernard Malamud*

I began to hear the message: *writing is rewriting.*

The Satisfactions of Revision

11   Slowly, almost without realizing it, and certainly without admitting it to any editor, I became addicted to revision. I found rewriting seductive. I saw—draft by draft—unexpected but significant meanings come clear; I heard—line-by-line—the music of my voice adapted to the purpose of the text.

12   Before, the first draft was that terrible combination of ambition and terror. I wanted to write the great story, article, poem, the one that had never been written before, the one that would establish a new standard for perfection.

13   And having set that impossible goal, I suffered—appropriately—fear raised to terror, anxiety multiplied by apprehension. But once I got something down, forced by deadline and hunger, I was not suspended between absolute perfection and total failure. I had a draft I could read and develop; I could roll up my sleeves and get to work.

Problems to Solve

14   I learned to be grateful because revision revealed problems to be solved and we are ultimately problem-solving animals. I had problems of subject, of meaning, of organization, of communication, of language. And the identified problem, exposed and defined by rereading and rewriting, usually presents possible solutions.

15   Oh, this piece of writing is terrible, awful, awful terrible, I can't write. Moan. Whimper. Wail. Sob. You've heard others; you've heard yourself; I've heard myself.

16   But rereading and rewriting lead you out of the swamp of self-pity. Now you can identify the problems, one at a time.

17   "This paper on the Great Depression is a mess," says the writer to the writer.

18   "OK, but what kind of mess?"

19   "I've got a lot of facts. Unemployment. The market. Stuff like that. Good stuff but it's all a jumble."

20   "What do you mean, a jumble?"

21   "There's no order. It isn't lined up. The reader wouldn't see the, what do you call it, sequence, the way one thing leads to another, the process that makes a depression inevitable. That's my point."

22   "Good. Now you know what to do."

23   "What?"

24   "Think about it. How do you make the sequence clear?"

25   "Maybe an outline. Perhaps subheads. An introduction that says what I'm trying to prove, then the steps to prove it, then a conclusion."

26   "Sounds good. Try it."

27   Inexperienced writers can solve, by common sense and their experience in other fields, most writing problems, and that process is satisfying. Most of us feel good when we solve a problem.

Exploration

28   The hard work of revision was fascinating because I was not correcting my copy. I was exploring my subject. Before the first draft I felt dumb. Now as I rewrote I discovered how much I knew. The writing gave me questions to ask, trails to explore.

29   Writing leads to more writing. Topics grow and split, increasing the subjects I have to write about. People ask me where I get my ideas—mostly from my writing. I explore one subject and see many others to explore. And I like the process of exploration—learning—that takes place when I rewrite and re-rewrite.

Discovery

30   Exploration leads to discovery and that is my principal motivation to write and rewrite. I surprise myself on the page. I do not write what I intend but what I had no intent of writing. There is always new territory I can perceive through the draft, new mountain ranges, great tidal inlets, cities, ships on the horizon of a type I have never seen.

31   I used to worry that there would be no new discoveries for me in writing. A day would come when the magic would be gone. I no longer worry about that. I have

been publishing for more than fifty years and yet, each morning at my desk, I am fifteen years old and the world is new. In fact, I have learned to be freer in my writing, to take more risks to explore close to—and beyond—the edge.

32   As I have learned the craft of revision, I have learned how to see the discoveries that used to lie hidden before my eyes. And through this same craft, I am able to develop those discoveries so I am saying more than I could have hoped to say when I began the draft. Sometimes the discoveries are large—this was not a book on revision when I began it—and others are small—the word *companioned*, which does not yet appear in the dictionary, is just right for a line of poetry I have written:

> Now I live most alone with others, companioned
> by silence and the long road at my back,
> mirrored by daughters . . .

33   Each of the discoveries is satisfying in its own way; each contains a surprise and there is something on the page that was not there before. I have the feeling of accomplishment someone else gets from lifting a fresh loaf of bread from the oven, slowly playing in a rainbow trout, sinking a three-pointer, building a shelf that is true and strong.

Memory

34   I have a poor memory until I write. The act of writing brings back—in context—the revealing details of childhood in the 1920s, combat in the 1940s, high school in the 1930s, the police-headquarters press room in 1950, the night I spent alone on Uncle Don's boat in 1943, the abandoned village I "discovered" in the New Hampshire woods in 1938, the intensive-care ward in which my daughter died in 1977, the trip I took in the Scandinavian Arctic in 1989, the summer I learned to swim, 1936.

35   If I were to write about any of those events, I would recover from that enormous memory bank in my brain sights, sounds, smells, tastes, phrases; I would see actions and reactions; recover feelings and thoughts I had at the time. And I will remember many things I never knew I observed and stored away, for my brain is recording more than I am aware of at any moment, including this one.

36   Rewriting mobilizes these resources within the brain, makes them worthwhile as the act of writing gives them meaning. I don't know what I remember—and its importance—until I start a draft and see before me a rediscovered world.

Awareness

37   I am never bored because I am always writing and rewriting in my head and in my daybook. I am an observer of my own life, a scholar of what I feel and see and hear and care about. I tend to my anger and my sense of humor; I try to make sense of the life I am living and the lives that surround me.

38   Rewriting multiplies my awareness. Sitting in a traffic jam, I watch those who talk and sing to themselves or act out scenes in which they, at last, tell off the boss as if they had privacy in a car. Waking at night and having trouble going back to sleep, I

revise yesterday's pages in my head. Sitting in the parking lot, I try to describe shoppers' walks and make mental notes on how each walk reveals anxiety, satisfaction, despair, pleasure, love, hate. Sitting in a boring meeting or class, I take my daybook and revise a poem, a paragraph, the opening of an article—or the ending.

39   And when what I observe seems predictable, I ask the question Bob Cormier, a wonderfully inventive writer, asks: "What if?" What if the butcher took the cleaver and . . . What if that housewife took the groceries and drove to Dayton, Ohio . . . What if the fifty-year-old man in the three-button suit leaned over and kissed the high-school-aged supermarket sacker girl putting the groceries in the station wagon . . . What if she were his daughter—his daughter that had been placed for adoption at birth; his baby sitter; his partner's daughter; his child bride; his . . . What if, what if, what if?

40   My awareness on the page increases my awareness when I am not writing; my awareness of my world, of myself reacting to that world, increases my awareness when I am writing. This circle of awareness increases the richness of my life.

Connection

41   The information we collect connects, almost on its own, with other information. It seems driven to make meaning. Revision connects fragments of information that we thought were unrelated. And it is from these unexpected relationships that new meanings are born. In writing, two and seven and a bag of fresh chocolate-chip cookies add up to four. A quotation, an image, a statistic, a feeling that seem unrelated reveal an unexpected meaning when they meet in a draft.

42   The writer rewriting is a magnet for information. Facts, observations, ideas, citations, actions performed and actions unperformed, answers, questions all are collected and then, in the rewriting, join in producing insight, conclusion, theory, idea, thesis, proof.

Pattern

43   Marge Piercy made me see anew the profound importance of pattern when she said:

> I think that the beginning of fiction, of the story, has to do with the perception of pattern in event, of the large rhythms in things like birth, growth, decline and death, and the short rhythms like the excitement of searching for things and finding them, the repetition of the sexual pattern, these are things that we experience again and again as having dramatic shape. At the basis of fiction is a desire to find meaningful shape in events, in the choices people make.

44   And this is just as true of nonfiction, history essay and lab report, term paper and blue-book exam, book review and paper of literary criticism. It is pattern that reveals and contains meaning.

45   The biologist looks through the microscope, the astronomer looks through the telescope, the accountant through the spread sheet, the historian through colonial records, the coach through the team's stats, the writer through the draft, all seeking patterns that reveal meaning, that carry within them implication.

Music

46   One of the great enjoyments of rewriting is that it allows me to hear the music of what I read, the music of others and the music of my own drafts, at first faint, and then with tuning, strong and clear.

47   Voice is most likely the element that keeps you reading, that makes you care about what is being said, that makes you trust the writer. The music—or voice of the text—underlies and supports the meaning of what you have to say and it is the music from my first draft that tells me the meaning of what I have written. As I listen to the music of the draft, I begin to understand the meaning of the text and as I hear how it will sound in the reader's ear I learn how to revise for that reader so the meaning will be heard.

48   There is enormous satisfaction in revising or tuning the music of a draft. Change the word, the pauses between words, the beat, the length of the line, all the elements that communicate the music of the text, and the message of the text comes clear.

Communication

49   A benefit of revision is communication. Heather McHugh said, "I began to write because I was too shy to talk, and too lonely not to send messages." Writing is an antidote to loneliness.

50   I was—am—shy. As a child I hid in the closet when company came; now I say I am out of town when the invitation to the cocktail party arrives. But by writing I found that what Kafka said—"A book should serve as the axe for the frozen sea within us"—was true.

51   I write and meet readers—you—whom I have never seen, will probably never see. I play in many games as a writer. For example, I dropped out of high school twice, then flunked out in part because I thought the way writing was taught was stupid. Now through writing, I have had my say about how writing should be taught and have earned the "compliment" of having those who taught the way I was taught calling my methods stupid. But now I am not a disenfranchised drop-out, I am an empowered participant and although not everyone, thank goodness, shares my views, they all hear them because I have revised and revised them until they can be heard.

The Adventure of Thought

52   I am fascinated by spiders—at a distance. They weave their webs of their own lives it seems and I think I weave in language the meanings of my own life. Plato said, "The life which is unexamined is not worth living." I agree and I have examined and re-examined my life by writing.

53   Rewriting is thinking. There is satisfaction in making meaning of what has happened to you, what is happening to you, integrating reading, study, research, observation, feeling, reaction until you come up with some possible answers—and some good, tough questions that need more thinking and rethinking.

54   Writing is the most disciplined form of thinking; writing is the fundamental tool of the intellectual life. Write your life down and you can stand back and study it, learn

from it. Writing demands precision of language, logical structure, documentation, focus. Writing is a fascinating discipline of mind.

The Pleasure of Craft

55   Above all else, the act of revision is central to the pleasure of making. When we build a house, bake a batch of Christmas cookies, cut a cross-country ski trail through the woods, write an essay, we add to the world.

56   And in the making we lose ourselves. Writing is my hobby and my obsession. Before I sit down to write I put on a compact disc and turn up the volume, but when I become lost in the writing and rewriting I no longer hear the music or know if it stops; I forget the time, the place, who I am going to meet for lunch, what errands I will run that afternoon. I forget my worries, fears, problems when I am in the work. As Bernard Malamud said, "If it is winter in the book, spring surprises me when I look up."

57   Do not minimize this gift. The joy—yes, joy—of crafting a text under my hand and with my ear is a daily satisfaction to me. I am so involved in the task that I achieve concentration and that is the reason we do those activities that give us the most pleasure. Casting for a trout, painting a picture or a house, building a shelf, creating a great soup, conducting an experiment in the lab, constructing an arterial bypass to the heart or to downtown, we are lost in the making. Our life achieves, for the moment, a healing concentration of effort.

58   These are a few of the satisfactions of revision. As a first-draft writer I stand back from the actual writing process. When I revise, I am totally involved. I am playing the game of making meaning with language and as someone who has played the games of football and hockey, the game of jumping out of airplanes, the terrible "game of war," I find rewriting the most exciting game of all.

The Craft of Revision

59   The craft of revision gives us experience within the writing act. Reading about writing—or being talked to about writing—tells us what the writing experience *may* be; reading written writing allows us to imagine what its writing *may* have been like; writing, reading, and revising allow us to experience the writing act. We go backstage and see how the printed text is made and learn the craft of revision that precedes publication. We learn to write by rewriting.

60   Each writing problem is not solved the same way. As we gain experience in revision, we build up a repertoire of solutions that we can try when we confront an old, familiar problem—or a new one.

61   Our attitude changes as we rewrite successfully. We do not see problems as obstacles but rather as opportunities. We are problem-solving animals and rewriting is the skill of solving written-language problems. When we realize that we can solve problems in our writing, that we have an inventory of solutions to try, and when we learn that we can combine and adapt, even improvise solutions, then writing becomes a game and we do not so much work as play.

62   And we begin to read in a different way, picking up new moves from pages written by others. Once we know the problems behind the page that are invisible to ordinary

writers, we can begin to recognize when the writer faced those problems and be fascinated by their solution. Failure stops being failure. The solution that works and the one that does not work are both experiments in meaning and from the "failed" experiment we may learn how to try one that will work.

The Process of Revision

63 Revision is a logical process. The overwhelming task of revising an essay—or a book—is based on a sequence of decisions. Certain problems have to be solved before other problems. The sequence can be understood and adapted to the rewriter's way of thinking, working, and writing as well as to the particular writing task.

64 But to adapt it is necessary first to understand the basic process. This means that tasks that the experienced rewriter may do simultaneously have to be broken down for the inexperienced writer to understand and practice. . . . It is important to have an overview of the complete process.

Draft to Explore

65 We can't rewrite until we have a draft that explores the territory where there may be a subject. The writer has to lower the standards that may cause paralysis and write a rough draft that moves across the territory. This draft may be close to free writing, usually when the writer has not thought much about the territory to be explored, or it may be focused and look like a finished draft, especially when the writer has thought critically about the subject over an extensive period of time.

66 This is a time for honesty: The first draft may be finished. Rewriting is not a virtue, it is an essential process—most of the time for most writers.

Read to Discover

67 After we have completed a draft we should read it not so much for what we intended to write but for what we did not intend to write. The act of writing is the act of thinking, and if we are lucky our page will move beyond our intentions. When I read my drafts, I read for surprise.

68 Sometimes I am aware of the surprise when I am drafting the text and follow it, developing its possibilities as I write. My reading allows me to stand back and consider the surprise: Is this what I want to say? Other times the surprise may be hidden in a turn of voice, an unexpected word or phrase, a trail of evidence I was not aware of as I wrote. These surprises must be spotted and their implications considered: Is this the road I want to travel in the next draft?

69 Usually there are both obvious and hidden surprises in the text. If I do not see them, the reader will and be confused. I must read and deal with them by elimination or development. The real mistake is to see the surprises as mistakes. The unexpected—what you said as different from what you planned to say—is not an error. It is what happens when we write. The act of writing reveals possibilities of thought and presentation. If I knew what I was going to say in advance of writing, I would not bother to write and rewrite.

70   Of course, you have the final word. During revision you decide what you want to say and how you want to say it, but I have learned that you disregard the direction the text wants to take at a price. The text leads and the wise writer follows it if possible.

Revise for Meaning

71   After the reading has revealed the primary meaning of your text, you revise to make that meaning clear. Effective writing has focus. Everything in the draft must lead to that meaning or follow it. It is usually a good idea to write that meaning down. Such a line may or may not be in the text but it will be a North Star to guide you through the revision.

72   Inexperienced writers usually plunge in when revising and start to correct the language. It is a waste of time to work on the language line-by-line unless the meaning is clear to the reader.

73   Doesn't this attention to one dominant meaning lead you to throw good stuff away? Yes, a good draft might be measured by the amount of good material that has to be discarded. A powerful, rich draft grows from abundant soil. Besides, you can save the discarded good stuff for another day.

Revise for Audience

74   Now that you know what you want to make clear through revision, you should stand back and read it as a reader will. Again, you must not read what you intended to have in the draft, but what is actually on the page and what will be in the reader's mind. Does the rewriter become a mind reader? Yes. You can train yourself to read your text as a stranger. My trick is to imagine a specific reader. I pick someone I know who is intelligent but ignorant of my subject and uninterested in knowing about it.

75   I often role play, walking around my desk the way that reader walks, trying to sit as that reader would sit, reading as that reader would read, hastily, with a critical eye. I mark up the draft as that reading tells me what needs to be added, what must be moved to anticipate the reader's questions, what needs to be developed, what needs to be cut.

Revise for Order

76   When I know what I want to say and to whom I want to say it, I can reconsider the shape and sequence of the draft.

77   First I have to consider the form or genre of the draft. Is it appropriate to the message and the message receiver? I may decide the memo needs to become a familiar letter or a more formal report; the book review may become a literary essay. And, of course, if the form is assigned and I have no choice, I must make sure that I know and respond to the readers' expectations when they confront that form. The distance the writer stands from the subject and the documentation the reader expects is not the same for a familiar letter as it is for a term paper.

78   When the form is established I can pay attention to the structure with the draft. Do my arguments anticipate the reader's responses and deal with them in the order

they will occur to the reader? Do my points move forward in a logical sequence? Does the structure of the draft support my dominant meaning?

Revise for Evidence

79   Now that we know the focus, the reader, the form and structure, we must make sure that we have the evidence to support that meaning. We should not depend on one form of evidence but have as much variety as possible within the traditions of the genre in which we are writing.

80   Most of us fall into a pattern of documentation. I tend to use—and overuse— personal anecdotes; another writer almost always uses statistics; another uses scholarly quotations. We must develop an inventory of evidence so that we can choose the particular documentation that is appropriate to the meaning we are communicating and that will persuade the reader we are attempting to reach.

Revise for Voice

81   And now we come to the magic of voice—that element of writing that unites meaning, order, evidence, and reader. This final stage of the revision process includes editing and more; it involves following the traditions of language or breaking them for good reason; it involves listening to and tuning the voice of the text.

82   As we read the text word-by-word, line-by-line, we must make sure that each word, the spaces between the words, the punctuation, all the elements of language work in harmony, that they are accurate, clear, and graceful.

83   Working with voice is the ultimate satisfaction for writers as we sit at the workshop bench, messing with the basic materials of our craft. After working with voice we can understand what the historian Barbara Tuchman said:

> Nothing is more satisfying than to write a good sentence. It is no fun to write lumpishly, dully, in prose the reader must plod through like wet sand. But it is a pleasure to achieve, if one can, a clear running prose that is simple yet full of surprises. This does not just happen. It requires skill, hard work, a good ear and continued practice, as much as it takes Heifetz to play the violin.

84   And it is a profound form of play.

Questions on Content

1. In his opening paragraph Murray describes three beliefs that he held for years before learning how wrong they were. To what extent do you subscribe to the same or similar beliefs?

2. Define *voice*. Why does Murray place such importance on it?

3. Discuss what Murray means by each of the following:

    A. "I was not correcting my copy, I was exploring my subject" (paragraph 28).

B. People ask me where I get my ideas—mostly from my writing" (paragraph 29).

C. "Each morning at my desk, I am fifteen years old and the world is new" (paragraph 31).

D. "I have a poor memory until I write" (paragraph 39).

E. "Rewriting multiplies my awareness" (paragraph 38).

Questions on Structure and Style

4. This selection is from the opening chapter of Murray's textbook, *The Craft of Revision*. Describe the tone. Is it unusual for a textbook? Is it appropriate for a student audience?

5. Discuss the purpose and effectiveness of Murray's opening paragraph.

6. What is the effect of the expert opinions Murray cites in paragraph 10?

7. Murray compares the writing act to such unlikely things as music and spider webs. Discuss the effectiveness of such figures.

Assignments

1. Select a paper that you have written. Revise the paper carefully by following Murray's suggestions. Be prepared to discuss the experience.

2. Write a description of your writing process from freewriting to revision and editing. Try to imitate Murray's style by being personal, informal, and anecdotal.

Concision

Joseph M. Williams

Explanations, especially when offered on paper, work best when they're specific and brief. Although student writers often hear reminders to be specific, brevity hardly seems desirable when most assignments include a length requirement. Moreover, whenever we doubt the clarity of what we've stated, our tendency is to add words—to say yet more. In the following selection from his book *Style: Ten Lessons in Clarity and Grace,* Joseph M. Williams shows why saying *less,* not more, provides one key to clarity. Achieving "Concision" (the title of Williams's Lesson 8) requires that we recognize weak and bloated language, which at first might not always look that way to us. Williams teaches at the University of Chicago.

■ **J O U R N A L   P R O M P T** *In the selection that follows, Joseph M. Williams describes ways to prune wordiness. As an example, he prunes the following thirty-one word sentence to six words: "In my personal opinion, it is necessary for all of us not to miss the opportunity to think over in a careful manner each and every suggestion that is offered us." Prune this sentence on your own before glancing at Williams's selection.*

Clarity, Grace, and Concision

1 You are a long way toward clarity when you match characters to your subjects and actions to your verbs and when you structure your sentences to focus your readers' attention on the right sequence of topics. But even when you do all that, your readers may still think that you are a long way from grace if you write like this:

> In my personal opinion, it is necessary for all of us not to miss the opportunity to think over in a careful manner each and every suggestion that is offered us.

This writer matched most of her agents and actions with subjects and verbs, but in more words than her readers needed: Every opinion is personal, so we can cut *personal.* And since this statement is obviously opinion, *in my opinion,* as well. *It is necessary* means *must. Us* implies *all. Think over* means *consider. In a careful manner* means *carefully. Each and every* is redundant. A suggestion is by definition offered, so neither do we need *that is offered.* And since the negative *not miss* negates itself, we can change the sentence to an affirmative. What's left is a leaner, more straightforward sentence. If not obviously elegant, it has at least the quality of compression, a quality that in Marianne Moore's judgement, is style's first grace:

✓ We must consider each suggestion carefully.

To get to that sentence, I applied five principles of economy:

1. Delete words that mean little or nothing.
2. Delete words that repeat other words.
3. Delete words whose meaning your reader can infer from other words.
4. Replace a phrase with a word.
5. Change unnecessary negatives to affirmatives.

2   Unfortunately, these principles are easier for me to state than for you to follow, because the only way to identify and prune wordiness is to inch your way through every sentence, word by word. That's hard work. It helps a bit, though, to know generally what to look for. (Don't worry about discriminating among these categories; use them just as a way to think about concision systematically.)

1. Delete Meaningless Words

3   Some words are verbal tics that we use as unconsciously as we clear our throats:

kind of	particular	certain
virtually	basically	given
actually	really	various
individual	generally	practically

Productivity **actually** depends on **certain** factors that **basically** involve psychology more than any **particular** technology.

✓ Productivity depends more on psychology than on technology.

Here's the point: Don't use words whose meaning adds nothing to the sentence.

---

2. Delete Doubled Words

4   Early in the history of English, writers began to pair a native English word with a French or Latin word, because a borrowed word sounded more learned than the native one. Among the common pairs today:

full and complete	hope and trust	any and all
true and accurate	each and every	basic and fundamental
hopes and desires	first and foremost	various and sundry

Here's the point: When you use a familiar pair of adjectives, your readers probably need only one of them.

---

3. Delete What Readers Infer

5   This is the most common redundancy.

Redundant Modifiers

6   Often, the meaning of a word implies its modifier:

completely finish	**past** history	**various** different
basic fundamentals	**future** plans	**personal** beliefs
final outcome	**true** facts	**consensus** of opinion
terrible tragedy	**free** gift	**each** individual

> Do not try to *anticipate* **in advance** those events that will **completely** *revolutionize* society because **past** *history* shows that it is the **eventual** *outcome* of minor events that **unexpectedly** *surprises* us more.

> ✓ Do not try to *anticipate revolutionary* events because *history* shows that the *outcome* of minor events *surprises* us more.

Perhaps the most common redundancy is a preposition implied by its verb:

continue **on**	return **back** to	penetrate **into**	circle **around**

> *Here's the point:* When a word implies its modifier, drop the modifier.

Redundant Categories

7   Every word implies the name of its general category, so you can usually cut the word for the category. Compare:

> During that *period* of **time,** the *membrane* **area** became *pink* in **color** and *shiny* in **appearance.**

> ✓ During that *period,* the *membrane* became *pink and shiny.*

8   Sometimes, when we eliminate the category, we must change an adjective into an adverb:

> The holes must be aligned in an *accurate* **manner.**

> ✓ The holes must be aligned *accurately.*

Sometimes we must change an adjective modifying a deleted category into a noun:

> The **educational** *process* and public **recreational** *activities* are the responsibility of the **county** *government.*

> ✓ The **county** is responsible for **education** and public **recreation.**

Here are some general nouns (boldfaced) often used redundantly:

large in **size**	*round* in **shape**	*honest* in **character**
unusual in **nature**	of a *strange* **type**	**area** of mathematics
of a *bright* **color**	at an *early* **time**	in a *confused* **state**

> ***Here's the point:*** When a general category word is attached to a specific modifier, drop the category word.

General Implications

9   This kind of wordiness is a general version of the others, but it is harder to spot because it can be so diffuse:

> Imagine someone trying to learn the rules for playing the game of chess.

Learning implies *trying, playing* a *game* implies *rules, chess* is a kind of *game.* More concisely.

> ✓ Imagine someone learning the rules of chess.

> ***Here's the point:*** When one word implies others, cut the others.

Unnecessary Explanation

10   In technical writing for an informed audience, writers assume their readers have a good deal of knowledge.

> The basic type of verb stem results from rearrangement of the phonemic content of polysyllabic forms so that the initial CV of the first stem syllable is transposed with the first CV of the second stem syllable.

The writer didn't define *verb stem, phonemic content, stem syllable,* or *CV* because she assumed that anyone reading that professional journal would know. On the other hand, a student reading his first linguistics textbook would probably need a definition even of *phonetic transcription:*

> To study language scientifically, we need some kind of phonetic transcription, a system to write a language so that visual symbols consistently represent segments of speech.

> ***Here's the point:*** Don't tell your readers what you are *certain* they already know.

4. Replace a Phrase with a Word

11 This kind of redundancy is the most difficult to prune, because a writer needs a large vocabulary and the wit to use it. For example,

> As you carefully read what you have written to improve wording and catch errors of spelling, punctuation, and so on, the thing to do before anything else is to see whether you could use sequences of subjects and verbs instead of the same ideas expressed in nouns instead of verbs.

That is,

✓ As you edit, first replace nominalizations with clauses.

I compressed six phrases into six words:

carefully read what you have written	→	edit
the thing to do before anything else	→	first
see where	→	find
use X instead of Y	→	replace
sequences of subjects and verbs	→	clauses
nouns instead of verbs	→	nominalizations

12 I can offer no principle to help you recognize phrases that you can replace with a word, much less give you that word. I can point out only that we often can, and that we should be on the alert for opportunities to do so—which is to say, try.

13 Here are some common phrases you can watch for (note that some of these also let you revise a nominalization into a verb; they are indicated by italicized nominalizations and verbs):

the reason for
due to the fact that
owing to the fact that
in light of the fact that   } because, since, why
considering the fact that
on the grounds that
this is why

We must explain **the reason for** the *delay* in the meeting.

✓ We must explain **why** the meeting is *delayed*.

despite the fact that
regardless of the fact that   } although, even though
notwithstanding the fact that

Despite the fact that the data were checked, errors occurred.

✓ **Even though** the data were checked, errors occurred.

$$\left.\begin{array}{l}\text{in the event that}\\\text{if it should transpire/happen that}\\\text{under circumstances in which}\end{array}\right\}\quad \text{if}$$

In the event that the information is ready early, contact this office.

✓ **If** the information is ready early, contact this office.

$$\left.\begin{array}{l}\text{on the occasion of}\\\text{in a situation in which}\\\text{under circumstances in which}\end{array}\right\}\quad \text{when}$$

In a situation in which a class is closed, you may petition for admission.

✓ **When** a class is closed, you may petition for admission.

$$\left.\begin{array}{l}\text{as regards}\\\text{in reference to}\\\text{with regard to}\\\text{concerning the matter of}\\\text{where . . . is concerned}\end{array}\right\}\quad \text{about}$$

I should now like to say a few words **concerning the matter of** money.

✓ I should now like to say a few words **about** money.

$$\left.\begin{array}{l}\text{it is crucial that}\\\text{it is necessary that}\\\text{there is a need/necessity for}\\\text{it is important that}\\\text{it is incumbent upon}\\\text{cannot be avoided}\end{array}\right\}\quad \text{must, should}$$

There is a need for more careful *inspection* of all welds.

✓ You **must** *inspect* all welds more carefully.

$$\left.\begin{array}{l}\text{is able to}\\\text{is in a position to}\\\text{has the opportunity to}\\\text{has the capacity for}\\\text{has the ability to}\end{array}\right\}\quad \text{can}$$

We are in a position to make you a firm offer.

✓ We **can** make you a firm offer.

it is possible that
there is a chance that   } may, might, can, could
it could happen that
the possibility exists for

It is possible that nothing will come of these preparations.

✓ Nothing **may** come of these preparations.

prior to
in anticipation of
subsequent to   } before, when, as, after
following on
at the same time as
simultaneously with

Prior to the *end* of the training, you should apply for your license.

✓ **Before** your training *ends,* you should apply for your license.

increase in   } less/fewer, better/worse
decrease in more

There has been an ***increase*** in the number of university *applications.*

✓ ***More*** people are *applying* to universities.

We have noted a ***decrease*** in the number of errors.

✓ We have noted *fewer* errors.

Here's the point: Look for the word that says the same thing as a phrase or clause.

---

5. Change Negatives to Affirmatives

14   When you express an idea in a negative form when a positive form would suffice, you have to use an extra word: *not different* → *same.* But more important, you may also force your readers to infer your meaning through a kind of algebraic computation. These two sentences mean much the same thing, but the affirmative is more direct:

Do not write in the negative.

✓ Write in the affirmative.

15   Do not translate a negative into an affirmative if you want to emphasize the negative. (Is that such a sentence? I could have written, *Keep a negative sentence when. . . .*) But you can rewrite most negatives, some almost formulaically:

not different → similar	not many → few	not remember → forget
not notice → overlook	not include → omit	not consider → ignore
not the same → different	not often → rarely	not have → lack
not allow → prevent	not admit → deny	not accept → reject

16   Some verbs, conjunctions, and prepositions are implicitly negative:

Verbs: *preclude, prevent, lack, fail, doubt, reject, avoid, deny, refuse, exclude, contradict, prohibit, bar*

Conjunctions: *except, unless*

Prepositions: *without, against, lacking, absent, but for*

17   As complex as simple multiple negatives can be, you will thoroughly baffle your readers if you combine them with these implicitly negative verbs, conjunctions, and prepositions. Compare these:

Except when applicants have **failed to** submit applications **without** documentation, benefits will **not** be **denied.**

✓ You will receive benefits only if you submit your documents.

✓ To receive benefits, submit your documents.

18   And when you combine these negatives with passives and nominalizations, your readers will find such sentences almost incomprehensible:

There should be no submission of payments without due notification of this office, unless the payment does not exceed $100.

This sentence relates two events, one a precondition for the other. First change nominalizations into verbs and passives into actives:

Do not submit payments if you have not notified this office, unless you are paying less than $100.

Now revise the negatives into affirmatives:

✓ Submit payments to this office only if you are paying less than $100.

✓ If you submit more than $100, notify this office first.

Which do you put first—the outcome or the condition? That depends on what you think your reader has in mind. Reading these sentences, the reader would have in mind the idea of submitting payments. So begin with what your readers know and move to what they do not.

Here's the point: To be direct, choose the affirmative.

---

19   Having emphasized concision so relentlessly as the first grace of style, here at the end of this lesson I should qualify what I have urged: Readers don't like graceless redundancy, but a style so concise, so tight, so compact that it has no soft edges at all can seem gracelessly brusque. I can't tell you when that happens. That's why you must pay such close attention to what your readers think, because your readers know something that you don't: They know how it feels to be your reader.

Questions on Content

1. One of Williams's five principles of economy is to change unnecessary negatives to affirmatives. Summarize the reasons for this advice.

2. The author describes some meaningless words as "verbal tics" (paragraph 3). Explain what he means.

3. What does Williams mean by *doubled words* and *redundant modifiers*? Try to think of examples other than those he offers.

Questions on Structure and Style

4. Discuss the clarity of Williams's presentation. Did you find it helpful and clear? Did anything confuse you? Be specific.

5. Is Williams's prose concise? Discuss the economy of his writing as well as his use of concrete examples.

Assignments

1. Familiarize yourself with the five principles of economy that Williams lists in his opening paragraph. Revise an essay you have written following these principles. Remember, this is hard work. Take your time. The author says, "Inch your way through every sentence word by word" (paragraph 2).

2. Working in groups, write a letter of advice to future students who will enroll in this composition course. Focus your advice on Williams's five principles of economy. Restate the principles in your own words, and try to find illustrations of the principles in your writing.

Computers and Writing

Sharon Cogdill

Word processing is not writing, but it plays an important role for many writers. In the following essay, written especially for *About Language*, Sharon Cogdill illuminates the sometimes critical, often surprising ways in which word processing affects writing, especially student writing. As she points out, technological change has always alarmed, as well as fascinated, anyone who treasures language. Cogdill is a writer, editorial consultant, and teacher of writing. She writes with a gold-tipped fountain pen and a computer.

■ **J O U R N A L   P R O M P T** *List ways that computers and word-processing technology have helped your writing process. Can you think of ways such technology might cause problems for writers?*

1   If you ask writers why they use word processing, they will tell you that it makes them write better; but if you press them to explain how, they will say that the physical act of writing goes so much faster on a keyboard, that word processing makes their writing look so good, that revision is so much easier on a word processor. Word processing offers powerful advantages, but the tool you use when you write is only a tool. Like all powerful tools, a computer can make writers much more efficient than they are without it. It can do huge damage, however, in the hands of somebody who doesn't know how to use it: the same qualities that make it powerful also make it dangerous.

2   The physical act of writing or drafting is only one small part of a complex set of recursive phases: prewriting or planning, writing or drafting, rewriting or revising, editing, and publishing. Computers have brought increased speed and efficiency to the writing or drafting phase and thereby made a difference to writers, especially in their attitudes about the work that has to be done. With some training and practice, people can keyboard much faster than they can write by hand: a speed of seventy-five words per minute, not out of the question for most people, seems much closer to the speed of thought than is the rate at which they can legibly write. The training required to keyboard at this rate is not much different from what high schools used to (and probably still) teach in typing classes, except that even young men too concerned about their masculinity to type find nothing threatening or embarrassing about keyboarding.*

3   Although such speed and efficiency are undeniably attractive, they do have disadvantages. Most good writing takes thought and care—and precise selection of

---

* Marcia Peoples Halio, "Student Writing: Can the Machine Maim the Message?" *Academic Computing*, January 1990: 16. This article has generated quite a bit of controversy, and Halio has had to retract significant portions of it. See, for example, Dave Debronkart, "Platform Hysteria," *Personal Publishing*, January 1991: 14–15.

384

words. Writing on a keyboard leads some people to do little more than free associate, trying to get down in black and white (or green or amber) the river of their consciousness. This kind of freewriting is fun to do. Sometimes it helps you decide what you want to write about or what order you should handle topics in, and occasionally it gives you one or two sentences you can use, but it does not give you what most writers think of as finished writing. Sitting at the keyboard and doing a mind dump mostly gives you chat, something less thoughtful and careful than finished writing should be, something more conversational and linear, something private and personal. When I first started writing seriously, I wrote whatever I could and then went back and cut out and rewrote what didn't work; but now I want to go slower and write down less, so there are fewer streams and masses of words to untangle later.

4   All writers who use a computer fall in love with the neatness, the orderliness, brought to their pages by the screen and the cursor. Second graders think of themselves as serious writers when they see their handwritten stories turned into typeset and bound "books," and the lesson carries over into their reading. When they hear a story they like, they'll say, "Who *wrote* that book?" and they'll remember the names of authors, like Maurice Sendak and Herman Melville (the Classic Comics *Moby-Dick* has been in print for decades). There are many children in the United States who have very high test and I.Q. scores but who cannot get comfortable reading and writing. When they are allowed to use the computer or a typewriter for their homework, they have a less painful time with school. The neatness afforded by the computer is more acceptable to these children than their own spiky, awkward handwriting, and their attitude improves: they like writing better, they like English better, they like school better.

5   Because word processing makes writing look so good, however, it can turn writers' attention from what they are saying to how the words appear on the page. This drive to the superficial is fueled by the computer as well as the writer, and some computers may be worse than others. For example, some people believe that students who use Macintoshes choose less profound topics and use less sophisticated language than IBM users.* Right now, *if* this is true, we can only guess why. (It could be that students oriented more to the graphical than to the textual may select the Mac; or that, since every character matters when you're "talking" to DOS the unfriendliness of the IBM interface may encourage students to be more precise in their language; or that the smaller Mac screen may limit writers' scope.) I think the focus on the superficial is encouraged by the WYSIWYG (what you see is what you get) quality of the Mac screen. WYSIWYG on any computer encourages writers to treat their words as meaningless shapes and to think only about the appearance of the pages instead of about their content.

6   Students are not the only writers who get superficial on a computer. Full-grown authors fall into the same trap. Writers can make an enormous contribution to the production of their books if their manuscript is on disk as well as paper, but only if the manuscript pages are *not* filled with formatting. It costs publishers money to unformat fancy pages, just as it costs authors time to format them: time spent tabbing

* Halio, 17.

and centering instead of turning thinking into language, time spent making beautiful title pages and illustrations instead of putting words on paper or screen, time spent junking up the files with control codes and escape sequences instead of writing.

7   Writerly avoidance behaviors are perfectly understandable; some are even potentially useful (like cleaning off your desk or washing the ceilings). Up against a difficulty and a blinking cursor, any writer will fiddle with the appearance of the writing. Dozens of formatting options can keep writers from writing, and all of them make the pages look nicer: headlines, graphics, headers and footers, special typefaces, boldface, italics, margins, tab settings, special indents for lists and examples, and decorative devices for the title page. The danger is twofold: time spent on the surface is time taken away from the depth, and neat, decorated pages look like finished pages to a vulnerable writer.

8   The fact is that good writing is not the same as good decorating or even good editing. Really bad writing can be spelled, punctuated, edited, and formatted perfectly, and really good writing doesn't necessarily look good. Once I read a gripping autobiography childishly printed in pencil in a spiral notebook. The author had written it day after day sitting on a pillow on top of the electric skillet as dinner cooked for her family. She misspelled *some* and *very* and *while*. The only words she consistently spelled right were the ones she had looked up and memorized because their written form had power in her life: *paranoid schizophrenic, electroshock therapy, thirteen voluntary hospitalizations*. Though I had to read it out loud to be able to understand it, her book was wonderfully written: it was alive and thoroughly realized. Every idea had a beginning, a middle, and an end.

9   In spite of the lure of its speed and the temptation it presents to focus on the surface, no tool on earth is better than a word processor in the hands of an experienced writer—one who knows how to make revisions that improve the writing. Such knowledge comes only with doing lots of writing, showing other people your writing, and reading theirs.

10   I can remember when I finally learned to revise, when it finally occurred to me that I couldn't get by any longer on the flash method of writing—waiting to get started until the pain of not writing was worse than the pain of writing, then having one great (I hoped) idea, writing the paper, typing it, turning it in. I remember realizing that I had to come up with a flash for every paragraph instead of a flash for every paper and that I would have to take several days (or longer!) to give the flashes enough time. I realized that I would have to break open essays I thought I had finished and let new ideas grow where there had been gaps before—never gaps in the typed page, on the surface of the writing, but gaps in the ideas, in the deep structure of the sentences and paragraphs. This kind of revising is more than fixing words and spelling and punctuation. Although some sentences may be just fine and need little changing, others may need a lot of work, and whole paragraphs may need to go in where there used to be a word or a paragraph break or a parenthetical aside.

11   Nearly all writers I know use computers, and they all print out their documents to revise them. Computers give you infinitely expandable space: the whole world can fit between two letters. Infinitely expandable space is exactly what you need when you're revising, but you can't tell you need that kind of space until you read the hard

copy. You can't tell if you have left out an idea or some description that says exactly what happens, or if your sequence is jumbled, written the way you thought of things instead of the way the reader needs to follow them. You can't tell if you need to collapse paragraphs into sentences, sentences into phrases, phrases into words. You can't see the structure of your writing until you look at it on paper, until you read it as a reader, until you have a sense of it as a whole. Because it's neat and there is no scribbling between the lines, a printout is not the end of the writing process—it's a beginning, a clean copy that will show, with enough handwriting on it, enough boxes and arrows and deletions and insertions, all the things you're capable of fixing this time, right this minute.

12   Studies show that students who write exclusively on the keyboard and revise exclusively on the screen write worse papers than students who take their time getting started and revise on hard copy.* It makes sense. When writers look at their writing in whatever material form it takes, they are looking at it through a window. If you are looking at an 8½-by-11-inch piece of paper, then that is the size of your window. The screens of computer monitors nearly always show far fewer words than you see on an 8½-by-11-inch piece of paper. The smaller the window, the smaller the scale of revision: writers move smaller chunks of text shorter distances on the screen than they do on paper.† With a pen and an 8½-by-11-inch window (or a group of windows side by side), writers make larger changes, moving a clump of sentences from the bottom of a paragraph to the top, putting a paragraph from the middle of a paper at the end, turning an introduction into a conclusion. Good writers use a word processor to implement the changes they make with a pen.

13   Revising on the screen does make your *editing* better. Looking at your writing on the screen leads you to fix the little things, the lower order concerns (things the size of a word or smaller), especially if you run your file through a spell checker. But unless you print your writing out to see it as a reader will, through the bigger window, you will miss many of the higher order concerns (at the level of the sentence, paragraph, essay). You will miss the places where the thinking needs work, and that's where most unsuccessful writers fail: not on the grammar, which can be fixed, but on the development and full expression of their thoughts.

14   Actually, the standard 8½-by-11-inch window may itself be too small. There's certainly nothing in nature that makes that size necessary: an arbitrary accident related to paper manufacture is what makes it the norm. Jack Kerouac used to complain about the restrictions imposed by normal typing paper, and he experimented with typing his novels on continuous rolls of paper. Kerouac's experiments were thought eccentric and impractical, which they were, and not really designed to make revising easier, but they show that Kerouac had insight into what he needed in order to "see" his writing, to get a sense of it as a whole. Eudora Welty lays all her paragraphs out on her dining room table so that she can see them all at once, not merely

---

* Gail E. Hawisher, "The Effects of Word Processing on the Revision Strategies of College Freshmen," *Research in the Teaching of English*, May 1987: 157.
† Jean Lutz, "A Study of Professional and Experienced Writers Revising and Editing at the Computer and with Pen and Paper," *Research in the Teaching of English*, December 1987: 407.

in order, and she pins them together with dressmaker's pins. Some people have said that the size of her dining room table, with all the leaves in place, has an effect on the size of her stories. Laying stories out this way achieves another end as well: Welty can see her story uninterrupted by page breaks, she can see its continuousness, its independence of its current form. This continuousness is the reason Kerouac gave for typing his work onto rolls of paper: not only was the window too small, but the breaks were arbitrary, unplanned, unrelated to aesthetic coherence.*

15   In spite of the many dangers of writing with a word processor, I think writers have to learn to counteract the dangers rather than give up the tool. Writing has always benefited from technological change. In fact, it has always been on the cutting edge of technology, and important advances in literacy have always had deep, structural implications for society and history. People have objected to every important advance in writing technology since the end of the 1400s, and the objections they have made have been the same. They objected when Gutenberg introduced moveable type, making the mass production of books possible for the first time in the history of humanity. They objected when printing was automated. They objected when steel pen points replaced quills barely 150 years ago; they objected when typewriters became popular a century ago. Now they are raising the same objections about word processors (and their chassis, computers): that they are noisy, unnatural (or at least inorganic), mechanical, and dehumanizing; that they make writing too easy; that they contribute to a decline in standards (or to the decline of civilization as we know it); that they present some unnamed danger to our reproductive systems (this one was offered as a reason women shouldn't learn to use typewriters, and it may be true about computers); that they separate us from the natural way of doing things.

16   These reasons, and the dangers word processing poses to the writing process, are not enough to make me turn off the computer and go back to writing with a quill. The technologies of writing have never come cheap. With every innovation in the history of literacy, we have lost distinctive qualities of the old ways of writing and publishing—qualities that are closer to nature, that are more handmade. Each innovation has made writing easier and less exclusive and reading faster and less expensive, until now we have enough books for everyone to own and to read.

17   Computers are like table saws and cars and telephones. There's no question about the damage they do—to our peace of mind, to our environment—but people will not give up their cars or power tools or telephones until something better comes along. For all the ill that technology brings, it can be democratizing. It can give unimportant people—isolated individuals—more scope, efficacy, and presence. Cars have done this, telephones have done it, and computers have done it. It is not enough to believe in computers and defend them against all criticism; it is not enough to hate computers and deny everything but the damage they do. We have to listen to the prophets who see the fall of western civilization in the flickering glow of a CRT and

---

* Jack Kerouac was one of the most important writers of the Beat movement, which hit its zenith in the 1950s and 1960s in the United States. Kerouac died before anybody had a personal computer. Eudora Welty writes fiction in Jackson, Mississippi.

separate their truths from their doomsaying, doomsaying that has attended every single one of these technological innovations. We as writers need to learn to control some of the ill effects of word processing by getting away from the computer at critical moments, but to ask us to give up our computers is to stand knee-deep in the tide of technological change and order it back.

Questions on Content

1. Cogdill suggests that although computers help writers, they also introduce new difficulties. Does this surprise you? Do you agree? What are some of the difficulties Cogdill talks about?

2. How, according to Cogdill, has writing always benefited from technological change?

3. Cogdill suggests that "good writing is not the same as good decorating or even good editing" (paragraph 8). Explain what she means.

4. Writers tend to think that word-processing makes revision easier. Do you agree? Does Cogdill?

5. What is the meaning of the word *window* in paragraph 12? How did Jack Kerouac and Eudora Welty respond to the problem presented by too small a window?

6. What are the differences between editing and revising?

7. Cogdill contends that word processing will make some writers worse. Explain her position.

Questions on Structure and Style

8. What is the thesis of this selection? Is it implied or stated directly?

9. How effective is Cogdill's use of parallel structure in paragraph 15? Can you find other examples?

10. Discuss Cogdill's use of transitions between paragraphs and between sections of the essay.

11. Discuss the effectiveness of Cogdill's conclusion.

12. How does the author's tone affect her presentation? Exactly what is the tone? Where is it especially noticeable?

Assignments

1. Respond to the following in terms of your own writing habits:

   A. "The same qualities that make it [a computer] powerful also make it dangerous" (paragraph 1).
   B. "Sitting at the keyboard and doing a mind dump mostly gives you chat, something less thoughtful and careful than finished writing should be, something more conversational and linear, something private and personal" (paragraph 3).
   C. "Because word processing makes writing look so good, . . . it can turn writers' attention from what they are saying to how the words appear on the page" (paragraph 5).
   D. "The smaller the window, the smaller the scale of revision" (paragraph 12).
   E. "Revising on the screen does make your *editing* better" (paragraph 13).

2. Interview several people for whom writing is an important part of their professional lives. What do they think is the ideal writing tool? What do they call their most important tool? Are their opinions very strong, or do they have doubts about loving or hating computers? Try to discover how word processing has helped and/or hurt their writing. Mention the problems of adjusting to a computer. Report your findings in a well-developed essay.

ADDITIONAL ASSIGNMENTS AND RESEARCH TOPICS

1. Some faculty members at your college no doubt have written for publication. There may also be other writers in your community. Find one of these writers, and in an interview ask the following questions (and others):

   A. Why do you write? For money? Professional advancement? Personal satisfaction?
   B. What aspect of writing was the most difficult to master? What aspect is still the most difficult?
   C. What aspects of writing seemed difficult at first but now come naturally?
   D. Who gave you the greatest help in learning to write well?
   E. Does reading other people's work play a role in your own writing?
   F. What writing habits do you follow? (For example, at what time of day do you most often write; do you write first drafts in longhand or on a typewriter or computer?)
   G. What role does revision play in your writing process?
   H. Who is your most reliable critic?
   I. Is there a type of writing you have never tried but would like to try?
   J. What advice can you give to a student of writing?

   Report your findings either in an essay or in an oral report to your class.

2. Interview three classmates, asking them to describe their writing processes. Then compose an essay comparing the processes, referring to the authors in this chapter.

3. Write an essay analyzing your own writing habits. Find papers you wrote in high school or in previous college courses, and use them as research material. How do the papers exemplify the writing process you relied on in the past? How would you proceed differently now?

4. Writers need to eliminate sexist language because language shapes our attitudes toward other people and the world generally. Maxine Hairston points out that as long as we have a male-centered language, breaking other male-centered patterns in our culture will be difficult. As she says,

   > We no longer live in a world in which almost all doctors, engineers, police, judges, and pilots are men, or one in which all telephone operators, nurses, and teachers are women, and in order to describe our present-day world accurately, writers have to use language carefully. If they don't, they are likely to offend, and therefore lose, many of their readers.*

   Eliminating sexist implications from your writing is not difficult. Once you become conscious of the problem, you'll find that with a little thought you can

---

* Maxine Hairston, *Contemporary Composition* (Boston: Houghton Mifflin, 1986), 253.

indeed write clear and nondiscriminatory prose. Hairston offers the following guidelines for doing so:

A. When you can, use plural forms. Often this is the simplest way to solve the problem. For example, change "A speaker who hopes to be taken seriously must do his homework and get his facts straight" to "Speakers who hope to be taken seriously must do their homework and get their facts straight." Change "The driver who gets three speeding tickets will lose his license for a month" to "Drivers who get three speeding tickets will lose their licenses for a month."

B. When you cannot use plural pronouns in a sentence, you have three options for solving your problem. First, you can write *he or she* and *him or her* when you need to use a pronoun. Second, you can write *he/she* or *him/her* when you need to use a pronoun. Third, you can alternate between using *he* and *she* or *him* and *her*; that is, for some examples use *he* and for other examples use *she*.

C. If you can, substitute *person* or *people* for *man* or *men*, respectively. You can also just leave out *man* or *men* in some phrases. For instance, instead of writing, "The man who chooses to go into politics must be prepared to compromise," write "The person who goes into politics must be prepared to compromise." Instead of using *policeman*, use *police*; instead of using *Frenchmen*, use *the French*.

D. Sometimes you can substitute *one* or *anyone* for *he* or *she* or *man* or *woman*. For example, instead of writing, "If a man is enterprising and lucky, he can become a millionaire," write "If one is enterprising and lucky, one can become a millionaire." Or instead of writing, "The woman who doesn't smoke usually has fewer wrinkles," write "Anyone who doesn't smoke usually has fewer wrinkles."

E. When you can, instead of identifying people by their gender, identify them by their roles or their actions. Instead of using *mailman*, use *mail carrier*; instead of using *fireman*, use *firefighter*. Instead of writing, "Housewives who buy groceries in supermarkets should consider food co-ops," write "Shoppers who buy groceries in supermarkets should consider food co-ops." Instead of writing, "Men who invest in real estate must know their tax laws," write "Real estate investors must know their tax laws."

F. Avoid using language that stereotypes certain professions or jobs as male or female. For instance, don't automatically use *he* and *him* as pronouns when referring to engineers, judges, surgeons, or legislators and use *she* and *her* as pronouns when referring to teachers, secretaries, or nurses. Avoid classifying people into traditional roles by writing sentences such as this: "Even when they are in junior high school, girls can earn money baby-sitting and boys can earn money mowing lawns."

G. Avoid special female designations if you can. For example, it isn't necessary to use *poetess* or *songstress*; *poet* and *singer* are better.

H. Avoid stereotyping people by supposedly sex-linked traits. For example, do not describe women as frivolous, emotional, or intuitive and men as stalwart, rugged, or logical. Also avoid mentioning a woman's appearance unless in the same circumstances you would mention a man's.

I. Refer to women by their own names, such as Mary Scott Webster or Julia Martin, rather than as Mrs. John Webster or Mrs. James Martin. Mention their marital status only if that information is important to your readers and only if you also refer to men's marital status; that is, don't say Ruth Collins is divorced unless under the same circumstances you would mention that Jack Collins is divorced.

J. Be consistent when you refer to people by their last names; that is, if you write *Faulkner* and *Capote*, also write *Didion*, not *Joan Didion*; if you write *Reagan*, also write *Thatcher*, not *Margaret Thatcher*.

(1) Keeping Hairston's guidelines in mind, pay attention to the prose that you encounter in textbooks, newspapers, and magazines, as well as the language of radio and television broadcasts. Keep a journal in which you record instances of sexist language, and also note efforts to avoid sexist language. Collect data for a few days, and then describe your findings in an essay.

(2) Using Hairston's guidelines, eliminate any sexist implications from the following sentences:*

(a) A driver who wants to keep his insurance rates low must be careful that he doesn't get traffic tickets for moving violations.

(b) If a professor wants his students to respect him, he will always come to class prepared.

(c) Men who choose to go into politics in this country need tremendous stamina and a talent for communication.

(d) A woman can prevent premature aging by always protecting her skin from the sun.

(e) Statistics show that policemen who receive training in interpersonal communication and stress management have less job burnout.

(f) Engineers who work abroad must often be separated from their wives for long periods of time.

(g) Faculty wives are a traditional source of cheap labor in many colleges.

(h) President Reagan and Mrs. Thatcher conferred about economic problems frequently last year.

(i) The chief witness for the defense was a pretty blonde divorcée.

---

* Maxine Hairston, *Contemporary Composition* (Boston: Houghton Mifflin, 1986), 258.

Writing and Documenting: A Brief Guide

I. Essay Writing and Revising

The selections in Chapter 8 emphasize various aspects of the writing process—from discovering a topic to revising a draft, from being precise to being concise. The chapter demonstrates that writers don't think of everything all at once; rather, they move recursively in stages from planning to drafting to revising. Good writing is made, not born, and making good writing is every writer's true job. However, once you have made an acceptable draft, there's still work to do. What follows is a checklist for a developed essay—the final part of the process before you submit your essay to an audience.

Since this is a brief guide, we address only the most common problems writers face. These problems are targeted in the checklist that follows.

Revision Checklist

☐ Does the paper follow essay form?

☐ Do the openings and closings perform as they should?

☐ Is the title appropriate?

☐ Are quotations used correctly?

☐ Are transitions smooth and logical?

☐ Is manuscript form correct?

☐ Are paragraphs unified?

☐ Are paragraphs coherent?

☐ Are paragraphs adequately developed?

☐ Is diction appropriate throughout?

☐ Is the writing concise?

☐ Are there grammatical errors?

☐ Are punctuation marks used correctly?

☐ Is spelling correct?

☐ Does the paper follow essay form?

No single formula can describe the shape of an essay, but you should be able to answer the following basic questions:

What am I writing about?	Introduction
What point(s) do I want to make?	Thesis
Have I explained the point(s) I want to make?	Development
Have I come to appropriate closure?	Conclusion

☐ Do the openings and closings perform as they should?

The introductory paragraph should incite your readers' interest, and the conclusion should satisfy it. An introductory paragraph should perform at least two tasks: (1) it should catch the attention of your readers and make them want to read further, and (2) it should announce what the essay is going to be about. In addition, the thesis statement generally appears or is implied in the introductory paragraph.

Among the most effective means for catching the interest of your readers are the following: a direct quotation, an anecdote, a question, an unusual fact or statistic, or an unusual statement.

The conclusion should sum up major points that have been presented in the essay. It also can bring the essay full circle by referring to something that was mentioned in the opening. Note how the following opening and closing paragraphs by Virginia Woolf work together to interest the reader and to reach appropriate closure:

> No one perhaps has ever felt passionately towards a lead pencil. But there are cir-cumstances in which it can become supremely desirable to possess one; moments when we are set upon having an object, an excuse for walking half across London between tea and dinner. As the fox hunter hunts in order to preserve the breed of foxes, and the golfer plays in order that open spaces may be preserved from the builders, so when the desire comes upon us to go street rambling a pencil does for a pretext, and getting up we say: "Really I must buy a pencil," as if under cover of this excuse we could indulge safely in the greatest pleasure of town life in winter—rambling the streets of London.

> • • •

> That is true: to escape is the greatest of pleasures; street haunting in winter the greatest of adventures. Still as we approach our own doorstep again, it is comforting to feel the old possessions, the old prejudices, fold us round; and the self, which has been blown about at so many street corners, which has been battered like a moth at the flame of so many inaccessible lanterns, sheltered and enclosed. Here again is the usual door; here the chair turned as we left it and the china bowl and the brown ring on the carpet. And here—let us examine it tenderly, let us touch it with reverence—is the only spoil we have retrieved from all the treasures of the city, a lead pencil.

> —Virginia Woolf

☐ Is the title appropriate?

Ideally, your title, your introduction, and your conclusion should work together. A good title is more than just a label such as one might put on a file drawer. Good titles should be brief, informative, and engaging. For example, the title for Virginia Woolf's essay from which we've included the opening and closing paragraphs is "Street Haunting." The title of the model student essay that is presented later in this guide, "The Language of Doctors: A Personal Experience," is informative, brief, and inter-esting. Frequently, titles are written after completing the essay because, more often than not, they develop from the thesis statement.

☐ Are quotations used correctly?

Unless you've been assigned a research project involving secondary sources, it's unlikely you will use direct quotations often. However, quotations do serve important purposes. They create a sense of immediacy with reputable figures who agree with you, they provide relief from the sound of your voice, they give the appearance of not distorting what others have said, and they enhance your authority by displaying your knowledge of literature that is relevant to your topic.

☐ Are transitions smooth and logical?

Good writing is coherent when sentences and paragraphs are logically connected. You use transitions to create coherence by showing the relationships between one idea and the next as you move from sentence to sentence and paragraph to paragraph. Writers should be aware of the following transitional devices:

1. Transitional words and phrases (*consequently, for example, in addition, however,* and *on the other hand*).
2. Pronoun reference. Use clear pronoun references to refer to nouns in a previous sentence or paragraph.
3. Repetition of key terms.
4. Parallelism (similar ideas expressed in similar constructions).

☐ Is manuscript form correct?

Writing begins to make an impression on readers the moment they look at a manuscript. The following guidelines for correct manuscript form may be helpful:

1. Use 8½-by-11-inch 20-pound bond paper.
2. Type or print on one side of the sheet only.
3. Include your name, the course name and number, your instructor's name, and the date at the top left corner of the first page.
4. Leave a margin of at least 1 inch on all 4 sides of the paper.
5. Center the title.
6. Indent the first line of each paragraph 5 spaces (½ inch).
7. Use your name and page number as the header on all pages after page 1.
8. Double-space all text.
9. Check with your instructor about specific requirements for the title page.

☐ Are paragraphs unified?

Most paragraphs should contain a topic sentence or controlling idea. The topic sentence is generally the first sentence of a paragraph (or the second, following a transitional sentence). Each sentence that follows should stick to the topic and not discuss irrelevant issues. As you examine your draft, ask yourself how each sentence relates to the central idea. In the model student essay that begins on page 403, note how each sentence relates to the controlling idea: medical language is impersonal.

☐ Are paragraphs coherent?

In a paragraph, coherence means that the sentences flow logically. Each idea follows from the one before it. A paragraph should not be a sequence of isolated sentences that the reader must link together.

In the model essay note how *medical language* and *another purpose* relate to preceding paragraphs. Note the use of parallel structure, the pronoun *this,* and the repetition of *impersonal language.*

☐ Are paragraphs adequately developed?

A paragraph is adequately developed when it presents sufficient details, examples, and illustrations to support the topic sentence. Each paragraph must be judged independently, and the amount and method of development are often determined by the scope of the topic sentence.

☐ Is diction appropriate throughout?

Correct diction means using language appropriate to the audience. There are no absolute rules for correct diction. In general, use language that your audience is willing to understand and accept. Doing so usually means avoiding slang, regionalisms, and unnecessarily technical terms.

☐ Is the writing concise?

Joseph Williams treats concise writing in depth in Chapter 8. He affirms that good writing is precise and concise. You achieve both objectives when you substitute exact words and phrases for empty words and needless repetition. For example, use *because* rather than *due to the fact that* and *soon* rather than *in the near future.*

☐ Are there grammatical errors?

Among the most common sentence-level errors are comma splices, fused sentences, and lack of agreement between subjects and verbs and between pronouns and antecedents.

1. **Comma splice.** A common type of run-on sentence is the comma splice, in which two or more independent clauses are joined by a comma without a coordinating conjunction (*and, but, or, nor, for, so,* and *yet*). Here's an example of a comma splice:

   The audience applauded, the critics did not.

2. **Fused sentence.** A fused sentence occurs when a writer puts no mark of punctuation and no coordinating conjunction between independent clauses. Here is an example of a fused sentence:

   The audience applauded the critics did not.

3. **Subject and verb agreement.** A verb must agree with its subject in person and number. Singular subjects take singular verbs, and subjects in the third person take verbs in the third person, as shown in the following examples:

   Every morning a group of dogs gathers on the sidewalk.

   A bus carrying a large group of students stops in front of my house every morning.

   Each of the students carries a green book bag.

4. **Pronoun and antecedent agreement.** Each pronoun should agree with its antecedent in person and number, as shown in the following example:

   Each student and faculty member should take her seat so the conference can begin.

☐ Are punctuation marks used correctly?

Although correctness is important for all marks of punctuation, writers have the most difficulty with commas, semicolons, colons, and dashes.

Commas signal brief pauses within sentences.

1. Use commas to separate independent clauses joined by a coordinating conjunction.

   Seattle is the largest city in Washington, and it is the gateway to Alaska and the Far East.

2. Use commas to separate elements in a series.

   Successful tennis players are those who practice all year, concentrate on each match, and challenge players better than themselves.

3. Use commas after introductory elements.

   In other words, you did not wash the windows.

   Unfortunately, the pilings were rotten.

4. Use commas to separate nonrestrictive elements (modifiers that are not essential to the meaning of the sentence).

   The Wheeler House, which is the oldest house in town, is open for visitors.

5. Use commas to set off direct quotations and arbitrary words.

   "A stitch in time saves nine," she said.

   No, I cannot "substitute" for you this weekend.

6. Use commas to set off transitional words and parenthetical elements.

The book, as you can see, has missing pages.

The mayor's behavior, for example, did not help local politicians.

Semicolons join independent clauses and separate elements in a complex series.

1. Use semicolons to join independent clauses that are not joined by a comma and coordinating conjunction.

The redwood tree thrives in the damp climate near the Pacific Ocean; it rarely grows farther than fifty miles inland.

Rock music is played all over the world; however, Americans still play more rock than anyone else.

2. Use semicolons to separate items in a series when some or all of the items contain commas.

The finalists for the most valuable player are Jane, who struck out ten batters; Ruby, who hit the winning home run; and Sue, who had five singles and a double.

Colons introduce lists, explanations, and formal quotations. They also separate titles and subtitles.

1. Use colons to introduce a list.

The instructor found three weaknesses in Evan's paper: diction, punctuation, and coherence.

2. Use colons to introduce an explanatory statement.

According to the swimming coach, there was only one thing we could do to win the meet: place in three of the last four events.

3. Use colons to formally introduce a quotation.

When the senator was recognized, he made his position clear: "Under no circumstances will I support the majority."

4. Use colons to separate titles and subtitles.

The title of the model essay is "The Language of Doctors: A Personal Experience."

Dashes separate and emphasize nonessential information and signal changes in thought. Form a dash with two unspaced hyphens.

Cardiologists recommend that young people--and middle-aged people, for that matter--do aerobic exercises.

The Reformation was a religious movement--social and political as well--that gave birth to Protestantism.

☐ **Is spelling correct?**

Correct spelling is important on all final drafts. Take the time to proofread your papers carefully. Even if you're a good speller, use your word processor's spell-check program, but remember that no computer program truly understands anything, including spelling. Make frequent use of your dictionary.

A Sample Student Essay

The following essay illustrates many of the recommendations offered in the revision checklist, as well as other important aspects of essay writing.

Assignment: The language of doctors often is criticized for being too technical for the general public to understand. In an essay of about 500 words, support the opposite opinion. Point out the virtues of medical language.

1. Correct manuscript form is reflected in double-spacing throughout, centered title, and one-inch margins on left and right sides and on top and bottom of the page.

2. A colon separates the title and subtitle.

3. All paragraphs are indented five spaces (one tab), and double-spacing continues between paragraphs.

4. The opening three sentences attract the interest of the reader and lead to the thesis.

5. The comma following *either* in sentence three precedes the coordinating conjunction *and* and separates two independent clauses.

6. The conjunctive adverb *however* is a transitional device, followed by a comma, that connects contrasting thoughts.

7. The thesis statement announces the central idea of the essay, reveals the writer's attitude, and prepares the reader for the content of the essay.

8. The short opening sentence provides a transition between paragraphs one and two.

9. The second sentence is the topic sentence. It announces the controlling idea of the paragraph.

10. The writer's diction sounds natural ("the stakes are too high" and elsewhere) and is appropriate for a general audience.

1

Nathaniel Evans
English 101-120
October 23, 1998
Professor Sunega

2   The Language of Doctors: A Personal Experience

3   When I think about the language that doctors
use, I can think only of the confusing technical
terms that I heard after my grandmother suffered a
4   heart attack. As her doctor described her condition
to my parents in her hospital room, they listened
carefully but later complained that they hadn't
understood the doctor at all. I hadn't understood one
5   word either, and I thought that his complicated
explanation was supposed to tell us mainly that the
doctors knew a great deal about medical care, and
6   that we did not. However, if I look at this encounter
from the doctor's standpoint, I see less disturbing
7   reasons why a doctor might use language that patients
(and their families) do not understand. These reasons
cannot excuse thoughtlessness, but they do cast my
grandmother's doctor, and maybe all doctors, in a
different light.
8   Medical language has a major strength. It's
9   precise, and precision seems especially valuable
when discussing anatomy and pharmacology and other
complicated topics that doctors discuss on the job
every day. For example, consider the consequences of
misidentifying a heart valve when reading an x-ray.
Each valve has a unique name composed of Latin terms.
10 Radiologists use these names because the stakes are
too high to do otherwise. All doctors rely on the

11. The rhetorical question further serves to engage the reader.

12. The pronoun *this* provides a transition between paragraphs two and three.

13. The short, simple sentence provides sentence variety and emphasizes an important point.

14. The repetition of *perhaps* is an example of parallel structure that contributes to paragraph coherence.

15. This opening sentence provides a smooth transition between paragraphs three and four as well as leading to the topic sentence.

16. The parallel repetition of *it lets* adds coherence to this paragraph.

17. The comma after *patients* separates contrasting ideas.

18. The dash following *paralysis* emphasizes the sentence element that follows.

19. The comma separates coordinate adjectives.

Evans 2

precision of medical language for the same reason.
We might complain that language so precise sounds
impossibly technical, but any unfamiliar vocabulary
sounds confusing. Imagine that you've never seen an
automobile. Wouldn't terms like "transmission" and
"accelerator" sound just as imposing and confusing
as "auricle" and "ventricle"?

This was just the sort of vocabulary that my
grandmother's doctor used. It was precise. Perhaps
the doctor, after many hours on the job, simply
spoke to us as he was accustomed to speaking.
Perhaps his explanation, if offered in our living
room and not in a hospital, would have relied more
on our vocabulary and less on his.

Medical language probably has another purpose
for doctors, at least sometimes. Medical language is
impersonal. It lets a doctor treat patients, not
people. It lets a doctor handle a difficult case of
paralysis--instead of trying to help someone's
father walk again. This difference in the way that
we describe a doctor's job, compared with the
doctor's description, reflects our very different
responsibilities. Doctors make decisions with
extremely serious consequences. Using impersonal,
scientific language to distance themselves from
their patients probably becomes necessary at times
if a doctor hopes to remain clear-headed enough to
offer help.

Instead of trying to impress us, perhaps my
grandmother's doctor was just using language this
way. Maybe offering his complex analysis of his

20. The concluding paragraph echos the main idea of the essay, and it allows the essay to sound completed, not merely at an end.

21. The final assertion ("He should have been more thoughtful") itself sounds thoughtful because the author, while maintaining his position firmly, also sounds reasonable ("but maybe at the time . . .").

Evans 3

patient's condition actually made it possible for
him to say anything at all to us.

20   Although I can't forget the confusion and
anger caused by my grandmother's doctor, I no longer
see only the worst possible motive behind his use of
21   language that helped us so little. He should have
been more thoughtful, but maybe at the time we all
were doing the best that we could.

II. The Documented Essay

The documented essay, also called the research or term paper, constitutes one of the most familiar assignments that students face. The sample documented essay appearing later in this section illustrates points highlighted in the following revision checklist. The checklist addresses those aspects of the documented essay that most often prove troublesome for writers.

Revision Checklist

☐ Do I understand the purpose of the documented essay?

☐ Have I avoided plagiarism?

☐ Have I documented sources according to standard form?

☐ Have I prepared the Works Cited list according to standard form?

☐ Have I used only appropriate abbreviations?

☐ Have I used correct Works Cited form if citing two or more works by the same author?

☐ Have I identified inclusive page numbers correctly?

☐ Do I understand the purpose of the documented essay?

The documented essay differs from other writing assignments because its thesis is supported by your own ideas as well as by evidence drawn from outside sources. This evidence, which most often takes the form of quotations, paraphrasings, and summaries, offers your readers relevant data and the authoritative opinions of others.

Data consist of factual items generally considered free from bias. These include statistics (for example, voting records and population figures) and historical information (names, places, and dates). Authoritative opinions originate with other people whose ideas support the assertion contained in your own thesis, thereby enhancing its credibility.

Note that not all opinions should be considered authoritative or equally authoritative. For example, if your thesis deals with the cost of medical care, the opinions of doctors and hospital administrators will carry more weight than the opinions of police officers, who might provide emergency medical care at accident scenes but otherwise seem remote from the issues raised by your thesis.

One hallmark of the documented essay is its reliance on a systematic, standard form for presenting all evidence and identifying sources. Several systems exist, each one designed to serve the needs of different academic disciplines. The system described here, created by the Modern Language Association (MLA) of America and last revised in 1995, is the one used most often in the humanities.

☐ Have I avoided plagiarism?

Plagiarism occurs when you use other people's information or ideas but fail to identify this material as having originated with someone else. Using a quotation without documenting its source, or "borrowing" an idea, including even the organizational strategy someone else has used, constitute the two most common forms of plagiarism.

Remember that plagiarism lies not in what you *intend* but in what you actually *do*. Even when the result of an honest mistake, plagiarism usually destroys credibility overall. An author either careless or dishonest enough to plagiarize creates distrust in readers, who inevitably doubt the reliability of the entire presentation.

Remember also that intentional plagiarism actually defies logic. One purpose of any documented essay is to make clear your own authority on a topic by demonstrating your study of research material. For this reason alone, acknowledging all sources is very much to your advantage.

☐ Have I documented sources according to standard form?

Evidence almost always is documented by using a parenthetical citation and a corresponding Works Cited entry.

In the text of your essay and immediately following the evidence, place within parentheses the minimum information that unambiguously ties the evidence to a specific entry in the Works Cited list. This Works Cited entry provides full publication information. The sample documented essay that appears later in this section illustrates the relationship between the parenthetical citation and Works Cited entry, which should be treated as a pair.

Note that the parentheses should contain only the minimum information required to link evidence with its corresponding Works Cited entry. Sometimes the minimum requires both an author and page number. Your essay might state, for example:

```
Even when no other remedy exists, no reputable economist
would recommend war as a solution to economic depression
(Miller 247).
```

The same sentence also could be written:

```
As Edwin Miller stresses, even when no other remedy
exists, no reputable economist would recommend war as a
solution to economic depression (247).
```

In both cases the Works Cited entry is:

```
Miller, Edwin. Economic Patterns of the Twentieth
     Century. New York: Dietrich, 1996.
```

The amount of parenthetical information varies, sometimes considerably. For example, if your essay includes evidence from two works by the same author, each work will have its own Works Cited entry, so parenthetical references to this author must make clear which of the author's works is being cited:

```
Even when no other remedy exists, no reputable economist
would recommend war as a solution to economic depression
(Miller, Patterns 247).
```

The book's title is abbreviated to create the unambiguous reference with minimum information.

A few other examples of parenthetical Works Cited pairings are presented here:

```
Dogs not only enjoy our company; as John Winokur states,
"dogs have been eager accomplices in all manner of human
endeavor from war to frisbee" (xv).
```

```
Winokur, Jon. Introduction. Mondo Canine. Ed. Jon
     Winokur. New York: Dutton, 1991. xiii-xvi.
```

This citation identifies only the introduction to an anthology of readings from many sources. The introduction was written by the anthology's editor.

```
Historian Francis Parkman says of La Salle, "Nature had
shaped him for other uses than to teach a class of boys
on the benches of a Jesuit school" (728).
```

```
Parkman, Francis. La Salle and the Great West. 1884.
     France and England in North America. Vol. 1. New
     York: Library of America, 1983. 2 vols.
```

The source, *La Salle and the Great West,* was published originally in 1884 and forms part of the series *France and England in North America*. The entire series was re-published in two volumes in 1983, with *La Salle and the Great West* appearing in volume 1. If citing the entire series, the entry would read:

```
Parkman, Francis. France and England in North America.
     1883. 2 vols. New York: Library of America, 1983.
```

```
At its start in 1944, the G.I. Bill entitled any veteran
with ninety days of service to one year of college
(Haydock 54).
```

```
Haydock, Michael D. "The G.I. Bill." American History
    Sept./Oct. 1996: 52+.
```

The article, which appears in a bimonthly magazine, begins on page 52 and continues on nonconsecutive pages.

☐ Have I prepared the Works Cited list according to standard form?

The Works Cited page of a documented essay should include every source you document in the text of the paper and any source referred to in notes. Do *not* document sources you examined while researching but did not use when writing the paper itself.

Entries are listed alphabetically by author or, if no author is listed, by the first important word of the source's title. Double-space entries, and indent each line of each entry five spaces *except* the first line. Use only one space, not two, after each period within the entries.

☐ Have I used only appropriate abbreviations?

A selection of the most common standard abbreviations appears below. Never make up your own abbreviations if standard versions already exist.

ch.	chapter
dir.	directed by, director
diss.	dissertation
ed(s).	editor(s), edition(s)
et al.	and others
GPO	Government Printing Office
narr.	narrated by, narrator
n.d.	no date
n. pag.	not paginated
p., pp.	page, pages
rev.	reviewed by, review
trans.	translated by, translator
vol(s).	volume(s)
UP	University Press

Publisher's names are shortened when the reader is likely to recognize the names and not be confused. For example, Houghton Mifflin Company should be listed as "Houghton"; Prentice-Hall becomes "Prentice."

☐ Have I used correct Works Cited form if citing two or more works by the same author?

Replace the author's name with three unspaced hyphens followed by a period; then list the entries alphabetically according to the first important words in the titles. For example:

Theroux, Paul. <u>The Family Arsenal</u>. Boston: Houghton,
    1976.

---. <u>Kowloon Tong</u>. Boston: Houghton, 1997.

☐ Have I identified inclusive page numbers correctly?

The hyphen separates inclusive pages numbers (167-89). Note also that page numbers are identified using only the minimum number of digits required for clarity (*not* 167-189 in this example). The plus sign after the page number (32+) denotes a source that does not continue on consecutive pages, for example, a source interrupted by full-page advertisements or "Continued on page 103" or elsewhere in an issue.

Typical Works Cited Entries

The following examples illustrate only the most common types of sources cited in documented essays. Additional examples can be found in the sample documented essay that concludes this section. For complete information about citation forms, consult a college writing handbook or the *MLA Handbook for Writers of Research Papers* (1995).

Books

Book with one author:

Cronkite, Walter. <u>A Reporter's Life</u>. New York: Knopf,
    1996.

Book with two or three authors:

Parker, Page, and Lois N. Dietz. <u>Nursing at Home</u>. New
    York: Crown, 1980.

The name of only the first author is reversed. Use *and* before only the last name listed if there are three authors.

Book with more than three authors:

Alexander, Anne, et al. <u>Surgical Responsibility and the</u>
    <u>Medical Curriculum</u>. Saint Louis: Neville, 1991.

Later edition:

>   Schneier, Bruce. <u>Applied Cryptography</u>. 2nd ed. New York:
>   Wiley, 1996.

Book with a translator:

>   García Márquez, Gabriel. <u>One Hundred Years of Solitude</u>.
>   Trans. Gregory Rabassa. New York: Avon, 1970.

Work in more than one volume:

>   Smith, Page. <u>A New Age Now Begins</u>. 2 vols. New York:
>   McGraw, 1976.

The preceding listing cites the entire set of a multivolume work. To cite only one volume of a multivolume work, use this form:

>   Smith, Page. <u>A New Age Now Begins</u>. Vol. 1. New York:
>   McGraw, 1976. 2 vols.

Book with an editor:

>   Hawthorne, Nathaniel. <u>The Scarlet Letter</u>. Ed. Ross C.
>   Murfin. Boston: Bedford-St. Martin's, 1991.

The hyphen separates a division, or imprint, of a publisher (in this case, Bedford Books) from the publisher itself (St. Martin's Press).

Selection from an edited anthology:

>   Tindall, William York. "The Symbolism of W. B. Yeats."
>   <u>Yeats: A Collection of Critical Essays</u>. Ed. John
>   Unterecker. Englewood Cliffs, NJ: Prentice, 1963.
>   43-53.

Because the selection appears on consecutive pages, inclusive page numbers for the entire selection are cited.

Introduction, preface, foreword, or afterword:

>   Plumb, J. H. Introduction. <u>Oscar Wilde</u>. By Louis
>   Kronenberger. Boston: Little, Brown, 1976. vii-x.

Encyclopedia or almanac entry:

>   "Lincoln, Abraham." <u>The Encyclopedia Americana</u>. 1993
>   edition.

If entries are arranged alphabetically, no volume or page numbers are needed.

Newspapers

Article or column:

```
Richard, Paul. "The Memorial's Old Deal." Washington Post
     27 Apr. 1997: G6.
```

The articles *the, a,* and *an* are dropped from the names of newspapers. If the newspaper is divided into sections and page numbers include the sections, use the form just shown. If the paper is divided into sections but printed page numbers do not identify sections, use the following form:

```
"Little New in Latest County Offer." New City Messenger
     [Hartford] 18 Nov. 1983, sec. B: 1+.
```

Note also that the newspaper's name does not identify the city, so the city is included in brackets.

Editorial or letter to the editor:

```
"Michigan Expelling God." Editorial. Wall Street Journal
     17 June 1997: A18.
Whitley, Brenda. Letter. USA Today 9 Apr. 1997: 10A.
```

Magazines and Journals

Article in a monthly magazine:

```
Oppenheimer, Todd. "The Computer Delusion." The Atlantic
     July 1997: 45+.
```

Article in a weekly magazine:

```
Jeffrey, Don. "BMG Launches Wasabi." Billboard 26 July
     1997: 8+.
```

Article in a journal paginated by volume:

```
Rosenbloom, Peter. "Endgame in Zaire." Current History 96
     (1997): 200-05.
```

Article in a journal paginated by issue:

```
Rauch, Ellen. "Continuing Education Round-Up." Eastern
     Region News 29.1 (1994): 7.
```

The decimal point separates the volume and issue (in this example, volume 29, issue 1).

Electronic Sources

Material from an on-line service:

```
"NEA's Portrait of a Public School Teacher: White,
     Female, Aging." Education Week 9 July 1997: n. pag.
     Online. CompuServe, 20 July 1997.
```

The unpaginated, unsigned article appears in the on-line version of a weekly print journal, in this case in the July 9, 1997, issue. The article was accessed on July 20, 1997.

Newsgroup posting:

```
Fermi, Rick. "Latest Thai Data Likely Flawed." 12 July
     1997. Online posting. Newsgroup sci.med.physics.
     Usenet. 22 July 1997.
```

World Wide Web sources:

```
"Why Is Sea Surface Temperature So Important to Fishing?"
     12 June 1997: n. pag. Online. Internet. 3 Aug. 1997.
     Available WWW: http://www.sstol.com/faq.htm.
```

The unsigned, unpaginated source appears on a WWW page dated June 12, 1997, and accessed on August 3, 1997.

Material obtained through FTP and Gopher:

```
Blackstock, Steve. "LZW and GIF Explained." 1 Dec. 1992.
     Online. Internet. 5 August 1997. Available Gopher:
     wiretap.spies.com/Library/Techdoc/Misc/lzwexp.txt.
```

The article, dated December 1, 1992, was accessed on August 5, 1997.

Other Sources

Pamphlet:

```
Neck Exercises for a Healthy Neck. Daly City, CA:
     Krames, 1990.
```

Treat pamphlets as books. In this example, the publisher's location includes the state (California) only because the city's name is not immediately recognizable.

Government publications:

```
National Bureau of Standards. Care of Books, Documents,
     Prints and Films. Washington: GPO, 1971.
```

A Sample Documented Essay

The short documented essay that follows illustrates many of the points emphasized in the revision checklist, as well as other important aspects of this type of writing assignment.

<u>Assignment: In a documented essay of about five hundred words, examine one important aspect of American regional dialects.</u>

1. Although MLA style does not require a title page, your instructor may require one. The sample provided here illustrates the title page format expected by most instructors. Note in particular the essay's title. Capitalize the first word, last word, and all other words in the title *except* articles (*a, an, the*), prepositions, coordinating conjunctions, and *to* in infinitives. Do *not* underline your essay's title, capitalize every letter in it, or set it between quotation marks.

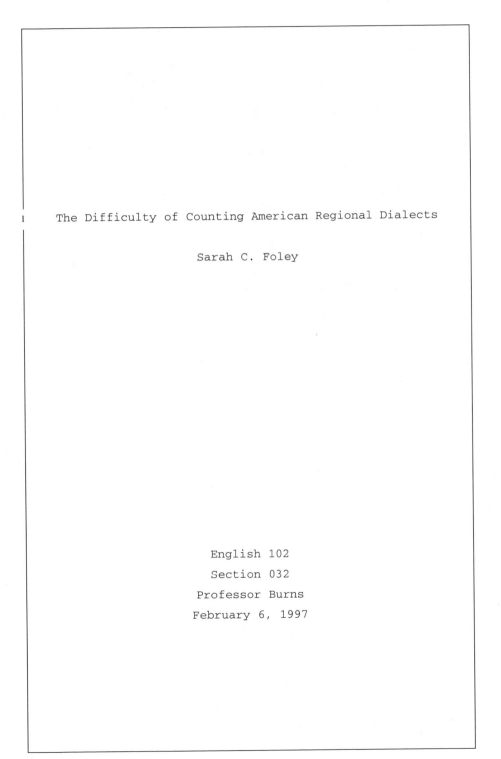

The Difficulty of Counting American Regional Dialects

Sarah C. Foley

English 102
Section 032
Professor Burns
February 6, 1997

2. The first three sentences engage the reader and lead into the thesis. The author also avoids an abrupt opening.

3. The thesis sentence, or controlling idea, limits the focus and prepares readers for the supporting ideas that follow.

4. All quotations, including this one, are discussed in the present tense ("Claiborne *states*"), not the past.

5. In the parenthetical citation, the author's name is not included because it is mentioned in the text.

6. Inclusive page numbers are identified using the minimum number of digits required for clarity (*not* "279–280").

7. The author interprets the evidence; she does not simply report it.

8. The transition creates coherence by linking the new topic (disagreement over which standard is most reliable) with the preceding one (disagreement over which standards actually exist).

Foley 1

The Difficulty of Counting American Regional Dialects

Many of us who attend college away from home are surprised when others point out (often incorrectly) that we sound as if we come from New York, or the South, or some other area of the country. We also discover that many unfamiliar ways of speaking English seem perfectly normal for others. Exactly how many American regional dialects exist? This simple-sounding question actually is quite difficult because any answer depends on how dialects are counted, and different methods lead to very different totals.

As Robert Claiborne states, "How many American dialects exist depends largely on whom you're reading, and whether they focus on phonetics, vocabulary or both" (240). These two standards of measurement, which linguists often call phonological and lexical (Fromkin and Rodman 279-80), obviously look at different aspects of the language people use. However, some linguists also refer to a third standard, the syntactical, which identifies regional differences in the ways that words are arranged in sentences (Fromkin and Rodman 282). If experts themselves do not always agree on the same standards of measurement, measuring anything, including American regional dialects, becomes much more complicated.

Linguists also disagree about which standard is most reliable. The importance of vocabulary, which Claiborne calls "the fun part of dialectology"

9. The source is a personal interview. See the Works Cited list for its corresponding entry.

10. Note how smoothly the author incorporates the evidence into her own sentence.

11. The plus sign after the page number (69+) denotes a source that does not continue on consecutive pages.

12. The ellipsis (". . .") indicates that words in the original source have been omitted in the quotation.

13. This is a good transitional paragraph.

14. The opening sentence of the paragraph incorporates both a direct quotation and a paraphrasing. Because of its placement at the end of the sentence, the parenthetical page reference indicates that both the quotation and paraphrasing come from page 240.

Foley 2

(240), might seem obvious. For example, other people similar to us in age and economic background might order large sandwiches and call them "hoagies" instead of the "grinders" that everyone ordered back home. As one student puts it, "Sometimes ordering lunch can make you feel like a foreigner" (Goldman). However, Claiborne also says that regional differences in vocabulary are not always clear-cut and actually "throw little light on regional differences in American speech" (240).

In a contrasting view, Walt Wolfram maintains that differences in the use of words such as <u>pail</u> and <u>bucket</u> sometimes are in fact clear and important enough to deserve careful study (69+). In such cases these differences can be marked on maps as isoglosses, which set apart zones of usages (71). In general, according to Wolfram, "lexical items . . . serve as indicators of more broadly based historical and cultural foundations upon which regional dialects rest, and their significance should not be dismissed cavalierly" (76). Once again, if the experts disagree, in this case on the reliability of standards, then using those standards to count anything becomes difficult.

And just how difficult?

Speaking of the American dialects, Claiborne declares that "the minimum number is seven," with some scholars identifying more than a dozen on the Atlantic seacoast alone (240). Wolfram speaks of two to two hundred, depending on "how thinly a dialectologist chooses to slice the pieces of

15. The source is a videocassette. See the Works Cited list for its corresponding entry.

dialect from the language pie" (67). Estimates that
vary so greatly make clear that regional dialects
are not like cars or voters and simply cannot be
studied the same way.

   If counting regional dialects seems difficult,
we should not be surprised. Our speech reveals the
many ways that we deal with the world, and even
within communities accents vary (<u>American Tongues</u>).
Because so many language possibilities exist,
the most rewarding approach to studying regional
dialects most likely involves concentrating on
careful listening rather than counting.

16. The Works Cited list begins on a new page with its heading centered beneath a one-inch top margin.

17. The citation identifies a videocassette.

18. The work cited is a book with one author. The book is published by an imprint (New York Times Books) of a major publishing house (Random House). The hyphen (Times Books-Random) denotes this relationship.

19. The citation identifies a book with two authors.

20. The citation identifies a personal interview.

21. The work cited is a book with one author.

Foley 4

16   Works Cited

17   <u>American Tongues</u>. Dir. Louis Alvarez and Andrew
          Kolker. Narr. Polly Holliday. Videocassette.
          Center for New American Media, 1986.
18   Claiborne. Robert. <u>Our Marvelous Native Tongue</u>. New
          York: Times Books-Random, 1983.
19   Fromkin, Victoria, and Robert Rodman. <u>An Introduc-
          tion to Language</u>. 5th ed. Fort Worth: Harcourt,
          1993.
20   Goldman. Susan. Personal interview. 29 May 1997.
21   Wolfram, Walt. <u>Dialects and American English</u>.
          Englewood Cliffs, NJ: Prentice, 1991.

Glossary of Rhetorical and Linguistic Terms

Acronym   An acronym is a word formed from the first or first few letters of a sequence of words. Examples include AIDS (Acquired Immune Deficiency Syndrome) and laser (light amplification by stimulated emission of radiation).

Americanism   An Americanism is a word, phrase, or usage that originated in or is unique to the United States. *Bamboozle* and *buckaroo* are among many Americanisms from the Far West. For further discussion of Americanisms, see Bryson (p. 179).

Analogy   An analogy is a comparison that clarifies one thing by likening it to something more familiar. In essays, analogies help explain difficult or abstract concepts. The human circulatory system, for example, might be likened to the plumbing system of a house.

Bilingual Education   Bilingual education is an educational approach in which students are instructed in their primary language, even if that language is not the language of the majority of people in their locale. This approach has become controversial, especially in the American Southwest, where the large Hispanic population is often taught in Spanish. Bilingual education is discussed in several of the selections in Chapter Five, "Language and Cultural Diversity."

Cause-and-Effect Analysis   Cause-and-effect analysis is a strategy of expository writing that examines the relationships between the why (cause) and the what (effect). For example, a writer might examine the causes and effects of King Lear's madness or of the fall of the Berlin Wall.

Chunking   Chunking is the technique of segmenting your writing to make it easier for readers to follow. Long units of writing should be broken into parts so that they will be easier for readers to process. See Hairston's "Holding Your Reader" (p. 349).

Classification   Classification is a strategy of expository writing in which the writer places an object or person in a group of similar objects or persons and then focuses on characteristics that distinguish the subject from the larger category. For example, a writer might explain why the language of the Deep South or of New York City can be categorized as a dialect.

Cliché   A cliché is a trite expression, once original, that has lost its power to surprise because of overuse. "Between a rock and a hard place" and "on a wing and a prayer" are among many possible examples.

Colloquial Language   Colloquial language is language that is informal and only appropriate to speech; for example, "The kids felt the council's decision was not a good deal." Since it tends to be informal, colloquial language should be used in writing only to represent speech.

Comparison and/or Contrast   Comparison and/or contrast is a writing strategy that explores the similarities and differences among persons, places, or things. Comparisons usually focus on similarities, and contrasts examine differences. Comparisons must be balanced and logical. For example, a writer might compare and contrast tractors and horses as farming aids.

Concision   Concision is the practice of compressing writing to eliminate unnecessary and meaningless words, phrases, and repetitions. Effective writing is concise; concise writing should reflect the quality of compression. See Williams, "Concision" (p. 375).

Conclusion   Conclusion, or closing, refers to the sentences or paragraphs that bring an essay to an end. The conclusion should satisfy readers by growing organically from the material that precedes and giving a sense of completion. A conclusion often refers back to the essay's opening, identifying broader implications of the thesis, asks a rhetorical question, or makes a memorable statement. (See *Essay Form.*)

Connotation/Denotation   Connotation refers to the meanings often implied in a word or expression. Connotation includes all of the emotional overtones suggested by a word. Denotation refers to the strict definition of a word, such as is found in dictionaries. For example, *underweight, thin,* and *skinny* all share the same denotation, but their connotations differ greatly.

Definition   Definition is a writing strategy that sets forth the essential meanings or properties of something. In paragraphs or essays, definitions are extended to expand on basic meaning. For example, a definition of a regional dialect might discuss its sound, vocabulary, and history.

Denotation   See *Connotation/Denotation.*

Description   Description is a writing strategy and one of the four traditional modes of discourse. (The others are argument, exposition, and narration.) Description most often appeals to the senses by showing how a person, thing, or place looks, sounds, tastes, feels, and/or smells. Description can be objective (factual) or subjective (impressionistic).

Dialect   A dialect is a variety of a language (usually spoken) that distinguishes the speech of a given region. Dialectical differences occur in pronunciation, vocabulary, and grammar. For example, the speech heard in Birmingham, Alabama, is quite distinct from that heard in Portland, Maine.

Diction   Diction refers to a writer's (or speaker's) choice of words. Diction can be abstract or concrete, fresh or clichéd, formal or informal. Diction generally reflects the writer's choice of words for their connotative and denotative value (see *Connotation/Denotation*). Most writers choose words that are appropriate for their audience and purpose as well as lively and concrete.

Division and Classification   See *Classification.*

Encomium   An encomium is a formal expression of lofty praise associated with elegies and tributes.

Eponym An eponym is a word taken from the name of a real or fictitious person or product. Examples of eponyms include *sandwich* (from the Earl of Sandwich) and *Xerox* (from the photocopiers sold by the Xerox Corporation).

Essay Form An essay is a short, nonfiction, prose composition with a structural pattern of introduction/body/conclusion. The introduction usually serves the rhetorical purpose of stating a thesis and the stylistic purpose of opening discussion and leading the reader into the presentation—often with direct quotes, anecdotes, questions, interesting facts or statistics, or unusual statements. The body consists of groups of ideas (topics and supporting evidence) that explain why the thesis is true. The conclusion usually serves the rhetorical purpose of reaffirming (not necessarily restating) the thesis and the stylistic purpose of closing the discussion.

Etymology Etymology is the study of the origin and history of words. For example, the etymology of *language* reveals that the word comes from the Old French word *langue* (for tongue or language) and before that from the Latin *lingua* (tongue). Most dictionaries provide etymologies of words in brackets or parentheses before the definitions. The *Oxford English Dictionary* provides the most complete and accurate English etymologies.

Euphemism A euphemism is a word or phrase that is substituted for another that is considered offensive or disquieting. For example, *white meat* and *dark meat* are euphemisms for *breast* and *leg* that first came into use at a time when it was considered inappropriate to mention anatomical terms at the dinner table. For further discussion, see Murphy's "The E Word" (p. 117).

Evidence Evidence consists of facts, statistics, and examples that support a general thesis or assertion. In writing, evidence provides the reader with some proof of accuracy.

Figurative Language Figurative language consists of colorful and imaginative words and phrases sometimes used in a nonliteral sense. Among the most common figures of speech are similes, metaphors, personification, and hyperbole.

Hyperbole Hyperbole is intentional exaggeration, as in, for example, "The golfer drove the ball into the next county."

Idiom Idioms are expressions with arbitrary meanings different from those suggested by the words themselves. *Ran across, all thumbs,* and *plug away at* are examples. People tend to learn the idioms of their native language naturally, but idioms often confuse nonnative speakers.

Introduction An introduction is the first impression a writer makes, and for that reason alone it is important. Introductions should announce the subject and the essay's focus—to tell why readers ought to be interested in the topic, to make clear the essay's purpose and the writer's point of view, and often to suggest the pattern the essay will follow. (See *Essay Form* and *Thesis Statement*.)

Jargon Jargon is the specialized language of an occupation or profession. For example, doctors often use the word *stat* to mean "immediately," although the general public uses other terms.

Lead   The lead is the opening of a piece of writing. The most important sentence in any piece of writing is the first; if it is dull, you may lose your readers. See the Introduction as well as Hairston's "Holding Your Reader" (p. 349).

Lexicography   Lexicography is the art or process of compiling a dictionary. See Bryson (p. 94) for a discussion of lexicography and the English language.

Linearity   Linearity is a quality in writing that enables readers to move in a straight line without having to stop or reread to discover the writer's meaning. See Hairston's "Holding Your Reader" (p. 349).

Metaphor   A metaphor is a comparison that equates two objects implicitly, that is, without use of a connecting word; for example, "Throughout the trauma the child was a brick."

Neologism   A neologism is a newly coined word or expression or a new meaning for an existing word. For example, just as *motel* resulted from the joining of *motor* and *hotel*, *infotainment* (from *information* and *entertainment*) has appeared recently to categorize such television shows as *Geraldo* and *America's Most Wanted*. Not all neologisms consist of such combinations, as the computer term (and neologism) *executable* illustrates.

Onomastics   Onomastics is the study of the meaning and origin of names. This topic is addressed in detail in Chapter One, "Names and Naming."

Onomatopoeia   Onomatopoeia is the imitation of a sound in the word used to identify it. *Cuckoo, buzz, tinkle,* and *chickadee* are examples of onomatopoeic words.

Opprobrium   An opprobrium is a name or label that indicates shame or disgrace.

Orthography   Orthography is the study of correct spelling according to a system of established usage. The sounds of a language are represented with literal symbols that are called graphemes (letters).

Paradox   A paradox is an apparent contradiction that is nevertheless generally true. For example, "The more you've got, the less you have" points out a paradox.

Paragraph   A paragraph is a written unit of thought that usually contains a topic sentence and evidence to support it. Occasionally, a paragraph may be as short as one sentence, to create emphasis or to serve as a transition joining one paragraph to another.

Parallelism   Parallelism is the use of obviously systematic or similar wording or sentence structure to create emphasis. For example, note the use of the infinitives in the following: "Writing teachers want their students to organize their thoughts, to supply specific information, and to write in complete sentences." Parallel structure usually enhances clarity because it is consistent and balanced.

Paraphrase   A paraphrase is a reiteration, in new wording, of an idea originating with someone else. A paraphrase can be as long as the original but should not be confused with a quotation, which restates an author's words exactly, or a summary, which condenses a long passage into a much shorter form.

Patronym   A patronym is a name that is directly derived from a parent or ancestor. For example, *Johnson* was originally from "son of John." See Hook's "From a World Without Surnames" (p. 4) for a complete discussion of the sources of surnames.

Personification   Personification is the assignment of human traits to something nonhuman; for example, "The doors seemed to have ears."

Phonology   Phonology is the study of a unified sound system in which each symbol represents a single sound in a language. For example, there are three sounds in *through,* so its phonetic representation consists of three symbols, as opposed to the seven letters in the conventional spelling. The International Phonetic Alphabet has become the most frequently used phonetic system.

Process Analysis   Process analysis is a writing strategy that explains how to do something. Sometimes a process analysis consists of step-by-step directions for achieving desired results. For example, a writer might describe how to rig a sail for a windsurfer.

Propaganda   Propaganda is information, accurate or inaccurate, used to sway public opinion. Propaganda is regularly employed to elicit public support for political causes (tax reform, for example), social causes (discouraging smoking), or any effort that will benefit from such support. See "Types of Propaganda" (p. 291) for a detailed discussion.

Pun   A pun is a play on words, either on different senses of the same word (as in "Grave men near death") or on different pronunciations of a word ("The content will make you content").

Racist Language   Racist language is language that suggests consciously or otherwise the superiority of one race or ethnic group over another or that unfairly draws distinctions among racial groups. The topic of racist language is addressed in many of the selections in Chapter Two, "Gender, Race, and Language Conflict."

Regionalism   A regionalism is a word or expression that is characteristic of a particular geographic area. Regionalisms are colorful, but they should be avoided in writing intended for general use. For detailed discussion of regionalisms, see Bryson (p. 179).

Sexist Language   Sexist language is language that stereotypes a person or group based on gender differences or suggests the superiority of one gender over the other. See Nilsen (p. 49) for a discussion of sexist language. See also Hairston's suggestions for avoiding sexist language (p. 392–393).

Simile   A simile is a comparison of two unlike things connected with *like* or *as* or other words that link explicitly; for example, "She watched him like a cat."

Slang   Slang is language that commonly originated in the speech of a minority group or subculture and is usually narrow, flippant, and meaningful only to a special audience. Slang unites those who employ it, while excluding outsiders.

Standard English   Standard English consists of the conventional vocabulary and usage of educated speakers and writers of English. Standard English does not include slang, vulgarisms, regionalisms, and other constructions that are considered undignified or unorthodox by those seeking a language acceptable to a general audience.

Summary   See *Paraphrase*.

Thesis Statement   A thesis statement is an assertion containing the central idea of an essay. Usually positioned early in the essay, the thesis statement narrows the topic, makes an assertion (thereby revealing an attitude) about the topic, and sometimes indicates how the essay will be organized.

Tone   The tone is the prevailing sound of a speaker's or writer's language, which might be labeled playful, ironic, neutral, and so on. Pinker's "Baby Born Talking . . ." (p. 141) is a good example of an author's use of a playful and ironic tone.

Topic Sentence   A topic sentence is a statement of the main point of a paragraph. It is often the first sentence of the paragraph (or the second, following a transitional sentence), although it may occasionally be placed at the end of a paragraph to vary paragraph structure or for dramatic effect. The topic sentence is supported by evidence, such as examples, that make the paragraph concrete and convincing.

Transition   A transition is a link between two ideas in a piece of writing. Transitions often consist of stock words and expressions that identify how ideas are related. For example, *as a result* indicates a cause-and-effect relationship; *however* indicates that one idea contrasts with another. Transitions can also consist of demonstrative terms (*this, that, these, those,* and *such*), relative pronouns (*who, which, where,* and *that*), or repeated or parallel wording (*the first reason, the second reason, another reason*).

Credits

Klose, Robert. "This Dad Gives His Son a Rarity: Grammar Lessons," by Robert Kose. *Boston Globe,* September 4, 1996. Copyright © 1996. Reprinted by permission of the author.

Lamott, Anne. From *Bird by Bird* by Anne Lamott. Copyright © 1994 by Anne Lamott. Reprinted by permission of Pantheon Books, a division of Random House, Inc.

Lawrence, Barbara. "Four-Letter Words Can Hurt You." Copyright © 1973 by The New York Times Co. Reprinted by permission.

Lutz, William. "Empty Eggs: The Doublespeak of Weasel Words." Adapted from *Doublespeak* by William Lutz. Copyright © 1989 by Blonde Bear, Inc. Reprinted by permission of HarperCollins Publishers, Inc.

MacNeil, Robert. From *Wordstruck* by Robert MacNeil. Copyright © 1989 by Neely Productions, Ltd. Used by permission of Viking Penguin, a division of Penguin Books USA, Inc.

Milward, C. M. "The Story of Writing" from *A Biography of the English Language* by Celia M. Milward, copyright © 1989 by Holt, Rinehart, and Winston. Reprinted by permission of the publisher.

Milward [within Milward]. Adapted from Roland Siegrist, ed., *Prehistoric Petroglyphs and Pictographs in Utah.* Copyright © 1972. Used by permission of Utah State Historical Society.

Murphy, Cullen. "The E Word" by Cullen Murphy, *The Atlantic Monthly*, September 1996, pp. 16, 18. Reprinted by permission of the author.

Murray, Donald M. Excerpt from *The Craft of Revision* by Donald M. Murray, copyright © 1991 by Holt, Rinehart and Winston, reprinted by permission of the publisher.

Pace Nilsen, Alleen. "Sexism in English: A 1990s Update." Copyright © Alleen Pace Nilsen, 1990. Reprinted by permission of the author.

Parshall, Gerald. "Words with Attitude," by Gerald Parshall, *U.S. News & World Report,* June 27, 1994, pp. 61–64, 67. Copyright © 1994 U.S. News & World Report. Reprinted by permission.

Pinker, Steven. Text, pp. 262–76 from *The Language Instinct* by Steven Pinker. Copyright © 1994 by Steven Pinker. By permission of William Morrow & Company, Inc.

Pollak, Felix. "Aesthetics" is reprinted from *Ginkgo* by Felix Pollak, Copyright © 1973 by Felix Pollak, reprinted by permission of The Elizabeth Press.

Postman, Neil. From *The End of Education* by Neil Postman. Copyright © 1995 by Neil Postman. Reprinted by permission of Alfred A. Knopf Inc.

Quindlen, Anna. "The Name Is Mine." Copyright © 1987 by The New York Times Co. Reprinted by permission.

Raymo, Chet. "Playing the Name Game by Other Rules" by Chet Raymo, *The Boston Globe*, October 10, 1994, p. 26. Reprinted by permission of the author.

Reidy, Chris. From "Think About It: Things Go Better with Quark?" by Chris Reidy, *The Boston Globe*, February 25, 1997, pp. D1, D15. Reprinted courtesy of The Boston Globe.

Roberts, Paul. "A Brief History of English" from *Understanding English* by Paul Roberts. Copyright © 1958 by Paul Roberts. Reprinted by permission of Addison-Wesley Education Publishers, Inc.

Rodriguez, Richard. From *Hunger of Memory* by Richard Rodriguez. Reprinted by permission of David R. Godine, Publisher, Inc. Copyright © 1982 by Richard Rodriguez.

Savan, Leslie. "Yadda, Yadda, Yadda," by Leslie Savan, *Time*, December 16, 1996, p. 88. © 1996 Time Inc., reprinted by permission.

Smitherman, Geneva. Excerpted from *Black Talk*. Copyright © 1994 by Geneva Smitherman. Reprinted by permission of Houghton Mifflin Company. All rights reserved.

Stegner, Wallace. From *Good-Bye to All T__t!* by Wallace Stegner. Copyright © 1965 by Wallace Stegner. Copyright renewed © 1993 by Wallace Stegner. Reprinted by permission of Brandt & Brandt Literary Agents, Inc.

Stewart, Doug. "Flame Throwers." Reprinted by permission of OMNI, © 1992 Omni Publications International, Ltd.

Tannen, Deborah. From *You Just Don't Understand* by Deborah Tannen, Ph.D. Copyright © 1990 by Deborah Tannen, Ph.D. By permission of William Morrow & Company, Inc.

Index

"Aesthetics" (Pollak), 41

"Americanization is Tough on 'Macho'" (Del Castillo Guilbault), 238–239

"American Names" (Benét), 44–45

Anderson, Chris, "Freewriting," 338–343

Angelou, Maya, *I Know Why the Caged Bird Sings* (excerpt), 20–24

"Aria: A Memoir of a Bilingual Childhood" (Rodriguez), 227–236

August, Eugene R., "Real Men Don't: Anti-Male Bias in English," 68–76

"Baby Born Talking—Describes Heaven" (Pinker), 141–151

Baldwin, James, "On Black English," 87–89

Barry, John A., "Techniques of Coinage," 330–332

Bernays, Anne
  and Justin Kaplan, "A Strange Kind of Magick Bias" (Kaplan & Bernays), 13–18
  and Justin Kaplan, "Names in the Melting Pot," 241–244

Benét, Stephen Vincent, "American Names," 44–45

Bird by Bird: Some Instructions on Writing and Life (excerpt) (Lamott), 345–348

Bolton, W. F., "Putting American English on the Map," 29–36

Boorstein, Daniel J., "The Rhetoric of Democracy," 258–266

"A Brief History of English" (Roberts), 168–177

Bryson, Bill
  "Old World, New World," 179–190
  "Order Out of Chaos," 94–105

"*C'est* What?" (Yemma), 326–328

Cobb, Nathan, "Gender Wars in Cyberspace!" 316–319

Cogdill, Sharon, "Computers and Writing," 384–389

"Computers and Writing" (Cogdill), 384–389

"Concision" (Williams), 375–383

Crystal, David, "Vanishing Languages," 210–217

Cummings, E. E., "next to of course god america i," 298

Del Castillo Guilbault, "Americanization Is Tough on 'Macho,'" 238–239

Dodge advertisement, 284

Elyssa, Tara, "Learning English Good," 246–253

"Empty Eggs: The Doublespeak of Weasel Words" (Lutz), 268–276

"English Belongs to Everybody" (MacNeil), 128–131

Esquire advertisement, 311

"The E Word" (Murphy), 117–120

"Everything Had a Name" (Keller), 136–139

"Flame Throwers" (Stewart), 314–315

Ford advertisement, 285

"Four-Letter Words Can Hurt You" (Lawrence), 110–112

"Freewriting" (Anderson), 338–343

"From African to African American" (Smitherman), 82–85

"From a World Without Surnames" (Hook), 4–10

Frum, David, "Just Call Me Mister," 26–27

"Gender Wars in Cyberspace!" (Cobb), 316–319

"Getting Close to the Machine" (Ullman), 321–324

"Good-bye to All T__t!" (Stegner), 114–115

Goodman, Ellen, "Unprotected Sex Talk," 288–289

Hairston, Maxine C., "Holding Your Reader," 349–363

"Holding Your Reader" (Hairston), 349–363

Hook, J. N., "From a World Without Surnames," 4–10

I Know Why the Caged Bird Sings (excerpt) (Angelou), 20–24

Institute for Propaganda Analysis, "Types of Propaganda," 291–295

Jeep advertisement, 283

"Just Call Me Mister" (Frum), 26–27

Kaplan, Justin
  and Anne Bernays, "A Strange Kind of Magick Bias" (Kaplan & Bernays), 13–18
  and Anne Bernays, "Names in the Melting Pot," 241–244

Keller, Helen, "Everything Had a Name," 136–139

Kennedy, John F., "Inaugural Address," 300–302

King, Robert D., "Should English Be the Law?" 218–226

Klose, Robert, "A Rarity: Grammar Lessons from Dad," 107–108

Lamott, Anne, *Bird by Bird: Some Instructions on Writing and Life* (excerpt), 345–348

Lawrence, Barbara, "Four-Letter Words Can Hurt You," 110–112

"Learning English Good" (Elyssa), 246–253

Lutz, William, "Empty Eggs: The Double-speak of Weasel Words," 268–276

MacNeil, Robert, "English Belongs to Every-body," 128–131

Millward, C. M., "The Story of Writing," 196–204

Murphy, Cullen, "The E Word," 117–120

Murray, Donald M., "Writing Is Rewriting," 364–373

"Names in the Melting Pot" (Kaplan & Bernays), 241–244

"The Name Is Mine" (Quindlen), 79–80

"next to of course god america i" (Cummings), 298

Nilsen, Alleen Pace, "Sexism in English: A 1990s Update," 49–57

"Old World, New World" (Bryson), 179–190

"On Black English" (Baldwin), 87–89

"Order Out of Chaos" (Bryson), 94–105

Parshall, Gerald, "Words with Attitude," 122–126

Pinker, Steven, "Baby Born Talking—Describes Heaven," 141–151

"Playing the Name Game by Other Rules" (Raymo), 38–40

Pollak, Felix, "Aesthetics," 41

Postman, Neil, "The Word Weavers/The World Makers," 154–166

"'Put Down That Paper and Talk to Me!': Rapport-Talk and Report-Talk" (Tannen), 60–66

"Putting American English on the Map" (Bolton), 29–36

Quindlen, Anna, "The Name Is Mine," 79–80

"A Rarity: Grammar Lessons from Dad" (Klose), 107–108

Raymo, Chet, "Playing the Name Game by Other Rules," 38–40

Reagan, Ronald, "First Inaugural Address," 304–307

"Real Men Don't: Anti-Male Bias in English" (August), 68–76

Reidy, Chris, "Things Go Better with Quark?" 278–280

"The Rhetoric of Democracy" (Boorstin), 258–266

Roberts, Paul, "A Brief History of English," 168–177

Rodriguez, Richard, "Aria: A Memoir of a Bilingual Childhood," 227–236

Savan, Leslie, "Yadda, Yadda, Yadda," 193–194

"Sexism in English: A 1990s Update" (Nilsen), 49–57

"Should English Be the Law?" (King), 218–226

Smitherman, Geneva, "From African to African American," 82–85

Stegner, Wallace, "Good-bye to All T__t!" 114–115

Stewart, Doug, "Flame Throwers," 314–315

"The Story of Writing" (Millward), 196–204

"A Strange Kind of Magick Bias" (Kaplan & Bernays), 13–18

Tannen, Deborah, "'Put Down That Paper and Talk to Me!': Rapport-Talk and Report-Talk," 60–66

"Techniques of Coinage" (Barry), 330–332

"Things Go Better with Quark?" (Reidy), 278–280

"Two Presidential Speeches" (Kennedy & Reagan), 300–307

"Types of Propaganda" (Institute for Propaganda Analysis), 291–295

Ullman, Ellen, "Getting Close to the Machine," 321–324

"Unprotected Sex Talk" (Goodman), 288–289

"Vanishing Languages" (Crystal), 210–217

Williams, Joseph M., 375–383

"Words with Attitude" (Parshall), 122–126

"The Word Weavers/The World Makers" (Postman), 154–166

"Writing Is Rewriting" (Murray), 364–373

"Yadda, Yadda, Yadda" (Savan), 193–194

Yemma, "*C'est* What?" 326–328